The Liberty of Non-Citizens

Indefinite Detention in Commonwealth Countries

Rayner Thwaites

• H A R T •
PUBLISHING

OXFORD AND PORTLAND, OREGON
2014

Published in the United Kingdom by Hart Publishing Ltd
16C Worcester Place, Oxford, OX1 2JW
Telephone: +44 (0)1865 517530
Fax: +44 (0)1865 510710
E-mail: mail@hartpub.co.uk
Website: http://www.hartpub.co.uk

Published in North America (US and Canada) by
Hart Publishing
c/o International Specialized Book Services
920 NE 58th Avenue, Suite 300
Portland, OR 97213-3786
USA
Tel: +1 503 287 3093 or toll-free: (1) 800 944 6190
Fax: +1 503 280 8832
E-mail: orders@isbs.com
Website: http://www.isbs.com

Hart Publishing is an imprint of Bloomsbury Publishing Group plc

British Library Cataloguing in Publication Data
Data Available

ISBN: 978-1-84946-431-4

Typeset by Hope Services, Abingdon
Printed and bound in Great Britain by
Lightning Source UK Ltd

ACKNOWLEDGEMENTS

The book has benefited from many conversations with friends and colleagues.

It is developed from my 2010 doctoral thesis at the University of Toronto. My thanks at the completion of that process also apply to the current work. My gratitude to my doctoral committee bears reiteration, to David Dyzenhaus, Karen Knop and Audrey Macklin, for the generosity with which they engaged with my arguments and with me. Thanks to Kent Roach for comments as internal examiner. In the book I also endeavour, with mixed success, to address the thought-provoking questions of my external examiner, Clive Walker.

David Dyzenhaus and Matthew Lewans nudged me on transforming the thesis into a book, for which, thanks. Campbell McLachlan advised me through the book proposal process and beyond. He has been a constant interlocutor throughout. Your office visits and invitations to lunch were always welcome. Thanks to Janet McLean for comments on the proposal. Thanks also to the two anonymous reviewers engaged by Hart. The book benefits from their suggestions on how to better structure and present the material.

The work on the book was done while I was on the law faculty at Victoria University of Wellington, New Zealand. The faculty allowed me to organise matters so as, twice, to have a semester free of teaching during work on the book. More fundamentally, the faculty was a remarkably supportive and congenial environment in which to work. I will miss you.

Victoria University provided a Research Establishment Grant and further funding. This enabled me to engage Daniel Hunt and Cathy Nijman. Daniel and Cathy prepared research memoranda on many and various points, pressed me on my prose and treatment of the material, and worked on the style and referencing of the manuscript. Your involvement made the work much easier, and more companionable, than it would otherwise have been.

The book covers three national jurisdictions. In respect of each, I am grateful to 'local informants' of knowledge and expertise who were able to set me right on numerous points when I stumbled, or simply missed the point. For constructive comments my thanks to: Eric Adams, Elisa Arcioni, Matthew Groves, Emily Hammond, Max Harris, Tom Hickman, John Ip, Derek McKee, Campbell McLachlan, Kim Rubenstein and the Hon Mr Justice Walker. Particular thanks are due to Matthew, Emily, Tom and Campbell for comments which resulted in sizeable changes to the material covered, or to the presentation of the argument. I am, of course, solely responsible for the book's shortcomings.

Hart Publishing has been a pleasure to deal with. To all at Hart, and to Ruth Massey for copy editing, thanks.

At a number of points, reference is made to the legal position 'at the time of writing'. This is June 2013, when the manuscript was submitted.

The book is dedicated to my partner, Emily Hammond, and kids, Arlo and April. You bring me joy.

Rayner Thwaites
Wellington
November 2013

CONTENTS

Acknowledgements v
Table of Cases xi
Table of Legislation and Constitutional Provisions xix
Table of Conventions, Treaties etc xxv

Introduction

1 Introduction 3
1.1 Introduction 3
1.2 Shared Principles 12
1.3 Two Judicial Responses to Indefinite Detention of Non-Citizens 15
1.4 'Nationality-Differentiated Risk-Acceptability'? 20
1.5 Criticisms of 'Nationality-Differentiated Risk-Acceptability' 25
1.6 A Shared Commonwealth Legal Tradition? 28
1.6.1 Choice of Jurisdictions 28
1.6.2 Structural Differences 30
1.7 Plan of the Book 33

Australia

2 Limits on Immigration Detention 37
2.1 Introduction to the Australian Chapters 37
2.2 The Australian Legal Context 39
2.2.1 The Constitution and Federal Legislative Power 39
2.2.2 Common Law on Statutory Authority for Administrative Detention 44
2.3 *Lim* 46
2.3.1 *Lim* Introduced 46
2.3.2 The Separation of Judicial Power and Non-Citizens 48
2.3.3 Non-Citizens' Vulnerability to Removal and the Separation of Powers 50
2.3.4 Conclusions on *Lim* 54
2.4 *Al Masri* 55
2.4.1 *Al Masri* Introduced 55
2.4.2 *Al Masri* at First Instance 57
2.4.3 *Al Masri* in the Full Court of the Federal Court 59
2.4.4 Conclusions on *Al Masri* 63

3 Indefinite Detention of Aliens 65
3.1 Introduction to *Al-Kateb* 65
3.2 The Majority on Interpretation of the Detention Provisions 67
3.3 The Majority on the Constitutionality of Indefinite Detention 71
3.4 The Minority – Gleeson CJ 78
3.5 The Minority – Gummow and Kirby JJ 82
3.6 The Relevance of International Law to Interpretation 87
3.7 The Conditions of Detention 91
3.8 Conclusions on *Al-Kateb* 95

4 *Al-Kateb* Contested 99
4.1 Introduction 99
4.2 Administrative Measures 100
4.3 The *Offshore Processing Case* 103
4.4 *Plaintiff M47: Al-Kateb* Reconsidered (by some) 109
4.4.1 *Plaintiff M47* Introduced 109
4.4.2 *Al-Kateb* should be Overruled 111
4.4.3 *Al-Kateb* should be Upheld 113
4.4.4 The Majority 116
4.5 Conclusion 118

United Kingdom

5 Prohibitions, Derogations and Deference 123
5.1 Introduction to the United Kingdom Chapters 123
5.2 *Hardial Singh* 126
5.3 *Chahal* 128
5.3.1 *Chahal* on Deportation 130
5.3.2 *Chahal* on Detention 132
5.4 The Legislative Response to *Chahal*: SIAC 135
5.5 The Human Rights Act 1998 137
5.6 *Rehman* and SIAC's Review Function 138
5.7 Derogations in the European Convention on Human Rights 142

6 *Belmarsh* in the United Kingdom Courts 145
6.1 The Measures at Issue in *Belmarsh* 145
6.2 Introduction to the *Belmarsh* Litigation 147
6.3 The Case before SIAC 149
6.3.1 Introduction 149
6.3.2 Proportionality and Discrimination 150
6.3.3 Conclusions on the SIAC Judgment 154
6.4 *Belmarsh* in the Court of Appeal 156
6.4.1 Lord Woolf CJ – the Erasure of Discrimination 156
6.4.2 Brooke LJ – the Alien as Enemy 161
6.4.3 Conclusions on *Belmarsh* in the Court of Appeal 162
6.5 The Certification Proceedings 163

6.6 *Belmarsh* in the House of Lords 164
6.6.1 The Existence of a Public Emergency 164
6.6.2 The Strictly Required Criterion 165
(a) Rejection of a Case-by-Case Analysis 166
(b) Deference 167
(c) The Applicable Standard of Review 171
6.6.3 Discrimination 173
(a) The Immigration Context 173
(b) Use of International Law 176
6.6.4 The Declaration of Incompatibility 179
6.7 Conclusion 182

7 The Periphery of Indefinite Detention 185
7.1 Introduction 185
7.2 *Belmarsh* in the European Court of Human Rights 186
7.2.1 Introduction to *A v United Kingdom* 186
7.2.2 The ECtHR on Article 5(1) 188
(a) 'action is being taken with a view to deportation' 188
(b) The Fair Balance Argument 190
(c) The ECtHR's Findings on the Facts 191
7.2.3 Conclusions on *A v United Kingdom* 192
7.3 The Legislative Response to *Belmarsh* 193
7.4 Substance – The Extent of the Obligations Imposed 196
7.4.1 The Effect of Control Orders 196
7.4.2 Court-Imposed Limits on the Obligations 199
7.5 Procedure – The Development of the Control Order Regime 202
7.6 The Change to TPIMs 207
7.7 The Position of Non-Citizens 210
7.8 Development of the *Hardial Singh* Principles 215
7.8.1 Confirmation and Elaboration of the Principles 215
7.8.2 The Consequences of Breach of a Public Law Duty 219
7.9 Conclusion 220

Canada

8 The Charter and Security Certificates 225
8.1 Introduction to the Canadian Chapters 225
8.2 Citizenship in the Constitution 226
8.3 Section 15 of the Charter 227
8.4 Section 7 of the Charter 230
8.4.1 Relationship between Section 7 and Section 1 of the Charter 230
8.4.2 *Singh* 232
8.4.3 *Chiarelli* 234
8.5 The Security Certificate Regime 237
8.6 *Suresh* 239

8.7 Federal Court Decisions Preceding *Charkaoui* 244
8.7.1 Decisions on Deportation to Torture 245
8.7.2 Consequences of the *Suresh* Exception 246
8.7.3 Review of Detention 248

9 *Charkaoui*'s Procedural Solution 251
9.1 *Charkaoui* Introduced 251
9.2 Submissions of the Parties and Interveners 253
9.3 Section 7 Analysis of the Statutory Procedure 255
9.4 Unanswered Questions 259
9.4.1 Substantive Limits on Indefinite Detention? 259
9.4.2 Discriminatory against Non-Citizens? 262
9.5 The Court's Use of Comparative Authority 263
9.5.1 'Reasonably Necessary for Deportation Purposes' 263
9.5.2 'The IRPA . . . Does Not Authorise Indefinite Detention'? 266
9.6 Deportation to Torture and the *Suresh* Exception 268
9.7 The Missing Proportionality Analysis 270
9.8 Conclusions on *Charkaoui* 271
9.8.1 Principled Minimalism? 271
9.8.2 Commonalities between *Charkaoui* and *Suresh* 272
9.9 Bill C-3 274
9.10 Exits from the Security Certificate Regime 276
9.10.1 *Charkaoui II* 276
9.10.2 Exit 1 – Mr Charkaoui 279
9.10.3 Exit 2 – Mr Almrei 280
9.11 Conclusion 282

Conclusion

10 Conclusion 287
10.1 Introduction 287
10.2 Divergent Responses to a Common Issue 288
10.2.1 The Decisions of Courts of Other States 288
10.2.2 The Influence of International Law 291
(a) Australia – The Point of Entry for International Law 292
(b) The United Kingdom – The Meaning of Treaty Texts 293
(c) Canada – How Seriously are International Law Obligations Taken? 295
10.3 The Purpose(s) of Detention 296
10.3.1 'Segregation from the Community' or 'Dangerousness' 296
10.3.2 'Detention Pending Removal' 298
10.3.3 The Rights-Protecting Approach 299
10.4 Non-Citizens in Times of Threat 300
10.5 The Importance of Membership 301
10.6 The Integration of Rights and Immigration Control 305
10.7 Conclusion 306

Bibliography 309

Index 319

TABLE OF CASES

Australia

Al–Kateb v Godwin [2004] HCA 37, (2004) 219 CLR 562........ 8, 10, 14, 16–17, 21, 25, 27, 30, 33, 37–38, 44–46, 48, 52, 54–56, 60, 64–91, 93–101, 103, 106–07, 109–19, 154, 162, 170, 179, 189, 265, 287–90, 292–93, 296–99, 302–04, 307

Al Masri v Minister for Immigration & Multicultural & Indigenous Affairs [2002] FCA 1009, (2002) 192 ALR 609 (*Al Masri,* First Instance).. 56–58, 64, 66, 81, 98

Al Masri v Minister for Immigration & Multicultural & Indigenous Affairs [2002] FCA 1099 (*Al Masri,* Re–detention) 58, 62, 98

American Dairy Queen (Q) Pty Ltd v Blue Rio Pty Ltd [1981] HCA 65, (1981) 147 CLR 677..45

Annetts v McCann [1990] HCA 57, (1990) 170 CLR 596......................................106

Australian Communist Party v Commonwealth [1951] HCA 5, (1951) 83 CLR 1 (*Communist Party Case*)................................ 44, 82–85, 90–91, 93, 298

Australian Education Union v General Manager of Fair Work Australia [2012] HCA 19, (2012) 296 ALR 625..113

Behrooz v Secretary, Department of Immigration & Multicultural & Indigenous Affairs [2004] HCA 36, (2004) 219 CLR 486.................................. 66, 74, 76, 79, 85, 87–88, 91–94

Bolton, Re, ex parte Beane [1987] HCA 12, (1987) 162 CLR 514...............44–46, 70

Coco v R [1994] HCA 15, (1994) 179 CLR 427 ....45–46, 70

Coleman v Power [2004] HCA 39, (2004) 220 CLR 1 70

Commonwealth v Progress Advertising & Press Agency Co Pty Ltd [1910] HCA 28, (1910) 10 CLR 457 45

Communist Party Case. See *Australian Communist Party v Commonwealth*

Cunliffe v Commonwealth [1994] HCA 44, (1994) 182 CLR 272 51

Daniels Corporation International Pty Ltd v Australian Competition & Consumer Commission [2002] HCA 49, (2002) 213 CLR 543.........45–46, 70–71

Dickson v R [2010] HCA 30, (2010) 241 CLR 491 112

Durham Holdings Pty Ltd v New South Wales [2001] HCA 7, (2001) 205 CLR 399...45

Electrolux Home Products v Australian Workers Union [2004] HCA 40, (2004) 221 CLR 309..81, 113

John v Federal Commissioner of Taxation [1989] HCA 5, (1989) 166 CLR 417...111

Jones v Dunkel [1959] HCA 8, (1959) 101 CLR 298 58
K–Generation Pty Ltd v Liquor Licensing Court [2009] HCA 4, (2009) 237 CLR 501 113
Kioa v West [1985] HCA 81, (1985) 159 CLR 550 .... 37, 39, 49, 60, 70
Kirk v Industrial Relations Commission of New South Wales [2010] HCA 1, (2010) 239 CLR 531 44
Koon Wing Lau v Caldwell [1949] HCA 65, (1949) 80 CLR 533 45
Lacey v Attorney–General of Queensland [2011] HCA 10, (2011) 242 CLR 573 113
Leghaei v Director General of Security [2005] FCA 1576 (*Leghaei,* First Instance) 118
Leghaei v Director General of Security [2007] FCAFC 37 (*Leghaei,* Appeal) 118
Lim (Chu Kheng) v Minister of Immigration, Local Government & Ethnic Affairs [1992] HCA 64, (1992) 176 CLR 1 .... 13, 15, 23, 31, 37, 43–44, 46–56, 59–60, 64, 72–76, 79–80, 82–85, 92, 95, 114, 116, 292, 299
Little v Commonwealth [1947] HCA 24, (1947) 75 CLR 64 .... 50, 84
Lo Pak, Ex parte (1888) 9 NSWLR 221 .... 19, 44, 287, 307
Malaysian Declaration Case. See *Plaintiff M70/2011 v Minister of Immigration & Citizenship*
Minister for Immigration & Ethnic Affairs v Teoh (1995) 183 CLR 273 292
Minister for Immigration & Multicultural & Indigenous Affairs v Al Khafaji [2002] FCA 1369 66
Minister for Immigration & Multicultural & Indigenous Affairs v Al Khafaji [2004] HCA 38, (2004) 219 CLR 664 .... 66, 91
Minister for Immigration & Multicultural & Indigenous Affairs v Al Masri [2003] FCAFC 70, (2003) 126 FCR 54 (Full Court of the Federal Court of Australia) 23, 37–38, 48, 55–57, 59–64, 66, 73, 76, 98, 111, 126, 154, 289, 292–93, 300
Momcilovic v R [2011] HCA 34, (2011) 245 CLR 1 .... 17, 38
Musgrove v Chun Teeong Toy [1891] AC 272 (PC) 27, 39–40
NAAV v Minister for Immigration [2002] FCA 443, (2002) 123 FCR 298 .... 39, 112
Nolan v Minister for Immigration & Ethnic Affairs [1988] HCA 45, (1988) 165 CLR 178 49
Offshore Processing Case. See *Plaintiff M61/2010E v Commonwealth*
Patterson, ex parte Taylor, Re [2001] HCA 51, (2001) 207 CLR 391 41
Plaintiff M47/2012 v Director General of Security [2012] HCA 46, (2012) 86 ALJR 1372 .... 15, 17, 94, 99, 103, 109–16, 119, 207, 289, 303
Plaintiff M61/2010E v Commonwealth [2010] HCA 41, (2011) 243 CLR 319 (*Offshore Processing Case*) 99, 103–08, 119
Plaintiff M70/2011 v Minister of Immigration & Citizenship [2011] HCA 32, (2012) 244 CLR 144 (*Malaysian Declaration Case*) 99, 119
Plaintiff S10/2011 v Minister for Immigration & Citizenship [2012] HCA 31 .... 108, 119

Plaintiff S157/2002 v Commonwealth [2003] HCA 2, (2003) 211 CLR 476 .... 45, 60–61
Polites v Commonwealth [1945] HCA 3, (1945) 70 CLR 60 88
Potter v Minahan [1908] HCA 63, (1908) 7 CLR 277 .... 42, 45–46, 70
R v Davey, ex parte Freer [1936] HCA 58, (1936) 56 CLR 381 41
R v Director General of Social Welfare, ex parte Henry [1975] HCA 62, (1975) 133 CLR 369 42
R v MacFarlane, ex parte O'Flanagan and O'Kelly [1923] HCA 39, (1923) 32 CLR 518 42
R v Wilson, ex parte Kisch [1934] HCA 50, (1934) 52 CLR 234 41
Robtelmes v Brenan [1906] HCA 58, (1906) 4 CLR 395 .... 39, 69
Ruddock v Vadarlis [2001] FCA 1329, (2001) 110 FCR 491, 180 ALR 1 (*The Tampa*) 39, 104
Saaed v Minister for Immigration & Citizenship [2010] HCA 23, (2010) 241 CLR 252 113
SBEG v Commonwealth of Australia [2012] FCAFC 189 .... 93–95, 103
SHDB v Goodwin [2003] FCA 300 .... 65, 114
SHFB v Goodwin [2003] FCA 29 56
SHFB v Goodwin [2003] FCA 294 66
Singh v Commonwealth [2004] HCA 43, (2004) 222 CLR 322 .... 42, 49
Tampa (The). See *Ruddock v Vadarlis*
Thomas v Mowbray [2007] HCA 33, (2007) 233 CLR 307 83
Victorian Council for Civil Liberties v Minister for Immigration & Multicultural Affairs [2001] FCA 1297 104
Wentworth v NSW Bar Association [1992] HCA 24, (1992) 176 CLR 239 45
Woolley, ex parte Applicants M276/2003 (by their next friend GS), Re [2004] HCA 49, (2004) 210 ALR 369 .... 42, 76, 86–87, 116, 303
Zheng v Cai [2009] HCA 52, (2009) 239 CLR 446 .... 112, 119

Refugee Review Tribunal

Al Masri decision, 5 December 2001 57

Canada

Ahani v Canada (Minister of Citizenship & Immigration) 2002 SCC 2, [2002] 1 SCR 72 242
Almrei v Canada [2005] FC 355, (2005) 262 FTR 7 (*Almrei, Second Danger Opinion*) 246–47
Almrei v Canada (Minister of Citizenship & Immigration) [2005] FC 1645, (2005) 270 FTR 1 (*Almrei, Second Application for Release*) 244, 251, 262, 269

Almrei v Canada (Minister of Citizenship & Immigration) [2005] FCA 54, 251 DLR (4th) 13 252
Almrei, Re 2009 FC 3, (2009) 337 FTR 160 ....249, 264
Almrei, Re (2009) FC 1263, [2011] 1 FCR 163 (*Almrei 2009 Reasonableness Decision*) 141, 279–82, 290–91
Andrews v Law Society of British Columbia [1989] 1 SCR 143 228–29
Attorney–General for Canada v Cain [1906] AC 542 ....24, 26–27, 51
Canada (Employment & Immigration) v Chiarelli [1992] 1 SCR 711 ....227, 229, 234–38, 244, 254, 256–57, 273, 277
Canada (Minister of Citizenship & Immigration) v Mahjoub [2004] 1 FC 493 248
Canada (Minister of Citizenship & Immigration) v Mahjoub [2005] FC 1596, (2005) 270 FTR 101 (*Mahjoub, Second Application for Release*) 248–49, 264, 267, 269, 297
Canada (Minister of Citizenship and Immigration) v Mahjoub [2009] FC 439 250
Charkaoui [2004] FCA 421, 247 DLR (4th) 405 251–52
Charkaoui, Re (2005) FC 149, (2005) 261 FTR 1 ....237, 277
Charkaoui, Re [2005] FC 258, (2005) 252 DLR (4th) 601 (*Charkaoui, Fourth Application for Release*) 249, 251
Charkaoui, Re (2006) FCA 206, (2006) 272 DLR (4th) 175 277
Charkaoui, Re (2009) FC 1030, [2010] 4 FCR 448 (*Charkaoui 2009*) 279–80
Charkaoui v Canada (Minister of Citizenship & Immigration) [2007] SCC 9, [2007] 1 SCR 350 (*Charkaoui*) 10, 17, 21, 30, 33, 118, 204, 225–27, 230–32, 234, 238–39, 243–49, 251–53, 255–82, 287–91, 295, 298–301, 307
Charkaoui v Canada (Minister of Citizenship & Immigration) [2008] SCC 38, [2008] 2 SCR 326 (*Charkaoui II*) 202, 256, 276–82
Chiarelli v Canada (Minister of Employment & Immigration) [1990] 2 FC 299, 67 DLR (4th) 697 (*Chiarelli* FCA) 236
Corbiere v Canada (Minister of Indian & Northern Affairs) [1999] 2 SCR 203 228
Cunningham v Tomey Homma [1903] AC 151 226
Dunsmuir v New Brunswick [2008] SCC 9, [2008] 1 SCR 190 242
Egan v Canada [1995] 2 SCR 513 228–29
Godbout v Longueuil (City) [1997] 3 SCR 844 231
Harkat, Re [2005] FC 393, (2005) 261 FTR 52 252
Harkat v Canada (Minister of Citizenship & Immigration) [2005] FCA 285 252
Harkat v Canada (Minister of Citizenship & Immigration) [2006] FC 628, [2007] 1 FCR 321 (*Harkat, Second Application for Release*) 249, 251
Jaballah, Re [2006] FC 1230, (2006) 148 CRR (2d) 1 (*Jaballah, Second Reasonableness Decision*) 247–48, 268
Jaballah v Canada (Minister of Public Safety & Emergency Preparedness) [2007] FC 379, (2007) 296 FTR 1 (*Jaballah, Third Application for Release*) 249

Lavoie v Canada 2002 SCC 23, [2002] 1 SCR 769 228–29
Law Society of BC v Mangat 2001 SCC 67, [2001] 3 SCR 113 226
Libman v Attorney–General of Quebec [1997] 3 SCR 569 .... 166, 170
Mahjoub v Canada (Minister of Citizenship & Immigration) [2005] FC 156, (2005) 261 FTR 95 (*Mahjoub, First Danger Opinion*) 245, 247
Mahjoub v Canada (Minister of Citizenship & Immigration) [2006] FC 1503, [2007] 4 FCR 247 (*Mahjoub, Second Danger Opinion*) 246–247
Mahjoub v Canada (Minister of Citizenship & Immigration) [2007] FC 171, (2007) 309 FTR 72 (*Mahjoub, Third Application for Release*) 248–49, 261, 267, 269
Medovarski v Canada (Minister of Citizenship & Immigration) 2005 SCC 51, [2005] 2 SCR 539 .... 236, 256
Miron v Trudel [1995] 2 SCR 418 229
New Brunswick (Minister of Health and Community Services) v G(J) [1999] 3 SCR 46 230
R v Lyons [1987] 2 SCR 309 .... 237, 262
R v Oakes [1986] 1 SCR 103 .... 166, 227, 232, 257, 294
R v Swain [1991] 1 SCR 933 231–32
RJR MacDonald Inc v A–G Canada [1995] 3 SCR 199 .... 150, 170
Sahin v Canada (Minister of Citizenship & Immigration) [1995] 1 FC 214 .... 249, 265–66
Singh v Canada (Minister of Employment & Immigration) [1985] 1 SCR 177 .... 232–34, 237, 243, 254, 256–57
Suresh v Canada (Citizenship & Immigration) [2002] SCC 1, [2002] 1 SCR 3 .... 140, 226, 231, 238–48, 254, 267–69, 272–74, 281, 291, 295
Thomson Newspapers v Canada (Director of Investigation & Research) [1990] 1 SCR 425 237
Union Colliery v Bryden [1889] AC 580 226
Withler v Canada (Attorney–General) 2011 SCC 12, [2011] 1 SCR 396 254

European Court of Human Rights

A v United Kingdom (2009) 49 EHRR 29 .... 21, 118, 134, 148, 163–64, 170, 175, 180–81, 186–93, 202, 204–07, 289, 293, 295
Belgian Linguistic Case (No 2) (1968) 1 EHRR 252 174
Chahal v United Kingdom (1997) 23 EHRR 413 .... 123, 126, 128–37, 139, 145, 153–54, 157, 188, 190, 192–93, 203, 206, 217, 240, 258, 267–68, 289, 291, 293, 295
Cruz Varas v Sweden (1992) 14 EHRR 1 130
Guzzardi v Italy Series A no 39 (1981) 3 EHRR 333 .... 194, 200
Handyside v United Kingdom (1976) 1 EHRR 727 144
James v UK Series A no 98 (1986) 8 EHRR 123 144

Klass v Germany (1979) 2 EHRR 214..131
Leander v Sweden (1987) 9 EHRR 433..131
McCann v United Kingdom (1995) 21 EHRR 97 144
Mikolenko v Estonia, App no 10664/05 (ECtHR, 8 Oct 2009) 133
Saadi v Italy (2009) 49 EHRR 30.. 130, 193, 241, 295
Saadi v United Kingdom (2008) 47 EHRR 17 ....134, 295
Silvers v United Kingdom (1983) 5 EHRR 439 144
Soering v United Kingdom (1989) 11 EHRR 439 130
Vilvarajah v United Kingdom (1992) 14 EHRR 248 130

United Kingdom

A v Secretary of State for the Home Department [2002] EWCA Civ 1502, [2004] QB 335 (*Belmarsh*, Court of Appeal)............................... 25, 138, 140, 145, 153, 156–62, 179, 182–83, 189–91, 210
A v Secretary of State for the Home Department [2002] HRLR 45) (*Belmarsh*, SIAC) 138, 140, 147–51, 153–55, 172, 184, 190
A v Secretary of State for the Home Department [2004] EWCA Civ 1123..............20
A v Secretary of State for the Home Department [2004] UKHL 56, [2005] 2 AC 68 (*Belmarsh*)..................................3, 10–11, 17, 21, 23, 25, 27–28, 30, 33, 91, 123–26, 130, 134, 137–48, 150, 153, 155, 157–58, 162–82, 184–86, 189, 191–94, 199, 205, 210, 212–14, 217, 220–21, 228, 254–55, 260, 266–68, 270, 273–75, 281, 287–91, 293, 297–98, 300–02, 305–07
Al Rawi v Security Service [2011] UKSC 34, [2012] 1 AC 531 207
Amin v Brown [2005] EWHC (Ch) 1670...25
Associated Provincial Picture Houses Ltd v Wednesbury Corp [1948] 1 KB 223 ....150, 218, 306
Belmarsh litigation. See *A v Secretary of State for the Home Department*
Brown v Stott [2000] UKPC D3, [2001] 2 WLR 817 152
CA v SSHD [2010] EWHC 2278(QB)...198
Entick v Carrington (1765) 19 St Tr 1030..124
G v Secretary of State for the Home Department [2004] UKSIAC 2/2002, Bail Application SCB/10 163
Hardial Singh. See *R v Governor of Durham Prison, ex parte Singh*
Home Office v Tariq [2011] UKSC 35, [2012] 1 AC 542......................................207
Huang v Secretary of State for the Home Department [2007] UKHL 11, [2007] 2 AC 167 ....150, 165–66
International Transport Roth GmbH v Secretary of State for the Home Department [2002] EWCA Civ 158, [2003] QB 728 168
John v Rees [1970] Ch 345...206
Johnstone v Pedlar [1921] 2 AC 263...24, 26–27
Khawaja v Secretary of State for the Home Department [1984] 1 AC 74....... 174–75

Leach v Money (1765) 3 Burr 1692 124
Liversidge v Anderson [1942] AC 206 44
Padfield v Minister of Agriculture, Fisheries and Food [1968] AC 997 .... 218, 306
R v Director of Public Prosecutions, ex parte Kebilene [1999] UKHL 43, [2000] 2 AC 326 167
R v Governor of Durham Prison, ex parte Singh [1983] EWHC 1 (QB), [1984] 1 All ER 983 (*Hardial Singh*) 15, 58, 61, 125–27, 133, 153, 156–57, 162, 185, 214–19, 255, 264–66, 273–74, 289–90, 300–01, 306
R v Home Secretary, ex parte Khawaja [1984] AC 74 .... 44, 60
R v Secretary of State for the Home Department, ex parte Chahal, unreported (10 November 1995) 129
R v Secretary of State for the Home Department, ex parte Daly [2001] UKHL 46, [2001] 2 AC 532 150
R v Secretary of State for the Home Department, ex parte Hosenball [1977] 3 All ER 452 237
R v Secretary of State for the Home Department, ex parte Pierson [1997] UKHL 37, [1998] AC 539 .... 46, 79
R v Secretary of State for the Home Department, ex parte Saadi [2002] UKHL 41, [2002] 4 All ER 785 126
R v Secretary of State for the Home Department, ex parte Simms [1999] UKHL 33, [2000] 2 AC 115 .... 45–46, 79
R v Secretary of State for Transport, ex parte Factortame Ltd [1989] UKHL 1, [1990] 2 AC 85 31
R (Anam) v Secretary of State for the Home Department (No 2) [2012] EWHC 1770 (Admin) 216, 218
R (BB) v Special Immigration Appeals Commission [2012] EWCA Civ 1499 213
R (Clays Lane Housing Cooperative Ltd) v Housing Corp [2004] EWCA Civ 1658 144
R (I) v Secretary of State for the Home Department [2002] EWCA Civ 888, [2003] INLR 196 .... 127, 215–16, 218, 266
R (Kambadzi) v Secretary of State for the Home Department [2011] UKSC 23, [2011] 1 WLR 1299 .... 153, 185–86, 215–16, 218–19, 221
R (Lumba) v Secretary of State for the Home Department [2011] UKSC 12, [2012] 1 AC 245 .... 48, 127, 134, 153, 185–86, 215–19, 221, 266, 299, 306
R (Mahmood) v Secretary of State for the Home Department [2000] EWCA Civ 315, [2001] 1 WLR 840 150
R (Omar Othman) v SIAC [2012] EWHC 2349 214
RB (Algeria) v Secretary of State for the Home Department [2009] UKHL 10, [2010] 2 AC 110 .... 173, 213
Secretary of State for the Home Department v AE [2008] EWHC 585 (Admin) 204
Secretary of State for the Home Department v AF [2008] EWHC 453 (Admin) 204

Secretary of State for the Home Department v AF [2009] UKHL 28, [2010] 2 AC 269 .... 118, 202, 204–07, 213, 289, 293
Secretary of State for the Home Department v AN [2008] EWHC 372 (Admin)....... 204
Secretary of State for the Home Department v AP [2008] EWHC 2001 (*AP, First Instance*) 201
Secretary of State for the Home Department v AP [2010] UKSC 24, [2011] 2 AC 1 .... 201, 214
Secretary of State for the Home Department v CC and CF [2012] EWHC 2837 (Admin) 208
Secretary of State for the Home Department v JJ [2008] 1 AC 385........194, 198–201
Secretary of State for the Home Department v MB [2007] UKHL 46, [2008] 1 AC 440 .... 132, 202–07, 213, 278, 289
Secretary of State for the Home Department v Rehman [2001] UKHL 47, [2003] 1 AC 153 .... 126, 136, 138–42, 151, 159, 167–68, 241, 243, 281, 290–91, 298
Somersett v Stewart (1772) 20 St Tr 1 124
Wheeler v Leicester City Council [1985] UKHL 6, [1985] AC 1054 46

Other Commonwealth Countries

de Freitas v Permanent Secretary of Ministry of Agriculture, Lands and Housing [1998] UKPC 68, [1999] 1 AC 69............ 150, 165–66, 171–72, 294
Matadeen v Pointu [1998] UKPC 9, [1999] 1 AC 98 20
Tan Te Lam v Superintendent of Tai A Chau Detention Centre [1996] UKPC 5, [1997] AC 97 .... 58, 84, 126, 255
Zaoui v Attorney–General [2005] 1 NZLR 577 (NZCA and NZSC)............ 10

United States of America

Clark v Martinez, 543 US 371 (2005) 7
Demore v Kim, 538 US 510 (2003) 8
Korematsu v United States, 323 US 214 (1944) 90
Korematsu v United States, 584 F Supp 1406 (1984)............ 91, 170
Marbury v Madison, 5 US (1 Cranch) 137 (1803) 44
Railway Express Agency Inc v New York, 336 US 106 (1949)......... 158, 174, 210, 214
Shaughnessy v United States, ex rel Mezei, 345 US 206 (1953) ... 6, 9, 69, 78, 97, 179
United States v Carolene Products, 304 US 144 (1938) 228
United States v Shaughnessy, 195 F 2d 964 (2d Cir 1952)............ 69, 97
Zadvydas v Davis, 533 US 678 (2001) 4–10, 12, 15–16, 26, 29, 58, 61, 74, 76–78, 80, 82, 154, 179, 189, 255, 259–60, 264–66, 273–74, 289–90, 296–98, 300–01, 303

TABLE OF LEGISLATION AND CONSTITUTIONAL PROVISIONS

Australia

Australian Citizenship Act 1948 (Cth) ... 41
Australian Citizenship Act 1973 (Cth) ... 41
Australian Security Intelligence Organisation Act 1979 (ASIO Act 1979) ... 109, 115–16
s 4 ... 109–10, 116
s 36 ... 110
Charter of Human Rights and Responsibilities Act 2006 (Vic) ... 38
Communist Party Dissolution Act 1950 (Cth) ... 83
Constitution ... 31, 37, 39–41, 43, 49, 56, 59, 66, 83–84, 88, 226
Ch III ... 43, 51, 72, 75–76, 83–85, 96
s 7 ... 40
s 24 ... 40
s 34 ... 40
s 41 ... 43
s 44(i) ... 40
s 51 ... 40,43
s 51(vi) ... 83
s 51(xix) ... 40–42, 49, 72–76, 86–87
s 51(xxvi) ... 49
s 51(xxvii) ... 40–42
s 51(xxxi) ... 43
s 51(xxxix) ... 83
s 61 ... 83
s 75 ... 106
s 75(v) ... 106
s 80 ... 43
s 92 ... 43
s 109 ... 40
s 116 ... 43
s 117 ... 40, 43
Human Rights Act 2004 (ACT) ... 38
Immigration Restriction Act 1901 (Cth) ... 41–42

Judiciary Act 1903 (Cth)
s 40 66
Magistrates Court Act 1991 (South Australia) 92
Migration Act 1958 (Cth) 37–39, 41, 47, 53, 55–57, 65–67, 71, 73, 78–79, 82, 92, 95, 99, 102, 104–05, 108, 117, 119, 298
Division 4B 47–48, 52–54
s 54P 48, 52–53
s 54Q 48
s 54R 52, 54
Division 4C 55
Part 8C 101
s 31 100
s 46A 105–06, 108
ss 72–73 100
s 88 47–48
s 189 .... 52, 56, 67, 106, 111, 113
s 195A 100, 106, 108
s 196 .... 56, 58, 61, 63, 66–67, 71, 111, 113
s 197A 91
s 197AB 94, 102
s 198 .... 56–58, 61, 67, 71, 73, 81, 113
s 199 .... 56, 61, 67
s 200 .... 56, 61
s 486L–N 102
s 486O 101–02
s 486P 102
Migration Amendment Act 1992 47
Migration Amendment Act (No 4) 1992 (Cth) 48
Migration Amendment (Detention Arrangements) Act 2005 100–02
Migration Amendment (Excision from the Migration Zone) Act 2001 104
Migration Amendment (Unauthorised Maritime Arrivals and Other Measures) Act 2013 104
Migration Reform Act 1992 .... 55, 65
s 13 55
Migration Regulations 1994 (Cth) 100, 105, 109, 116–17
reg 2.20(12) 100
reg 2.20A 100
Sch 2 [Visa] Subclass 070 .... 38, 100

Canada

Canada Evidence Act 1985
s 38 258

Canadian Bill of Rights 1960 233–34
s 1(a) 234
s 2(e) 233–234
Canadian Charter of Rights and Freedoms 17, 32–33, 225–27, 229–34, 237, 240, 242–43, 248, 253, 257–58, 260–61, 263–64, 269, 272–74, 287, 290, 295
s 1 .... 32, 227, 229–32, 234, 236, 240, 242, 252, 257, 259, 270, 274
s 3 226
s 6 .... 227, 229, 233, 235
s 7 .... 32, 227, 230–37, 240–43, 252–57, 259, 261–62, 272, 274, 277–78, 291
s 9 252–53
s 10 .... 252, 273
s 12 .... 252–55, 261–62, 266
s 15 .... 32, 227–30, 235, 252–54, 262–63, 266, 270, 272
s 23 227
s 33 .... 227, 242
Canadian Security Intelligence Service Act 1984(CSIS Act 1984) 235, 258, 277
s 12 277
Citizenship Act RSC 1985 226
Constitution Act 1867 226
s 91(25) 226
s 95 226
Immigration Act 1976 .... 233, 235
Immigration Act 1985 239
s 53(1)(b) 239
Immigration and Refugee Protection Act 2001 (IRPA 2001) 235, 238–39, 244, 249, 251–52, 254, 256, 258, 261, 263, 266–67, 287
Pt 1, Division 9 238
s 77(1) 238
s 78 238
ss 80–81 238
s 82 .... 238, 249, 252
s 83 238
s 84 .... 238, 248, 262–63
s 95 239
s 115 239,244–45
IRPA 2001 as amended 2008 .... 249, 252, 274–75, 279–80, 282
s 79 280
s 82 .... 249, 252
s 83 279
s 85 .... 275, 279

European Union

European Communities Act 1972
s 2 31

United Kingdom

Anti-Terrorism, Crime and Security Act 2001
(ATCSA 2001) 146–47, 152–53, 157, 180–81, 190, 202, 213, 266
Pt 4 .... 146–47, 154, 157, 161, 163–64, 166, 168, 172, 177, 180–82, 185–86, 188, 193–95, 197–99, 202, 204, 210–11, 214
s 21 146
s 22 .... 146, 175
s 23 .... 146, 148, 167, 179, 266, 268
ss 25–26 147
s 30 .... 147–48, 166, 168–69
British Nationality Act 1981
s 40 212–13
Habeas Corpus Act 1640 44
Habeas Corpus Act 1679 44
Habeas Corpus Act 1816 44
Human Rights Act 1998 (HRA 1998) 31–32, 124–26, 137–40, 146–48, 155, 168–69, 176, 181–82, 200, 293
s 1 .... 31, 137, 148
s 2 .... 137, 206, 293
s 3 .... 31–32, 137, 203, 207
s 4 .... 31–32, 137, 179–82, 207
s 6 137
s 7 180
s 8 180
s 10 .... 32, 181
s 14 147–48
Immigration Act 1971 .... 128, 146, 212, 214–15, 219, 266
Sch 2, para 22(1) 213
Immigration, Asylum and Nationality Act 2006
s 56 212
Justice and Security Act 2013 207
Nationality Immigration and Asylum Act 2002
s 4(1) 212
Prevention of Terrorism Act 2005 (POTA 2005) 181, 185, 193–94, 196–97, 202–03, 208, 211, 214, 221
s 1 193
s 2 195

s 3 195
s 9 198
s 13 196
s 14 195
s 15 195
s 16 186
Sch 1 195
para 4(3) 203
Special Immigration Appeals Commission Act 1997 (SIAC Act 1997) 135, 137–39
s 3 213
s 4 .....138, 139
s 6 136
s 7 .....136, 138, 147
Sch 1
Art 1 136
Art 5 136
Sch 3 213
Terrorism Act 2000 .....151, 193
Terrorism Prevention and Investigation Measures Act 2011 (TPIM Act 2011) 193, 207–09, 211, 213–14, 220–21, 304
s 1 208
s 5 208
s 20 195
Sch 1 208
Sch 5 208

Statutory Instruments

Human Rights Act 1998 (Designated Derogation) Order 2001, SI 2001/3644 (Derogation Order) 146–147, 164, 167, 179
Rules of Court
r 76.29(8) 203
Special Immigration Appeals Commission (Procedure) Rules 2003, SI 2003/1034 (SIACR 2003) 136
r 36 136
r 47 136

United States of America

Constitution 4–10, 265
Fifth Amendment 5, 8, 77
Immigration and Nationality Act 8 USC §1101 *et seq* 8 USC §1231(a)(6) 4

TABLE OF CONVENTIONS, TREATIES ETC

Convention for the Protection of Human Rights and Fundamental Freedoms 1950 (ECHR) 31, 63, 123, 125, 128–32, 137, 139, 142, 145–48, 152, 155, 158, 160, 170, 174, 178, 180–82, 184, 186, 191–94, 203, 205, 213, 268, 291, 293

- Art 3 .... 123, 130–32, 134, 140, 146, 161, 186, 191–93, 212, 268
- Art 5 .... 31, 63, 137, 152, 154, 164, 179, 182, 187, 191, 194, 196, 199–01
- Art 5(1) 123, 125, 129, 132–34, 146–48, 156, 163, 186, 188, 190–92, 200
- Art 5(1)(c) 133
- Art 5(1)(f) 31, 125, 132–34, 145, 148, 152–53, 164, 180, 186–93, 268
- Art 5(4) 134–35, 186, 192, 204–05
- Art 6 .... 137, 199, 203, 205, 213
- Art 6(1) 199, 204
- Art 8 .... 23, 131, 201
- Art 8(1) 201
- Art 8(2) 131
- Arts 8–11 131
- Art 13 .... 129, 131–32, 134–35, 186
- Art 14 .... 31, 123, 151–52, 154–55, 157, 164, 173–74, 179, 182, 184, 186, 188
- Art 15 .... 142, 144, 147–49, 155–56, 164–65, 169, 171, 178, 182, 184, 186, 293
- Art 15(1) 142, 148, 164
- Art 15(2) 146
- Art 46 31
- Protocol 11 129

Convention on the Rights of the Child 1989 87

Convention relating to the Status of Refugees 1951 (Refugee Convention) 47, 87, 97, 108–09, 178, 233

- Art 1A(2) 233
- Protocol relating to the Status of Refugees 1967 .... 47, 97, 108, 233

Convention on the Status of Stateless Persons 1954 178

Convention against Torture and Other Cruel, Inhuman or Degrading Treatment 1984 .... 242, 255, 295

- Art 3 .... 240, 242

Geneva Conventions 177

International Convention on the Elimination of All Forms of Racial Discrimination 1965 177

Art 8 ... 177
International Covenant on Civil and Political Rights 1966
(ICCPR) ... 62, 87, 133, 178
Art 2 ... 178
Art 4 ... 178
Art 9 ... 62–63, 87, 133
Art 26 ... 178
UNCERD General Recommendation 30 on Discrimination Against
Non-Citizens ... 255
UN Declaration on the Human Rights of Nationals Who are Not Nationals
of the Country in which They Live 1985 ... 178

Introduction

1

Introduction

The claim to equality before the law is in a substantial sense the most fundamental of the rights of man.

Hersch Lauterpacht, *An International Bill of the Rights of Man* (1945)[1]

'The power to admit, exclude and expel aliens was among the earliest and most widely recognized powers of the sovereign state', and the power remains 'undoubted'. But unless [it] is understood to be a constitutional principle, or the instrument of constitutional principle, the power will crumble, eroded by newly enforceable constitutional principles of equality before the law, and by rights as ancient as liberty (immunity from coercion or imprisonment) . . .

John Finnis, *Law Quarterly Review* (2007)[2]

1.1 Introduction

The executive issues a removal order against a non-citizen, who is then detained pending removal. But that person cannot be removed. There may be a legal restriction on his or her return to the country of nationality, or there may be no other country prepared to accept him or her. What then? Is detention still authorised? In this book I consider judicial responses to this question in Australia, the United Kingdom and Canada, and the legal implications and reverberations of those responses.

The key judicial decisions discussed and analysed in this book postdate 11 September 2001. They have exposed a deep divergence of opinion between final courts of appeal which share a common legal heritage, particularly on issues of liberty and equality as fundamental as those considered here. My purpose is to analyse these cases in terms of both judicial method and the underlying legal principles relied upon by the courts. My central argument is that at heart the decisions

[1] *A v Secretary of State for the Home Department* [2004] UKHL 56, [2005] 2 AC 68 (*Belmarsh*) [45] (Lord Bingham), citing Hersch Lauterpacht, *An International Bill of the Rights of Man* (New York, Columbia University Press, 1945).

[2] John Finnis, 'Nationality, Alienage and Constitutional Principle' (2007) 123 *LQR* 417, 417 (footnotes omitted).

in these cases turned on judicial views on a set of issues concerning the scope of the liberty interest in democratic societies.

The issues traversed in the cases have achieved currency and gained urgency in the period since 11 September 2001. The judicial divergences that have emerged between the national courts in this period appear stark when examined in the context of a legal family that has been accustomed to sharing a great deal.[3] But there is little that is new or unique about the current dilemmas Commonwealth courts are facing in this field. The issues with which the courts are grappling concern older, and persisting, questions about the nature and place of the rights of non-citizens within our societies. I start, therefore, with an examination of a case which predated, by just a few months, the events of 11 September 2001. The case, *Zadvydas*,[4] was a judgment of a common law final court of appeal outside the Commonwealth, namely the United States Supreme Court. But the reasoning in the *Zadvydas* judgments, of both the majority and minority, clearly exposes the fault lines of a jurisprudential conflict subsequently ventilated, in very different ways, in the three Commonwealth final courts of appeal. The decision serves as a point of reference in those Commonwealth decisions.

In *Zadvydas*, the United States Supreme Court consolidated two cases of detention, concerning Mr Zadvydas and Mr Kim Ho Ma, for argument and decision. At issue before the United States Supreme Court was the question whether authorisation to detain beyond a statutory 90-day 'removal period' was subject to an implied limitation that the detention be no longer than reasonably necessary to effect removal to another country.[5] The relevant statutory provision read:

> An alien ordered removed who is inadmissible under section 1182 of this title, removable under section[s] . . . or who has been determined by the Attorney-General to be a risk to the community or unlikely to comply with the order for removal, may be detained beyond the removal period and, if released, shall be subject to the terms of supervision in paragraph (3).[6]

Mr Zadvydas, of alleged Lithuanian parentage, came to the United States in 1948, aged 8, from a displaced persons camp in Germany. He had a substantial criminal record. In 1994 the Immigration and Naturalization Service (INS) ordered his deportation to Germany. Germany refused to accept him as a non-German national. Lithuania denied his application for Lithuanian citizenship. The Fifth Circuit had held that Mr Zadvydas's detention 'did not violate the Constitution because his eventual deportation was not "impossible", good-faith efforts to remove him from the United States continued, and his detention was subject to periodic administrative review'.[7]

[3] Canada is a mixed jurisdiction, with Quebec a civil law jurisdiction. The Scottish legal system combines common and civil law elements.

[4] *Zadvydas v Davis*, 533 US 678 (2001).

[5] ibid, 706.

[6] Immigration and Nationality Act, 8 USC §1231(a)(6).

[7] *Zadvydas* (n 4) 685.

Mr Kim Ho Ma was born in Cambodia in 1977, and came to the United States aged 7 from refugee camps in Thailand and the Philippines. Following a conviction for manslaughter he was sentenced to 38 months' imprisonment, and released into immigration custody after serving two years. A Federal District Court determined that there was no 'realistic chance' that Cambodia would accept Mr Ma. The Ninth Circuit had concluded that the statute did not authorise detention for more than a 'reasonable time' beyond the 90-day statutory removal period. It had further held that what amounted to a 'reasonable time' was to be determined with reference to the statute's purpose of facilitating removal. The government appealed Mr Ma's case to the Supreme Court.

The Court split 5:4 on the question of whether the statute authorised indefinite detention pending removal. Breyer J delivered the Opinion of the Court.[8] Kennedy J and Scalia J each delivered a dissenting judgment.[9] The *Zadvydas* judgments chart divergent understandings of the liberty interests of non-citizens and of the nature of the immigration power.

Breyer J, writing the Opinion of the Court, anchored his reasons in the Due Process Clause of the Fifth Amendment, which provides in part: 'No person shall . . . be deprived of . . . liberty . . . without due process of law.' He reasoned that to interpret the statute to allow indefinite detention would 'raise a serious constitutional problem'.[10] Accordingly, 'interpreting the statute to avoid a serious constitutional threat, we conclude that, once removal is no longer reasonably foreseeable, continued detention is no longer authorized by statute'.[11]

Breyer J's starting premise was that government detention violates the Due Process Clause unless it is ordered in a criminal proceeding with adequate procedural protections, or there is a special justification that outweighs the constitutionally protected interest in freedom from physical restraint.[12] The only such justification for detention appropriately confined to non-citizens is 'ensuring the appearance of aliens at future immigration proceedings'.[13] This justification is often referred to in the *Zadvydas* judgments by the shorthand of 'flight risk'.

Breyer J also addressed the government's argument that there was a second 'special justification', distinct from and independent of the objective of facilitating removal, for indefinite detention measures confined to non-citizens – 'preventing danger to the community',[14] or 'the dangerousness rationale'.[15] He acknowledged that dangerousness might serve as a rationale for indefinite administrative detention, of both citizens and non-citizens, but only in special circumstances, and those special circumstances were not present in *Zadvydas.* Critically, the Court held that the special circumstances required to establish the

[8] Stevens, O'Connor, Souter and Ginsburg JJ joined the Opinion of the Court delivered by Breyer J.
[9] Thomas J joined Scalia J's judgment. Rehnquist CJ joined Kennedy J's judgment.
[10] *Zadvydas* (n 4) 699.
[11] ibid.
[12] ibid, 690.
[13] ibid.
[14] ibid.
[15] ibid, 691.

dangerousness rationale were not made out simply because the detainee was a dangerous non-citizen subject to removal.

The Court held that a dangerousness rationale for detention is only applicable where a statute is confined to an especially dangerous class, and that was not the case here. Further, where the detention is potentially indefinite, there are additional requirements. The dangerousness rationale only justifies indefinite detention if there is 'some other special circumstance . . . that helps to create the danger'.[16] The Court and dissents disagreed on whether alienage amounts to a 'special circumstance' sufficient to justify indefinite detention on 'dangerousness' grounds. The Court stated that it does not. An alien detainee's removable status 'bears no relation to a detainee's dangerousness'.[17] The Court held that alienage, or an alien's vulnerability to removal, does not supply an additional factor sufficient to establish the dangerousness rationale for indefinite detention.

Breyer J also addressed a third, distinct government argument that 'alien status itself can justify indefinite detention'.[18] This argument was derived from *Shaughnessy v Mezei*,[19] a 1953 case in which Mr Mezei, a non-citizen seeking return to the United States where he had lived for 25 years, was denied entry, and detained for years pending ultimately unsuccessful attempts at removal. Breyer J distinguished *Shaughnessy* on the basis that the detainees in the present case had effected entry into the United States. They were not subject to the 'no-entry' fiction operative in *Shaughnessy*. The detainees' legally acknowledged presence effected a change in their legal position sufficient to distinguish *Shaughnessy*.[20]

In the result, the Court interpreted the statute to authorise detention only for as long as removal was reasonably foreseeable.[21] This reading flowed from the Court's understanding of the statute's 'basic' purpose as being to 'assur[e] the alien's presence at the moment of removal'.[22] The immigration statute only per-

[16] ibid, 691.

[17] ibid, 691–92.

[18] ibid, 692.

[19] *Shaughnessy v United States; ex rel Mezei*, 345 US 206 (1953). Mr Ignatz Mezei was the husband of a United States citizen and had resided in the United States for 25 years. He returned to visit his mother in Romania, spending time in Hungary. On his return to the United States, the Attorney-General ordered that Mr Mezei be excluded without a hearing, based on confidential information. He tried repeatedly to leave the United States, but because no country would take him he remained in detention in the New York City Harbour. For subsequent historical evidence indicating that the Attorney-General's suspicions about Mr Mezei were misguided, and based on what was suspected to be weak and questionable evidence at the time, see Charles D Weisselberg, 'The Exclusion and Detention of Aliens: Lessons from the Lives of Ellen Knauff and Ignatz Mezei' (1995) 143 *University of Pennsylvania Law Review* 933.

[20] The Court's acceptance of a distinction between the liberty interest of those who have lawfully entered the United States and those who have entered unlawfully is criticised in Scalia's dissent. For further criticism of this point from a different perspective see T Alexander Aleinikoff, 'Detaining Plenary Power: The Meaning and Impact of *Zadvydas v Davis*' (2002) 16 *Georgetown Immigration Law Journal* 365, 366, 373–78; Linda Bosniak, 'A Basic Territorial Distinction' (2002) 16 *Georgetown Immigration Law Journal* 407.

[21] *Zadvydas* (n 4) 699.

[22] ibid.

mitted detention to that end.[23] To hold otherwise would be to treat the 'alien's removable status' as determinative of liberty rights.[24]

Kennedy J, in dissent, held that to interpret the statute as contended for by the Court 'defeats the statutory purpose and design'.[25] He held that the statutory text was intractable, and so the Court was not at liberty to choose between a constitutionally questionable and a constitutionally acceptable interpretation. His disagreement with the Court centred on his response to the argument for dangerousness as a rationale for the indefinite detention of non-citizens.

For Kennedy J, protection of the community is a freestanding justification for the indefinite detention of non-citizens: 'The authority to detain beyond the removal period is to protect the community, not to negotiate the aliens' return.'[26] Outlining a dangerousness rationale for the indefinite detention of non-citizens, Kennedy J stated: 'The risk to the community exists whether or not the repatriation negotiations have some end in sight; in fact, when the negotiations end, the risk may be greater.'[27] His rationale for indefinite immigration detention was grounded in his characterisation of the immigration power: 'the motivation to protect the citizenry from aliens determined to be dangerous is central to the immigration power itself.'[28]

Kennedy J's position distinguished between the detention of dangerous non-citizens and equally dangerous citizens. He provided reasons for a lack of equivalence between the two classes. He noted that non-citizens in immigration custody may well have '[u]nderworld and terrorist links' that are 'overseas, beyond our jurisdiction to impose felony charges'.[29] He also emphasised the United States' vulnerability to 'hostile' overseas interests making 'strategic' use of their nationals. He portrayed judicially mandated release based on the prospects of removal as playing into the hands of such interests, enabling them to 'force dangerous aliens upon us' by refusing their return.[30]

But at base, Kennedy J held that the reason for distinguishing between citizens and aliens was that 'a removable alien does not have the same liberty interest as a citizen does'.[31] He stated: 'The Court cannot bring itself to adopt this established proposition.'[32] More accurately, Kennedy J and the Court were in fundamental disagreement as to the nature of the 'established proposition' Kennedy J referred to. The Court agreed that a non-citizen is vulnerable to removal in a way a citizen is not, and may have his or her liberty limited to facilitate removal. Yet it did not

[23] ibid, 697. Aff'd *Clark v Martinez*, 543 US 371 (2005), 378, 386.
[24] *Zadvydas* (n 4) 691–92.
[25] ibid, 707.
[26] ibid, 708.
[27] ibid. See also 709.
[28] ibid, 713.
[29] ibid, 714.
[30] ibid, 711–12.
[31] ibid, 717.
[32] ibid.

consider that 'removable status' in and of itself, absent a reasonably foreseeable prospect of removal, sufficed to authorise detention of non-citizens.[33]

Kennedy J objected to the Court's view that authority to detain might turn on a judicial review of the viability of removal. He held that the Court's interpretation 'causes systemic dislocation in the balance of powers', raising serious concerns about 'the Court's own view of its proper authority'.[34] The courts should not intrude into 'sensitive negotiations with foreign powers'.[35] In a phrase that surfaced in subsequent Commonwealth judgments, Kennedy J indicted judicial evaluation of the prospects of removal as putting 'foreign relations . . . into judicially supervised receivership'.[36] Removal negotiations were characterised as a matter of delicate foreign relations in which the courts have no business getting involved.

Kennedy J did not deny that the Due Process Clause has a bearing on the legality of immigration detention. As 'persons within our jurisdiction', Mr Zadvydas and Mr Ma were entitled to its protections.[37] Kennedy J held that the Due Process Clause precludes 'arbitrary or capricious' detention.[38] By this, Kennedy J meant that such 'detention cannot be justified as punishment nor can the confinement or its conditions be designed in order to punish'.[39] '[A]rbitrary and capricious' detention can be avoided by procedural means. Kennedy J held that the necessary protections were supplied by the procedures used to determine 'removable status' and the internal administrative procedures for review of detention. He did, however, leave open the possibility that the constitutional protection against 'arbitrary and capricious' detention might mean that the adequacy of procedures and judicial safeguards for establishing that detention is justified could be tested by a habeas court.[40]

In summary, Kennedy J saw dangerousness as a freestanding rationale for an indefinite detention regime confined to non-citizens, independent of a justification for government detention based on 'effectuating an alien's removal'.[41] He portrayed the dangerousness rationale as provided for by statute and unaffected by constitutional considerations. Further, he characterised the likelihood of removal as a matter for executive evaluation. In his view, judicial review of the prospects of removal went beyond the Court's 'proper authority'.[42]

Scalia J agreed with Kennedy J's interpretation of the statute but took a more radical position on the possibility of court-ordered release. Scalia J held that there

[33] The categories of non-citizens who could be detained under the relevant statutory provision extended well beyond the dangerous. Kennedy J addressed his judgment to the cases of Mr Zadvydas and Mr Ma before the Court: see *Zadvydas* (n 4) 725.

[34] ibid, 705.

[35] ibid.

[36] ibid, 712, 725. See *Al-Kateb v Godwin* [2004] HCA 37, (2004) 219 CLR 562, [285] (Callinan J).

[37] *Zadvydas* (n 4) 718.

[38] ibid, 721.

[39] ibid.

[40] This was left open in *Zadvydas* (n 4) 724–25. And see *Demore v Kim*, 538 US 510 (2003), 532–33 (Kennedy J).

[41] *Zadvydas* (n 4) 697 (Opinion of the Court).

[42] ibid, 705.

are no situations in which the courts can order the release of a non-citizen pending removal. Where authorisation to be in the United States ends, so does any constitutional right to liberty.

> [The] claim can be repackaged as freedom from 'physical restraint' or freedom from 'indefinite detention,' . . . but it is at bottom a claimed right of release into this country by an individual who concededly has no legal right to be here. There is no such constitutional right.[43]

He held that the binary of authorised/unauthorised is determinative of a non-citizen's liberty. The absence of a 'legal right to be here' is conclusive. Contrary to the Court, in dissent Scalia J reasoned that there is no difference between the situation of the inadmissible alien 'stopped at the border' in *Shaughnessy*,[44] and an alien subject to a final order of removal. Neither has any right of release into the country.[45]

To summarise, the Court's interpretation of the statutory power to detain pending removal was driven by constitutional concerns about indefinite, non-punitive detention grounded in a dangerousness rationale. The Court held that authority to detain is defined and limited by the purpose of facilitating removal. The Court provides for release on conditions and return to custody where those conditions are violated.[46] For Kennedy J, the Constitution mandates procedural review, which is afforded by existing internal administrative processes. Scalia J viewed judicially mandated release as conclusively precluded by the fact that the aliens in question had no right to be in the United States.

Before leaving *Zadvydas*, I note one troubling legacy of the Opinion of the Court, namely the Court's provisional allowance for a 'terrorism exception' to its reasoning. The Court stated that it did not 'consider terrorism or other special circumstances where special arguments might be made for forms of preventive detention and for heightened deference to the judgments of the political branches with respect to matters of national security'.[47] The Court's caveat raised the question whether, when pressed, the courts would expand their understanding of the purposes of immigration detention, such that a foreign terrorist suspect would be held in immigration detention despite the absence of any real prospect of removal in the reasonably foreseeable future.

Kennedy J criticised the Court for the incoherence the terrorism exception introduced into its analysis. He reasoned that the Court's terrorism exception appeared to base authority to detain on an assessment of risk, independent of any consideration of the prospects of removal. But such an exercise was exactly what was precluded by the Court's reasoning.[48] 'The Court ought not to reject a

[43] ibid, 702–03.

[44] *Shaughnessy v Mezei* (n 19). To speak of Mr Mezei as 'stopped at the border' is to invoke the US 'entry fiction'.

[45] *Zadvydas* (n 4) 703.

[46] ibid, 699–700.

[47] ibid, 696.

[48] ibid, 714–15. See also Aleinikoff (n 20) 378–79.

rationale in order to deny power to the Attorney General and then invoke the same rationale to save its own analysis.'[49] I agree with Kennedy J's criticism of the Court on this point. He squarely raised a question that is central to the subsequent Commonwealth jurisprudence on indefinite detention. To what extent do national security concerns license the expansion of an 'immigration' rationale for detention? The central tenet of my argument, based on a critical analysis of the case law, is that, contra Kennedy J, there is no justifiable basis for a 'terrorism exception' of the form suggested by the Court.

This book centres on how the highest appellate courts in Australia, the United Kingdom and Canada have responded to government claims to possess a power to detain non-citizens indefinitely. In these countries (and others),[50] the issue of the legality of the indefinite detention of non-citizens has generated some of the key public law decisions of the last decade. *Al-Kateb*, the *Belmarsh* decision and *Charkaoui* continue to be central to discussions about public law and rights in these jurisdictions.[51] Their legal significance and consequences extend well beyond the subject matter of indefinite detention pending removal.

These decisions outline a continuum of legal positions on the legality of the indefinite detention of non-citizens. The High Court of Australia upheld the indefinite detention of any non-citizen subject to a removal order.[52] The United Kingdom House of Lords held that indefinite detention pending removal was incompatible with enacted rights.[53] The Supreme Court of Canada subjected indefinite detention to procedural constraints, without condemning it as an unlawful violation of a non-citizen's rights.[54]

The decisions starkly evidence the tension between a right to liberty, coupled with a principle of equality before the law, and a commitment to the differential treatment of citizens and non-citizens that is central to border control. The decisions are polarising in their effect. Government claims to legal authority to indefinitely detain non-citizens in the jurisdiction without lawful authority, and more so judicial rulings upholding those claims, have been registered with shock. The High Court of Australia's *Al-Kateb* decision was and is the most dramatic manifestation of this. Its prominence as a spectacular failure of rights protection appears undiminished as the years go by.[55] The shock goes not simply to the sense

[49] *Zadvydas* (n 4) 715.

[50] For another example within the Commonwealth see *Zaoui v Attorney-General* [2005] 1 NZLR 577 (NZCA and NZSC).

[51] *Al-Kateb* (n 36); *Belmarsh* (n 1). Belmarsh is the name of the prison where the detainees were held. *Charkaoui v Canada (Minister of Citizenship and Immigration)* 2007 SCC 9, [2007] 1 SCR 350.

[52] *Al-Kateb* (n 36). Some statutory regimes, such as the Australian Migration Act 1958, distinguish between 'removal' and 'deportation' provisions. This distinction is not relevant to my argument, and throughout the book the terms are used interchangeably.

[53] *Belmarsh* (n 1).

[54] *Charkaoui* (n 51).

[55] See, for example, the prominence and frequency of references to the *Al-Kateb* decision in arguments for a bill of rights, particularly in the context of the Australian National Human Rights Consultation held in 2009: see National Human Rights Consultation Committee, *Report on the Consultation into Human Rights in Australia* (September 2009), 267–69. See also, eg, Caroline Henkels, 'Mandatory Detention of Asylum Seekers in Australia: Would a Bill of Rights Make a Difference?'

that a long-hallowed civil right – the right to personal liberty – has been effaced. There is a sense that something not easily reducible to any isolated right, a conception of human dignity or humanity, affirmed in the idea that those subject to the law should be entitled to its protection, has been undermined. A similar assessment of the incompatibility of indefinite detention pending removal with fundamental justice is conveyed in the stature and constitutional significance the *Belmarsh* decision has attained.[56]

An opposing evaluation is offered by those who see the viability of immigration control, and beyond that the modern liberal democratic state, undermined by successful legal challenges to the indefinite detention of non-citizens.[57] The legal authority of the government to accord different, and more attenuated, rights protections to non-citizens, to the extent contemplated in the measures under challenge, is seen as integral to border control and the constitution and proper functioning of the community. This concern with border control may draw on a deeper affirmation of the importance of a distinction between citizen and non-citizen.[58]

In each of the jurisdictions studied, I argue for the availability and desirability of an interpretation of the legal materials that precludes the indefinite detention of non-citizens. Detention is lawful if it is proportionate to the infringement of the detainee's liberty interest, as judged against the purpose of facilitating the non-citizen's removal.[59] Indefinite detention fails this proportionality test and as such is an unlawful infringement of a non-citizen's rights. The law of Australia and Canada, as well as the United Kingdom, had and has ample legal resources to support a ruling that indefinite detention is unlawful. Such a ruling on indefinite detention best serves the idea of law as an effective limit on power. Immigration powers to admit, exclude and expel non-citizens can, and do, persist in jurisdictions that firmly reject indefinite detention. What is needed is better integration of these immigration powers with the rights of non-citizens, not the denial of meaningful rights to non-citizens.

If the law of Australia, Canada and the United Kingdom support a judgment that indefinite detention is unlawful, the question arises as to why this assessment has not prevailed in every jurisdiction. The full particulars of the answer lie in numerous legal debates within each jurisdiction, the subject matter of this book. But underlying these particulars, the answer lies in deep-seated assumptions

(2006) 4 *Human Rights Research Journal* 1; Alice Rolls, 'Avoiding Tragedy: Would the Decision of the High Court in *Al-Kateb* have been Any Different if Australia had a Bill of Rights like Victoria?' (2007) 18 *Public Law Review* 119; Janina Boughey, 'The Use of Administrative Law to Enforce Human Rights' (2009) 17 *Australian Journal of Administrative Law* 25; Hon Michael McHugh AC, 'A Human Rights Act, the Courts and the Constitution' (2009) 11 *Constitutional Law and Policy Review* 86; Dan Meagher, 'The Significance of *Al-Kateb v Godwin* for the Australian Bill of Rights Debate' (2010) *Constitutional Law and Policy Review* 15.

[56] See ch 5, s 5.1 and ch 6, s 6.7.

[57] Finnis (n 2), discussed in ss 1.4 and 1.5 below.

[58] ibid.

[59] A 'broad-brush' concept of proportionality is employed here. It is sketched in s 1.3 below.

about the legal significance of a person not being a citizen. These assumptions shape judicial reasoning in the central case studies and throughout the relevant jurisprudence. I argue that what grounds the divergences in legal reasoning within each jurisdiction is the 'intellectual frame of mind with which we approach constitutional questions regarding regulation of aliens'.[60] A judge's understanding of citizenship, or more particularly the legal position of non-citizens, serves as the 'intellectual filter'[61] through which arguments about the legality of non-citizens' detention are run, rendering the government arguments for indefinite administrative detention deeply disturbing to some judges' conception of the rule of law, and untroubling to others.

This chapter provides the foundation for the subsequent legal discussion and analysis in chapters two to nine. An initial aspect of this groundwork is a discussion in section 1.2 of the shared principles that inform the legal analysis in each jurisdiction. Two opposing judicial positions that define the fault lines of the debate on the legality of indefinite detention are outlined in section 1.3. Sections 1.4 and 1.5 consider a developed, and influential, attempt to justify a stark hierarchy of liberty rights between citizens and non-citizens, namely that offered by John Finnis in a 2007 article in the *Law Quarterly Review*.[62] Section 1.6 explains my choice of jurisdictions and outlines some of the basic differences between them. Section 1.7 provides the plan of the book.

1.2 Shared Principles

The law in Australia, the United Kingdom and Canada recognises principles of liberty and equal protection of the law. I argue that indefinite detention pending removal is incompatible with these constitutional principles. Detention in the absence of criminal conviction, and disproportionate to a legitimate non-punitive purpose, infringes the liberty rights of non-citizens.

The starting point is a general prohibition on administrative detention, and in particular long-term or indefinite administrative detention. Any exception to this general prohibition calls for special justification, as required by the Court in *Zadvydas*. Turning to thc particulars of immigration detention, the starting premise is that a non-citizen subject to a removal order retains a right to liberty. A non-citizen's liberty right is not conclusively revoked by the issuance of a removal order. It is, however, qualified in a way that a citizen's right to liberty is not. In Australia, the United Kingdom and Canada, the courts have held that non-citizens' rights to liberty and equal protection of the law are respectively qualified

[60] T Alexander Aleinikoff, 'Citizens, Aliens, Membership and the Constitution' (1990) 7 *Constitutional Commentary* 9, 25–26 fn 62. For the purposes of discussion, 'alien' is synonymous with 'non-citizen'.

[61] ibid, 25–26 fn 62.

[62] Finnis (n 2).

and shaped by non-citizens' vulnerability to removal. 'While an alien who is actually within this country enjoys the protection of our law, his or her status, rights and immunities under that law differ from the status, rights and immunities of a . . . citizen in a variety of important respects.'[63] The most important respect in which an alien's 'status, rights and immunities' diverge from those of a citizen is 'the vulnerability of the alien to exclusion or deportation'.[64] Corresponding to this vulnerability on the part of a non-citizen is a government power of deportation. Ordinarily, a non-citizen against whom a valid deportation decision is issued can be legally removed from the jurisdiction, the usual destination being his or her country of citizenship. Primarily, the cases analysed in this book address circumstances in which there is a legal, or practical, impediment to removal, leading to indefinite detention. Judicial attempts to integrate a non-citizen's vulnerability to removal with the principle of equal protection of the law generate the jurisprudence under discussion.

I argue that detention measures confined to non-citizens pending removal are only legitimate to the extent that they are proportionate to the goal of facilitating removal. As Wilsher has identified, in order for proportionality analysis to enter the picture, value judgments have to be made about the legitimate purposes of immigration detention.[65] Key considerations here are one's conception of equality of persons and its application to non-citizens. The area of controversy is not whether governments are allowed to discriminate between citizens and non-citizens 'unfairly'. No one claims that they are. What is in dispute is what amounts to 'unfair' discrimination. The difference between the judgments on this question, namely what amounts to 'unfair' discrimination, is dependent on how the government purpose of immigration control is understood and, more particularly, its relation with constitutional principles of liberty. Judges who give sanction to indefinite detention pending removal reason that immigration purposes justify such detention. I argue that the putative immigration purposes that sustain detention without prospect of removal both negate any meaningful liberty interest on the part of the non-citizen and radicalise the distinction between the liberty rights of citizens and non-citizens, in a direct challenge to the concept of equality before the law.

By way of contrast, detention for the purpose of facilitating removal can be rendered compatible with the continuing subsistence of the detainee's liberty right. This compatibility is ensured by way of proportionality analysis. I have adopted a relatively 'pared back' concept of proportionality in this book, requiring that detention be 'reasonably necessary' to achieve that purpose. This captures the basic link between proportionality and fundamental rights,[66] and accommodates

[63] *Chu Kheng Lim v Minister of Immigration, Local Government and Ethnic Affairs* [1992] HCA 64, (1992) 176 CLR 1, [26] (Brennan, Deane and Dawson JJ).

[64] ibid.

[65] Daniel Wilsher, *Immigration Detention: Law, History, Politics* (Cambridge, Cambridge University Press, 2012) 335. Wilsher talks of '*reasonable* goals' rather than legitimate purposes.

[66] On proportionality as the logical corollary of the recognition of fundamental rights see Paul Craig, *Administrative Law*, 7th edn (London, Sweet & Maxwell, 2012) para 21-017.

the case law from the United Kingdom, Canada and Australia.[67] This test, while 'broad-brush', is sufficient to delineate the primary differences in judicial approach to indefinite detention pending removal. In adopting this minimalist conception of proportionality, directed to the permissible duration of detention, I do not mean to suggest that it is adequate to ensure the legality of detention pending removal.[68] Nor do I disagree that the concept of proportionality is inevitably shaped by matters of local context – namely text, doctrine, the vagaries of the cases in which its form is hammered out, and the prevalent legal and political culture.[69]

A commitment to equality exerts pressure on the legal analysis at two points. It informs the identification of the permissible purposes of immigration detention, as introduced above, and it underpins the proportionality analysis. Stated baldly, equality of treatment requires that differences in treatment be sufficiently clearly related to legitimate government purposes.[70] That is, there must be an adequate connection between a legitimate purpose and the class of persons affected. The adequacy of this connection is tested by means of a proportionality analysis. To frame the issue in rule of law terms, a commitment to the rule of law entails, at a minimum, that the government cannot discriminate unfairly between persons 'by selective application of general principles it claims to honour'.[71] In this book, I show how the judgments that give legal sanction to indefinite detention pending removal are characterised by the selective application of general legal principles.

In the cases discussed, judges take a position on a continuum. At one end of the continuum are those who hold indefinite detention of non-citizens to be unjustifiably discriminatory. They hold that legitimate immigration purposes do not authorise indefinite detention, which accordingly amounts to arbitrary and discriminatory treatment of non-citizens. At the other pole are judges who sanction indefinite detention as an unproblematic instance of non-citizens' 'exceptional' vulnerability to removal.

In the following section, I provide an initial outline of two competing judicial responses to the indefinite administrative detention of non-citizens. Throughout

[67] More particularly, this broad-brush account of proportionality accommodates Australia, where the relevant constitutional test of proportionality is whether a measure is 'reasonably capable of being seen as necessary' to immigration processing or removal: see further ch 2, pp 50–52. In Australia (and Canada) proportionality is usually discussed in the constitutional context, as opposed to an administrative law setting. See eg Susan Kiefel, 'Proportionality: A Rule of Reason' (2012) 23 *Public Law Review* 85 (with reference to Australia).

[68] In particular, I do not directly address the proportionality of the initial decision to detain. It is considered indirectly, by reason of its relationship to the proportionality of the time spent in detention. Indefinite detention will be harder to sustain where a person is detained 'regardless of personal circumstances, regardless of whether he or she is a danger to the [national] community, and regardless of whether he or she might abscond': *Al-Kateb* (n 36) [29] (Gleeson CJ). For an application of proportionality to immigration detention in its entirety see Wilsher (n 65) ch 7.

[69] See eg Claudia Geiringer, 'Sources of Resistance to Proportionality Review of Administrative Power under the New Zealand Bill of Rights Act 1990' (2013) 11 *New Zealand Journal of Public and International Law* 123.

[70] TRS Allan, *Constitutional Justice: A Liberal Theory of the Rule of Law* (Oxford, Oxford University Press, 2001) 3.

[71] ibid, 2.

the book, I analyse the jurisprudence on indefinite administrative detention of non-citizens with reference to these two responses.

1.3 Two Judicial Responses to Indefinite Detention of Non-Citizens

The case studies I consider are, for the most part, instances of detention of non-citizens subject to a removal order.[72] I am centrally concerned with *direct* challenges to claims of legal authority to detain non-citizens indefinitely – that is, challenges to the power to detain in the circumstances as opposed to challenges to the deportation decision on which detention is predicated. To the extent that I address the scope of the power to deport, I do so to consider its implications for authority to detain.

In these cases, judges responded to indefinite detention pending removal in one of two ways. All judges held that authority to detain was based, at least in part, on the premise that it facilitated deportation. However, they differed on what amounted to a sufficient connection between detention and deportation. Judges who ruled against the legality of indefinite detention adopt a variant of the proposition that only a real prospect of removal in the reasonably foreseeable future justifies detention of a non-citizen subject to a removal order. They held that the relevant statutory provisions did not authorise indefinite detention, or that they did, but were therefore incompatible with enacted rights. Conversely, judges who upheld a statutory power of indefinite duration reasoned that the *possibility* of removal sufficed to justify immigration detention.

The first type of judicial response, illustrated by the Opinion of the Court in *Zadvydas*, holds that indefinite administrative detention of non-citizens is not sufficiently connected to the legitimate government purpose of facilitating removal. This type of judicial response implements what I call a 'rights-protecting' model of immigration detention, where the right protected is liberty. In the clearest instances of this model, detention is not reasonably necessary for deportation unless deportation is 'reasonably foreseeable'; that is, there has to be a real prospect of removal in the reasonably foreseeable future.[73] Where a court or independent tribunal reaches an adverse decision on the viability of removal, the connection between detention and deportation is held to be too tenuous to

[72] Some of the cases do not fit this characterisation. See eg *Lim* (n 63) and *Plaintiff M47/2012 v Director General of Security* [2012] HCA 46, (2012) 86 ALJR 1372, in which the decisions were addressed to detention during processing of an application for a visa (in the latter case only on the reasoning of the majority).

[73] See eg *Zadvydas* (n 4) 699 (Opinion of the Court). This reasonable foreseeability requirement is, in Commonwealth jurisprudence, most famously associated with the case of *Hardial Singh*: *R v Governor of Durham Prison, ex parte Singh* [1984] 1 All ER 983. See ch 5, s 5.2 and, for a development of the *Hardial Singh* principles in later British jurisprudence, ch 7, s 7.8.

support an authority to detain. Thus, the rights-protecting model applies a proportionality requirement to the duration of detention for deportation purposes.

The second type of judicial response, illustrated by the dissents in *Zadvydas*, sanctions the indefinite administrative detention of non-citizens. This type of response implements what I call a 'rights-precluding' model of immigration detention, where the right precluded is the right to liberty of a non-citizen against whom a deportation order has been issued. Under this model, detention is authorised provided the government is making efforts to remove the non-citizen and as long as removal remains a future prospect. A bona fide attempt to remove the non-citizen is all that is required of the detaining government, which is presumed to be doing its best in a world of complicated international relations. On this model, the judicial role in review of authority to detain is, at most, to ensure that the government continues to pursue removal in good faith.

Judges who apply the rights-precluding model may also adopt a second justification for indefinite administrative detention of non-citizens, namely removal from the 'community'. The more tenuous the possibility of removal, the more prominent this second justification becomes. In rare cases, such as the dissenting judgment of Kennedy J in *Zadvydas*, judges openly rely upon isolation from, or protection of, the national community as an independent rationale for the indefinite administrative detention of non-citizens.[74] Where the rights-precluding model is adopted, use is usually made of both the first and second justifications, with the second reinforcing the first.

The prospects of removing a non-citizen will often be uncertain. The rights-protecting and rights-precluding models of immigration detention represent two different responses to this uncertainty. The judges agree that there is no current reasonable prospect of removal. They disagree as to what constitutes a sufficient justification for detention. On the rights-protecting model, a court is prepared to order release on the basis that it is not satisfied that there is any prospect of removal in the reasonably foreseeable future. It is *possible* that circumstances will change such that the non-citizen will be able to be removed, but in the meantime, it is not appropriate for the non-citizen to be detained. Where the prospects of removal are doubtful, it is the state's authority to hold a non-citizen in immigration detention that gives way.

Conversely, judges who align with the rights-precluding model give determinative weight to the possibility that circumstances might change. Even if there are no present prospects of removal, things may look very different in the future.[75] The rights-precluding judge is not prepared to rule against authority to detain as long as there remains a *possibility* of removal. The existence of a future possibility of

[74] See eg *Al-Kateb* (n 36) [45] (McHugh J), [247], [255] (Hayne J) (Heydon J concurring). See ch 3, s 3.3.

[75] *Al-Kateb* (n 36) [229] (Hayne J): 'the most that could ever be said in a particular case where it is not now, and has not been, reasonably practicable to effect removal, is that there is *now* no country which will receive a particular non-citizen whom Australia seeks to remove, and it cannot *now* be predicted when that will happen.'

removal, being necessarily speculative, can be very hard, if not impossible, for a detainee to refute. Underlying this position is the view, sometimes express and sometimes implicit, that the citizenry should not bear any risk associated with a non-citizen's continued presence. The citizenry does not need to tolerate risks from non-citizens and can place a non-citizen in indefinite detention to avoid any such risk.

The two models subscribe to the same underlying constitutional values of liberty and equal treatment. It is not the presence or absence of legal values that defines them, but the application of those values. Exponents of both approaches understand themselves to be upholding core values of legality. I argue, however, that the rights-precluding model applies general principles selectively to uphold indefinite detention.

Nor do the models lead to diametrically opposed results. This can be illustrated by an initial comparison between the House of Lords' decision in *Belmarsh* and the Canadian Supreme Court case of *Charkaoui.* For reasons elaborated in chapters six and nine respectively, I characterise *Belmarsh* as a rights-protecting decision, and *Charkaoui* as a rights-precluding decision. This characterisation is based on the respective court's determination on the substantive rights at issue. *Belmarsh* held that indefinite administrative detention pending removal is discriminatory against non-citizens and is incompatible with Britain's rights commitments. *Charkaoui* held that such detention is not in itself discriminatory nor otherwise in contravention of the Canadian Charter. However, *Charkaoui* also put in place a 'procedural solution' to indefinite detention that did assist some of the detainees. To the extent that *Charkaoui*'s procedural protections substitute for substantive limits, leading to 'exit' from the detention regime, there is a degree of convergence in result between the two models.

Why would a judge work within a rights-precluding model? Each judge works with 'a *personal* conception of the nature of the law, society and the state'.[76] The choice of model reveals fault lines in thinking about law and the rule of law.[77] I argue that, in the key cases on indefinite detention, the legal materials present a number of 'constructional choices', choices that can usefully be characterised as a choice between the two models outlined.[78] The meaning of the statutory text at issue in these cases was not 'intractable',[79] but emerged from an interactive process of interpretation that moved between the text and 'the political point of legal order'.[80]

To understand the conception of the rule of law associated with each model, I refer to the categories employed by David Dyzenhaus in *The Constitution of Law*,[81]

[76] David Feldman, 'Public Law Values in the House of Lords' (1990) 106 *LQR* 246, 246.

[77] ibid. See also Max Harris, 'Public Law Values in the House of Lords – In an Age of Counter-Terrorism' (2011) 17 *Auckland University Law Review* 119.

[78] On the phrase see *Momcilovic v R* [2011] HCA 34, [50] (French CJ). The phrase is adopted in the submissions of the plaintiff in *Plaintiff M47/2012* (n 72). On *Plaintiff M47* see ch 4, s 4.4.

[79] cf *Al-Kateb* (n 36) [241] (Hayne J).

[80] David Dyzenhaus, *The Constitution of Law: Legality in a Time of Emergency* (Cambridge, Cambridge University Press, 2006) 8.

[81] ibid.

namely judges who ascribe to a substantive conception of the rule of law on the one hand, and constitutional positivists on the other. These categories speak to different conceptions of the judicial role. A judge adopting a substantive conception of the rule of law does not see their interpretive duty as

> first to determine the content of the positive law without relying on their own moral sensibilities and, second, to apply that content. Rather, their duty is to determine the content of the law in accordance with the aspirations of (ideal) legal order.[82]

For such judges a key function of the law is to act as a windbreak: 'The law restrains and civilises power.'[83] An integral element of the judge's role is to ensure, to the best of her or his ability, that the law performs this function. In doing so, the judiciary draws on a substantive conception of the rule of law. The content of that ideal can be briefly outlined:

> [L]egislation must be capable of being interpreted in a way that it can be enforced in accordance with the requirements of due process: the officials who implement it can comply with a duty to act fairly, reasonably and in a fashion that respects the equality of all those who are subject to the law and independent judges are entitled to review the decisions of these officials to check that they do so comply.[84]

The judicial role requires judges to clearly and publicly state when there is a departure from substantive legality, looking to 'a kind of justice located within the law, justice in the administration of the law'.[85] The rights-protecting model of immigration detention is a doctrinal expression of this substantive conception of legality. Conversely, adoption of the rights-precluding model tends to align with what Dyzenhaus identifies as 'constitutional positivism'.[86]

Constitutional positivists view it as democratically illegitimate, absent a clear endorsement in the constitutional or statutory text, for courts to introduce into legal analysis a 'cross-current of judicial opinion' protective of rights.[87] Nor is it simply a matter of textual endorsement. A constitutional positivist will be uneasy when there is explicit endorsement of an abstract ideal such as liberty or equality in the constitutional or statutory text, responding by narrowing and confining the scope of such liberty. The role thrust upon them by such provisions is in tension with an understanding of the judicial role as the application of determinate legal rules. They deny or downplay the need for recourse to substantive legality as part of the interpretive exercise.[88]

'Constitutional positivism' is a compromise between an understanding of law as the application and interpretation of determinate legal rules and a common law

[82] ibid.

[83] Murray Gleeson, *The Rule of Law and the Constitution: Boyer Lectures* (Sydney, ABC Books, 2000) 1.

[84] Dyzenhaus (n 80) 12–13.

[85] ibid, 12.

[86] ibid, 22, 68–71.

[87] AV Dicey, *Lectures on the Relation between Law and Public Opinion in England during the Nineteenth Century*, 2nd edn (London, Macmillan, 1904) 398.

[88] Dyzenhaus (n 80) 70.

legal order whose shape and nature are not fully captured by that understanding.[89] In the absence of a substantive conception of legality to guide adjudication on detention of non-citizens, judges have recourse to a range of proxies for legislative intent. In the areas of immigration and national security these proxies involve an assumption that judicial review, to the extent that it has any purchase at all, should be minimal. Statutory powers are read broadly against background assumptions that government should have a relatively free hand in the immigration area.

Judges who are constitutional positivists in the area of non-citizens' rights are not constitutional positivists in all matters. A judge who openly draws on a substantive conception of legality with respect to some subjects may hold that such an approach has little or no application when it comes to immigration and national security. In those areas, his or her reasoning becomes more insistent on implementation of a constitutional positivist position, and on efforts to expunge, as legally irrelevant, the influence of rights on the interpretive process.

In the cases analysed in this book, a judge's choice of constitutional positivism, or a more substantive conception of legality, correlates with his or her view of the legal subject. A judge's view of the legal subject has implications for the understanding of 'fairness, reasonableness and equality' he or she brings to their work.[90] For a judge working with a more substantive conception of legality, the meaning of these concepts is likely to be heavily influenced by the idea of the individual as a bearer of rights as this idea has been developed in the post-World War II human rights project. This human rights project reinforces a pre-existing common law tradition that held that those who are answerable to the law are entitled to its protection.[91] The common law on alienage, immigration and security is complex and contradictory. The human rights project powerfully reinforces those aspects of the common law attentive to the human autonomy of the detainee.

A rights-precluding judge works with a much 'thinner' legal subject.[92] The availability of procedural protections and rights tends to turn on a 'classification exercise'.[93] Citizens get rights or protections, non-citizens do not. 'Reliance upon on/off status or classifications . . . eliminate[s] possible inquiries as to the impact of decisions on individuals, in particular, impacts that intensify with time.'[94] The individual detainee's plight disappears from view, except perhaps to note their contribution to their own predicament; 'what matter[s], instead, [is] expedience in executing the administration's program'.[95]

There is no stark dichotomy of normative considerations underlying the rights-precluding and rights-protecting models. Rather, each model tends more or less strongly towards opposite normative poles. Nevertheless, the above account of

89 ibid, 69.

90 ibid, 13.

91 See Windeyer J's judgment in *Ex parte Lo Pak* (1888) 9 NSWLR 221, 245.

92 On the 'thin' legal subject see Robert Leckey, *Contextual Subjects: Family, State and Relational Theory* (Toronto, University of Toronto Press, 2008) ch 5.

93 ibid, 173.

94 ibid.

95 ibid.

contrasting models furnishes an initial set of coordinates with which to begin mapping the case law.

1.4 'Nationality-Differentiated Risk-Acceptability'?

In this section I move from outlining models of judicial response to indefinite detention to consider the normative stance on citizenship that underpins them. The models address distributive questions. To what degree do non-citizens share in the liberty interests and attendant protections of citizens? To what extent and for what reasons are they excluded from such protections? The models are a set of legal commitments that inform a judge's response to the central concern of this book, namely the relative priority and weight to be accorded to a state's power 'to admit, exclude and expel aliens' on the one hand, and constitutional principles of liberty and equality on the other.

The literature on the indefinite administrative detention of non-citizens returns to the idea that 'The problem of the indefinitely "irremovable" foreigner . . . is a boundary problem of the intersection of . . . two building blocks of our constitutional scheme'.[96] The building blocks are the state's power to 'admit, exclude and expel aliens' on the one hand, and constitutional principles of liberty and equality on the other.[97] The central difference between the two models of immigration detention introduced above is the priority they accord to these 'building blocks'.

In the rights-protecting model, legal authority to detain a non-citizen subject to a removal order is defined by the purpose of facilitating removal. If the non-citizen's removal is frustrated, that purpose no longer obtains and cannot be used to justify detention. The model accepts that authority to detain non-citizens is subject to legal qualification. These legal qualifications emanate, by a variety of doctrinal routes, from a non-citizen's liberty interest.

Conversely, the rights-precluding model tends to emphasise that it is integral to a state's sovereign power to decide who enters, and remains in, its territory. Any qualification of this power is seen as a threat to the state. As noted in the second epigraph quoted at the beginning of this chapter, the fear is that, if qualified, the state's sovereign power will 'crumble, eroded by newly enforceable constitutional

[96] Finnis (n 2) 445; see also 417. See *A v Secretary of State for the Home Department* [2004] EWCA Civ 1123. [234] (Laws J): 'First, we are dealing, as I said at the outset, with the tension between two constitutional fundamentals: the abhorrence of executive detention and the State's duty to safeguard its citizens and its own integrity.' For reference to equality as a 'building block of democracy' see *Matadeen v Pointu* [1998] UKPC 9, [1999] 1 AC 98, 109, [8] (Lord Hoffmann). For other express academic statements registering this tension, though drawing different conclusions from Finnis, see eg Linda Bosniak, *The Citizen and the Alien: Dilemmas of Contemporary Membership* (Princeton, Princeton University Press, 2006) 38; Catherine Dauvergne, 'Security and Migration Law in the Less Brave New World' (2007) 16 *Social & Legal Studies* 533, 545; Kate Nash, *The Cultural Politics of Human Rights: Comparing the US and UK* (Cambridge, Cambridge University Press, 2009) ch 3.

[97] Finnis (n 2) 417.

principles of equality before the law, and by rights as ancient as liberty (immunity from coercion and imprisonment)'.[98] Any resident non-citizen is simply a 'guest' and the host is free to revoke the invitation at will. Deportation is a refusal by the government to harbour persons it does not want. Tension between a state's powers of exclusion and expulsion of non-citizens and constitutional rights is avoided by denying that non-citizens subject to a removal order hold these rights.

In this section, I consider John Finnis's justification for the rights-precluding model, set out in his 2007 article 'Nationality, Alienage and Constitutional Principle'.[99] I focus on Finnis for a number of reasons. He analyses the three decisions – *Al-Kateb*, *Belmarsh* and *Charkaoui* – at the centre of the discussion of the legality of indefinite detention in their respective jurisdictions. While his analysis of the legal positions that result from each of these decisions is, I think, correct, his evaluation of those positions is the antithesis of my own. I argue for a 'rights-protecting' approach to detention pending removal, as that approach is outlined in section 1.3 above. Finnis defends the contrary 'rights-precluding' approach. In the course of doing so, Finnis articulates clearly the moral/political rationale for the sharp distinction between the liberty rights of citizens and non-citizens expressed in the rights-precluding approach. In this he makes explicit what is often only implicit in the rights-precluding judgments and provides me with a foil. Moreover, the position he adopts is not 'academic' in the pejorative sense. His position has shaped government argument in the courts. The imprint of his 2007 article is evident in the United Kingdom's legal argument before the European Court of Human Rights in *A v United Kingdom*, the final instalment of the *Belmarsh* litigation.[100] In that case, the United Kingdom ran a new argument, not advanced at any stage of the domestic *Belmarsh* litigation. The government adopted Finnis's line of argument.[101]

Finnis argues that a citizen's right to be protected against risk trumps a non-citizen's right to liberty. He further argues that a lower tolerance for the risks posed by non-citizens is necessary to define a group, those with formal legal citizenship, amongst whom can develop the solidarity that enables the social goods of the modern liberal democratic state.

Finnis's paper is, centrally, an argument for the existence of a 'constitutional principle' which he labels 'nationality-differentiated risk-acceptability'. This constitutional principle is argued to justify the legal position that I have called the rights-precluding model. The principle's formulation comes to rest in Finnis's statement that

[98] ibid.

[99] ibid. Some of the following analysis of Finnis's article draws on Rayner Thwaites, 'The Security of Citizenship? Finnis in the Context of the United Kingdom's Citizenship Stripping Provisions' in Fiona Jenkins et al, *Allegiance and Identity in a Globalised World* (Cambridge, Cambridge University Press, forthcoming 2014).

[100] *A v United Kingdom* (2009) 49 EHRR 29.

[101] See ch 7, s 7.2.

> the presence in the community of an alien who, individually considered, can fairly be said to present some genuine *risk*, even relatively slight, to the rights of others, or to national security, public safety, the prevention of crime, the protection of health or morals or maintenance of l'ordre public, or to anything else of 'public interest in a democratic society', *need not be accepted.*[102]

Such risk can permissibly be obviated by detention ancillary to removal, which is unambiguously taken to extend to indefinite immigration detention.[103]

There are three components to Finnis's argument for his constitutional principle: it has explanatory force in relation to current law (the explanatory argument); it has historical support (the historical argument); and there is a compelling normative case for the principle (his rationale for the rights-precluding model). I propose to address the explanatory and historical arguments here, in the Introduction. But the more fundamental question is whether the underlying principle he advances for the rights-precluding approach is defensible. That question is best assessed when the judgments that are informed by, and the judgments that reject, that principle have been considered. In chapter ten, drawing on the study of the judgments and broader legal developments in the book, I argue for the rejection of Finnis's principled basis for the rights-precluding approach.

The judgments I categorise as rights-precluding see immigration as governed by a set of assumptions that do not operate in the general law: expansive conceptions of executive power, minimal judicial review and the attenuated operation of constitutional norms protective of the individual. These background assumptions tend to permeate the reasoning in rights-precluding judgments. In the judicial reasoning considered in this book they are largely implicit. Finnis makes them explicit, foregrounding a candidate for a principle that underlies and encapsulates these assumptions – his constitutional principle of nationality-differentiated risk-acceptability.

The constitutional status of the principle is central to Finnis's account. He states that 'constitutional principles and rights prevail over ordinary norms of statutory interpretation; the presumption that statutes do not overturn these rights and principles qualifies the ordinary subordination of common law to parliamentary authority'.[104] In other words, his constitutional principle is equivalent to fundamental common law rights. It is presented as functioning in the same way as such rights in statutory interpretation. The difference is that what is being asserted is not an individual's right or liberty, but a right on the part of a state – the right to exercise a power to exclude, admit and deport aliens.

Finnis makes clear that the reason for arguing that his concept has the status of 'constitutional principle' is to ensure equivalence between the state right asserted

[102] Finnis (n 2) 423.

[103] The requirement of individual consideration would seem to rule out mandatory detention regimes, such as that which has operated in Australia since 1992, though the breadth of the grounds for removal from the community gives rise to some uncertainty on this point.

[104] Finnis (n 2) 417.

and fundamental common law rights of individuals. As emphasised in the epigraph, the power to admit, exclude and expel aliens needs to have the status of constitutional principle if it is to avoid erosion by the current constellation of fundamental rights.[105]

At a number of points in the case law, particularly in relation to the Australian material, the nature of the argument between the rights-protecting and rights-precluding judges initially appears to turn on acceptance or rejection of the legitimacy of constitutional values sourced in the common law. On this characterisation of the debate, rights-protecting judges allow for a constitutionalism that does not originate in statutory or constitutional text, but which forms a set of background assumptions against which those texts are read. And on this characterisation, rights-precluding judges insist on express statutory or constitutional endorsement of normative values. In the absence of such endorsement, such values are to be expunged from judicial reasoning as lacking the necessary democratic legitimacy.

What can be learned from Finnis's account is that the conventional way the debate is depicted, as outlined in the preceding paragraph, misstates the real conflict at a level of principle. Finnis argues for the acceptance of 'nationality-differentiated risk-acceptability' as a constitutional counterweight to common law presumptions in favour of rights. This is not an argument against the legal relevance of values in interpretation. It is an argument for a different set of values. Finnis's account suggests that it is not so much the presence or absence of common law values in the interpretive framework that is at issue; rather, it is the content of those common law values.

Finnis's case for the constitutional status of his principle is in the first instance developed through an argument for its historical grounding. The historical argument is directed at showing how the principle coheres with, and grows out of, the common law legal orders in question. In making this argument, Finnis acknowledges a prominent common law tradition with which his constitutional principle had to contend. He notes: 'foreigners within the realm (speaking always of non-enemy aliens) enjoy the subject's common law right to freedom from every act of a government servant or agent which if done by a private person would be a tort.'[106] On this characterisation of the common law position, the question is not

[105] See n 2. The two principles nominated by Finnis in the second epigraph to this chapter, 'equality' and 'liberty', were central to the reasoning in *Belmarsh* (n 1). Finnis goes on to make additional reference to Art 8 of the Convention for the Protection of Human Rights and Fundamental Freedoms, 4 November 1950, 213 UNTS 211, Eur TS 5 (ECHR), on respect for private and family life. United Kingdom government proposals to limit Art 8 review were included in the Queen's Speech 2013 (Parliament, 8 May 2013).

[106] Finnis (n 2) 419. For a discussion of the contemporary legal significance of this principle see Karen Knop, 'Citizenship, Public & Private' (2008) 71 *Law & Contemporary Problems* 309. Statements that the non-citizen (or the non-enemy alien) was not an outlaw were intended to encapsulate this principle. The term, and concept, 'outlaw' is employed repeatedly in the contemporary case law, in order to reject the concept: see eg *Lim* (n 63) and *Minister for Immigration & Multicultural & Indigenous Affairs v Al Masri* [2003] FCAFC 70, (2003) 126 FCR 54, discussed in ch 2, ss 2.3 and 2.4 respectively.

'does the non-citizen have a right to remain?', but 'did the respondent/defendant have legal authority to remove him?'[107]

Finnis accepts that positive statutory authority was at one point in time required for any such action, referring to Dicey's position that if foreign anarchists suspected of plotting to blow up the Houses of Parliament could not be put on trial, there was 'no means of arresting them, or of expelling them from the country'.[108] He then states: 'But when Dicey last passed this passage for the press in 1908, the law had begun to leave him behind.'[109] Finnis argues that his principle rose to prominence in the twentieth century. The legal form it took was unclear. He submits that this principle was inherent in a pre-existing prerogative of expulsion which has simply been given statutory support. In that way the twentieth century statutes are enlisted as a source of constitutional principle.

In relation to the argument from the prerogative, Finnis maintains that the Privy Council decisions of *Attorney-General for Canada v Cain*[110] and *Johnstone v Pedlar*[111] had supplied 'constitutional foundations' for the expulsion of suspected foreign terrorists. These authorities either left open, or adverted to, the possible existence of a relevant prerogative power. He supplements his case for a prerogative of expulsion with reference to Holdsworth.[112] The central theme of his account is that since the beginnings of the twentieth century there has been an increasingly vigorous assertion of a 'power of the State' to expel, and that the rise of this power has clarified or confirmed what was previously ambiguous – that is, that the presence of a non-citizen within the jurisdiction is conditional on their proper conduct. A non-citizen is liable to removal or exclusion for 'recalcitrant failure to assimilate his conduct, in matters of weight, to the particular conceptions of common and public good that are embodied in our constitution and law'.[113] On Finnis's account, the presumption had shifted from the need for statutory authority to remove (in the absence of which forcible removal would be false imprisonment) to a presumption of authority to remove.

The argument from legislation holds that twentieth-century immigration statutes defined a 'constitutional scheme' with 'two legal constitutional principles, each resting on a moral-constitutional principle'.[114] Of these 'legal constitutional principles', the first is that non-enemy aliens present within the realm have all the rights and obligations of citizens, subject to their vulnerability to removal; the second is that a citizen cannot be excluded from the realm. The moral-

[107] Knop (n 106). See also Christopher Vincenzi, 'Aliens and the Judicial Review of Immigration Law' [1985] *PL* 93, 96–97.

[108] Finnis (n 2) 419, citing AV Dicey, *Introduction to the Study of the Law of the Constitution*, 1st edn (1885) 239–40; 7th edn (1908) 226–27.

[109] Finnis (n 2) 420.

[110] *Attorney-General for Canada v Cain* [1906] AC 542.

[111] *Johnstone v Pedlar* [1921] 2 AC 263.

[112] Finnis (n 2) 420 fn 17, citing Holdsworth, *History X*, 393–400.

[113] ibid, 418.

[114] ibid, 422.

constitutional principle on which these legal principles are said to rest is 'nationality-differentiated risk-acceptability'.

As a closing point, Finnis suggests that the detention of foreign terrorist suspects should be conceptualised in terms of the wartime detention of enemy aliens. He develops this point with reference to the foreign terrorist suspects before the House of Lords in *Belmarsh*. He does not claim that the foreign terrorist suspects in *Belmarsh* were 'enemy aliens'.[115] He does, however, suggest a possible analogy between the indefinite administrative detention of foreign terrorist suspects and the wartime internment of foreign nationals. In his final footnote on detention, appended to a statement that the constitutional principle warrants non-citizens being 'kept apart from the community by humane detention or control', Finnis writes:

> The liability of enemy aliens – a category not considered in this article, and hitherto conceived of as nationals of a state at war with ours – to statutorily authorised detention in time of war might be understood as a form which that liability to removal reasonably takes when circumstances prevent (or make unreasonable) actual removal.[116]

This characterisation prepares the way for wartime internment as a precedent for detention of non-citizens subject to removal orders. This use of wartime internment cases is a recurrent tendency in the rights-precluding judgments on detention of non-citizens.[117]

1.5 Criticisms of 'Nationality-Differentiated Risk-Acceptability'

Finnis derives a general principle of nationality-differentiated risk-acceptability from the existence of powers of expulsion and immigration detention in relation to non-citizens on the one hand, and the prohibition on the banishment of citizens on the other. The principle is then fed back into the analysis to license expansive readings of the relevant powers over non-citizens. A basic problem with this reasoning is that the generalisation Finnis arrives at to explain those legal positions – his moral-constitutional principle of nationality-differentiated risk-acceptability – has at least one competing justification that also claims to explain the same set of facts: that offered under the rights-protecting model. The

[115] ibid, 419. Finnis noted, with reference to Coke, that 'the supposed incapacity of aliens to pursue personal actions at law was limited . . . to enemy aliens: subjects of a state at war with the crown'. For a contemporary reaffirmation of the incapacity of enemy aliens to pursue personal actions, with an emphasis on the view that 'there is no warrant for extending it [the status of enemy alien] to modern armed conflict not involving war in the technical sense', see *Amin v Brown* [2005] EWHC (Ch) 1670, [46].

[116] Finnis (n 2) 445 fn 109.

[117] See *Al-Kateb* (n 36) [55]–[61] (McHugh J); *A v Secretary of State for the Home Department* [2002] EWCA Civ 1502, [2004] QB 335, [112]–[131] (Brooke LJ).

competing explanation might be stated this way: the nation does not have to accept from foreigners the same degree of risk it accepts from its nationals, and may obviate the risk posed by foreigners by their deportation, to the extent that another country can be found to which it is appropriate to remove the non-citizen, and this removal, and processes ancillary to it, does not disproportionately impinge on the non-citizen's fundamental rights. Finnis's concern is that under the weight of these qualifications, the power to admit, exclude and expel aliens 'will crumble'. But he does not offer any reason why we should think of the power as brittle in this way.[118] The better view is simply that the power has to accommodate the principle that legislation should be interpreted consistently with fundamental rights, whether that obligation is sourced in common law, international human rights jurisprudence or constitutional doctrine.

Turning to his historical argument, as outlined above, Finnis's derivation of his constitutional principle appears to have two bases: an argument from the prerogative and an argument from legislation. What links the two arguments is the idea that the relevant legislation inherited and continued a set of understandings about the appropriate division of constitutional responsibilities in immigration. The argumentative utility of keeping in play the idea that the rights of exclusion or expulsion may be, or even just may have been, prerogative powers is that it lends weight to those powers,[119] making them seem like part of the order of things, since time immemorial.[120] Further, it links immigration with major prerogative powers in the area of defence and foreign policy, colouring it as an area in which extensive deference to the executive is appropriate, a position already encountered in Kennedy J's judgment in *Zadvydas*.[121]

An initial problem with Finnis's argument is that the case for the existence of any prerogative of expulsion or exclusion in the last 300 years is weaker than he suggests.[122] The decisions that he held provide the 'constitutional foundations' for the expulsion of foreign terrorists, *Attorney-General for Canada v Cain* and *Johnstone v Pedlar*,[123] are best regarded as simply having announced a new exclusionary principle that had not previously existed at common law:[124]

> the position from an historical examination of the cases appears to be that there are no cases supporting the existence of this supposed prerogative for more than 200 years

[118] This response to Finnis developed through a conversation with Audrey Macklin. See also Gerald Neuman, *Strangers to the Constitution* (Princeton, Princeton University Press, 1996) 124.

[119] See Ian A Macdonald QC and Ronan Toal, *MacDonald's Immigration Law & Practice*, 7th edn (London, LexisNexis, 2008) para 1.8.

[120] See also James AR Nazfiger, 'The General Admission of Aliens under International Law' (1983) 77 *American Journal of International Law* 804, 805.

[121] See s 1.1.

[122] Finnis (n 2) 420: 'The issues, decided and undecided, rest today where the Privy Council left them in 1906 and 1921: there is constitutional authority, whether by prerogative or not, to exclude an alien in the interests of the community's well-being.'

[123] *Cain* (n 110); *Johnstone* (n 111).

[124] Robert Plender, *International Migration Law*, 2nd edn (Dordrecht, Martinus Nijhoff, 1988); Nazfiger (n 120); Vincenzi (n 107).

> after the revolutionary settlement of 1688. Then, in 1891, came *Musgrove v Chun Teeong Toy*, and, in 1906, *Attorney-General for Canada v Cain*. All of the dicta supporting the prerogative [and this includes the relevant dicta from *Johnstone v Pedlar*], in so far as any authority is provided, are based, either directly or indirectly, upon those two cases or upon Blackstone.[125]

But 'prerogatives, by their very nature, must be both of ancient origin and in receipt of continuing judicial recognition'.[126] Finnis also cites Holdsworth in support of a prerogative of exclusion and expulsion.[127] He does not record that 'many important constitutional writers have denied or doubted the existence of any prerogative in relation to friendly aliens, including Coke, Hale, Brougham, . . . Erskine May, Clarke, Craies, Oppenheim and de Smith'.[128]

Turning to Finnis's argument from statute, his derivation of broad 'legal constitutional principles' from an extensive, complex, and frequently amended statutory scheme is fraught with difficulty.[129] But there is a more basic problem. The reason why these statutes should have determined, or continue to determine, the content of unwritten constitutionalism is left undeveloped. The point can be made by a comparison between Finnis and the central object of his criticism, the majority of the House of Lords in *Belmarsh*.

In *Belmarsh*, Lord Bingham, like Finnis, allowed a 'historic right of sovereign states over aliens entering or residing in their territory', stating: 'Historically, this was the position.' Lord Bingham continued: 'But a sovereign state may by international treaty restrict its absolute power over aliens within or seeking to enter its territory, and in recent years states have increasingly done so.'[130] Both Finnis and Lord Bingham overplay the contrast between 'the historical position' and the legal position established under international treaty obligations. The difference is that where Lord Bingham reports his understanding of the historical position and supplies reasons for its adjustment and change, Finnis exerts himself to establish a

[125] Vincenzi (n 107) 105. See also at 97–98, 101–04.

[126] ibid, 105. Finnis quotes a statement from the 1906 Privy Council decision of *Cain* that is in turn, in its entirety, a quotation from Vattel. In a detailed historical analysis of how the statements of Vattel and other publicists of international law were used in foundational United States authorities on immigration law of the late 19th and early 20th centuries, Nazfiger concluded that 'the proposition that a state has the right to exclude all aliens is of recent origin', and where this proposition was recited it often amounted to no more than an unsupported maxim: Nazfiger (n 120) 807. The foundational United States authorities criticised by Nazfiger were influential in the development of early 20th-century Australian immigration jurisprudence, quoted by members of the *Al Kateb* majority: see ch 3, s 3.2.

[127] Finnis (n 2) 420 fn 17.

[128] Vincenzi (n 107) 105. The ellipsis is for Dicey, whom Finnis acknowledges held a contrary view.

[129] For a contemporary extra-judicial statement cautioning against talk of 'purpose' at the level of a complex statute, as opposed to the level of the relevant provisions, see Murray Gleeson, 'The Meaning of Legislation: Context, Purpose and Respect for Fundamental Rights' (2009) 20 *Public Law Review* 26. For a discussion critical of selective utilisation of the policies and principles underlying immigration legislation, see Ninette Kelley, 'Rights in the Balance: Non-Citizens and State Sovereignty under the *Charter*' in David Dyzenhaus (ed), *The Unity of Public Law* (Oxford, Hart Publishing, 2004) 253, 266–67.

[130] *Belmarsh* (n 1) [69] (Lord Bingham).

reasoned foundation for reinvigoration of the historical position.[131] Attitudes toward the prerogative change, the nature (and existence) of constitutional principles shifts. What is needed is an argument as to why change should be embraced or resisted.

This section has endeavoured to show that questions about the differential treatment of non-citizens cannot be resolved by a particular reading of history. In particular this is because, as Lord Bingham suggested in *Belmarsh*, this ignores a major current of change within the constitutional framework. The result is that the argument for a clear hierarchy between the liberty rights of citizens and non-citizens, to the detriment of the latter, stands or falls at a more fundamental level of principle. I return to that argument in chapter 10, the Conclusion, following an analysis of the cases. For present purposes I simply register that his argument is one against the current trajectory of legal change, as he perceives it.

1.6 A Shared Commonwealth Legal Tradition?

1.6.1 Choice of Jurisdictions

My choice of jurisdictions is informed by what they share. Underlying the divergence in their constitutional frameworks is common membership of the common law family of the Commonwealth. In legal terms, the jurisdictions share much: 'They make similar assumptions about legal goals and values; they employ similar legal terms and concepts; they draw broadly on the same theorists, including AV Dicey; and they use similar legal techniques.'[132] Doctrinally, the jurisdictions branched out from a common base. The judgments analysed in this book recurrently make use of judgments in other common law jurisdictions with no discussion or reference to comparative law methodology.

Nonetheless, the relevant legal debates are clearly framed by specific elements of the constitutional and legal context in each of the three countries. Care has to be taken with assumptions of homogeneity.[133] The different national legal systems have necessarily diverged. A key 'catalyst' for that divergence is the influence of

[131] Further, in so doing, Finnis glosses over the potential, and highly relevant, complexities of 'the historical position', in particular the nexus between powers of deportation and detention. Even during the heyday of expansive executive discretion over immigration in the first half of the 20th century, it was far from clear that commentators of that period shared Finnis's confidence that a right of deportation was accompanied by extensive powers of immigration detention. On the courts' hostility to interference with personal liberty under immigration statutes, see eg John Willis, 'Statute Interpretation in a Nutshell' (1938) 16 *Canadian Bar Review* 1, 22–23; Moffatt Hancock, 'Discharge of Deportees on Habeas Corpus' (1936) 14 *Canadian Bar Review* 116.

[132] Cheryl Saunders, 'Constitution as Catalyst: Different Paths within Australasian Administrative Law' (2012) 10 *New Zealand Journal of Public and International Law* 143, 146.

[133] ibid.

the various national constitutional frameworks (introduced in the next section).[134] In this work, I continue within the common law tradition of referring to other common law jurisdictions without a comparative law methodology, mindful that this exercise calls for greater care than in the past. Where relevant, the use and misuse of foreign authority, including amongst the three jurisdictions studied, is discussed.

The United States has diverged from this Commonwealth unity to an extent that removes it from the common law family of the British Commonwealth. The relevant institutional and legal assumptions that operate within the United States are distinct from many of those shared between Australia, the United Kingdom and Canada,[135] and while there are references to United States material in the work (this chapter opened with *Zadvydas*), I do not make the United States an object of study.

A second reason for the selection of jurisdictions is my argument that, on analysis, the reasons for the differences between the rights-precluding and rights-protecting judgments are explained not by differences in the written constitutional frameworks, but on the more fundamental level of judicial approaches to questions of principle. Different judicial attitudes to non-citizens, immigration and the judicial role do more explanatory work in this area than the particulars of the doctrinal or constitutional framework in which the issues arise. There are alignments in judicial positions cutting across the three national jurisdictions that 'transcend in importance orthodox distinctions based on':[136] (a) a federal constitution but no enacted bill of rights (Australia), (b) an enacted but not entrenched bill of rights (the United Kingdom), and (c) a federal constitution and an entrenched bill of rights (Canada).[137] I am as interested in differences in judicial approach within a given jurisdiction as I am in differences between jurisdictions. In this, the work is as much a comparison of judges, or more accurately judgments, as it is of courts or jurisdictions.[138]

As introduced above, I argue that the jurisprudence is structured by two different judicial responses to the prospect of indefinite immigration detention: one leading to a finding that such detention is unlawful and one allowing for it. *Both* lines of judicial response were available in both Australia and the United Kingdom,

[134] The concept of 'catalyst' is intended to convey that the constitutional framework does not mandate a particular doctrinal development or outcome in a linear fashion, but may nonetheless be a key reason for those developments: ibid, 157.

[135] For succinct summaries of relevant distinctions between the United States on the one hand and the British Commonwealth on the other, see HP Glenn, *Legal Traditions of the World*, 3rd edn (Oxford, Oxford University Press, 2007) 248–55; Peter Cane, '2. The Institutional Framework of Public Administration' in Peter Cane, *Administrative Law*, 5th edn (Oxford, Oxford University Press, 2011) 22–46. The contrast in Cane is between public law under a presidential system and that under Westminster systems.

[136] Dyzenhaus (n 80) 5.

[137] ibid. Section 1.6.2 provides an introductory outline of these distinctions.

[138] Vicki C Jackson and Jamal Greene, 'Constitutional Interpretation in Comparative Perspective: Comparing Judges or Courts?' in Tom Ginsburg and Rosalind Dixon (eds), *Comparative Constitutional Law* (Cheltenham, Edward Elgar, 2011) 599.

as evidenced by the existence of both rights-protecting and rights-precluding judgments. I argue that Canadian law contained the legal resources to support the rights-protecting model. Conversely, I outline the legal arguments that led the Canadian Supreme Court to give legal sanction to a rights-precluding approach in *Charkaoui*.

A third reason for the choice of jurisdictions is that the key cases on the legality of indefinite detention from these jurisdictions provide clear examples of three distinct points on the continuum of judicial responses to the issue. In *Al-Kateb*, a majority of the High Court of Australia upheld the legality of the indefinite detention of non-citizens, subject to the most marginal constitutional or legal constraints. The decision constitutes a clear example of a rights-precluding decision. In contrast, the UK House of Lords' decision in *Belmarsh* constitutes a clear example of the rights-protecting approach. The House of Lords ruled that detention for the purpose of deportation was necessarily of limited duration. The relevant statutory provisions were characterised as national security provisions and the decision to confine the detention provisions to non-citizens was held to be discriminatory. While the decision left the validity of the law unaffected, it clearly stated that the relevant statutory provisions were incompatible with the United Kingdom's rights commitments.

In *Charkaoui*, the Canadian Supreme Court postponed any decision on the lawful duration of detention of a non-citizen subject to a deportation order. The Court instead relied on procedural constraints to address any future violation of rights on a case-by-case basis. The legality of indefinite detention was upheld at the same time as procedural reforms required by the court inaugurated a series of legal developments that have placed the detention regime under increasing pressure. As I outlined in section 1.3 in the course of introducing the models, I contend that 'the procedural solution' mandated by the Canadian Supreme Court is rights-precluding. It is nonetheless qualitatively distinct from *Al-Kateb* in the level of legal protection provided to the detainees.

The issues of statutory and constitutional interpretation covered in this book arise in a diverse range of legal contexts and circumstances. The two models of immigration detention outlined above supply the jurisprudence with a constant pattern despite this diversity. This pattern amidst diversity grounds my claim that more than any particular rights framework what matters are judicial understandings of the legal position of non-citizens, understandings available in each of the jurisdictions considered.

1.6.2 Structural Differences

This book centres on legal developments in the indefinite administrative detention of non-citizens subject to a removal order in Australia, the United Kingdom and Canada. Here I introduce the legal framework in each jurisdiction, focusing on the presence or absence of enacted or entrenched guarantees of personal liberty.

Australia has a federal constitution (Constitution),[139] conferring enumerated heads of legislative power on the national government. Legislation can be invalid as contrary to the Constitution. There is neither an entrenched nor an enacted national bill of rights. The Constitution has been construed to imply a separation of judicial and non-judicial powers at the federal level. One implication of the separation doctrine is the general proposition that a person can only be detained by order of a court. This proposition is subject to exceptions, one of which is immigration detention. The issue that arises is whether administrative detention of a non-citizen subject to a removal order, where there is no real prospect of removal, can be justified as immigration detention, so falling within the exception. Constitutional reasoning has a direct bearing on statutory interpretation by way of a presumption that Parliament did not intend to pass beyond constitutional bounds.[140]

The United Kingdom has a statutory bill of rights,[141] the Human Rights Act 1998 (HRA 1998). The HRA 1998 gives effect to rights under the European Convention on Human Rights (ECHR),[142] including a right to liberty (Article 5) that is subject to an express exception for deportation purposes (Article 5(1)(f)).[143] The question that arises is whether administrative detention where there is no real prospect of removal can be justified as being for deportation purposes, and so fall within the exception to the liberty right. If detention in such circumstances is not 'with a view to deportation' this has the further consequence that the primary justification for confining the detention measures to non-citizens is not present. In the absence of an alternative justification, the measures would contravene the prohibition on discrimination under the HRA 1998.[144] In the United Kingdom, legislation cannot be invalidated.[145] The United Kingdom is also a State Party to the ECHR and is accordingly bound by decisions of the European Court of Human Rights (ECtHR).[146] The HRA 1998 gives legislative sanction to the courts adopting a strong interpretive approach to ensure compatibility with Convention rights (section 3). Where legislation cannot be interpreted consistently with Convention rights, the courts can issue a declaration of incompatibility (section 4). A declaration formally conveys

[139] Commonwealth of Australia Constitution Act 1900 (UK) (63 & 64 Vict c 12) (Constitution).

[140] *Lim* (n 63) 14 (Mason CJ).

[141] On the meaning of the 'United Kingdom': 'Technically, "United Kingdom" refers collectively to the three legal systems of England and Wales (which together constitute a single system), Scotland and Northern Ireland. "Great Britain" (or "Britain") refers collectively to England and Wales, and Scotland': Peter Cane, *Administrative Tribunals and Adjudication* (Oxford, Hart Publishing, 2009) 1 fn 2.

[142] See n 105.

[143] Under the HRA 1998, rights adopted from the ECHR and protocols have been given a statutory footing as 'Convention rights': HRA 1998, s 1. Among these Convention rights is that to liberty and security of the person (ECHR, Art 5). Under that article, an exception is made to the prohibition on deprivation of liberty for 'the lawful arrest or detention . . . of a person against whom action is being taken with a view to deportation': Art 5(1)(f).

[144] ECHR, Art 14.

[145] European Community law does, however, take precedence over inconsistent national law: European Communities Act 1972, s 2; *R v Secretary of State for Transport, ex parte Factortame Ltd* [1989] UKHL 1, [1990] 2 AC 85.

[146] ECHR, Art 46.

the court's view that a measure is incompatible with the relevant Convention right. Legislation found incompatible with a Convention right remains in full force and effect. Since one of the primary purposes of the HRA 1998 is to provide a successful litigant with a remedy, courts will strive to interpret legislation compatibly with Convention rights. Section 3 is the only means by which Convention rights can be protected without further intervention by Parliament or the government.[147] But the practical effect of a declaration should not be overlooked. Where a declaration of incompatibility has become final in its entirety,[148] Parliament has remedied the incompatibility identified, either by primary legislation or by a remedial order under section 10 of the HRA 1998,[149] or has taken steps to do so.[150]

Canada has both a federal constitution and an entrenched bill of rights, the Canadian Charter of Rights and Freedoms (Charter).[151] Liberty is a protected interest under the Charter and detention is precluded unless it is imposed 'in accordance with the principles of fundamental justice' (section 7) or 'can be demonstrably justified in a free and democratic society' (section 1). A legislative provision that infringes a Charter right and is not justified under section 1 will be invalid. A question that arises in the Charter context is whether detention of a non-citizen subject to a deportation order, in circumstances where there is no real prospect of removal, infringes section 7. If it is found to do so, then a further question arises as to whether it is justified under section 1. To the extent that the administrative detention of non-citizens in these circumstances is not authorised by the purpose of facilitating deportation, an alternative reason for its confinement to non-citizens is needed. In the absence of a satisfactory reason, the detention will be found to be discriminatory, in contravention of the equality right in section 15. As in the Australian context, constitutional reasoning has a direct bearing on statutory interpretation by way of a presumption that legislation complies with constitutional norms.

Finally, although there is no single common law position on statutory interpretation, the common law of each jurisdiction studied recognises a presumption against the legislative abrogation of personal liberty. This presumption can support an interpretive approach whereby a statutory power of detention for the

[147] I say 'or the government' as s 10 HRA 1998 provides for a 'fast-track' procedure whereby primary legislation may be amended by ministerial order, available when a s 4 declaration of incompatibility is issued.

[148] Meaning that the declaration was not subject to appeal, in whole or in part.

[149] See n 147 on s 10 HRA 1998.

[150] See Ministry of Justice, *Responding to Human Rights Judgments: Report to the Joint Committee on Human Rights on the Government Response to Human Rights Judgments 2011–2012* (Cm 8432, 2012) annex A. The Ministry of Justice noted that, in the period between 2 October 2000 when the HRA 1998 entered into force and 31 July 2012, 27 declarations were made, 19 of which became final in their entirety (ie the declaration is not subject to appeal, in whole or in part). Of those 19, 11 have been remedied by later primary legislation, three have been remedied by remedial order under s 10 HRA, four related to provisions that had already been remedied by primary legislation at the time of the declaration, and the last was under consideration to determine how to remedy the incompatibility.

[151] Canadian Charter of Rights and Freedoms, Part I of the Constitution Act, 1982, being Schedule B to the Canada Act 1982 (UK), c 11 (Charter).

purposes of deportation will be read as not extending to indefinite detention, unless indefinite detention is explicitly provided for.[152]

1.7 Plan of the Book

The book falls into three Parts, divided by jurisdiction: Australia (chapters two to four), the United Kingdom (chapters five to seven), and Canada (chapters eight and nine). Within each part, discussion centres on a particular case study, namely the leading authority of the highest appellate court on the legality of indefinite detention pending removal: *Al-Kateb*, *Belmarsh* and *Charkaoui* respectively. In Part I on Australia, chapter two provides legal context, including key decisions, relevant to understanding and evaluating the High Court of Australia's decision in *Al-Kateb*. *Al-Kateb* is analysed in chapter three. And chapter four considers subsequent Australian legal developments that speak to the legacy of that decision or bear on its evaluation. The same pattern of analysis of the leading authority on indefinite detention, flanked by preceding context and subsequent developments, is repeated in relation to both the British and the Canadian Parts. This simple pattern belies a considerable difference in the materials consulted for each jurisdiction, a function of the different legal contexts and circumstances in which each decision was decided. In Part II, chapter five provides the legal context for the *Belmarsh* litigation. The *Belmarsh* litigation before the Special Immigration Appeals Commission, the Court of Appeal and the House of Lords is the subject of chapter six. Chapter seven addresses the wider periphery of immigration detention in the United Kingdom, in particular the regimes of preventive constraint known as control orders and terrorism prevention and investigation measures. In Part III, on Canada, chapter eight outlines relevant Charter jurisprudence on non-citizens, and litigation on the relevant detention regime, that preceded *Charkaoui*. Chapter nine analyses *Charkaoui* and subsequent cases on the Canadian detention regime.

Chapter ten, the Conclusion, brings together the findings of my review. Close analysis of the reasoning of the courts on the legality of indefinite detention pending removal, and related issues, enables me to return in the Conclusion to the underlying questions of principle posed at the outset. The answer to those questions is of practical import to non-citizens subject to indefinite detention pending removal. It bears on how courts adjudicate on whether such detainees should be released. It also speaks to a more general interest in determining the nature and scope of liberty rights in democratic societies. Who can be interned to protect who from what and for what reasons? The book holds a mirror up to the process of reasoning in final courts of appeal. It provides insights into the factors that lead

[152] Or if the provisions would be rendered wholly inoperative if not read as providing for indefinite detention.

judges to come to very different views on what is, in the final analysis, the same question. It also serves to illuminate a central dilemma about who is entitled to benefit from the rights that democratic societies pledge themselves to enshrine and protect.

Australia

2

Limits on Immigration Detention

> Since aliens who are unlawfully within Australia are not outlaws but enjoy, in common with every other person in Australia, the equal protection of Australia's laws, the principle of construction to which we have referred is not to be excluded simply because the subject matter of a statute is the detention of aliens. It is a principle of universal application.
>
> Black CJ, Sundberg and Weinberg JJ, *Al Masri*, Full Court of the Federal Court of Australia (2003)[1]

2.1 Introduction to the Australian Chapters

In *Al-Kateb v Godwin*, the High Court of Australia determined by majority that the Migration Act 1958 (Cth) authorised the indefinite administrative detention of a non-citizen who had no right to be in Australia.[2] It further determined that the Australian Constitution (Constitution)[3] supported federal legislation for the indefinite detention of non-citizens who do not enjoy a statutory right to be in Australia. The *Al-Kateb* majority judgment provides a clear example of the rights-precluding model of immigration detention. The judgment sanctioned legislation for the indefinite detention of non-citizens, subject to only the most minimal judicial supervision.

The *Al-Kateb* majority found that, even in the absence of any explicit provision to that effect, the Migration Act 1958 authorised the indefinite detention of a non-citizen who, through no fault of her or his own, could not be removed. *Al-Kateb* was a controversial decision.[4] The Court's decision has become a reference point

[1] *Minister for Immigration & Multicultural & Indigenous Affairs v Al Masri* [2003] FCAFC 70, (2003) 126 FCR 54, [114]. This quote references the 1992 Australian High Court decision of *Chu Kheng Lim v Minister for Immigration, Local Government and Ethnic Affairs* [1992] HCA 64, (1992) 176 CLR 1, 19, which in turn refers back to *Kioa v West* [1985] HCA 81, (1985) 159 CLR 550, 631(Deane J).

[2] *Al-Kateb v Godwin* 2004 HCA 37, (2004) 219 CLR 562. Majority: McHugh, Hayne, Heydon and Callinan JJ; Dissenting: Gleeson CJ, Gummow and Kirby JJ.

[3] Commonwealth of Australia Constitution Act 1900 (UK) (63 & 64 Vict, c 12) (Constitution).

[4] Immediately following the decision in *Al-Kateb*, the Federal President of the Labor Party, the Australian Democrats and the Greens called for a bill of rights to override the Migration Act 1958: see Meaghan Shaw, 'Ban Indefinite Detention: Lawrence', *The Age* (Melbourne, 12 August 2004), www.theage.com.au/articles/2004/08/11/1092102523200.html. The Greens' media release stated that the

in contemporary debate about the adequacy of human rights protections in Australia.[5] It marks a spectacular failure of rights protection.

McHugh J, a member of the *Al-Kateb* majority, pronounced the result in the case 'tragic',[6] but held that there was nothing the Court could do in the continuing absence of a national bill of rights in Australia.[7] For the reasons given in the next chapter, I do not agree with this assessment. The judges in *Al-Kateb* were faced with a genuine 'constructional choice'.[8] I argue that the *Al-Kateb* minority were correct in their judgment that Australian law supports a different interpretation of the Migration Act 1958, and were also correct in their further assessment of the constitutional limits applying to the detention of non-citizens pending removal.

In this chapter I outline pertinent features of the legal context, to better appreciate the legal reasoning in *Al-Kateb*. In addition, in order to show the alternative approach open to the High Court in *Al-Kateb*, I here discuss an earlier case determined in the Federal Court of Australia. The judgments of the Federal Court in *Al Masri*[9] and the minority judgments in *Al-Kateb* substantiate my claim that Australian law provides resources to better protect the liberty of non-citizens.

legislative provisions 'make every immigration detention centre in Australia another Guantanamo Bay': 'Bill of Rights: One Way to Defeat Indefinite Detention' (6 August 2004). There was also back-bench disquiet within the governing Liberal-National Coalition, leading to the creation, in late March 2005, of a new visa class allowing some unsuccessful asylum seekers whose removal from Australia was not reasonably practicable to be released from detention unless and until it became practicable to remove them: Migration Regulation 1994 (Cth), Sch 2 [Visa] Subclass 070. On 'removal pending' bridging visas see ch 4, s 4.2.

[5] See the prominence and frequency of references to *Al-Kateb* in the National Human Rights Consultation: National Human Rights Consultation Committee, *Report on the Consultation into Human Rights in Australia* (September 2009), www.ag.gov.au/RightsAndProtections/HumanRights/TreatyBodyReporting/Pages/HumanRightsconsultationreport.aspx. For relatively early instances of an extensive, and largely negative, response from the academy and the profession, see eg Arthur Glass, '*Al-Kateb* and *Behrooz*' (Gilbert + Tobin Centre of Public Law 2005 Constitutional Law Conference, Sydney, 18 February), www.gtcentre.unsw.edu.au.html; Dennis Rose, 'The High Court Decision in *Al Kateb* and *Al Khafaji*: A Different Perspective' (2005) 8(3) *Constitutional Law and Policy Review* 58; Matthew Zagor, 'Uncertainty and Exclusion: Detention of Aliens and the High Court' (2006) 34 *Federal Law Review* 127. For a positive evaluation of the majority's reasoning, see James Allan, '"Do the Right Thing" Judging? The High Court of Australia in *Al-Kateb*' (2005) 24 *University of Queensland Law Journal* 1.

[6] *Al-Kateb* (n 2) [31] (McHugh J).

[7] Australia does not have a bill of rights binding on the federal government (the level of government with legislative power over 'aliens' and 'immigration'): see ch 1, s 1.6.2. The Australian Capital Territory and the State of Victoria have adopted a charter of rights: see Human Rights Act 2004 (ACT) and Charter of Human Rights and Responsibilities Act 2006 (Vic).

[8] The phrase is taken from *Momcilovic v R* [2011] HCA 34, (2011) 245 CLR 1, [50] (French CJ).

[9] *Minister for Immigration & Multicultural & Indigenous Affairs v Al Masri* [2003] FCAFC 70, (2003) 126 FCR 54.

2.2 The Australian Legal Context

2.2.1 The Constitution and Federal Legislative Power

In the absence of a national bill of rights in Australia, the constitutional requirements regarding the exercise of federal legislative power and the separation of federal judicial power assume particular importance in any discussion of the legality of administrative detention. Immigration legislation used to be skeletal in nature, containing little more than a broad conferral of substantially unfettered powers on the executive. It is now highly prescriptive, imposing numerous obligations on immigration officials.[10] This shift occurred in response to changes in judicial attitudes toward the legal regulation of executive discretions.[11]

From the foundational authorities of Australian immigration law, dating from the late nineteenth and early twentieth centuries, executive power over immigration has required statutory authorisation. In the foundational case for Australia on the government's power to exclude aliens, *Musgrove v Toy*,[12] the Privy Council held that legislation gave the executive its power to exclude aliens. The Court's interpretation of the statute in question was transparently shaped by an assumption that there is expansive executive power over immigration. Nonetheless, the Court ascribed the power to statute, based on particular, contentious, rules of statutory interpretation.[13] In Australia, courts have not, with one exception,[14] acknowledged extra-statutory executive power to exclude aliens, whether derived from the historical prerogative or from any notion of inherent executive power. Australian jurisprudence on the state's power of exclusion has always been a jurisprudence of statutory interpretation.[15]

[10] See eg French J in *NAAV v Minister for Immigration* [2002] FCA 443, (2002) 123 FCR 298, [399]: 'The most recent changes to the *Migration Act* are the latest in a long series of over 100 amending Acts since it was enacted in 1958 . . . it is a statute replete with official powers and discretions, tightly controlled under the Act itself and under the Regulations by conditions and criteria to be satisfied before those powers and discretions can be exercised.'

[11] More particularly, changes to the procedural rights of migration applicants: see Mark Aronson, Bruce Dyer and Matthew Groves, *Judicial Review of Administrative Action*, 3rd edn (Sydney, Law Book Co, 2004) 381–84; Mary Crock, *Immigration and Refugee Law in Australia* (Sydney, Federation Press, 1998) 279–83. Both accounts focus on the seminal case of *Kioa* (n 1).

[12] *Musgrove v Toy* [1891] AC 272 (PC).

[13] Namely that payment tendered is not equivalent to payment; and imposition of a penalty in respect of an act implicitly prohibits that act. For another reading of *Musgrove* that does not treat it as relying on prerogative powers see *Ruddock v Vadarlis* [2001] FCA 1329, (2001) 110 FCR 491, [10] (Black CJ) (*Tampa*); cf [112] and [186] (Beaumont and French JJ respectively). For an academic analysis favouring Black CJ's reading see Geoffrey Lindell, 'Reflections on the Tampa Affair' (2002) 4(2) *Constitutional Law and Policy Review* 21. The foundational Australian case on a right to deport aliens, *Robtelmes v Brennan* [1906] HCA 58, (1906) 4 CLR 395, similarly required that the power have a statutory foundation: see 401 and 403 (Griffith CJ).

[14] cf *Ruddock v Vadarlis* (n 13). On the context see pp 103–04.

[15] The foundational authorities of immigration law in the Anglo-American legal world date from the late 1880s and early 1890s: see Robert Plender, *International Migration Law*, 2nd edn (Dordrecht,

Given that executive powers in the immigration context flow from federal legislation, the Constitution's grants of legislative power are the logical starting point for a discussion of the constitutional limits on those powers. Australia came into existence as a political and legal entity through the federation of British colonies under the Constitution.[16] The Constitution divides legislative powers between federal Parliament and Australian state legislatures. This division is achieved by enumerating the subject matters on which federal Parliament can legislate. Federal legislation is only valid to the extent that it can be grounded in one of these heads of power. Unlike in Canada, there is no list of enumerated state or provincial powers. The power of the state legislatures is subject to external limits imposed by the Constitution, including the requirement that in the event of inconsistency between (valid) federal and state legislation, federal legislation will prevail.[17] But as a matter of internal limits, the power of state legislatures is plenary.[18] The heads of federal legislative power most relevant to the discussion are section 51(xix) and (xxvii): '51. The Parliament shall, subject to this Constitution, have powers to make laws for the peace, order and good government of the Commonwealth with respect to: . . . (xix) Naturalization and aliens' and '(xxvii) Immigration and emigration'. In common usage, these are referred to as the aliens power and the immigration power respectively.

The Constitution does not provide for Australian citizenship.[19] In constitutional terms, Australian citizenship is no more than a 'mere legal inference' from the constitutional text.[20] Instead, phrases such as 'people of the Commonwealth'[21] and 'subject of the Queen'[22] are employed, reflecting the 'political realities' at

Martinus Nijhoff, 1988) 2; see also James AR Nazfiger, 'The General Admission of Aliens under International Law' (1983) 77 *American Journal of International Law* 804, 807. This holds true for Australian jurisprudence, with *Musgrove* (n 12) dating from 1891. Before this time any power on the part of the relevant states to exclude aliens was not expressed as a power over immigration. The immediate catalyst for the American and Australian case law of this period was Chinese emigration.

[16] The Australian Constitution was an Act of the British Parliament. The text was predominantly drafted during a series of conventions in the 1890s attended by delegates of the various colonies that went on to become states, and adopted by voters in those colonies in referenda held in the period 1898–1900.

[17] s 109 of the Constitution, headed 'Inconsistency of Laws', states: 'When a law of a State is inconsistent with a law of the Commonwealth, the latter shall prevail, and the former shall, to the extent of the inconsistency, be invalid.'

[18] There are caveats to the plenary power of the state legislatures, but they are not relevant to this study.

[19] s 44(i) provides that citizenship of a foreign power is a disqualification from serving as a Commonwealth Parliamentarian. Concepts of membership of the community are also contained in ss 34 and 117.

[20] See Kim Rubenstein, *Australian Citizenship Law in Context* (Sydney, Law Book Co, 2002) 38. The phrase is taken from an exasperated utterance by one of the constitutional drafters, John Quick, provoked by the continued rejection of a constitutional definition of citizenship: see Kim Rubenstein, 'Citizenship and the Constitutional Convention Debates: A Mere Legal Inference' (1997) 25 *Federal Law Review* 295, 295.

[21] The phrase 'people of the Commonwealth' appears in s 24 providing for the electors of the House of Representatives. Section 7, which provides for the electors for the Senate, refers to the 'people of the State'.

[22] s 34 provides that to qualify for the House of Representatives a prospective member must be 'a subject of the Queen'. See also s 117.

Federation.[23] The new community post-Federation was not defined by an Australian nationality distinct from a British one, and Australian citizenship only came into existence with the entry into force of the Australian Citizenship Act 1948 (Cth).[24] Until then, the main *legal* distinction was between British subjects and aliens. However, there operated a 'de facto administrative Australian citizenship', which distinguished between those British subjects who could be deported and those who could not.[25] The main mechanism of this de facto administrative Australian citizenship was the infamous dictation test.[26] The test provided that persons would be prohibited from landing, or deported, if they failed to write out a passage of 50 words in a European language as dictated by the officer.[27] A concise account of the dictation test was offered by the High Court in 1936: 'It was merely a convenient and polite device . . . for the purpose of enabling the Executive Government of Australia to prevent the immigration of persons deemed unsuitable because of their Asiatic or non-European race.'[28]

The judgments discussed in this chapter focus on the aliens power. Reliance on the aliens power, as opposed to the immigration power, to regulate immigration is a relatively recent phenomenon. For more than seven decades after Federation the immigration power was the primary head of power relied upon to authorise immigration legislation.[29] It was assumed that a British subject could not be an alien so that grounding legal authority in the aliens power would leave a 'huge

[23] 'Political realities' is Kirby J's phrase from *Re Patterson, ex parte Taylor* [2001] HCA 51, (2001) 207 CLR 391, [270]. The omission of citizenship is not because the concept did not form part of the legal lexicon of the time. The issue of Australian citizenship was a subject of heated debate during the constitutional conventions, and a conscious decision was made to exclude it from the constitutional text: Kim Rubenstein, 'Citizenship and the Centenary – Inclusion and Exclusion in 20th Century Australia' (2000) 24 *Melbourne University Law Review* 576, 580. A prominent reason for the absence of Australian citizenship in the Constitution was the difficulty involved in devising a formulation that preserved the racially exclusionary features desired: see Rubenstein, *Australian Citizenship Law in Context* (n 20) ch 2. Rubenstein discusses a range of other obstacles to the inclusion of citizenship in the Constitution, including indeterminacies arising from: attempts to transplant citizenship into a legal system that had not employed the status; an individual's status as simultaneously a member of a colony, the British Empire and the new nation; and the lack of agreement as to what, if any, rights and responsibilities flowed from citizenship.

[24] The Act was originally named the Nationality and Citizenship Act 1948 (Cth) but was renamed by the Australian Citizenship Act 1973 (Cth).

[25] David Dutton, *Citizenship in Australia: A Guide to Commonwealth Government Records* (Canberra, National Archives of Australia, 1999) 13.

[26] The dictation test was abolished by the Migration Act 1958. The White Australia policy continued to be implemented in the absence of this particular statutory mechanism, and was only unequivocally abolished under the Whitlam government which came to power in 1972, although steps taken prior to that time can be characterised as 'dismantling' the policy: see Gwenda Tavan, *The Long, Slow Death of White Australia* (Melbourne, Scribe Publications, 2005).

[27] Immigration Restriction Act 1901 (Cth), ss 3(a), 7 and 14. A Czech dissident, Egon Kisch, proved to be fluent in so many European languages that the officer was reduced to administering a test in Scottish Gaelic. The High Court held the resulting decision to deport him unlawful on the grounds that Scottish Gaelic was not a 'European language' within the meaning of the Act: *R v Wilson, ex parte Kisch* [1934] HCA 50, (1934) 52 CLR 234.

[28] *R v Davey, ex parte Freer* [1936] HCA 58, (1936) 56 CLR 381, 386 (Evatt J for the Court).

[29] See Crock, (n 11) 20–23. See also Tony Blackshield and George Williams, *Australian Constitutional Law & Theory*, 4th edn (Sydney, Law Book Co, 2010) 939, 946–47.

gap',[30] preventing the deportation of those from elsewhere in the British Empire travelling on British passports. The Immigration Restriction Act 1901 (Cth) was based on the immigration power.

Under the immigration power, it was the High Court that came to define who could freely enter and remain, and who could be excluded and removed. The High Court addressed the question of who was subject to the immigration power with reference to the concept of 'community': 'The ultimate fact to be reached as a test whether a given person is an immigrant or not is whether he is or is not at that time a member of the Australian community.'[31] The concept (membership of the Australian community) lacks the legal specificity of connecting factors such as domicile, residence, personal presence or citizenship.[32] This lack of specificity may, as a matter of history, have been the point. For its intelligibility, the concept of 'community' relied on certain widespread assumptions concerning the habits and mores, and particularly ethnic composition, of the Australian populace. 'Community' was an indeterminate legal concept well suited to support the 'de facto administrative citizenship' of early racially informed immigration policy.

The shift to reliance on the aliens power was responsive to judicial decisions holding that an 'immigrant' could be 'absorbed' into the Australian community, so passing beyond the scope of the immigration power.[33] According to the Australian courts, alienage can only be displaced by a formal grant of citizenship, not by gradual absorption. As such it remains more amenable to government control than the status of immigrant. The move to legislate under the aliens power was enabled by the enactment of national citizenship laws and the related decline of the assumption that a British subject could not be an alien.[34] The scope of the aliens power essentially came to rest on the statutory concept of citizenship. The existence of a constitutional concept effectively defined by statute raises problems of its own.[35] Primary among these problems is Parliament's ability to define a concept that is intended to define its power.

[30] *R v MacFarlane, ex parte O'Flanagan and O'Kelly* [1923] HCA 39, (1923) 32 CLR 518, 556 (Isaacs J).

[31] *Potter v Minahan* [1908] HCA 63, (1908) 7 CLR 277, 308 (Isaacs J). While Isaacs J was in dissent on the issue of what constituted membership of the community, he was at one with the majority in holding that the limits of the immigration power were determined by who was, and who was not, a member of the community.

[32] See *Re Woolley, ex parte Applicants M276/2003 (by their next friend GS)* [2004] HCA 49, (2004) 210 ALR 369, [135]–[148] (Gummow J).

[33] The shift of bureaucratic and legislative focus to the aliens power is usually dated from the High Court's decision in *R v Director General of Social Welfare, ex parte Henry* [1975] HCA 62, (1975) 133 CLR 369, in which the majority endorsed the view that an individual could cease to be an immigrant upon being 'absorbed' into the community. See also Blackshield and Williams (n 30) 939, 946–47.

[34] There are, however, conflicting modern High Court decisions on whether alienage and citizenship are the only possible classes of subjects, or whether there exists a third class of British subjects who are neither aliens nor citizens. The binary classification appears to have prevailed: see *Singh v Commonwealth* [2004] HCA 43, (2004) 222 CLR 322.

[35] See Michelle Foster, 'Membership in the Australian Community: *Singh v Commonwealth* and its Consequences for Australian Citizenship Law' (2006) 34 *Federal Law Review* 161; Sydney Tilmouth, 'Citizenship as a Constitutional Concept: *Singh v Commonwealth of Australia* and *Rasul v Bush, President of the United States*' (2005) 26 *Australian Bar Review* 192.

The exercise of legislative power under the Constitution is subject to some substantive limits, prominent among them those derived from the separation of federal judicial power. The Constitution makes limited explicit textual provision for individual rights,[36] and these are not relevant to immigration detention. However, the courts have held that the Constitution implies a separation of judicial power, which is in turn a source of rights protection. The first three chapters of the Constitution are structured to reflect a tripartite division between parliament (Chapter I), the executive (Chapter II) and the judiciary (Chapter III). However, the strictest separation is that of federal judicial power from the other branches of government. Australian judges sometimes refer to the requirements of the separation of federal judicial power as the 'requirements of Chapter III'. The statement in section 51 that the listed heads of legislative power are 'subject to this Constitution' has served as the textual basis for reading the heads of federal legislative power as subject to these separation of powers requirements.

Chapter III requirements for the exercise of legislative power are central in Australian jurisprudence on the constitutionality of the indefinite detention of non-citizens. More particularly, a key issue in Australian jurisprudence on immigration detention is whether the administrative detention of aliens is invalid for inconsistency with separation of powers constraints on administrative detention. For reasons I will discuss in the context of *Lim*,[37] the separation of judicial power has been held to support the implication of a general freedom from administrative detention, subject to certain judicially recognised exceptions.[38] In *Lim*, the Court recognised an exception for the administrative detention of aliens for an immigration purpose (ie, consideration of an application for entry, or effecting removal of an alien who has no right to remain). The Court's analysis focused on whether the indefinite detention of non-citizens subject to a removal order falls within this immigration exception to the constitutional freedom from administrative detention. In determining whether a detention power falls within this exception, or is precluded by a general freedom from administrative detention, the Court employed a criterion of proportionality.

Australian courts claim the right to strike down legislation that is invalid for inconsistency with the Constitution. This claim rests on the status of the Constitution as 'supreme' law. As evidence of the supremacy of the Constitution the courts point to covering clause 5, which provides in part: 'This Act, and all laws made by the Parliament of the Commonwealth under the Constitution, shall be binding on the courts, judges, and people of every State and every part of the Commonwealth.' The courts consider it axiomatic that it is their role to

[36] These are the civil and political freedoms of the right to vote (s 41), trial by jury (s 80), freedom of religion (s 116) and the rights of out-of-state residents (s 117); and the economic freedoms of interstate trade and commerce (s 92) and acquisition of property on just terms (s 51(xxxi)).

[37] *Lim* (n 1).

[38] See the more detailed discussion of the case law in section 2.3 below.

pronounce on the constitutional validity of legislation: This is a question of law to be determined by the courts under the constitutional separation of powers.[39]

2.2.2 Common Law on Statutory Authority for Administrative Detention

It is a fundamental common law principle that statutory authority is required for executive detention.[40] This legal principle is a venerable one, dating back to the habeas corpus statutes of the seventeenth century.[41] The remedy of habeas corpus played a key ideological role in the English political and legal struggles between Crown and Parliament, serving as a vehicle for discussion of the extent to which the executive could imprison a person without being called to account in the common law courts.[42] The writ was promoted by Parliament and directed at assertions of inherent authority by the Crown. The law of habeas corpus has long been central in immigration jurisprudence. The remedy sought by an alien in some form of immigration detention, from the foundational authorities of the late nineteenth century to the present day in Australia, has been an order in the nature of habeas corpus directing his or her release.[43] Further, it would now appear that the remedy of habeas corpus has been 'constitutionalised'.[44]

The remedy of habeas corpus itself influences the way legislation that purports to authorise detention is interpreted. Habeas corpus encapsulates the principle that every imprisonment is prima facie illegal at common law.[45] It makes vivid the principle that the respondent has the burden of justifying the applicant's detention.[46] The conflict within the Australian authorities examined in this chapter

[39] The Court here acknowledged the influence of *Marbury v Madison* 5 US (1 Cranch) 137 (1803). See eg *Australian Communist Party v Commonwealth* [1951] HCA 5, (1951) 83 CLR 1, 262–63 (Fullagar J).

[40] *Lim* (n 1) 13 (Mason CJ), 19 (Brennan, Deane and Dawson JJ) and 63 (McHugh J); *Re Bolton, ex parte Beane* (1987) 162 CLR 514, 528 (Deane J).

[41] The Habeas Corpus Act 1640 set out to curtail the prerogative power to commit a person to detention: see RJ Sharpe et al, *The Law of Habeas Corpus*, 3rd edn (Oxford, Oxford University Press, 2011) 15. With the Habeas Corpus Act 1679, which set out to remedy various procedural deficiencies that had allowed for evasion of the writ, it took on its modern form: ibid, 16–17. See also FW Maitland, *The Constitutional History of England* (Cambridge, Cambridge University Press, 1919) 314. The Habeas Corpus Act 1816 gave a statutory footing to the application of the Habeas Corpus Act 1679 to non-criminal cases: see AV Dicey, *The Law of the Constitution*, 8th edn (London, Macmillan, 1915) 133.

[42] See Matthew Groves, 'Chapter 14 – Habeas Corpus' in Mark Aronson, Bruce Dyer and Matthew Groves (eds), *Judicial Review of Administrative Action*, 3rd edn (Sydney, Law Book Co, 2004) 754–55. See also Sharpe (n 39) ch 1; David Clark and Gerard McCoy, *The Most Fundamental Legal Right: Habeas Corpus in the Commonwealth* (Oxford, Clarendon Press, 2000).

[43] See eg *Ex parte Lo Pak* (1888) 9 NSWLR 221; *Al-Kateb* (n 2) [24] (Gleeson CJ). For an account of what lies behind the phrase 'an order in the nature of habeas corpus', see DJ Clark, 'Jurisdiction and Power: Habeas Corpus and the Federal Court' (2006) 32 *Monash University Law Review* 275.

[44] *Kirk v Industrial Relations Commission of New South Wales* [2010] HCA 1, (2010) 239 CLR 531, [98] (French CJ, Gummow, Hayne, Crennan, Kiefel and Bell JJ).

[45] See *Liversidge v Anderson* [1942] AC 206, 245 (Lord Atkin); *R v Home Secretary, ex parte Khawaja* [1984] AC 74, 110, 112–14 (Lord Scarman) and 122–23 (Lord Bridge).

[46] There is an evidential burden on the applicant at the first *ex parte* stage to cast doubt on the propriety of his or her detention, and the legal burden of proof shifts to the respondent at the show cause stage.

turns on what is required by way of justification. The degree of substantive justification required affects the construction of the relevant statutory provisions.

The primary way in which the common law impacts on the indefinite detention of non-citizens is by way of a common law presumption in favour of liberty. In Australian law 'statutory provisions are not to be construed as abrogating important common law rights, privileges and immunities in the absence of clear words or a necessary implication to that effect'.[47] The High Court's support for this presumption is traced to *Potter v Minahan*,[48] and it has been affirmed on numerous occasions,[49] including by the majority in *Al-Kateb*.[50] One justification for the presumption is that it makes parliaments accountable for action under statutory authority that infringes fundamental privileges or immunities. Lord Hoffmann's statement of this justification in *R v Secretary of State for the Home Department, ex parte Simms* has been influential in contemporary judgments:

> The principle of legality means that Parliament must squarely confront what it is doing and accept the political costs. Fundamental rights cannot be overridden by general or ambiguous words. This is because there is too great a risk that the full implications of their unqualified meaning may have passed unnoticed in the democratic process. In the absence of express language or necessary implication to the contrary, the courts therefore presume that even the most general words were intended to be subject to the basic rights of the individual.[51]

The presumption acknowledges that the common law is not entrenched against legislation. Australian courts recognise that they lack power to 'disapply' legislation on the ground that it is inconsistent with a fundamental common law right.[52] Where legislation makes provision for the criteria for exercising a power, as in *Al-Kateb*, the question is whether it is possible to construe the statutory criteria in a way that accommodates the right.

While the High Court applied the common law presumption as early as 1908, its use of the presumption increased starting in the late 1980s. As the High Court stated in 2002:

[47] *Daniels Corporation International Pty Ltd v Australian Competition & Consumer Commission* [2002] HCA 49, (2002) 213 CLR 543, [11] (Gleeson CJ, Gaudron, Gummow and Hayne JJ).

[48] *Potter* (n 31) 304 (O'Connor J).

[49] For instances prior to *Al-Kateb*, see eg *Coco v R* [1994] HCA 15, (1994) 179 CLR 427; *Wentworth v NSW Bar Association* [1992] HCA 24, (1992) 176 CLR 239, 252 (Deane, Dawson, Toohey and Gaudron JJ); *Re Bolton, ex parte Beane* (n 40) 523 (Brennan J); *American Dairy Queen (Q) Pty Ltd v Blue Rio Pty Ltd* [1981] HCA 65, (1981) 147 CLR 677, 682–83 (Mason J); *Commonwealth v Progress Advertising & Press Agency Co Pty Ltd* [1910] HCA 28, (1910) 10 CLR 457, 464 (O'Connor J). See also *Koon Wing Lau v Caldwell* [1949] HCA 65, (1949) 80 CLR 533, 581 (Dixon J).

[50] *Al-Kateb* (n 2) [241] (Hayne J) (McHugh and Heydon JJ concurring). See further ch 3, s 3.2. See also Dan Meagher, 'The Common Law Principle of Legality in the Age of Rights' (2011) 35 *Melbourne University Law Review* 449.

[51] *R v Secretary of State for the Home Department, ex parte Simms* [1999] UKHL 33, [2000] 2 AC 115, 131. See also *Plaintiff S157/2002 v Commonwealth* [2003] HCA 2, (2003) 211 CLR 476, [30] (Gleeson CJ); *Al-Kateb* (n 2) [19] (Gleeson CJ dissenting); *Daniels* (n 49) [104]–[108] (Kirby J).

[52] *Durham Holdings Pty Ltd v New South Wales* [2001] HCA 7, (2001) 205 CLR 399, [7] (Gaudron, McHugh, Gummow and Hayne JJ): 'the existence of the presumption [against legislative abrogation of that fundamental common law right] suggests that the power, against the exercise of which the presumption operates, indeed exists.'

> It is now well settled that statutory provisions are not to be construed as abrogating important common law rights, privileges and immunities in the absence of clear words or a necessary implication to that effect. That rule, the expression of which can be traced to *Potter v Minahan* [1908] . . . is a rule which . . . has been strictly applied by this Court since the decision in *Re Bolton; Ex parte Beane* [1987].[53]

Australian courts' revival of the presumption in and after the 1980s paralleled English developments. In 1985, in his dissenting judgment in *Wheeler v Leicester City Council*,[54] Browne-Wilkinson LJ asserted that there are substantive standards of legality to be applied at common law. This proposal was rejected by the House of Lords on appeal, but the idea slowly gained traction in the English jurisprudence, reaching its high point in *Simms*.[55] The developed modern English jurisprudence on common law presumptions and the principle of legality has exerted considerable influence on the Australian law of statutory interpretation.

2.3 *Lim*

2.3.1 *Lim* Introduced

Prior to *Al-Kateb*, the leading High Court authority on the constitutionality of immigration detention was *Chu Kheng Lim v Minister for Immigration, Local Government and Ethnic Affairs*.[56] *Lim*'s discussion of the constitutional separation of powers doctrine is important for subsequent case law. *Lim* established that the separation doctrine imposes limits on the duration of immigration detention. In *Lim*, these constitutional limits were formulated in terms of a proportionality test directed at the link between detention and the relevant immigration purpose (whether removal or admissions 'processing'). *Lim* posed a reasonable necessity test for the legality of immigration detention: was detention 'reasonably capable

[53] *Daniels* (n 47) [11] (Gleeson CJ, Gaudron, Gummow and Hayne JJ). *Re Bolton, ex parte Beane* (n 42) was also a case concerned with the existence of a statutory authority to detain.

[54] *Wheeler v Leicester City Council* [1985] UKHL 6, [1985] AC 1054. In *Coco* four members of the High Court endorsed *Wheeler*: see *Coco* (n 49) 437–438 (Mason CJ, Brennan, Gaudron and McHugh JJ).

[55] *Simms* (n 51). See also Lord Browne-Wilkinson's reprise of the idea 12 after *Wheeler* in *R v Secretary of State for the Home Department, ex parte Pierson* [1997] UKHL 37, [1998] AC 539. On the latter occasion he returned to the idea better armed with legal and academic authority, drawing the following conclusion at 575: 'I think the following proposition is established. A power conferred by Parliament in general terms is not to be taken to authorise the doing of acts by the donee of the power which adversely affect the legal rights of the citizen or the basic principles on which the law of the United Kingdom is based unless the statute conferring the power makes it clear that such was the intention of Parliament.' On the development of British jurisprudence on common law rights from *Wheeler* to *Simms*, see Tom Hickman, *Public Law after the Human Rights Act* (Oxford, Hart Publishing, 2010) 103–08.

[56] *Lim* (n 1).

of being seen as necessary for the purposes of deportation or to enable an entry application to be made and considered' (reasonable necessity test)?[57]

The plaintiffs in *Lim* were Cambodian nationals who had arrived in Australia by boat in late 1989 and early 1990 without government authorisation, and subsequently applied for refugee status.[58] They were detained on arrival. For authority to detain, the government initially relied on the Migration Act 1958, section 88 of which provided that a person could be held in detention until the vessel on which they arrived left its last Australian port. This 'turn-around' provision assumed that an 'illegal entrant' would leave Australia on the vessel in which he or she had arrived, and in any case could not be kept in detention after that particular vessel had left its last port of call in Australia. The period of detention was limited to the duration of the ship's stay in Australia. The section was not well suited to the circumstances of the plaintiffs in *Lim*. There was no prospect of the plaintiffs returning in the vessels in which they had arrived. Furthermore, the usual timing involved in the turn-around approach was not consistent with any tenable assessment time for a claim for refugee status. Nonetheless, the government's actions followed the assumption initially developed in the context of this 'turn-around' scenario, namely that the plaintiffs would remain in detention until removed, or formally processed and admitted.[59] The detention regime at issue in *Lim*, unlike most other decisions considered in this book, was detention during admissions processing, not 'pending deportation'.

The applicants spent more than two years in detention while their applications for refugee status were considered. The applications were rejected, but the decisions to reject them were set aside by the Federal Court, and referred back to a delegate of the Minister for redetermination. At the time the rejection decisions were set aside, applications for orders for release were set down for hearing. The government responded by enacting legislation to provide for the applicants' ongoing detention. This amending legislation was given royal assent the day before the Federal Court of Australia was due to hear argument on the applications for release.[60] It inserted a new 'Division 4B' into the Migration Act 1958 which established a class of 'designated persons' whose definition encompassed the Cambodian plaintiffs. A person falling within the class of 'designated persons'

[57] ibid, 10 (Mason CJ), 33 (Brennan, Deane and Dawson JJ), 58 (Gaudron J), 65–66, 71 (McHugh J).

[58] For the wider political and legal context see Mary Crock, 'A Legal Perspective on the Evolution of Mandatory Detention' in Mary Crock (ed), *Protection or Punishment: The Detention of Asylum Seekers in Australia* (Sydney, Federation Press, 1993) 25. For an account of the litigation see Mary Crock, 'Climbing Jacob's Ladder: The High Court and the Administrative Detention of Asylum Seekers in Australia' (1993) 15 *Sydney Law Review* 338. The legal status of refugee can be found in the Convention relating to the Status of Refugees, 28 July 1951, 189 UNTS 150 and Protocol relating to the Status of Refugees, 31 January 1967, 606 UNTS 267.

[59] Australian immigration law still contains many other provisions, policies and practices which effectively provide for an initial screening and 'turnaround': see eg Savitri Taylor, 'Sovereign Power at the Border' (2005) 16 *Public Law Review* 55, 69–71.

[60] The Federal Court had adjourned the hearing of their application for release to 7 May 1992. Two days prior to the plaintiffs' scheduled court appearance, on 5 May 1992, the Federal Parliament passed the Migration Amendment Act 1992. The legislation passed both Houses of Parliament in less than an hour and received royal assent the following day.

was to remain or be placed in custody until either removed from Australia or granted an entry permit. Division 4B introduced mandatory immigration detention into the Australian legal system. Critically, it also contained some limits on detention. It placed a fixed temporal limit of 273 days (nine months) on immigration detention. It also contained a provision, section 54P(1), which provided that an officer must remove a detainee from Australia as soon as practicable if the detainee asked the Minister, in writing, to be removed.[61]

The legislation stipulated that the count towards the 273-day limit excluded days where matters beyond the control of the Department of Immigration, Local Government and Ethnic Affairs impacted on the processing of the application, such as delays in the provision of information or, critically, court proceedings.[62] In September 1993, some nine months after the High Court's judgment in *Lim*, many of the plaintiffs remained in detention under Division 4B. The stated temporal limit of 273 days had yet to expire because their cases had been before the courts, and were thus held to be out of the control of the Department.[63]

After the government secured passage of the legislation, the Federal Court proceedings were adjourned *sine die*. The plaintiffs subsequently brought a constitutional challenge to the validity of the amending legislation in the High Court.

In *Lim*, the High Court held that the amendments introduced as Division 4B authorised the plaintiffs' detention. Insofar as it wanted to insulate the plaintiffs' detention from legal challenge, the government was well advised to rush Division 4B through Parliament. The Court held that the provision relied on prior to the enactment of Division 4B, section 88, did not authorise long-term detention. Furthermore, in the absence of the freshly enacted Division 4B, 'the continued detention of each plaintiff in custody . . . was unlawful'.[64] In response to the High Court's ruling that the plaintiffs had been held for years without legal authority, the plaintiffs issued writs seeking damages for the tort of false imprisonment. However, any such compensation was effectively foreclosed by special legislation setting the rate of damages payable for the wrongful detention at a dollar a day.[65]

2.3.2 The Separation of Judicial Power and Non-Citizens

In the following discussion I focus on the joint judgment of Brennan, Deane and Dawson JJ (the joint judgment), which supplied the ratio of the case.[66] The sub-

[61] Further, it contained requirements that a non-citizen be removed from Australia 'as soon as practicable' if he or she either failed to apply for an entry permit within two months, or had had such application refused and exhausted appeals and reviews of that decision: ss 54Q and 54P(2) and (3) of the Migration Act 1958, respectively.

[62] Migration Act 1958, s 54Q.

[63] There is a tension here with the idea that a person is asserting his or her legal *rights* before the court: see *R (on the application of Lumba) v Secretary of State for the Home Department* [2011] UKSC 12, [2012] 1 AC 245, [111]–[121], [144].

[64] *Lim* (n 1) 22 (Brennan, Deane and Dawson JJ), 64 (McHugh J).

[65] See Migration Amendment Act (No 4) 1992 (Cth).

[66] For subsequent judicial recognition that the joint judgment supplies the ratio of the decision, see *Al-Kateb* (n 2) eg [127]–[133], [139] (Gummow J), [251]–[252] (Hayne J); *Al Masri* (n 1) [53]–[63].

stantive reasons in the *Lim* joint judgment commenced with the following observation:

> Under the common law of Australia and subject to qualification of an enemy alien in time of war, an alien who is within this country, whether lawfully or unlawfully, is not an outlaw. Neither public official nor private person can lawfully detain him or her or deal with his or her property except under or in accordance with some positive authority conferred by law.[67]

While in terms directed to the need for statutory authority to detain a non-citizen, the comment is indicative of the view that adjudication on the detention of non-citizens draws on constitutional norms of general application.

The *Lim* joint judgment held that the legislation fell within the scope of the aliens power.[68] If the plurality had stopped there, the aliens power would confer effectively unlimited legislative power over aliens.[69] However, the bare characterisation of the head of power was only the first step in the reasoning. The judges then turned to restraints on legislative power within 'our system of government', namely the separation of federal powers.

A separation of powers analysis turns on the content given to the concepts of 'judicial', 'legislative' and 'executive' power. The *Lim* joint judgment defined judicial power with reference to past practice. The judges drew on historical instances of functions within or without the scope of judicial power.[70] The most important historical exemplar of a judicial function was held to be the 'essentially and exclusively judicial' function of 'the adjudgment and punishment of criminal guilt'.[71] Administrative detention for the purposes of punishment would usurp an exclusively judicial power. Here the joint judgment emphasised that 'the Constitution's concern is with substance and not mere form':

> it would, for example, be beyond the legislative power of the Parliament to invest the Executive with an arbitrary power to detain citizens in custody notwithstanding that

[67] *Lim* (n 1) 19 [footnotes omitted]. The quoted passage in turn refers back to *Kioa* (n 1) 631 (Deane J).

[68] *Lim* (n 1) 25. The definition of 'alien' in 51(xix) of the Constitution relied upon by the High Court in *Lim* was established in the 1988 case of *Nolan*, which treated 'alien' in s 51(xix) of the Constitution as synonymous with 'non-citizen': see the joint judgment in *Lim* (n 1) 25–26, referring to *Nolan v Minister for Immigration and Ethnic Affairs* [1988] HCA 45, (1988) 165 CLR 178, 183 (Mason CJ, Wilson, Brennan, Deane, Dawson and Toohey JJ). This binary opposition was reaffirmed, after a number of twists and turns in the High Court jurisprudence, in *Singh* (n 34).

[69] While Gaudron J formed part of the majority, she adopted a minority interpretation of the scope of the aliens power. Gaudron J argued that the aliens power should *not* be read as conferring unlimited legislative power over aliens. She argued that the heads of legislative power defined with reference to persons 'falling within a particular class or answering a particular description', such as the aliens power under s 51(xix) or the race power under s 51(xxvi), called for an analysis distinct from that applied to powers 'to legislate for a stated topic or for a stated purpose' – for example bankruptcy, marriage or immigration: see *Lim* (n 1) 54 58 (Gaudron J).

[70] See the discussion of the definition of 'judicial power' as an Australian constitutional term in Simon Evans, 'The Meaning of Constitutional Terms: Essential Features, Family Resemblance and Theory Based Approaches' (2006) 29 *University of New South Wales Law Journal* 207, 227–30.

[71] *Lim* (n 1) 27.

> the power was conferred in terms which sought to divorce such detention in custody from both punishment and criminal guilt.[72]

The Court's concern was with legislation inflicting punishment without any conviction in the ordinary sense of judicial proceedings, in other words a Bill of Pains and Penalties.[73] A Bill of Pains and Penalties would infringe the separation of powers by substituting a legislative judgment of guilt for the judgment of the courts exercising federal legislative power.[74] This offends against the rule of law requirements that offences are to be framed generally, and anyone accused of an offence is to be tried in a court of law. Unquestioning acceptance of government statements that a power is or is not punitive would lend itself to easy evasion of that constitutional requirement.

In light of the close historical association between detention and punishment, the joint judgment treated an executive power of detention as prima facie unconstitutional in the absence of a justified rational connection with a legitimate, non-punitive purpose.[75] It placed the onus on the government to justify the detention without implying punishment or criminal guilt.[76] The joint judgment in *Lim* assumed that detention is punishment unless the government can show it to be a reasonable means to a legitimate, non-punitive end.

2.3.3 Non-Citizens' Vulnerability to Removal and the Separation of Powers

The reasoning in the joint judgment sought to balance the principle – namely that administrative detention is prima facie contrary to the separation of powers, against the exception – derived from the requirements of immigration control. It held that, certain exceptions aside, Australian *citizens*, at least in times of peace,[77] enjoy 'a constitutional immunity from being imprisoned by Commonwealth authority except pursuant to an order by a court in the exercise of the judicial power of the Commonwealth'.[78] Attention then turned to the exceptions.[79] In

[72] ibid.

[73] See the judgment of McHugh J in *Lim* (n 1) 69–71. He defined the elements of such a Bill as '(1) directed to an individual or particular group of individuals (2) which punishes that individual or individuals (3) without the procedural safeguards involved in a judicial trial': 70.

[74] *Lim* (n 1) 70 (McHugh J).

[75] See Leslie Zines, *The High Court and the Constitution*, 5th edn (Sydney, Federation Press, 2008) 282–93, in particular 288–89.

[76] See Stephen McDonald, 'Involuntary Detention and the Separation of Judicial Power' (2007) 35 *Federal Law Review* 25, 31.

[77] The judgment cites *Little v Commonwealth* [1947] HCA 24, (1947) 75 CLR 64 as authority for this caveat. That case held that a detention order issued against a citizen was not reviewable except on grounds of bad faith. See David Dyzenhaus, 'Cycles of Legality in Emergency Times' (2007) 18 *Public Law Review* 165, 181.

[78] *Lim* (n 1) 28–29.

[79] These exceptions included committal to custody pending trial (but allowing for bail) and involuntary detention on grounds of mental illness or infectious disease. The justification for detention in these cases was practical and direct, involving an assessment of flight risk, self-harm, or the need for

considering the application of the constitutional immunity to aliens, the joint judgment stated:

> While an alien who is actually within this country enjoys the protection of our law, his or her status, rights and immunities under that law differ from the status, rights and immunities of an Australian citizen in a variety of important respects.[80]

The most important difference 'lies in the vulnerability of the alien to exclusion or deportation'.[81] The joint judgment stated that the effect of the alien's vulnerabilities 'is significantly to diminish the protection which Chapter III of the Constitution provides . . . against imprisonment otherwise than pursuant to judicial process'.[82] These vulnerabilities are taken to be a matter of international law, 'an incident of sovereignty over territory'.[83] The authority cited for this proposition was the 1906 Privy Council decision of *Attorney-General (Canada) v Cain*.[84] The joint judgment extracted from that 1906 decision the proposition that 'the power to expel or deport a particular alien, and the associated power to confine under restraint to the extent necessary to make expulsion or deportation effective, were seen as *prima facie* executive in character'.[85] The idea that 'an alien is not an outlaw' and the constitutional immunity derived from the separation of powers confronted a countervailing common law tradition of executive control over immigration.

There was a general constitutional immunity from administrative detention, and a permitted exception to it in the form of immigration detention. The question for resolution was whether the detention provisions fell under the constitutional immunity, or under a permitted exception. In the contemporaneous case of *Cunliffe v Commonwealth*, Brennan J stated: 'The cases in this category arise because legislative power is restricted by a limitation, the law in its effect and operation infringes on the limitation and it is necessary to ascertain whether the purpose or object of the law nevertheless falls within the power.'[86] Critically, the question of whether the detention provisions fell within the immigration exception was assessed with reference to the connection between detention and legitimate immigration purposes. These purposes were facilitating deportation and considering an entry application (the latter sometimes referred to as 'processing').

quarantine. Other exceptions to the constitutional immunity applicable to citizens rested primarily on tradition: the powers of Parliament to punish for contempt and of military tribunals to punish for breach of military discipline.

[80] *Lim* (n 1) 29.

[81] ibid.

[82] ibid.

[83] ibid.

[84] *Attorney-General (Canada) v Cain* [1906] AC 542, 546, quoting Vattel, *Law of Nations* (1758), bk 1, s 231; bk 2, s 125, and quoted in *Lim* (n 1) 29–30. See ch 1, pp 26–27.

[85] *Lim* (n 1) 30.

[86] *Cunliffe v Commonwealth* [1994] HCA 44, (1994) 182 CLR 272, 323 24 (Brennan J). For discussions of proportionality in the Australian constitutional context, see eg Bradley Selway QC, 'The Rise and Rise of the Reasonable Proportionality Test in Public Law' (1996) 7 *Public Law Review* 212; Jeremy Kirk, 'Constitutional Guarantees, Characterisation and the Concept of Proportionality' (1997) 21 *Melbourne University Law Review* 1.

The joint judgment elaborated on the connection between detention and immigration purposes in terms of the reasonable necessity test introduced earlier. The detention provisions would be valid if they were 'reasonably capable of being seen as necessary for the purposes of deportation or to enable an entry application to be made and considered'.[87] The test is one of proportionality, allowing the Court to grapple with the question of whether a measure authorising immigration detention overreached itself as a disproportionate means to otherwise legitimate ends. Leslie Zines observes that, 'in view of the fact that the difference between punitive and non-punitive detention is not always as clear as that between chalk and cheese, proportionality would appear to be a useful criterion to use'.[88]

The content of the proportionality test employed is best ascertained through its application to the facts of the case. In its reliance on what was 'reasonably *capable* of being *seen* as necessary' (emphasis added), the test is, on its face, a highly deferential one.[89] And indeed, in *Lim* the joint judgment applied it in a highly deferential fashion, holding that the system of mandatory detention introduced by Division 4B met its requirements.[90] The joint judgment did not require any form of individualised assessment as to whether extended detention was 'reasonably necessary' for an assessment of immigration status, or removal. It allowed for extended detention based on a government officer's 'reasonable suspicion' that a person fell within the category of aliens designated by the legislation.[91] It did not require that this decision to place the non-citizen in detention be subject to review, or that there be periodic review of detention during the period authorised.

The High Court's conclusion that the mandatory detention regime was constitutional rested on various limitations contained in the scheme. The decision does not leave a clear message regarding the outer temporal limit of immigration detention, as the time limit was treated as part of a package of limitations. The joint judgment's statement on constitutionality took the form of a counterfactual. It held that a limit of 273 days, following a period of unlawful detention, *would not* have been sufficient without the request for release provision. It is not clear whether *with* the request for removal provision (and without a prior period in unlawful detention) detention in excess of 273 days would be constitutional.[92]

[87] *Lim* (n 1) 33.

[88] Zines (n 77) 289.

[89] In *Al-Kateb*, the Human Rights and Equal Opportunity Commission (HREOC) submitted that the majority test from *Lim* 'accords too much deference to Parliament'. 'The test should be whether detention is reasonably necessary to make an assessment of the status of the person (health, security, migration) and/or for removal or deportation to then be effected': Submissions of the Human Rights and Equal Opportunity Commission Seeking to Intervene, [37], www.humanrights.gov.au/legal/submissions_court/intervention/khafaji.html.

[90] A provision of the scheme was struck down, but it was 'clearly severable' from the scheme as a whole and did not affect the validity of any other provision, or undermine the scheme's operation: *Lim* (n 1) 37. See the discussion of s 54R, the provision struck down, in the text to n 100.

[91] Migration Act 1958, s 189.

[92] *Lim* (n 1) 32–35.

What is clear is that the request for removal provision was critical to the constitutionality of the detention regime.[93]

The request for removal section provided that an officer must remove a detainee from Australia as soon as practicable if the detainee asked the Minister, in writing, to be removed. It was held to 'set . . . the context in which the other provisions' of the mandatory detention regime operated,[94] transforming what would otherwise be involuntary detention into a species of 'voluntary' detention, since it is within the detainee's power 'to bring his or her detention in custody under Division 4B to an end at any time'.[95] The moment detainees relinquish the attempt to enter Australia, and request removal, their continued detention is only authorised 'for the limited period involved, in the circumstances of the particular case, in complying with the statutory requirement of removal "as soon as practicable"'.[96] The reasoning in *Lim* was predicated on the assumption that the detainees, by way of the request for removal provision, had it within their power to bring their detention to an end. It was in essence a 'prison with three walls' argument. The reasoning on the request for removal provision was that, while the plaintiffs were presently barred from release into Australia, the 'fourth wall' remained open. They were always free to leave.[97]

McHugh J offered the fullest explanation of why the request for removal provision was critical to the constitutionality of the detention regime. He emphasised the provision's importance, stating that the ability to request removal, and so release, was 'vital' to the constitutionality of the scheme. He conceded, given the plaintiffs' application for refugee status, that voluntary removal was not a 'real choice', but continued:

> But for the purpose of the doctrine of the separation of powers, the difference between involuntary detention and detention with the concurrence or acquiescence of the 'detainee' is vital. A person is not punished if, after entering Australia without permission, he or she chooses to be detained in custody pending the determination of an application for entry rather than to leave the country during the period of determination.[98]

In *Lim*, McHugh J held that it is imperative that the detention is in some sense 'chosen' by the detainee. The constitutional permissibility of immigration detention relies on an understanding that those coming to Australia have chosen to submit themselves to state control, and that authority for their ongoing detention is connected with the detainees' 'decision' to remain, as deduced from the absence of a request for removal. McHugh J's reasoning illustrates that the request for

[93] ibid, 33. The joint judgment held that the 273-day limit and the requirement that a person be removed from Australia as soon as practicable after refusal of an entry application 'would not . . . have gone far enough were it not for the provision of section 54P(1)'.

[94] ibid.

[95] ibid, 34.

[96] ibid.

[97] At the time of hearing and judgment, the plaintiffs had yet to have their applications for refugee status determined by a delegate of the Minister responsible for the Migration Act 1958.

[98] *Lim* (n 1) 72.

removal provision is central to his separation of powers analysis because it preserves the detainees' agency, even if as a matter of legal fiction.

Incidentally, the *Lim* majority did hold that one provision of Division 4B contravened the separation of powers. Section 54R provided that a court was not 'to order the release from custody of a designated person'. The majority in *Lim* held that a law that purports to direct a court in unqualified terms that any person whom the Commonwealth executive has imprisoned cannot be released is invalid. As section 54R was such a law it constituted 'an impermissible intrusion into the judicial power' and was struck down.[99]

The joint judgment's reasoning on section 54R also illustrates the centrality of the request for removal provision to the separation of powers analysis. The joint judgment gave, as an example of a situation in which legal authority to detain would be spent (but section 54R still directed the Court not to order release), a situation in which a detainee is held in custody 'in disregard' of a request for removal.[100] The joint judgment's use of this example was premised on a request for removal being an *effective* means of securing release from detention.

2.3.4 Conclusions on *Lim*

Lim allowed for extended mandatory detention of persons in the absence of any individualised assessment. Detention was based on an officer's 'reasonable suspicion' that the detainee fell within the requisite statutory category. There was no requirement for periodic review of detention. It is only in the light of the subsequent ruling in *Al-Kateb* that *Lim* appears, in relative terms, to be protective of liberty.

Lim is clear authority that immigration detention is subject to a proportionality requirement. A non-citizen can be detained for purposes incidental to his or her immigration processing and/or removal. The purposive link between detention and removal is to be assessed by testing whether the detention provisions are 'reasonably capable of being seen as necessary for the purposes of deportation'.[101]

The following features of *Lim* are particularly salient to an evaluation of the subsequent case law on detention of non-citizens. First, the separation of powers demands that any purpose of immigration detention is necessarily *limited*. There is then the question of how the limit is to be determined. The starting premise of the joint judgment in *Lim* was that detention other than by court order contravenes the separation of powers. Detention is prima facie punishment unless it can be shown to be a reasonable means to a legitimate end. A proportionality test is employed to determine whether detention is precluded by the constitutional

[99] Mason CJ, Toohey and McHugh JJ held that s 54R could be read down to avoid invalidity. The minority agreed that the majority's reading of the provision, if unavoidable, was such as to render the provision in contravention of the separation of powers.

[100] *Lim* (n 1) 36.

[101] ibid, 10 (Mason CJ), 33 (Brennan, Deane and Dawson JJ), 58 (Gaudron J), 65 66, 71 (McHugh J).

immunity, or falls within the exception. The reasonable necessity test is employed to assess whether an infringement of a non-citizen's liberty is proportionate to the requirements of admission and/or removal.

The other key feature of the *Lim* decision is the legal significance attached to the request for removal provision. As stated in the joint judgment, it set the context for the detention regime.[102] By providing that it always lay within a detainee's power to secure his or her own removal, the request for removal provision enabled a characterisation of detention as 'with the concurrence or acquiescence' of the detainee.[103] It is 'vital' to the separation of powers that a detainee is able to secure his or her own release.[104]

After *Lim*, amendments to the Migration Act 1958, entering into effect on 1 September 1994, introduced detention provisions in the form of those challenged in *Al-Kateb* and the following case, *Al Masri*. The Migration Reform Act 1992 also removed the 273-day detention limit noted in *Lim*.[105]

2.4 *Al Masri*

2.4.1 *Al Masri* Introduced

Starting in 2002, a series of challenges to indefinite immigration detention were brought in the Federal Court of Australia. The challenges were brought by non-citizens who did not have a legal right to be in Australia and had formally requested removal, but whose removal could not be effected because no other State had agreed to receive them. The government maintained that its authority to continue to hold these individuals in immigration detention, for an indefinite period, was not impugned by the fact that there were difficulties in effecting their removal.

The question arose as to whether the 'reasonable necessity' test from *Lim* was satisfied where there was no real likelihood of the request being fulfilled by the government. Was the request for removal provision to be understood as necessarily directed in a 'genuine, and realistic, sense towards removal' from Australia?[106] Any argument such as that advanced by McHugh J in *Lim*, that the request for removal provision served to preserve the detainees' agency, giving them a choice as to whether to remain in detention, was predicated on that request having practical effect.

[102] ibid, 33 (Brennan, Deane and Dawson JJ).

[103] ibid, 72 (McHugh J); see also 34 (Brennan, Deane and Dawson JJ).

[104] ibid, 72 (McHugh J).

[105] Migration Reform Act 1992, s 13, inserting a new 'Division 4C – Detention of unlawful non-citizens' into the Migration Act 1958.

[106] *Al Masri* (n 1) 79.

There was a divergence of opinion in the Federal Court on the legality of indefinite detention of the non-citizens.[107] A temporary resolution was reached when the Full Court of the Federal Court handed down judgment in *Minister for Immigration & Multicultural & Indigenous Affairs v Al Masri*.[108] Applying *Lim*, the Full Court reasoned in accordance with the rights-protecting model of immigration detention. The Court's decision was framed as an exercise in statutory interpretation, based on a common law presumption against the abrogation of liberty. The reasoning was informed by the need for detention to have a temporal limit if it is to meet the requirements of the constitutional separation of powers, and buttressed by international human rights law. The Court determined that where there is no real prospect of removal in the reasonably foreseeable future, the rationale of detention is frustrated and, accordingly, authority to detain is suspended.

The Federal Court's judgment in *Al Masri* represented the Australian legal position for less than 16 months. The High Court of Australia handed down judgment in *Al-Kateb* in August 2004. In that case the High Court majority held that the Migration Act 1958 authorised detention for as long as the government had the *intention* of removing the detainees, even if removal was not practicable for an indefinite period. While the majority did not openly distinguish *Lim*, they undermined the constitutional limits outlined in that case, holding that even if the separation of powers did supply a constitutional immunity from executive detention, its impact on immigration detention was precluded by the operation of the aliens power. The *Al-Kateb* majority's interpretation of the statute and the Constitution constitutes a clear example of a rights-precluding approach to detention of non-citizens subject to removal. As made explicit by some members of the *Al-Kateb* majority, their reasoning was responsive to, and a rejection of, the rights-protecting reasoning of the Full Court of the Federal Court in *Al Masri*.

The statutory scheme for detention of non-citizens pending removal, the subject of *Al Masri* and *Al-Kateb*, centred on sections 189, 196 and 198 of the Migration Act 1958. Section 189 provided in part:

> 189 Detention of unlawful non-citizens
>
> (1) If an officer knows or reasonably suspects that a person in the migration zone (other than an excised offshore place) is an unlawful non-citizen, the officer must detain the person.

Section 196 provided in part:

> 196 Period of detention
>
> (1) An unlawful non-citizen detained under section 189 must be kept in immigration detention until he or she is:
>
> (a) removed from Australia under section 198 or 199; or
> (b) deported under section 200; or

[107] Contrast *Al Masri v Minister for Immigration & Multicultural & Indigenous Affairs* [2002] FCA 1009, (2002) 192 ALR 609 (*Al Masri* (first instance)) and *SHFB v Goodwin* [2003] FCA 29.

[108] *Al Masri* (n 1).

(c) granted a visa.

Section 198 provided in part:

198 Removal from Australia of unlawful non-citizens

(1) An officer must remove as soon as reasonably practicable an unlawful non-citizen who asks the Minister, in writing, to be so removed.

The central issue in both cases was whether the above provisions of the Migration Act 1958 providing for mandatory detention authorised the indefinite, possibly permanent, administrative detention of a person who had requested removal, where there was no real prospect that that request could be effected in the reasonably foreseeable future.[109]

2.4.2 *Al Masri* at First Instance[110]

The reasoning in the first instance decision highlights the factual and evidential issues that characterise the Australian case law on the indefinite administrative detention of non-citizens. Mr Al Masri, a Palestinian from the Gaza Strip, arrived in Australia without a visa in June 2001 and was placed in immigration detention. His application for refugee status was not granted and he made a written request to be returned to Gaza in early December 2001.[111] The Australian government was unable to secure his entry into the Gaza Strip transiting via Israel, Egypt or Jordan. On being approached, Syria refused his removal to that country. Mr Al Masri commenced a proceeding against the Minister, seeking an order in the nature of habeas corpus for release from detention. The Full Court's judgment stated: 'The delay and uncertainty about [his] . . . removal caused him to suffer anxiety and depression and also led to self-harm, resulting in him being admitted to hospital.'[112]

Although it was not a national security case, government claims of confidentiality, and attendant understandings of what was required by way of government justification for detention, informed the litigation in *Al Masri*. The government acknowledged that there was nothing in the evidence expressing a view as to the likelihood of Mr Al Masri's removal, but submitted that active efforts were being made to secure his removal and he was not being 'left to languish' in detention.[113] The Minister suggested that revealing the 'full details' of factual information as to the prospects of Mr Al Masri's removal would be likely to prejudice that removal.

[109] See *Al Masri* (n 1) [2].

[110] *Al Masri* (first instance) (n 107). I was Associate to the judge at first instance, Justice Merkel, during hearing and judgment.

[111] He was unsuccessful before the delegate of the Minister charged with making a decision whether to grant a protection visa recognising refugee status and on review before the Refugee Review Tribunal. He did not challenge the Tribunal's decision, but instead requested that he be returned to Gaza on the day of the Tribunal's decision, 5 December 2001.

[112] *Al Masri* (first instance) (n 107) [8].

[113] ibid, [48].

The trial judge, Merkel J, commented: 'No basis was put forward for that view. In any event, something less than the "full details" of the relevant communications may well have sufficed.'[114] In the absence of any evidence as to the present prospects of the applicant's removal, Merkel J held that the Minister had failed to discharge the burden on him to prove that Mr Al Masri's continued detention was lawful. In particular, Merkel J held that as the Minister had not placed information available to him before the court, it was open to him to infer that that information would not assist the Minister's case.[115] This inference effectively required the Minister to provide reasons justifying the continued authority to detain.

Merkel J made a factual finding that Mr Al Masri's removal from Australia was 'not reasonably practicable at the present time as there is no real likelihood or prospect of removal in the reasonably foreseeable future'. He held that the better reading of section 196, supported by section 198, is that detention is authorised only where the Minister is taking steps to secure removal, and there is a real likelihood or prospect of removal in the reasonably foreseeable future.[116] In arriving at this reading, he drew on comparative authorities favouring an implied limitation on immigration detention of this form. Two authorities he relied upon recur repeatedly in the jurisprudence: the decision of the Queen's Bench in *Hardial Singh*,[117] and that of the US Supreme Court in *Zadvydas*.[118] Merkel J ordered Mr Al Masri's immediate release from detention, subject to reporting conditions and a duty to comply with arrangements to facilitate his removal.

Some two weeks after the decision, Mr Al Masri was taken back into immigration detention on the basis that the Minister was now in a position to secure his removal. Mr Al Masri was removed from Australia several days later.[119] After he had left Australia the first instance decision was upheld on appeal in the unanimous decision of the Full Court, discussed below.[120]

[114] ibid, [51].

[115] ibid, [52]. In Australia this is known as a *Jones v Dunkel* point after the decision of the same name: [1959] HCA 8, (1959) 101 CLR 298.

[116] *Al Masri* (first instance) (n 107) [38].

[117] *R v Governor of Durham Prison, ex parte Singh* [1984] 1 All ER 983 (*Hardial Singh*). On *Hardial Singh* see ch 5, s 5.2. Merkel J also addressed the Privy Council's endorsement of the 'Hardial Singh principles' in *Tan Te Lam v Superintendent of Tai A Chau Detention Centre* [1997] AC 97.

[118] *Zadvydas v Davis*, 533 US 678 (2001). On *Zadvydas* see ch 1, s 1.1.

[119] *Al Masri v Minister for Immigration & Multicultural & Indigenous Affairs* [2002] FCA 1099 (*Al Masri* (re-detention)). In *Al Masri* (first instance) (n 107) [24], Merkel J held that the Minister was not precluded from taking Mr Al Masri back into detention when his removal was imminent.

[120] As noted, the appeal to the Federal Court was heard after Mr Al Masri had already been removed from Australia. Mr Al Masri's lawyers brought a motion to dismiss the appeal on discretionary grounds, on the basis that determination of the appeal was of no practical significance to him. The motion was refused on the basis of the Minister's submission that determining the appeal was necessary to determine the adverse costs order against the Minister at first instance. The Court also noted the convenience of determining the present appeal given that the orders of the trial judge had been relied upon in applications for release in other proceedings.

2.4.3 *Al Masri* in the Full Court of the Federal Court[121]

The joint reasons of the Full Court of the Federal Court in *Al Masri* intertwined constitutional law, common law, comparative and international law on the legality of indefinite administrative detention. The decision was grounded in principles of statutory interpretation, elaborated in the shadow of constitutional invalidity. The initial 32 paragraphs of the reasons were devoted to considering the constitutional constraints on immigration detention, with pride of place accorded to *Lim*. These constitutional considerations were held to 'point very strongly to the need and foundation for a limitation' on the power to detain in the form of a requirement that there be a 'real likelihood or prospect of removal in the reasonably foreseeable future'.[122] However, the 'presumption of constitutionality', that is, the presumption that statutes should be interpreted consistently with the Constitution as far as it is possible to do so, was not relied upon. The Court concluded that the central issue in the appeal could be determined on the basis of common law presumptions concerning fundamental rights and freedoms.

The Court began its elaboration of the common law presumption in favour of liberty by engaging extensively with comparative common law authority on immigration detention. These comparative authorities were discussed 'as indicative of the approach taken by courts in the common law tradition to the construction of statutes providing for administrative detention'.[123] They were considered as part of the reasoning leading to the Court's conclusions on construction of the statutory provisions. By way of contrast, it was only *after* it stated its conclusions on construction that the Court turned to consider Australia's international obligations. These international obligations were introduced as fortifying the Court's conclusions on statutory interpretation. In what follows I sketch the strands of the Court's reasoning, introduced above, with particular attention to their mutual influence.

The Court began its reasoning with reference to the presumption in favour of constitutionality. Central to the Court's reading of *Lim* was the understanding that the request for removal provision has to be directed in 'a genuine and realistic sense towards removal' from Australia if it is to serve its constitutional function.[124] The Court stated that in *Lim* the 'scales were tilted in favour of validity' by the request for removal provision, by reason of that provision's 'presumed practical effect'.[125] The Court held that for the request for removal provision to do the constitutional work assigned to it by the reasoning in *Lim*, it must be true that 'it always lies within

[121] *Al Masri* (n 1). The bench of the Full Court of the Federal Court was comprised of Black CJ, Sundberg and Weinberg JJ.

[122] ibid, [81].

[123] ibid, [96]. While the quoted phrase is attributed to the trial judge, it is clearly the view of the Full Court.

[124] ibid, [79].

[125] ibid, [63] and [61] respectively.

the power of a designated person to bring his or her custody to an end'.[126] On the government's reading of the legislation, this was no longer the case.

In considering the second, common law, presumption, the Court adopted Gleeson CJ's formulation in *Plaintiff S157*:

> courts do not impute to the legislature an intention to abrogate or curtail fundamental rights or freedoms unless such an intention is clearly manifested by unmistakable and unambiguous language. General words will rarely be sufficient for that purpose. What courts look for is a clear indication that the legislature has directed its attention to the rights or freedoms in question, and has consciously decided upon abrogation or curtailment.[127]

As in *Lim*, the discussion of immigration detention was framed with reference to common law authorities protective of liberty. However, in *Al Masri*, in the context of the common law presumption, the discussion of these authorities was focused directly on the alien's liberty interest at common law, rather than (as in *Lim*) framed with reference to constitutional jurisprudence on the nature of judicial power.

The Court in *Al Masri* was confident of the presumption's place in the law. A section of its judgment entitled 'liberty and the common law' begins:

> The principle against the imputation of an intention to curtail fundamental rights is sometimes criticized on account of uncertainty about the rights to which it applies. This may be so at the margins, but there can be no question that the right to personal liberty is among the most fundamental of all common law rights.[128]

The Court added: 'It is also among the most fundamental of the universally recognised human rights.'[129] The status of the right at international law (with particular emphasis on its universality) was advanced in support of its legitimacy as a common law right.[130]

Much of the discussion of the right to liberty at common law was dedicated to showing, by way of common law precedent, that 'the common law's concern for the liberty of individuals extends to those who are within Australia unlawfully'.[131] A

[126] ibid, [61], quoting *Lim* (n 1) 34.

[127] *Plaintiff S157* (n 51) [30]. *Plaintiff S157* was a decision on a privative clause that sought to abolish judicial review of migration decisions as far as that was constitutionally possible. While the High Court upheld the constitutional validity of the privative clause, it held that it was not effective to protect decisions involving 'jurisdictional error' from judicial review. The Court reasoned that decisions effected by this error are not recognised in law as decisions at all, rather they are 'purported decisions'. Accordingly they were not decisions 'made under the Act' and were not caught by the privative clause. The decision effectively neutralised the government's attempt to end judicial review of immigration decisions. In *Plaintiff S157* and *Al-Kateb*, Gleeson CJ wrote a separate judgment relying on the principle of legality, and avoiding constitutional reasoning.

[128] *Al Masri* (n 1) [86].

[129] ibid.

[130] On international law as a means of updating common law rights, see eg David Dyzenhaus, Murray Hunt and Michael Taggart, 'The Principle of Legality in Administrative Law: Internationalisation as Constitutionalisation' (2001) 1 *Oxford University Commonwealth Law Journal* 5; Mayo Moran, 'Authority, Influence and Persuasion: *Baker*, Charter Values and the Puzzle of Method' in David Dyzenhaus (ed), *The Unity of Public Law* (Oxford, Hart Publishing, 2004).

[131] There are statements to this effect in *Kioa* (n 1), the joint judgment in *Lim* (n 1), and Lord Scarman's judgment in *Khawaja* (n 45): see *Al Masri* (n 1) [114].

large part of the Court's development of the common law presumption was by way of comparative authority, including reference to *Hardial Singh* and *Zadvydas*.[132] In concluding an extended review of these comparative authorities, the Court made the statement that appears as this chapter's epigraph. Unauthorised aliens are not 'outlaws' but 'in common with every other person in Australia' enjoy 'the equal protection of Australia's laws'. The presumption against the curtailment of fundamental freedoms is 'a principle of universal application'.[133]

Immigration detention was treated as just another regulatory power, operating in the same common law environment as other government regulatory powers. The starting presumption was not that the government must have the power to detain a non-citizen who has no right to remain. Rather, it was that such detention infringes a non-citizen's liberty right, where the extent of that infringement called for justification. Further, the relevant common law context was seen as shared between the national jurisdictions, a repository of principle that each could draw on.

Having outlined the case for strong constitutional and common law presumptions against indefinite detention, the Court's attention shifted to the question of whether those presumptions were rebutted. Here, dictated by the principle of legality, the question the Court asked was: 'Had the legislature directed its attention to the possibility of indefinite detention?'[134] Section 196 provides that an unlawful non-citizen is to be kept in detention 'until' he or she is removed under section 198 or 199, deported under section 200,[135] or granted a visa.[136] The Court asked how much weight this word 'until' could bear. Had Parliament directed its attention to the possibility that none of the three listed events might occur?[137] The possibility that detention might be 'for the rest of a person's life' needed to be 'squarely confronted'.[138] In construing the statute, the Court acknowledged textual features that militated for the proposition that Parliament had directed its attention to the possibility of indefinite detention, and textual features which indicated that it had not. The Court held that the better reading was that Parliament had not attended to such a possibility.[139] The Court's resolution of the conflicting statutory signals was underwritten by its position that 'when the demands of certainty and liberty come into conflict, the tradition of the common law is to lean towards liberty'.[140]

[132] *Al Masri* (n 1) [114] referencing *Hardial Singh* (n 117) and *Zadvydas* (n 118).

[133] *Al Masri* (n 1) [114].

[134] The formulation of the presumption the Court adopts, taken from *Plaintiff S157* (n 51), contains two requirements: (i) has the legislature directed its attention to the rights or freedoms in question? and (ii) has it consciously decided on abrogation or curtailment? See the quotation in the text accompanying n 127. The Court's reasoning focused on the first requirement.

[135] The distinction in statutory terminology was between the 'removal' of 'unlawful' non-citizens and the 'deportation' of non-citizens convicted of serious crimes.

[136] See the provision, quoted in the text preceding n 111.

[137] *Al Masri* (n 1) [119].

[138] ibid, [117].

[139] ibid, [119]–[132].

[140] ibid, [129].

The government argued that an implied temporal limitation would result in the release of those 'who had no right to be . . . in Australia'.[141] The Court agreed that it would be releasing those with no right to remain, but did not accept that this involved a contradiction. It rejected the equivalence at the heart of the government's case between the absence of a right to remain and the absence of a right to liberty. An unlawful non-citizen released from detention remained vulnerable to deportation. This was demonstrated by Mr Al Masri's circumstances. He was re-detained a fortnight after his release by order of the trial judge and shortly thereafter removed from Australia. His earlier release from detention did not confer a right to remain.[142]

The government proceeded to raise a number of policy issues. It focused on the uncertainty that court-ordered release could introduce into its management of immigration. In response, the Court relied on the comparative authorities to demonstrate the practicality of a temporal limitation. The decades of governmental practice in other jurisdictions were taken to suggest that such difficulties are 'likely to be more apparent than real'.[143] More fundamentally, it was in response to this line of government argument that the Court stated its preference for liberty over (administrative) certainty.[144]

The final government objection was pernicious in the circumstances. It argued that court-ordered release raised the prospect of 'release into the community of persons who might pose a threat to the safety of others, or to national security'.[145] The Court resisted this attempt to inject national security concerns into the debate. Such persons would comprise only an exceptional subset of those to whom the limitations on detention might ever apply. The Court observed that this category would only pose a problem if the person could not otherwise be detained. The judges noted that Australian criminal law, and that of other countries to which the individual might be extradited, provided for detention. And they noted that the legislature could enact specific provisions to address security concerns.

Only after reaching its conclusions on the construction of the statute did the Court turn to consider Australia's international obligations, arguing that these obligations support their conclusions on other grounds, via the presumption that statutes are to be interpreted, as far as their language permits, in conformity with international law. The Court focused on the international jurisprudence on Article 9 of the International Covenant on Civil and Political Rights (ICCPR).[146]

[141] ibid, [125]–[128].

[142] The trial judge sanctioned his re-detention prior to removal as consistent with the purpose of the power: see *Al Masri* (re-detention) (n 119).

[143] *Al Masri* (n 1) 129.

[144] See text to n 140.

[145] *Al Masri* (n 1) 131.

[146] International Covenant on Civil and Political Rights (adopted 19 December 1966, entered into force 23 March 1976) 999 UNTS 171 (ICCPR). The Court also discussed commentary on the provision and the views of the United Nations Human Rights Committee, stating: 'Although the views of the Committee lack precedential authority in an Australian court, it is legitimate to have regard to them as the opinions of an expert body established by the treaty to further its objects' (*Al Masri* (n 1) 148). For

Article 9(1) provides:

> Everyone has the right to liberty and security of the person. No one shall be subject to arbitrary arrest or detention. No one shall be deprived of his liberty except on such grounds and in accordance with such procedure as are established by law.

The central theme of the international law discussion was the requirement that a deprivation of liberty not only be prescribed by law, but the law and its application in a given case must not be arbitrary. The notion of 'arbitrariness' found in the international materials includes detention which in the individual case was 'unproportional' or 'unjust'.[147] The Court concluded that the interpretation contended for by the government would be arbitrary detention within the meaning of Article 9(1). The Court also had recourse to jurisprudence on Article 5 of the European Convention on Human Rights (ECHR)[148] that supported its conclusions on Article 9 of the ICCPR. The ECHR jurisprudence was treated as comparative law. The Court concluded its review of international law by holding that to read section 196 conformably with Australia's obligations under Article 9(1) of the ICCPR, authority to detain could 'not extend to a time when there is no real likelihood or prospect in the reasonably foreseeable future of a detained person being removed and thus released from detention'.[149]

International human rights jurisprudence was held to 'fortify' the conclusion arrived at by means of the common law presumption and the presumption of constitutionality, namely that the general words should be read as subject to an implied temporal limitation.

2.4.4 Conclusions on *Al Masri*

The Full Court in *Al Masri* relied on a common law presumption against the curtailment of fundamental freedoms. This was reinforced by an argument that the provisions should be read as subject to an unexpressed exception so as to avoid contravening the separation of powers. These readings were supported by a presumption of compliance with international law. Further, the elaboration of the common law presumption made extensive use of comparative common law authority. The reasoning from these various sources was mutually reinforcing. They required that the duration of immigration detention be proportionate to the legitimate immigration purpose of facilitating removal.

Despite these sources of law pulling together, there is a clear hierarchy between them. While any ruling on constitutional invalidity is effectively kept in reserve,

a review of relevant decisions of the United Nations Human Rights Committee see Daniel Wilsher, *Immigration Detention: Law, History, Politics* (New York, Cambridge University Press, 2012) 157–66.

[147] *Al Masri* (n 1) [152].

[148] Convention for the Protection of Human Rights and Fundamental Freedoms (opened for signature 4 November 1950, entered into force 3 September 1953) 213 UNTS 211, Eur TS 5 (ECHR).

[149] *Al Masri* (n 1) [155].

the prospect of such invalidity shadows the reasoning as a whole. At the other end of the continuum, the presumption in favour of conformity with international law is reduced to a supporting role, brought in after the heavy lifting had been done by constitutional and common law considerations.

The judges situated the law's antipathy towards indefinite administrative detention in the overlap of these sources of interpretive influence. What do the common law and international law arguments add to the constitutional argument drawn from *Lim*? Perhaps most importantly, in their focus on the nature of the harm, the common law and international law jurisprudence draws attention to what the constitutional separation of powers analysis is centrally *for* – the protection of the legal subject. In addition, these sources reaffirm the commitment to extend the law's protection to all within the jurisdiction, whether there lawfully or unlawfully. This frames immigration detention as a limited exception to constitutional norms, not a distinct domain in which such norms do not apply. Finally, the understanding of arbitrariness contained in the international human rights jurisprudence, carrying with it a requirement of proportionality, echoes and augments the constitutional exercise of determining whether a given instance of executive detention falls within the constitutional immunity from executive detention, or a purposive exception to it. In binding together these different strands, the Court's judgment in *Al Masri* brought to the surface the way in which the separation of powers arguments in *Lim* were motivated by a concern to protect the liberty of the legal subject.

An application for special leave to appeal *Al Masri* to the High Court of Australia was refused on 14 August 2003.[150] However, the High Court decision discussed in the next chapter, *Al-Kateb*, was in effect, if not in fact, an appeal from *Al Masri*.[151]

The *Al Masri* decision of the Full Court of the Federal Court had no practical effect on Mr Al Masri's circumstances. As noted above, he had already been removed from Australia.[152] It did, however, lead to the release of about 12 others. Amongst them was a Mr Al-Kateb,[153] who was apparently driven from the immigration detention centre into the regional South Australian town of Port Augusta, where he and some others were left without money in the town square.[154]

[150] Transcript of Proceedings, *Minister for Immigration and Multicultural and Indigenous Affairs v Al Masri* (High Court of Australia, Gummow, Kirby and Hayne JJ, 14 August 2003).

[151] For references to *Al Masri* see *Al-Kateb* (n 2) [234]–[238] (Hayne J), [3] and [23] (Gleeson CJ), [300] (Callinan J, referring to *Al Masri* (first instance) (n 109)).

[152] In August 2008, it was reported in the Australian media that Mr Al Masri had been shot dead in the Gaza Strip. See Paul Bibby et al, 'Deported Refugee Shot Dead' *Sydney Morning Herald* (Sydney, 2 August 2008), www.smh.com.au/news/world/deported-refugee-shot-dead/2008/08/01/1217097536265.html.

[153] *Al-Kateb* (n 2) [107] (Gummow J): Mr Al Kateb was released by consent order of the Federal Court (Mansfield J) made on 17 April 2003, two days after the decision in *Al Masri* (n 1), delivered on 15 April.

[154] See David Marr, 'Escape from a Life in Limbo' *Sydney Morning Herald* (Sydney, 27 October 2007), www.smh.com.au/news/national/escape-from-a-life-in-limbo/2007/10/26/1192941339538.html.

3

Indefinite Detention of Aliens

> The power with respect to both heads [aliens and immigration] extends to preventing aliens entering or remaining in Australia except by executive permission. But if the heads of power extend so far, they extend to permitting exclusion from the Australian community – by prevention of entry, by removal from Australia, *and* by segregation from the community by detention in the meantime.
>
> Hayne J, *Al-Kateb*, High Court of Australia (2004)[1]

> The possibility that a person, regardless of personal circumstances, regardless of whether he or she is a danger to the community, and regardless of whether he or she might abscond, can be subjected to indefinite, and perhaps permanent, administrative detention is not one to be dealt with by implication.
>
> Gleeson CJ in dissent, *Al-Kateb*, High Court of Australia (2004)[2]

3.1 Introduction to *Al-Kateb*

Mr Al-Kateb had been denied a visa and had been in detention since December 2000 pursuant to Australia's legislative regime for the mandatory detention of unlawful non-citizens.[3] He was a Palestinian who had been born and resided most of his life in Kuwait. Mr Al-Kateb's long-term residency in Kuwait did not guarantee permanent residence, and it was not contested that he was a stateless person. In mid-2002 he requested removal to Kuwait or, failing that, to Gaza.[4] The Immigration Department was unable to secure his removal to either of those locations or to any third country, and continued to hold him in detention. In 2003, Mr Al-Kateb brought an application for habeas corpus to the Federal Court and sought a declaration that he was being unlawfully detained.

On 3 April 2003, the trial judge, von Doussa J, dismissed Mr Al-Kateb's application.[5] Von Doussa J found that Mr Al-Kateb's removal from Australia was 'not

[1] *Al-Kateb v Godwin* 2004 HCA 37, (2004) 219 CLR 562, [255]. See also [247] (Heydon J concurring).

[2] ibid, [21].

[3] Migration Act 1958. The form of the relevant provisions was introduced by the Migration Reform Act 1992, entering into effect on 1 September 1994.

[4] *SHDB v Goodwin* [2003] FCA 300, [5] (Von Doussa J).

[5] ibid, [5].

reasonably practicable at the present time as there is no real likelihood or prospect of removal in the reasonably foreseeable future'.[6] However, he disagreed with Merkel J's first instance ruling in *Al Masri* that detention pending removal was subject to an implied temporal limitation.[7] Von Doussa J held that, as long as the government was making all reasonable efforts to secure Mr Al Kateb's removal, his detention met legislative and constitutional requirements. On the basis that authority to detain hinged on governmental intention, the prospects of removal were legally irrelevant. Mr Al-Kateb lodged an appeal from von Doussa J's judgment, which appeal was removed to the High Court.[8]

Mr Al-Kateb was released from detention two weeks later, following the decision of the Full Court of the Federal Court in *Al Masri*.[9]

The High Court heard argument in Mr Al-Kateb's appeal over two days in November 2003. It reserved judgment for almost 10 months. In August 2004, the Court held, by a majority of four of seven judges, that section 196 of the Migration Act 1958 required Mr Al-Kateb's indefinite detention until such time as he could be removed or was granted a visa.

Mr Al-Kateb's challenge to the government's power to detain him presented two broad issues. The first was whether the Migration Act 1958 required the detention of non-citizens present in Australia without a visa who had requested removal, where removal was not practicable. The second issue was whether, if the Migration Act 1958 did so require, it was consistent with the Constitution. The *Al-Kateb* majority (McHugh, Hayne, Callinan and Heydon JJ) held that the legislation authorised the indefinite detention of unlawful non-citizens and that it was constitutional. The minority (Gleeson CJ, Gummow and Kirby JJ) held that the Migration Act 1958 did not authorise detention of a non-citizen whose removal was impracticable. Gummow and Kirby JJ further held that such legislation would be contrary to the separation of powers.

[6] ibid, [9].

[7] ibid, [10], incorporating by reference his comments in the judgment of the same day in *SHFB v Goodwin* [2003] FCA 294. On the primary decision in *Al Masri* see ch 2, s 2.4.2.

[8] This occurred on an application by the Commonwealth Attorney-General under the Judiciary Act 1903 (Cth), s 40. This s 40 removal to the High Court was accompanied by the removal of another case, *Minister for Immigration and Multicultural and Indigenous Affairs v Al Khafaji* [2002] FCA 1369, which resulted in the High Court decision of *Minister for Immigration and Multicultural and Indigenous Affairs v Al Khafaji* [2004] HCA 38, (2004) 219 CLR 664. A third case heard and delivered at the same time was *Behrooz v Secretary, Department of Immigration and Multicultural and Indigenous Affairs* [2004] HCA 36, (2004) 219 CLR 486. On *Behrooz* see s 3.7.

[9] *Minister for Immigration & Multicultural & Indigenous Affairs v Al Masri* [2003] FCAFC 70, (2003) 126 FCR 54. See ch 2, p 64.

3.2 The Majority on Interpretation of the Detention Provisions

To reiterate, the relevant provisions of the Migration Act 1958 stated as follows:

> 189 Detention of unlawful non-citizens
>
> (1) If an officer knows or reasonably suspects that a person in the migration zone (other than an excised offshore place) is an unlawful non-citizen, the officer must detain the person.
>
> 196 Period of detention
>
> (1) An unlawful non-citizen detained under section 189 must be kept in immigration detention until he or she is:
>
> (a) removed from Australia under section 198 or 199; or
> (b) deported under section 200; or
> (c) granted a visa.

Next, section 198 provided in part:

> 198 Removal from Australia of unlawful non-citizens
>
> (1) An officer must remove as soon as reasonably practicable an unlawful non-citizen who asks the Minister, in writing, to be so removed.

The Act provided that a person was to be held in detention 'until' one of three specified events occurred: removal, deportation or the grant of a visa (section 196). A person in Mr Al-Kateb's position, who had requested removal, was to be removed 'as soon as reasonably practicable' (section 198).

The Migration Act 1958 did not provide for what was to occur if those terminating events did not eventuate. The *Al-Kateb* majority held that the Act mandated that a non-citizen be held in detention indefinitely, possibly permanently, until one of those events occurred. The possibility that none of those events might ever occur was treated as legally irrelevant. The majority held that the statutory language was 'intractable in its provision for indefinite detention in the circumstances'.[10]

The government argued that the phrase 'reasonably practicable' in section 198 blunted any argument that the purpose of removal could be frustrated, which would in turn suspend authority to detain. It submitted that what matters is that the executive keeps trying to carry out its duty to remove a non-citizen, by taking such reasonable steps as it can to achieve what is not, presently, reasonably practicable. As expressed at the hearing:

> *McHugh J*: Ultimately, you have to go so far as to contend that, in a particular case, you may be able to keep a person in immigration detention for the rest of that person's life,

[10] *Al-Kateb* (n 1) [241] (Hayne J).

> so long as you have the purpose of preventing the person moving into the Australian community and for the purpose of deporting the person.
>
> *Mr Bennett [Australian Solicitor General]*: Yes, that is one of the legitimate purposes and the purpose of deporting which, as I say, is a purpose as to which, by necessity, one can never say never.[11]

The majority endorsed the government's submission. Hayne J gave the leading judgment on statutory construction.[12] He stated:

> the most that *could* ever be said in a particular case where it is not *now*, and has not been, reasonably practicable to effect removal, is that there is now no country which will receive a particular non-citizen whom Australia seeks to remove, and it cannot *now* be predicted when that will happen . . . That is not to say that it will *never* happen.[13]

The majority position was that authority to detain rested on the government's intention to remove the non-citizen.[14] There was minimal scope for judicial scrutiny of the appropriateness of the measures adopted in the light of the ends to which they were directed.[15] In setting store by the government's good faith efforts to remove the detainee, even where such efforts were best assessed as futile, the majority treated the time the detainee spent in detention as legally irrelevant.

The majority held that the general words of the statute, providing for detention until one of the three nominated events occurred, made it unmistakably clear that indefinite detention was provided for. Up to this point in its reasoning, the majority seemed to follow a general interpretive approach which denies that common law rights form part of the context in which statutory meaning is determined. And there are other aspects of the majority reasoning that support this reading. In the last paragraph of his reasons, Hayne J quoted the following passage from a dissenting judgment of Learned Hand J in the United States Second Circuit:

> Think what one may of a statute . . . when passed by a society which professes to put its faith in [freedom], a court has no warrant for refusing to enforce it. If that society

[11] *Behrooz v Secretary DIMIA, SHDB & Godwin, MIMIA v Al Khafaji* [2003] HCA Trans 456 (12 November 2003), www.austlii.edu.au/au/other/HCATrans/2003/456.html. See Juliet Curtin, '"Never Say Never": *Al-Kateb v Godwin*' (2005) 27 *Sydney Law Review* 355.

[12] McHugh and Heydon JJ agreed with Hayne J's reasoning on statutory interpretation: see *Al-Kateb* (n 1) [33] and [303] respectively. McHugh J, however, devoted three paragraphs of his reasoning to statutory interpretation, stating at [33] that 'the words of the three sections are too clear to read them as being subject to a purposive limitation or an intention not to affect fundamental rights'. Callinan J held at [298]: 'The statutory language is clear and unambiguous . . . It requires detention of aliens until such time as they are granted a visa or removed.'

[13] *Al-Kateb* (n 1) [229].

[14] Hayne J allowed that the relevant purpose would be spent where it was 'reasonably practicable' to remove a non-citizen but the government did not do so: see *Al-Kateb* (n 1) [251]. Callinan J appeared to go further: 'It would only be if the respondents [the government] formally and unequivocally abandoned that purpose that the detention could be regarded as being no longer for that purpose': *Al-Kateb* (n 1) [299].

[15] See Arthur Glass, '*Al-Kateb* and *Behrooz*', Gilbert + Tobin Centre of Public Law 2005 Constitutional Law Conference, Sydney, 18 February 2005, www.gtcentre.unsw.edu.au.

> chooses to flinch when its principles are put to the test, courts are not set up to give it derring-do.[16]

This runs directly counter to the rationale for the principle of legality. However, I argue that the majority's interpretation did not repudiate the common law presumption against abrogation of common law rights.[17] Such an approach would be inconsistent with the position on common law presumptions in Australian law. Rather, the majority's interpretation was driven by substantive considerations particular to non-citizens, and in particular to understandings of the 'rights' of non-citizens.

Hayne J's reasons opened with an examination of the history of the regulation of immigration to Australia. He cited and quoted early twentieth-century authorities on legislative power with respect to immigration. Amongst these he quoted, and endorsed, the following passage from *Robtelmes v Brenan*:

> The power to make such laws as Parliament may think fit with respect to aliens must surely, if it includes anything, include the power to determine the conditions under which aliens may be admitted to the country, the conditions under which they may be permitted to remain in the country, and the conditions under which they may be deported from it. I cannot, therefore, doubt that the Commonwealth Parliament has under that delegation of power authority to make any laws that it may think fit for that purpose; and it is not for the judicial branch of the Government to review their actions, or to consider whether the means that they have adopted are wise or unwise.[18]

Hayne J reviewed the legislative evolution of the mandatory detention regime and the current scheme of the Act. He concluded that the principal feature of the legislative regime was that it addressed persons who were detained because they were not authorised to remain in the country.[19] The statutory provisions were read against this understanding of the immigration context and an aligned understanding of the overall scheme of the legislation. It is this understanding that explains why the majority saw the general words of the statute as 'intractable' in providing for indefinite detention.

Hayne J accepted the rule of Australian statutory interpretation that provisions should not be construed as abrogating important common law rights in the

[16] *United States v Shaughnessy*, 195 F 2d 964 (2d Cir 1952), 971, quoted in *Al-Kateb* (n 1) [269] (Hayne J), with the substitution in square brackets inserted by Hayne J. As noted by Hayne J, 'the decision of the Second Circuit Court of Appeals, from which Judge Hand dissented, was reversed by the Supreme Court of the United States' in *Shaughnessy v United States; ex rel Mezei* (1953) 345 US 206 (*Shaughnessy v Mezei*).

[17] Of the judges under consideration, McHugh J arguably came closest, or at least was the most explicit, in reasoning from a general interpretive position that left little space for the operation of the presumption. He clearly exemplified the 'constitutional positivist' position as characterised by Dyzenhaus: see David Dyzenhaus, *The Constitution of Law: Legality in a Time of Emergency* (Cambridge, Cambridge University Press, 2006); see also ch 1, pp 17–19. Nonetheless, I argue that at key points in his legal reasoning McHugh J relies on particular understandings of the legal position of non-citizens that are not dictated by any such interpretive position.

[18] *Al-Kateb* (n 1) [203] (Hayne J), citing *Robtelmes v Brenan* [1906] HCA 58, (1906) 4 CLR 395, 404. See also *Al-Kateb*, [74] (McHugh J).

[19] *Al-Kateb* (n 1) [210], [211].

absence of clear words or necessary implication.[20] Two years before judgment in *Al-Kateb* was delivered, Hayne J joined the majority judgment in *Daniels Corporation International Pty Ltd v Australian Competition & Consumer Commission*, which stated:

> It is now well settled that statutory provisions are not to be construed as abrogating important common law rights, privileges and immunities in the absence of clear words or a necessary implication to that effect. That rule, the expression of which can be traced to *Potter v Minahan* [1908] . . . is a rule which . . . has been strictly applied by this Court since the decision in *Re Bolton; Ex parte Beane* [1987].[21]

In *Al-Kateb*, Hayne J cited this passage from *Daniels*.[22] He also cited the High Court decision in *Coco v R*.[23] The leading judgment in *Coco* held that the presumption of legality is only overridden by express words or necessary implication.[24] In expanding on the latter phrase, the High Court held that a presumption would be overridden by necessary implication where 'necessary to prevent the statutory provisions from becoming inoperative or meaningless'.[25]

Further, in *Daniels*, the Court had held that in order to apply common law rights it was *not* necessary to first find a lack of clarity in the statutory words themselves.[26] In *Daniels*, the common law presumption formed part of the context in which the Court decided on the meaning of the relevant provision.[27] *Daniels* was a decision on legal professional privilege. The statutory provisions at issue in that decision clearly covered documents in relation to which legal profes-

[20] ibid, [241].

[21] *Daniels Corporation International Pty Ltd v Australian Competition & Consumer Commission* [2002] HCA 49, (2002) 213 CLR 543, [11] (Gleeson CJ, Gaudron, Gummow and Hayne JJ). The second case referred to in the extract, *Re Bolton, ex parte Beane* [1987] HCA 12, (1987) 162 CLR 514, was also a case of statutory authority to detain. In *Re Bolton* a former US serviceman had been arrested in Australia under a purported statutory authority to arrest deserters from foreign forces. He was granted habeas corpus, in part on the basis that the legislation was to be read in light of the common law presumption in favour of fundamental freedoms and that when so read, it did not authorise his detention. The timing of the resurgence of common law presumptions in favour of fundamental freedoms in the late 1980s is consistent with a range of other changes to Australian administrative law in the 1980s that can broadly be characterised as reflecting a rights orientation: eg *Kioa v West* [1985] HCA 81, (1985) 159 CLR 550; ch 2, pp 45–46.

[22] *Al-Kateb* (n 1) [241].

[23] *Coco v R* [1994] HCA 15, (1994) 179 CLR 479. The case concerned statutory authority to enter premises to install a listening device. The relevant fundamental common law right was the right of a person in possession of premises to exclude others from those premises.

[24] The lead judgment was that of Mason CJ, Brennan, Gaudron and McHugh JJ.

[25] *Coco* (n 23) [8].

[26] *Daniels* (n 21) [85]–[105]. The lead judgment was signed by Gleeson CJ, Gaudron, Gummow and Hayne JJ. The comparison between *Al-Kateb* and *Daniels* was first suggested in Dennis Rose, 'The High Court Decisions in *Al-Kateb* and *Al Khafaji*: A Different Perspective' (2005) 8(3) *Constitutional Law and Policy Review* 58.

[27] Another decision in which presumptions in favour of fundamental rights were relied upon by a member of the majority in *Al-Kateb* was *Coleman v Power* [2004] HCA 39, (2004) 220 CLR 1 (here with reference to freedom of speech), in which Hayne J made use of the principle: *Coleman* [188]. It is, however, a less provocative comparator for *Al-Kateb* than *Daniels* (n 21), in that in *Coleman* the principle was relied upon to give a narrow construction to a broad and imprecise public order offence, rather than to ground an unexpressed exception.

sional privilege could be claimed. Nevertheless, the provisions were held not to apply to those documents in the absence of clear and unambiguous words to the contrary. In other words, in that decision, the legislative provisions were held to be subject to an *unexpressed exception* to preserve the privilege.

Nonetheless, in *Al-Kateb*, Hayne J spoke for the majority when he stated that 'the words [of sections 196 and 198] are . . . intractable' and displaced the general principle that statutory provisions should not be construed as interfering with fundamental rights. He held that reading the Act in context gave rise to a necessary implication that indefinite detention was authorised.

When *Al-Kateb* is viewed in the context of the unexpressed exception read into the statute in *Daniels*, the majority's interpretation does not look like the simple unfolding of a *general* interpretive approach that keeps common law presumptions out of sight until the meaning of the statute is determined. Rather, I argue that the *Al-Kateb* majority drew the necessary implication abrogating rights from an understanding that the underlying statutory purpose was to exclude non-citizens present without authorisation from the community. The crucial premise for the majority's statutory reasoning was an expansive understanding of the purposes of immigration detention. It is the statutory purpose, as understood by the majority, that points irresistibly to the conclusion that indefinite detention is intended.

The majority drew the necessary implication, that the detention of a non-citizen in Australia without permission was to continue even if removal was not viable, from reading the Migration Act 1958 in light of an assumption that segregating non-citizens from the community pending removal was a permissible and distinct purpose of immigration detention. Read in the light of this purpose, the general words of the statute were understood to point irresistibly to the conclusion that indefinite detention was contemplated. Reading an implied temporal limitation into the statute would have frustrated this purpose and so the limitation was rejected.

The statutory purpose identified by the *Al-Kateb* majority, segregating non-citizens from the community pending their removal, effectively effaced any right to personal liberty for a non-citizen in Australia without permission. That the majority held that a non-citizen had no right to liberty, whether understood in terms of a constitutional immunity derived from the separation of powers or otherwise, became explicit in their reasoning on the constitutional validity of the indefinite detention of unauthorised non-citizens, discussed in the next section.

3.3 The Majority on the Constitutionality of Indefinite Detention

Al-Kateb also raised the question of whether a statute authorising indefinite detention of non-citizens was constitutional. The constitutional argument centred on the nature and scope of an implied constitutional immunity from administrative detention. The constitutional immunity derived from the separation of federal judicial power. As stated in *Lim*, subject to certain exceptions, Australian citizens, in peace-time, enjoy 'a constitutional immunity from being imprisoned by Commonwealth authority except pursuant to an order by a court in the exercise of the judicial power of the Commonwealth'.[28] Immigration detention constituted one of the relevant exceptions. Whether a given detention power fell within the immigration exception was determined by asking if it was 'reasonably capable of being seen as necessary for the purposes of deportation'.[29]

By way of contrast, the *Al-Kateb* majority held that the aliens power directly authorised detention pending deportation.[30] Detention was held to be authorised under this head of legislative power as long as it was directed at the exclusion of non-citizens from the national community.[31] The majority held that where a valid removal decision had been made concerning a non-citizen, there was authority to detain the non-citizen under the aliens power. The detention was held to fall within the 'immigration' exception to the implied constitutional right. The viability of deportation was constitutionally irrelevant. The majority's rights-precluding approach denied that a non-citizen subject to a removal order had a liberty interest that influenced adjudication on the scope of the aliens power.

The majority's argument for the constitutionality of indefinite immigration detention in *Al-Kateb* was framed in response to *Lim*. Without expressly overruling *Lim*, the majority undermined the substantive limits on immigration detention central to that decision, derived from the separation of powers. They questioned the very existence of a constitutional immunity from executive detention and expanded the scope of the immigration exception to it. The shift from *Lim* to *Al-Kateb* reflects a shift of weight, from the protections derived from the separation of powers on the one hand, to the power conferred by the aliens power on the other.[32]

In *Lim*, the primary purposes of immigration detention were understood to be facilitating consideration of an application for admission, and removal. Executive detention was prima facie precluded by a constitutional immunity derived from the separation of powers. An exception to this constitutional immunity was allowed on the basis that detention could legitimately be employed to facilitate the primary purposes of processing and removal. The detention provisions under consideration in *Lim* were 'saved' by the request for removal provision. This provision was held to transform the nature of detention. The fact that a non-citizen detainee could always request removal was held to mean that continued detention

[28] *Chu Kheng Lim v Minister of Immigration, Local Government and Ethnic Affairs* [1992] HCA 64, (1992) 176 CLR 1.

[29] ibid, 33.

[30] *Al-Kateb* (n 1) [41] (McHugh J), [247] (Hayne J).

[31] On the qualification that the separation of powers did not apply to detention under the aliens power in its 'exclusionary' operation see *Al-Kateb* (n 1) [259]–[260] (Hayne J).

[32] See Leslie Zines, *The High Court and the Constitution*, 5th edn (Sydney, Federation Press, 2008) 288 on the issue of the weight given the protections of Ch III.

was a matter of his or her 'concurrence or acquiescence'.[33] This position reflected an assumption that a request for removal would lead to removal, and so release from detention. As put by the Full Court of the Federal Court in *Al Masri*, in *Lim* 'the scales were tilted in favour of [constitutional] validity'[34] by the presumed 'practical effect'[35] of the request for removal provision.

The majority's interpretation of the Migration Act 1958 in *Al-Kateb* drained the request for removal provision of any such practical effect. Section 198's role in enabling a detainee to secure his or her own release from detention became contingent on the conditions for removal, outside the detainee's control, lining up in an auspicious fashion. On the authority of *Lim*, the question is how the *Al-Kateb* majority arrived at the conclusion that the detention provisions, so read, were constitutional.

In assessing the key precedent before him, *Lim*, Hayne J expressed doubt as to the existence of any constitutional immunity, on the basis that it is difficult to identify when and where it operates, given that the class of exceptions is not closed.[36] Hayne J's scepticism assumes that the constitutional immunity is a rule, weakened by exceptions, whereas it is better seen as a principle. A principle may be outweighed in certain circumstances, but may nonetheless still inform judicial attitudes to executive detention.

At the core of the majority's constitutional reasoning in *Al-Kateb* was the view that the aliens power precluded any constitutional immunity from executive detention.[37] The aliens power was taken to define a zone of legislative and executive power unaffected by constraints on executive detention applicable elsewhere in the law. Hayne J held that detention pursuant to the aliens and immigration powers in their 'exclusionary' operation did 'not infringe the limitations on power which follow from the separation of judicial powers from legislative or other powers'.[38] This was a qualitative shift from *Lim*.

Lim held that administrative detention is contrary to the separation of powers, unless it can be shown to be a reasonable means to a legitimate end. The reasonable necessity test in *Lim* was a means of assessing whether the connection between detention and the core powers of immigration processing and/or deportation was sufficient for it to fall within an exception to the general prohibition on administrative detention. One started from the assumption that detention was not authorised, and then sought to establish a sufficient connection with the head of power. In *Al-Kateb*, the majority started from the contrary assumption, that the aliens power confers a blanket power to detain unauthorised aliens. This move radicalised the exceptional legal circumstances of immigration detention. Immigration detention was no longer an exception to a constitutional immunity. Rather it was

[33] *Lim* (n 28) 72 (McHugh J). See the discussion in ch 2, pp 52–54.
[34] *Minister of Immigration & Multicultural & Indigenous Affairs v Al Masri* [2003] FCAFC 70, (2003) 126 FCR 54, [63].
[35] ibid, [61].
[36] *Al-Kateb* (n 1) [258].
[37] On the aliens power see ch 2, s 2.2.1.
[38] ibid, [260].

an exceptional regime of legislative and executive power, effectively independent of the normal operation of the separation of powers principles.

The independence of immigration detention from considerations derived from the separation of judicial power aligns closely with judicial attitudes toward the personal liberty of non-citizens. In a statement reminiscent of Scalia J in *Zadvydas*, Hayne J stated: 'Nor is there any judgment made against a person otherwise entitled to be at liberty in the Australian community. The premise for the debate is that the non-citizen does not have permission to be at liberty in the community.'[39] The liberty of non-citizens is, to use the language of Scalia J in *Zadvydas*, 'totally extinguished' by the removal order.[40]

The *Al-Kateb* majority acknowledged that it was introducing a more radical interpretation of federal power to legislate with respect to aliens than previously recognised. Hayne J commented that the power was not to be read 'in quite so confined a manner as is implicit in the joint reasons in [*Lim*]'.[41] Hayne J held that the Court in *Lim* had overlooked a valid purpose for which the aliens power can be exercised,[42] namely 'segregation' of non-citizens from the 'Australian community':

> The power with respect to both heads [aliens and immigration] extends to preventing aliens entering or remaining in Australia except by executive permission. But if the heads of power extend so far, they extend to permitting exclusion from the Australian community – by prevention of entry, by removal from Australia, *and* by segregation from the community by detention in the meantime.[43]

Hayne J's reasoning here is indicative of patterns of reasoning in support of a rights-precluding approach to immigration detention more generally. One begins with the power to exclude and deport. One then generalises from these powers to a far more sweeping power to exclude from the '[national] community'. Legal questions are then approached in the light of this more general power, licensing expansive and exclusionary readings of the powers of immigration detention. The power to segregate from the community obviates any need to assess detention for proportionality with the purposes of processing or removal. It applies to any non-citizen in the relevant statutory class simply by virtue of the fact that her or his presence in the territory is not authorised. The segregation rationale is a blunt and complete answer to any claim to liberty by the non-citizen detainee.

[39] ibid, [254]; see also [211] (Hayne J). The relevant passage from Scalia J's judgment in *Zadvydas v Davis*, 533 US 678 (2001) is 703–04: 'This claim can be repackaged as freedom from "physical restraint" or freedom from "indefinite detention", but it is at bottom a claimed right of release into this country by an individual who concededly has no legal right to be here. There is no such constitutional right.' See ch 1, s 1.1.

[40] *Zadvydas* (n 39) 704 (Scalia J).

[41] *Al-Kateb* (n 1) [255]; see also [227]–[228].

[42] The two primary purposes of detention are to assess immigration status and to facilitate removal.

[43] *Al-Kateb* (n 1) [255]; see also *Behrooz* (n 8) [171] (Hayne J). *Behrooz* was the companion case to *Al-Kateb*, heard at the same time and with judgment delivered on the same day. On *Behrooz* see s 3.7 below.

Hayne J provided no authority for what amounted to a jurisprudential shift of wide-ranging significance. The new purpose of 'segregation from the community' was simply seen as the unfolding of the exclusionary logic of the authorities. He slid from exclusion at the border and removal from Australian territory, to exclusion and removal from the Australian community. This is a remarkable hardening of the jurisprudence, converting the absence of a right to remain into the absence of a right to liberty.

Hayne J's reasoning on the scope of the aliens power did not attract clear majority support in *Al-Kateb*. This was because one member of the majority, Callinan J, held that he did not need to decide whether there was a rationale for detention distinct from facilitating deportation.[44] This was something of a technicality, though, as Callinan J went on to agree with prudential reasons for the view that the aliens power supports legislation for the purpose of the segregation of non-citizens from the Australian community.[45] Heydon J concurred with Hayne J, and McHugh J also endorsed the power to legislate to segregate aliens from the community: 'As long as the purpose of detention is to make the alien available for deportation or to prevent the alien from entering Australia *or the Australian community*, the detention is non-punitive' (emphasis added).[46]

The *Al-Kateb* majority's recognition of a 'segregation' purpose for the aliens power uncoupled immigration detention from the protections implied from the separation of judicial power. It did this by creating a new type of non-punitive detention (immigration detention for the purposes of segregation), and asserting that non-punitive administrative detention is by definition categorically compatible with the separation of judicial power. The impact of this shift is vividly illustrated by comparing McHugh J's reasons in *Lim* and *Al-Kateb*. In both cases, McHugh J reasoned that punitive administrative detention infringes the separation of powers. In *Lim* he held that the detention regime did not contravene the separation of powers because the non-citizen always had it within his or her power to effect release from detention by requesting removal from Australia. In essence, in *Lim*, McHugh J relied on the 'prison with three walls' argument to square immigration detention with the requirements of the separation of powers.[47] Further, in *Lim* he had suggested: 'If a law authorising the detention of an alien went beyond what was reasonably necessary to effect the deportation of that person, the law might be invalid because it infringed Ch. III of the Constitution.'[48]

In *Al-Kateb*, McHugh J approved a more radical purpose for legislative power with respect to aliens – the segregation of aliens from the community. It follows from this purpose that detention lies at the core of the aliens power, and is not ancillary to it:

[44] *Al-Kateb* (n 1) [289].

[45] ibid, [289]: 'If it were otherwise, aliens having exhausted their rights to seek and obtain protection as non-citizens would be able to become de facto citizens.'

[46] *Al-Kateb* (n 1) [45].

[47] *Lim* (n 28) 72.

[48] ibid, 65.

> The power to detain aliens is not an incidental power . . . Such laws . . . deal with the very subject of aliens. They are at the centre of the power, not at its circumference or outside the power but directly operating on the subject matter of the power.[49]

The 'reasonably capable of being seen as necessary' test from *Lim* was a means of assessing whether an ancillary power, detention, was justified as sufficiently related to the 'core' power of deportation. By placing detention pending removal at the core of the aliens power, McHugh J removed any need to justify its connection with the head of power, obviating the need for any proportionality test.

A few months after *Al-Kateb*, in *Re Woolley*, McHugh J suggested that the majority in *Al-Kateb* had signalled the end of the 'reasonably necessary' test for the validity of detention pending removal.[50] In *Re Woolley* he stated that what mattered, post-*Al-Kateb*, was the character of a law's purpose. If the purpose of a law could be characterised as non-punitive, then it did not infringe the separation of powers.[51] Applying this understanding, the *Al-Kateb* majority's identification of a new 'non-punitive' purpose for immigration detention completely uncoupled immigration detention from separation of powers concerns.

The *Al-Kateb* majority advanced a supporting prudential justification for its position that there is a valid legislative power to 'segregate' aliens: were this not a valid legislative purpose, this 'would mean that [non-citizens], by their illegal and unwanted entry, could become *de facto* Australian citizens'.[52] While Callinan J held that he did not need to decide whether the aliens power extended to a purpose of exclusion from the Australian community, he nevertheless agreed that if such a power were not 'constitutionally acceptable' it might lead to irremovable non-citizens becoming de facto citizens.[53]

The spectre of 'de facto citizenship' overlooks, amongst other things, an alien's continuing vulnerability to deportation. As described in the preceding chapter, Mr Al Masri was released and then subsequently re-detained shortly prior to his removal from Australia, attesting to the practical reality of the distinction between a right to release and a right to remain.[54] On the reasoning in *Al Masri*, representative of the rights-protecting approach outlined in chapter one, the power to detain for the purpose of removal was only suspended where there was no real prospect of removal. Should the government subsequently establish that there was a real prospect of removal in the reasonably foreseeable future, a power of detention was available to ensure the non-citizen's availability for removal.[55] The majority's

[49] *Al-Kateb* (n 1) [39].

[50] *Re Woolley, ex parte Applicants M276/2003 (by their next friend GS)* [2004] HCA 49, (2004) 210 ALR 369, [71].

[51] See also *Behrooz* (n 8), discussed in s 3.7.

[52] *Al-Kateb* (n 1) [46] (McHugh J). Recall the response of the Full Court in *Al Masri* (n 34) (or that of the majority in *Zadvydas*) to the suggestion that release would amount to *de facto* citizenship. The majority rejected the suggestion that release into the community, while still remaining liable to removal, was equivalent to having a right to remain: see ch 2, p 62.

[53] *Al-Kateb* (n 1) [189] (Callinan J).

[54] See ch 2, p 58.

[55] A continuing line of debate between rights-precluding and rights-protecting judges centres on whether there is a power to release on terms and conditions. In *Al-Kateb* (n 1) see eg [24]–[28] (Gleeson CJ), arguing for such a power; [242]–[243] (Hayne J), arguing against.

conflation of release with admission to membership is discussed further below. Further, Hayne J noted that detainees share responsibility for their detention, which is attributable to their decision to enter Australia without authorisation.[56] This language of fault jars in the context of a case concerned with a person who 'through no fault of his own or of the authorities . . . cannot be removed'.[57]

The majority viewed their interpretation as supported by case law, drawing on circumstances from different eras and circumstances. McHugh J drew on detention cases from World War II to argue that detention of unauthorised non-citizens is 'no more an exercise of judicial power than is a law requiring enemy prisoners-of-war to be detained in custody until they are deported from Australia'.[58] He treated the ambit of the defence power in wartime as a fitting analogy for the effect of the aliens power on separation of powers limitations. More generally, he drew on wartime detention cases to support the proposition that 'indefinite detention at the will of the Executive, and according to its opinions, actions and judgments' is not foreign to Australia's constitutional arrangements.[59]

In considering how the *Al-Kateb* majority arrived at a new immigration purpose of 'segregation from the community', the *Zadvydas* minority judgments are a strong contender for influence. There are notable similarities between the *Al-Kateb* majority's position on 'segregation from the community' and the reasoning of the minority justices in *Zadvydas*. In his dissenting judgment in *Zadvydas*, Kennedy J referred to the 'community' 21 times, almost invariably with reference to the risk posed to it by dangerous non-citizens, or conversely the need to protect the community. Kennedy J's concerns with protection of the community, and the need for the executive to have a free hand in the removal of aliens to better effect that protection, surfaced in the majority judgments in *Al-Kateb*, in Callinan J's judgment by way of direct quotation from *Zadvydas*.[60]

As for 'exclusion', it is Scalia J's refusal to countenance any right to liberty on the part of an alien with no 'right to be here' that best aligns with the majority position in *Al-Kateb*. Central to Scalia J's judgment was the equivalence between an inadmissible alien at the border, whose 'continued exclusion' did not deprive him of any right, and 'an alien under final order of removal' who 'stands on an equal footing with an inadmissible alien' in possessing no right to remain.[61] For

[56] See *Al-Kateb* (n 1) [261], [268] (Hayne J). On the *Al-Kateb* majority's rhetoric (in the classical sense) with respect to non-citizens see Matthew Zagor, 'Judicial Rhetoric and Constitutional Identity: Comparative Approaches to Aliens' Rights in the United Kingdom and Australia' (2008) 19 *Public Law Review* 271, 282.

[57] *Al-Kateb* (n 1) [21] (Gleeson CJ, dissenting).

[58] ibid, [47] and [55]–[61].

[59] ibid, [55] and [55]–[61].

[60] ibid, [284]. Callinan J stated: 'Not only because of the absence of the complication of a constitutional provision in Australia such as the Fifth Amendment, but also because, in my respectful opinion, they were both more orthodox expressions of constitutional principle and practical reality, I would prefer the opinions of the minority Justices [in *Zadvydas*],' before quoting with approval paragraphs from the dissents in that decision.

[61] *Zadvydas* (n 39), 703 (Scalia J).

Scalia J, non-citizens in both categories fell within the exclusionary logic of *Shaughnessy v Mezei*.[62] Hayne J referred to the aliens power in its 'exclusionary' operation and, more fundamentally, with the rest of the *Al-Kateb* majority, effectively endorsed Scalia J's reasoning.[63] Hayne J chose to close his judgment in *Al-Kateb* with quotations from the United States litigation that concluded with *Shaughnessy v Mezei*. The phrase 'exclusion from the Australian community', and more fundamentally the way the majority used that concept, aligns closely with the dissents in *Zadvydas*. It is plausible that the 'background influence' of the *Zadvydas* dissents obscured some of the particulars of the Australian context in Hayne J's reasoning.[64]

In light of the majority's acceptance of segregation from the community as a valid purpose of detention under the aliens power, it is not surprising that they also accepted a subjective test of whether detention was for the purpose of removal. For the majority, the premise on which statutory authority to detain was held to rest, namely the executive's intention to remove the non-citizens, was close to unfalsifiable in any particular case.[65] Once a person is validly taken into detention, the executive's ongoing legal authority to detain is effectively impervious to legal challenge. The majority viewed immigration as an area in which the legislature can, and has, granted sweeping powers of detention to the executive, and the executive can exercise those powers subject to only the most marginal judicial supervision.

3.4 The Minority – Gleeson CJ

Gleeson CJ held that the Migration Act 1958 was 'silent'[66] on whether detention could continue where a detainee had requested removal but 'removal is not possible in the circumstances which prevail at the time and which are likely to prevail

[62] ibid.

[63] Hayne J referred to the aliens and immigration powers not infringing the separation of powers in their 'exclusionary' operation: *Al-Kateb* (n 1) [260]. It was not clear whether this qualifier was an additional constitutional constraint, and if so what it added, and on what basis. On the similarities between Hayne J's reasoning and that of Scalia J in *Zadvydas*, compare *Al-Kateb* at [254]: 'The premise for the debate is that the non-citizen does not have permission to be at liberty in the community'; see also [219].

[64] On 'background influence' in comparative law see Brun-Otto Bryde, 'The Constitutional Judge and the International Constitutionalist Dialogue' in Sir Basil Markesinis and Jorg Fedtke (eds), *Judicial Recourse to Foreign Law: A New Source of Inspiration?* (Oxford, Routledge, 2006) 295, 298.

[65] *Al-Kateb* (n 1) [231] (Hayne J): 'Because there can be no certainty about whether or when the non-citizen will be removed, it cannot be said that the Act proceeds from a premise (that removal will be possible) which can be demonstrated to be false in any particular case.' Callinan J took matters a step further: 'It would only be if the respondents [ie the government] formally and unequivocally abandoned that purpose that the detention could be regarded as being no longer for that purpose': *Al-Kateb*, [299].

[66] ibid, [18].

in the foreseeable future'.[67] He rejected the government's submission that 'the terms of the statute are general, but tolerably clear, and if there is silence on the particular problem raised by the case of the appellant, that is only because it is sufficiently covered by the general words'.[68] Gleeson CJ's response to the government's submission was this:

> The possibility that a person, regardless of personal circumstances, regardless of whether he or she is a danger to the community, and regardless of whether he or she might abscond, can be subjected to indefinite, and perhaps permanent, administrative detention is not one to be dealt with by implication.[69]

Such an egregious infringement of a fundamental right could only be provided for by express words. In setting out his interpretive approach, Gleeson CJ referred to Australian authorities for the presumption against abrogation of 'certain human rights or freedoms (of which personal liberty is the most basic)', and to well-known contemporary expressions of the 'principle of legality' and its rationale in contemporary United Kingdom jurisprudence.[70]

Gleeson CJ held that the power of indefinite detention proposed was too grave a violation of personal liberty to be provided for other than by express words. He read the statute as subject to an unexpressed exception to the effect that where removal was not reasonably practicable, authority to detain for the purposes of removal was suspended.

Gleeson CJ's interpretation of the power avoided the constitutional problem of punitive administrative detention: 'So characterised, the power . . . does not involve an invalid attempt to confer on the Executive a power to punish people who, being in Australia, are subject to, and entitled to the protection of, the law.'[71] As a result of his interpretation of the statute, he did not need to consider the constitutionality of the detention provisions. However, while Gleeson CJ's reasoning relied on statutory interpretation, he did reference constitutional cases in delineating the permissible purposes of immigration detention. In determining that the statute did not implicitly abrogate the detainees' freedom from indefinite administrative detention, Gleeson CJ also had to determine whether segregation of unlawful non-citizens from the community constituted a freestanding purpose of immigration detention, distinct from facilitating removal. Gleeson CJ's presentation of the purpose of the power of immigration detention took the constitutional discussion in *Lim* as its starting point. He held, with reference to *Lim*, that the Migration Act 1958's

[67] ibid, [1]. See also [13], [14] and [21].

[68] ibid, [21].

[69] ibid.

[70] ibid, [19]. Gleeson CJ cited passages from Lord Hoffmann's judgment in *R v Secretary of State for the Home Department, ex parte Simms* [1999] UKHL 33, [2000] 2 AC 115, and from Lord Steyn's judgment in *R v Secretary of State for the Home Department, ex parte Pierson* [1997] UKHL 37, [1998] AC 539.

[71] *Al-Kateb* (n 1) [4]. Cf Gleeson CJ's reasoning in *Behrooz*: see s 3.7.

> scheme of mandatory immigration detention is a valid law with respect to aliens on the basis . . . that a limited authority to detain an alien in custody is conferred as an incident of the executive powers of excluding and removing aliens.[72]

Gleeson CJ clearly reaffirmed the view expressed by the joint judgment in *Lim* that immigration detention is an incidental or secondary power, justified by its role in facilitating removal. This can be contrasted with McHugh J's statement in *Al-Kateb* that the power to detain aliens is 'at the centre of the power . . . directly operating on the subject matter of the power'.[73] As such it does not stand in need of justification with reference to its role in facilitating removal.

The disagreement between Gleeson CJ and McHugh J here is a reprise of the distinction in *Zadvydas* between the majority and the minority as to the purpose and nature of immigration detention.[74] Fundamentally, the policy of the Act is limited by the scope of federal power to legislate with respect to aliens. For Gleeson CJ, the power to detain is necessarily incidental to removal in legislation enabled by the aliens power.

The basic difference between Gleeson CJ in dissent and the majority is that the latter reasoned that common law presumptions do not apply where the subject matter is the detention of non-citizens. In contrast, Gleeson CJ held that such presumptions are principles of universal application. Underlying this difference are contrasting views on whether a non-citizen who does not have permission to remain retains a right to liberty.

For Gleeson CJ, the mandatory nature of the detention scheme made it more difficult to imply a power of indefinite detention. Gleeson CJ focused on the fact that mandatory detention is blind to context. The arbitrariness of the detention measures, their lack of attention to whether, in any given case, detention was a reasonable means of securing the nominated ends, made any claim that a power of indefinite detention was necessarily implied harder to sustain. Mr Al-Kateb's circumstances raised the prospect that an individual 'regardless of personal circumstances, regardless of whether he or she is a danger to the Australian community, and regardless of whether he or she might abscond' could be subjected to indefinite detention.[75] Gleeson CJ stated:

> In a case of uncertainty, I would find it easier to discern a legislative intention to confer a power of indefinite administrative detention if the power were coupled with a discretion enabling its operation to be related to the circumstances of individual cases, including, in particular, danger to the community and likelihood of absconding.[76]

[72] *Al-Kateb* (n 1) [4].

[73] ibid, [39]. For the full extract see the text to n 49.

[74] *Zadvydas* (n 39) 713 (Kennedy J): 'the motivation to protect the citizenry from aliens determined to be dangerous is central to the immigration power itself.'

[75] *Al-Kateb* (n 1) [21].

[76] ibid, [22]. At [29] Gleeson CJ deferred the issue of the power of the courts to impose conditions or restraints on a non-citizen who posed a danger to the community, or who could not be removed because her country of nationality or other potential receiving countries regarded her as a dangerous person.

Gleeson CJ's suggestion of individualised assessment creates space for a human rights analysis of the problem. A discretion could be shaped to require that detention be capable of being justified as necessary, and a proportionate means of ensuring a legitimate aim.[77]

For Gleeson CJ, the role of a court in statutory interpretation is to construe the legislation in its best light with reference to shared commitments to protect the rights of persons:

> A statement concerning the improbability that Parliament would abrogate fundamental rights by the use of general or ambiguous words is not a factual prediction, capable of being verified or falsified by a survey of public opinion. In a free society, under the rule of law, it is an expression of legal value, respected by the courts, and acknowledged by the courts to be respected by Parliament.[78]

Gleeson CJ's dissenting judgment in *Al-Kateb* is a vivid exposition, and use, of the 'principle of legality'. It describes an understanding of the judiciary as having an obligation to protect certain fundamental legal values. The protection of these fundamental values is understood to be a collaborative project as between Parliament and the courts. Where Parliament wants to depart from these values, the principle of legality requires that it direct its attention to the freedom in question, here the freedom from indefinite detention, and consciously decide to abrogate that freedom by express words. On Gleeson CJ's account the legislature must unequivocally take responsibility where it decides to reject the 'working hypothesis' that it intends to respect fundamental freedoms.[79]

Gleeson CJ rejected the idea that authority to detain could rest on the government's *intention* to remove the relevant non-citizen. He stated that the primary purpose of detention, namely facilitating removal, is 'objective': 'What is in question is the purpose of detention, not the motives or intention of the Minister, or the officers referred to in section 198.'[80] Purpose is a judicially ascertainable fact independent of the executive's intention. It is ultimately for the judiciary to determine whether removal is reasonably practicable, and if it is not, to order release until such time as it is. Such release could be on conditions, including that the releasee notify the department of any change of address, and reporting conditions such as had been ordered by the trial judge in *Al Masri*.[81]

[77] Ben Saul, 'Australian Administrative Law: The Human Rights Dimension' in Matthew Groves and HP Lee, *Australian Administrative Law: Fundamentals, Principles and Doctrines* (Melbourne, Cambridge University Press, 2007) 50, 62. In relation to 'danger to the community', to fall within the rights-protecting model outlined in ch 1, the duration of detention would still need to be defined by the purpose of removal, even if the need for it in the individual case turned on questions of 'danger'.

[78] *Al-Kateb* (n 1) [20].

[79] *Electrolux Home Products v Australian Workers Union* [2004] HCA 40, (2004) 221 CLR 309, [21] (Gleeson CJ).

[80] *Al-Kateb* (n 1) [17].

[81] The power of a court to impose conditions on release was a central point of contention between the dissents and the majority. Gleeson CJ held that a remedy of the nature of habeas corpus was inherently adaptable, and the imposition of conditions was not antithetical to the remedy: *Al-Kateb* (n 1) [23]–[28]. Hayne J held that there was no statutory basis for the imposition of such conditions: [242]–[244].

3.5 The Minority – Gummow and Kirby JJ

Gummow J arrived at the same legal position as Gleeson CJ, but he emphasised a presumption in favour of constitutional validity rather than the common law presumption against the abrogation of fundamental freedoms. Gummow J's constitutional analysis (adopted by Kirby J) was centrally concerned with the need for court-determined limits on the authority to detain, defined with reference to the purpose of detention *and distinct* from government statements of intention. Kirby J held that Gummow J's constitutional reasoning was 'further supported . . . by considerations of international law and the common law presumption in favour of personal liberty'.[82]

On Gummow and Kirby JJ's view, the Migration Act 1958, as interpreted by the government, encountered a 'serious constitutional problem'.[83] Gummow J cited *Lim* as authority for the proposition that the aliens power is subject to separation of powers considerations.[84] Accordingly, 'the power of the Parliament to authorise the administrative detention of aliens is not at large . . . the power does not extend to authorise detention for any purpose selected by the Parliament'.[85] The separation of powers sets limits on the legally permissible purposes of immigration detention, and the legislative powers take their character from these purposes.

The central target of Gummow J's reasoning was the majority view that authority to detain rested on 'an executive opinion as to the continued viability of a purpose of deportation'.[86] He concluded his reasoning on statutory construction with a caustic rejoinder to the majority, stating:

> The point of present importance for the appellant is that the continued detention of this stateless person is not mandated by the hope of the Minister, triumphing over present experience, that at some future time some other State may be prepared to receive the appellant.[87]

Gummow J introduced into the constitutional reasoning an element that was absent from the other judgments, namely the 'constitutional fact' doctrine from *Australian Communist Party v Commonwealth* (*Communist Party Case*).[88] He held that the government's position was inconsistent with this doctrine, because it left key 'constitutional facts', on which authority to detain rested, to be determined by executive officials.

[82] *Al-Kateb* (n 1) [150].

[83] This was an explicit reference to the interpretive approach of the majority Opinion in the United States Supreme Court decision of *Zadvydas* (n 39) 690: *Al-Kateb* (n 1), [159], [193] (Kirby J); see also [118] (Gummow J).

[84] *Al-Kateb* (n 1) [110].

[85] ibid, [131].

[86] ibid, [88].

[87] ibid, [125].

[88] *Australian Communist Party v Commonwealth* [1951] HCA 5, (1951) 83 CLR 1 (*Communist Party Case*).

In the *Communist Party Case*, the Australian High Court invalidated the Communist Party Dissolution Act 1950 (Cth). The decision is almost universally regarded as one of Australian constitutionalism's 'greatest triumphs'.[89] Amongst other matters, the legislation challenged in that case banned the Communist Party and allowed the executive on executive determination to 'declare' that an individual was a communist and was engaged in, or was likely to engage in, activities prejudicial to the security and defence of Australia. Declared persons could not be employed by the Commonwealth or by a Commonwealth authority. They could not hold office in a union in an industry declared by the executive to be 'vital to the security and defence of Australia'. As noted in the previous chapter, the Australian federal government has limited legislative powers. It can only exercise those powers explicitly or impliedly conferred by the Constitution. The central issue in the *Communist Party Case* was: who gets to decide the scope of those powers?

The operative provisions of the Communist Party Dissolution Act 1950 were preceded by a long preamble containing nine 'recitals'. These recitals stated that the powers principally relied upon were the defence power, the express incidental power, and the executive power.[90] They went on to summarise the case against the Communist Party and, most importantly, asserted that the measures taken in the Act were necessary for Australia's defence and security and the execution and maintenance of its Constitution and laws, thereby seeking to ground the Act's operative provisions in the heads of power listed above.

The majority of the Australian High Court held that the Parliament could not recite itself into power.[91] The judiciary had the final word on whether legislation was within power, and the Parliament could not validly base legislation on its own declaration (or that of an executive official) of the existence of a fact which was a precondition to its power to legislate. The judiciary had to establish that the necessary 'constitutional fact' actually existed.[92] With reference to the Communist Party Dissolution Act 1950, it was for the judiciary to determine whether there was any factual connection between the declared bodies and persons and security. Such a factual connection was necessary to bring the legislation under the defence power.

In *Al-Kateb*, Gummow J linked the 'constitutional fact' doctrine to the High Court's judgment in *Lim* that the constitutional validity of immigration detention, under separation of powers principles grounded in Chapter III of the

[89] George Winterton, 'The Communist Party Case' in HP Lee and George Winterton (eds), *Australian Constitutional Landmarks* (Cambridge, Cambridge University Press, 2003) 108, 108. Cf Callinan J's comments in *Thomas v Mowbray* [2007] HCA 33, (2007) 233 CLR 307, [532]–[533], [583]–[589]. For Kirby J's rejoinder to Callinan J see *Thomas v Mowbray*, [386]. My description of the *Communist Party Case* draws on Winterton's account.

[90] Commonwealth of Australia Constitution Act 1900 (63 & 64 Vict c 12), ss 51(vi), 51(xxxix) and 61 respectively (Constitution).

[91] *Communist Party Case* (n 88) 206 (McTiernan J), 263, 265 (Fullagar J).

[92] ibid, 193 (Dixon J), 206 (McTiernan J), 222, 225, 226 (Williams J), 258, 263 (Fullagar J), 272–75 (Kitto J).

Constitution, depends on the 'continued viability of the purpose of deportation or expulsion'. Gummow J explained that 'the continued viability of the purpose of deportation' is the 'constitutional fact' required for constitutional authority to detain Mr Al-Kateb.[93] Gummow J summed up his reasoning in the following statement:

> The continued viability of the purpose of deportation or expulsion cannot be treated by the legislature as a matter purely for the opinion of the executive government. The reason is that it cannot be for the executive government to determine the placing from time to time of that boundary line which marks off a category of deprivation of liberty from the reach of Ch III. The location of that boundary line itself is a question arising under the *Constitution* or involving its interpretation, hence the present significance of the *Communist Party Case*. Nor can there be sustained laws for the segregation by incarceration of aliens without their commission of any offence requiring adjudication, and for a purpose unconnected with the entry, investigation, admission and deportation of aliens.[94]

Gummow J's reasons foregrounded the 'constitutional fact' doctrine, but the doctrine is largely adjectival to the *Lim* judgment on the scope and nature of detention under the aliens power. In a sense, then, it is not surprising that the majority largely ignored Gummow J's analysis. McHugh J stated that the *Communist Party Case*, central to the reasoning of Gummow and Kirby JJ, did not assist Mr Al-Kateb.[95] This was despite the fact that McHugh J fully agreed with the constitutional fact doctrine,[96] and the merits and importance of the *Communist Party Case.*[97] As was the case with the legal relevance of common law presumptions, both the majority and the dissenting judges understood themselves to be bound by the same rule – here the constitutional fact doctrine from the *Communist Party Case*. The difference between the majority and minority rested on different understandings of constitutional power to detain aliens. The difference can be highlighted when Gummow J's reasoning is represented as a syllogism:

i any finding of fact necessary for the constitutional validity of a law or executive act is to be made by a court ('the constitutional fact' point); and

[93] cf *Tan Le Tam* [1997] AC 97. The Privy Council held that the question of whether detention was 'pending removal' was a jurisdictional fact to be determined the courts.

[94] *Al-Kateb* (n 1) [140]. Gummow J finished that paragraph by registering a caveat to the preceding proposition, by way of a quote from the joint judgment in *Lim* (see *Lim* (n 28)) which noted that the Court had deferred any consideration of wartime detention under the defence power. In *Lim*, the quoted passage, and the judgment referred to – *Little v Commonwealth* [1947] HCA 24, (1947) 75 CLR 64, concerned the wartime detention of citizens.

[95] *Al-Kateb* (n 1) [50] (McHugh J).

[96] ibid, [44] (McHugh J): 'Even a law whose object is purely protective will infringe Ch III if it prevents Ch III courts from determining some matter that is a condition precedent to authorising detention.'

[97] See eg McHugh J, 'The Strengths of the Weakest Arm', Australian Bar Association Conference, Florence, 2 July 2004: 'It is difficult to believe that Australia would have been as politically free a country as it is today if the High Court had upheld the validity of the legislation challenged in the *Communist Party Case.* If that legislation had survived, its legacy must have influenced the way that we give effect to political rights and freedoms.' Kirby J noted McHugh J's extra-judicial praise of the *Communist Party Case* in *Al-Kateb* (n 1) [149].

ii the constitutional validity of detention for the purpose of removal relies on removal remaining a viable option (the '*Lim*' point); therefore
iii it is for the courts to determine whether removal remains a viable option.

The majority accepted the first point. But they disagreed with the second, holding the viability of removal irrelevant to the constitutionality of detention pending deportation.[98] As discussed above, they held that when detention was authorised under the aliens power, separation of powers concerns were effectively precluded. The constitutionality of detention rests on the fact a non-citizen has no permission to be in Australia, and the government intends to remove him or her.

While the majority did not expressly respond to Gummow J on this point, the form of their response is evident from their reasoning. They would say that, to use his words, they *had* determined 'the placing . . . of that boundary line which marks off a category of liberty from the reach of Ch III'.[99] They simply differed on the placement of that boundary line. They held that the relevant purpose allows for detention for as long as the government intends to remove, even if that intention can never be put into practice. Thus, the majority saw no tension between the position they adopted and the requirements of the *Communist Party Case*. On their view, the *Communist Party Case* would have had legal relevance if the legislation barred the courts from determining whether a person is an unauthorised non-citizen.

Nevertheless, Gummow J's reasoning from the constitutional fact doctrine serves to highlight that the majority's position gave Parliament and the executive effectively uncontrolled power over aliens. On the majority view there is no law-free area de jure. Accordingly, they were untroubled by, or could do nothing about, the fact that there is a law-free area de facto because the detention power is of such staggering generality that it provides 'no constraint or none for which accountability may be made'.[100]

Gummow J also engaged with the majority position that the aliens power supports legislation to 'segregate' aliens from the community. As noted earlier, Hayne J made reference to the aliens power extending to 'permit exclusion from the Australian community'.[101] McHugh J also suggested that the purpose of preventing an alien from entering 'the Australian community', as distinct from entering Australia, suffices to render detention non-punitive, and so constitutional.[102] The conflation of the power to exclude at the border with a power to exclude those

[98] The dependence of the doctrine of the *Communist Party Case* on the judicial identification of 'constitutional facts' is also highlighted in *Behrooz* (n 8). In that case, delivered on the same day, Kirby J referenced the doctrine but Gummow J did not do so. Kirby J held that the constitutionality of detention may rest on the conditions of detention, and accordingly the conditions of detention are a constitutional fact, for determination by the courts. Gummow J joined the majority in *Behrooz* in holding the conditions of detention to be legally irrelevant to authority to detain. See s 3.7 above.

[99] *Al-Kateb* (n 1) [140]; see text at n 94.

[100] Colin Warbrick, 'The European Response to Terrorism in an Age of Human Rights' (2004) 15 *European Journal of International Law* 989, 1000.

[101] *Al-Kateb* (n 1) [255]. The relevant passage from the judgment is reproduced in the text to n 43.

[102] ibid, [45] (McHugh J).

within Australia from the community was central to the majority reasoning in the case.

In his dissent in *Al-Kateb*, and then again in a judgment delivered two months later, *Re Woolley*,[103] Gummow J criticised the *Al-Kateb* majority position that the aliens power supports legislation to 'segregate' aliens from the community. Gummow J's central objection was to the majority's conflation of a lack of membership with a lack of rights. In *Al-Kateb*, he rejected the suggestion that statements in the case law going to lack of *membership* in the community of a non-citizen present without lawful authority 'support a system of segregation by incarceration without trial for any offence and with no limit of time or a limit fixed only by an executive opinion as to the ultimate possibility of their removal from Australia'.[104] He held that one should not treat judicial statements on who is and is not a member of the community as addressed to who can and cannot be detained. The strong correlation between membership and rights in the reasoning of the *Al-Kateb* majority is central to the rights-precluding approach more generally. Gummow J was troubled by the authoritarian implications of a rule that a non-citizen without a right to remain thereby has no right to liberty. When he revisited the issue in *Re Woolley*, he stated: 'The reference to "exclusion" [in the phrase "exclusion from the 'Australian community'"] may also be an Orwellian euphemism.'[105]

In addition, Gummow J objected to the majority's reliance on the term 'community', which had been central in defining the scope of the immigration power in the heyday of the White Australia policy, before the advent of a legal status of national citizenship. Gummow J's references were the historical considerations referred to in chapter two, on the judicial construction of 'community' to define the reach of the immigration power, and the shift to reliance on the aliens power.[106] Gummow J concluded his review of the term 'community' in Australian constitutional discourse with the following statement: 'Here is a political idea whose time has come and gone. Still less is it a sound constitutional doctrine to construe the aliens power by reference to notions of "protection" of the "Australian community" by excluding aliens from "membership" of that community.'[107] Here, there was an objection to use of 'Australian community' based on the racialised use of the term in early immigration cases.[108] There was also an analytic objection that concerns about 'community' and 'membership', issues once relevant to the immigration power, were transferred onto the aliens head of power, to which they were not relevant.[109]

The purpose of the shift to the aliens head of power was, at least in part, to avoid the prospect that by absorption an immigrant might become part of the

[103] *Re Woolley* (n 50).
[104] *Al-Kateb* (n 1) [92].
[105] *Re Woolley* (n 50) [137].
[106] See ch 2, s 2.2.1.
[107] *Re Woolley* (n 50) [146].
[108] ibid, [141], [142].
[109] ibid, [147], [148]. See ch 2, s 2.2.1.

community and cease to be an immigrant, passing beyond the reach of the immigration power. Under the aliens power, presence in the community does *not* lead to legal membership via any concept of absorption.[110] Presence in 'the community' and membership of that community are kept distinct. Hayne J's use of the concept of the 'Australian community' in relation to the aliens power suggested, or at least risked, analytic confusion.

In *Re Woolley* Hayne J was moved to respond to Gummow J's criticism, but he did so in a way that talked past it. He objected that he did not mean to invoke the separate communities that evolved in the British Empire in the late nineteenth and early twentieth centuries, or to invoke the prospect of absorption under the immigration power.[111] He stated that he simply meant to describe the operation of the legislation. The statutory detention powers served to segregate non-citizens who did not have permission to remain in Australia from the Australian community. Hayne J did not address Gummow J's underlying concern that, in his application of these ideas in his constitutional reasoning, Hayne J had confused the questions of who is, or is not, a member of the community with who can be physically present in it. Gummow J's underlying objection was to the assumption that the absence of a right to remain equates to the absence of a right to liberty.

3.6 The Relevance of International Law to Interpretation

Al-Kateb is also well-known in Australia for illustrating judicial frustration at the absence of judicially enforceable rights. In his judgment McHugh J called Mr Al-Kateb's position tragic,[112] and used the case as a platform to advocate for the need for an Australian Bill of Rights 'which substantially adopts the rules found in the most important of the international human rights instruments'.[113] However, he held that he could not, in his judicial capacity, do anything other than give legal sanction to Mr Al-Kateb's indefinite detention. His position in *Al-Kateb*, and the related immigration detention cases of that period,[114] present as an unusually

[110] See ibid, [147]–[148] and more generally [137]–[148].

[111] See ibid, [223].

[112] *Al-Kateb* (n 1) [31].

[113] ibid, [73].

[114] Two months after *Al-Kateb* was decided, McHugh J concluded, in relation to children held in immigration detention, that Australia's mandatory immigration detention regime was probably 'arbitrary' as that term is understood in relevant international human rights instruments. He there suggested that 'periodic judicial review of the need for detention, some kind of defined period of detention and the absence of less restrictive means of achieving the purpose served by detention of unlawful non-citizens' might be required if the regime was to avoid breaching 'the Refugees Convention, the ICCPR or the Convention on the Rights of the Child': *Re Woolley* (n 50) [114], and see more generally [107]–[116]. Cf Hayne J's understanding of the prohibition on 'arbitrary' detention under Art 9 of the International Covenant on Civil and Political Rights (adopted 19 December 1966, entered into force 23 March 1976) 999 UNTS 171 (ICCPR): *Al-Kateb* (n 1) [238]. See also *Behrooz* (n 8).

clear case of a judge with a conception of his role that compelled him to acquiesce in what he regarded as 'tragic' circumstances.

McHugh J outlined his conception of the judicial role in an extensive, point-by-point exchange with Kirby J, centring on the proper use of international law. This exchange has become well-known, both in Australia and internationally, as an unusually open judicial staging of two opposed attitudes as to the proper influence of international law in the domestic courts. At the end of that exchange, following a debate on the proper influence of international law – in particular international human rights law – on interpretation, McHugh J stated:

> Under the aliens power, the Parliament is entitled to protect the nation against unwanted entrants by detaining them in custody. As long as the detention is for the purpose of deportation or preventing aliens from entering Australia or the Australian community, the justice or wisdom of the course taken by Parliament is not examinable in this or any other domestic court. It is not for the courts, exercising federal jurisdiction, to determine whether the course taken by Parliament is unjust or contrary to basic human rights.[115]

For McHugh J, human rights considerations are only legally relevant if expressly endorsed by the legislature or included in the Constitution by way of amendment.

In contrast, Kirby J argued that it was time for Australian law to revisit the position, set down in a judgment of Dixon CJ in 1945,[116] that international law is not a proper influence on constitutional interpretation. Kirby J argued that there should be an interpretive principle favouring consistency with international law, and particularly the international law of human rights and fundamental freedoms. In saying this, he did not dispute the traditional dualism of domestic and international law, and the need for incorporation for international law to become part of Australian municipal law.[117] He argued for a broadening of the contextual and historical materials essential to develop an evolving understanding of what the Constitution means and how it operates to 'add a reference to one of the most important legal developments that is occurring and to which national constitutions must adapt, namely the growing role of international law, including the law relating to human rights and fundamental freedoms'.[118] Kirby J's proposal that recourse be had to international law in constitutional interpretation has not gained wider acceptance in the High Court. I am less interested in the rights and wrongs of his particular proposal, than in the light the debate casts on the place of international human rights law and values in judicial interpretation more generally.[119]

[115] *Al-Kateb* (n 1) [74]. See the text to n 18.

[116] *Polites v Commonwealth* [1945] HCA 3, (1945) 70 CLR 60, 78 (Dixon J) cited in *Al-Kateb* (n 1) [171].

[117] *Al-Kateb* (n 1) [179].

[118] ibid, [183].

[119] In the companion case of *Behrooz,* Kirby J bracketed the question of whether the Constitution can be construed by reference to international law, moving straight to its place in statutory interpretation: *Behrooz* (n 8) [127].

Kirby J's view was that international human rights law constitutes a legitimate and valuable part of the interpretive context. The relevant precedent dates from 1945. Then, a judge might legitimately have conceived of international law as having no bearing on the constitutionality of the indefinite administrative detention of non-citizens. Kirby J's point was that this was not a tenable position to adopt in 2004.[120]

McHugh J's unease with the use of international law in interpretation did not stop with constitutional interpretation. He only grudgingly accepted, as 'too well established to be repealed now by judicial decision', the orthodox position that a *statute* should, so far as is possible, be construed to conform with international law.[121] McHugh J was concerned that affording international law a place in interpretation is likely to introduce a divergence in the way the text was understood by the parliamentarians enacting the legislation and the way judiciary charged with interpreting it understand it. He expressed concern for the position of legislators, who

> would be surprised to find that an enactment had a meaning inconsistent with a meaning they thought it had because of a rule of international law which they did not know and could not find without the assistance of a lawyer specialising in international law.[122]

Saddled by precedent and practice with the rule that statutes should, so far as is possible, be read consistently with international law, McHugh J tried to make the most of a bad situation by only allowing international law a role where there was evident ambiguity on the face of the statute. Much of McHugh J's opposition to the place of international law in constitutional interpretation replicated his doubts about statutory interpretation. In the case of constitutional interpretation, these doubts were uncomplicated by contrary precedents.

Informing the debate between Kirby and McHugh JJ was a difference as to the purposes for which international human rights is to be employed in judicial reasoning and law. The distinction between the two judges came to be expressed in the language of 'rules' and 'principles'. For McHugh J, the difference between a rule and a principle is the level of abstraction at which it is expressed.[123] McHugh J allowed that 'political, social and economic developments since 1900' could be taken into account in construing constitutional provisions.[124] However, he held that international human rights treaties supply 'rules' of international law and that

> Rules are too specific to do no more than provide insight into the meanings of the constitutional provisions. Either the rule is already inherent in the meaning of the provision or taking it into account alters the meaning of the provision.[125]

[120] *Al-Kateb* (n 1) [172].

[121] ibid, [65]. Heydon J expressly reserved his position on whether the statutory provisions in question should be interpreted consistently with treaties to which Australia is a party: see *Al-Kateb* (n 1) [303].

[122] *Al-Kateb* (n 1) [65].

[123] ibid, [68] fn 64.

[124] ibid, [71].

[125] ibid.

In the form of rules, McHugh J understood international human rights to be in competition with legislative intention, a competing and illegitimate source of normativity.

Kirby J responded that while the 'tangible manifestation' of international human rights law 'exists in the form of "rules" and discourse', they also constitute 'political, social or economic developments, [and] the principles they express can *influence* legal understanding'.[126] At issue was the legitimacy of international human rights influence on municipal law. McHugh J saw little opening for such influence. The legislature, or constitutional convention, was the source of normativity in the legal system, with the judiciary's role being to implement rules emanating from those sources. For Kirby J, legal values are a legitimate part of the interpretive context and international human rights law is a valuable reference point for those values. Over and above the particular rules of international human rights law, I understand Kirby J to be referencing the underlying aspirations of international human rights – that is, its commitment to equality of persons and the concept that everyone, regardless of legal status, has rights. How such aspirations work to substantiate the position of the legal subject as rights-bearer has to be evaluated case by case.[127]

The exchange between McHugh J and Kirby J in *Al-Kateb* makes explicit McHugh J's opposition to a substantive legality that would cut across the legislature's intention, understood in terms of the meaning the legislator 'thought it [the statute] had'. In *Al-Kateb*, Gleeson CJ's use of the principle of legality furnishes the clearest example of what a defence of that substantive conception would involve. McHugh J's constitutional positivism demands the rejection of international human rights as an interpretive influence, to the extent that this can be squared with the authorities. It is also uncomfortable with normativity sourced in common law or constitutional doctrine.[128]

It is arguable that McHugh J's affirmation of World War II internment precedents highlights the practical significance of his approach to international law. He referred to the precedents to show that indefinite detention is compatible with Australia's constitutional arrangements.[129] McHugh J stated that he could see no reason why the High Court would strike down similar regulations should Australia again find itself at war.[130] Kirby J responded that while he accepted that there existed Australian authorities which supported arbitrary and unrestricted detention by the executive in time of war, these cases were the Australian equivalent of *Korematsu*,[131] and, like *Korematsu*, should now be regarded as

[126] ibid, [173].

[127] For substantiated scepticism regarding the correlation between judicial reference to rights and attentiveness to rights claimants see Fleur Johns, 'Human Rights in the High Court of Australia, 1976–2003: The Righting of Australian Law' (2005) 33 *Federal Law Review* 287.

[128] On constitutional positivism see ch 1, s 1.3.

[129] *Al-Kateb* (n 1) [55] (McHugh J). McHugh J was quoting [146] (Kirby J).

[130] ibid, [61].

[131] The decision referred to was *Korematsu v United States*, 323 US 214 (1944). In that decision the United States Supreme Court deferred to the military's assessment that military imperatives required

incorrect; 'we should be no less embarrassed by the local equivalents'.[132] Kirby J continued:

> I do not doubt that if Australia were faced with challenges of war today, this Court, strengthened by the post-War decision in the *Communist Party Case*, and other cases since, would approach the matter differently than it did in the decisions which McHugh J has cited with apparent approval. Respectfully, I regard them as doubtful authority in the light of legal developments that occurred after they were written.[133]

For Kirby J the World War II internment cases, and indefinite detention of non-citizens pending removal, were fundamentally antithetical to the post-World War II rights project. The basic aspirations of this project, at least in terms of opposition to indefinite detention at the will of the executive, or racial categorisation, are values to which all are now assumed to be committed. By way of contrast, McHugh J viewed reference to international human rights not as a registering a shift in underlying 'political [and] social developments' but as a competing source of rules without democratic foundation.[134]

3.7 The Conditions of Detention

Arguments in *Al-Kateb* did not touch on the detention conditions, or the pressure they might put on the punitive/non-punitive distinction. But these issues arose in the companion case of *Behrooz*.[135] A consideration of *Behrooz* alongside *Al-Kateb* conveys the extent to which the current Australian understanding of authority to detain is resistant to legal challenge. Mr Behrooz left the Woomera Immigration Detention Centre in the outback of South Australia on or around 18 November 2001. Escape constituted an offence under section 197A of the Migration Act 1958, and Mr Behrooz was charged with escape.[136] In his defence, Mr Behrooz sought to argue that the conditions of his detention were punitive, that punitive detention was not authorised by the Act, and accordingly escape from such detention did not contravene the Act.[137] Consistent with this legal strategy, he sought

the wartime internment of ethnic Japanese living on the West Coast of the United States. Internment was pursued on the basis that ethnicity raised suspicions of disloyalty.

[132] ibid, [163]. See also reference to *Korematsu* as 'a caution that in times of distress the shield of military necessity and national security must not be used to protect governmental actions from close scrutiny and accountability' in the House of Lords *Belmarsh* decision: *A v Secretary of State for the Home Department* [2004] UKHL 56, [2005] 2 AC 68, [41] (Lord Bingham), citing *Korematsu v United States*, 584 F Supp 1406 (1984), [21]; see ch 6, p 170.

[133] *Al-Kateb* (n 1) [165].

[134] ibid, [71].

[135] The High Court of Australia heard three cases at the same time, with judgments delivered on the same day: *Al-Kateb* (n 1), *Behrooz* (n 8) and *Al Khafaji* (n 8).

[136] Migration Act 1958, s 197A: 'A detainee must not escape from immigration detention'; 'Penalty: imprisonment for 5 years.'

[137] See eg *Behrooz* (n 8) [4], [17] (Gleeson CJ), [31] (McHugh, Gummow and Heydon JJ), [66] (Kirby J).

and obtained witness summonses seeking the production of documentary material going to the conditions at the detention centre.[138] The government sought to set aside his summonses on the basis that the information sought was irrelevant and served no useful forensic purpose. By a majority of six of seven judges the High Court upheld the government's application to set the witness summonses aside. Kirby J dissented.

The *Behrooz* majority's starting proposition was that administrative detention for the purposes of the visa processing, or removal, of a non-citizen is non-punitive, and as such does not contravene the constitutional separation of powers. As Gleeson CJ explained:

> there is no warrant for concluding that, if the conditions of detention are sufficiently harsh, there will come a point where the detention itself can be regarded as punitive, and an invalid exercise of judicial power. Whatever the conditions of detention, the detention itself involves involuntary deprivation of liberty. For a citizen, that alone would ordinarily constitute punishment. But for an alien, the detention is an incident of the exclusion and deportation to which an alien is vulnerable.[139]

In *Behrooz*, the formal nature of the punitive/non-punitive distinction, that is, its divorce from any correlation with the reality of detention, is readily apparent. The label 'punitive' was held inapplicable by reason of the purposes of immigration detention, which purposes could not be impugned with reference to the conditions of immigration detention.

Central to the government's argument and the majority's reasoning was a distinction between 'lawful authority to detain and the means by which the detention is achieved or enforced, including the conditions of detention'.[140] No one contended that the Migration Act 1958 authorises detention in inhuman or intolerable conditions. What was in dispute was the remedy for any such state of affairs. The question was whether redress, at least in part, lay in the denial of the legality of detention, or exclusively in the possibility of other proceedings, notably negligence, to challenge the alleged mistreatment.

The *Behrooz* majority held that legal authority to detain is impervious to the conditions in which detainees are held.[141] This holding was softened by the accompanying message: 'An alien does not stand outside the protection of the civil and criminal law.'[142] The availability of other avenues of legal redress was emphasised:

[138] The witness summons was sought under the Magistrates Court Act 1991 (South Australia). Mr Behrooz was successful before the magistrate in having the summons issued. A judge of the South Australian Supreme Court granted the government's application to have the summons set aside on the basis stated in the text. A majority of the Full Court of the Supreme Court of South Australia declined leave to appeal.

[139] *Behrooz* (n 8) [21] (Gleeson CJ). The authority relied upon by Gleeson CJ in the last three sentences of this extract is *Lim* (n 28): see *Behrooz* [20] (Gleeson CJ). Cf Kirby J's reference to *Lim* in *Behrooz* [117]–[124].

[140] *Behrooz* (n 8) [46] (McHugh, Gummow and Heydon JJ), [75] (Kirby J).

[141] ibid, [21] (Gleeson CJ), [53] (McHugh, Gummow and Heydon JJ), [174] (Hayne J), [218] (Callinan J).

[142] ibid, [21] (Gleeson CJ).

'If an officer in a detention centre assaults a detainee, the officer will be liable to prosecution, or damages. If those who manage a detention centre fail to comply with their duty of care, they may be liable in tort.'[143] On the majority reasoning, the extent to which a detained alien enjoys the protection of the law rests on his or her ability to access these alternatives to a challenge to authority to detain. The utility to detainees of such legal actions are considered later in this section, with reference to *SBEG*, a recent negligence case in the Full Court of the Federal Court of Australia.[144]

Kirby J's dissent in *Behrooz* was directed not to the remedy of release, but to that of removal from the conditions of detention, or defence to the charge of escape.[145] He emphasised that the issues fell to be considered in the context of an application for summary relief, counselling restraint in striking out the action. He was adamant that the legal and constitutional character of detention could not be determined by the label adopted by Parliament or the description afforded by the executive.[146] He drew on the *Communist Party Case* in making this point.[147] He reasoned that it was not for Parliament or the executive to conclusively determine what constitutes 'immigration detention'.[148] As in *Al-Kateb*, the relevance of the *Communist Party Case* to the legal dispute in *Behrooz* turned on whether a particular state of affairs was seen as a condition precedent to the legality of detention. Kirby J was prepared to entertain the possibility that the conditions of detention might cause detention to pass beyond the purposes provided for in the Act, namely 'holding, processing, admitting or expelling "unlawful" alien entrants'.[149] Further, as a constitutional matter, he stated that the conditions of detention might cause detention to pass beyond the purposes for which Parliament could provide without contravening the separation of powers.[150] Accordingly, he held the conditions of detention to be a constitutional fact for determination by the Court. In contrast, as noted above, the other members of the Court held that the conditions of detention were legally irrelevant to authority to detain.

Kirby J criticised the majority's reliance on collateral remedies, stating that this effectively deprived the plaintiff of any ability to answer the charge against him, and was divorced from the realities of immigration detention: 'People confined in immigration detention are ordinarily likely to be impecunious, powerless, with limited command of the English language and, in a place as remote as Woomera, with extremely restricted access to legal assistance.'[151] Kirby J concluded that, allowing for the possibility that the conditions of detention are 'inhuman, intolerable,

[143] ibid.
[144] *SBEG v Commonwealth of Australia* [2012] FCAFC 189.
[145] *Behrooz* (n 8) [131]; see also [104] (Kirby J).
[146] ibid, [123] (Kirby J).
[147] *Behrooz* (n 8) [107]–[111] (Kirby J); *Communist Party Case* (n 88). See n 98.
[148] *Behrooz* (n 8) [106]–111].
[149] ibid, [120], [122] (Kirby J).
[150] ibid.
[151] ibid, [136].

degrading and unhealthy', a possible defence to escape founded in these conditions should not be foreclosed.[152]

The legal position regarding detention pending removal, and immigration detention more generally, that emerges from *Al-Kateb* and *Behrooz* is that once validly admitted to immigration detention, a non-citizen may have no basis to challenge legal authority to detain, notwithstanding an unimplemented request for removal, indefinite and perhaps permanent detention, and intolerable conditions.

By way of a coda to *Behrooz*, I consider the recent case of *SBEG*,[153] which concerned a negligence action brought by an individual suffering under the conditions of immigration detention. Australia had recognised the appellant in *SBEG* as a refugee, but he remained in detention as he had been issued with an adverse security assessment by the Australian Security Intelligence Organisation (ASIO).[154] The appellant advanced medical evidence that features of his continued detention were having an adverse impact on his mental health.[155] With reference to *Behrooz*, he argued that the Commonwealth owed him a duty of care,[156] and that pursuant to that duty it should place him in circumstances conducive to his mental health. In particular he argued that the Minister should exercise his power to make a 'residence determination'.[157] This would allow the appellant to reside in the community pending the determination of his application for a protection visa.[158] With reference to the appellant's adverse security assessment, the Minister had declined to consider the exercise of this power.[159] The grounds for the adverse security assessment were not known to the appellant or the Court. The primary judge had determined that the adverse security assessment was properly the subject of public interest immunity and there had been no appeal from that decision.[160] This was the context in which the applicant's action for removal from 'an environment of incarceration' was considered.

At the centre of the Court's reasoning was the following proposition: 'The risk of harm to the detainee is not the only matter to be considered in assessing whether reasonable care has been exercised: a consideration which must be

[152] ibid, [139] (Kirby J).

[153] *SBEG* (n 144).

[154] The class of persons currently in indefinite detention by reason of an ASIO adverse security assessment is the subject of ch 4, s 4.4, where the issue is addressed in the context of a study of the Australian High Court's decision in *Plaintiff M47/2012 v Director General of Security* [2012] HCA 46, (2012) 86 ALJR 1372 (*Plaintiff M47*).

[155] There is systemic evidence the adverse health implications of long-term immigration detention are widespread amongst detainees: see eg Melissa Bull et al, 'Sickness in the System of Long-Term Immigration Detention' (2013) 26 *Journal of Refugee Studies* 47, discussed in ch 4, pp 102–03.

[156] *SBEG* (n 144) [51] (Keane CJ, Lander and Siopis JJ), referencing *Behrooz* (n 8) [21] (Gleeson CJ), quoted from in part in the text to n 143.

[157] Migration Act 1958, s 197AB.

[158] The immediate reason the application was still pending was the decision of the High Court in *Plaintiff M47* (n 154), discussed in ch 4, s 4.4. The power to make 'residence determinations' was part of a package of reforms introduced in 2005: see ch 4, s 4.2.

[159] *SBEG* (n 144) [27] (Keane CJ, Lander and Siopis JJ).

[160] ibid, [68].

addressed is the need to ensure effective detention in accordance with law.'[161] The government argued that the need for 'effective detention', consequent on the issue of the adverse security assessment, had not been challenged, and the requirements of 'effective detention' were incompatible with the relief sought.[162]

The Court agreed. It held that there is a qualitative difference between anything that might meet the definition of 'detention' under the Migration Act 1958 and the placement requested by the appellant. Any detention would involve the appellant's involuntary restraint and it was the appellant's ability to come and go as he pleased that was argued to be critical to his mental health. The Court held that the form of 'detention' the appellant sought would be so benign as to pass outside the meaning of 'detention' under the Act.[163] Any assessment of the duty of reasonable care owed by the Commonwealth had to take into account the need for compliance with the statutory requirements of immigration detention.[164] In summary, the Commonwealth's duty of care could not be given practical content that addressed the relevant harm. Its duty of care was secondary to the mandatory detention regime and so could not afford redress to a person suffering by reason of prolonged and indefinite detention.

3.8 Conclusions on *Al-Kateb*

Following the hurried introduction of mandatory immigration detention considered in *Lim*,[165] the detention of non-citizens during processing and removal was largely unconstrained. There was no requirement of individualised assessment of the need for detention, or any requirement of periodic review of the need for detention. Since 2005, this has been qualified by the existence of an Ombudsmen review process, discussed in the next chapter.[166] The Ombudsman's review relates to long-term detainees, who have been in detention for a period of over two years, and includes the power to issue non-binding recommendations.

Lim did, however, provide some limits. It held that a request for removal was not to be a matter of legal indifference, but would have an effect on continuing authority to detain. The majority in *Al-Kateb* were dismissive of the constitutional limits in *Lim*, while not overruling them. They were also dismissive of any requirement for unequivocal statutory words to authorise a practice as destructive of

[161] ibid, [19].
[162] ibid, [47].
[163] ibid, [64].
[164] ibid, [69]: 'In these circumstances, it may be accepted that the respondent owed the appellant a duty to take reasonable care for his safety in detention; but to say that is not to advance the appellant's case very far when regard is had to the appellant's adverse security assessment. And in any event, the assessment of reasonable care takes place in the context of the need for compliance with the statutory requirement of immigration detention.'
[165] *Lim* (n 28).
[166] See ch 4, s 4.2.

human autonomy as indefinite, possibly permanent, administrative detention. In the case of both constitutional and statutory interpretation, the *Al-Kateb* majority drew on an expansive view of the purposes of the government's power over immigration and aliens. This expansive conception of immigration purposes denuded common law statutory presumptions, the separation of powers under Chapter III of the Constitution, and the constitutional fact doctrine of anything but the most marginal role in protecting the liberty of non-citizens.

I argue that it is not the rules applied, stated at the level of 'a constitutional immunity from administrative detention subject to exceptions', or 'a presumption against the abrogation of fundamental rights', that differentiate the majority and minority judgments in *Al-Kateb*, but the way in which those rules were applied to non-citizens. The difference is registered in the weight accorded the aliens power as against the constitutional immunity derived from Chapter III, or the government's purpose of immigration control as against the presumption against abrogation of liberty. Where decisive weight is accorded to the aliens power, or the government's purpose of immigration control, unauthorised non-citizens are placed outside the normal, generally applicable, legal protections. A lack of membership, designated by the double absence of citizenship status and immigration authorisation, is equated with a lack of rights. It is this absence of a right to liberty that forms the starting premise of a judge working within the rights-precluding model.

Where weight is accorded to the protective rationale of the constitutional immunity or the common law presumption, detention to facilitate a non-citizen's removal is subject to meaningful limits. Legal authority to detain pending removal is held to depend on the viability of removal, and the viability of removal is a question for the courts. The judges who accord weight to doctrines and presumptions protective of rights emphasise their universal nature. The exceptions arising from a non-citizen's vulnerability to removal are acknowledged, but are integrated with persisting rights of non-citizens. They are held not to completely preclude the operation of these rights-protective doctrines.

The rights-precluding approach seen in the *Al-Kateb* majority is attributable to two underlying impulses: first, a particular understanding of law and the judge's role; and second, and determinatively, a particular understanding of immigration powers and the legal position of non-citizens. As to the former, the majority in *Al-Kateb* exhibited a proclivity to treat law as a classification exercise, with the judicial role being the application of determinate rules. This style of legal thought seems more inclined to treat the absence of a right to remain as an 'off-switch', rendering liberty rights inapplicable. This approach evidences a distrust of evaluative judgment in judicial reasoning, which extends to a distrust of any exercise that involves determining the *extent* of a power's lawful exercise, such as is involved in a proportionality assessment of detention pending removal.

This distrust of evaluative judgment in judicial reasoning does not herald value-free adjudication. The second element in the majority reasoning is an expansive understanding of what constitutes a legitimate immigration power, and acceptance of a stark distinction between the rights of citizens and those of non-citizens. The legal order in which the rights-precluding judges find themselves contains legal doctrines protective of liberty. These features of the legal system are squared with the indefinite detention of non-citizens by denying that they apply to such detention.

The closing passages of Hayne J's judgment convey both his disavowal of any conception of a judicial role in putting society's commitment to rights and freedoms to the test, and his conviction that the non-citizen present without permission has no right to liberty. Both views are conveyed by way of quotation from one of the high-water marks of the plenary power doctrine in the United States, the *Shaugnessy v Mezei* litigation. I placed the first quotation in section 3.2, as indicating Hayne J's ambivalence to the principle of legality.[167] The second of Hayne J's quotations from Learned Hand J reads thus:

> An alien, who comes to our shores and the ship which bears him, take the chance that he may not be allowed to land. If that chance turns against him, both know, or, if they do not, are charged with the knowledge, that, since the alien cannot land, he must find an asylum elsewhere; or, like the Flying Dutchman, forever sail the seas. When at his urgence we do let him go ashore – *pendente lit e* so to say – we may give him whatever harbourage we choose, until he finds shelter elsewhere if he can.[168]

The insouciance expressed in this quote as to the detainee's position is the more arresting in that in both *Al-Kateb* and the judgment from which the quote was taken, the individuals and deporting governments had made concerted efforts 'to find asylum elsewhere', but were unable to do so. Both litigants suffered from prolonged detention as a substitute for departure. For both, 'harbourage' was a euphemism for indefinite, involuntary detention.

Learned Hand J's remark is an eloquent distillation of the view that rights are for members, and non-citizens are conditional members. Where permission to be here is withheld, so are rights. The quote is indifferent to any obligations a state may owe to a non-citizen seeking entry, an issue relevant to a country that is signatory to the Refugee Convention.[169] More immediately, any legal issues raised by the non-citizen's continuing detention and presence are avoided by the analogy with someone 'stopped at the border'.[170]

For the applicant in both cases, *Shaugnessy* and *Al-Kateb*, release from detention was only effected when the relevant detainees were eventually released into the country that had subjected them to prolonged detention in an effort to exclude them. The litigants came to reside in America and Australia respectively. As noted

[167] For the quotation see the text to n 16.

[168] *United States v Shaughnessy* (n 16), 971 quoted in *Al-Kateb* (n 1) [269] (Hayne J).

[169] Convention relating to the Status of Refugees (adopted 28 July 1951, entered into force 22 April 1954) 189 UNTS 150; Protocol relating to the Status of Refugees (adopted 31 January 1967, entered into force 4 October 1967) 606 UNTS 267 (Refugee Convention and Protocol).

[170] Use of the quotation is incongruous in *Al-Kateb*. Australian law contains no equivalent to the 'entry' fiction central to *United States v Shaughnessy* (n 16), making references to the alien who is 'not allowed to land' inapposite.

at the end of the preceding chapter, Mr Al-Kateb had been released from detention following the Full Court's *Al Masri* decision. He sat through the hearings on his case in November 2003.[171] Following the High Court's decision, he was not taken back into detention, but remained 'free' subject to conditions under a bridging visa granted by the Immigration Minister, in the exercise of her discretion.[172] In late 2007, Mr Al-Kateb was granted leave to remain in Australia indefinitely. As last reported, he was working with a firm of environmental designers in Canberra.[173]

Mr Al-Kateb's presence in the Australian 'community', before, during and after the verdict that authorised his indefinite detention, strongly suggests that the power was not actually needed in the case on which it was argued. What appears to be crucial from the government perspective is that it possess the power to hold a non-citizen in indefinite detention. The power, and conversely the absence of legal restrictions, becomes the goal.

Together, the three dissenting judges in *Al-Kateb* (and the four federal court judges delivering judgment in the *Al Masri* litigation) applied legal and constitutional doctrines through which the 'general belief that human rights and fundamental freedoms should ultimately be protected' was registered in the Australian legal system.[174] By way of contrast, the majority approach ran counter to the notion that constitutionalism helps to restrain our excesses.[175]

[171] See David Marr, 'Escape from a Life in Limbo' *Sydney Morning Herald* (Sydney, 27 October 2007), www.smh.com.au/news/national/escape-from-a-life-in-limbo/2007/10/26/1192941339538.html.

[172] ibid.

[173] ibid.

[174] John Basten, 'Book Review of *The Ultimate Rule of Law* by David M Beatty' (2005) 29 *Melbourne University Law Review* 930, 938.

[175] Glass (n 15).

4

Al-Kateb Contested

> It is . . . not correct . . . to characterise *Al-Kateb* as a decision 'rest[ing] upon a principle carefully worked out in a significant succession of cases'.
>
> Bell J, *Plaintiff M47*, High Court of Australia (2012)[1]

4.1 Introduction

In this chapter, I study aspects of the wider Australian debate on the detention of non-citizens under the Migration Act 1958. This provides further context for an assessment of *Al-Kateb* and the position of non-citizens in long-term immigration detention in Australia, as a matter of practice and law.[2] In section 4.2, I examine administrative measures introduced after *Al-Kateb* to alleviate the harshness of the Australian detention regime. In section 4.3, the *Offshore Processing Case*, a 2010 decision of the Australian High Court, is discussed.[3] The decision suggests that in recent years the Australian government's immigration policy has been operating in a more legally constrained space than it did previously.[4] The High Court's reasoning in the *Offshore Processing Case* provides an interesting counterpart to *Al-Kateb*. The High Court held that the effect of the processes under challenge on the liberty interests of unlawful non-citizens gave rise to procedural fairness obligations. In section 4.4, the 2012 case of *Plaintiff M47* is considered.[5] It directly raised the issue of the legality of indefinite detention pending removal. In *Plaintiff M47* four members of the High Court of Australia found it unnecessary to revisit *Al-Kateb*. The three judges who addressed the status of *Al-Kateb* disagreed on whether it should be overruled. The decision testified to the uncertain status of *Al-Kateb* within Australian law.

[1] *Plaintiff M47/2012 v Director General of Security* [2012] HCA 46, (2012) 86 ALJR 1372, [526] (*Plaintiff M47*).

[2] *Al-Kateb v Godwin* 2004 HCA 37, (2004) 219 CLR 562.

[3] *Plaintiff M61/2010E v Commonwealth* [2010] HCA 41, (2011) 243 CLR 319 (*Offshore Processing Case*).

[4] See also *Plaintiff M70/2011 v Minister of Immigration and Citizenship* [2011] HCA 32, (2012) 244 CLR 144 (*Malaysian Declaration Case*).

[5] *Plaintiff M47* (n 1).

4.2 Administrative Measures

Arguably, the greatest gains in ameliorating the harshness of the Australian immigration detention regime have been achieved through administrative measures introduced by Parliament. A number of practical means of monitoring and ameliorating long-term detention have been introduced following *Al-Kateb.*

In 2005, reportedly in response to community pressure and pressure from backbench members of its own party,[6] the government created a new temporary visa class, the 'removal pending bridging visa'.[7] This visa enables those in long-term detention to be released, including those who have been refused refugee status but cannot return to their country of origin. It enables a Minister to release a detainee where certain criteria are met, the most important of which are that the Minister is satisfied that a non-citizen's removal from Australia is not reasonably practicable, and the non-citizen will do 'everything possible' to facilitate their removal from Australia.[8] Bridging visas, and in particular the removal pending bridging visa, qualify the binary opposition between detention of the unauthorised non-citizen and liberty of the authorised. The grant of a bridging visa enables a person to become a lawful non-citizen, even though he or she does not possess a substantive visa.[9]

A removal pending bridging visa is evidently of great benefit to the recipient, conferring liberty upon the detainee. It also leaves the Minister's discretion regarding the liberty of the detainee almost completely unfettered. A detainee cannot initiate an application for a removal pending visa. Only those persons given 'an invitation in writing' by the Minister can apply.[10] The relevant section conferring power to grant the bridging visa 'if the Minister thinks that it is in the public interest' is specified as a non-compellable power to be exercised by the Minister personally.[11]

The introduction of this bridging visa ameliorates the mandatory scheme for indefinite detention. However, it does not vindicate detainees' right to liberty.[12]

[6] See eg Louise Dodson, 'Set them Free: PM's Big Shift on Boat People' *Sydney Morning Herald* (Sydney, 23 March 2005); Elizabeth Colman and Steve Lewis, 'PM Eases Stance on Detainees' *The Australian* (Sydney, 23 March 2005).

[7] Migration Regulations 1994 (Cth), Sch 2 [Visa] Subclass 070.

[8] Migration Act 1958, s 31; Migration Regulations 1994, reg 2.20(12). On a complexity of the second criterion mentioned, that the non-citizen should do 'everything possible' to facilitate their removal, see William Maley, 'Freedom a Mirage for Some Detainees', Australian Policy Online, http://apo.org.au/commentary/freedom-mirage-some-detainees.

[9] Migration Act 1958, s 73. Bridging visas can only be granted to those who satisfy the relevant criteria (ss 72, 73). On the bridging visa regime, and the legislative scheme post-*Al-Kateb* more generally, see Matthew T Stubbs, 'Arbitrary Detention in Australia: Detention of Unlawful Non-Citizens under the Migration Act 1958 (Cth)' (2006) 25 *Australian Year Book of International Law* 273, 277–79.

[10] Migration Regulations 1994, reg 2.20A.

[11] Migration Act 1958, s 195A, inserted by the Migration Amendment (Detention Arrangements) Act 2005.

[12] cf Dan Meagher, 'The Significance of *Al-Kateb v Godwin* for the Australian Bill of Rights Debate' (2010) 12(1) *Constitutional Law and Policy Review* 15, 20 fn 58, though see his tentative agreement

Indeed, by granting a bridging visa the courts and the government do not concede that the detainee has any right to liberty. Whether a non-citizen is released from administrative detention under a bridging visa remains a matter 'for the opinion of the executive government'.[13] It is a mechanism of potential utility to the detainee, but being the recipient of an uncompellable ministerial discretion may not be experienced in the same way as being able to assert one's rights. More straightforwardly, the distinction between ministerial discretion and rights is critical for those the government has decided are to remain in lengthy, indefinite detention.

In a further development of considerable practical significance, in 2005 Parliament conferred a new Immigration Ombudsman function on the Commonwealth Ombudsman.[14] This change responded to the mistaken immigration detention of Ms Cornelia Rau and the detention and removal of Ms Alvarez Solon, both Australian citizens suffering from mental health problems.[15] The scandal attending these cases coincided with a wider debate on immigration detention (some of it attributable to *Al-Kateb*). The Rau and Alvarez cases were followed by the referral to the Commonwealth Ombudsman of 247 cases in which an individual's records had been marked 'not unlawful', meaning either that he or she should not have been detained, or that he or she could no longer be detained. The Ombudsman investigated whether all or any part of the person's detention was unlawful or wrongful.[16] These referrals resulted in the Ombudsman releasing six consolidated public reports and two on individual cases.[17] The systemic failures in immigration administration disclosed in these reports resulted in an extensive reform programme in the immigration portfolio, commencing in 2005, an element of which was the creation of the specialist role of Immigration Ombudsman, with new statutory powers and resources.[18]

A critical component of the Ombudsman's review function is the power to conduct detention review. Upon receipt of a report from the Secretary of the Department of Immigration and Citizenship, the Ombudsman is required to give the Minister an assessment of the appropriateness of arrangements for the person's detention.[19] The Ombudsman is provided with a report within 21 days of

with the statement that the grant of a visa to Mr Al-Kateb did not prove that Australian democracy protects rights, on the same page.

[13] *Al-Kateb* (n 2) [140] (Gummow J).

[14] These reforms to the Ombudsman's role were contained in a new Part 8C of the Migration Act 1958, inserted by the Migration Amendment (Detention Arrangements) Act 2005.

[15] Mick Palmer, *Inquiry into the Circumstances of the Immigration Detention of Cornelia Rau: Report* (Commonwealth of Australia, July 2005); Neil Comrie, *Inquiry into the Circumstances of the Vivian Alvarez Matter*, Report No 03/2005 (Canberra, Commonwealth Ombudsman, September 2005).

[16] John McMillan, *Lessons for Public Administration: Ombudsman Investigation of Referred Immigration Cases* (Canberra, Commonwealth Ombudsman, August 2007), 2.

[17] For the reports into the referred immigration cases see www.ombudsman.gov.au/reports/investigation/2006 and www.ombudsman.gov.au/reports/investigation/2007.

[18] The legislative component of the reforms was implanted by the Migration Amendment (Detention Arrangements) Act 2005.

[19] Migration Act 1958, s 486O.

a person having been in detention for two years and, if the person remains in detention, at six monthly intervals thereafter.[20] The Ombudsman's assessment may include non-binding recommendations regarding the person's detention, and must include a statement which the Minister is to table in Parliament within 15 days of receipt.[21] These statements are generally in the form of a report of three to four pages

> dealing with the circumstances of a person's detention, visa claims and litigation, their health, family issues, attitude to detention or removal, problems occurring in detention, and the Ombudsman's recommendations on matters such as detention arrangements and whether the grant of a visa should be considered.[22]

The statements, together with the Minister's tabling statement, are available on the Ombudsman's website.[23] In addition, the Ombudsman's office makes regular visits to detention centres. These measures significantly enhance the transparency and awareness of, and accountability for, long-term detention in Australia.

The statutory review requirement implicitly acknowledges two years as a lengthy period of detention, and signals in principle opposition to indefinite detention.[24] The considerable achievements of the Immigration Ombudsman in relation to immigration detention may be attributable in part to the non-binding nature of its review and recommendations. The Office functions by negotiation and recommendation rather than legal demand. But these features of the Ombudsman's functions also represent the limitations of such detention review: 'people may still be detained – even indefinitely – at the discretion of the department and the minister.'[25]

The 2005 amendments to the Migration Act 1958 also made provision for 'residence determinations', which confer a power on the minister to determine that it is in the public interest that a non-citizen reside at a specified place other than a detention centre.[26]

The Ombudsman's reports have provided an important source of information about immigration detention. Researchers have drawn on this material to address the relationship between immigration detention and 'various dimensions of

[20] See ibid, s 486L–N (setting out the government's reporting obligations).

[21] ibid, ss 486O and 486P.

[22] Mary Durkin and John McMillan, 'External Scrutiny of Immigration Administration: The Changing Role of the Commonwealth and Immigration Ombudsman', National Administrative Law Forum, Surfers Paradise, June 2006, 'Procedure and Format of Reports'.

[23] See www.ombudsman.gov.au/reports/immigration-detention-review.

[24] Durkin and McMillan (n 22), 'Two Year Detention Review – Issue and Themes'. See also the government's seven key immigration detention values announced on 29 July 2008. Value 4 reads: 'Detention that is indefinite or otherwise arbitrary is not acceptable and the length and conditions of detention, including the appropriateness of both the accommodation and the services provided, would be subject to regular review.' See www.immi.gov.au/media/fact-sheets/82detention.htm.

[25] Petro Georgiou, 'Protection should be Paramount' *The Age* (Melbourne, 31 July 2008). Petro Georgiou MP was commenting on the government's announcement, several days earlier, of seven key 'detention values', including '4. Detention that is indefinite or otherwise arbitrary is not acceptable'.

[26] Migration Act 1958, s 197AB.

mental and physical health and well-being'.[27] A recent systemic review of the Ombudsman's reports confirms earlier studies finding a link between the length of detention and poor health. In 54 per cent of cases reviewed, detention was identified as causing, being among the causes of, or exacerbating, mental and physical health problems.[28] The *SBEG* case (analysed in chapter three, section 3.7) is a concrete instance of the connection. Running throughout the review is evidence of the corrosive effect of immigration detention on detainees' health. A central element of the harm is the detainees' loss of autonomy over most aspects of their lives.[29] Another arresting finding in the report is that 'more than 85 per cent of the long-term detainees described in the reports analysed as part of this study were eventually provided with permanent protection'.[30] Long-term detention not only has stark adverse effects on the mental and physical health of detainees but is largely pointless, as judged against the ostensible goal of removal. In the vast majority of cases, it is a process by which significant harm is inflicted on future members of the Australian community.

4.3 The *Offshore Processing Case*[31]

The *Offshore Processing Case* provides an interesting counterpart to the ruling in *Al-Kateb*. The existence of a liberty interest on the part of a non-citizen in immigration detention played a central role in the Court's reasoning.

Since the arrival of Mr Al-Kateb and Mr Al Masri in Australia without visas, in mid-December 2000 and June 2001 respectively, the Australian regime for the processing and detention of non-citizens has been shaped by the advent of 'offshore processing'. This is part of the relevant background to the *Offshore Processing Case* and *Plaintiff M47*. The offshore processing regime emerged from the extraordinary events surrounding the *Tampa*, a Norwegian commercial vessel.[32] The *Tampa* rescued 433 persons from a distressed boat bound for Australian territory. The rescuees intended to enter Australian territorial waters and apply for refugee status. Following a fraught series of exchanges with the Australian government, the boat entered Australian waters and was boarded by members of the Australian Special Air Services regiment. After a series of ultimately unsuccessful legal

[27] Melissa Bull et al, 'Sickness in the System of Long-Term Immigration Detention' (2013) 26 *Journal of Refugee Studies* 47, 47. The study consisted of an 'examination of 419 cases of detention exceeding 24 months recorded by the Commonwealth Ombudsman over the period of July 2005 [to] March 2009' (49).

[28] Bull et al, ibid, 58. They also detailed that poor health caused delays in the removal process and in proceeding with required immigration processes, so lengthening detention.

[29] See eg ibid, 63.

[30] See eg ibid, 59.

[31] *Offshore Processing Case* (n 3).

[32] For an account of the *Tampa* episode see David Marr and Marian Wilkinson, *Dark Victory* (Sydney, Allen & Unwin, 2003).

challenges to the Australian government's actions in the Federal Court,[33] the rescuees, who had been transferred to another boat, were taken to the Pacific Island of Nauru, where their applications for refugee status were processed by Australian officials.

The above events unfolded in the context of a Federal election in which refusing the rescuees access to Australian territory was perceived as a vote-winner for the incumbents (who went on to win the election), and was fused in the public imagination with the campaign slogan 'we will decide who comes to this country and the circumstances in which they come'.[34] The election campaign spanned the terrorist attacks of 11 September 2001. The first instance ruling of the Australian Federal Court against the legality of the government's actions was handed down on 11 September 2001. At the time the first instance ruling in the *Tampa* case was delivered, the Australian Prime Minister was visiting the Eastern Seaboard of the United States. The terrorist attack on New York fell in the interval between delivery of the first instance judgment in *Tampa* and the Prime Minister's scheduled press conference on that decision. The appeal, in which a majority of the Full Court of the Federal Court upheld the government position, was delivered a week later. The *Tampa* episode was retrospectively validated, and the future diversion of unauthorised arrivals to Pacific countries for immigration processing put on a legislative footing, in a package of six Acts which received royal assent on 27 September 2001, for the most part entering into effect that day.[35] These Acts put in place the statutory framework at the centre of the *Offshore Processing Case*. The central conceit of the new statutory arrangements was the legal fiction of a 'migration zone' that was different from, and smaller than, Australian sovereign territory.[36] Various Australian islands, namely those where unauthorised non-citizens arriving by boat were most likely to make contact with Australian territory, were excised from the Australian 'migration zone'.[37] Anyone arriving on these islands, termed 'excised offshore places', without a valid visa was an unlawful entrant and an 'offshore entry person'. Offshore entry persons could be transferred to a declared country, Nauru or Papua New Guinea. This transfer procedure was the central device of the 'Pacific Solution'. These arrangements were designed to prevent offshore entry persons, a class anticipated to encompass the vast majority of arrivals by boat, from accessing the provisions of the Migration Act 1958 and its procedures for merits and judicial review.

Following a change of government at the 2007 national election, the incoming Labor administration adopted a policy of not exercising the power to transfer off-

[33] *Victorian Council for Civil Liberties v Minister for Immigration & Multicultural Affairs* [2001] FCA 1297 (11 September 2001); *Ruddock v Vadarlis* [2001] FCA 1329, 180 ALR 1 (18 September 2001).

[34] John Howard, 'Election Policy Speech' (City Recital Hall, Sydney, 28 October 2001), http://australianpolitics.com/2001/10/28/john-howard-election-policy-speech.html.

[35] *Offshore Processing Case* (n 3) [29].

[36] More recently, the Australian Parliament has legislated to exclude the entirety of Australia from the (Australian) migration zone: Migration Amendment (Unauthorised Maritime Arrivals and Other Measures) Act 2013.

[37] Migration Amendment (Excision from the Migration Zone) Act 2001.

shore entry persons to other countries.[38] Instead, future unauthorised boat arrivals would be held on the Australian territory of Christmas Island pending a decision by the Minister as to whether or not to exercise a non-delegable, non-compellable power under section 46A(2) of the Migration Act 1958 to 'lift the bar' that prevented offshore entry persons from applying for refugee status. This shift did not mean that the government had accepted the application of the Migration Act 1958, merits review, or the normal application of the traditional grounds of judicial review to offshore entry persons.

The relevant processing of 'offshore entry persons' was conducted on what the government understood to be an extra-statutory footing, in part by a private provider named Wizard People Pty Ltd.[39] The Australian Department of Immigration developed two procedural manuals, for 'Refugee Status Assessment' (RSA) and 'Independent Merits Review' (IMR). The Migration Act 1958 and Australian case law were presented as guidelines for the private provider. The RSA manual stated: 'the Migration Act, the Migration Regulations 1994 . . . and Australian case law on the interpretations of the definition of a refugee and "protection obligations" do not apply', though 'officers should be guided by these as a matter of policy'.[40]

The extra-statutory processing regime was linked to Australia's immigration system through the Minister's discretion to 'lift the bar' on visa applications from offshore entry persons. The bar was set out at subsection 46A(1) of the Migration Act 1958. Subsection 46A(2) stated in part: 'If the Minister thinks it is in the public interest to do so, the Minister may . . . determine that subsection (1) does not apply . . .' Subsection 46A(7) (the 'no-consideration' clause) provided:

> The Minister does not have a duty to consider whether to exercise the power under subsection (2) in respect of any offshore entry person whether the Minister is requested to do so by the offshore entry person or by any other person, or in any other circumstances.

If at the RSA or IMR stage an officer concluded that Australia's protection obligations were engaged, a recommendation would go to the Minister to that effect, seeking her or his agreement that the bar in section 46A(1) should be lifted, pursuant to section 46A(2). If the officer concluded that Australia did not have protection obligations to the applicant, no recommendation would go to the Minister. An applicant had an opportunity to address a negative decision at the first RSA stage and on merits review. Subject to the officer's further assessment of whether any other international treaty obligations were engaged, a negative decision on merits review led to commencement of the removal process.

[38] There has since been a resumption of the policy of offshore processing, with any asylum seeker arriving in Australia after 13 August 2012 transferred to a Regional Processing Centre in Nauru or Papua New Guinea (Manus Island): see Janet Phillips and Harriet Spinks, *Immigration Detention in Australia* (Parliamentary Library Background Note, updated 20 March 2013), 18–19.

[39] Wizard People conducted the merits review portion of the process: *Offshore Processing Case* (n 3) [50].

[40] ibid, [42].

The plaintiffs in the *Offshore Processing Case* had been through the RSA and IMR processes, and at both stages the reviewers had concluded that they were not persons to whom Australia owed protection obligations. The plaintiffs challenged these decisions on procedural fairness grounds, in the High Court's original jurisdiction under section 75(v) of the Constitution.[41]

Under Australian law a duty of procedural fairness arises where a statute 'confers power to destroy, defeat or prejudice a person's rights, interests or legitimate expectations'.[42] In the *Offshore Processing Case*, the government argued that there was no obligation to afford procedural fairness because what was at issue was the discretionary power to confer a right. The Court disagreed. It held that the inquiries under challenge directly engaged 'the rights and interests of the plaintiffs to freedom from detention at the behest of the Australian executive'.[43] The plaintiffs' rights were directly affected 'by the decision to consider the exercise of those powers [to lift the bar on grant of a visa, or issue a residence determination]' *because it prolonged their detention.*[44] Here, the obligations of procedural fairness arise from the effect of the processing on the plaintiffs' liberty.[45] In its discussion, the Court repudiated the language of fault used by the majority in *Al-Kateb*: 'even if it were the fact that individuals were content to have detention prolonged [as a price of eventual entry to Australia], that must not obscure that what was being done . . . had the consequence of depriving them of their liberty.'[46]

A second feature of the Court's reasoning was its holding that the duration of detention was determined by decision-making under statute. This involved rejecting the government's submission that 'detention of an offshore entry person was permitted while the officer detaining the person awaited the possibility of the exercise of power under s 46A or s 195A'.[47] The Court responded:

> Several points may be made about this proposition. First, the existence of any relevant possibility is wholly within the control of the Executive. It follows that the period of an individual's detention would be wholly within the control of the Executive. Second, deciding whether there is a relevant possibility of the exercise of power under s 46A or s 195A would require some prediction of the likelihood of the exercise of a personal non-compellable power . . . Such a construction of the relevant provision should not be adopted unless no other construction is reasonably open . . .[48]

[41] ibid, [51]. Section 75(v) of the Constitution states: 'In all matters . . . (v) in which a writ of Mandamus or prohibition or an injunction is sought against an officer of the Commonwealth; the High Court shall have original jurisdiction.'

[42] ibid, [74], citing *Annetts v McCann* [1990] HCA 57, (1990) 170 CLR 596, 598 (Mason CJ, Deane and McHugh JJ).

[43] ibid, [9].

[44] ibid, [76].

[45] ibid, [75]. See Mary Crock and Daniel Ghezelbash, 'Due Process and Rule of Law as Human Rights: The High Court and the "Offshore" Processing of Asylum Seekers' (2011) 18 *Australian Journal of Administrative Law* 101, 108–09.

[46] *Offshore Processing Case* (n 3) [76]; cf *Al-Kateb* (n 1) [261], [268] (Hayne J).

[47] *Offshore Processing Case* (n 3) [64]. Section 195A confers power on the Minister to grant visas to persons in detention under s 189.

[48] ibid, [65].

The Court commented:

> It is not readily to be supposed that a statutory power to detain a person permits continuation of that detention at the unconstrained discretion of the Executive. Yet a proposition of that kind lay at the heart of the submissions advanced on behalf of the Commonwealth and the Minister.[49]

The Court's characterisation of the government position in the above extracts generates a dissonance with the majority reasoning in *Al-Kateb*. In the *Offshore Processing Case*, the High Court lambasted the idea that a person can continue in detention 'at the unconstrained discretion of the executive'.[50] There were two components to this characterisation of the government's position by the Court in the *Offshore Processing Case*: the means of obtaining release were completely within the control of the executive; and no predictions could be made as to whether, or when, those means would be utilised by the government.[51] These components also served to characterise the power of detention pending removal given legal sanction in *Al-Kateb*. There is the distinction that, in *Al-Kateb*, the ability to effect a detainee's removal from Australia is not 'wholly within the control of the [Australian] executive'. It is dependent on the cooperation of foreign governments. But in a situation where the Australian government cannot effect removal, *Al-Kateb* illustrated that the detainee may be entirely dependent on the government to obtain release. Absent removal, *Al-Kateb* means that any remaining prospect of the detainees' release is 'wholly within the control of the executive'.[52]

On the second point, the unpredictability of the detainees' circumstances, the same can be said of the power of detention pending removal given legal sanction in *Al-Kateb*. In his dissent in *Al-Kateb* Gummow J accurately characterised the majority's understanding of that power as 'mandated by the hope of the Minister . . . that at some future time some other State may be prepared to receive the appellant'.[53] In *Al-Kateb*, as in the *Offshore Processing Case*, the detainee could make no prediction as to the possibility or timing of release.

The government had submitted that detention was permitted while awaiting the possible exercise of a discretionary power. The High Court held that this characterisation of the arrangements should not be adopted while another was reasonably open. The Court reasoned that the government construction involved an 'irreducible tension between the exercise of a power to detain in a way that prolongs detention, because inquiries are being made, and those inquiries having no statutory foundation'.[54] The High Court preferred a construction that avoided this tension. The alternative construction advanced by the Court rested on a positive ministerial decision to consider exercising the power to lift the bar in the case of

[49] ibid, [64].
[50] ibid.
[51] ibid, [65].
[52] ibid.
[53] *Al-Kateb* (n 2) [125] (Gummow J).
[54] *Offshore Processing Case* (n 3) [66].

every offshore claimant. Above, I noted the 2008 ministerial announcement to the effect that all future unauthorised arrivals would be processed on the Australian territory of Christmas Island.[55] The High Court treated this announcement, coupled with the decision to use the RSA procedures, as a *decision to consider* exercising the s 46A power to lift the bar in the case of every 'offshore' claimant.[56] In addition, the High Court regarded sections 46A and 195A (regulating access to processing and release from detention, respectively) as 'the only statutory powers that could be engaged to avoid breaching Australia's international obligations', in particular the Refugee Convention and Protocol.[57] The entirety of the purportedly 'extra-statutory' review process was given a statutory foundation. Once the review process was held to have a statutory foundation, the principles governing the application of judicial review were said to be 'well established'.[58]

Both plaintiffs established a breach of procedural fairness. The High Court issued a declaration that the decision-makers had made an error of law in not treating the Migration Act 1958 and decisions of Australian courts as binding, and had further failed to observe procedural fairness.

The decision in the *Offshore Processing Case*, a unanimous decision of the High Court of Australia, is welcome, in that it helps to ensure that the executive does not evade legal accountability in its exercise of coercive power over non-citizens. Its interpretation of the Migration Act 1958 assumed and so affirmed Australia's commitment to the Refugee Convention and Protocol. The decision led to improved procedural protections.[59] The High Court's rejection of 'detention at the unconstrained discretion of the executive' was not hollow, but directed to ensuring that processing decisions were made according to law, with attendant obligations of procedural fairness. The lawfulness of the detention was not challenged, and the reality of detention continued, though on a new legal footing.

[55] See text following n 38 above.

[56] *Offshore Processing Case* (n 3) [37]–[40]. The importance of the ministerial announcement in the *Offshore Processing Case* is underscored by the fact that the absence of such an announcement was used to distinguish that case from the circumstances in *Plaintiff S10/2011 v Minister for Immigration and Citizenship* [2012] HCA 31, [41]–[47], [49] (French CJ and Kiefel J). In the absence of such an announcement it was held that the Minister could not be said to have made a decision to consider whether to exercise his powers. The contrast was between a system of assessment and review 'knitted' into the relevant statutory power by a ministerial announcement that he would consider exercising the power in every case, the situation in the *Offshore Processing Case*, and a departmental process anterior to exercise of statutory powers, but which did not constitute or evidence their exercise: *Plaintiff S10/2011*, [49] and [47] respectively.

[57] *Offshore Processing Case* (n 3) [40]. The need for Australia to give effect to its international obligations was central to the court's reasoning: see eg [27], [103]. See the Convention relating to the Status of Refugees (adopted 28 July 1951, entered into force 22 April 1954); Protocol relating to the Status of Refugees (adopted 31 January 1967, entered into force 4 October 1967) 606 UNTS 267 (Refugee Convention and Protocol).

[58] *Offshore Processing Case* (n 3) [73].

[59] See Department of Immigration and Citizenship, 'Changes to Refugee Status Determination', www.immi.gov.au/visas/humanitarian/_pdf/faq-changes-to-refugee-status.pdf. 'The Protection Obligations Determination process replaces the existing Refugee Status Determination process used for irregular maritime arrivals. The changes are in response to the High Court's decision of 11 November 2010 that all irregular maritime arrivals are able to seek judicial review of a negative assessment of their claims for refugee status.'

4.4 *Plaintiff M47: Al-Kateb* Reconsidered (by some)

4.4.1 *Plaintiff M47* Introduced

The issue of the legality of indefinite detention returned to the Australian High Court in the context of challenges to the detention of refugees who had received an adverse security clearance from the Australian Security and Intelligence Organisation (ASIO). The High Court delivered judgment in *Plaintiff M47* in October 2012.

The plaintiff in *Plaintiff M47* was a Tamil refugee from Sri Lanka.[60] It was agreed that he was a refugee within the meaning of Article 1A of the Refugee Convention.[61] On 18 October 2009 he was one of approximately 80 asylum seekers intercepted by an Australian customs vessel, the *Oceanic Viking*.[62] The plaintiff entered Australia lawfully and, as an irregular entrant without a valid visa,[63] has been detained on Christmas Island since 30 December 2009.[64] The Australian Department of Immigration and Citizenship recognised him as a refugee, but this did not automatically result in a 'protection visa'. In addition to refugee status, another criterion had to be satisfied for the grant of such a visa, namely 'Public Interest Criterion 4002'. This criterion required as follows: 'The applicant was not assessed by the Australian Security Intelligence Organisation to be directly or indirectly a risk to security, within the meaning of section 4 of the Australian Security Intelligence Organisation Act 1979' (ASIO Act 1979). The definitions section of the ASIO Act 1979 (section 4) provides in part:

> 'security' means:
>
> (a) the protection of, and of the people of, the Commonwealth and the several States and Territories from:
>
> i. espionage;
> ii. sabotage;
> iii. politically motivated violence;
> iv. promotion of communal violence;
> v. attacks on Australia's defence system; or
> vi. acts of foreign interference;
>
> whether directed from, or committed in, Australia or not; and

[60] My account of the factual context draws on Ben Saul, 'Dark Justice: Australia's Indefinite Detention of Refugees on Security Grounds under International Human Rights Law' (2012) 13 *Melbourne Journal of International Law* 685.

[61] *Plaintiff M47* (n 1) [155] (Hayne J). None of the provisions for denying refugee status on security grounds contained within the Refugee Convention was held to be applicable: Refugee Convention (n 57) arts 1F, 32 and 33(2).

[62] *Plaintiff M47* (n 1) [366] (Crennan J).

[63] He entered Australia lawfully on a 'special purpose' visa, which expired on the day of entry, rendering him eligible for detention: see ibid, [369] (Crennan J).

[64] ibid, [463] (Bell J).

(aa) the protection of Australia's territorial and border integrity from serious threats; and

(b) the carrying out of Australia's responsibilities to any foreign country in relation to a matter mentioned in any of the subparagraphs of paragraph (a) or the matter mentioned in paragraph (aa).

A refugee issued with an adverse security assessment was notified by letter that he or she had been assessed by the ASIO to pose a direct (or indirect) risk to security within the meaning of section 4. 'No further details, allegations, particulars of evidence or reasons for such conclusions were provided to the refugees in their letters.'[65]

The plaintiff was issued with an adverse security assessment.[66] As a consequence,[67] he was held in detention pending removal. Section 36 of the ASIO Act 1979 specifies that certain procedural protections that apply to Australian citizens, permit residents and special purpose visa holders do not apply to other non-citizens. Among the procedural protections not required for such non-citizens are a statement of reasons, and merits review before the Australian Administrative Appeals Tribunal.

The Australian government had made clear that it would abide by its *non-refoulement* obligations and had no intention of returning the plaintiff to his country of nationality.[68] Bell J provided the fullest account of the viability of plaintiff's removal, summing up as follows: 'Conscientious endeavours to find a third country that is willing to receive the plaintiff have been pursued by DIAC for not less than two years and eight months to no avail.'[69] She drew the inference that 'the removal of the plaintiff from Australia is not likely to be practicable in the foreseeable future'.[70]

In *Plaintiff M47*, four of seven members of the High Court found it unnecessary to consider *Al-Kateb*. These four judges held that the regulation that prescribed security clearance as a criterion for a protection visa was ultra vires.[71] Consequently, the plaintiff's application for a protection visa remained to be determined and he remained lawfully detained during processing. It followed, for these four judges, that 'the arguments advanced by the parties about overruling or distinguishing the decision in *Al-Kateb v Godwin* and about the constitutional limits of the power to detain unlawful non-citizens need not be examined'.[72]

[65] Saul (n 60) 693.

[66] He was issued with two adverse security assessments, one in 2009 and one in 2012. The judgments focused on the 2012 assessment as substituting for the earlier assessment.

[67] There is no legal requirement that an unauthorised non-citizen against whom ASIO has issued an adverse security assessment be detained. But in practice the Department has treated the existence of an adverse security assessment as determinative of the need for detention: Saul (n 60) 697.

[68] *Plaintiff M47* (n 1) [99]–[100] (Gummow J).

[69] ibid, [524], and see [519]–[524] (Bell J). DIAC is the Department of Immigration and Citizenship. See also [145]–[148] (Gummow J). A reluctance on the part of other countries to accept a person refused admission on security grounds may provide at least a partial explanation for Australia's lack of success.

[70] ibid, [524] (Bell J).

[71] On the reasons the Court gave to regard the criterion as ultra vires see the text to n 112 below.

[72] *Plaintiff M47* (n 1) [226] (Hayne J). See also [72] (French CJ), [404] (Crennan J), [460] (Kiefel J).

In the discussion that follows, I focus on the reasoning of the three judges who upheld the validity of the regulatory provision that made the security assessment a criterion for grant of a visa. These judges did determine whether sections 189 and 196 of the Migration Act 1958 authorised detention where removal was not likely to be practicable in the foreseeable future. Gummow and Bell JJ held that those provisions did not authorise the plaintiff's detention, and stated that *Al-Kateb* should be overruled.[73] Heydon J applied *Al-Kateb*, and ruled that the plaintiff's detention should be authorised.[74]

In the following sections I consider the minority judgments in favour of overruling *Al-Kateb* and Heydon J's defence of the authority and reasoning of *Al-Kateb*.

4.4.2 *Al-Kateb* should be Overruled

The government submitted that leave should not be given to re-open the decision in *Al-Kateb*. Leave to re-open a decision is not likely to be granted if the decision 'rests upon a principle carefully worked out in a significant succession of cases'.[75] Bell J responded:

> Differing interpretations of the detention power under s 196(1)(a) had been adopted by judges at first instance in the Federal Court. Those differing approaches were ventilated and analysed in *Al Masri*. The Full Court of the Federal Court concluded that the power to detain under s 196(1)(a) was subject to implied limitation in circumstances in which there was no real likelihood of removal in the reasonably foreseeable future. This Court, by a slim majority, rejected that interpretation in *Al-Kateb*. It is therefore not correct for the purposes of the first of the *John* considerations to characterise *Al-Kateb* as a decision 'rest[ing] upon a principle carefully worked out in a significant succession of cases'.[76]

This comment highlights the contingency of the legal position in *Al-Kateb*, resting on a slim majority and unsupported by further High Court authority.[77] In *Plaintiff M47* Gummow and Bell JJ built on the minority judgments in *Al-Kateb*. But there was a shift in the reasoning, with greater emphasis on the principle of legality. It constituted a distinct change of emphasis for Gummow J, and a reorientation of the constitutional focus of the *Al-Kateb* minority. Gummow J reiterated his *Al-Kateb* reasoning on the interpretation and constitutionality of the provisions.

[73] In this Gummow J reiterated the position set out in his dissenting judgment in *Al-Kateb*, with the differences noted in this chapter. Bell J is a post *Al-Kateb* appointment to the High Court.

[74] Heydon J had concurred with Hayne J's reasons in *Al-Kateb*, and applied the reasoning that supported that decision, with the developments noted in this chapter.

[75] *John v Federal Commissioner of Taxation* [1989] HCA 5, (1989) 166 CLR 417, 438–39 (Mason CJ, Wilson, Dawson, Toohey and Gaudron JJ).

[76] *Plaintiff M47* (n 1) [526] in part quoting *John* (n 75) 438.

[77] On a speculative note, the reasoning on the part of the majority, on a question added to the special case during hearing, with the result that *Al-Kateb* did not need to be considered, may also evidence its continuing contestability.

However, a central theme of Gummow J's exposition was that the components of Gleeson CJ's position in *Al-Kateb* had been reaffirmed and become 'better understood' in the years since that decision.[78]

Gummow J objected to an understanding of statutory intention as a 'factual prediction' of the collective mental state of the legislators. He noted that what has become 'better understood' since *Al-Kateb* is that the phrase 'legislative intention' and cognate expressions are 'indicative of the constitutional relationship between the arms of government respecting the making, interpretation and application of laws'.[79] He cited an influential statement from a 2009 High Court decision, *Zheng v Cai*:

> It has been said that to attribute an intention to the legislature is to apply something of a fiction. However, what is involved here is not the attribution of a collective mental state to legislators . . . Rather, judicial findings as to legislative intention are an expression of the constitutional relationship between the arms of government with respect to the making, interpretation and application of laws. As explained in *NAAV* . . . the preferred construction by the court of the statute in question is reached by the application of rules of interpretation accepted by all arms of government in the system of representative democracy.[80]

This passage from *Zheng v Cai* has since been endorsed by a unanimous bench of all seven judges of the High Court.[81] The *Zheng v Cai* formulation leaves considerable latitude as to what the relevant 'constitutional relationship' is. But it rejects the view that the judiciary's role is simply to act as the legislature's agent. The interpretive exercise will necessarily move back and forth between the text and a judge's understanding of the legal and constitutional order. In *Plaintiff M47*, Gummow J's central point was that the common law legal order in which the court is situated incorporates certain rules of interpretation defensive of liberty. These presumptions against the abrogation of rights are 'rules of interpretation accepted by all arms of government in the system of representative democracy'.[82] The *Zheng v Cai* formulation allows for the legitimacy of judicial interpretation of statutes constituting a 'cross-current of opinion' in a representative democracy.[83] In *Plaintiff M47*, Bell and Gummow JJ adopted the principle of legality offered by Gleeson CJ in *Al-Kateb*.[84]

Gummow and Bell JJ's adoption of the principle of legality as the foundation for a challenge to *Al-Kateb* is consistent with the ascendency of that principle in

[78] *Plaintiff M47* (n 1) [118] (Gummow J).

[79] ibid.

[80] ibid, citing *Zheng v Cai* [2009] HCA 52, (2009) 239 CLR 446, [28].

[81] *Dickson v R* [2010] HCA 30, (2010) 241 CLR 491, [32].

[82] *Zheng v Cai* (n 80) [28].

[83] On the characterisation of the passage in *Zheng v Cai* as having affinities to AV Dicey's attempts to reconcile parliamentary sovereignty and the rule of law see Cheryl Saunders, 'Constitution as Catalyst: Different Paths within Australasian Administrative Law' (2012) 10 *New Zealand Journal of Public and International Law* 143, 152. On this aspect of Dicey more generally see Tom Hickman, 'Constitutional Dialogue, Constitutional Theories and the Human Rights Act 1998' [2005] *PL* 306.

[84] *Plaintiff M47* (n 1) [528] (Bell J), quoting *Al-Kateb* (n 2) [20] (Gleeson CJ). See ch 3, s 3.4.

the Court.[85] On numerous occasions since 2009,[86] the Court has quoted Gleeson CJ's statement on the status of the presumption against legislative abrogation of rights:

> The presumption is not merely a common sense guide to what a Parliament in a liberal democracy is likely to have intended; it is a working hypothesis, the existence of which is known to both Parliament and the courts, upon which statutory language will be interpreted. The hypothesis is an aspect of the rule of law.[87]

Both Gummow and Bell JJ made the 'requirement of express authorisation to abrogate fundamental rights' central to the legacy of the dissents in *Al-Kateb*, referring to it as 'what was then and has remained the doctrine of the Court which provides strongest guidance in resolving the issue of construction presented by the interaction between ss 189, 196 and 198'.[88]

Gummow J provided as a justification for not following the *Al-Kateb* majority the fact that they 'erred in a significant respect in the applicable principles of statutory construction'.[89] He held that the principle of legality clearly applied, and applied at the time of *Al-Kateb*, and led to a different construction of the relevant provisions than that arrived at by the *Al-Kateb* majority. Bell J implied that the reason for this was that the principles were applied selectively, and erroneously taken to have no application to non-citizens.[90]

4.4.3 *Al-Kateb* should be Upheld

Like Gummow and Bell JJ, Heydon J upheld the validity of the security clearance criterion under the legislation and confronted the question of whether, in the circumstances, there was authority to hold the plaintiff in detention pending removal.

Heydon J found that the detention was not 'indefinite'. He held that the factual premise in *Al-Kateb*, namely the finding that removal from Australia was 'not reasonably practicable . . . as there [was] no real likelihood or prospect of removal

[85] See Dan Meagher, 'The Common Law Principle of Legality in the Age of Rights' (2011) 35 *Melbourne University Law Review* 449.

[86] See eg *K-Generation Pty Ltd v Liquor Licensing Court* [2009] HCA 4, (2009) 237 CLR 501, [47] (French CJ); *Saaed v Minister for Immigration and Citizenship* [2010] HCA 23, (2010) 241 CLR 252, [15] (French CJ, Gummow, Hayne, Crennan and Kiefel JJ); *Lacey v Attorney-General of Queensland* [2011] HCA 10, (2011) 242 CLR 573, [43] (French CJ, Gummow, Hayne, Crennan, Kiefel and Bell JJ); *Australian Education Union v General Manager of Fair Work Australia* [2012] HCA 19, (2012) 296 ALR 625, [30] (French CJ, Crennan and Kiefel JJ). On the very different view of the prospects for the principle of legality in Australia as they appeared in 2008 see Matthew Zagor, 'Judicial Rhetoric and Constitutional Identity: Comparative Approaches to Aliens' Rights in the United Kingdom and Australia' (2008) 19 *Public Law Review* 271, 283.

[87] *Electrolux Home Products v Australian Workers Union* [2004] HCA 40, (2004) 221 CLR 309, [21].

[88] *Plaintiff M47* (n 1) [119] (Gummow J). See also [532] (Bell J).

[89] ibid, [121] (Gummow J). Both he and Bell J made mention of the fact that neither McHugh or Callinan JJ considered the principle of legality in *Al-Kateb*.

[90] ibid, [532] (Bell J).

in the reasonably foreseeable future',[91] was missing in *Plaintiff M47*. He effectively adopted a presumption that a real likelihood or prospect of removal existed. It was for the plaintiff to surmount the evidential difficulties to prove a negative. He must discharge the 'burden of persuasion that a real likelihood or prospect of removal does not exist'.[92] Heydon J's account has the curious effect of reading the legal reasoning of the *Al-Kateb* majority back into the factual premises that gave rise to *Al-Kateb*. This has the effect of making it unclear, as a practical matter, when those factual premises will arise again. The apparent divergence in factual findings between Bell and Gummow JJ on the one hand and Heydon J on the other rests on different legal understandings of immigration detention. Heydon J nonetheless went on to address the substantive arguments for re-opening *Al-Kateb*, reasoning both that it was inappropriate to re-open the decision, and that the majority position in it was correct.

Heydon J opened his reasons by citing a 'penetrating question' from McHugh J in oral argument in *Al-Kateb*: 'How can you claim a right of release into the country when you have no legal right to be here?'[93] Consistently with their positions in *Al-Kateb*, where Gummow and Bell JJ (the latter a post-*Al-Kateb* appointment) supported and developed the minority judgments in *Al-Kateb*, Heydon J restated and defended the majority position in that decision. Like the majority in *Al-Kateb*, he expressed doubts about the separation of powers analysis of the joint judgment in *Lim*,[94] without going so far as to overrule that decision.[95] Heydon J gave considerable space to criticism of the proposition, taken from *Lim*, that the separation of powers precludes involuntary detention by the executive except in 'exceptional cases'. But he departed from, or developed, the majority position in *Al-Kateb* in one important respect. In response to the question of whether the separation of powers analysis contained in the joint judgment in *Lim* should stand, Heydon J stated:

> It is not necessary to decide that question. It is sufficient to decide that, since the exceptions to the principle Brennan, Deane and Dawson JJ stated are not closed, another should be added: the detention of unlawful non-citizens who threaten the safety or welfare of the community because of the risks they pose to Australia's security.[96]

Heydon J's proposed new category is akin to the 'segregation from the community' rationale offered by Hayne J in *Al-Kateb* and endorsed by McHugh and

[91] *SHDB v Goodwin* [2003] FCA 300, [9] (Von Doussa J).

[92] *Plaintiff M47* (n 1) [354] (Heydon J).

[93] ibid, [228], quoting *Al-Kateb* (n 2) 565. Gummow J responded: 'The issues which arise are not answered simply by a response to a rhetorical question asking how the plaintiff may claim release from detention in the absence of a "legal right" to be present in this country': [88].

[94] *Chu Kheng Lim v Minister of Immigration, Local Government and Ethnic Affairs* [1992] HCA 64, (1992) 176 CLR 1.

[95] On this aspect of the majority reasoning in *Al-Kateb* see ch 3, pp 71–74.

[96] *Plaintiff M47* (n 1) [346] (Heydon J). Heydon J's proposal of a new category presumed the question in dispute in *Plaintiff M47*. All the High Court had before it was a non-reviewable ASIO assessment addressed to a regulatory criterion struck down by a majority of the Court.

Heydon JJ in that decision.[97] The segregation rationale is a corollary of a blinkered focus on the proposition that a non-citizen 'has no right to be here'. The distinction between Heydon J's 'threat' rationale in *Plaintiff M47* and Hayne J's 'segregation' rationale in *Al-Kateb*, is that the latter did not articulate, or explicitly rest on, the notion that threats from non-citizens need not be tolerated. The facts of *Plaintiff M47* explicitly raised the security issues that were absent in *Al-Kateb*. Heydon J took the opportunity to make clear what was arguably implicit in the *Al-Kateb* majority reasoning, namely that an executive determination of threat by itself constitutes sufficient justification for detention of a non-citizen. The new exception to the constitutional immunity from executive detention proposed by Heydon J recalls Finnis's concept of 'nationality-differentiated risk-acceptability', introduced in chapter one[98] – that is, the idea that the distinction between citizens and non-citizens suffices to justify the indefinite detention of the latter when they present

> some genuine risk, even relatively slight, to the rights of others, national security, public safety, the prevention of crime, the protection of health or morals or the maintenance of l'ordre public, or to anything else of 'public interest in a democratic society' . . .[99]

Critically, for Heydon J, detention ancillary to deportation encompassed indefinite detention predicated on an executive determination of threat.

Ideas informing the 'segregation' and 'threat' rationales are brought to the surface in Heydon J's explicit analogy between detention of non-citizens and quarantine. He asked: 'Why is it not possible to detain a person assessed to be a risk to Australia's security because that person is a threat to public health in a different way?'[100] The person assessed to be a threat to 'security' in the broad sense of the ASIO Act 1979 is a contagion, not to be allowed into contact with the community. The position outlined by Heydon J expressed a fundamental and pervasive discontinuity between the rights of citizens and those of non-citizens.

To understand this point it is necessary to note the breadth of the concept of 'security' under the ASIO Act. In the course of concluding her judgment Bell J stated:

> The Special Case has been conducted upon acceptance that the plaintiff is not a person about whom there are reasonable grounds for regarding as a danger to the security of Australia. Nor is he a person who having been convicted of a serious crime constitutes a danger to the Australian community.[101]

It is not necessary to show that the subject of the adverse assessment poses any direct or indirect threat to Australia to satisfy the definition of security in the ASIO Act 1979.[102] Plaintiff M47 had been issued an adverse security assessment

[97] See ch 3, s 3.3.
[98] See ch 1, s 1.4.
[99] John Finnis, 'Nationality, Alienage and Constitutional Principle' (2007) 123 *LQR* 417, 423.
[100] *Plaintiff M47* (n 1) [346] (Heydon J).
[101] ibid, [534].
[102] See ibid, [433] (Kiefel J).

because the concept of 'security' as defined in the ASIO Act 1979 extends to 'the carrying out of Australia's responsibilities to any foreign country' with respect to any of the matters listed in the definition of security as threats to Australia.[103] Heydon J was well aware of the extent of the definition of security applied in security assessments,[104] but held that the sovereign right of nations to exclude non-citizens extended 'particularly to preventing their entry on security grounds'.[105] He expressly adverted to the fact that the 'security' denying entry may encompass the security of the country from which the refugee has successfully sought asylum.[106] To the extent that a notion of 'protection of the Australian community' is operative here, it is operative in the most attenuated fashion.

Heydon J's judgment is notable also for its finding of proportionality between detention and deportation. In *Lim*, the joint judgment had held that the test for ascertaining whether an instance of Commonwealth detention was precluded by a constitutional immunity against administrative detention, or fell within a permitted exception to that immunity, was to ask whether it was 'reasonably necessary' to a legitimate immigration purpose. Those purposes were processing and removal.[107] Heydon J did not deny the continuing existence of the 'reasonably necessary' test post-*Al-Kateb*.[108] Rather, he held that it was met. He applied the 'never say never' logic of Hayne J's reasoning on statutory interpretation in *Al-Kateb*:[109] 'Deportation may be impossible to achieve quickly. But the end is deportation. The means – detention until deportation is reasonably practicable – is reasonably proportionate to that end.'[110] One can allow that proportionality review can be applied with different intensities, but in Heydon J's reasoning the requirement does no work at all. On his view, detention of *any* length will necessarily be proportionate because one can 'never say never'.

4.4.4 The Majority

During the course of the hearing in *Plaintiff M47*, a new question was added to the Special Case before the Court, asking whether the provision in the regulations that designated an ASIO security assessment as a criterion for the grant of a protection visa was ultra vires. Four members of the court, French CJ, Hayne, Crennan and Kiefel JJ, answered this question in the affirmative. As a result of this holding, there was no valid decision on the plaintiff's application for a protection visa. As noted in section 4.4.1, the majority ruled that while his application was

[103] Australian Security Intelligence Organisation Act 1979, s 4, definition of 'security', (b), quoted above in pp 109–10.
[104] *Plaintiff M47* (n 1) [319] (Heydon J).
[105] ibid, [322] (Heydon J).
[106] ibid, [325] (Heydon J).
[107] *Lim* (n 94) 33 (Brennan, Deane and Dawson JJ).
[108] cf McHugh J in *Re Woolley* (n 45).
[109] *Al-Kateb* (n 2) [229].
[110] *Plaintiff M47* (n 1) [348] (Heydon J).

pending, Plaintiff M47 was validly detained for the purpose of *processing*, obviating the need to consider the authority of *Al-Kateb*. His detention continued, but under a different rationale.

The majority held that the relevant regulatory provision was invalid on the basis that it was inconsistent with the scheme of the Act. It was inconsistent with the Minister's own discretions under the Migration Act 1958 and his or her responsibility for decisions precluding review. The inconsistencies between the regulatory provision and the statutory scheme arose from the breadth of 'security' under an ASIO security assessment. The definition of 'security' employed by the impugned regulatory criterion was 'wider in scope than [relevant statutory criteria for ministerial powers] and sets no threshold level of threat necessary to enliven its application'.[111] This meant that the government could have recourse to public interest criterion 4002 in every case to which the other statutory 'security' provisions might apply. The criterion rendered other statutory provisions addressed to security redundant. The High Court was concerned that the criterion 'subsumed' the Minister's own discretions under the statute, replacing them with an ASIO decision.[112] Further, the statutory security provisions rendered redundant were attended by procedural protections that did not accompany the ASIO assessments, including provision for merits review before the Australian Administrative Appeals Tribunal.

If one focuses on the invalidation of the regulation prescribing public interest criterion 4002, against the background of the preceding paragraph, the majority decision might appear to be a gain for procedural fairness. The invalidation deprived the government of a regulatory 'back-route' by which it could avoid statutory mechanisms attended by greater procedural protections. However, if one focuses on the harm of continued detention, the majority's reasoning is no more than a re-categorisation exercise, deferring any question on the temporal limits of detention of non-citizens under the Migration Act 1958.

In terms of procedures, an initial point is that the Commonwealth conceded that it owed the plaintiff an obligation of procedural fairness by reason of the 'dramatic effect' the security assessment had on his liberty.[113] But the decision did little to advance the procedural fairness obligations to non-citizens. It was tightly focused on the particular circumstances of the case, and did not address the dearth of procedural protections attending ASIO assessments. A majority, five of seven members of the Court, held that there had been no denial of procedural fairness on the facts.[114] This finding rested entirely on oral assertions at the plaintiff's interview, absent any more complete summary of statement and reasons. With reference to the transcript of the interview, it was held that his questioning was

[111] ibid, [71] (French CJ).

[112] ibid.

[113] ibid, [246] (Heydon J), [497] (Bell J).

[114] ibid, [140]–[144] (Gummow J), [244]–[253] (Heydon J), [378]–[380] (Crennan J), [413]–[415] (Kiefel J), [491]–[505] (Bell J). The other two members of the bench, French CJ and Hayne J, held that it was not necessary to answer the question of procedural fairness: [73] (French CJ), [160], [226] (Hayne J).

'copious'.[115] It stretched over a period of five hours from 9.30 am, with three breaks of between 10 and 25 minutes spaced at intervals during the five-hour period.[116] He was accompanied by a lawyer, whom he could have consulted during the breaks, and was given opportunities to explain inconsistencies and obscurities.[117] The plaintiff's case was that three key allegations were not put to him.[118] The record of interview was said to show that he was alerted to the allegations against him, and could not be said to have been 'left in the dark'.[119] It was further stated: 'Notably absent from the plaintiff's case was any indication of what additional material he might have adduced had the interviewing officers put the allegations to him in terms.'[120]

The majority's focus on the particular facts of the case avoided addressing the inadequacy of the procedural protections attending adverse security assessments more generally.[121] Ben Saul notes that the High Court did not take the opportunity to overrule an earlier Federal Court authority, *Leghaei*,[122] which held that disclosure obligations were met by the ASIO Director General giving his genuine consideration to the issue.[123] In *Leghaei* it was held that where the ASIO Director General determined that no disclosure was possible, that was the end of the matter. In such cases 'the content of procedural fairness is reduced, in practical terms, to nothingness'.[124] The position in *Leghaei* affords much more minimal procedural protections for non-citizens in the security context than has been held necessary in decisions delivered in the United Kingdom and Canada.[125]

4.5 Conclusion

2005, the year after *Al-Kateb*, saw the introduction of a range of administrative means by which long-term detainees could be released from immigration detention, and the introduction of systematic review of long-term detention (of over two years) by the Commonwealth Ombudsman. These measures are to be wel-

115 ibid, [248](Heydon J).
116 ibid, [252] (Hedyon J).
117 ibid.
118 ibid, [247] (Heydon J), [499] (Bell J).
119 ibid, [502] (Bell J) and see [248]–[253] (Heydon J), [500]–[504] (Bell J).
120 ibid, [502] (Bell J).
121 On the inadequacies of the procedures attending adverse ASIO security assessments more generally see Saul (n 60) 725–27, 729.
122 ibid, 725, with reference to *Leghaei v Director General of Security* [2005] FCA 1576 (*Leghaei*, first instance), upheld by the Full Court of the Federal Court in *Leghaei v Director General of Security* [2007] FCAFC 37 (*Leghaei* appeal).
123 *Leghaei*, first instance (n 122) [86].
124 ibid, [88] aff'd in *Leghaei* appeal (n 122) [43]–[55].
125 See the discussion of *A v United Kingdom* (2009) 49 EHRR 29 and *Secretary of State for the Home Department v AF (AF No 3)* [2009] UKHL 28, [2010] 2 AC 269 in ch 7, s 7.5, and the discussion of *Charkaoui v Canada (Minister of Citizenship and Immigration)* 2007 SCC 9, [2007] 1 SCR 350 in ch 9, s 9.3.

comed, but that welcome is muted by reason of the government's retention of sweeping powers over the liberty of detainees. Non-citizens' liberty remains exposed to the political winds, without effective statutory or other legal protections. This can be seen in the cases of refugees subject to an ASIO adverse security assessment who cannot be removed to another country, such as the plaintiff in *Plaintiff M47*.

Conversely, the *Offshore Processing Case* placed significant legal constraints on government conduct.[126] In contrast to the *Al-Kateb* majority, the Court in the *Offshore Processing Case* acknowledged the non-citizen's liberty interest, putting that interest at the centre of its reasoning concerning the claim of denial of procedural fairness. The *Offshore Processing Case* saw the Court rein in a government attempt to evade judicial scrutiny of migration processing by conducting it outside the Migration Act 1958. The Court reasoned that the power was instead 'knitted' back into the statute,[127] and that the Act's procedural fairness obligations applied. While this may seem remote from the legal issue in *Al-Kateb*, which concerned the scope of a substantive duty under statute, the fact remains that the Court in the *Offshore Processing Case* was squarely opposed to any assumption that the duration of detention under statute might be contingent on an uncontrolled executive discretion. The central objection to the decision in *Al-Kateb* is that, in the not uncommon event that removal could not be effected, decisions on release from detention are left to uncontrolled executive discretion.

The judgments of Gummow and Bell JJ in *Plaintiff M47* saw common law presumptions, and the view that legislative intention is 'an expression of the constitutional relationship between the arms of government with respect to the making, interpretation and application of laws' come to the fore.[128] This constitutionalism is central to arguments that *Al-Kateb* should be overturned, as illustrated in their minority judgments in *Plaintiff M47*.

Plaintiff M47 confirms *Al-Kateb*'s unsettled and contingent status in Australian law at the time of writing.

[126] See also the *Malaysian Declaration Case* (n 4).
[127] *Plaintiff S10* (n 56) [49]. See n 56 above.
[128] *Plaintiff M47* (n 1) [118] (Gummow J), citing *Zheng* (n 80) [28].

United Kingdom

5

Prohibitions, Derogations and Deference

The prohibition provided by Article 3 . . . against ill-treatment is equally absolute in expulsion cases . . . In these circumstances, the activities of the individual in question, however undesirable or dangerous, cannot be a material consideration.

Chahal, European Court of Human Rights (1996)[1]

The introduction of a right to appeal to an independent commission in these cases means that the commission will be in a position to overturn decisions made personally by the Secretary of State. Of course, any such decisions taken by the commission will be unwelcome to the Secretary of State, but it is an essential aspect of complying with the *Chahal* judgment that the commission should be able to take decisions, rather than only make non-binding recommendations in the manner of the three advisers who formerly acted in such cases.

Mr Mike O'Brien, Parliamentary Under-Secretary of State, House of Commons, 26 November 1997[2]

5.1 Introduction to the United Kingdom Chapters

The House of Lords' decision in *Belmarsh* lies at the centre of my discussion of the United Kingdom material.[3] By a majority of eight of nine judges, the House of Lords quashed an order that purported to derogate from the right to liberty under Article 5(1) of the European Convention on Human Rights (ECHR),[4] and declared a statutory provision authorising indefinite immigration detention to be incompatible with both Article 5(1) and the prohibition against discrimination under Article 14.

[1] *Chahal v United Kingdom* (1997) 23 EHRR 413, para 80.

[2] Mike O'Brien, Parliamentary Under-Secretary of State for the Home Department, on the Third Reading of the Special Immigration Appeals Commission Bill, HC Deb 26 November 1997, vol 301, col 1033.

[3] *A v Secretary of State for the Home Department* [2004] UKHL 56, [2005] 2 AC 68 (*Belmarsh*). Belmarsh was the name of the prison where the detainees were held.

[4] Convention for the Protection of Human Rights and Fundamental Freedoms (opened for signature 4 November 1950, entered into force 3 September 1953) 213 UNTS 211, Eur TS 5 (ECHR).

Probably the most famous decision decided under the Human Rights Act 1998 (HRA 1998) to date, *Belmarsh* was hailed as a historic beacon in the judicial defence of liberty, both on the national[5] and international stage.[6] It has been received as a vindication of the HRA 1998, and commentators have gone so far as to call it 'the most powerful judicial defence of liberty since *Leach v Money* (1765) 3 Burr 1692 and *Somersett v Stewart* (1772) 20 St Tr 1'.[7] Those sceptical about the HRA 1998 and concerned that fundamental rights provide a cover for judicial aggrandisement have nonetheless received *Belmarsh* as a remarkable instance of courts rising to the challenge of protecting individual liberty in the face of competing government claims.[8] A leading text on human rights in the United Kingdom refers to it in 60 paragraphs, more than any other decision.[9] Internationally, it is held up as the leading exemplar of a new assertion of judicial competence and legitimacy to review security measures post-9/11, on the part of national courts from prominent democratic states.[10] Where there is criticism of *Belmarsh*, much of it has the characteristic of being indirect, arguing for the decision's futility in the light of what followed rather than criticising the reasoning itself.[11]

Belmarsh's prominence rests first and foremost on the view that it was a striking, and welcome, assertion of judicial legitimacy to review national security measures. It is seen as a bold departure from an Anglo-American tradition of giving decisive weight to the government position in reviewing matters of national security.[12] I share this evaluation of the decision. The interaction between national security and immigration was central to the decision in *Belmarsh*. My analysis

[5] David Feldman, 'Case and Comment: Proportionality and Discrimination in Anti-Terrorism Legislation' [2005] *Cambridge Law Journal* 271; Keith Ewing, 'The Futility of the Human Rights Act: A Long Footnote' (2005) 37 *Bracton Law Journal* 41; Adam Tomkins, 'Readings of *A v Secretary of State for the Home Department*' [2005] *PL* 259.

[6] Eyal Benvenisti, 'United We Stand: National Courts Reviewing Counterterrorism Measures' in Andrea Bianchi and Alexis Keller (eds), *Counterterrorism: Democracy's Challenge* (Oxford, Hart Publishing, 2008) 251.

[7] Feldman (n 5) 273. For another invocation of 18th century comparators see Ewing (n 5) 42, who described *Belmarsh* as 'perhaps the most important decision since *Entick v Carrington* (1765) [19 St Tr 1030]', in part because 'the House of Lords stood up so convincingly to the Executive'. See also Conor Gearty, 'Human Rights in an Age of Counter-Terrorism: Injurious, Irrelevant or Indispensable?' (2005) 58 *Current Legal Problems* 25, 37.

[8] See eg Adam Tomkins, 'The Rule of Law in Blair's Britain' (2007) 26 *University of Queensland Law Journal* 255, 279.

[9] See Jack Beatson et al, *Human Rights: Judicial Protection in the United Kingdom* (London, Sweet & Maxwell, 2008) Table of cases.

[10] Benvenisti (n 6).

[11] Keith Ewing and Joo-Cheong Tham, 'The Continuing Futility of the Human Rights Act' [2008] *PL* 668; Tomkins (n 8). For commentary that is directly critical of the reasoning in *Belmarsh* see John Finnis, 'Nationality, Alienage and Constitutional Principle' (2007) 123 *LQR* 417; David Campbell, 'The Threat of Terrorism and the Plausibility of Positivism' [2009] *PL* 501.

[12] In a review of executive measures for managing terrorism and protecting national security in Britain and several of its colonies from 1905 to 2007, David Bonner stated that *Belmarsh* 'represents a marked but welcome departure from a traditional judicial attitude of extreme deference to executive opinion when the red flag of national security is waved': David Bonner, *Executive Measures, Terrorism and National Security: Have the Rules of the Game Changed?* (Aldershot, Ashgate, 2007) 292. See also Benvenisti (n 6); Tomkins (n 8) 279.

emphasises the latter, placing the decision in the context of domestic, European and comparative common law on the indefinite administrative detention of non-citizens.[13] The decision is most often feted for delivering a 'most eloquent and magisterial judicial rebuke' to the Attorney-General's claim to submissive deference from the courts.[14] My interest is in what that rebuke enabled, namely a clear-sighted denunciation of a discriminatory measure trading on associations between foreigner and threat.

The events on which these chapters centre are the United Kingdom's anticipatory derogation from Article 5(1) of the ECHR and the subsequent enactment of legislation providing for the indefinite administrative detention of non-citizens pursuant to powers of immigration detention. These actions were justified with reference to the threat posed by Al-Qaeda terrorists, as manifest in the terrorist attacks of 11 September 2001.

The next chapter details the domestic *Belmarsh* litigation before the Special Immigration Appeals Commission (SIAC), the Court of Appeal and the House of Lords.[15] It charts the interaction between the weight given to the government's evaluation of what counter-terrorism steps were needed, the weight given to the liberty of non-citizens, and the proportionality standard and its application. This interaction shifts at each level of the litigation.

The legal framework for the *Belmarsh* litigation was the ECHR as viewed through the lens of the HRA 1998. More particularly, the litigation centred on the legality of the United Kingdom's derogation from Article 5(1)(f) of the ECHR. Article 5(1)(f) constitutes the exception to the right to liberty relevant to non-citizens held pending removal. Article 5(1) states: 'Everyone has the right to liberty and security of person. No one shall be deprived of his liberty save in the following cases and in accordance with a procedure prescribed by law.' The article then sets out an exhaustive list of exceptional circumstances in which an individual may be deprived of their liberty, including, at 5(1)(f), 'the lawful arrest or detention of a person . . . against whom action is being taken with a view to deportation or extradition'. As noted above, the United Kingdom sought to derogate from Article 5(1) in order to enable the indefinite detention of non-citizens against whom a removal order had been issued. In this chapter I explain why it did so, and more generally the legal setting in which the issues in *Belmarsh* arose for consideration.

I first consider in section 5.2 the *Hardial Singh* decision.[16] This short judgment set down principles that have since defined English law on detention pending

[13] The closest equivalent in terms of focus is John Finnis's article 'Nationality, Alienage and Constitutional Principle' (n 11). His evaluation of *Belmarsh* is effectively the antithesis of my own. For an analysis of his reasoning see ch 1, ss 1.4–1.5; ch 6, p 180. See also ch 7, s 7.2.

[14] Lord Steyn, '2000–2005: Laying the Foundations of Human Rights Law in the United Kingdom' (2005) 4 *European Human Rights Law Review* 349, 350.

[15] The litigation before the British courts, in distinction to the case the litigants argued before the European Court of Human Rights.

[16] *R v Governor of Durham Prison, ex parte Singh* [1983] EWHC 1 (QB), [1984] 1 All ER 983 (*Hardial Singh*).

removal. The decision of the European Court of Human Rights (ECtHR) in *Chahal* is then outlined in section 5.3. This decision did more to shape the legal context for the derogation and indefinite detention measures, and so the *Belmarsh* litigation, than any other. In *Chahal*, the ECtHR set the legal parameters for deportation and immigration detention that govern the European and United Kingdom jurisprudence studied. As detailed in section 5.4, *Chahal* also transformed the domestic institutional landscape for review of national security decisions, serving as the spur for the development of SIAC. The procedural innovations introduced with the creation of SIAC, notably the role of special advocate, have continued to be central to legal debates over review of national security, both in the United Kingdom and beyond.[17] Section 5.5 introduces the HRA 1998.

In the final two sections, I introduce fault lines in approaches to deference and to derogation from rights that characterise the legal argument and judicial reasoning in the *Belmarsh* litigation. I approach the issue of deference through an analysis of the House of Lords' earlier national security decision in *Rehman*,[18] focusing on tensions in Lord Hoffmann's reasoning. In section 5.7, I outline two different understandings of what it means to derogate from a right, and provide an initial account of their implications for the legal reasoning in *Belmarsh*.

5.2 *Hardial Singh*

If it is accepted that detention of a non-citizen issued with a deportation order is ancillary to deportation, how is that relationship, between detention and deportation, to be understood? When is detention 'reasonably necessary for deportation purposes'? The starting point for English discussions of this issue is the decision of *Hardial Singh*. *Hardial Singh* is a short judgment of a single judge, Woolf J, in the Queen's Bench Division from 1984. It takes up only six pages in the reports. The principles governing the limits of authority to hold an individual in detention pending deportation are commonly referred to as the *Hardial Singh* principles in English[19] and other Commonwealth authorities.[20] In 2011, more than a quarter of a century after *Hardial Singh*, members of the House of Lords stated that the

[17] See eg the discussion of the Canadian security certificate regime in ch 9.

[18] *Secretary of State for the Home Department v Rehman* [2001] UKHL 47, [2003] 1 AC 153.

[19] The principles established in this case were approved by the Privy Council in *Tan Te Lam v Superintendent of Tai A Chau Detention Centre* [1996] UKPC 5, [1997] AC 97, 111–12 and by the House of Lords in *R v Secretary of State for the Home Department, ex parte Saadi* [2002] UKHL 41, [2002] 4 All ER 785, 793 (Lord Slynn). For a list of cases in which the *Hardial Singh* principles played an operative part in the decision see Alex Goodman and Justin Leslie, 'The Limits of Detention: Case Law Since *Hardial Singh*' [2010] *Judicial Review* 242.

[20] See eg the endorsement of the *Hardial Singh* principles in *Minister for Immigration & Multicultural & Indigenous Affairs v Al Masri* [2003] FCAFC 70, (2003) 126 FCR 54 (Full Court of the Federal Court of Australia), discussed in ch 2, pp 60–61. *Al Masri* lists and discusses common law authorities drawing on those principles.

case's principles on the limits of detention have been 'accepted without question' since they were delivered.[21]

Mr Singh was an Indian national. He entered the United Kingdom lawfully in 1977 and was granted indefinite leave to remain. He was subsequently convicted in relation to two burglary offences in 1980 and 1982 and in March 1983 the Secretary of State ordered his deportation on 'conducive to the public good' grounds. He was not released on the day set down for his parole in July 1983 but remained in the prison pursuant to a power to detain pending deportation. Mr Singh had been detained under the immigration power for nearly five months at the time of judgment. The United Kingdom government had not obtained the necessary travel documents from India and led no evidence that Mr Singh's removal was imminent.

The detention provisions considered in *Hardial Singh* contained no express limitation of time. With reference to the purpose of detention, Woolf J held that there is an implied temporal limitation on authority to detain. He held that authority to detain is limited to the period reasonably necessary to facilitate deportation. The power can only be exercised in relation to detention pending removal; 'It cannot be used for any other purpose'. Detention is limited to a period 'reasonably necessary for that purpose'.[22] Woolf J went on to state that if it is apparent that the government 'was not going to be able to operate the machinery provided in the Act' for removal within a reasonable period, it should not exercise its power of detention.[23] The focus is on the need for an official invested with statutory authority not to misuse that authority.

Woolf J put the onus on the government to provide evidence that there is a real prospect of removal within a reasonable time. In the absence of such evidence, Woolf J's position was that a judge should order release. If removal is not a real prospect, the purpose of detention no longer obtains and so cannot be used to justify that detention.[24] Additionally, the government is to exercise 'reasonable expedition' in ensuring removal.[25]

The judgment was concerned with implicit limits on a widely drawn statutory discretion. These limits were derived from the statutory purpose, namely facilitating removal.[26] The *Hardial Singh* principles provide an articulation of the limits

[21] *R (WL) (Congo) v Home Secretary* [2011] UKSC 12, [2012] 1 AC 245 (*Lumba*), [199] (Baroness Hale); see also [174] (Lord Hope). Cf Lord Phillips in dissent, arguing for the need to challenge the orthodox formulation of the principles. Lumba was the name of the lead claimant.

[22] *Hardial Singh* (n 16) 985 (Woolf J).

[23] ibid.

[24] Woolf J did not direct release, but granted a limited adjournment of three days, on the basis that the government had only received the applicant's affidavit the previous day and that 'a very short period of additional detention' was not such an injustice as to deny the government the opportunity to file further evidence: *Hardial Singh* (n 16) 988 (Woolf J). For a restatement of the *Hardial Singh* principles see *R (I) v Secretary of State for the Home Department* [2002] EWCA Civ 888, [2003] INLR 196 [46] (Lord Dyson).

[25] *Hardial Singh* (n 16) 985 (Woolf J).

[26] This represents the current orthodoxy as expressed in *Lumba* (n 21) eg [174] (Lord Hope); cf Lord Phillips in dissent.

on detention pending removal that has come to shape British understandings of the nature and scope of that power.[27]

5.3 *Chahal*

Central to the legal developments surrounding indefinite detention of non-citizens in the United Kingdom is the interaction between two distinct legal orders: that of the United Kingdom and the Council of Europe. The intervention of the ECtHR has been a driving force in domestic legal developments. In this chapter, this dynamic centres on the ECtHR's decision in *Chahal v United Kingdom*.[28] *Chahal* established the relevance of the ECHR to circumstances where the deportee faces a real risk of torture or ill-treatment on return.

In August 1990, the Home Secretary served notice of an intention to deport Mr Chahal on the basis that his continued presence was unconducive to the public good for reasons of national security. Mr Chahal was alleged to be involved with Sikh extremist groups. On the day Mr Chahal was served with notice of an intention to deport, he applied for political asylum in the United Kingdom on the basis that he would face torture and persecution if returned to India. He was detained for deportation purposes under the Immigration Act 1971, and he remained in detention up to the time of judgment of the ECtHR on 15 November 1996, more than five years later.

The national security elements in his case had the consequence that Mr Chahal had no right of appeal from the deportation decision.[29] The decision was instead subject to a non-statutory advisory procedure[30] – the 'three wise men'. Under this procedure Mr Chahal was

> given an opportunity to make written and/or oral representations to an advisory panel, to call witnesses on his behalf, and to be assisted by a friend, but he is not permitted to have legal representation before the panel. The Home Secretary decides how much information about the case against him may be communicated to the person concerned. The panel's advice to the Home Secretary is not disclosed, and the latter is not obliged to follow it.[31]

[27] 'subsequent cases have applied the principles to the whole range of administrative powers of detention which can be applied to immigrants facing removal or expulsion': Goodman and Leslie (n 19) 242.

[28] *Chahal v United Kingdom* (1997) 23 EHRR 413 (*Chahal*).

[29] The general right to appeal a deportation order under s 15(1) of the Immigration Act 1971 was excluded by s 15(3) if the grounds for a non-citizen's deportation 'was that his deportation is conducive to the public good as being in the interests of national security or of the relations between the United Kingdom and any other country or for other reasons of a political nature'.

[30] House of Commons, *Statement of the Changes in Immigration Rules* (HC 251, 1990) para 157.

[31] *Chahal* (n 28) para 60.

Following review by the panel, the Home Secretary signed an order for Mr Chahal's deportation. The High Court and Court of Appeal rejected Mr Chahal's challenges to the decision to refuse asylum, and to the deportation order.[32]

At that time the ECHR provided for a two-tiered system of rights protection. Applicants went first to the European Commission, and if the matter was not resolved at that stage, they could progress to the ECtHR.[33] In the event that the Commission could not settle a matter it had determined to be admissible, it was charged with issuing a report on the established facts, and an opinion on whether there had been a violation of the ECHR. In a report of June 1995,[34] the Commission expressed the opinion that Mr Chahal's return to India would constitute a violation of the ECHR.[35] The Commission ruled that the United Kingdom courts' power of review in relation to the decision to deport was too restrictive to meet the requirements of an 'effective remedy' under Article 13. Further, the proceedings against Mr Chahal were not pursued with the requisite speed to justify his continued detention.[36]

Armed with the European Commission's report, Mr Chahal brought an application in the domestic courts for temporary release pending the decision of the ECtHR, by way of habeas corpus and judicial review. In reviewing the decision to detain, the Divisional Court judge stated:

> I have to look at the decision of the Secretary of State and judge whether, in all the circumstances, upon the information available, he has acted unlawfully, or with procedural impropriety, or perversely to the point of irrationality. I am wholly unable to say that there is a case for such a decision, particularly bearing in mind that I do not know the full material on which the decisions have been made . . . [I]t is obvious and right that in circumstances the Executive must be able to keep secret matters which they deem necessary to keep secret . . . There are no grounds, in my judgment, for saying or even suspecting that there are not matters which are present in the Secretary of State's mind of that kind upon which he was entitled to act.[37]

The above statement is quoted in full in the ECtHR's judgment in *Chahal.* It is a remarkable statement of the 'traditional' approach to judicial review in the area of national security, characterised by an unquestioning trust in the executive, not tempered by any requirement of verification. It serves as a useful indicator of the distance travelled by the English courts in national security matters between the

[32] ibid, paras 40–42. Leave to appeal to the House of Lords was refused.

[33] The European Commission was abolished by Protocol 11 to the European Convention on Human Rights, which entered into force on 1 November 1998.

[34] The Commission's opinion is reproduced in *Chahal* (n 28) 437–54.

[35] Nuala Mole, *Asylum and the European Convention on Human Rights*, 4th edn (Strasbourg, Council of Europe, 2007) 40: 'The report of the Commission in *Chahal* marked a departure from the Commission's earlier approach to the government's assessment of the situation in the country of destination. The Commission was impressed by the evidence submitted by the applicants as to the situation in India.'

[36] Under Art 5(1) of the ECHR.

[37] *Chahal* (n 28) para 43, citing *R v Secretary of State for the Home Department, ex parte Chahal*, unreported (10 November 1995) (McPherson J).

mid-1990s and the *Belmarsh* litigation of 2002–04, a change effected in part by *Chahal* itself.

The importance of *Chahal* for ECHR jurisprudence is twofold. It clearly establishes that the ECHR imposes an absolute prohibition on deportation to torture. And it suggests limits on the duration of immigration detention and sets requirements for the review of that detention. The case was heard by the Grand Chamber of the ECtHR, a bench of 19 judges.

5.3.1 *Chahal* on Deportation

The relevant provision of the ECHR in relation to torture or ill-treatment is Article 3, which provides: 'No one shall be subjected to torture or to inhuman or degrading treatment or punishment.' This provision was held to place an implied obligation on a Contracting State not to deport an individual when there were substantial grounds for believing that there was a real risk of torture or other treatment, contrary to Article 3, by the receiving country.[38] The United Kingdom government accepted this implied obligation in its pleadings before the ECtHR.[39]

The bulk of the ECtHR's reasoning on deportation is addressed to the effect of national security concerns on the implied obligation not to deport. The United Kingdom argued that national security concerns counselled against an absolute prohibition on deportation to torture. It was consistently unsuccessful on this score. It contended that there was an implied limitation on Article 3 in national security cases, allowing for deportation even where there was a real risk of treatment contrary to Article 3 by the receiving state. In the alternative, the United Kingdom argued for a 'balancing approach' that weighed various factors including the threat to United Kingdom security in considering whether to deport. In relation to this second submission, the government argued that the ability to deport to a real risk of torture should be assessed against a sliding scale. The greater the doubt about a risk of ill-treatment, the more weight should be given to national security.

The majority of the Grand Chamber rejected these government submissions.[40] The majority made clear that Article 3 imposes an absolute prohibition on deportation to a real risk of torture, irrespective of the victim's conduct: 'the activities of

[38] *Chahal* (n 28) para 74. For this implied obligation, the ECtHR cited its earlier decisions in *Soering v United Kingdom* (1989) 11 EHRR 439; *Cruz Varas v Sweden* (1992) 14 EHRR 1; and *Vilvarajah v United Kingdom* (1992) 14 EHRR 248. The obligation not to deport an individual to torture is sometimes referred to as the 'extraterritorial application' of Art 3. In *Chahal*, 7 of the 19 judges dissented on the extraterritorial application of Art 3 to expulsion cases. See now *Saadi v Italy* (2009) 49 EHRR 30, in which the extraterritorial application of Art 3 received unanimous support from the Grand Chamber.

[39] The United Kingdom had contested this implied obligation before the European Commission.

[40] More recently, the United Kingdom advanced these same submissions in *Saadi v Italy* (n 38) where they met with unanimous rejection by the ECtHR: see paras 138–42.

the individual in question, however undesirable or dangerous, cannot be a material consideration.'[41] In emphasising the absolute nature of Article 3, the ECtHR contrasted it with other provisions of the ECHR, stressing that Article 3 contains no exceptions and is non-derogable in the event of a public emergency. The ECtHR then engaged in an extended consideration of the risk of ill-treatment in Mr Chahal's case, with the majority concluding that 'the order for his deportation to India, if executed, would constitute a violation of Article 3'.[42]

Later in the judgment, the ECtHR considered whether the applicants had been provided with the 'effective remedy' required by Article 13. Article 13 states: 'Everyone whose rights and freedoms as set forth in this Convention are violated shall have an effective remedy before a national authority notwithstanding that the violation has been committed by persons acting in an official capacity.' The United Kingdom argued that in past national security cases the ECtHR had read the requirement for an 'effective remedy' as requiring 'a remedy that is as effective as can be', given the need to rely on secret information.[43] The ECtHR responded that those earlier cases were concerned with the qualified rights contained in Articles 8 and 10 of the ECHR, where the Court was obliged to have regard to the national security claims advanced by the government.[44] The ECtHR stated that in relation to Article 3, Article 13 requires that there be independent scrutiny of whether there are substantial grounds to believe that the applicant faces a real risk of torture in the receiving country.[45] It reiterated: 'This scrutiny must be carried out without regard to what the person may have done to warrant expulsion or to any perceived threat to the national security of the expelling state.'[46] The ECtHR held that the English courts had not carried out such scrutiny. Rather, they had balanced the risk to Mr Chahal against the danger to national security. The ECtHR held that judicial review of the decision to deport, as then practised in the United Kingdom, was not an effective remedy in respect of Mr Chahal's complaint under

[41] *Chahal* (n 28) para 80. See also the view of the Commission at para 104: 'While it is accepted that this may result in undesirable individuals finding a safe haven in a Contracting State, the Commission observes that the State is not without means of dealing with any threats posed thereby, the individual being subject to the ordinary criminal laws of the country concerned', quoted in *Chahal* (n 28) para 70.

[42] This holding was adopted by 12 votes to 7. The seven in dissent on this point adopted the United Kingdom's argument for a 'fair balance' between risk of torture for the applicant, and the risk to national security posed by the applicant: see *Chahal* (n 28) 481–85.

[43] The cases in question were *Klass v Germany* (1979) 2 EHRR 214 and *Leander v Sweden* (1987) 9 EHRR 433.

[44] *Chahal* (n 28) para 150. The rights in Arts 8–11 are subject to similar exceptions. For example, Art 8(2) (Right to respect for private and family life) reads: 'There shall be no interference by a public authority with the exercise of this right except such as is in accordance with the law and is necessary in a democratic society in the interests of national security, public safety or the economic well-being of the country, for the prevention of disorder or crime, for the protection of health or morals, or for the protection of the rights and freedoms of others.'

[45] The ECtHR clarified that such independent scrutiny did not have to be provided by a court, the effectiveness of the remedy depending on the powers and guarantees afforded by the reviewing body: *Chahal* (n 28) para 152.

[46] ibid, para 151.

Article 3,[47] and accordingly there was a violation of Article 13 in conjunction with Article 3.[48]

In a passage that has achieved a small measure of fame through its influence on subsequent legal developments, the ECtHR noted the interveners' submission that Article 13 'required at least that some independent body should be appraised of all the facts and evidence and entitled to reach a decision that would be binding on the Secretary of State'.[49] In this connection, the Court noted a Canadian approach whereby the confidentiality of national security material was maintained by allowing for a security-cleared counsel to act in the interests of the applicant, instructed by the court rather than the applicant him- or herself. This security-cleared counsel is allowed to cross-examine witnesses and generally test the strength of the state's case.[50] The ECtHR referred to the possibility of employing such an approach to counterbalance the procedural unfairness caused by a lack of full disclosure in national security cases. In a point of some importance for later jurisprudence, the Court did not, however, express any opinion as to whether the procedures central to the 'Canadian approach', notably the security-cleared counsel, would in themselves satisfy the requirements of the ECHR.[51]

5.3.2 *Chahal* on Detention

Article 5(1) of the ECHR provides that 'Everyone has the right to liberty and security of the person', and then sets out an exhaustive list of exceptional circumstances in which an individual may be deprived of their liberty, including, at 5(1)(f), 'the lawful arrest or detention of a person . . . against whom action is being taken with a view to deportation or extradition'.

The European Commission had concluded that the proceedings against Mr Chahal had not been pursued with the requisite speed and accordingly his deten-

[47] ibid, para 153. At para 154, the ECtHR listed additional criticisms of the advisory panel procedure: the lack of entitlement to legal representation; the provision of only an outline of the grounds for the deportation decision; and the fact that the panel had no power of decision, its advice was not binding on the Home Secretary, and was not disclosed.

[48] This holding was unanimous.

[49] ibid, para 144.

[50] ibid. As has been recorded since, the Court wrongly attributed this procedure to the Federal Court of Canada, when it was in fact a self-generated procedure of the Canadian Security Intelligence Review Committee (SIRC): see Rayner Thwaites, 'Deportation on National Security Grounds' (LLM thesis, University of Toronto, 2004) app 1; John Ip, 'The Rise and Spread of the Special Advocate' [2008] *PL* 717, 719; Audrey Macklin, 'Transjudicial Conversations about Security and Human Rights' in Mark Salter (ed), *Mapping Transatlantic Security Relations: The EU, Canada and the War on Terror* (Oxford, Routledge, 2010) 212, 218–21; David Jenkins, 'There and Back Again' (2011) 42 *Columbia Human Rights Law Review* 279, 289–312. At the time of the *Chahal* hearing and judgment the SIRC procedure was only employed where the non-citizen to be deported from Canada was a permanent resident. The Canadian SIRC procedure for review of decisions to deport on grounds of national security, praised in *Chahal*, ceased to be employed in Canada in relation to any deportation decisions in 2002.

[51] See the discussion of the jurisprudence on the fairness of the procedures under the regime of 'control orders' in ch 7, s 7.5, in particular *Secretary of State for the Home Department v MB* [2007] UKHL 46, [2008] 1 AC 440.

tion had ceased to be justified. The ECtHR did not adopt the Commission's holding on this point. The ECtHR made clear that there is nothing in the text of Article 5(1)(f) that requires a connection between detention and the detainee's conduct. Authority to detain does not depend on it being 'reasonably considered necessary' to prevent the non-citizen from committing an offence or fleeing.[52] Further, the Court held that under Article 5(1)(f) it is immaterial whether the underlying decision to deport can be justified under Convention law.[53]

The ECtHR held that the only requirement relevant to detention pending deportation is that 'action is being taken with a view to deportation'. This requirement was interpreted in the following passage:

> any deprivation of liberty under Article 5(1)(f) will be justified only for as long as deportation proceedings are in progress. If such proceedings are not prosecuted with due diligence, the detention will cease to be permissible under Article 5(1)(f). It is thus necessary to determine whether the duration of the deportation proceedings was excessive.[54]

Chahal's reading of Article 5(1)(f) invites independent review of whether deportation proceedings are in progress, whether they are being pursued with due diligence, and whether the overall period of detention has become excessive in duration.[55] These requirements mean, at least in principle, that a state cannot treat the mere formal issuance of a deportation order as a sufficient basis for immigration detention.

These requirements were applied to the facts of the case in a very deferential fashion. The majority discounted the period during which Mr Chahal was held in compliance with a request from the European Commission that he not be deported. It considered only a period of some three and a half years from August 1990 to March 1994, during which domestic proceedings were afoot. Stressing the applicant's interest in careful consideration of his case by the courts, the ECtHR concluded that this period of detention was not excessive and that there was no violation of Article 5(1) on account of any lack of diligence by the national

[52] A contrast is drawn with the wording of Art 5(1)(c) which provides that detention in cases of bail pending charge is only authorised where 'reasonably considered necessary' to prevent the commission of an offence or fleeing: *Chahal* (n 28) para 112. *Chahal*'s reading of Art 5(1)(f) was affirmed in *A v United Kingdom* (2009) 49 EHRR 29, 625, para 164, as discussed in ch 7, s 7.2. The ECtHR's reading of Art 5(1)(f) in *Chahal* is in marked contrast with the jurisprudence of the Human Rights Committee on the analogous provision of the International Covenant on Civil and Political Rights (adopted 16 December 1966, entered into force 23 March 1976) 999 UNTS 171, Art 9 (ICCPR). Under Art 9 of the ICCPR, detention will be considered 'arbitrary' 'if it is not necessary in all the circumstances of the case, for example to prevent flight or interference with evidence: the element of proportionality becomes relevant in this context': *A v Australia* No 560/1993, para 9.2. On the relevant jurisprudence of the United Nations Human Rights Committee see Daniel Wilsher, *Immigration Detention: Law, History, Politics* (Cambridge, Cambridge University Press, 2012) 157–66.

[53] *Chahal* (n 28) para 112.

[54] ibid, para 113.

[55] On a later shift in the ECtHR jurisprudence from the 'due diligence' test to one analogous to the *Hardial Singh* principles, turning on a 'realistic prospect of removal', see *Mikolenko v Estonia*, App no 10664/05 (ECtHR, 8 Oct 2009) para 68. See further Wilsher (n 52) 150–57.

authorities.[56] The key point for the *Belmarsh* litigation discussed in the next chapter is the interaction of the requirements *Chahal* placed on Article 5(1)(f) with its holding that Article 3 places an absolute prohibition on deportation to torture. Where Article 3 bars deportation, the necessary government 'action' required to animate the exception to liberty in Article 5(1)(f) cannot occur, with the result that the detention is a deprivation of liberty, infringing Article 5(1).

Article 5(1)(f) allows for the '*lawful* arrest or detention . . . of a person against whom action is being taken with a view to deportation' (emphasis added). The ECtHR held that 'lawfulness' requires not only that detention be prescribed by law, but also that arbitrary detention is avoided.[57] It held that 'in the context of Article 5(1)' the advisory panel procedure met any charge of arbitrariness that might render Mr Chahal's detention unlawful. A majority of the ECtHR concluded that Mr Chahal's detention did not violate Article 5(1) of the ECHR.[58]

Chahal eschews any clear proportionality test as to the duration of detention. What it does do is impose clear requirements on the *review* of that same detention. The procedural requirements attending Mr Chahal's detention were analysed with reference to Article 5(4) of the ECHR,[59] which states:

> Everyone who is deprived of his liberty by arrest or detention shall be entitled to take proceedings by which the lawfulness of his detention shall be decided speedily by a court and his release ordered if the detention is not lawful.

The ECtHR concluded that there *was* a violation of the procedural requirements of Article 5(4). The conjunction of the ECtHR's rulings on Articles 5(1) and 5(4) is unsatisfactory. In its Article 5(1) analysis, the Court defused the charge of arbitrary detention with reference to the available procedures. It then went on, in its Article 5(4) analysis, to pronounce those same procedures inadequate.[60] On the nature of the inadequacy under Article 5(4), the ECtHR reasoned that 'the domestic courts were not in a position to review whether the decisions to detain Mr Chahal and to keep him in detention were justified on national security grounds', and the advisory panel was not a 'court' for the purposes of Article 5(4).[61] It continued:

[56] cf *Lumba* (n 21) [111]–[121], [144]. See ch 7, s 7.8.

[57] This drew on Convention jurisprudence on what was required for a measure to be 'lawful'. See more recently *A v United Kingdom* (n 52) para 164; *Saadi v United Kingdom* (2008) 47 EHRR 17, paras 67 and 67–74.

[58] By 13 votes to 6.

[59] The ECtHR held that the complaint that national security grounds had prevented the domestic courts from considering whether detention was lawful and 'appropriate' should be considered under Art 5(4) rather than under Art 13, on the basis that Art 5(4) was a more specialised instance of the general requirements of Art 13: see *Chahal* (n 28) paras 124–26.

[60] See also, in a partial dissent going to the ECtHR's finding of no violation of Art 5(1), Judges Martens and Palm's statement that 'the Court finds that [the advisory panel procedure] does not meet the requirements of Article 5(4) and of Article 13 . . . We find it difficult to understand why it did not draw the same conclusion in the context of Article 5(1)(f)': ibid, 484, para 4.

[61] ibid, para 130.

> The Court recognises that the use of confidential material may be unavoidable where national security is at stake. This does not mean, however, that the national authorities can be free from effective control by domestic courts whenever they choose to assert that national security and terrorism are involved.[62]

In comments that parallel those discussed above in relation to Article 13 and review of the decision to deport, the ECtHR went on to state that it 'attached significance' to the development of 'a more effective form of judicial control . . . in cases of this type' in Canada. The ECtHR stated that the Canadian example 'illustrates that there are techniques which can be employed which both accommodate legitimate security concerns about the nature and source of intelligence information and yet accord the individual a substantial measure of procedural justice'.[63] It concluded that there had been a violation of Article 5(4).[64]

5.4 The Legislative Response to *Chahal*: SIAC

In *Chahal*, the ECtHR rejected the proposition that 'national authorities can be free from effective control by the domestic courts whenever they choose to assert that national security and terrorism are involved'.[65] The ECtHR's position was given content through its identification of the deficiencies in the United Kingdom procedures, and the alternative example of the Canadian procedure. Under the Canadian arrangement outlined by the ECtHR, the authority's evidence was examined in the absence of the affected individual or his or her legal representative. Counsel with security clearance was charged with representing the affected individual's interests, and was able to cross-examine any witness for the government and generally assist to test the strength of the government case.[66]

In response to *Chahal*, the United Kingdom Parliament enacted the Special Immigration Appeals Commission Act 1997.[67] Those promoting the bill presented SIAC as addressing the ECtHR's concerns over procedural fairness, while utilising the means suggested by the Court, with reference to Canadian procedures, to preserve confidentiality. SIAC was presented as the 'independent body . . . appraised of all the facts and evidence and entitled to reach a decision

[62] ibid, para 131.

[63] ibid.

[64] This holding was unanimous.

[65] *Chahal* (n 28) para 131 (in the discussion of authority to detain); see also paras 151–55 (re decision to deport).

[66] ibid, para 144. On the Canadian example, the SIRC process (see n 50), see further Murray Rankin, 'The Security Intelligence Review Committee: Reconciling National Security with Procedural Fairness' (1989–90) 3 *Canadian Journal of Administrative Law & Practice* 173.

[67] Special Immigration Appeals Commission Act 1997 (SIAC Act 1997). See John Greenway on the Special Immigration Appeals Commission Bill, SC Deb (D), 11 November 1997: 'It is a simple but fundamental point that this legislation would not be before us now were it not for the European Court's decision in the *Chahal* case.'

which would be binding on the Secretary of State' demanded by the ECtHR in *Chahal*.[68]

SIAC was and is composed of panels of three, appointed by the Lord Chancellor,[69] consisting of a High Court judge, a judge with experience in immigration matters, and a layperson possessing a high-level security clearance who has experience in analysing intelligence.[70] SIAC is able to consider both 'open' and 'closed' material, though neither those subject to its decisions nor their legal representatives can see the closed material. Instead, this closed material is disclosed to one or more 'special advocates'. A 'special advocate' is appointed to represent the certified individual's interests in any hearing from which the individual and her or his legal representatives are excluded.[71] In a critical limitation on his or her role, a special advocate can meet with the certified individual whose interests he or she represents before receiving the government evidence, but thereafter any communication from the special advocate to the certified individual has to be authorised by SIAC.[72] A 'special advocate' does not act on the instructions of the certified individual and cannot seek his explanation of the government evidence. The functions of the special advocate are to test whether greater disclosure is warranted and to challenge the government's case as best they can in the absence of instructions from the certified individual. SIAC is only bound to communicate its reasons for decision to the parties 'if and to the extent that it is possible to do so without disclosing information contrary to the public interest'.[73] In practice, SIAC issues both an 'open' and a 'closed' judgment in respect of each of its decisions. Both the government and the certified individual can appeal SIAC's determinations to the Court of Appeal, but only on a question of law.[74]

The creation of SIAC marked a fundamental shift from the situation that had previously obtained in the United Kingdom. As noted above, prior to *Chahal* the

[68] See *Chahal* (n 28) para 144.

[69] SIAC Act 1997, sch 1, Art 1.

[70] The requirement that members meeting the first two requirements listed be on the panel is contained in the SIAC Act 1997, sch 1, Art 5.

[71] SIAC Act 1997, s 6. Most of the substantive detail regarding SIAC's operation was left to the rules of procedure: see Special Immigration Appeals Commission (Procedure) Rules 2003, SI 2003/1034 (SIACR 2003).

[72] SIACR 2003, r 36. Upon being notified of any such request for communication, SIAC has to notify the Secretary of State, who then has a period of time to make an objection, which is to be considered by SIAC. If SIAC rules for disclosure, the government is not bound to disclose if it elects not to rely on the material that is the subject of the ruling.

[73] ibid, r 47.

[74] SIAC Act 1997, s 7. There was more parliamentary debate on the provision concerning appeal from SIAC than on any other aspect of the legislation. The debate on this issue provides a snapshot of the then prevalent expectations of the courts in the national security field. The legislation as initially introduced made no provision for any appeal, with the Labour government portraying the corresponding conclusiveness of a decision by SIAC as expressive of the rule of law. The opposition Conservatives, worried that SIAC would not give appropriate weight to government security concerns, pushed for the Minister, and not the certified individual, to have a broad right of appeal to the courts. It was assumed that the courts would 'correct' any lack of deference on the part of SIAC. The opposition view of the courts' response to SIAC was vindicated by the *Rehman* decision (see this chapter, s 5.6). The eventual position whereby both parties could appeal on an issue of law (SIAC Act 1997, s 7) was a compromise: see Thwaites (n 50) 76–81.

Secretary of State's decision to deport a non-citizen on grounds of national security was not subject to independent scrutiny leading to a binding decision.[75] Those promoting the SIAC bill understood it to be an essential part of complying with *Chahal* that SIAC would be able to make decisions binding on the Secretary of State.[76] They presented the Secretary of State's subjection to binding review as a significant advance in human rights terms.[77]

5.5 The Human Rights Act 1998

On 2 October 2000, between the enactment of the SIAC Act 1997 and the *Belmarsh* litigation, the HRA 1998 entered into force.[78] Under the HRA, the United Kingdom Parliament created a new and general ground of illegality by making it unlawful for any public authority to act incompatibly with 'Convention rights' (section 6).[79] As the courts are themselves a public authority, they must develop and apply the law compatibly with Convention rights. In addition, the HRA 1998 requires that all legislation be read compatibly with Convention rights 'so far as it is possible to do so' (section 3). Where legislation cannot be read compatibly with Convention rights, the courts may issue a declaration of incompatibility (section 4).

The legal framework that structured the *Belmarsh* litigation was that of the ECHR viewed through the lens of the HRA 1998. There is necessarily a supranational aspect to jurisprudence under the HRA 1998. The rights in the HRA 1998 are drawn from the ECHR. Section 2 of the HRA 1998 provides that a court determining a question that arises in connection with a right under the HRA 1998 'must take into account' any judgment of the ECtHR relevant to the proceedings. The HRA 1998 is not an 'incorporation statute'. It does not incorporate the rights under the ECHR into United Kingdom law, rather it 'gives effect' to them as domestic statutory rights created by the HRA 1998.[80]

As is evident in the discussion of the House of Lords' reasoning in *Belmarsh*, the HRA 1998 was not intended, or received, as 'just another statute'. It was intended to promote a shift to a greater focus on rights across the three branches of government, including a shift in the judicial role. In the closing words of his

[75] See text to nn 30 and 31.

[76] See Mike O'Brien, Parliamentary Under-Secretary of State for the Home Department, on the Third Reading of the Special Immigration Appeals Commission Bill, HC Deb 26 November 1997, vol 301, col 1033. The passage can be found at the beginning of this chapter at n 2.

[77] See Lord Williams of Mostyn, HL Deb 5 June 1997, vol 580 col 752: 'it is intended that the decision should bind the Home Secretary. I respectfully suggest that this is a very significant advance in human rights terms.'

[78] The main provisions of the HRA 1998 entered into force on 2 October 2000 (ie not every provision).

[79] 'Convention rights' are defined for the purposes of the HRA 1998 in s 1(1) and include Arts 2–12 and 14 of the ECHR, in addition to several articles from protocols to the ECHR.

[80] See Beatson (n 9) paras 1-69–1-76.

Tom Sargant Memorial Lecture on 16 December 1997, the then Lord Chancellor, Lord Irvine of Lairg, said:

> This Bill [HRA 1998] will therefore create a more explicitly moral approach to decisions and decision-making; will promote both a culture where positive rights and liberties become the focus and concerns of legislators, administrators and judges alike; and a culture in judicial decision making where there will be a greater concentration on substance rather than form.[81]

5.6 *Rehman* and SIAC's Review Function

The *Belmarsh* litigation commenced with an appeal to SIAC. SIAC's approach to review in that decision was informed by the House of Lords' decision in *Rehman*,[82] delivered some nine months earlier.[83] In addition to its impact on SIAC's reasoning, *Rehman* is discussed here as a contrast to the House of Lords' *Belmarsh* decision, on the issue of deference in the area of national security.

Rehman is a pre-HRA 1998 case. The Secretary of State decided to deport a foreign national, Mr Rehman, from the United Kingdom on the basis that it was conducive to the public good on grounds of national security. Mr Rehman was accused of supporting terrorist activities on the Indian sub-continent. He appealed to SIAC. This was a full appeal, reviewing the Secretary of State's decision on the law and his findings of fact.[84] SIAC overturned the Secretary of State's decision. It held that a threat to national security had to be a direct threat to the United Kingdom. It further held that the Secretary of State had failed to satisfy a high civil standard of proof in establishing that Mr Rehman was a threat to national security. The House of Lords overturned SIAC on both holdings. The House of Lords' reasoning on the second point, namely how SIAC should understand its review function, is of particular relevance to the discussion in this chapter and the next.

The House of Lords noted a number of indicators that SIAC's rulings were entitled to deference. Their lordships acknowledged that the legislation supported the conferral of a full appellate jurisdiction on SIAC. The SIAC Act 1997 provided as follows:

[81] Lord Irvine of Lairg, 'The Development of Human Rights in Britain under an Incorporated Convention on Human Rights', Tom Sargant Memorial Lecture, Law Society Hall, London, December 1997, www.roughjusticetv.co.uk/irvine.htm.

[82] *Rehman* (n 18).

[83] See *A v Secretary of State for the Home Department* [2002] HRLR 45 (*Belmarsh* (SIAC)), [15], [16], [21]. See also *A v Secretary of State for the Home Department* [2002] EWCA Civ 1502, [2004] QB 335 (*Belmarsh* (Court of Appeal)), [81] (Brooke LJ).

[84] SIAC Act 1997, s 4(1)(a). Section 7(1) then provided for an appeal from SIAC to the Court of Appeal on 'any question of law material to' the Commission's determination.

> The Special Immigration Appeals Commission on an appeal to it under this Act – (a) shall allow the appeal if it considers – . . . (ii) where the decision or action involved the exercise of a discretion by the Secretary of State or an officer, that the discretion should have been exercised differently . . .[85]

Lord Hoffmann commented that 'The amplitude of [SIAC's] jurisdiction is emphasised by the express power to reverse the exercise of a discretion'.[86] Further, the reasons referred to SIAC's membership and procedures as supporting its expertise and its ability to determine questions of law and fact in the realm of national security.[87] The relevance of the demands of the HRA 1998 to SIAC's appellate functions was noted.[88]

Nonetheless, the House of Lords read down this statutory conferral of jurisdiction on SIAC with reference to 'a common sense recognition of the nature of the issue [national security] and the difference in the decision making processes and responsibilities of the Home Secretary and the Commission'.[89] As put by Lord Hoffmann, 'the question is not the extent of the Commission's appellate jurisdiction. It is whether the particular issue can be properly decided by a judicial tribunal at all.'[90] The House of Lords recast SIAC's role to bring it into conformity with a traditional, deferential approach to government decision-making in matters of national security. The creation of SIAC was a legislative experiment, sparked by *Chahal*, to introduce a new level of accountability into national security. The reasoning in *Rehman* marked a reassertion of a traditional approach to deference to government decision-making in the area of national security.[91]

Lord Slynn stated that whereas *past* events have to be proven to the civil standard, the government is best placed to evaluate *future risk*, with that task falling to the Secretary of State:

> He is entitled to have regard to preventative and precautionary principles rather than wait until directly harmful activities have taken place, the individual in the meantime remaining in this country. In doing so he is not merely finding facts but forming an executive judgment or assessment.[92]

What was at issue was an evaluation of risk the Secretary of State was best placed to perform. All members of the House of Lords supported the proposition that evidence of future risk does not have to be proven to a civil standard in the same way as evidence of present or past facts. Lord Slynn and Lord Steyn put this in terms of according due weight to the Secretary of State's assessment and conclusions.[93] Lord

[85] ibid, s 4(1)(a)(ii).
[86] *Rehman* (n 18) [58] (Lord Hoffmann). See also [26] (Lord Slynn), [30]–[31] (Lord Steyn).
[87] ibid, [30] (Lord Steyn).
[88] ibid, [30] (Lord Steyn).
[89] ibid, [58] (Lord Hoffmann). On the superior expertise of the Minister see also [26] (Lord Slynn).
[90] ibid, [52] (Lord Hoffmann).
[91] See David Dyzenhaus, 'Intimations of Legality amid the Clash of Arms' (2004) 2 *International Journal of Constitutional Law* 244, 260–62.
[92] *Rehman* (n 18) [22] (Lord Slynn). The sole dissenter in *Belmarsh*, Lord Walker, also explicitly adopted a 'precautionary' approach: see *Belmarsh* (n 3) [197].
[93] *Rehman* (n 18) [26] (Lord Slynn), [31] (Lord Steyn).

Hoffmann went further, holding that the Secretary of State's determination as to whether deportation was in the interests of national security could not 'ordinarily' be interfered with if it could 'reasonably be entertained'.[94] In its *Belmarsh* judgment, SIAC quoted and referred to Lord Hoffmann's statements on this issue.[95] *Rehman* has been treated as authority for a deferential approach to the government's national security decision-making *generally*. Nonetheless, it is notable that their lordships were all careful to frame their conclusions with reference to the government's power of deportation in the public good. Their reasons were addressed to the deportation power.[96]

Lord Hoffmann explicitly based his reasoning on the separation of powers, which is taken to demand a compartmentalisation of judicial, executive and legislative functions. Where a matter of national security is entrusted to the executive, the courts are not to interfere: 'Under the constitution of the United Kingdom and most other countries, decisions as to whether something is or is not in the interests of national security are not a matter for judicial decision.'[97] The idea that national security should largely be free from judicial scrutiny complements the view that, in this area, accountability should be through the political process. Lord Hoffmann's postscript to *Rehman* is a well-known expression of the appropriateness of political, as opposed to legal, forms of accountability, in dire matters of national security.[98]

Lord Hoffmann's statements on the primacy of political, as opposed to legal, accountability in matters of national security need to be placed alongside his position on judicial review of certain rights. He commented, *obiter*, on the appropriate approach to the issue of whether a deportee might be subject to torture in violation of Article 3. This, Lord Hoffmann stated, is an issue 'which at no point lie[s] within the exclusive province of the executive'.[99] In relation to some questions, accountability is primarily political, in others it is within the exclusive province of the courts.

[94] ibid, [57]. Lord Clyde adopted the reasons of Lord Hoffmann. Lord Hutton adopted the reasons of Lords Slynn, Steyn and Hoffmann.

[95] See *Belmarsh* (SIAC) (n 83) [15]. See also *Belmarsh* (Court of Appeal) (n 83) [81] (Brooke LJ).

[96] *Rehman* (n 18) [22], [15] (Lord Slynn), [29] (Lord Steyn).

[97] ibid, [50]. The clearest application of Lord Hoffmann's approach to national security was his holding that SIAC was 'not entitled to differ from the opinion of the Secretary of State' as to whether the promotion of terrorism in a foreign country by a British resident was contrary to national security: [53].

[98] ibid, [62] (Lord Hoffmann): 'I wrote this speech some three months before the recent events in New York and Washington. They are a reminder that in matters of national security, the cost of failure can be high. This seems to me to underline the need for the judicial arm of government to respect the decisions of minsters of the Crown on the question of whether support for terrorist activities in a foreign country constitutes a threat to national security. It is not only that the executive has access to special information and expertise in these matters. It is also that such decisions, with serious potential results for the community, require a legitimacy which can only be conferred by entrusting them to persons responsible to the community through the democratic process. If the people are to accept the consequences of such decisions, they must be made by persons whom the people have elected and whom they can remove.' This speech was quoted with approval by the Canadian Supreme Court in *Suresh v Canada (Citizenship and Immigration)* [2002] SCC 1, [2002] 1 SCR 3, [33] and [31]. *Suresh* is discussed in ch 8, s 8.6.

[99] *Rehman* (n 18) [54] (Lord Hoffmann).

The problem with this demarcation of zones of deference and intense scrutiny is that they are likely to overlap. The rights that trigger intensive scrutiny are likely to be at issue in cases of national security. The analysis Lord Hoffmann provided is one where the perceived infringement of a particular right catapults the analysis from complete deference to the most demanding standard of review. There are practical problems with this abrupt shift from marked deference to intense review, arising from the intermingling of factors going to the risk of torture and national security concerns. The same issues arise in relation to the Canadian case law on security certificates, and I explore them in that context in chapter eight.[100]

The House of Lords' approach to deference in *Rehman* is often contrasted with the majority's approach in *Belmarsh*.[101] Murray Hunt's analysis of deference in 'Sovereignty's Blight' provides a means of delineating the contrasting approaches.[102] The reasoning in *Rehman*, certainly that of Lord Hoffmann, evidences a 'spatial' approach to deference. By way of contrast, the reasoning of the majority in *Belmarsh* displays a more contextualised approach, termed 'due deference' by Hunt. The 'spatial' approach contemplates that there are particular subject matters in respect of which a decision-maker is effectively immune from judicial review.[103] Certain subject areas, such as national security, are seen as not amenable to judicial determination.[104] It is in effect, a (non-)justiciability doctrine.

As adverted to above, a key problem with the spatial approach is that issues of rights and national security are not so easily separated out for different treatment. The spatial approach provides little guidance on how to accommodate the high level of scrutiny appropriate to infringements of fundamental rights with the view that certain areas of decision-making are effectively non-justiciable. Questions about deportation to torture, liberty or non-discrimination are likely to arise in areas in which the courts have traditionally been reluctant to intervene in the decisions of primary decision-makers, such as national security.[105] As expressed by Hunt:

> Because rights and values are transcendent of context, cases cannot be neatly classified into categories according to the kind of subject matter they raise, and then a particular standard of review applied to them. This means that the relevant features which pull in different directions as far as the intensity of review is concerned are often present in the same case.[106]

[100] See ch 8, s 8.7.1.

[101] See eg *Re Almrei* 2009 FC 1263 (Canadian Federal Court), [102] (Mosley J), discussed in ch 9, pp 281–82. See also Beatson et al (n 9) paras 3-254, 3-269; Roger Masterman, *The Separation of Powers in the Contemporary Constitution: Judicial Competence and Independence in the United Kingdom* (Cambridge, Cambridge University Press, 2011) 98–99.

[102] Murray Hunt, 'Sovereignty's Blight: Why Contemporary Public Law Needs the Concept of "Due Deference"' in Nicholas Bamforth and Peter Leyland (eds), *Public Law in a Multi-Layered Constitution* (Oxford, Hart Publishing, 2003) 337. Hunt does not discuss *Rehman*, and could not discuss *Belmarsh* given the timing. It is his framework that is applied.

[103] ibid, 345.

[104] ibid.

[105] ibid, 347.

[106] ibid. See also David Mullan, 'Deference from *Baker* to *Suresh* and Beyond' in David Dyzenhaus (ed), *The Unity of Public Law* (Oxford, Hart Publishing, 2004) 21.

In contrast to the spatial approach, a contextualised approach to deference copes better with a situation characterised by contrary indicators of the appropriate intensity of review. A contextualised approach is less prone to oscillation between complete deference and its total absence, which Lord Hoffmann's reasons in *Rehman* prefigured. It allows for variable standards of review within a given case, addressed to the particular decision under review. The weight attached to the decision-maker's views is determined by the institutional and democratic considerations pertinent to a particular decision and its effect on rights. The application of such a contextualised approach is developed, in the context of the House of Lords' reasoning in *Belmarsh*, in the next chapter.

5.7 Derogations in the European Convention on Human Rights

The ECHR makes provision in Article 15 for derogation from rights in a time of 'public emergency'. The inclusion of such derogation provisions in the ECHR and other prominent international human rights treaties acknowledges that when governments perceive 'threats to the life of the nation' they are likely to take action that seriously impinges on rights. Derogation provisions simultaneously acknowledge the inevitability of 'exceptional measures' and put in place criteria against which the legality of the derogation can be reviewed.

For a derogation to be lawful under Article 15(1) of the ECHR, it must meet three criteria:

i there must be a 'public emergency threatening the life of the nation';
ii the derogating measures must be 'strictly required by the exigencies of the situation'; and
iii they are not to be 'inconsistent with [the relevant state's] other obligations under international law'.

These three criteria lie at the centre of the *Belmarsh* litigation and are discussed in the next chapter. Before entering into a discussion of the litigation, I outline the limitation and derogation models developed by Tom Hickman to explore what it means to derogate from a right.[107] These models delineate certain differences between the government argument in *Belmarsh* and the reasoning of the *Belmarsh* majority. Beyond that, the models assist more generally in understanding the context for the legal reasoning in *Belmarsh*, a context in which rights had, purportedly, been derogated from, but a relatively 'thick' conception of legality remained in place.

[107] Tom R Hickman, 'Between Human Rights and the Rule of Law: Indefinite Detention and the Derogation Model of Constitutionalism' (2005) 68 *MLR* 655. While Hickman developed the models with reference to *Belmarsh*, he uses them to criticise the House of Lords' reasoning on the first criterion for lawful derogation under Art 15 of the ECHR, the existence of a public emergency.

Hickman introduces the two models against the background of a third – the 'extra-legal measures' model.[108] This model argues against accommodating executive responses to emergencies within the legal framework. It does so on the grounds that attempts to 'legalise' executive responses to emergencies are both futile and counter-productive.[109] They are futile in that there will always be uncontrolled executive action in response to an emergency. They are doubly counter-productive in that they both impose restraints on the executive precisely when it most needs a free hand, and risk causing lasting damage to the legal system's fundamentals in their attempts to accommodate the exceptional.

Of the two approaches to derogation considered by Hickman, the limitation model is the more vulnerable to the charges of being futile and counterproductive.[110] As its name suggests, it treats a derogation as simply another limitation on rights. Rights obligations that are derogated from still apply; it is simply that their scope is diminished. A clear example of such an approach is furnished by the government argument in *Belmarsh* that the derogation merely enabled an extension of the detention power by way of a corresponding limitation on the right to liberty. The limitation model feels the bite of criticisms from the extra-legal measures perspective. Rights obligations are brought into disrepute when diminished by extensive limitation.

The alternative, the 'derogation' model, holds that a derogation does not just limit a right; it releases a state from its obligation to observe that right.[111] The central feature of the model is that it sees a derogation as sanctioning a departure from a rights obligation, but not from legality.[112] A derogation from rights obligations still falls to be assessed against substantive, and strictly applied, criteria for lawfulness. The space opened up between rights and legality softens the criticism from the extra-legal measures quarter.[113] A derogation allows a state to pursue its advertised course of action without having to justify itself with reference to the right, and the legal understanding of the right is in turn insulated, at least to a degree, from the exceptional turn of events. The derogation model remains firmly distinct from the 'extra-legal measures' model in that fundamental criteria of legality still apply to the executive's action. The importance of these criteria was testified to by the House of Lords' decision in *Belmarsh*.

That a derogation releases a state from a rights obligation, rather than simply limiting that obligation, raises the stakes considerably. The standard of review applied in assessing the lawfulness of a derogation needs to be higher than the standard of review for infringement of a right. It is appropriate that the ability to

[108] See Oren Gross, 'Chaos and Rules: Should Responses to Violent Crises Always be Constitutional?' (2003) 112 *Yale Law Journal* 1011. Hickman also references chapters from Martin Loughlin's *The Idea of Public Law* (Oxford, Oxford University Press, 2004). My description and understanding of the 'extra-legal measures' model refers to Gross's article.

[109] Hickman (n 107) 658.

[110] ibid.

[111] ibid.

[112] ibid, 659. See eg ch 6, p 155.

[113] ibid, 660.

suspend a right be more tightly circumscribed than the ability to limit it. The ECtHR case law reflects this in associating the 'strictly required' criterion in Article 15 of the ECHR with an 'indispensability' standard higher than 'necessity'.[114] The difference between necessity and the higher 'indispensability' standard is that the latter, more onerous test requires the government to show that it has considered the alternatives, and no less intrusive possibility exists.[115]

An assessment of the *Belmarsh* litigation needs to appreciate the difference between questions about the scope of the relevant Convention rights and questions about the standards for lawful derogation. The central question addressed in the litigation was whether indefinite administrative detention of non-citizens was 'strictly required by the exigencies of the situation'. The right to liberty was not directly at issue; rather the question was whether the government's suspension of the right to liberty was arbitrary.

[114] See *Handyside v United Kingdom* (1976) 1 EHRR 727, para 48; *Silvers v United Kingdom* (1983) 5 EHRR 439, para 97; *McCann v United Kingdom* (1995) 21 EHRR 97, para 149. See also Beatson et al (n 9) paras 2-176–2-186.

[115] See eg *James v UK* A 98 (1986), 8 EHRR 123, para 51 and the discussion in *R (Clays Lane Housing Cooperative Ltd) v Housing Corp* [2004] EWCA Civ 1658, [21]–[22]. See also Hickman (n 107) 666.

6

Belmarsh in the United Kingdom Courts

If the Secretary of State's decision as to what the exigencies of the situation strictly required stands (as I think it must), then the argument based on discrimination falls away.

Chadwick LJ, *A v Secretary of State for the Home Department, Court of Appeal* (2002)[1]

In the present case I see no escape from the conclusion that Parliament must be regarded as having attached insufficient weight to the human rights of non-nationals.

Lord Nicholls, *A v Secretary of State for the Home Department, House of Lords* (2004)[2]

6.1 The Measures at Issue in *Belmarsh*

Prior to the events of 11 September 2001, a number of foreign nationals were known to the United Kingdom authorities (ie, MI5) whom it wished to deport but could not, due to the real risk of torture on return to their country of nationality and the legal significance of this fact as a bar to removal following *Chahal*.[3] The bar on deportation arguably frustrated the precondition for immigration detention under Article 5(1)(f) of the European Convention on Human Rights (ECHR), namely the taking of action 'with a view to deportation'. Subsequent to the terrorist attacks of 11 September 2001, the United Kingdom government renewed its efforts to remove these foreign nationals from the community. In doing so it had to address the incompatibility with the ECHR of both deportation to a real risk of torture, and indefinite detention of a non-citizen subject to a

[1] *A v Secretary of State for the Home Department* [2002] EWCA Civ 1502, [2004] QB 335 (*Belmarsh* (Court of Appeal)), [153].

[2] *A v Secretary of State for the Home Department* [2004] UKHL 56, [2005] 2 AC 68 (*Belmarsh*), [81].

[3] *Chahal v United Kingdom* (1997) 23 EHRR 413.

removal order. It responded by using the derogation provisions in the ECHR,[4] introduced in the previous chapter.

The government sought to derogate from Article 5(1) in anticipation of the enactment of indefinite detention provisions. Its decision to detain rather than deport was shaped by the architecture for lawful derogation in the ECHR. The government had to work around the fact that the prohibition on deportation to torture under Article 3 was 'non-derogable'.[5] The ECHR drafters had concluded that states were not to be released from their obligations with respect to the prohibition on torture in any circumstances. However, the derogation provisions did allow for detention without trial in a time of public emergency. The government could derogate from Article 5(1), and did so on the grounds that there existed, in the form of Al-Qaeda, a terrorist threat that constituted a 'public emergency threatening the life of the nation'.[6]

The legislation served by the derogation was the Anti-Terrorism, Crime and Security Act 2001 (ATCSA 2001). The ATCSA 2001 was introduced into Parliament the day after the Derogation Order had been tabled. Section 23 of the ATCSA 2001 provided for 'international terrorist suspects' to be taken into indefinite immigration detention.

The indefinite detention regime under challenge in the *Belmarsh* litigation was contained in Part 4 of the ATCSA 2001 ('Immigration and Asylum'). Section 21(1) provided that the Secretary of State could issue a certificate with respect to a named individual if she or he 'reasonably':

(a) believes that a person's presence in the United Kingdom is a threat to national security, and
(b) suspects that the person is a terrorist.

A person so certified could be deported or, should his or her removal or departure from the United Kingdom be prevented, detained.[7] The power of detention applied to all instances in which the power of deportation was frustrated. A deportation order could be issued despite the fact that the non-citizen's removal was frustrated for the indefinite future (due to either a 'point of law' or a 'practical consideration').[8] Section 23 provided for a certified individual to be detained under the Immigration Act 1971 'despite the fact that his removal or departure from the United Kingdom is prevented (whether temporarily or indefinitely)'.

[4] Convention for the Protection of Human Rights and Fundamental Freedoms (opened for signature 4 November 1950, entered into force 3 September 1953) 213 UNTS 211, Eur TS 5 (ECHR).

[5] ECHR (n 4) Art 15(2).

[6] The United Kingdom sent a *note verbale* to the Secretary General of the Council of Europe, pursuant to its obligation under the ECHR to keep him informed of any derogation. To register a 'designated derogation' under the HRA 1998, the government tabled a domestic derogation order before the UK Parliament on 11 November 2001: Human Rights Act 1998 (Designated Derogation) Order 2001, SI 2001/3644 (Derogation Order). The *note verbale* to the Secretary General was scheduled to Art 2 of the Derogation Order.

[7] Anti-Terrorism, Crime and Security Act 2001 (ATCSA 2001), ss 22–23.

[8] ibid, s 22.

Part 4 of the ATCSA 2001 added to the Special Immigration Appeals Commission's (SIAC's) jurisdiction. It provided for two avenues of appeal, in relation to 'certification' and 'derogation matters' respectively, giving rise to two lines of litigation. Under the first, a person certified to be a 'suspected international terrorist' could appeal that certification decision.[9] In relation to the second avenue of appeal, section 30(1) defined a 'derogation matter' as:

(a) a derogation by the United Kingdom from Article 5(1) of the Convention on Human Rights which relates to the detention of a person where there is an intention to remove or deport him from the United Kingdom, or
(b) the designation under section 14(1) of the Human Rights Act 1998 (c. 42) of a derogation within paragraph (a) above.

SIAC had exclusive jurisdiction over derogation matters.[10] My focus is almost exclusively on the second line of litigation, bearing on the legality of the derogation. On derogation matters, Parliament had provided for appeal on a question of law from SIAC to the Court of Appeal.[11] As will be seen, the Court of Appeal and the House of Lords adopted different readings of what constituted a 'question of law' that could be overturned on appeal.

6.2 Introduction to the *Belmarsh* Litigation

The ATCSA 2001 came into force on 4 December 2001. On 17 or 18 December 2001, the first of the applicants was certified, and detained shortly thereafter, with the other applicants similarly certified and detained in the weeks and months that followed. A number of those detained challenged their detention as incompatible with their Convention rights under the Human Rights Act 1998 (HRA 1998). They argued that the derogation did not meet the requirements of the ECHR and that in the absence of a lawful derogation their detention was incompatible with Article 5(1). They sought the quashing of the Derogation Order and a declaration of incompatibility under the HRA 1998 in respect of the detention provisions.

In considering the litigation on the derogation, attention must be paid to the concessions made by the government and how these shaped the proceedings. In the domestic proceedings, the legal debate centred on the criteria for lawful derogation set out in Article 15 of the ECHR. The government reserved the issue of

[9] ibid, s 25. See also s 26 on review of certification by SIAC.

[10] ibid, s 30(2). Section 30 was an attempt to manage the potential legal challenges to the derogation. 'Since it is contained in a statutory instrument, the designated derogation would have been open to judicial review. In addition, it might have been contended by anyone who was detained that the action was unlawful because it was incompatible with human rights': *A v Secretary of State for the Home Department* [2002] HRLR 45 (*Belmarsh* (SIAC)), [9].

[11] ATCSA 2001, s 30(3), provided the rules for appeal from SIAC set out in s 7 of the SIAC Act 1997 applied (s 30(3)(b) of the ATCSA qualified the application of s 7 of the SIAC Act to 'derogation matters' with the words 'with any modification which the Commission considers necessary').

whether or not the detention provisions would infringe Article 5(1)(f) of the ECHR in the absence of the derogation.[12] The government conceded that if the derogation was held not to be lawful, then section 23 of the ATCSA 2001 was incompatible with Article 5(1) of the ECHR.

The government further conceded that the validity of the derogation in domestic law depended on whether the derogation to which it gave effect at international law was lawful under Article 15 of the ECHR.[13] The HRA 1998 appears to adopt the derogation regime in the ECHR in providing for 'designated derogations' from Convention rights in sections 1(2) and 14.[14]

As noted in the previous chapter, for a derogation to be lawful it must meet the following three criteria under Article 15(1):

(i) there must be a 'public emergency threatening the life of the nation';
(ii) the derogating measures must be 'strictly required by the exigencies of the situation'; and
(iii) they are not to be 'inconsistent with [the relevant state's] other obligations under international law'.

My discussion focuses on the second of these criteria, namely the issue of whether the measures were 'strictly required'. This book centres on the discriminatory and disproportionate nature of indefinite detention measures confined to non-citizens, and these issues are most directly addressed under the second criterion.

The detainees' fortunes were reversed at each stage of the domestic proceedings. As required by section 30 of the ATCSA 2001, the detainees' challenge to the derogation and legislation was first heard by SIAC. The appellants were successful in obtaining a declaration of incompatibility from SIAC, but this remedy was overturned by the Court of Appeal, before being reinstated by a majority of the House of Lords. An appreciation of the earlier decisions is needed to properly understand the House of Lords' reasoning. In addition, the majority positions at each level of the litigation contrast three highly distinct ways in which a proportionality test can be applied to national security concerns, with very different consequences. The litigation as a whole is an interesting case study of the relationship between deference, standards of review, and rights.

Most of the litigants in the domestic *Belmarsh* litigation also made a subsequent application to the European Court of Human Rights (ECtHR), admitted, heard and determined by that body. The ECtHR's decision, handed down in February

[12] Years later, before the Grand Chamber of the ECtHR, the United Kingdom government did run the argument that in the absence of a derogation, the detention provisions were consistent with Art 5(1)(f): see *A v United Kingdom* (2009) 49 EHRR 29, and the discussion in ch 7, s 7.2. The United Kingdom government's argument was unsuccessful.

[13] *Belmarsh* (SIAC) (n 10) [12], [38]. For an argument that this concession was correctly made see Jack Beatson et al, *Human Rights: Judicial Protection in the United Kingdom* (London, Sweet & Maxwell, 2008) para 1-115.

[14] Section 1(2) of the HRA 1998 provides that the statutory rights under the HRA 1998 are to have effect subject to any 'designated derogation'. This phrase is defined in s 14 as 'any derogation by the United Kingdom from an Article of the Convention . . . which is designated for the purposes of this Act in an order made by the Secretary of State'.

2009, essentially confirmed the House of Lords' reasoning, although there was some variation in the argument on the substantive legality of detention. The decision also marked a substantial intervention by the ECtHR on the procedural rights of terrorist suspects subject to executive orders. I discuss that decision in chapter seven.[15]

6.3 The Case before SIAC

6.3.1 Introduction

The first decision in the domestic litigation was *A v Secretary of State for the Home Department*.[16] Delivered less than a year after the terrorist attacks of 11 September 2001, SIAC unanimously held that the required rational connection between national security purposes and the detention measures under challenge was lacking. The rock on which the government case foundered was the decision to confine the measures to non-citizens, given evidence that the threat was posed by both non-citizens and citizens. The measures were under-inclusive, in only responding to a subset of those posing a threat. This deficiency was also registered in the holding that the measures were discriminatory on grounds of nationality. In these respects, SIAC's decision anticipated the later decision of the House of Lords.

SIAC's reasoning contrasts with that of the House of Lords in its acceptance of the government view that a power of indefinite detention was required. SIAC's underlying objection was that the detention measures *did not go far enough in protecting national security*. It acknowledged that its reasoning pointed to an expansion of the power of indefinite detention to encompass citizens as well as non-citizens.

SIAC made an *effective* response to the threat its exclusive concern, with little overt regard for the liberty rights of non-citizens. The problem perceived by SIAC was that the detention measures did not constitute an effective response. The measures' primary deficiency was a lack of rational connection between objective and means, rather than a lack of proportionality in any broader sense. In this, SIAC reasoned that it was the perceived distortions that the decision to target non-citizens had on the government's pursuit of its objectives, rather than any disregard of non-citizens' rights, that was fatal to the measures.

SIAC's reasoning on the Article 15 requirement, that a derogation be 'strictly required' by the exigencies of the situation, was loose. It considered broad arguments: less intrusive measures were available; and there was no rational

[15] Section 7.2.
[16] *Belmarsh* (SIAC) (n 10).

connection between the measures adopted and the end sought to be achieved.[17] It did not refer to any particular jurisprudential basis for a proportionality analysis, except to observe that the interveners had urged that at least '*Daly* standards' should apply – that is, the link between the measures adopted and the objective should be rigorously scrutinised.[18] The 'at least' is a reference to the fact that the 'strictly required' standard is more demanding than ordinary proportionality. As discussed in chapter five, the ECtHR's 'strict necessity' standard requires no less intrusive means of securing the aim exists.[19] It is clear that SIAC did not adhere to this standard. The members of SIAC cited with approval a judicial statement in the Supreme Court of Canada:

> the tailoring process seldom admits of perfection and the courts must accord some leeway to the legislator. If the law falls within a range of reasonable alternatives, the courts will not find it overbroad merely because they can conceive of an alternative which might better tailor objective to infringement.[20]

6.3.2 Proportionality and Discrimination

The proportionality test adopted by the House of Lords in the *Belmarsh* litigation requires that, in determining whether a measure is arbitrary or excessive, a court should ask if:

> (i) the legislative objective is sufficiently important to justify limiting a fundamental right; (ii) the measures designed to meet the legislative objective are rationally connected to it; and (iii) the means used to impair the right or freedom are not more than is necessary to accomplish these objectives.[21]

SIAC first considered the last of these questions: the argument that there were less intrusive means. Its treatment of this criterion saw the unravelling of the 'ordinary' proportionality test by dint of deference to the government on national security (and certainly did not rise to any higher standard of 'strict necessity' appropriate to

[17] ibid, [39].

[18] ibid, [40]. The standard of 'rigorous' scrutiny is described in *R v Secretary of State for the Home Department, ex parte Daly* [2001] UKHL 46, [2001] 2 AC 532; see in particular at [26]–[27] where Lord Steyn stated that proportionality is the appropriate standard for review of Convention rights, as distinct from any variation on the traditional standards based on *Associated Provincial Picture Houses Ltd v Wednesbury Corp* [1948] 1 KB 223. The *Wednesbury* standard Lord Steyn rejected was: 'When anxiously scrutinising an executive decision that interferes with human rights, the court will ask the question, applying an objective test, whether the decision-maker could reasonably have concluded that the interference was necessary to refer to one or more of the legitimate aims recognised by the Convention': *R (Mahmood) v Secretary of State for the Home Department* [2000] EWCA Civ 315, [2001] 1 WLR 840, [40] (Lord Phillips MR).

[19] See ch 5, pp 143–44.

[20] *Belmarsh* (SIAC) (n 10) [44], citing *RJR MacDonald Inc v A-G Canada* [1995] 3 SCR 199, 342 (McLachlin CJ). In *Belmarsh* (n 2), Lord Hope criticised SIAC's adoption of this standard.

[21] *de Freitas v Permanent Secretary of Ministry of Agriculture, Lands and Housing* [1998] UKPC 68, [1999] 1 AC 69, [25] (Lord Clyde for the Court). For the recognition of this formulation of proportionality by the House of Lords see *Belmarsh* (n 2) [30] (Lord Bingham); *Huang v Secretary of State for the Home Department* [2007] UKHL 11, [2007] 2 AC 167, [19] (Appellate Committee).

the derogation context). SIAC's approach to proportionality was consistent with the view that 'the serious potential results'[22] of a terrorist attack meant that *any measure of additional protection* secured would justify even such a grave rights violation as indefinite preventive detention. An incremental gain in safety was held to justify the imposition of draconian measures. The most evident source of this precautionary logic was *Rehman*, quoted repeatedly in SIAC's reasons.[23]

The detainees submitted that there were measures falling short of indefinite detention without charge available to achieve the desired objectives, citing the range and breadth of criminal offences under the Terrorism Act 2000, and the possible use of telephone intercept evidence. SIAC was unconvinced, taking the position that as long as the challenged measures conferred 'additional protection' they could be said to be 'strictly required'. SIAC found that the measures did afford 'additional protection'. It accepted the government's statement that there were some individuals whose neutralisation would not be assisted by the criminal and evidential provisions (or proposed provisions) identified by the detainees. SIAC effectively held that it was not necessary to adopt less intrusive anti-terrorism measures if this would lead to any decline in effectiveness.

Because it did not question the need for indefinite preventive detention, SIAC did not approach the differential treatment of non-citizens from the other direction. The members of SIAC did not raise the question of why, if indefinite detention was not necessary for those terrorist suspects who were citizens, it was said to be necessary at all.

SIAC held that the requirement of rational connection was not met. There was an insufficient rational connection between the national security purposes of the detention measures and the decision to confine them to non-citizens. SIAC did not hold that there was no rational connection, but rather that the connection was insufficient. The members of SIAC accepted that the detention measures advanced the protective ends to which they were directed to an extent. They simply held that the decision to utilise immigration measures meant that the detention provisions were not properly and fully directed at the threat, and were skewed in a discriminatory way.

SIAC's objection was not that the detention measures were unjustifiably burdensome, but that a fundamental error had been made in how they were tailored to the threat. The 'strictly required' argument was treated as simply replicating the discrimination argument. SIAC's ruling that it was irrational to confine the detention measures to non-citizens simply incorporated its reasoning on the Article 14 discrimination violation.[24] Turning to SIAC's reasoning on the alleged discrimination, Article 14 of the ECHR provides:

[22] *Secretary of State for the Home Department v Rehman* [2001] UKHL 47, [2003] 1 AC 153, [62] (Lord Hoffmann). This case is discussed in ch 5, s 5.6.

[23] *Belmarsh* (SIAC) (n 10) [15], [16], [21].

[24] ibid, [52]: 'We find it convenient to consider the arguments on this issue [that the measures are irrational in that they are confined to non-citizens] together with those relating to Article 14 of the Convention [on discrimination], which we do . . . below.'

> The enjoyment of the rights and freedoms set forth in this Convention shall be secured without discrimination on any ground such as sex, race, colour, language, religion, political or other opinion, national or social origin, association with a national minority, property, birth or other status.

Relying on ECtHR jurisprudence, SIAC held that a successful derogation from Article 5 did not render it unnecessary to consider Article 14 (from which there had been no derogation). The ATCSA 2001 allowed only for the indefinite detention of *foreign* terrorist suspects. It was submitted that because the detainees could not be removed from the jurisdiction, they were in an analogous position to suspected international terrorists who were nationals. Accordingly, the distinction the Secretary of State had drawn between foreign nationals and British nationals was discriminatory.

In response, the Attorney-General made two submissions. First, the measures in the ATCSA 2001 formed part of immigration control, and in that field it was legitimate to distinguish between British nationals and others. Second, there were objective reasons for focusing on foreign nationals as they constituted the predominant source of the threat. SIAC's wording of the government's 'immigration control' argument was that the ATCSA 2001 'is intended to protect the United Kingdom population to the same extent that it would be protected by expulsion in circumstances where the Convention rights of the detainee do not permit expulsion'.[25] The government presented the administrative detention of non-citizens as a straight substitute for expulsion. The proposal was that the power to detain non-citizens was as wide as the power to expel, with both being aspects of a more general power to protect the citizenry.

The government argued that while the ATCSA 2001 did extend the power of immigration detention beyond what Article 5(1)(f) of the ECHR permitted, it did not change the nature of immigration detention in any fundamental respect. Immigration detention was argued to be a manipulable category, expanding in times of threat to support the differential treatment of non-citizens. This position manifests the limitation model of derogation outlined in chapter five, section 5.7 and is an indication of that approach's ability to undermine the integrity of limited exceptions to rights.

A second line of argument pursued by the government was to extrapolate from earlier, general judicial statements to the effect that the search for a 'fair balance' 'between the general interest of the community and the personal rights of the individual' was inherent in the ECHR as a whole.[26] The government submitted that the ATCSA 2001 achieved a 'fair balance' between the state's interest in 'being able to protect its population from malevolent aliens' and the 'main interest' of those aliens in not being deported to torture.[27] This argument for a 'fair balance' between state protection and deportation to torture recurred throughout the

[25] ibid, [83].
[26] ibid, [88], citing *Brown v Stott* [2000] UKPC D3, [2001] 2 WLR 817, 836 (Lord Bingham).
[27] ibid, [88].

Belmarsh litigation.[28] The argument is a good indicator of the danger of the balance metaphor.[29] By locating the issue of indefinite detention somewhere on scales defined by the legitimate aim of protecting the population on one side and deportation to torture on the other, the government sought to sidestep discussion of indefinite detention as itself a rights violation, instead presenting it as a reasonable accommodation.

SIAC's response to these government submissions was terse and to the point. It accepted that the government was entitled to a 'degree of deference' with regard to how to pursue the legitimate aim of protection against terrorism, and continued:

> We further accept that the measures in the [ATCSA] form part of immigration control, but we have more difficulty in understanding why, in response to the threat of terrorism from suspected international terrorists it was considered necessary or even appropriate to focus on immigration control.[30]

SIAC treated the stated objectives of the measures, rather than the immigration characterisation, as fundamental. It was accordingly sceptical of the proposition that the stated security considerations justified the decision to rely on immigration.

Further, SIAC rejected the submission that the ATCSA 2001 simply extended Article 5(1)(f) without changing its nature in any fundamental respect. In doing so, it affirmed a rights-protecting view of immigration detention: 'Critically underlying any normal and lawful action within Article 5(1)(f) is the prospect within a reasonable time of the detainee being transferred to a place where he or she will be at liberty.'[31] SIAC supported this statement with the passage from *Chahal* stating that immigration detention is predicated on deportation proceedings being prosecuted with due diligence and is not to be excessive in duration.[32] While the SIAC judgment referred to *Chahal*, the phrase 'reasonable time' did not appear in *Chahal*. This language suggests that *Chahal* was read against *Hardial Singh*.[33]

SIAC then turned to consider the proposition underlying the government's distinction between citizens and non-citizens, namely that aliens have no general right to be in the country – at large among the population – even when they

[28] See eg *Belmarsh* (Court of Appeal) (n 1) [28] (Lord Woolf CJ). Here Lord Woolf CJ outlined the Secretary of State's case.

[29] There is a considerable literature on the danger of the balance metaphor in the national security context. See eg Jeremy Waldron, 'Security and Liberty: The Image of Balance' (2003) 11 *Journal of Political Philosophy* 191.

[30] *Belmarsh (SIAC)* (n 10) [92].

[31] ibid, [93].

[32] See ch 5, p 133.

[33] *R v Governor of Durham Prison, ex parte Singh* [1983] EWHC 1 (QB), [1984] 1 All ER 983 (*Hardial Singh*). On the relationship between *Chahal* and the *Hardial Singh* principles see now *R (WL) (Congo) v Home Secretary* [2011] UKSC 12, [2012] 1 AC 245 (*Lumba*), [30] (Lord Dyson), [199] (Baroness Hale); and *R (Kambadzi) v Secretary of State for the Home Department* [2011] UKSC 23, [2011] 1 WLR 1299, [58], [59] (Lord Hope), [76] (Baroness Hale), [94] (Lord Brown). *Lumba* and *Kambadzi* are discussed in ch 7, s 7.8.

cannot be removed.[34] SIAC responded: 'That seems to us to be an over simplification. The effect of the decision in *Chahal*, as we understand it, is that if the alien cannot be deported he must be allowed to remain.'[35] SIAC continued:

> A person who is irremovable cannot be detained or kept in detention simply because he lacks British nationality. In order to detain him there must be some other justification, such as that he is suspected of having committed a criminal offence. If there is to be an effective derogation from the right to liberty enshrined in Article 5 in respect of suspected international terrorists – and we can see powerful arguments in favour of such a derogation – the derogation ought rationally to extend to all irremovable suspected international terrorists. It would properly be confined to the alien section of the population only if, as the Attorney General contends the threat stems exclusively or almost exclusively from that alien section.[36]

In relation to the 'empirical' argument for a focus on aliens, raised by the last sentence of the above quotation, namely that foreigners were the exclusive, or near exclusive, source of the threat, SIAC made the following finding, critical to the litigation as a whole:

> But the evidence before us demonstrates beyond argument that the threat is not so confined. There are many British nationals already identified – mostly in detention abroad – who fall within the definition of 'suspected international terrorists', and it was clear from the submission made to us that in the opinion of the respondent there are others at liberty in the United Kingdom who could be similarly so defined.[37]

SIAC concluded that the measures were clearly discriminatory on grounds of national origin, and so in violation of Article 14 of the ECHR.

6.3.3 Conclusions on the SIAC Judgment

In its concluding comments, SIAC effectively proposed that the indefinite immigration detention regime put in place by Part 4 was simply 'unlegalisable' in the circumstances. It stated that merely scheduling a derogation to Article 14 'would not assist' because there was no reasonable relation between means and aims. That is, the decision to confine detention to non-citizens is not 'just' a discrimination problem, but raises an insoluble problem of rational connection, fatal to meeting the criteria for a lawful derogation.[38] SIAC's reasoning has the consequence that at least certain forms of discriminatory treatment cannot be provided

[34] cf the majority reasons in *Al-Kateb v Godwin* [2004] HCA 37, (2004) 219 CLR 562, discussed in ch 3, ss 3.2–3.3. See also the dissenting judgments in *Zadvydas v Davis*, 533 US 678 (2001), discussed in ch 1, s 1.1.

[35] *Belmarsh* (SIAC) (n 10) [94]. This proposition is reminiscent of the reasoning in *Minister for Immigration & Multicultural & Indigenous Affairs v Al Masri* [2003] FCAFC 70, (2003) 126 FCR 54, discussed ch 2, p 62.

[36] *Belmarsh* (SIAC) (n 10) [94]. Compare the first two sentences of this extract with *Zadvydas* (n 34) 691–92 (Opinion of the Court). See ch 1, s 1.1.

[37] *Belmarsh* (SIAC) (n 10) [95].

[38] ibid, [96].

for by derogation from the ECHR.[39] To reiterate, a finding that a measure is discriminatory will also signal issues about whether there is a rational connection between aims and means, and vice versa. The absence of a rational connection means that the 'strictly required' criterion for a lawful derogation is not met.

SIAC's reasoning on discrimination and the strictly required criterion clearly demonstrates the distance between the derogation model under the ECHR and the 'extra-legal measures' model.[40] The extra-legal measures model advocates stepping outside the constraints of legality in times of emergency. The derogation model seeks to clarify how one can suspend a right without stepping outside the bounds of legality. On SIAC's reasoning, even accepting the need, borne of emergency, to suspend the right to liberty to allow for administrative detention, government action still needs to be justifiable against legal criteria and, if arbitrary, denied legal sanction.

SIAC's acceptance of the need for indefinite preventive detention, and its holding that the sole flaw with the measures was that they were under-inclusive (where this is registered as a violation of both Article 14 and the strictly required criterion under Article 15), means that its judgment points to an expansion of the detention power. SIAC issued a declaration of incompatibility under the HRA 1998. In its concluding substantive paragraph SIAC stated: 'We recognise, of course, that such a declaration may be of little if any assistance to the appellants should Parliament decide to deal with the discrimination which we perceive to exist by extending the power of detention to nationals.'[41]

To the extent that the House of Lords' decision in *Belmarsh* is criticised as endangering national security on the basis of a misplaced regard for the rights of foreign terrorist suspects, SIAC's reasoning shows how a concern with the effective implementation of national security objectives may achieve the same result. SIAC did not base its decision on the effect of the measures on the liberty of foreign terrorist suspects. It held that any gain in security would justify the detention measures. But the government failed to explain the rational connection between its stated national security objective of meeting the threat from Al-Qaeda, and its decision to detain only non-citizens. The measures were under-inclusive.

SIAC was deferential to the government in that it did not question the government's claim that indefinite detention measures were necessary to meet the threat. At the next stage of the litigation, the Court of Appeal deepened the deference shown by SIAC and effectively removed independent judicial review of the rational connection requirement. The House of Lords and the ECtHR built on SIAC's factual finding that the measures were under-inclusive. Both courts broadened and strengthened the proportionality analysis, with the result that the need for indefinite preventive detention, whether directed at non-citizens, or at everyone within the jurisdiction, was questioned.

[39] See also *Belmarsh* (n 2) [60] (Lord Bingham).
[40] On the two models see ch 5, s 5.7.
[41] *Belmarsh* (SIAC) (n 10) [96].

6.4 *Belmarsh* in the Court of Appeal

The detainees did not have long to enjoy their legal success. SIAC's judgment was handed down on 30 July 2002, and on 25 October of that year the Court of Appeal reversed the decision, ruling for the government.[42] The Court of Appeal judgments were, collectively, notable for their deferential stance. There was a division of labour between the judgments. Lord Woolf CJ developed the implications of a deferential approach and the argument for the measures as immigration measures. Brooke LJ presented the more sweeping claim that, even outside the immigration context, in time of war or public emergency detention measures confined to non-citizens find support in international law.[43]

6.4.1 Lord Woolf CJ – the Erasure of Discrimination

Lord Woolf CJ's judgment is notable in the jurisprudence on the indefinite detention of non-citizens discussed in this book as the most explicit instance of deference to the government undermining the claim that such detention is discriminatory. He held that the derogation was lawful. His reasoning on the second criterion for a lawful derogation under Article 15 of the ECHR can be summarised as follows: the detention measures were strictly required because the Secretary of State said they were. He then appears to hold that because the measure was strictly required, it did no more than was necessary, and so it was not discriminatory. Such reasoning evidences a fundamental confusion. The need for a measure might establish that a discriminatory measure is nonetheless justified. But it is hard to see how it directly removes the claimed discrimination.[44]

Lord Woolf CJ adopted a range of additional points raised by the government to buttress the argument that indefinite immigration detention is not discriminatory. In this last exercise he was joined by Brooke LJ, who engaged in a review of international law, concluding that 'democratic states are entitled to detain non-nationals on national security grounds in time of war or other public emergency'.[45]

Lord Woolf CJ was clear that in the absence of a derogation, the detention measures violated Article 5(1) of the ECHR. In addressing the question of how long it was appropriate to detain a non-citizen subject to a deportation order, he revisited his earlier decision in *Hardial Singh*, stating that a consequence of that decision was that a non-citizen subject to a deportation order cannot be detained under the immigration legislation 'if it is known that a deportation is not

[42] *Belmarsh* (Court of Appeal) (n 1).

[43] The third judgment, of Chadwick LJ, was supportive of points already made in the other judgments, and is noted where relevant.

[44] See the submissions for Liberty recorded in the Queen's Bench report: *Belmarsh* (Court of Appeal) (n 1) 344.

[45] ibid, [130] (Brooke LJ).

possible'.[46] He then turned to *Chahal* and, as SIAC did, summarised its effect using the language of *Hardial Singh*.[47] On grounds of national security, the Secretary of State could 'detain pending deportation a person who did not have the right of abode in this country if he was in the position to carry out the deportation within a reasonable time but not otherwise'.[48] Lord Woolf CJ stated that the intention of the derogation and Part 4 of the ATCSA 2001 was to do 'no more than' reverse the legal effects of *Chahal* on the scope of immigration detention.[49]

SIAC had held that the questions of whether the measures were 'strictly required' and whether they were discriminatory were two sides of the same coin. In its reasoning the Court of Appeal separated these questions, and it treated SIAC as having reached divergent conclusions on the two issues. The Court held that SIAC's ruling against the government had rested on the discrimination point under Article 14 alone. All members of the Court of Appeal stated that SIAC had found *for* the government on the question of whether the measures were strictly required.[50] This is not a supportable reading of SIAC's judgment.[51] There was pressure on the Court of Appeal to read SIAC's judgment as they did on this point, as detailed in the following paragraph.[52]

All members of the Court of Appeal treated the question of whether the measures were 'strictly required' as a question of fact. Under the ATCSA 2001, SIAC's derogation decisions could only be appealed on a question of law. On the Court of Appeal's approach to proportionality, it would appear to follow that no appeal could lie from any determination by SIAC that the measures were not 'strictly required'. The only way for the judges of the Court of Appeal to get around this, consistent with their stated approach to proportionality, was to simply deny that SIAC had found against the government on the 'strictly required' criterion. Whatever the reason for the Court of Appeal's misreading of SIAC's judgment, it had the effect that a decision that was notably deferential to SIAC's findings as a matter of doctrine was anything but deferential in practice.

Lord Woolf CJ quoted and endorsed the following famous judicial statement of Justice Robert Jackson of the United States Supreme Court:

[46] ibid, [16] (Lord Woolf CJ), citing *Hardial Singh* (n 33).

[47] For this point in relation to SIAC see text to n 33 above.

[48] *Belmarsh* (Court of Appeal) (n 1) [17] (Lord Woolf CJ).

[49] ibid, [27] (Lord Woolf CJ), and also [17], [23] and [31]. See also Brooke LJ at [92]: 'The Government made no secret of the fact that one purpose of the measure was to reverse the effect of [*Hardial Singh and Chahal*].'

[50] *Belmarsh* (Court of Appeal) (n 1) [35] (Lord Woolf CJ), [91] (Brooke LJ), [147], [150] (Chadwick LJ).

[51] See the discussion of the SIAC judgment at pp 150–52. See also *Belmarsh* (n 2) [173] (Lord Rodger) beginning: 'Unfortunately, the Court of Appeal misconstrued the decision of SIAC. It by no means constituted a finding of fact in favour of the Secretary of State which foreclosed further consideration of the issue . . .'

[52] The Court of Appeal was not alone in its misreading of SIAC's judgment. Lord Bingham (but not the other members of the majority in *Belmarsh*) shared in the same erroneous reading of SIAC's judgment. See the discussion in the text to n 137 below.

> equality is not merely abstract justice. The framers of the Constitution knew, and we should not forget today, that there is no more effective guaranty against arbitrary and unreasonable government than to require that the principles of law which officials would impose upon a minority must be imposed generally. Conversely, nothing opens the door to arbitrary action so effectively as to allow those officials to pick and choose only a few to whom they will apply legislation and thus to escape the political retribution that might be visited upon them if larger numbers were affected. Courts can take no better measure to assure that laws will be just than to require that laws be equal in operation.[53]

This passage is a succinct, and famed, expression of an instrumental argument for equality. This instrumental argument for equality has been influential in scholarship on the appropriate response to coercive counterterrorism measures, in particular those directed at non-citizens.[54] A persisting puzzle in relation to Lord Woolf CJ's judgment is his endorsement of the above passage at the start of a judgment that is deaf to its message.[55]

Lord Woolf CJ was of the view that the Secretary of State's reliance on immigration detention was to be welcomed as confining to a minimum the number of persons affected by special powers of detention.[56] There were two components to his position. First, consistent with the position adopted by SIAC, deference to the Minister required Lord Woolf CJ to accept that the indefinite preventive detention of the foreign terrorist suspects was needed. From this starting point, the probable outcome of a successful discrimination argument would be the extension of the detention powers to citizens. Lord Woolf CJ treated the idea that the ECHR might require that 'more extensive' action be taken as a *reductio ad absurdum* of the detainees' discrimination argument.[57] However, the idea that equality might demand 'more extensive' allocation of a burden was the central message of the passage from Jackson J's judgment in *Railway Express*, which Lord Woolf CJ quoted.[58]

Where Lord Woolf CJ deepened the deference shown by SIAC was in holding that he must find that 'no more than' the indefinite preventive detention of *foreign* terrorist suspects was necessary. He afforded decisive weight to the Secretary

[53] *Belmarsh* (Court of Appeal) (n 1) [7] (Lord Woolf CJ), quoting *Railway Express Agency Inc v New York*, 336 US 106 (1949), 112–13. Lord Woolf CJ also quoted this passage in a public address to the British Academy, 10 days before the Court of Appeal delivered judgment in *Belmarsh*: see Lord Woolf, 'Human Rights: Have the Public Benefited?', British Academy, Thanks-Offering to Britain Fund Lecture, 15 October 2002, www.britac.ac.uk.

[54] See Neal Katyal, 'Equality in the War on Terror' (2007) 59 *Stanford Law Review* 1365, 1370. This article can be understood as a development of the message conveyed by Jackson J in the text to n 53. Katyal's thesis is discussed in ch 7, s 7.7.

[55] cf *Belmarsh* (n 2) [46] (Lord Bingham).

[56] *Belmarsh* (Court of Appeal) (n 1) [39] (Lord Woolf CJ).

[57] ibid, [49] (Lord Woolf CJ): 'Such a result would not promote human rights . . . There would be an additional intrusion into the rights of nationals so that their position would be the same as non-nationals . . .' See also [53] (Lord Woolf CJ).

[58] cf *Belmarsh* (n 2) [68] (Lord Bingham): 'Any discriminatory measure . . . cannot be justified on the ground that more people would be adversely affected if the measure applied generally.' Note that Lord Woolf CJ sought not to justify discrimination, but to argue that there was no discrimination.

of State's determination as to the extent of the measures necessary for national security:

> Whether the Secretary of State was entitled to come to the conclusion that action was only necessary in relation to non-national suspected terrorists, who could not be deported, is an issue on which it is impossible for this court in this case to differ from the Secretary of State.[59]

If the Secretary of State was of the view that detention of foreigners 'will achieve all that is required', the Court could not demur. Adopting the government's logic, he accepted that compliance with the 'strictly required' criterion for lawful derogation *demanded* that the measures be confined to non-citizens:

> No doubt, by taking action against nationals as well as non-nationals the action from a security point of view would have been more effective. Equally, if the non-nationals were detained notwithstanding the fact that they wanted to leave the country, the action would be more effective. However, on his assessment of the situation, the Secretary of State was debarred from taking more effective action because it was not strictly necessary.[60]

Admirable in his restraint, the Secretary of State had chosen to subject only non-citizens to indefinite detention, allowing them to leave the country if they wished. The Secretary of State's decision is characterised as follows: 'it is only persons who fall within that class [ie, foreigners] who need to be detained in order to meet the emergency.'[61] The Court of Appeal held that it could not go behind this ministerial assessment. The rationale for deference offered is one familiar from *Rehman*, namely the Minister's superior institutional competence in matters of future risk assessment.[62] In reviewing the legality of a derogation from rights, in particular the central requirement of rational connection, as a result of its own reasoning the court was reduced to performing a rubber stamping exercise.

It was this reading of the 'strictly required' criterion that allowed Lord Woolf CJ to reverse the legal significance of SIAC's key factual finding, namely that the threat was not confined to aliens. This finding led SIAC to conclude that confining the measures to non-citizens was under-inclusive, and discriminatory. Lord Woolf CJ countered that SIAC's position was an 'over-simplification because the Secretary of State has come to the conclusion that he can achieve what is necessary by either detaining or deporting only the terrorists who are aliens'.[63] It was 'impossible to differ' from the Secretary of State on the question of whether the detention of non-citizens was all that was strictly required. And if it was strictly required, then there was a match between means and aims such that the measure was not discriminatory. Lord Chadwick, in agreement, stated: 'If the Secretary of State's decision as to what the exigencies of the situation strictly required stands (as I

[59] *Belmarsh* (Court of Appeal) (n 1) [40] (Lord Woolf CJ).
[60] ibid, [45] (Lord Woolf CJ).
[61] ibid, [153] (Chadwick LJ).
[62] On *Rehman* (n 22) see ch 5, s 5.6.
[63] *Belmarsh* (Court of Appeal) (n 1) [47] (Lord Woolf CJ).

think it must), then the argument based on discrimination falls away.'[64] Lord Woolf CJ's argument did not justify discrimination; it made it disappear. While 'the exigencies of the situation' might supply a justification for discrimination, transparency is not served by adopting a deferential approach to the existence of discrimination.

Further, Lord Woolf CJ's reasoning up-ended the review appropriate to derogations. In the ECHR jurisprudence, the grave consequence of a derogation, namely the suspension of a state's obligations with respect to the right derogated from, is held to warrant a 'strictly required' standard more stringent than 'ordinary' proportionality.[65] But Lord Woolf CJ went in the opposite direction, reasoning that the deference traditionally held to be appropriate in the area of national security extended to a deferential assessment of the criteria for lawful derogation. In so doing, his reasoning constituted an instance of a judicial attempt to scale back an innovative means of maintaining a regime of legality (here the criteria for lawful derogation) where there was claimed to be a public emergency. The derogation process was made to conform to a restrictive model of judicial review in the area of national security.

Lord Woolf CJ's arguments from deference were by themselves sufficient to decide the case against the detainees. However, he went on to argue that, in any case, there was an 'objective justification' for the differential treatment of non-citizens.[66] In examining this additional justification, the way his deferential approach was underwritten by a rights-precluding approach to immigration detention becomes apparent. For Lord Woolf CJ, a government *intention* to remove a non-citizen was all that was needed for authority to detain, irrespective of whether that intention could be implemented:

> There is a rational connection between their detention and the purpose which the Secretary of State wishes to achieve. It is a purpose which cannot be applied to nationals, namely detention pending deportation, irrespective of when that deportation will take place.
>
> The fact that detention cannot take place immediately does not mean that it ceases to be part of the objective.[67]

He concluded that there was no discrimination because the non-citizens in detention were not in an analogous position to citizens. The reasons loosely marshalled in support of this conclusion recur in the jurisprudence on indefinite detention of non-citizens. There was the hope that 'the regular review of their positions, which the legislation requires, will result in their detention being of limited duration'.[68] And there was the hard-edged distinction between citizens, who possess a 'right of abode', and non-citizens who can only claim a lesser 'right not to be removed' if

[64] ibid, [153] (Chadwick LJ).
[65] See the discussion of derogations in ch 5, s 5.7.
[66] *Belmarsh* (Court of Appeal) (n 1) [50] (Lord Woolf CJ).
[67] ibid, [52]–[53] (Lord Woolf CJ).
[68] ibid, [51] (Lord Woolf CJ). See also [64] (Lord Woolf CJ).

removal exposes the non-citizen to the risk of treatment that contravenes Article 3 of the ECHR.[69]

Early in his judgment, Lord Woolf CJ stated that to understand the government's arguments that there was no unlawful discrimination, it was necessary to take into account the history and development of the rights of states to detain and exclude aliens at international law. He did not develop such an account himself, instead relying on the reasoning of Brooke LJ, discussed below.

6.4.2 Brooke LJ – the Alien as Enemy

In a significant departure from Lord Woolf CJ's reasoning, Brooke LJ stated that the proposition that 'foreign nationals generally have no right to be in this country and are subject to immigration control' would not suffice to justify indefinite detention measures confined to non-citizens.[70] The proposition, 'though legally accurate, would not, if it stood alone, justify the identification of foreign nationals as being appropriate for discriminatory treatment of the type contemplated by the derogation and Part 4 [of the ATCSA 2001]'.[71] The further considerations determinative for Brooke LJ were his assessment that SIAC went astray in its analysis of the threat posed by foreigners, and the results of his review of international law.

On the first topic, SIAC's analysis of the threat posed by foreigners, Brooke LJ held that SIAC had asked itself the wrong question. He stated that SIAC's factual finding that non-citizens did not constitute the exclusive, or almost exclusive, source of the threat did not address the real point at issue, which was the *qualitative* question of whether non-citizens were the 'predominant' source of the threat. Brooke LJ reasoned: 'five generals and their chiefs of staff may pose a more serious and immediate threat than 5,000 foot soldiers'.[72] The problem with Brooke LJ's reasoning, even if plausible in the abstract, was that it discounted SIAC's factual findings on a purely speculative basis. The Court of Appeal only had access to the 'open' evidence. SIAC had access to both the 'open' and 'closed' evidence. Brooke LJ's reliance on this point furnishes a further example, in addition to the Court of Appeal's misreading of SIAC's findings on proportionality, of the Court of Appeal taking issue with SIAC's findings on the assumption that SIAC had failed to give sufficient weight to government security concerns.

In his argument from international law, Brooke LJ is best understood as accepting a government argument to the effect that *even outside the immigration context*, national security justified targeting non-citizens. The legal position of

[69] ibid, [53], [56] (Lord Woolf CJ). This was in effect an adoption of the government's argument that indefinite detention constitutes a 'fair balance' between protection of the populace and deportation to torture: see text to n 26 above.

[70] The proposition is taken from a statement by Mr Whalley, authorised to give evidence on behalf of the Home Secretary, identifying reasons for confining the indefinite detention measures to non-citizens: See *Belmarsh* (Court of Appeal) (n 1) [102].

[71] ibid, [104] (Brooke LJ).

[72] ibid, [103] (Brooke LJ).

non-citizens in a time of public emergency was clearly presented as an exception to the development of restrictions on a state's power over non-citizens, structured ever more explicitly with reference to human rights norms and an accompanying proportionality analysis. Brooke LJ's account of the development of restrictions on state power over non-citizens is a concise characterisation of the international law position drawn on by Kirby J in dissent in *Al-Kateb*, and by Lord Bingham in *Belmarsh*:

> What emerges from the efforts of the international community to introduce orderly arrangements for controlling the power of detention of non-nationals is a distinct movement away from the doctrine of the inherent power of the state to control the treatment of non-nationals within its borders as it will towards a regime, founded on modern international human rights norms, which is infused by the principle that any measures that are restrictive of liberty, whether they relate to nationals or non-nationals, must be such as are prescribed by law and necessary in a democratic society. The state's power to detain must be related to a recognised object and purpose, and there must be a reasonable relationship of proportionality between the ends and the means.[73]

But then Brooke LJ introduced an exception:

> On the other hand, both customary international law and the international treaties by which this country is bound expressly reserve the power of a state in time of war or similar public emergency to detain aliens on grounds of national security when it would not necessarily detain its own nationals on those grounds.[74]

Brooke LJ concluded his review of international law with the following: 'the principle that democratic states are entitled to detain non-nationals on national security grounds in time of war or other public emergency is one which is very firmly established.'[75] I defer a discussion of Brooke LJ's reasoning on international law, replicated in the Attorney-General's submission in the House of Lords, to the analysis of the House of Lords' reasoning in *Belmarsh*.[76] There Lord Bingham considered, and rejected, the principle Brooke LJ held to be 'very firmly established'.

6.4.3 Conclusions on *Belmarsh* in the Court of Appeal

The Court of Appeal redrew the rationale for, and the practice of, immigration detention. The concept of immigration detention pending removal contained in the *Hardial Singh* principles was replaced by the understanding that immigration detention could, by way of derogation, be transformed into a general mechanism for the protection of citizens from non-citizens. The legal thinking that supported such an expansion had a number of mutually reinforcing strands. Centrally, there

[73] ibid, [130] (Brooke LJ). On Kirby J's characterisation of international law in *Al-Kateb* see ch 3, s 3.6. On Lord Bingham's characterisation of international law in *Belmarsh* see pp 176–79.
[74] ibid.
[75] ibid, [131] (Brooke LJ).
[76] See pp 176–79.

was the argument from deference voiced by Lord Woolf CJ, which held that it was impossible for the Court to question the Minister's claim that the situation required 'no more than' the detention of non-citizens. As what the government delivered was no more or less than what was strictly required, there was no discrimination. The claim of discrimination was also addressed directly with an 'objective justification' for differential treatment. A non-citizen against whom a deportation order had been issued had no right to be 'at large' within the community and on that basis was not in an analogous position to a terrorist suspect who is a British national. And finally, there is the more sweeping holding, developed by Brooke LJ, that differential treatment, including detention, of non-citizens is justified under international law in a time of public emergency or war. Each of these three strands was separated out, and rejected, by the majority of the House of Lords.

6.5 The Certification Proceedings

As noted in introducing the legislation, Part 4 of the ATCSA 2001 provided for two avenues of appeal, in relation to 'certification' and 'derogation' matters respectively.[77] The above decisions of SIAC and the Court of Appeal involved challenges to the lawfulness of the derogation from Article 5(1) of the ECHR, and the legislative provisions that relied on that derogation. In between the Court of Appeal's judgment, handed down on 25 October 2002, and the House of Lords' decision on 16 December 2004, the other statutory avenue of appeal was active, with numerous challenges to the individual certification decisions heard and determined by SIAC and the Court of Appeal.[78] Of the 16 individuals who brought challenges to their certification, only one had his certificate cancelled by SIAC.

In one of the certification proceedings, bail was granted to the applicant known as 'G' because of the damage that detention was inflicting on his mental health.[79] That the onerous conditions on G's release were adequate to meet security concerns was noted by both Lord Bingham in the House of Lords in *Belmarsh*,[80] and singled out for comment by the ECtHR in *A v United Kingdom*.[81] The system of 'control orders' introduced in response to the House of Lords' decision in *Belmarsh*, discussed in the next chapter, section 7.2, was modelled on the bail conditions granted by SIAC in *G*.[82]

[77] See p 147.

[78] For a thorough overview of these certification challenges before SIAC see the ECtHR's judgment in *A v United Kingdom* (n 12), under the heading '1. The Circumstances of the Case – D. The certification proceedings: the individual determinations', paras 29–77.

[79] *G v Secretary of State for the Home Department* [2004] UKSIAC 2/2002, Bail Application SCB/10.

[80] *Belmarsh* (n 2) [35] (Lord Bingham).

[81] *A v United Kingdom* (n 12) paras 78–81.

[82] See Joint Committee on Human Rights, *Counter-Terrorism Policy and Human Rights: Draft Prevention of Terrorism Act 2005 (Continuance in force of sections 1 to 9) Order 2006, Twelfth Report of*

6.6 *Belmarsh* in the House of Lords

In *Belmarsh*, a House of Lords majority reaffirmed SIAC's decision, overruling the Court of Appeal to hold that the detention measures were not 'strictly required' and were discriminatory.[83] The House of Lords quashed the Derogation Order and issued a declaration that the detention provisions contained in Part 4 of the ATCSA 2001 were incompatible with Articles 5 and 14 of the ECHR.

In evaluating the House of Lords' reasoning, regard has to be had to the government concessions, referred to in section 6.2. The government conceded that in the absence of a lawful derogation, the detention measures contravened Article 5(1)(f) of the ECHR.[84] The better view is that the members of the House of Lords did not rest their reasoning on this concession. They did, if not expressly, consider whether the detention measures were compatible with Article 5(1)(f) before considering the validity of the derogation. The majority held that the detention measures were not compatible with the immigration exception in Article 5(1)(f).[85] Further, the government accepted that the validity of the derogation in domestic law depended on the validity of the derogation to which it gave effect in international law, as assessed against the criteria in Article 15.[86]

6.6.1 The Existence of a Public Emergency

My account of *Belmarsh* focuses on the 'strictly required' criterion under Article 15 of the ECHR. With the famous exception of Lord Hoffmann, all members of the House of Lords held for the government on the first criterion, concerning the existence of a 'public emergency threatening the life of the nation'.[87] Lord Hoffmann held that this criterion had not been met, stating: 'The real threat to the life of the nation, in the sense of a people living in accordance with its traditional laws and political values, comes not from terrorism but from laws such as these.'[88]

Session 2005–06 (2005–06, HL 122, HC 915) 62 (Appendix 7, Annex 2). In a witness statement by Gareth Pierce, annexed to a submission from Liberty, a skeleton argument of the government was quoted on the proposals that became control orders: 'Those proposals will not include detention in prison but will allow controls of the sort effected by SIAC via bail in the case of G.'

[83] Lord Bingham, Lord Nicholls, Lord Hope, Lord Scott, Lord Rodger, Baroness Hale and Lord Carswell. Lord Hoffmann was the eighth member of the majority, but on a different basis from the other seven. He found that the first criterion for lawful derogation under Art 15(1), the existence of a public emergency, was not satisfied. Lord Walker was the sole dissenter.

[84] See *Belmarsh* (n 2) [51] (Lord Bingham).

[85] See ibid, [8]–[9] (Lord Bingham), [103]–[105] (Lord Hope), [155] (Lord Scott), [163] (Lord Rodger), [222] (Baroness Hale). See also [97] for Lord Hoffmann's comment to the same effect. In *A v United Kingdom* (n 12), the ECtHR stated that the House of Lords had concluded that the detention measures did not fall within the immigration exception set out in Art 5(1)(f): para 17, para 155.

[86] See s 6.2.

[87] *Belmarsh* (n 2) [95]–[96] (Lord Hoffmann).

[88] ibid, [97] (Lord Hoffmann).

The two criteria – the 'existence of a public emergency' and the 'strictly required' criterion – are not completely independent. The second criterion asks what is 'strictly required *by the exigencies of the situation*' (my emphasis), where this points toward an inquiry into the nature of the emergency.[89] The reasoning of the members of the House of Lords on what is 'strictly required' occurred against a backdrop of widespread scepticism about the existence of a public emergency. To ignore these reservations would be to ignore the considerations at work in the opinions. Among the seven members of the majority who held *for* the government on the existence of a public emergency, this holding was delivered 'not without misgivings' (Lord Bingham),[90] and 'not without hesitation' (Lord Rodger),[91] rising to 'very great doubt' on the part of Lord Scott.[92] Lord Scott stated:

> For my part I do not doubt that there is a terrorist threat to this country and I do not doubt that great vigilance is necessary . . . to guard against terrorist attacks. But I do have very great doubt whether the 'public emergency' is one that justifies the description of 'threatening the life of the nation'.[93]

A more developed consideration of how the *nature* of the emergency impacts on the consideration of the other criteria under Article 15 of the ECHR was provided by Lord Hope. He accepted that 'questions whether there is an emergency and whether it threatens the life of the nation are pre-eminently for the executive and for Parliament'.[94] But this did not preclude an inquiry into the nature of the emergency and how that bore on the measures required to meet it. Lord Hope noted that the present emergency is likely to continue for many years, rendering preventive detention that responds to the emergency indefinite and lengthy.[95] The nature of the emergency informed Lord Hope's understanding of the measures claimed to be 'strictly required'.

6.6.2 The Strictly Required Criterion

Lord Bingham wrote the leading judgment in *Belmarsh*, and I centre my account on it, drawing on other judgments where appropriate. He titled his discussion on the second criterion for lawful derogation 'Proportionality', and opened with a statement of the prevailing domestic British criteria for such analysis, from *de Freitas v Permanent Secretary of Ministry of Agriculture, Lands and Housing*.[96] The

[89] ibid, [116] (Lord Hope).
[90] ibid, [26] (Lord Bingham).
[91] ibid, [165] (Lord Rodger).
[92] ibid, [111]–[112].
[93] ibid, [154].
[94] ibid, [116] (Lord Hope).
[95] ibid, [122] (Lord Hope).
[96] *de Freitas* (n 21); approved in *Belmarsh* (n 2) [30] (Lord Bingham) and subsequently endorsed by five members of the House of Lords in *Huang v Secretary of State for the Home Department* (n 21) [19].

de Freitas criteria provide that, in determining whether an infringement of a right is arbitrary or excessive, the court must ask

> whether, (i) the legislative objective is sufficiently important to justify limiting a fundamental right; (ii) the measures designed to meet the legislative objective are rationally connected to it; and (iii) the means used to impair the right or freedom are no more than is necessary to accomplish the objective.[97]

Lord Bingham stated: 'This approach is close to that laid down by the Supreme Court of Canada in . . . *Oakes* . . . and [*Libman v Quebec*].'[98] I address the issue of Lord Bingham's adoption of an 'ordinary' proportionality test, rather than a heightened 'strict necessity' standard, in part (c) of this section.

(a) Rejection of a Case-by-Case Analysis

As noted above, Part 4 of the ATCSA 2001 provided for two grounds of appeal.[99] One related to challenges to individual certification decisions. These challenges necessarily involved detailed consideration of the evidence against the individual detainees. The second ground of appeal, under section 30, related to 'derogation matters'. This second ground of appeal went to the lawfulness of the detention power (via the lawfulness of a derogation from the otherwise applicable Convention right).

A feature of the government's argument in the *Belmarsh* litigation was its reiterated preference for matters to be considered on a case-by-case basis. The reasons for this are obvious. Any ruling against the government emerging from such an assessment would be limited to the particular case, with the government power to hold non-citizens in indefinite detention preserved.[100] Lord Nicholls succinctly summarised the House of Lords' response:

> Nor is the vice of indefinite detention cured by the provision made for independent review by [SIAC]. The commission is well placed to check that the Secretary of State's powers are exercised properly [a reference to the certification review process]. But what is in question on these appeals is the existence and width of the statutory powers, not the way they are being exercised.[101]

That it was the existence and width of the statutory powers that were at issue blunts objections that the House of Lords was too ready to assume that removal

[97] *de Freitas* (n 21) 80.

[98] In *Huang* (n 21) Lord Bingham made clear that the *de Freitas* test derives from Dickson CJ's judgment in *R v Oakes* [1986] 1 SCR 103. The doctrinal consequence is that the *de Freitas* test is seen to include the fourth element of proportionality spelt out in *Oakes*, namely that 'the impact of fundamental rights needs to be balanced against the interests of society'. Thus, even where a measure is the least intrusive way of securing an aim (and is rationally connected to that aim), it may still be found to be disproportionate.

[99] See p 147.

[100] The government's record in relation to the certification decisions that preceded the House of Lords' judgment was probably not a matter of indifference either. Of the 16 individuals who challenged their certification, only one had his certification cancelled by SIAC: see s 6.5 above.

[101] *Belmarsh* (n 2) [82] (Lord Nicholls). See also [141] (Lord Scott), [220] (Baroness Hale).

was in fact 'impossible' and that the link between detention and removal had been severed.[102] In *Belmarsh*, their lordships focused on the existence of a statutory power to hold a non-citizen in indefinite detention. They were not directly concerned with whether, in an individual case, the length of detention, and prospects of removal, combined so as to contravene Convention rights.

(b) Deference

Following the success of the strategy before the Court of Appeal, the Attorney-General 'directed the weight of his submission to challenging the standard of judicial review' to be applied to the question of whether the measures were strictly necessary.[103] As explained under the preceding heading, the deference at issue was that which the courts should show to Parliament. It was not the deference, or conversely, intensity of review, appropriate to review of executive decisions. The dispute between the detainees and the government was one between claims premised on the existence of a fundamental right to liberty, extending to non-citizens, and government insistence on a 'discretionary area of judgment properly belonging to the democratic organs of the state'.[104] The close scrutiny appropriate to rights was opposed to a conception of national security as largely immune from judicial review. The government's central argument for such immunity was that contained in Lord Hoffmann's postscript in *Rehman*: 'such decisions [on threats to national security], with serious potential results for the community, require a legitimacy which can only be conferred by entrusting them to persons responsible to the community through the democratic process.'[105] Lord Bingham responded as follows:

> the appellants are . . . entitled to invite the courts to review, on proportionality grounds, the Derogation Order and the compatibility with the Convention of section 23 and the courts are not effectively precluded by any doctrine of deference from scrutinising the issues raised.

The central theme of Lord Bingham's response to the Attorney-General was that the Court was implementing a constitutional – and hence fully democratic – mandate. After acknowledging the distinct institutional competences of the executive and the courts, Lord Bingham stated:

> But the function of independent judges charged to interpret and apply the law is universally recognised as a cardinal feature of the modern democratic state, a cornerstone of the rule of law itself. The Attorney-General is fully entitled to insist on the proper

[102] For such an objection see John Finnis, 'Nationality, Alienage and Constitutional Principle' (2007) 123 *LQR* 417, 424–29.

[103] *Belmarsh* (n 2) [37] (Lord Bingham).

[104] ibid. The phrase 'discretionary area of judgment' was first used in A Lester and D Pannick (eds), *Human Rights Law and Practice* (London, Butterworths, 1999). The phrase was then adopted by Lord Hope in *R v Director of Public Prosecutions, ex parte Kebilene* [1999] UKHL 43, [2000] 2 AC 326, 381 in a passage quoted by Lord Bingham at [39].

[105] *Rehman* (n 22) [56] (Lord Hoffmann).

> limits of judicial authority, but he is wrong to stigmatise judicial decision-making as in some way undemocratic.[106]

This stigma was held to be particularly inappropriate in the context of the general legislative conferral of jurisdiction contained in the HRA 1998,[107] and the more specific legislative conferral constituted by the right of appeal on 'derogation matters' under Part 4 of the ATCSA 2001.[108] Lord Bingham's judgment did not preclude the operation of democratic considerations in deference. But he rejected the proposition that they foreclose judicial scrutiny of certain subject matters, amongst them national security.

Lord Bingham quoted a statement by Professor Jowell that under the HRA 1998, 'The courts are charged with delineating the boundaries of a rights-based democracy'.[109] The short 'analysis' piece by Jowell from which the quotation was taken provides a useful means of developing Lord Bingham's understanding of the rationale for judicial review. While a judge may of course select a choice phrase that suits his or her purposes without regard for context, aspects of the relevant paragraph from Jowell resonate with the tenor of Lord Bingham's reasoning in *Belmarsh*. Jowell's subject is the 'democratic principle' expressed by Lord Hoffmann in the *Rehman* decision.[110] It is by way of response to Lord Hoffmann that Jowell states, with reference to the changes wrought by the HRA 1998:

> Even if . . . the HRA in no way intends any expectation of a changed constitutional order, the courts have no need to expose their jugular whenever Parliament or its agents speak on the matter of public interest. Parliament's continuing power to defy the courts' declarations on Convention rights does not impinge on the courts' power to define the scope of those rights. The courts are charged by Parliament with delineating the boundaries of a rights-based democracy. In doing so, they ought not in any way to be influenced by the fact that Parliament may in the end disregard their pronouncements. Nor should they prefer the authority of Parliament or other bodies on the ground that they represent the popular will, or are directly or indirectly accountable to the electorate.[111]

The quotation Lord Bingham adopted in *Belmarsh* nestles in the middle of this paragraph from Jowell.[112] In this paragraph Jowell retreats from the bolder statements he makes earlier in his article, which speak of a 'changed constitutional

[106] *Belmarsh* (n 2) [42] (Lord Bingham).

[107] ibid.

[108] ibid, [176] (Lord Rodger): 'If the provisions of section 30 of the [ATCSA 2001] are to have any real meaning, deference to the views of the Government and Parliament on the derogation cannot be taken too far.'

[109] ibid, [42] (Lord Bingham), citing Jeffrey Jowell, 'Judicial Deference: Servility, Civility or Institutional Capacity?' [2003] *PL* 592, 597.

[110] See ch 5, s 5.6.

[111] Jowell (n 109) 597.

[112] See also *Belmarsh* (n 2) [41] (Lord Bingham), citing *International Transport Roth GmbH v Secretary of State for the Home Department* [2002] EWCA Civ 158, [2003] QB 728, [27] (Simon Brown LJ): 'the courts' role under the [HRA 1998] is as the guardian of human rights. It cannot abdicate this responsibility.'

order'. Here, Jowell's emphasis is on indications of a broad legislative intent to provide for rights-based judicial review, in the form of the grants of jurisdiction contained in the HRA 1998. In *Belmarsh* this was conjoined with the grant of appeal rights in section 30 of the ATCSA 2001. The quoted paragraph outlines Jowell's conservative alternative to a 'changed constitutional order'. In its reference to the courts' role in 'delineating the boundaries' despite the fact that 'Parliament may in the end disregard their pronouncements', it aligns well with both the holding and the remedy in *Belmarsh.* At a number of points in the *Belmarsh* judgments, this understanding of the judicial role was supported by claims that in exercising judicial review under these provisions 'British courts are performing their traditional role of watching over the liberty of everyone within their jurisdiction, regardless of nationality'.[113]

The statements from *Belmarsh* on democratic grounds for judicial deference have garnered significant attention. Lord Bingham's 'most eloquent and magisterial judicial rebuke' to the Attorney-General's claim to submissive deference is famous, as is Lord Steyn's comment on it.[114] This attention to democratic grounds for deference should not obscure the reasoning on the issue of institutional competence.[115] In considering institutional competence, the majority's treatment of the first and second criteria under Article 15 of the ECHR, the 'public emergency' and 'strictly required' criteria, should be compared.[116] In addressing the question of the existence of a public emergency, Lord Bingham referred to a demarcation of functions between the courts and the political bodies. On the question of the existence of a public emergency, 'great weight should be given to the judgment of the Home Secretary, his colleagues and Parliament . . . because they were called on to exercise a pre-eminently political judgment'.[117] This weight was characterised as a matter of the institutional competence of the different institutions to make factual predictions as to what terrorists might do, when, and with what consequences.[118]

By way of contrast, the assessment of whether the measures were 'strictly required by the exigencies of the situation' centred on a logical analysis of the

[113] *Belmarsh* (n 2) [178] (Lord Rodger). See also eg [36], [48] (Lord Bingham). In addition, the whole tenor of Lord Hoffmann's judgment was that the government's declaration of emergency was antithetical to British traditions.

[114] Lord Steyn, '2000–2005: Laying the Foundations of Human Rights Law in the United Kingdom' (2005) 4 *European Human Rights Law Review* 349, 350.

[115] The close relationship between issues of institutional and democratic deference was attested to by Lord Bingham's cross-references in *Belmarsh* (n 2) between his central statement on the 'democratic principle' advanced by the Attorney-General at [42] and his statement at [29] in which he outlined the relative institutional competency of the political bodies on the question of the existence of a public emergency. As stated by Hunt: 'Questions of institutional competence are inseparable from deeper normative questions of institutional design.' Murray Hunt, 'Sovereignty's Blight: Why Contemporary Public Law Needs the Concept of "Due Deference"' in Nicholas Bamforth and Peter Leyland (eds), *Public Law in Multi-Layered Constitution* (Oxford, Hart Publishing, 2003) 337, 350.

[116] See Mark Elliott, *Administrative Law: Text and Materials*, 4th edn (Oxford, Oxford University Press, 2011) 273–78.

[117] *Belmarsh* (n 2) [29] (Lord Bingham).

[118] ibid.

relationship between the legislative objectives of the measures and their effects.[119] The government's attempted justification of the relationship between aims and effects was amenable to judicial analysis. The majority concluded that the government had not satisfactorily addressed the issues of rational connection that had earlier been determinative in SIAC's reasoning. If the threat emanated from both citizens and non-citizens, why were powers of indefinite detention only pursued in relation to the latter? And if the detainees posed a threat sufficient to justify their indefinite detention, why were they free to leave? The debate on these questions did not centre on matters of national security expertise. It turned on normative questions about the legal position of non-citizens and the nature of immigration detention.

Lord Bingham marshalled an array of factors that offset deference to the government in matters of national security, justifying scrutiny of the measures on proportionality grounds where indefinite detention was at issue. The points he raised in this connection included:

- the particular expertise of the courts in relation to the requirements of a fair trial;[120]
- the fact that the ECHR is predicated on national courts playing the primary role in protecting the rights under the convention;[121]
- the greater intensity of review required under a proportionality approach, as compared to the traditional Wednesbury unreasonableness standard;[122] and
- the need to learn from past instances in which national security has been used to shield the persecution of a minority from scrutiny. Here he quoted from a decision which overturned the original conviction of Mr Korematsu, a Japanese American detained in World War II, on the basis that the government had knowingly submitted false information to the court that had a material impact on the court's decision.[123]

The last of these points raises the question of the reliability and drivers of the political branches' decisions in matters of national security, and the need

[119] See Elliott (n 116) 276–77.

[120] On this point, weight was given to Canadian authority, ie *Libman v Attorney-General of Quebec* [1997] 3 SCR 569; and to La Forest J's dissent in *RJR MacDonald Inc v Attorney-General of Canada* [1995] 3 SCR 199.

[121] cf Lord Walker in dissent, who applied the European 'margin of appreciation' in the *domestic* context: *Belmarsh* (n 2) [196]–[197]. The ECtHR upheld the *Belmarsh* majority's understanding of the 'margin of appreciation' in *A v United Kingdom* (n 12) para 184: 'The doctrine of margin of appreciation has always been meant as a tool to define relations between the domestic authorities and the Court. It cannot have the same application to the relations between the organs of State at the domestic level.'

[122] *Belmarsh* (n 2) [39]–[41] (Lord Bingham). See also n 18 above.

[123] ibid, [41]. The decision quoted is *Korematsu v United States*, 584 F Supp 1406 (1984) (United States District Court, Northern District of California), in which a writ of *coram nobis* was issued, overturning Mr Korematsu's original conviction in 1944 on the basis outlined in the text. The passage Lord Bingham took from the 1984 *Korematsu* decision stated that the United States Supreme Court's 1944 decision stood 'as a caution that in times of distress the shield of military necessity and national security must not be used to protect governmental actions from close scrutiny and accountability'. The negative example of *Korematsu* was also cited by Kirby J in his dissent in *Al-Kateb* (n 34) [163].

to require that claims about the threat and the effectiveness of the response be justified.[124]

In addition, other members of the House of Lords explicitly advanced minority protection as a rationale for judicial review. Lord Hope stated:

> We are dealing with actions taken on behalf of society as a whole which affect the rights and freedoms of the individual. This is where the courts may legitimately intervene, to ensure that the actions taken are proportionate. It is an essential safeguard, if individual rights and freedoms are to be protected in a democratic society which respects the principle that minorities, however unpopular, have the same rights as the majority.[125]

The issue of minority protection underlay a range of other concerns and arguments in the judgments,[126] but here Lord Hope expressly raised it to address the legitimacy of judicial review.

A significant feature of the *Belmarsh* majority judgments, particularly that of Lord Bingham, is the extensive reference made to the decisions and reports of parliamentary committees, international bodies and officials. Lord Bingham firmly situated the House of Lords' reasoning within a wider range of concerns and issues raised by bodies other than the courts. The House of Lords' reasoning drew contributions from, and contributed to, a wider, shared concern with rights and the appropriate use of public power.

(c) *The Applicable Standard of Review*

For the reasons given in the preceding section, Lord Bingham rejected the government's arguments that the derogation should effectively be immune from judicial scrutiny. He applied the 'ordinary' proportionality standard from *de Freitas*. He should have applied a higher standard, as did other members of the court, appropriate to the derogation context. For the reasons given when discussing derogations in chapter five, section 5.7, the 'strict necessity' criterion under Article 15 of the ECHR is a heightened standard, under which a government's latitude to choose between different measures to achieve the stated aim is more restricted than under an 'ordinary' proportionality analysis. The 'strict necessity' standard requires that the government choose the least intrusive possibility, and so makes it extremely difficult for broadly framed powers to meet the criterion. This heightened standard was applied by other members of the majority.[127]

[124] cf Mark Tushnet, 'Defending *Korematsu*? Reflections on Civil Liberties in Wartime' in Mark Tushnet (ed), *The Constitution in Wartime: Beyond Alarmism or Complacency* (Durham, NC, Duke University Press, 2005) 124. For scepticism about the government's security claims in *Belmarsh* see the text to n 90 above and following.

[125] *Belmarsh* (n 2) [108] (Lord Hope). See also [237] (Baroness Hale).

[126] From the reasons why prohibitions on discrimination inject a 'vital' discipline into human rights law: ibid, [136] (Lord Hope), to the argument that a requirement that burdens be equally distributed constitutes an effective guard against democratic pathologies: [46] (Lord Bingham).

[127] ibid, [124] and [121] (Lord Hope). See also [155] (Lord Scott), [172] (Lord Rodger), [227], [231] (Baroness Hale).

Lord Bingham's adoption of this 'lower' proportionality standard did not, in the circumstances, make a difference. The government did not meet the lower standard. There was no need to determine whether less intrusive measures were available because the government did not offer any explanation of why suspected terrorists who were nationals were not subject to the indefinite detention power.[128] No evidence was offered to rebut the inference that less intrusive measures were effective in relation to British nationals. In these circumstances, the indefinite detention of non-citizens did not meet the requirements of an ordinary proportionality test.[129]

SIAC had held that the decision to confine the measures to non-citizens was irrational.[130] SIAC found against the government at the second stage of the *de Freitas* proportionality test. The majority of the House of Lords additionally found against the government at the third stage of the test: that is, the measures went further than was necessary to meet the legislative objective.

The starting point for the House of Lords, as for SIAC, was to consider the government's decision to use immigration measures to address the relevant security problem. Lord Bingham quoted from the view of a parliamentary committee: 'Some of these problems arise because Part 4 [of the ATCSA 2001] is an adaptation of existing immigration and asylum legislation, rather than being designed expressly for the purpose of meeting the threat from international terrorism.'[131] Contrary to SIAC, Lord Bingham held that the problem was not that the measures did not extend far enough, in not allowing for the detention of *all* international terrorist suspects, non-citizens *and* citizens. The problem was that, if the detention measures were not necessary for citizens who were international terrorist suspects, the government had provided no evidence to rebut the inference that they were not necessary for suspects who were non-citizens either.[132] This had the consequence that the legal objection to the derogation could not simply be addressed by extending the measures to citizens.

As an additional ground for finding both a lack of rational connection and a lack of proportionality between aim and means, the majority regarded the allowance for simple expulsion as a perplexing response to dangerous, international terrorists.[133] It potentially left the suspects free to operate outside the United Kingdom. The majority perceived that 'the choice of an immigration measure to address a security problem had the inevitable result of failing adequately to address that problem'.[134]

128 ibid, [78] (Lord Nicholls), [129] (Lord Hope).

129 See also Beatson (n 13) para 3-165.

130 *Belmarsh* (SIAC) (n 10) [52], [79]–[96].

131 *Belmarsh* (n 2) [34] (Lord Bingham), citing Privy Counsellor Review Committee, *Anti-Terrorism, Crime and Security Act 2001 Review: Report* (HC 2003–04, 100-I) para 186 (*Newton Committee Report*).

132 *Belmarsh* (n 2) [43] (Lord Bingham). See also [138] (Lord Hope), [158] (Lord Scott), [178], [183], [188]–[189] (Lord Rodger), [228], [231] (Baroness Hale). See also [97] (Lord Hoffmann).

133 ibid, [44] (Lord Bingham).

134 ibid, [43] (Lord Bingham).

The majority held that the detention powers were not rationally connected to tackling the threat from Al-Qaeda, in that they allowed international terrorist suspects who were citizens to go free, and for the freedom of non-citizen terrorist suspects post-expulsion. And further, the powers offended against the requirement that the means be 'no more than are necessary' to the aim. As Baroness Hale stated:

> The conclusion has to be that it is not necessary to lock up the nationals. Other ways must be found to contain the threat which they present. And if it is not necessary to lock up the nationals it cannot be necessary to lock up the foreigners. It is not strictly required by the exigencies of the situation.[135]

Lord Bingham had one final matter to deal with in relation to the 'strictly required' criterion. He saw himself as having to overcome a finding by SIAC *for* the government on the 'strictly required' criterion. As discussed in relation to the Court of Appeal's reasoning, this was an erroneous reading of SIAC's judgment on that criterion.[136] The same erroneous reading had markedly different consequences as between Lord Bingham and the Court of Appeal, due to Lord Bingham's rejection of the idea that proportionality was a question of pure fact, not amenable to review.[137] Lord Bingham held that the intensity of review involved where the question was one of indefinite detention without charge was sufficient to warrant a re-examination of SIAC's reasoning on proportionality. He held that to treat questions of proportionality as pure questions of fact (as the Court of Appeal purported to do) would effectively 'emasculate' the courts' duty to protect Convention rights by treating the judgment of the court at first instance as conclusively precluding further review.[138]

6.6.3 Discrimination

(a) The Immigration Context

The majority of Lord Bingham's reasoning was addressed to the question of whether the detention was discriminatory, in violation of Article 14 of the ECHR.

[135] ibid, [231] (Baroness Hale). See also [76] (Lord Nicholls), [129] (Lord Hope), [188] (Lord Rodger).

[136] See text to n 51 above and following.

[137] *Belmarsh* (n 2) [44] (Lord Bingham).

[138] ibid. The question of where review of proportionality falls on the law/fact continuum has continued to be a live issue in judicial review of SIAC and decisions in the national security area more generally. SIAC's reasoning on the strictly required criterion in *Belmarsh* was that it was *irrational* to limit the detention power to foreign terrorists: *Belmarsh* (n 2) [174] (Lord Rodger). In *RB (Algeria) v Secretary of State for the Home Department* [2009] UKHL 10, [2010] 2 AC 110, [71] (Lord Phillips) the House of Lords clarified that rationality review of a proportionality finding was permissible, because it was not a review of the weight given to the facts, but of the rationality of the conclusion arrived at. And see [73]: 'SIAC's conclusions could only be attacked on the ground that they failed to pay due regard to some rule of law, had regard to irrelevant matters, failed to have regard to relevant matters, or were otherwise irrational.'

The appellants had objected that the detention measures were discriminatory, as they singled out those without British nationality. The Attorney-General's primary line of response was that the measures were appropriately characterised as *immigration* detention, and accordingly it was entirely appropriate to draw a distinction between citizens and non-citizens.

The signal achievement of the House of Lords in *Belmarsh* was to treat the government's choice of immigration powers as a reviewable matter, and to reject the government's characterisation of the detention provisions as immigration measures. The majority resisted the government's account of the scope of the immigration exception to liberty. They further rejected the view that protection of the citizenry from non-citizens constitutes an independent rationale for the detention of aliens.

The reasoning on immigration had two aspects. The first was a focus on the government's stated national security objectives. The second was an affirmation of the value of equality before the law. In relation to the first aspect, Lord Bingham structured his reasons in terms of the aims and effects of the legislative provisions, following ECHR case law on the correct approach to Article 14.[139] In its consideration of the aims and effects of the legislative provisions, the House of Lords majority reasoned, as had SIAC, from the national security objectives relied upon by the government. The use of immigration law was a choice to be evaluated against those objectives. When so evaluated, the reliance on immigration measures presented as an arbitrary choice, motivated by considerations that detracted from attainment of the legislative objectives. Lord Bingham started from the proposition that the *aim* of the detention measures was to protect the United Kingdom from Al-Qaeda terrorism. The *effect* was to deprive only non-citizens of their liberty. In circumstances where the threat presented by suspected international terrorists did not depend on their nationality or immigration status, there was a mismatch between aim and effect that established discrimination.[140]

The second aspect of Lord Bingham's reasoning, namely the commitment to equality before the law, was rooted in national, comparative and international legal sources and traditions. He began with Hersch Lauterpacht's statement that 'The claim to equality before the law is in a substantial sense the most fundamental of the rights of man'.[141] He quoted the passage from Jackson J in *Railway Express*, already encountered in Lord Woolf CJ's judgment,[142] on the beneficial political effects of requiring that measures imposed on a minority be extended to the general population. The reasoning of the House of Lords majority was in accordance with Jackson J's message. Lord Bingham also quoted *Khawaja*'s affirmation that 'Every person within the jurisdiction enjoys the equal application of

[139] *Belmarsh* (n 2) [49] (Lord Bingham), quoting from the *Belgian Linguistic Case (No 2)* (1968) 1 EHRR 252, para 10.

[140] *Belmarsh* (n 2) [54] (Lord Bingham).

[141] ibid, [45], citing Hersch Lauterpacht, *An International Bill of the Rights of Man* (New York, Columbia University Press, 1945) 115.

[142] *Belmarsh* (n 2) [46] (Lord Bingham), citing *Railway Express* (n 53) 112–13. For the passage see text to n 53 above.

our laws. There is no distinction between British nationals and others.'[143] Lord Bingham drew on these sources, and other British and European cases, as evidence of the law's rejection of the government's proposition that an immigration characterisation constitutes full justification for the decision to detain only those terrorist suspects lacking British nationality.

The majority identified that the government's proposal was predicated on the understanding that non-citizens had lesser liberty rights than citizens, where this lesser position was a function of alienage, independent of any proportionate link with an immigration purpose. And they suggested that measures directed at non-citizens were chosen on the grounds that they were more politically sustainable. Lord Bingham referred to the report of the Newton Committee, established under section 122 of the ATCSA 2001 to review the Act's operation.[144] The Newton Committee had expressed concern about the limited efficacy of powers directed only at those terrorist suspects who were foreigners.[145] The Secretary of State had responded:

> While it would be possible to seek other powers to detain British citizens who may be involved in international terrorism it would be a very grave step. The Government believes that such draconian powers would be difficult to justify. Experience has demonstrated the dangers of such an approach and the damage it can do to community cohesion and thus to the support from all parts of the public that is so essential to countering the terrorist threat.[146]

This response by the Secretary of State served as something of a lightning rod for criticism of the government's position in the *Belmarsh* judgments.[147] The gist of these judicial responses had a precursor in the Joint Committee on Human Rights' response to the above, 'extraordinary' statement from the government:[148]

> The Government's explanation in its discussion paper of its reluctance to seek the same powers in relation to UK nationals appears to suggest that it regards the liberty interests of foreign nationals as less worthy of protection than exactly the same interests of UK nationals, which is impermissible under the Convention.[149]

[143] *Belmarsh* (n 2) [47] (Lord Bingham), quoting *Khawaja v Secretary of State for the Home Department* [1984] 1 AC 74, 111 (Lord Scarman).

[144] The Newton Committee made only one review under this provision: see n 131 above.

[145] *Newton Committee Report* (n 131).

[146] *Belmarsh* (n 2) [64] (Lord Bingham), citing Home Office, *Counter-Terrorism Powers: Reconciling Security and Liberty in an Open Society* (Cm 6147, 2004), para 36. The proposition that community cohesion was better served by measures whose operation was confined to non-citizens was explicitly raised as a 'new' argument by the government before the ECtHR in *A v United Kingdom* and rejected by that body as being without evidential basis: *A v United Kingdom* (n 12) para 188.

[147] See *Belmarsh* (n 2) [129] (Lord Hope), [188] (Lord Rodger).

[148] The Joint Committee on Human Rights is a committee of both Houses of Parliament comprising 12 members. Its terms of reference include consideration of matters relating to human rights in the United Kingdom (excluding individual cases). The aspect of the Committee's work most relevant to the discussion is its scrutiny of bills and legislation for their compatibility with human rights.

[149] *Belmarsh* (n 2) [65] (Lord Bingham), citing Joint Committee on Human Rights, *Anti-Terrorism, Crime and Security Act 2001: Statutory Review and Continuance of Part 4 (Sixth Report)* (2003–04, HL 38, HC 381), para 44. See [84] (Lord Nicholls) for a closely equivalent statement.

Lord Nicholls stated: 'In the present case I see no escape from the conclusion that Parliament must be regarded as having attached insufficient weight to the human rights of non-nationals.'[150]

(b) Use of International Law

Characterisation of the detention measures as immigration detention was not the government's sole answer to the charge that the measures were discriminatory. The Attorney-General advanced a 'more far-reaching submission'.[151] Expanding on a power to control entry and expulsion, the Attorney-General proposed that 'international law sanctions the differential treatment, including detention, of aliens in time of war or public emergency'.[152] This was a reprise of the argument central to Brooke LJ's reasons in the Court of Appeal.

In response to the Attorney-General's argument from international law, Lord Bingham drew on a range of legal materials for the contrary proposition, namely that preventive detention measures had to apply equally to citizens and non-citizens. Lord Bingham's openness to international and comparative law materials has been much remarked upon.[153] In *Belmarsh*, the central subject matter of his discussion was a thickening set of legal objections to discrimination, and in particular discrimination against non-nationals. In considering Lord Bingham's extensive recourse to international, and in particular European, law and sources, it is to be kept in mind that his analysis was directed towards the validity of the derogation under European law. The government had conceded that the European criteria governed the effectiveness of the derogation from statutory 'Convention rights' under the HRA 1998.[154]

Lord Bingham's discussion of international human rights law was directed at the need to ensure that a state's response to security threats was proportionate and general in application, and did not single out non-citizens. Lord Bingham quoted materials in support of the following propositions:

- counterterrorism measures must comply with a state's national and international human rights obligations;
- these rights are applicable to all individuals subject to a state's jurisdiction;
- any infringement of rights must be proportionate to a legitimate aim; and
- counterterrorism should not serve as a pretext for non-compliance with rights obligations and, in particular, discrimination against persons on grounds of national origin.[155]

[150] *Belmarsh* (n 2) [81] (Lord Nicholls). See also [84].
[151] ibid, [55] (Lord Bingham).
[152] ibid.
[153] See eg Mads Andenas and Duncan Fairgrieve 'There is a World Elsewhere – Lord Bingham and Comparative Law' in Mads Andenas and Duncan Fairgrieve (eds), *Tom Bingham and the Transformation of the Law: A Liber Amicorum* (Oxford, Oxford University Press, 2009) 831.
[154] See text to n 13 above.
[155] *Belmarsh* (n 2) [56]–[63] (Lord Bingham).

He finished by quoting long passages from the Concluding Observations on the United Kingdom (10 December 2003) of the Committee established under Article 8 of the Convention against Racial Discrimination.[156] The quoted comments were specifically directed at the indefinite detention provisions in Part 4 of the ATCSA 2001.[157] The Committee sought to draw the United Kingdom's attention to its obligations under the Convention against Racial Discrimination with respect to both the basic prohibition of discrimination and the requirement of proportionality.

It was against the background of the above international law material developing the principle of non-discrimination that Lord Bingham turned to consider the Attorney-General's international law argument, which had been decisive for Brooke LJ in the Court of Appeal. Lord Bingham stated at the outset:

> The first step in this argument was to assert the historic right of sovereign states over aliens entering or residing in their territory. Historically, this was the position . . . But a sovereign state may by international treaty restrict its absolute power over aliens within or seeking to enter its territory, and in recent years states have increasingly done so.[158]

This was not dissimilar to Brooke LJ's starting point. Brooke LJ was, however, swayed by what he took to be the countervailing message of authorities from times of war and public emergency.[159] Lord Bingham examined the particular instruments relied upon by the Attorney-General in this connection. The first of these was the provision under the Geneva Conventions for wartime internment. Lord Bingham's response was terse: 'It is not suggested that the United Kingdom is, in a legal sense, at war or involved in an armed conflict, and it has no bearing on these appeals.'[160] Stopping to consider the analogy with wartime internment, these cases are drawn from a conventional war context in which the army of one nation is pitted against another. They are predicated on nationality being relevant to the threat. But the relevance of nationality to the security threat was the central matter in dispute in the *Belmarsh* proceedings. Reliance on the wartime analogy reintroduced the relevance of nationality to the security threat in a way that avoided discussion and debate.[161]

[156] International Convention on the Elimination of All Forms of Racial Discrimination (opened for signature 21 December 1965, entered into force 4 January 1969) 660 UNTS 195.

[157] See also *Belmarsh* (n 2) [57] (Lord Bingham), citing the critical comments of the European Commissioner for Human Rights on Part 4 of the ATCSA 2001.

[158] *Belmarsh* (n 2) [69] (Lord Bingham). For a discussion of the 'historical position' outlined in this statement see ch 1, s 1.5.

[159] A notable feature of Brooke LJ's argument from international and comparative law is that, with the exception of wartime internment and two questionable United States immigration authorities, his examples address a power of expulsion, not detention, of non-citizens.

[160] *Belmarsh* (n 2) [69] (Lord Bingham).

[161] The contrast between Lord Bingham's conclusions on his review of international law and those of Brooke LJ correlated with their positions on how the distinction between citizen and non-citizen maps onto that between friend and enemy. Brooke LJ entered into his review of international law on the assumption that non-citizens are the 'predominant' source of the threat: see the discussion in the text at pp 161–62 above. Lord Bingham reviewed the material on the basis of SIAC's factual finding that the threat was from both non-nationals and nationals.

The problems with the Attorney-General's argument identified by Lord Bingham in *Belmarsh* can be categorised as follows. The Attorney-General:

- failed to take into account the existence of subsequent treaty obligations that impacted on earlier treaty provisions relied on by the government;[162]
- selectively took into account only certain provisions from a given treaty instrument;[163]
- failed to take into account qualifications in the international instruments relied upon;[164] and
- drew on unjustifiable, or at least very loose, analogies.

Lord Bingham's reasons evidence his understanding of treaty interpretation as a dynamic process.[165] He considered the interrelationship between the provisions in a treaty and between different treaty regimes as they change over time. His focus on the application of the treaties to changing circumstances led him to look at the statements of various committees, office holders and treaty bodies charged with ensuring the continued relevance and application of treaty obligations to see what they had said about the circumstances presently before the court and like circumstances. He concluded:

> The materials I have cited are not legally binding on the United Kingdom. But there is no European or other authority to support the Attorney-General's submission . . . These materials are inimical to the submission that a state may lawfully discriminate against foreign nationals by detaining them but not nationals presenting the same threat in a time of public emergency.[166]

[162] The Attorney-General relied on the allowance made by the Convention relating to the Status of Refugees (opened for signature 28 July 1951, entered into force 22 April 1954) 189 UNTS 150 for expulsion on grounds of national security. Lord Bingham's response was to say that it did not avail the Attorney-General to show that a course of action was permissible under the Refugee Convention if it was not permissible under the ECHR. The same comment was made in relation to the Attorney-General's reliance on a provision in the Convention on the Status of Stateless Persons (opened for signature 28 September 1954, entered into force 6 June 1960) 360 UNTS 117.

[163] The Attorney-General relied on the fact that the derogation provision in the International Covenant on Civil and Political Rights (adopted 19 December 1966, entered into force 23 March 1976) 999 UNTS 171 (ICCPR), Art 4, contained an absolute prohibition on discrimination on a range of grounds that did not include national origin. Lord Bingham's response was to point to Arts 2 and 26 of the ICCPR, which did embrace discrimination on grounds of nationality or immigration status. Lord Bingham held that the detention provisions would breach Arts 2 and 26 of the ICCPR, and so would fall foul of the third criterion for lawful derogation under Art 15 of the ECHR, 'other obligations under international law'.

[164] The Attorney-General noted that the UN Declaration on the Human Rights of Nationals Who are Not Nationals of the Country in which They Live (UN Doc A/RES/40/144 (1985)) sanctioned differential treatment of non-citizens. Lord Bingham stated that this was qualified in the instrument by the requirement that such treatment not be incompatible with a state's international legal obligations. He further held that such treatment was incompatible with the United Kingdom's obligations under the ECHR and ICCPR.

[165] On broader issues raised by the contrast between Brooke LJ and Lord Bingham, going to the evolution of treaties over time, see Campbell McLachlan, 'The Evolution of Treaty Obligations in International Law' in Georg Nolte (ed), *Treaties and Subsequent Practice* (Oxford, Oxford University Press, 2013) 69. At 74–76 McLachlan discusses the contrast between Brooke LJ's and Lord Bingham's judgments in the *Belmarsh* litigation.

[166] *Belmarsh* (n 2) [63] (Lord Bingham).

By way of contrast, the account of international law provided by Brooke LJ in the Court of Appeal proceedings, drawing on the government's argument, treated the various treaty provisions in relative isolation from other provisions in the treaty or other treaties, and conveyed little sense of the work done after a treaty has entered into force to ensure its continued relevance. The Court of Appeal did not incorporate into its frame of reference the work of the various treaty bodies and offices charged with overseeing a given treaty's application. To the extent that there was an attempt to integrate the various treaty provisions it tended to reduce to a statement of rule and exception. There were increasing human rights obligations on states with respect to their treatment of non-nationals, but these fell away in times of emergency, allowing for differential treatment.

On a point raised earlier regarding the use of inappropriate analogies, one of the authorities relied upon by both the Attorney-General and Brooke LJ was the notorious 1951 judgment of *Shaugnessy v Mezei.*[167] Lord Bingham bluntly stated that this was 'not a decision which would be followed by a European Court'.[168] He further noted that the United States 'entry fiction', whereby an individual in the United States territory may be deemed for legal purposes not to have effected an entry, does not obtain in British law.[169] In relation to United States authority more generally, Lord Bingham suggested a more wide-reaching divergence. He moved to distinguish the persuasive value of United States authority with reference to 'the heightened deference shown by United States courts to the judgments of the political branches with respect to national security'.[170]

Lord Bingham was unpersuaded there was any authority for the submission that in a time of public emergency a state can discriminate against non-nationals by detaining them, but not nationals posing the same threat.

6.6.4 The Declaration of Incompatibility

The House of Lords quashed the Derogation Order and issued a declaration that section 23 of the ATCSA 2001 was incompatible with Articles 5 and 14 of the ECHR 'insofar as it is disproportionate and permits detention of suspected international terrorists in a way that discriminates on the ground of nationality or immigration status'.

[167] *Shaughnessy v United States; ex rel Mezei*, 345 US 206 (1953). *Shaughnessy* was quoted with approval by Brooke LJ in *Belmarsh* (Court of Appeal) (n 1) [128]. See also Scalia J's dissent in *Zadvydas* (n 34), discussed in ch 1, p 9, and Hayne J's quotes from the *Mezei* litigation in *Al-Kateb* (n 34), discussed in ch 3, pp 77–78.

[168] *Belmarsh* (n 2) [69].

[169] For a statement of the non-applicability of the United States 'entry fiction' in the Australian context see *Al-Kateb* (n 34) [96]–[97] (Gummow J). See ch 3, pp 85–87.

[170] *Belmarsh* (n 2) [69]. This distinction between the United States and the United Kingdom was raised to distance the House of Lords from the implications of the United States Supreme Court's obiter comments in *Zadvydas* on a 'terrorism exception' to the prohibition on indefinite detention pending removal: see *Zadvydas* (n 34) 696. This *Zadvydas* 'terrorism exception' is discussed in ch 1, pp 9–10.

I present the House of Lords' majority judgment in *Belmarsh* as a robust legal defence of non-citizens. But how is this to be squared with the remedy awarded to the detainees? As Lord Scott stated, the effect of any declaration of incompatibility on the validity of the ATCSA 2001 'is nil'.[171] Legislation declared to be in breach of a Convention right remains in full force and effect. There is a very real sense in which section 4 does not confer 'real legal protection to the rights of the detainees'.[172]

The primary response to this objection was that a declaration was the only remedy available to the court. This contention can be usefully expanded upon by addressing an argument to the contrary. John Finnis charges that, in issuing a declaration of incompatibility under section 4 of the HRA 1998, the House of Lords 'passed up on an opportunity to give real legal protection to the rights of the detainees' by reading in certain restrictions under section 3.[173] His criticism of the House of Lords is predicated on the view that, even in the absence of a lawful derogation, the detention provisions were compatible with the ECHR.[174] Finnis argues that compatibility with Article 5(1)(f) of the ECHR required no more than that the Home Secretary 'satisfy SIAC that he had acted and was continuing to take action for the purpose of securing that they could and would lawfully be deported'.[175] A rejection of the proposition that Article 5(1)(f) of the ECHR accommodates indefinite detention, provided the government continues to pursue removal, leads to a rejection of Finnis's argument on remedy.[176]

The legislative measures in Part 4 of ATCSA 2001 cannot be rendered compatible with the ECHR in the absence of a lawful derogation. In these circumstances, interpretation runs out. In a legal system in which legislation cannot be invalidated as incompatible with rights, the House of Lords' remaining function was to record that, unprotected by a lawful derogation, the legislation was indeed incompatible with the right to liberty. This is continuous with the common law tradition.

A second response to the objection that the appellants were not afforded a remedy highlights both the practical effects of such declarations, and the way in which those effects are realised. Where a declaration of incompatibility has become final

[171] *Belmarsh* (n 2) [144] (Lord Scott). Lord Scott's statement is not, strictly speaking, accurate. While the validity of the legislation is unaffected, an individual could bring an action under s 7(1)(a) of the HRA 1998 for compensation under s 8. See Clive Walker, 'Prisoners of "War All the Time"' [2005] *European Human Rights Law Review* 50, 68.

[172] Finnis (n 102) 435, and see 429–35.

[173] ibid, 435.

[174] This was the argument run by the United Kingdom in *A v United Kingdom* (n 12). The United Kingdom's arguments in that case mirror Finnis's argument. See ch 7, s 7.2.

[175] Finnis (n 102) 435.

[176] For a response to Finnis consistent with that offered here see Clive Walker, 'The Threat of Terrorism and the Fate of Control Orders' [2010] *PL* 4, 9–12. TRS Allan has expressed sympathy with Finnis's position that the House of Lords' use of s 4 in *Belmarsh* was inappropriate: TRS Allan, 'Deference, Defiance and Doctrine: Defining the Limits of Judicial Review' (2010) 60 *University of Toronto Law Journal* 41, 57–59. Against Allan's suggestions, and for substantially the same reasons I disagree with Finnis, I do not believe that a compatible interpretation was available.

in its entirety,[177] Parliament has remedied the incompatibility identified, either by primary legislation or a remedial order under section 10 of the HRA 1998,[178] or has taken steps to do so.[179] In response to the House of Lords' declaration in *Belmarsh*, Parliament enacted the Prevention of Terrorism Act 2005. In introducing the second reading of the Prevention of Terrorism Bill, the Home Secretary stated that a 'motivating principle' behind the Bill was 'the need to meet the Law Lords' judgment'. He stated: 'we should not ignore the judgment or flout it, but act on it and try to put in place a regime that is both proportionate and not discriminatory.'[180] The legislative response to *Belmarsh*, control orders, and the mechanism that succeeded them, terrorism prevention and investigation measures, are addressed in chapter seven.

The issuance of a declaration in *Belmarsh* is very much of a piece with the continuance of a 'political constitution' in the United Kingdom.[181] Where Parliament legislates to address the incompatibility identified in a decision of the courts, this is not demanded by any binding judicial decision or constitutional invalidation, but is an exercise of parliamentary choice. This statement is qualified by considerations of possible constitutional convention and the interaction with the institutions of the Council of Europe. But Parliament's ability to ignore a declaration or to withdraw from the ECHR remains. *Belmarsh* was an impressive indication of how a court can inject a 'cross-current of opinion' into public consideration of measures affecting rights.[182] It challenged the government's sweeping, status-based distinction between the liberty rights of nationals and foreigners and powerfully re-affirmed the equality of persons before the law.

One evident motivation for repealing Part 4 of the ATCSA 2001 was that, following the House of Lords' ruling that the detention regime was discriminatory, the ongoing legal justification for the detention regime was decidedly unstable.[183] Detainees could still challenge the ATCSA 2001 in Strasbourg, where the ECtHR was likely to give considerable weight to the House of Lords' reasoning in support of a declaration. And the ECtHR did so, in its reasoning in *A v United Kingdom*.[184]

[177] By 'final in its entirety' I mean that the declaration was not subject to appeal, in whole or in part.

[178] s 10 of the HRA 1998 provides for a 'fast-track' procedure whereby primary legislation may be amended by ministerial order.

[179] See Ministry of Justice, *Responding to Human Rights Judgments: Report to the Joint Committee on Human Rights on the Government Response to Human Rights Judgments 2011–2012* (Cm 8432, 2012), annex A. The Ministry of Justice notes that, in the period between 2 October 2000 when the HRA 1998 entered into force and 31 July 2012, 27 declarations were made, 19 of which became final in their entirety (ie the declaration was not subject to appeal, in whole or in part). Of those 19, 11 were remedied by later primary legislation, three were remedied by remedial order under s 10 of the HRA, four related to provisions that had already been remedied by primary legislation at the time of the declaration, and the last was under consideration to determine how to remedy the incompatibility.

[180] Charles Clarke MP, HC Deb 23 February 2005, vol 431 cols 345–47.

[181] Carol Harlow, 'The Political Constitution Reworked' in Rick Bigwood (ed), *Public Interest Litigation* (Wellington, Lexis Nexis NZ, 2006) 189, 208–10.

[182] AV Dicey, *Lectures on the Relation between Law and Public Opinion in England during the Nineteenth Century*, 2nd edn (London, Macmillan, 1904) 398.

[183] See Charles Clarke MP, HC Deb 23 February 2005, vol 43, col 347.

[184] *A v United Kingdom* (n 12), discussed in ch 7, s 7.2.

This Grand Chamber decision, an application by the *Belmarsh* detainees, is discussed in the next chapter.

6.7 Conclusion

Having decided that certain foreign terrorist suspects should not be 'at large' in the United Kingdom, and anticipating problems with securing their removal, the government derogated from the ECHR's guarantee of personal liberty (Article 5) to avoid incompatibility with the ECHR. The government relied on the derogation in defending legal challenges under the HRA 1998 and ECHR to the provision on indefinite detention in the ATCSA 2001. The *Belmarsh* litigation focused on whether the conditions stated in the ECHR, Article 15 for a lawful derogation were met and whether the detention provisions were compatible with the Article 14 ECHR prohibition on discrimination.

The government's decision to confine the power of indefinite detention to non-citizens lay at the centre of the *Belmarsh* litigation. At issue was whether a power of indefinite detention, so confined, met the strict necessity test under Article 15. The government's primary justification for administrative detention measures confined to non-citizens was as follows:

> There is a rational connection between [the foreign terrorist suspects'] detention and the purpose which the Secretary of State wishes to achieve. It is a purpose which cannot be applied to nationals, namely detention pending deportation, irrespective of when that deportation will take place.[185]

Thus, the government's justification characterised the indefinite detention as detention for a deportation purpose. The government argued that its intention to remove a non-citizen was all that was required for authority to detain, irrespective of whether that intention could be implemented.[186] At the centre of the government's argument lay its claim that detention in the absence of any real prospect of removal in the reasonably foreseeable future could still be characterised as detention for the purposes of deportation, and legitimately be confined to non-citizens on that basis.

The government's argument, as portrayed by Lord Woolf CJ in the Court of Appeal,[187] was that the power to detain pending deportation was an available tool in the fight against terrorism, and one it wished to utilise. The pre-derogation legal limits on detention pending deportation rendered the power unfit for purpose, in that authority to detain rested on the ability to effect removal within a reasonable time and removal of the foreign suspects under consideration might not be possible. Accordingly, the government sought to expand the scope of

[185] *Belmarsh* (Court of Appeal) (n 1) [52] (Lord Woolf CJ) (outlining the Secretary of State's case).
[186] See eg ibid, [52]–[53] (Lord Woolf CJ).
[187] See ch 6, s 6.4.

'detention pending deportation' by derogation, so as to encompass indefinite detention. In the Court of Appeal, Lord Woolf CJ gave legal sanction to this approach. The category of detention pending deportation was treated as elastic, allowing it to be stretched to accommodate the national security needs of the government. This elasticity was a function of the ruling that the government's intention to remove the detainees, regardless of when, or whether, that intention could be put into effect, was sufficient to characterise detention as pending deportation.

Turning to Lord Woolf CJ's assessment of the measures in the light of national security objectives, he held that the factual finding that the threat was not confined to foreign terrorist suspects did not pose a problem. The Secretary of State had made an assessment that he need do 'no more than' detain non-citizens to meet the threat. Lord Woolf CJ held that if, in the Secretary of State's view, that was what was needed to meet the threat, then the derogation criterion was satisfied, a point on which it was 'impossible' for the Court to differ.[188] The Secretary of State was not bound to take the measure that was most effective to meet the threat;[189] he was entitled to focus on a subset of the threat, if that would, in his opinion, be adequate to the circumstances.

The essential point of difference between the Court of Appeal on the one hand, and SIAC and the House of Lords majority on the other, was that the latter bodies did not accept the government claim that detention pending removal was an elastic category that could be stretched to accommodate the government's national security policy. SIAC and the House of Lords held that the category of detention pending deportation required that deportation be a viable option. A power of detention that made the viability of deportation irrelevant to authority to detain was not detention pending deportation. The government's immigration rationale for confining the detention measures to non-citizens was rejected.

Accordingly, SIAC and the House of Lords majority focused on the government's national security objectives. Neither SIAC nor the House of Lords was dismissive of a possible security rationale for the derogation and detention measures. The difficulty they had with the government case was that they could not square the decision to confine the measures to non-citizens with the stated security objectives. If the threat emanated from both citizens and non-citizens, it was arbitrary to confine the response to non-citizens.

Underpinning both the rejection of the government's 'immigration' characterisation of the measures and the critical assessment of the government's national security justification was a commitment to the view that a non-citizen's vulnerability to removal only gave rise to a *limited* exception to the general equality of persons before the law. For this exception to have integrity there had to be an objective connection between detention and deportation, to be determined by judicial review of the viability of removal. The government contended that authority to hold a non-citizen in detention pending deportation rested on the

[188] *Belmarsh* (Court of Appeal) (n 1) [40] (Lord Woolf CJ).
[189] ibid, [45] (Lord Woolf CJ).

government's intention to deport. This claim was recognised, most clearly by the House of Lords, as effectively collapsing the category of detention pending deportation into a sweeping distinction between the liberty rights of citizens and non-citizens. The House of Lords' emphasis on the principles of equality of persons, non-discrimination and the liberty of non-citizens grounded its opposition to the stark hierarchy between liberty of citizens and non-citizens.

In the *Belmarsh* litigation, the degree and nature of deference shown to the government determined judgments on the proper scope of immigration detention. SIAC and the House of Lords[190] both held that a power of indefinite detention irrespective of the viability of removal was not detention for the purposes of deportation. Accordingly, they then assessed the detention provisions against national security purposes. In the light of a finding that the terrorist threat came from citizens and non-citizens, legislation to detain only foreign terrorist suspects was determined to be discriminatory, arbitrary and irrational.

These issues all played out in a context in which it was accepted that the legal reasoning could not appeal to the right to liberty under the ECHR,[191] as it was the lawfulness of the derogation from that right that was the subject of dispute. The legal dispute centred on the criteria for lawful derogation, and in particular on the requirement that the measures be 'strictly required by the exigencies of the situation'. The fact that legal argument in *Belmarsh* centred on the criteria for lawful derogation, and that indefinite detention of non-citizens did not meet these criteria, highlights that what is *legally* troubling about indefinite detention pending removal is not reducible to its impact on a liberty right, whether sourced in statute, treaty or constitution. Nor is the issue reducible to the infringement of a discrimination right. As stated by SIAC, if the government derogated from the prohibition on discrimination under Article 14 this 'would not assist';[192] the issue of whether the measures were 'strictly required' would remain. *Belmarsh*'s stature rests on its affirmation that the government cannot, consistent with the requirements of legality,[193] arbitrarily single out a particular group to bear a burden.

[190] With the exception of Lord Walker's dissent in the House of Lords. Lord Hoffmann decided against the government on the basis that the first criterion for lawful derogation under Art 15 of the ECHR, the existence of a public emergency, had not been established. He made clear that he doubted the legality of the detention power, whether confined to non-citizens or extended to citizens and non-citizens alike: *Belmarsh* (n 2) [97].

[191] Until the validity of the derogation was determined.

[192] *Belmarsh* (SIAC) (n 10) [96]: 'Merely scheduling such a derogation [to the prohibition on discrimination in Art 14] would not assist, however, for in any event there is not a reasonable relationship between the means employed and the aims sought to be pursued.'

[193] As manifest in the criteria for lawful derogation in Art 15 of the ECHR. See ch 5, s 5.7.

7

The Periphery of Indefinite Detention

. . . we remain extremely concerned about the impact of control orders on the subject of the orders, their families and their communities. There can be no doubt that the degree of control over the minutiae of controlees' daily lives, together with the length of time spent living under such restrictions and their apparently indefinite duration, have combined to exact a heavy price on the mental health of those subject to control orders.

Joint Committee on Human Rights,
Counter-Terrorism Policy and Human Rights (2010)[1]

7.1 Introduction

Belmarsh ruled conclusively against the legality of indefinite detention pending removal.[2] But around the periphery of that ruling a number of other practices and legal positions have emerged that raise related and troubling issues. *Belmarsh* led to the demise of Part 4 of the Anti-Terrorism, Crime and Security Act 2001 (ATCSA 2001). In its place, the Prevention of Terrorism Act 2005 (POTA 2005) inaugurated the control order regime. Extending to citizens and non-citizens alike, control orders were a muted form of indefinite detention. The story of control orders and their successors, terrorism prevention and investigation measures (TPIMs), and the legal parameters of their use is the central topic of this chapter, stretching from sections 7.3 to 7.6. The British government's redoubled efforts to deport non-citizens, one line of response to legal constraints on their detention, is the subject of section 7.7. The chapter begins and ends with influential cases on national security procedure and immigration detention generally. In section 7.2 I analyse *A v United Kingdom*,[3] the *Belmarsh* detainees' application to the European Court of Human Rights (ECtHR) – the final instalment of the *Belmarsh* litigation. In section 7.8, I discuss *Lumba* and *Kambadzi*,[4] which develop the *Hardial Singh*

[1] Joint Committee on Human Rights, *Counter-Terrorism Policy and Human Rights (Sixteenth Report): Annual Renewal of Control Orders Legislation 2010* (2010–12, HC 395, HL 64) (JCHR, 2010 Report), para 44.

[2] *A v Secretary of State for the Home Department* [2004] UKHL 56, [2005] 2 AC 68 (*Belmarsh*).

[3] *A v United Kingdom* (2009) 49 EHRR 29.

[4] *R v Governor of Durham Prison, ex parte Singh* [1983] EWHC 1, [1984] 1 All ER 983 (*Hardial Singh*); *R (on the application of Lumba) v Secretary of State for the Home Department* [2011] UKSC 12,

principles and explore the application of general legal principles to immigration detention.

7.2 *Belmarsh* in the European Court of Human Rights

7.2.1 Introduction to *A v United Kingdom*

On 21 January 2005, following the House of Lords' decision in *Belmarsh*, 11 of those detained under Part 4 of the ATCSA 2001 lodged an application with the ECtHR. They alleged that they had been unlawfully detained in breach of Articles 3, 5(1) and 14 of the European Convention on Human Rights (ECHR)[5] and had not had adequate remedies at their disposal, in breach of Articles 5(4) and 13. The applicants sought compensation for pecuniary and non-pecuniary damages sustained as a result of the violations. In the time between the filing of the application and the hearing before the ECtHR, Part 4 of the ATCSA 2001 was repealed,[6] and the derogation purporting to render indefinite detention under that Part compatible with the ECHR was revoked. The case was heard by the Grand Chamber of the ECtHR, comprising 19 judges. There, the United Kingdom sought to re-litigate the matters which had been decided against it in *Belmarsh*. The ECtHR resoundingly – with a unanimous judgment of 19 – affirmed the House of Lords' ruling that indefinite detention pending removal was incompatible with the ECHR.

The United Kingdom's argument before the ECtHR differed in a number of respects from that advanced in the domestic proceedings. The changes made to the arguments advanced in the domestic proceedings are consistent with the argument Finnis outlines in his 2007 *Law Quarterly Review* article, relevant aspects of which I discuss in chapter six.[7] In its first set of written observations to the Grand Chamber, the United Kingdom indicated that it would not re-litigate the decision on the lawfulness of the derogation under Article 15, 'but would leave that point as determined against them by the House of Lords'.[8] Instead, the government argued that a lawful derogation was unnecessary, and that the United Kingdom had only derogated out of abundance of caution. It argued that in the absence of a derogation, the applicants' detention was properly characterised as the 'lawful detention . . . of a person against whom action is being taken with a view to deportation', and so fell within the exception to the right to liberty contained in Article 5(1)(f) of the ECHR.

[2012] 1 AC 245; *R (Kambadzi) v Secretary of State for the Home Department* [2011] UKSC 23, [2011] 1 WLR 1299.

[5] Convention for the Protection of Human Rights and Fundamental Freedoms (opened for signature 4 November 1950, entered into force 3 September 1953) 213 UNTS 211, Eur TS 5 (ECHR).

[6] Prevention of Terrorism Act 2005 (POTA 2005), s 16.

[7] See p 180.

[8] *A v United Kingdom* (n 3) para 138.

The history of the United Kingdom's submissions to the ECtHR is of interest in charting the British government's evolving relationship with national and European courts. The government argument outlined in the preceding paragraph sidestepped the legality of the derogation and directly addressed the compatibility of indefinite detention with Article 5 of the ECHR. In response, the applicants submitted that 'it was abusive and contrary to the principle of subsidiarity for the Government to raise a novel argument before the Court and they should be estopped from doing so'.[9] The ECtHR dismissed this objection on the basis that the government's argument was not inconsistent with the position the government had adopted before the national courts. The ECtHR held that the government had clearly kept open the question of the application of Article 5, both in the text of the derogation and in the domestic proceedings. Further, the ECtHR held that the House of Lords had, in its reasons, 'expressly or impliedly' considered the question of whether the detention measures were compatible with Article 5(1)(f).[10] I share this reading of the reasoning of the House of Lords.[11] Their lordships had made their own evaluation of the compatibility of the measures with Article 5(1)(f).

At a late stage in the proceedings, the government amended its pleadings to re-litigate the validity of the derogation. Again, the applicants objected on the basis that it 'was abusive of the Government, so late in the proceedings before the Grand Chamber, to challenge the House of Lords' decision quashing the derogation'.[12] More fundamentally, in the applicants' view it would be inconsistent with the purpose of the ECtHR and the principle of subsidiarity to allow a government to seek to limit or derogate from the rights determined by its national courts by going to the ECtHR. The ECtHR was not established to enable governments to undermine the rights protections arrived at by their national courts. The applicants continued: 'Since the legislation had been revoked and the derogation withdrawn, the Government is in effect seeking to obtain from the Court an advisory opinion to be relied on potentially at some later stage.'[13] The ECtHR responded: 'The present situation is, undoubtedly, unusual in that Governments do not normally resort to challenging, nor see any need to contest, decisions of their own highest courts before this Court.'[14] Nonetheless, the ECtHR saw no reason why the government should not have a chance to raise all arguments open to it to defend the proceedings.

As the applicants correctly pointed out, the government's legal strategy was an attempt to circumvent its own highest court by obtaining an advisory opinion

[9] ibid, para 140.

[10] ibid, para 155. A majority of the House of Lords found, impliedly or expressly, that the measures were not compatible with Art 5(1)(f).

[11] See the second paragraph of ch 6, s 6.6.

[12] *A v United Kingdom* (n 3) para 142.

[13] ibid. The applicants further submitted that to 'allow the Government to proceed would impact substantially on the right of individual petition . . . by deterring applicants from making complaints for fear that Governments would try to upset the decisions of their own supreme courts'.

[14] ibid, para 157.

recognising a power to hold non-citizens in indefinite detention pending removal. The strategy was unsuccessful. A unanimous Grand Chamber of 19 reaffirmed, and arguably clarified and strengthened, the limits on immigration detention set down in *Chahal*.[15]

I divide my account of *A v United Kingdom* into its substantive and procedural reasoning. The ECtHR's reasoning on the right to liberty is discussed in the following section. I defer discussion of the ECtHR's holding on the procedure to be afforded to the detainees to section 7.5. The procedural holding is discussed in the context of control orders, the preventive detention regime that succeeded Part 4 of the ATCSA 2001. Part 4 of the ATCSA 2001 was repealed shortly after the application was lodged with the ECtHR in 2005. When that Court delivered judgment in February 2009, the legal regime most immediately affected by the ECtHR's procedural rulings was the control order regime then in force.

7.2.2 The ECtHR on Article 5(1)

(a) 'action is being taken with a view to deportation'

This section addresses the parties' submissions and the ECtHR's holding on the scope of immigration detention. The ECtHR's discussion of the legality of the derogation essentially adopted the approach of the majority of the House of Lords and so is not elaborated upon.[16]

Article 5(1)(f) of the ECHR provides:

> 5(1) Everyone has the right to liberty and security of person. No one shall be deprived of his liberty save in the following cases and in accordance with a procedure prescribed by law: . . .
>
> (f) the lawful arrest or detention of a person . . . against whom action is being taken with a view to deportation . . .

The United Kingdom's argument fixed on the phrase 'action being taken with a view to deportation'. The government argued that the phrase 'as a matter of ordinary language . . . covered the situation where a Contracting State wished to deport an alien, actively kept that possibility under review and only refrained from doing so because of contingent, extraneous circumstances'.[17] It was submitted that the required review included 'monitoring the situation' in the detainees' respective countries of origin.[18] Detention for the purpose of deportation required only that the government keep trying to remove the non-citizen. Detention continued to be for the purpose of deportation, and therefore authorised, for as long

15 *Chahal v United Kingdom* (1997) 23 EHRR 413. On *Chahal* see ch 5, s 5.3.

16 *A v United Kingdom* (n 3) para 192. The Court held that it did not need to consider the violation of the Art 14 discrimination provision separately, given its conclusion in relation to Art 5(1).

17 ibid, para 146.

18 ibid, para 147.

as the government continued to harbour the intention of removing the non-citizen and was monitoring the situation to that end. This position is similar to that adopted by the majority of the Australian High Court in *Al-Kateb.*[19]

The government began its submissions in support of the above reading of Article 5(1)(f) with the statement, 'States have a fundamental right under international law to control the entry, residence and expulsion of aliens.'[20] Its submissions continued: 'Clear language would be required to justify the conclusion that the Contracting States intended through the Convention to give up their ability to protect themselves against a risk to national security created by a non-national.'[21] This submission sees Finnis's principle of 'nationality-differentiated risk-acceptability' in operation.[22] Any diminution or qualification of a state's (immigration) power over non-citizens is characterised as the state 'giving up' the ability to protect itself against non-citizens. Accordingly, the onus lies with anyone asserting such a qualification. This effectively reversed the presumption against the abrogation of fundamental freedoms in the case of non-citizens, replacing it with a presumption in favour of a 'fundamental state right' over non-citizens.

The United Kingdom government here conflated the two lines of argument it had advanced in *Belmarsh*, namely authority to detain premised on an immigration rationale,[23] and authority to detain premised on the different position of non-citizens in time of emergency.[24] The government argued that the right to control the entry, residence and expulsion of aliens (immigration) *was* a state right to protection. The powers of exclusion and expulsion were treated as applications of a more sweeping right to protect itself against non-citizens.[25]

The applicants responded that 'merely keeping the possibility of deportation under review' did not amount to 'action . . . being taken with a view to deportation'.[26] It was merely 'action, unrelated to any extant deportation proceedings, that might make the deportation a possibility in the future'.[27] The applicants concluded: 'Detention pursuant to such vague and non-specific "action" would be arbitrary.'[28] The mere future possibility of removal was not enough; something more determinate and certain was required to sustain the necessary connection between detention and deportation.

[19] *Al-Kateb v Godwin* [2004] HCA 37, (2004) 219 CLR 562. This case is discussed in ch 3.

[20] *A v United Kingdom* (n 3) para 146.

[21] ibid.

[22] On the principle, see ch 1, s 1.4.

[23] See the discussion of Lord Woolf CJ's reasoning in *A v Secretary of State for the Home Department* [2002] EWCA Civ 1502, [2004] QB 335 (*Belmarsh (Court of Appeal)*) in ch 6, s 6.4.1.

[24] See the discussion of Brooke LJ's reasoning in *Belmarsh (Court of Appeal)* in ch 6, pp 161–62, and Lord Bingham's reasoning in *Belmarsh* (n 2) in ch 6, pp 176–79.

[25] For a similar proposition see Kennedy J's dissent in *Zadvydas v Davis*, 533 US 678, 713 (2001): 'the motivation to protect the citizenry from aliens determined to be dangerous is central to the immigration power itself': see ch 1, pp 7–8.

[26] *A v United Kingdom* (n 3) para 141.

[27] ibid.

[28] ibid.

In its reasoning on the proper scope of Article 5(1)(f), the ECtHR both reaffirmed and developed the reading given to that provision in *Chahal*.[29] As in *Chahal*, there was no requirement that the initial decision to detain be reasonably considered necessary to prevent a non-citizen committing an offence or fleeing.[30] But the section did impose limits on detention pending removal. The requirement that detention be 'lawful' gave rise to a prohibition on 'arbitrary' detention, with consequences for the legality of indefinite detention. The ECtHR stated: 'to avoid being branded as arbitrary . . . the length of the detention should not exceed that reasonably required for the purpose pursued.'[31] The ECtHR found a clear lack of fit between the United Kingdom's actions and the purpose of deportation: 'One of the principal assumptions underlying the derogation notice, the [ATCSA 2001] and the decision to detain the applicants was . . . that they could not be removed or deported "for the time being".'[32]

(b) The Fair Balance Argument

In addition, the United Kingdom resurrected its argument of 'fair balance', discussed in chapter six in the context of the Special Immigration Appeals Commission's (SIAC's) decision[33] and that of the Court of Appeal[34] in the domestic *Belmarsh* proceedings. Using the same language it had employed before SIAC, the government argued that Article 5(1)(f) had to be interpreted

> so as to strike a balance between the interests of the individual and the interests of the State in protecting the population from malevolent aliens. Detention struck that balance by advancing the legitimate aim of the State to secure the protection of the population without sacrificing the predominant interest of the alien to avoid being returned to a place where he faced torture or death. The fair balance was further preserved by providing the alien with adequate safeguards against the arbitrary exercise of the detention powers in national security cases.[35]

Again, as before SIAC, detention was presented as a reasonable accommodation, squaring protection of the public with a prohibition on deportation to torture.[36] The ECtHR was brusque in its response:

> The Court does not accept the Government's argument that Article 5(1) permits a balance to be struck between the individual's right to liberty and the State's interest in

[29] *Chahal* (n 15). Discussed in ch 5, pp 132–34.

[30] *A v United Kingdom* (n 3) para 164.

[31] ibid.

[32] ibid, para 167.

[33] *A v Secretary of State for the Home Department* [2002] HRLR 45 (*Belmarsh (SIAC)*) [88]. See the discussion in pp 152–53. In the SIAC judgment, by way of contrast with that of the ECtHR, the government's 'fair balance' argument was considered not as an argument for the scope of Art 5(1)(f), but as a potential rebuttal of the allegation that the measures were discriminatory. This illustrates the way an argument for an immigration characterisation functions as an argument against discrimination.

[34] *A v Secretary of State for the Home Department* [2004] QB 335 (*Belmarsh (Court of Appeal)*), [28].

[35] *A v United Kingdom* (n 3) para 148.

[36] The ECtHR made reference to the supporting submission based on the provision of adequate procedural safeguards, a submission not noted in SIAC's judgment.

> protecting its population from terrorist threat . . . If detention does not fit within the confines of the paragraphs [the exhaustive list of exceptions to Article 5(1) contained in 5(1)(a)–(f)] as interpreted by the Court, it cannot be made to fit by an appeal to the need to balance the interests of the State against those of the detainee.[37]

The structure of Article 5(1) as a right subject to enumerated, exhaustive exceptions assumed particular prominence, and the exception made for immigration detention under Article 5 was held to have its own integrity. The limits of the exception to Article 5(1) were set by a proportionate connection to facilitating removal, not determined by the needs of national security. A purported power of immigration detention in circumstances where there was no prospect of removal did not come within Article 5(1)(f) and so was held to violate Article 5(1).

(c) The ECtHR's Findings on the Facts

The ECtHR, like the House of Lords, held that the central issue was the compatibility with the ECHR of a *statutory power* of indefinite detention confined to non-citizens. The focus was on the compatibility of the *legislation* with the ECHR, as opposed to any government decision under it. Nonetheless, unlike the domestic bodies that issued decisions in the *Belmarsh* litigation, the ECtHR went on to consider the alternative line of inquiry, namely whether the United Kingdom's actions with respect to the applicants constituted sufficient 'action . . . being taken with a view to deportation' in terms of Article 5(1)(f). On the possibility of the detainees' removal, the applicants stated:

> it was clear that during the periods when the applicants' cases were being considered by SIAC on appeal (July 2002–October 2003), the Government's position was that they could not be deported compatibly with Article 3 and that no negotiations to effect deportation should be attempted with the proposed receiving States.[38]

That is, until October 2003, well after the decisions of SIAC and the Court of Appeal in the *Belmarsh* litigation discussed in chapter six, the United Kingdom government had not even entered negotiations to effect the removal of the detainees. Further, as the ECtHR stated, 'There is no evidence that during the period of the applicants' detention there was . . . any realistic prospect of their being expelled without this giving rise to a real risk of ill-treatment contrary to Article 3'.[39] The absolute prohibition on deportation to torture meant that on the facts of the individual cases there was no 'realistic prospect' of removal.[40] The ECtHR stated that it did not consider that 'the [United Kingdom's] policy of keeping the possibility

[37] *A v United Kingdom* (n 3) para 171.

[38] ibid, para 141. The appeals referred to above are those relating to individual exercise of certification, discussed in ch 6, s 6.5. This account of the facts is consistent with the government's submissions: 'from the end of 2003 onwards the Government [was] in negotiation with Algeria and Jordan, with a view to entering into memoranda of understanding that the applicants who were nationals of those countries would not be ill-treated if returned' (para 147).

[39] ibid, para 167.

[40] See also Clive Walker, 'The Threat of Terrorism and the Fate of Control Orders' [2010] *PL* 4, 12.

of deporting the applicants "under active review" was sufficiently certain or determinative to amount to 'action . . . being taken with a view to deportation'.[41] Accordingly, the ECtHR concluded that the United Kingdom had violated Article 5(1)(f) in respect of nine of the 11 applicants (the remaining two had left the United Kingdom).

In *Belmarsh*, the House of Lords had focused on the compatibility of the relevant statutory power with the ECHR, rejecting a case-by-case analysis of the detainees' position.[42] The ECtHR's conclusion on the way the powers were being exercised was that additionally, their detention was incompatible with the ECHR when assessed on a case-by-case basis.

7.2.3 Conclusions on *A v United Kingdom*

The ECtHR held that the right to liberty and security of the person of a number of the applicants had been violated, and this was not saved by a lawful derogation.[43] It ordered payment of what are best seen as token amounts in respect of these violations.[44] In its final, concentrated, paragraph of reasoning on compensation,[45] the ECtHR withdrew some of the sting of its judgment against the United Kingdom. In reducing the amount claimed by the applicants, the ECtHR gave indirect weight to the government's 'fair balance' argument, effectively accepting that the measures were taken in 'good faith'. The government was trying to respond to the terrorist threat while observing its obligations with respect to deportation to torture under Article 3. The ECtHR further reasoned that the replacement 'control order' legislation had met the 'core part' of the disproportionality finding going to discrimination. As the applicants had become subjects of the control order regime, this was taken to minimise the legal wrong they had suffered under discriminatory measures. The control order regime was taken by the ECtHR to illustrate that the applicants would have suffered some restriction of liberty even in the absence of the discrimination.

Stopping to situate *A v United Kingdom* within the development of the Strasbourg jurisprudence, the ECtHR's reasoning on detention pending removal in *Chahal* was critical to the United Kingdom's decision to derogate from Article 5(1) after 9/11. The derogation was to secure the detention of foreign terrorist suspects whom the government did not want at large in the community, but who were 'irremovable' by virtue of the ECtHR's interpretation of Article

[41] *A v United Kingdom* (n 3) para 167.

[42] See ch 6, pp 166–67.

[43] It further held, as explained in s 7.6 above, that in a number of instances, due to the extent of non-disclosure of the allegations against them, the review of detention had not met the requirements of Art 5(4) of the ECHR, which provides: 'Everyone who is deprived of his liberty by arrest or detention shall be entitled to take proceedings by which the lawfulness of his detention shall be decided speedily by a court and his release ordered if detention is not lawful.'

[44] *A v United Kingdom* (n 3) para 253: the amounts ranging from €3,900 to €1,700.

[45] ibid, para 252.

3 in *Chahal.* Subsequent to the House of Lords' *Belmarsh* decision, in *Saadi v Italy* the Grand Chamber of the ECtHR unanimously affirmed that involvement in terrorism did not affect the absolute prohibition on deportation to a real risk of torture under Article 3.[46] Then, in *A v United Kingdom*, a unanimous Grand Chamber held that the scope of legally permissible detention under Article 5(1)(f) could not simply be expanded to accommodate security concerns: 'If detention does not fit within the confines of the paragraphs as interpreted by the Court, it cannot be made to fit by appeal to the need to balance the interests of the State against those of the detainee.'[47]

In *A v United Kingdom*, the ECtHR, following the majority of the House of Lords in *Belmarsh*, rejected the proposal that immigration detention was an elastic category, expanding in times of threat to authorise preventive measures confined to non-citizens. The trajectory of the ECtHR jurisprudence has been to unanimously affirm the propositions contained in *Chahal*, namely that deportation to torture and indefinite detention pending removal are incompatible with the ECHR.

7.3 The Legislative Response to *Belmarsh*

There are a number of different strands to the government response to *Belmarsh*. The first of these is the most obvious and the most scrutinised and discussed: the regime of 'obligations' on terrorist suspects that replaced Part 4 of the ATCSA 2001. Those obligations took the form of control orders under the POTA 2005, and have now been replaced by TPIMs under the Terrorism Prevention and Investigation Measures Act 2011 (TPIM Act 2011). These regimes, imposing constraints on terrorist suspects on a preventive rationale, are discussed in sections 7.3–7.6.

In this section I introduce legislative developments in the United Kingdom subsequent to *Belmarsh*. The successor regime to detention under Part 4 of the ATCSA 2001 was the POTA 2005. It provided for 'control orders' which applied to both citizens and non-citizens. A control order was defined as 'an order against an individual that imposes obligations on him for purposes connected with protecting members of the public from a risk of terrorism'.[48] The legislation set out a lengthy list of obligations that could be imposed on the subject of a control order.[49] Some of these obligations are considered below in section 7.4 in discussing the effects of control orders.

[46] *Saadi v Italy* (2009) 49 EHRR 730, judgment delivered 28 February 2008.

[47] *A v United Kingdom* (n 3) para 171.

[48] POTA 2005, s 1(1). 'Terrorism' is given the same meaning as under the Terrorism Act 2000: see s 1(5).

[49] POTA 2005, s 1(4).

Immediately after they were released from detention under Part 4 of the ATCSA 2001,[50] the nine *Belmarsh* detainees who had remained in the United Kingdom became the subject of control orders under the POTA 2005.[51] The control orders continued the pattern of restrictive measures based on anticipatory risk assessment established by the detention measures in Part 4 of the ATCSA 2001.[52] In December 2011, the control orders were repealed and replaced by terrorism prevention and investigation measures (TPIMs). Notwithstanding their repeal, an introduction to the operation of control orders is necessary to evaluate legal developments consequent on the *Belmarsh* decision.

Control orders were devised with compatibility with the right to liberty in Article 5 of the ECHR in mind. They were of two kinds: 'non-derogating' and 'derogating'. Under a 'non-derogating' control order, the Home Secretary could impose restrictions on the controlled person's movements, activities, communications and associations with others, provided these restrictions did not amount to a 'deprivation of liberty' under Article 5 of the ECHR. Under a 'derogating' control order, greater restrictions, amounting to a 'deprivation of liberty' under Article 5 of the ECHR, were permitted. As the name suggests, the second type of control order required a derogation from the ECHR. At no point did the government resort to derogating control orders. As to what amounts to a 'deprivation of liberty', the phrase was to be understood with reference to the ECtHR's decision in *Guzzardi v Italy*, in which the ECtHR stated that Article 5

> is not concerned with mere restrictions on liberty of movement . . . In order to determine whether someone has been 'deprived of his liberty' within the meaning of Art 5, the starting point must be his concrete situation and account must be taken of the whole range of criteria such as the type, duration, effects and manner of implementation of the measure in question.[53]

The following account concerns non-derogating control orders. The Secretary of State could make a control order against an individual where she or he had reasonable grounds for suspecting that the individual was or had been involved in

[50] For a detailed account of the movement of the *Belmarsh* appellants from detention pursuant to Part 4 of the ATCSA to constraint in residences pursuant to control orders see the witness statements by Gareth Pierce, solicitor for a number of the men subject to the orders: Joint Committee on Human Rights, *Counter-Terrorism Policy and Human Rights: Draft Prevention of Terrorism Act 2005 (Continuance in force of sections 1 to 9) Order 2006* (2005–06, HL 122, HC 915) (JCHR, 2006 Report) 59–80 (an annex to 'Appendix 7: Submission from Liberty) (Pierce, Joint Committee Witness Statement).

[51] Two of the *Belmarsh* detainees secured release from detention by leaving for France and Morocco respectively.

[52] See Clive Walker, 'Keeping Control of Terrorists Without Losing Control of Constitutionalism' (2007) 59 *Stanford Law Review* 1395, 1402. For an (inconclusive) discussion of whether control orders are appropriately characterised as 'preventive' see Lucia Zedner, 'Preventive Justice or Pre-Punishment? The Case of Control Orders' (2007) 60 *Current Legal Problems* 174.

[53] *Guzzardi v Italy* Series A no 39 (1981) 3 EHRR 333, para 91. That this guidance does not provide any 'bright line' rule on whether conditions constitute a 'deprivation of liberty' under Art 5 is highlighted in the House of Lords' decision in *Secretary of State for the Home Department v JJ* [2008] 1 AC 385, discussed at pp 199–201.

terrorism related activity, and considered it necessary, for purposes connected with protecting the public from a risk of terrorism, to make a control order imposing obligations on the individual.[54] Here, a low evidentiary threshold for involvement in 'terrorism related activity' (the reasonable suspicion test) was coupled with a forward-looking assessment of the need for the obligations imposed (the necessity test).

Before issuing a control order, the Secretary of State had to obtain permission from a court to do so.[55] In exceptional circumstances he or she could issue a control order and subsequently seek to have it confirmed by a court.[56] In considering whether to grant the Secretary of State permission to issue a control order, or to confirm a control order that was granted without permission by reason of urgency, the court had only to determine whether or not the Secretary of State's decision that there were grounds to make an order was 'obviously flawed'.[57]

The inclusion of citizens within the control order regime meant that SIAC was no longer an appropriate venue for the review of orders. Accordingly, jurisdiction was vested in the High Court.[58] The process for High Court review continued to resemble the SIAC model, including the provision for special advocates.[59]

A control order only had effect for 12 months, but could be renewed any number of times.[60] In practice, this allowed for indefinite detention or, as put by one Minister, detention for 'an identifiable, limited period . . . on a continuous basis'.[61] The Report of the Independent Reviewer of Terrorism Legislation that followed the demise of the control order regime documented that the longest period in which a person had been subject to a control order was in excess of 55 months.[62] Persons subject to control orders could be shifted to TPIMs, further extending the period of detention and control. Of the individuals subject to control orders for more than two years, three were subject to a control order for four-to-five years, four for three-to-four years, and eight for two-to-three years.[63] In a number of cases, this time was additional to time already spent in detention under Part 4 of the ATCSA 2001.

[54] POTA 2005, s 2(1). On these two tests see Clive Walker, *Terrorism and the Law* (Oxford, Oxford University Press, 2011) para 7.29.

[55] POTA 2005, s 3(2).

[56] ibid, s 3(3).

[57] ibid, s 3(2) and (3).

[58] ibid, s 15. In Scotland jurisdiction was vested in the Court of Session.

[59] ibid, Sch. 1.

[60] ibid, s 2(4).

[61] Walker (n 54) para 7.114, quoting Baroness Scotland, HL Deb 7 March 2005, vol 670 col 515.

[62] David Anderson QC, *Control Orders in 2011: Final Report of the Independent Reviewer on the Prevention of Terrorism Act 2005* (London, The Stationery Office, 2012) para 3.47. On the position of the Independent Reviewer see POTA 2005, s 14, now replaced by the TPIM Act 2011, s 20.

[63] Anderson (n 62) para 3.47.

7.4 Substance – The Extent of the Obligations Imposed

7.4.1 The Effect of Control Orders

The POTA 2005 was pushed through Parliament in a rancorous debate that included the longest sitting in 99 years.[64] The debates are permeated with alarm at the use of draconian powers against British subjects. The statement of Frank Dobson MP is representative:

> I cannot and will not support any law that would allow a British citizen to be imprisoned without trial on the say-so of the Home Secretary. There is nothing personal about that: the present Home Secretary is a decent man. But no Home Secretary should have the power to deprive a fellow citizen of his or her liberty without having to lay convincing evidence before a court, and letting the court decide.[65]

This extract identifies one of the main concerns with the Bill: orders were issued by the Home Secretary, not a court.[66] These concerns led to provision for an increased level of judicial involvement in the process, the results outlined earlier in describing the POTA 2005 in section 7.3. Another concession afforded by the government was that the operative provisions would have to be renewed by an order of the Secretary of State, to be laid before Parliament and approved by a resolution of each House.[67] These 'renewal debates' were a regular occasion for the expression of disquiet at the effect of control orders on those subject to them, as described below.

A secondary theme of the debates on POTA 2005 was the recurrent objection that 'The Bill is a gross manipulation and distortion of the Law Lords' ruling'.[68] The charge was that the government

> had a choice. At the moment of reversal at the hands of the Lords, the Home Secretary could have ceased to derogate from article 5 of the convention on human rights and ceased to detain without trial, or he could have chosen to widen detention without trial so that all UK citizens could be banged up on his say-so.[69]

The objection was that the government chose to extend the power to citizens, rather than decline to renew such a power. The control orders were seen as a con-

[64] A 32-hour session extending from late morning on Thursday 10 March 2005.

[65] Frank Dobson, HC Deb 23 February 2005, vol 431 col 389. For other statements against the measures expressed in terms of their effect on British citizens, see eg Mr Betts, HC Deb 23 February 2005, vol 431 col 352; Mr Blunt, HC Deb 23 February 2005, vol 431 col 353; Mr Davis, HC Deb 23 February 2005, vol 431 cols 364–65; Sir Menzies Campbell, HC Deb 28 February 2005, vol 431 col 653; Robin Cook, HC Deb 28 February 2005, vol 431 col 715; Kenneth Clarke, HC Deb 28 February 2005, vol 431 col 726; Mr Blunt, HC Deb 28 February 2005, vol 431 cols 749–50.

[66] See eg Robin Cook, HC Deb 23 February 2005, vol 431 col 338.

[67] POTA, s 13(1)–(4).

[68] Robert Marshall-Andrews, HC Deb 23 February 2005, vol 431 cols 415–16.

[69] Boris Johnson, HC Deb 23 February 2005, vol 431 col 386.

tinuation and extension of the repressive measures contained in Part 4 of the ATCSA 2001. The government was characterised as responding to a rights-protective decision by removing the privilege of habeas corpus.[70]

From early in the life of the control order regime, there was an awareness of the adverse impact of such orders on those subject to them. This awareness was registered in legislative debates, amongst other fora, and was informed by judicial statements in cases on control orders, and parliamentary reports. By way of illustration, I refer to the reports of the Parliamentary Joint Committee on Human Rights, and the recurrent annual 'renewal debates',[71] brief and poorly attended as these debates were. The concerns expressed in these fora testified to persistent parliamentary disquiet at the measures.

Two central themes ran through the testimony to Parliament on the effects of control orders: the deterioration in the mental health of those subject to such orders, and the significant adverse effects of the measures on the controlee's wider family. Taking the latter, the impact of control orders on the families of controlees was registered in the report of the Joint Committee on Human Rights (JCHR) issued in February 2006, less than a year after the introduction of such orders. The report registers frequent disturbance of and access to premises without notice, restrictions on communications, the isolation of families resulting from the deterrent effect of the vetting process for visitors and social interaction, and 'mental suffering and anguish due to the fear of their home being searched, the controlled person rearrested, or their own social interactions monitored'.[72] The appendices to the report contain submissions to the JCHR, amongst them one from Liberty, annexed to which is a witness statement by Gareth Pierce, solicitor for a number of detainees and their families, addressing the impact of control orders on the wives and children of controlees.[73] Amongst other matters, Pierce records constant disruption by way of telephone calls, inquiries and visits from the police. These were often to check that the controlee was present where the electronic monitors had lost contact with the controlee's tag. These incursions were often at night, as that was during the curfew period when the controlee had to be at home.[74] The disruptions to two households were such that the husbands had requested separate accommodation away from the house, in one case in a psychiatric department, to ease the burden on their families.[75] The report from Liberty was referred to in the first renewal debates on the POTA 2005 in February 2006, with a Member stating, with reference to evidence on the mental health of controlees and the impact of the orders on their families, 'The evidence is not only

[70] See eg Douglas Hogg, HC Deb 23 February 2005, vol 431 col 386; Boris Johnson, HC Deb 23 February 2005, vol 431 cols 386–90.

[71] See text to n 67 above.

[72] JCHR, 2006 Report (n 50) para 85.

[73] ibid, 70–80 (Annex 3 to Appendix 7).

[74] ibid, 72–73.

[75] ibid, 73. Such requests have also occurred under the Canadian security certificate regime, where those released on conditions have asked to be re-detained to alleviate the pressure on their families: see ch 8, pp 249–50.

distressing, but well beyond what . . . Members assumed would be the impact when they agreed to the process'.[76]

In reviewing the operation of the control order regime at the time of its repeal, the Independent Reviewer made particular reference to an article by the wife of one of the controlees. He noted that the author had been referred to in a 2010 High Court judgment as 'an impressive witness and person', the truth of whose evidence was accepted 'without reservation'.[77] She wrote of the lack of privacy:

> The restrictions and monitoring of who may and may not enter your home, as well as times and places the detainee can leave their residence and what can and cannot be kept at their location results in the majority of the time being spent alone in the home and this pressure is immense on a marriage and on home life. You literally feel as though you are fighting a ghost and there never seems to be any light at the end of the tunnel. This hopelessness, anguish and extreme anxiety manifests itself in constant arguments, loneliness and in the case of our eldest child who has just turned four, Post-Traumatic Stress Disorder.[78]

A significant reason for the stress occasioned by compliance with the restrictions was that contravention of an obligation under a control order was an offence, punishable by up to five years' imprisonment.[79] If the government could successfully prosecute a controlee for breach of his conditions, it could incarcerate him.

Specific categories of obligation under control orders gave rise to parliamentary concern, including the absence of any time limit on the renewal of orders, the power to relocate the subject of a control order to another part of the country, the extent and duration of the curfew requirement, and the low evidentiary standard placed on the government, namely the requirement of a 'reasonable suspicion' of 'terrorism related activity'. In the 2009 renewal debates one member stated:

> For the most part, respondents were not allowed to meet by prearrangement any person not approved by the Home Secretary. They were required to wear tags. They were required to notify the monitoring authority before they left and when they returned. They were not allowed to have any communication equipment other than monitored fixed lines. The practical effect, of course, was that they could not work. It is therefore perhaps not surprising that Lord Bingham said that the control order system is a form of house arrest, but without the benefit of association with fellow prisoners. It is very bad indeed.[80]

As the years went on, the 'sheer interminability' of control orders became a matter of increasing concern.[81] With reference to the cases of those who had been shifted from detention under Part IV of the ATCSA 2001 to the control order regime, it was said:

[76] See John McDonnell, HC Deb 15 February 2006, vol 442 col 1518.

[77] Anderson (n 62) para 3.40, quoting *CA v SSHD* [2010] EWHC 2278, [3].

[78] ibid, para 3.39, citing an article in *Muslim Weekly* (16 December 2011).

[79] POTA 2005, s 9.

[80] See Douglas Hogg, HC Deb 3 March 2009, vol 488 col 755. The reference to Lord Bingham is to his judgment in *JJ* (n 53), discussed at pp 199–201 above.

[81] See Chris Huhne, HC Deb 3 Mar 2009, vol 488 col 752.

> As we now know from the *Belmarsh* cases and others, a control order can mean seven years, which, with proper remission taken into account, is equivalent to a 14 year prison sentence, yet not many terrorism offences carry that weight of penalty.[82]

In its 2010 report, the JCHR stated:

> we remain extremely concerned about the impact of control orders on the subject of control orders, their families and their communities. There can be no doubt that the degree of control over the minutiae of controlees' daily lives, together with the length of time spent living under such restrictions and their apparently indefinite duration, have combined to exact a heavy price on the mental health of those subject to control orders.[83]

On the basis, in part, that the unreformed control order system had led to 'more unjustifiable interferences with people's liberty, more harm to people's mental health and the life of their families' and 'even longer periods under indefinite restrictions', the 2010 report of the Joint Committee on Human Rights 'reached the clear view that the system of control orders is no longer sustainable'.[84]

The above statements are reasonably representative of the comments that recurred time and again in parliamentary debates, committee reports, court cases, the reports of international bodies and the statutory reports of the Independent Reviewer. They raise the concern that, for the detainee, the difference between indefinite detention under Part 4 of the ATCSA 2001 and onerous conditions indefinitely renewed under control orders might have been hard to discern.

7.4.2 Court-Imposed Limits on the Obligations

Non-derogating control orders were challenged in the courts on two main grounds: first, the extent of the conditions imposed pursuant to control orders, in particular whether they were so onerous as to amount to a violation of Article 5 of the ECHR; and second, the fairness of the procedures under which they were tested, where the focus was on whether the regime violated the right to a fair trial under Article 6 of the ECHR.[85]

Regarding the first set of concerns, going to the extent of the conditions imposed, the litigation on the control order regime was generated by the government seeing how close it could sail to the wind without actually requiring a derogation from Article 5. In *Secretary of State for the Home Department v JJ* the control order under challenge imposed an 18-hour curfew, coupled with the effective exclusion of

[82] See Andrew Dismore, HC Deb 3 Mar 2009, vol 488 col 758. '*Belmarsh* cases' is a reference to those detained under Part 4 of the ATCSA who then became ongoing controlees.

[83] JCHR, 2010 Report (n 1) para 44.

[84] ibid, paras 111, 112.

[85] Article 6 provides in part: '(1) In the determination of his civil rights and obligations or of any criminal charge against him, everyone is entitled to a fair and public hearing within a reasonable time by an independent and impartial tribunal established by law.'

social visitors.[86] Of the five judges sitting, two found that the conditions amounted to a deprivation of liberty contrary to Article 5,[87] and two found that they did not.[88] In the deciding judgment, Lord Brown stated that the Strasbourg jurisprudence effectively provided that 'these appeals fall to be decided as "a matter of pure opinion"'.[89] He held that the 18-hour curfew breached Article 5, and ventured to suggest that '12 or 14 hour curfews . . . are consistent with physical liberty'.[90] A 16 hour curfew, however, 'should be regarded as the absolute limit'.[91] The House of Lords quashed the control order as in breach of Article 5, and therefore outside the relevant power to issue a non-derogating order under the Act.

The result of the decision in *JJ* was that the curfew was reduced. The lines drawn on the permissible length of curfew seem relatively arbitrary, leaving intact an onerous system of restraints of indefinite duration, implemented in the absence of any charge, let alone conviction. In this respect, the decision is indicative of the difficulties of trying to deal with a fundamentally problematic legal regime with reference to a set of limited questions, going to the compatibility of certain features of that regime with particular rights.[92] If one is tasked with delineating the boundaries of 'deprivation of liberty' contained in Article 5 of the ECHR,[93] an indefinite 16-hour curfew may be the appropriate place to draw the line. But there is an evident danger that by entering into such line-drawing, legitimacy is being conferred on the legally troubling practice of indefinite preventive restrictions based on anticipatory risk assessment. Subsequent to the decision, the government increased a number of curfews to 16 hours, arguing that this had been given legal sanction in *JJ*.[94]

[86] *JJ* (n 53). During the six hours in which the controlled (and electronically tagged) persons were permitted to leave their residences, they were confined to restricted urban areas, which deliberately did not extend to any area in which they had previously lived. They were prohibited from meeting anyone by pre-arrangement without prior Home Office approval.

[87] Lord Bingham and Baroness Hale.

[88] Lord Hoffmann and Lord Carswell. Lord Hoffmann held that Art 5(1) was only breached by 'literal physical restraint': ibid, [36] (Lord Hoffmann).

[89] ibid, [102]. The phrase 'a matter of pure opinion' is taken from the ECtHR decision in *Guzzardi* (n 53). Compare this with Lord Bingham in *JJ* at [17]: 'The [ECtHR] acknowledges the difficulty attending the process of classification in borderline cases, suggesting that in such cases the decision is one of pure opinion or what may, rather more aptly, be called judgment.'

[90] *JJ* (n 53) [105].

[91] ibid.

[92] On this theme see Zedner (n 52).

[93] For criticisms of the court in *JJ* for not developing jurisprudence under the HRA 1998 more robust than that of Strasbourg, see Keith Ewing and Joo-Cheong Tham, 'The Continuing Futility of the Human Rights Act' [2008] *PL* 668, 685–88. On the relationship between Strasbourg jurisprudence and Convention rights under the HRA generally, see Jack Beatson et al, *Human Rights: Judicial Protection in the United Kingdom* (London, Sweet & Maxwell, 2008), paras 1-79–1-99.

[94] Joint Committee on Human Rights, *Counter-Terrorism Policy and Human Rights (Ninth Report): Annual Renewal of Control Orders Legislation 2008* (2007–08, HL 57, HC 356) (JCHR, 2008 Report), Appendix 2 (Letter dated 18 February 2008 from the Rt Hon Jacqui Smith MP, Home Secretary, Home Office), para 4: 'I believe the House of Lords judgment on control orders allows us to impose curfews of up to 16 hours when it is necessary and proportionate to do so. Following the House of Lords judgment, I assessed that it was necessary and proportionate to modify four control orders such that the curfews were increased to 16 hours.'

The majority reasoning in JJ did not treat curfew length as the sole criterion for a lack of liberty.[95] The decision was based on the cumulative effect of the requirements imposed on the controlee: long curfews, continuing for an indefinite period; the effective exclusion of social visitors; the fact of being restricted to an area outside anywhere they had previously lived; and the fact that the controlee's flat could be entered at any time. The effect was that 'their lives were wholly regulated by the Home Office, as a prisoner's would be, although breaches were much more severely punishable'.[96] Lord Bingham compared the conditions in *JJ* unfavourably with an open-air prison, stating that a controlee did not 'enjoy the association with others and access to entertainment facilities' that a prisoner would expect.[97]

The view that assessment of compliance with Article 5 necessarily involved a range of factors and was not reducible to the duration of the curfew was highlighted by the 2010 case of *AP*.[98] AP was subject to a control order with a 16-hour curfew. His order was then modified, requiring him to relocate to a town in the Midlands, some 150 miles from his family and friends in London. AP challenged this modification to his order. The judge at first instance, Keith J, found that AP's social isolation following his relocation was profound.[99] AP was in an unfamiliar area without contacts and the practical difficulty of family visits was considerable. Keith J held that the adverse impact on AP's family life, while not giving rise to a claim under Article 8 of the ECHR,[100] was a relevant consideration under Article 5. The overall effect of the social isolation arising from the relocation together with the curfew was held to be a 'deprivation of liberty' under Article 5. Overturned by a majority of the Court of Appeal, the United Kingdom Supreme Court unanimously upheld the judge at first instance.[101]

More pervasive in their influence on the control order regime than the occasional decisions of the highest appellate courts has been the steady stream of judicial decisions at High Court level on individual control orders, and particular measures imposed under those orders. Clive Walker notes that 'There are regularly over thirty hearings per year, they are heard in primary courts of justice, and their superintendence has required justification and regular reassessment by the

[95] Lord Bingham, Baroness Hale and Lord Brown formed the majority. Lord Hoffmann and Lord Carswell formed the minority. The minority view was that 'the concept of deprivation of liberty [should be confined] to actual imprisonment or something which is for practical purposes little different from imprisonment': *JJ* (n 53) [44] (Lord Hoffmann).

[96] ibid, [24] (Lord Bingham).

[97] ibid.

[98] *Secretary of State for the Home Department v AP* [2010] UKSC 24, [2011] 2 AC 1.

[99] *Secretary of State for the Home Department v AP* [2008] EWHC 2001 (*AP, First Instance*).

[100] Article 8(1) of the ECHR provides: 'Everyone has the right to respect for his private and family life, his home and his correspondence.' Keith J held that the interference with family life was justified and proportionate given the needs of national security.

[101] *AP* (n 98). The lead judgment was given by Lord Brown (with whom Lords Phillips, Saville, Walker and Clarke agreed). Lord Rodger and Sir John Dyson SCJ concurred. In its reasons, the Supreme Court emphasised the considerable expertise and experience of the few nominated judges who hear control orders appeals, not generally shared by the appellate courts, entitling their determinations to respect: see *AP* (n 98) [5], [20] (Lord Brown).

Home Office'.[102] Following a thorough review of the relevant jurisprudence, Walker concludes that the High Court's 'authority and legitimacy to face down the securitocracy has unquestionably surpassed the deferential approach adopted in response to previous executive security measures'.[103]

7.5 Procedure – The Development of the Control Order Regime

On the fairness of control order procedures, I refer to three interrelated decisions: *Secretary of State for the Home Department v MB*,[104] *A v United Kingdom*,[105] and *AF v Secretary of State for the Home Department (No 3)*.[106] These three decisions strengthened the disclosure requirements imposed upon control orders (and now TPIMs). The disclosure at issue is disclosure to the controlee. In focusing on disclosure to the controlee, the decisions have simultaneously tried to address the limitations of the special advocate.[107] The courts have held that while the orders are to be assessed against a civil standard, the procedural protections should be commensurate with the gravity of the potential consequences.[108] The heightened disclosure requirements attest to intelligence being subject to more demanding evidentiary requirements when it is used to justify coercive state action. The shift from a traditional deferential judicial approach to executive decision-making where national security is invoked is also registered in the judgments' recognition of the fallibility and limitations of intelligence.

The *MB* decision addressed two cases, those of MB and AF, consolidated for argument. In both cases, the issuance of non-derogating control orders was supported by an open statement made available to the controlee and a closed statement which was not. The common feature of both cases was the bare and unsubstantiated nature of the allegations revealed in the open statement. On their face, the statute and regulations precluded the judge from ordering disclosure even where she or he considered that this was essential to a fair hearing. To remedy this state of affairs, the House of Lords read down the relevant provisions

[102] Walker (n 54) para 7.97. For a summary of the case law see paras 7.74–7.99.

[103] ibid, para 7.98. The statement is by way of a comparison between High Court cases under the POTA 2005 and SIAC decisions on Part 4 orders under the ATCSA 2001 (noted in ch 6, s 6.6), amongst other measures. For a similar conclusion, addressed in part to the control order regime, to the effect that there has been a qualitative shift to more robust judicial review of executive national security decision-making, see Adam Tomkins, 'National Security and the Role of the Court: A Changed Landscape?' (2010) 126 *LQR* 543, 550–59.

[104] *Secretary of State for the Home Department v MB* [2007] UKHL 46, [2008] 1 AC 440.

[105] *A v United Kingdom* (n 3).

[106] *Secretary of State for the Home Department v AF (AF No 3)* [2009] UKHL 28, [2010] 2 AC 269.

[107] The institution of special advocate was introduced in ch 5, s 5.4.

[108] See *MB* (n 104) [24] (Lord Bingham). A similar point was made by the Canadian Supreme Court in *Charkaoui v Canada (Minister of Citizenship and Immigration)* [2008] SCC 38, [2008] 2 SCR 326, [53]: discussed in ch 9, s 9.10.1.

of the schedule to the POTA 2005 and ruled by inserting an implied limitation (italicised):

> Sch 1, para 4(3) Rules of court made in the exercise of the relevant powers must secure –
>
> . . .
>
> (d) that the relevant court is required to give permission for material not to be disclosed where it considers that the disclosure of the material would be contrary to the public interest *except where to do so would be incompatible with the right of the controlled person to a fair trial.*[109]

The result of the amendment was that a court could refuse permission to the Secretary of State to withhold closed material. This is not to say that the Secretary of State was required to serve the material. Rather, if the Secretary of State elected not to disclose, he or she had to face the prospect of a court ruling that the non-disclosed material could not be relied upon and consequently, without the requisite evidential foundation, that the decision to issue the control order was flawed and had to be quashed.[110]

In his dissenting judgment Lord Hoffmann, in apparent reliance on *Chahal*, held that 'in principle the special advocate procedure provides sufficient safeguards to satisfy Article 6'.[111] His lordship held that the existence of the special advocate procedure constituted a full answer to concerns about how to reconcile national security confidentiality with the requirements of a fair trial under the ECHR. His view was underwritten by the view that there could be no core requirement of disclosure in the national security area. Lord Hoffmann's position became that advocated by the government in subsequent litigation on control orders.

The implied limitation read in by the House of Lords was a function of the conviction that at some point non-disclosure becomes incompatible with a right to a fair trial. The central question in *MB*, and subsequent jurisprudence on disclosure under the control order and TPIM regimes, is: when is that point reached? The House of Lords' judgments in *MB* offered a range of responses to this question. One comment in *MB* which generated much argument in the lower courts was Lord Brown's statement that even where it was impossible to indicate sufficient of the Secretary of State's case to enable the suspect to make an effective challenge, this might be compatible with Article 6 where 'the judge can nevertheless feel quite sure that in any event no possible challenge could conceivably have

[109] The same limitation was applied to the relevant rule: r 76.29(8).

[110] See *MB* (n 104) [72], [68]–[73] (Baroness Hale). In the result, in *MB*, the majority of the House of Lords ordered that the cases be remitted to the Administrative Court for a final decision as to whether it was possible to confirm the control orders consistently with the right to a fair trial. If, on remittal, the judges concluded that the orders could not fairly be made, s 3 of the HRA 1998 was then to be invoked, with the legislation read in the light of implied limitation and further comments of the House of Lords.

[111] See *MB* (n 104) [54] (Lord Hoffmann). The better reading of *Chahal* is that the ECtHR did not express an opinion on whether special advocates ('the Canadian approach') would satisfy the requirements of the ECHR: see ch 5, p 132.

succeeded'.[112] I do not detail the divergent responses in *MB* and ensuing variations in the tests applied by the lower courts,[113] as they have been overtaken by subsequent legal developments. For the current legal position, one has to look to *A v United Kingdom* and *AF (No 3)*.

The discussion of *A v United Kingdom* in section 7.2 focused on the substantive limits on detention pending removal. In this section, I discuss the ECtHR's reasoning on Article 5(4), the aspect of *A v United Kingdom* that has impacted on the disclosure requirements under the preventive detention regimes. *A v United Kingdom* was a challenge to Part 4 of the ATCSA 2001. The House of Lords subsequently held, in *AF (No 3)*, that the ECtHR's comments in *A v United Kingdom* on the fairness of the national security procedures under Part 4 were applicable to the control order regime.

Article 5(4) of the ECHR states:

> Everyone who is deprived of his liberty by arrest or detention shall be entitled to take proceedings by which the lawfulness of his detention shall be decided speedily by a court and his release ordered if the detention is not lawful.

In *A v United Kingdom*, the relevant complaint under Article 5(4) concerned the fairness of the procedures for reviewing decisions to certify a non-citizen as a suspected international terrorist and, in particular, the deficiencies of the special advocate procedure. The critical step in the ECtHR's reasoning was that:

> in the circumstances of the present case, and in view of the dramatic impact of the lengthy – and what appeared at that time to be indefinite – deprivation of liberty on the applicants' fundamental rights, Article 5§4 must import essentially the same fair trial guarantees as Article 6§1 in its criminal aspect.[114]

Against this background, the ECtHR arrived at the following general conclusions on the part played by the special advocate procedure:

> The Court further considers that the special advocate could perform an important role in counterbalancing the lack of full disclosure and the lack of a full, open, adversarial hearing by testing the evidence and putting arguments on behalf of the detainee during the closed hearings. However, the special advocate could not perform this function in any useful way unless the detainee was provided with sufficient information about the allegations against him to give effective instructions to the special advocate.[115]

[112] See *MB* (n 104) [90] (Lord Brown). Cf [91] (Lord Brown): 'I cannot accept that a suspect's entitlement to a fair hearing is merely a qualified right capable of being outweighed by the public interest in protecting the state against terrorism.'

[113] Compare, for example, *Secretary of State for the Home Department v AF* [2008] EWHC 453 (Admin), Burnton J; with *Secretary of State for the Home Department v AN* [2008] EWHC 372 (Admin), Mitting J; and *Secretary of State for the Home Department v AE* [2008] EWHC 585 (Admin), Silber J.

[114] *A v United Kingdom* (n 3) para 217. Earlier in its judgment the ECtHR referred to the decision of the Canadian Supreme Court in *Charkaoui v Canada (Minister of Citizenship and Immigration)* 2007 SCC 9, [2007] 1 SCR 350 for the principle that 'a person whose liberty is in jeopardy must know the case to meet': *A v United Kingdom* (n 3) para 111. The passages from *Charkaoui* quoted by the ECtHR were precisely those used by Lord Bingham in *MB* (n 104) [53], [64].

[115] *A v United Kingdom* (n 3) para 220.

In clearly alluding to limitations on the ability of the special advocate to perform his or her functions, the ECtHR diverged from the view Lord Hoffmann expressed in *MB*, where he held that provision for a special advocate in and of itself met the requirements for a fair trial under the ECHR.[116] The ECtHR went on to state that while the question of whether 'sufficient information' is provided to make an 'effective' response must be decided on a case-by-case basis, it could discern three categories of case:

(a) where the evidence is to a large extent disclosed and the open material plays the predominant role in the reasons for decision;
(b) where the evidence is largely undisclosed, but the allegations contained in the open material are sufficiently specific to make an effective response;
(c) where the allegations in the open material consist purely of general assertions, and SIAC's decision is based 'to a decisive degree' on closed material.[117]

The ECtHR held that cases falling into the third category do not satisfy the procedural requirements of Article 5(4). Applying the above analysis, the ECtHR determined that the application of the SIAC procedures to four of the 11 applicants had violated Article 5(4) of the ECHR.[118] Conversely, in relation to the other applicants, the allegations were sufficiently specific to make an effective response, and so met the requirements of Article 5(4).[119] In *A v United Kingdom*, the ECtHR held that there is an irreducible core requirement of disclosure, even in cases involving national security confidentiality. Failure to meet that core requirement constitutes a violation of the right to a fair trial in Article 6. It remains for the judiciary to determine the disclosure this requirement demands in each case.

In *AF (No 3)*, the House of Lords confirmed the relevance of the procedural holdings in *A v United Kingdom* for control orders.[120] Like *Belmarsh*, *AF (No 3)* was heard by a committee of nine Law Lords. In the lead judgment Lord Phillips stated:

> On 19 February, a little over a week before the commencement of the appeal in the House, the Grand Chamber of the Strasbourg Court handed down its judgment in *A and others v United Kingdom* . . . This addressed the extent to which the admission of closed material was compatible with the fair trial requirements of article 5(4). The Secretary of State recognised that the judgment cut the ground from under her feet in so far as she had hoped to persuade the House to adopt the approach of Lord Hoffmann in *MB*. An amended case was filed on her behalf.[121]

[116] See text accompanying note 111 above.
[117] *A v United Kingdom* (n 3) para 220.
[118] In relation to two of these four applicants, the relevant allegation against them was that they had engaged in fund-raising for groups linked to Al-Qaeda. The ECtHR stated: 'However, in each case the evidence which allegedly provided the link between the money raised and terrorism was not disclosed to either applicant': ibid, para 223. In relation to the other two, the allegation was that they were members of named extremist groups. In these cases the open evidence was characterised as insubstantial, and the evidence on which SIAC relied was largely contained in the closed material (para 224).
[119] ibid, para 222.
[120] *AF (No 3)* (n 106) [57] (Lord Phillips).
[121] ibid, [44] (Lord Phillips).

The House of Lords understood itself to be bound to accept and apply the decision of the ECtHR in *A v United Kingdom*,[122] though there was evident reluctance to do so on the part of some members of the bench.[123]

The government characterised the ECtHR's reasons in *A v United Kingdom* as standing for the principle that a 'controlee must have a reasonable opportunity to make an effective challenge to the case made against him'. The government contended that the ECtHR's reasons should not, however, be read as laying down 'an inflexible principle that there can never be a fair trial if the basis of the Secretary of State's suspicion is to be found solely or to a decisive degree in the closed material'.[124] Lord Phillips was unpersuaded by the government's submissions. He held that the ECtHR had ruled that where

> the open material consists purely of general assertions and the case against the controlee is based solely or to a decisive degree on closed materials the requirements of a fair trial will not be satisfied, however cogent the case based on the closed materials may be.[125]

In elaborating on his reasons in support of the ECtHR's position, Lord Phillips stated:

> There are . . . strong policy considerations that support a rule that a trial procedure can never be considered fair if a party to it is kept in ignorance of the case against him. The first is that there will be many cases where it is impossible for the court to be confident that disclosure will make no difference. Reasonable suspicion may be established on grounds that establish an overwhelming case of involvement in terrorism-related activity but, because the threshold is so low, reasonable suspicion may also be founded on misinterpretation of facts in respect of which the controlee is in a position to put forward an innocent explanation. A system that relies upon the judge to distinguish between the two is not satisfactory, however able and experienced the judge.[126]

The decision provides a clear marker of the distance travelled from the 'traditional' view of the place of the judge in matters of national security.[127] Their lordships' reasoning proceeds from the assumption that it is the place of judicial review to verify whether there are grounds for the government's 'reasonable sus-

[122] As stated most fully by Lord Carswell in *AF (No 3)* (n 106) at [108]: 'section 2(1) of the [HRA 1998] requires the House to take any such judgment into account. Whatever latitude this formulation may permit, the authority of a considered statement of the Grand Chamber is such that our courts have no option but to accept and apply it.' See also [70] (Lord Hoffmann), [98] (Lord Rodger), [121] (Lord Brown).

[123] See ibid, [70] (Lord Hoffmann), [108] (Lord Carswell), and less pointedly [121] (Lord Brown).

[124] ibid, [52] (Lord Phillips).

[125] ibid, [59] (Lord Phillips). Contrast Lord Brown's statement in *MB* (n 108), text to n 116.

[126] *AF (No 3)* (n 106) [63] (Lord Phillips). This statement of Lord Phillips followed an extract from the classic passage on natural justice from Megarry J in *John v Rees* [1970] Ch 345, at the core of which is the statement: 'As everybody who has anything to do with the law well knows, the path of the law is strewn with examples of open and shut cases which, somehow, were not; of unanswerable charges which, in the event, were completely answered . . .'; cf the response of Lord Hoffmann to this passage at [73]: 'Most lawyers will have heard or read of or even experienced such cases but most will also know how rare they are. Usually, if evidence appears to an experienced tribunal to be irrefutable, it is not refuted.' Lord Hoffmann followed the 'rigid' approach of the ECtHR with great reluctance ([71]).

[127] For example, as expressed by the lower courts in the course of the *Chahal* litigation: see pp 128–30.

picion'. In *AF (No 3)*, a unanimous bench of nine Law Lords endorsed the ECtHR's view that the right to a fair trial mandates a 'core irreducible minimum' of disclosure to the controlee. The controlee 'must be given sufficient information about the allegations against him to give effective instructions to the special advocate'.[128] No party submitted that the reading down of the statutory provision upheld in *MB* should be revisited in light of the 'more marked' effect of that reading down following *AF (No 3)*.[129] The reading of the statute arrived at in *MB* remained in place.

AF (No 3), alongside *A v United Kingdom*, has come to serve as a benchmark of the disclosure that is appropriate where there are severe intrusions on rights.[130] In the United Kingdom, considerable jurisprudential energy has been devoted to delineating the areas where the disclosure requirements of *AF (No 3)* do and do not apply.[131]

7.6 The Change to TPIMs

The Liberal Democrats and Conservatives, the two parties that went on to form the Coalition government, had made clear their intention to 'scrap' control orders going into the 2010 election.[132] Shortly after their entry into government, a Review of Counter-Terrorism and Security Powers was released, which spoke of the need to rebalance security powers and civil liberties, 'restoring those liberties wherever possible', and devoted considerable attention to control orders.[133] In late 2011, following cursory parliamentary scrutiny,[134] the TPIM Act 2011 was passed.

[128] *AF (No 3)* (n 106) [81].

[129] ibid, [67] (Lord Phillips); see also [95] (Lord Scott). On the 'reading down' required by *MB* (n 108) see text to n 109 above. The absence of such submissions points to a practical reason why, under the HRA 1998, section 3 interpretation may be employed whether or not a section 4 declaration may in some sense be more appropriate.

[130] See eg *Submissions on Behalf of the Australian Human Rights Commission, Plaintiff M47/2012*, filed, High Court of Australia, 8 June 2012, paras 46, 49, 50, www.hcourt.gov.au/assets/cases/m47-2012/M47-2012_HRC.pdf. On these proceedings see ch 4, s 4.4.

[131] See eg *Home Office v Tariq* [2011] UKSC 35, [2012] 1 AC 542, in which it was held that the procedural requirements of *AF (No 3)* did not apply to security vetting in the employment context. *Tariq* appears to hold that the disclosure required by *AF (No 3)* is only necessary where the liberty of the subject is at issue. See now the Justice and Security Act 2013. The legislation is to be understood against the background of *Al Rawi v Security Service* [2011] UKSC 34, [2012] 1 AC 531. At issue in *Al Rawi* was the question whether the court would order a closed material procedure, that is, a procedure in which material was not disclosed to the affected person, at common law. A majority of the Court declined to make such an order. They made the uncontroversial point that it was open to Parliament to introduce such a procedure.

[132] Liberal Democrat Party Manifesto 2010, 94, issuu.com/libdems/docs/manifesto; Conservatives, *Resilient Nation: National Security Green Paper* (Policy Green Paper No 13, 2009), www.conservatives.com/news/news_stories/2010/01/~/media/30D1AC669FE746E5ABCE8EB7C5E068D4.ashx.

[133] Home Office, *Review of Counter Terrorism and Security Powers* (Cm 8004, 2011).

[134] See Clive Walker and Alexander Horne, 'The Terrorism Prevention and Investigations Measures Act 2011: One Thing but Not Much the Other? [2012] *Criminal Law Review* 421, 426–28.

The new TPIM regime, as compared with control orders, curtails the number and extent of the obligations that can be imposed on those subject to such orders. Crucially, one of the limits introduced is that an order can only continue in force for two years. The TPIM Act 2011 was not prompted by any particular legal ruling or obligation, but by continuing concern, ventilated in parliamentary fora and elsewhere, at the operation of control orders.

On 14 December 2011, the TPIM Act 2011 entered into force. Section 1 of that Act repealed the POTA 2005. The new Act addressed a number of the features of the control order regime that had given rise to great concern.[135] The extent and range of measures that can be imposed under a TPIM is more limited than was available under the POTA 2005. The changes include the following:[136]

- The power to relocate controlled persons to other towns and cities (invariably used to move Londoners out of London) was removed.
- The power to confine a controllee to a particular area was replaced by the more limited power to exclude him from a specified area or place.[137]
- Curfews, which could be up to 16 hours under the control order regime, were replaced with 'overnight residence measures'.[138] In the first year of the TPIM Act's operation, the overnight resident requirement never exceeded 10 hours.[139]
- Those subject to orders must be allowed to have a telephone, fixed line access to the internet and a mobile phone without internet access.[140] Subjects of control orders were rarely allowed to have computers.
- Police searches for the purpose of determining whether an individual is complying with a TPIM now require a judicial warrant.[141] This ends, or at least curbs, the power of the police to enter the residence at any time to ascertain whether the terms of the order are being contravened.[142]
- The evidentiary standard for 'terrorism related activity' has moved from 'reasonable suspicion' to 'reasonable belief'. The latter standard is held to require belief that something *is* the case, as opposed to the belief that it *may be* the case.[143]

A signal change effected in the move from control orders to TPIMs is the introduction of a two-year time limit.[144] A limit of this duration had been championed

[135] One parliamentary critic of control orders stated that the TPIM Bill 'starts to tackle some of the grossest abuses of human rights that existed under the control order system, but I would like it to go further': Tom Brake, HC Deb 7 June 2011, vol 526 col 88.

[136] The measures are exhaustively provided for in sch 1 to the TPIM Act 2011.

[137] ibid, sch 1, para 3.

[138] ibid, sch 1, para 1.

[139] David Anderson QC, *Terrorism Prevention and Investigation Measures in 2012: First Report of the Independent Reviewer on the Operation of the Terrorism Prevention and Investigation Measures Act* (London, The Stationery Office, 2013) para 5.18.

[140] TPIM Act 2011, sch 1, para 7(3).

[141] ibid, sch 5, para 8.

[142] See text to n 74 above.

[143] *Secretary of State for the Home Department v CC and CF* [2012] EWHC 2837 (Admin), [24], [23]–[29] (Lloyd Jones LJ).

[144] TPIM Act 2011, s 5. Two qualifications on this limit are that it does not take into account time a person may have spent subject to control orders, and a new TPIM can be issued where there is 'new

by Lord Carlile, the first Independent Reviewer of Terrorism Legislation,[145] and the idea was endorsed by the Joint Committee on Human Rights.[146] As initially promoted by both parliamentary and academic commentators, the idea of a maximum limit was linked to concerns about the impact of the measures and the need to incentivise other mechanisms. A time limit would serve 'both as an important safeguard of the liberty and mental health of the individuals concerned, and as a discipline on the investigative and enforcement authorities' to find evidence for prosecution within a reasonable time.[147] On the latter function, it was hoped that a time limit would convert the preventive measures into either a form of provisional-charge or provisional-deportation detention, allowing time for the gathering of evidence, or making of arrangements.[148]

Recent reports of the Independent Reviewer express doubts as to whether those held under the measures will ever be able to be prosecuted.[149] In the absence of hopes for such an 'exit' from the regime, commitment to a time limit becomes more explicitly normative: 'if secret intelligence cannot be transformed into evidence over time, or if the State fails to obtain new evidence, the preventive measures should cease.'[150] The view that preventive constraints that severely infringe rights on the basis of anticipatory risk assessment should be temporary, albeit of extended duration, is most convincingly registered by the introduction of the two-year limit in the TPIM Act 2011. That limit on a number of current TPIM subjects will 'definitively expire, without the possibility of extension or replacement, in January 2014'.[151]

terrorism related activity'. On the first qualification, all nine subjects served with the first batch of TPIMs in early 2012 had been subject to control orders at the expiry of that regime: Anderson (n 139) paras 4.4 and 4.15(g); and Anderson (n 62) para 4.11.

[145] See eg Lord Carlile QC, *Third Report of the Independent Reviewer Pursuant to Section 14(3) of the Prevention of Terrorism Act 2005*, 18 February 2008 (London, The Stationery Office, 2008) para 50, 51; Lord Carlile QC, *Sixth Report of the Independent Reviewer Pursuant to Section 14(3) of the Prevention of Terrorism Act 2005*, 3 February 2011 (London, The Stationery Office, 2011) para 55. Between these two reports the recommendation changed from a statutory presumption against extension beyond two years, except in exceptional circumstances, to a maximum of two years with renewal only where there was evidence of new terrorist activity.

[146] See JCHR, 2008 Report (n 94) para 87; Joint Committee on Human Rights, *Counter-Terrorism Policy and Human Rights (Fourteenth Report): Annual Renewal of Control Orders Legislation 2009* (2008–09, HL 37, HC 282), para 30.

[147] JCHR, 2008 Report (n 94) para 87.

[148] See ibid, para 86. See also Clive Walker, 'Keeping Control of Terrorists Without Losing Control of Constitutionalism' (2007) 59 *Stanford Law Review* 1395, 1458, 1463; Clive Walker, 'The Threat of Terrorism and the Fate of Control Orders' [2010] *PL* 4, 16.

[149] Anderson (n 62) para 5.18.

[150] Joint Committee on Human Rights, *Counter-Terrorism Policy and Human Rights (Fourteenth Report): Annual Renewal of Control Orders Legislation 2009* (2008–09, HL 37, HC 282), para 32, quoting Eminent Jurists Panel, International Commission of Jurists, *Assessing Damage, Urging Action: Report of the Eminent Jurists Panel on Terrorism, Counter-Terrorism and Human Rights* (International Commission of Jurists, 17 February 2009) 122.

[151] Anderson (n 139) para 4.16.

7.7 The Position of Non-Citizens

In his most recent annual review, the Independent Reviewer stated: 'The journey from indefinite detention (2001) through control orders (2005) to TPIMs (2011) has been in a liberalising direction.'[152] I share this assessment of the trajectory, though the 'liberalisation' started from a very low base and TPIMs retain many of the features that troubled critics of control orders. The Reviewer goes on to add 'the important caveat that British citizens as well as non-nationals have been subject to the latter two regimes'.[153] In evaluating the effects of the House of Lords' decision in *Belmarsh*, I am interested in whether the caveat concerning the extension of the preventive regime to citizens has contributed to the liberalising trajectory: starting with Part 4 of the ATCSA 2001 to control orders and now TPIMs.

The idea behind the claim is simple, even if substantiating it is not. An insistence on general application of the law, irrespective of citizenship status, enables non-citizens to achieve a measure of 'virtual representation' in the legislature.[154] It helps to ensure that it is in the interest of members of the electorate to avoid unduly harsh and disproportionate laws. Equality provides a measure of political protection for the vulnerable. It is an idea that is succinctly expressed in the passage from Jackson J's judgment in *Railway Express* that recurred through the *Belmarsh* litigation:

> equality is not merely abstract justice. The framers of the Constitution knew, and we should not forget today, that there is no more effective guaranty against arbitrary and unreasonable government than to require that the principles of law which officials would impose upon a minority must be imposed generally. Conversely, nothing opens the door to arbitrary action so effectively as to allow those officials to pick and choose only a few to whom they will apply legislation and thus to escape the political retribution that might be visited upon them if larger numbers were effected. Courts can take no better measure to assure that laws will be just than to require that laws be equal in operation.[155]

Contrary to indefinite detention under Part 4 of the ATCSA 2001, TPIMs (and previously control orders) apply equally to citizens and non-citizens. Preventive orders have received close scrutiny in judicial, parliamentary and other fora. The question is whether, and to what extent, the extension of the measures to citizens has been a factor contributing to that close scrutiny. The question of the *extent* of the contribution requires a fuller study than is afforded here. Nonetheless, a

[152] ibid, para 1.13.

[153] ibid, para 1.13.

[154] Neal Katyal, 'Equality in the War on Terror' (2007) 59 *Stanford Law Review* 1365, 1382.

[155] *Railway Express Agency Inc v New York*, 336 US 106, 112–13 (1949). The passage is quoted in *A v Secretary of State for the Home Department* [2002] EWCA Civ 1502, [2004] QB 335 (*Belmarsh (Court of Appeal)*), [7] (Lord Woolf CJ) and *A v Secretary of State for the Home Department* [2004] UKHL 56, [2005] 2 AC 68, [46] (Lord Bingham). The passage is also quoted by Katyal (n 154) 1370.

review of the parliamentary debates on the POTA 2005 and the TPIM Act 2011 discloses that the measures are repeatedly condemned for the severity of their effect on the liberties of British subjects. The extension of the measures to citizens played *a* role in the level of antipathy, and scrutiny, that the measures encountered.

The liberalising trend referred to above is paralleled by another: a steadily declining portion of controlees who are non-citizens. As recorded in the Independent Reviewer's report for 2011:

> Of the 52 men subject to control orders between 2005 and 2011, 24 were British citizens (including some with dual nationality) and 28 were foreign nationals. There was however a marked change in the use of control orders over their period of operation. Initially, control orders were used solely against foreign nationals who had previously been subject to detention under Part 4 of ATCSA 2001. By the end, the subject of each of the nine control orders in force was a British citizen.[156]

In 2005, the first year of the control order regime's operation, eight of the nine subjects of control orders in force at the year's end were non-citizens.[157] In 2009, of those subject to control orders, nine were citizens and three were non-citizens.[158] *All* of the subjects of control orders at the time that regime was replaced by the TPIM regime in late 2011 were citizens.[159]

A significant factor in the declining portion of controlees who were non-citizens has been an 'aggressive policy of deportations' following the London bombings of July 2005,[160] though that terrorist act was perpetrated by British nationals. Ten of those held under control orders exited the regime when they were issued with notices of intention to deport, and six of those were deported.[161] In the debates on the introduction of the TPIM Act 2011, statements on the incompatibility of preventive orders with British traditions of liberty were followed by exhortations to 're-inject energy into our decision to negotiate memorandums of understanding',[162] where these memorandums are to enable deportation by addressing concerns that a deportee faces a real risk of torture upon return. Conversely, in arguing against the continuance of preventive orders, the same voices that emphasised the need for increased use of deportation contended that control orders were 'supposed to apply only to foreign nationals. There are now no foreign national controlees – they are all UK residents. All the reasons we had these things in the first place have gone.'[163]

[156] Anderson (n 62) para 3.14.
[157] See Walker (n 54) 324 table 7.1 (drawing on Home Office Statements to Parliament).
[158] See ibid.
[159] Anderson (n 62) para 3.14.
[160] Walker (n 62) para 7.102.
[161] Anderson (n 62) para 3.50.
[162] Patrick Mercer, HC Deb 7 June 2011, vol 529 col 98. See also Dominic Raab, HC Deb 7 June 2011, vol 529 col 111: 'I would welcome further still measures to strengthen our deportation capacity'; Stephen Pound, HC Deb 5 September 2011, vol 532 col 112.
[163] Patrick Mercer, HC Deb 7 June 2011, vol 529 col 101; Stephen Pound, HC Deb 5 September 2011, vol 532 col 112.

Recourse to deportation has been accompanied, and facilitated, by a range of legislative and regulatory initiatives directed at facilitating deportation on grounds of national security. Together with exclusion, deportation is usefully thought of as comprising an 'exit model' of response to foreign terror suspects, additional to and alongside criminal prosecution and orders imposing preventive constraints.[164] The exit model comprises a package of measures directed at removing those of concern from the United Kingdom. Among its attractions for the government, it promises a relatively conclusive means of eliminating risk, and is attended by attenuated procedural protections as compared to the criminal law or under preventive orders.[165]

To outline several of the measures comprising the current 'exit model', in the wake of the London bombings a list of 'unacceptable behaviours' was published as guidelines for deportation or exclusion under the Immigration Act 1971 (UK).[166] The list is directed to the deportation and exclusion of those who, absent any proven criminality or any direct threat to security, are deemed to pose an indirect threat by way of the views they express.[167] This constitutes an extension of the 'not conducive to the public good' ground of deportation. Since late 2003, considerable attention has also been devoted to securing diplomatic assurances to deport to countries where there is a prima facie risk of torture.[168] Deportation with assurances is a direct response to the problem of the 'irremovable foreigner' that generated the *Belmarsh* jurisprudence on indefinite detention of non-citizens. Assurances on the part of the receiving state can render lawful a removal that would otherwise contravene the Article 3 prohibition on deportation to torture, or other rights. Further, the class of persons who may be swept up in the exit strategy is wider than commonly assumed, extending to current citizens. The expansion of government powers to unilaterally strip a citizen of that status means that current possession of British citizenship may no longer preclude future deportation,[169] provided it does not render the person stateless.[170] The relevant criterion for deprivation of citizenship replicates that for deportation. A British

[164] Clive Walker, 'The Treatment of Foreign Terror Suspects' (2007) 70 *MLR* 427. Walker also includes a fourth 'war model', but this has not had much traction in the United Kingdom.

[165] Walker (n 54) para 7.121.

[166] Home Office, 'Tackling Terrorism – Behaviours Unacceptable in the UK', press release 124/2005 (24 August 2005). See also Home Office, *Countering International Terrorism: The United Kingdom's Strategy* (Cm 6888, July 2006) 12.

[167] See Walker (n 164) 434–37; James Hampshire, 'Disembedding Liberalism? Immigration Policies and Security' in Terri E Givens, Gary P Freeman and David L Neal (eds), *Immigration Policy and Security* (New York, Routledge, 2009) 109, 123.

[168] See Walker (n 164) 441–50. Jennifer Tooze, 'Deportation with Assurances: The Approach of the UK Courts' [2010] *PL* 362, 376–85.

[169] British Nationality Act 1981, s 40 as amended by the Nationality Immigration and Asylum Act 2002, s 4(1) and the Immigration, Asylum and Nationality Act 2006, s 56. On changes to citizenship deprivation powers since 11 September 2001 see Rayner Thwaites, 'The Security of Citizenship? Finnis in the Context of the United Kingdom's Citizenship Stripping Provisions' in Fiona Jenkins et al, *Allegiance and Identity in a Globalised World* (Cambridge, Cambridge University Press, forthcoming 2014).

[170] British Nationality Act 1981, s 40(4).

citizen can be stripped of his or her citizenship where the Secretary of State is 'satisfied' that this is 'conducive to the public good'.[171]

In all its aspects, the exit model raises an issue of effectiveness, prominent in *Belmarsh.* To quote the Newton Committee,[172] in turn quoted by Lord Bingham in *Belmarsh:*[173]

> Seeking to deport terrorist suspects does not seem to us to be a satisfactory response, given the risk of exporting terrorism. If people in the UK are contributing to the terrorist effort here or abroad, they should be dealt with here. While deporting such people might free up British police, intelligence, security and prison service resources, it would not necessarily reduce the threat to British interests abroad, or make the world a safer place more generally.[174]

The objection raised there does not appear to have been persuasive to the relevant decision-makers. The preference manifest in current measures is that terrorist suspects are best dealt with elsewhere. A factor in that assessment may be the extensive powers and attenuated rights protections that attend the exit model as compared with prosecution or preventive orders.

In terms of legal constraints on the government's pursuit of a deportation strategy, key legal protections afforded in the context of TPIMs (or earlier, control orders) are not applicable to deportation. The procedural holdings of *MB* and *AF (No 3)* discussed in section 7.5, cumulatively requiring that the subject of the control order 'be given sufficient information about the allegations against him to give effective instructions to the special advocate',[175] do not have direct application to deportation orders.[176] Further, rights protections in relation to both the risk and the severity of rights infringements by the receiving state that will block deportation are more limited than those that apply to rights infringements within the ECHR's territorial jurisdiction.[177]

SIAC has the power to grant bail from immigration detention in cases where individuals are held pending deportation on grounds of national security.[178] The

[171] ibid, s 40.

[172] The ATCSA 2001 provided for the appointment of a committee of Privy Counsellors to review the entire Act within two years.

[173] *Belmarsh* (n 2) [34]; see also [33] (Lord Bingham).

[174] Privy Counsellor Review Committee, *Anti-Terrorism, Crime and Security Act 2001 Review: Report* (HC 2003–04, 100-I), para 195.

[175] *AF (No 3)* (n 106) [81].

[176] See *RB (Algeria) v Secretary of State for the Home Department* [2009] UKHL 10, [2010] 2 AC 110, [178] (Lord Phillips) on the non-applicability of Art 6 of the ECHR to deportation; cf [88] (Lord Phillips).

[177] In relation to Art 6 of the ECHR see *RB v Algeria* (n 181) [106]–[141] (Lord Phillips). And see Mark Elliott, 'United Kingdom: The "War on Terror", UK-Style – The Detention and Deportation of Suspected Terrorists' (2010) 8 *International Journal of Constitutional Law* 131, 138–45. Elliott criticises *RB (Algeria)* for the degree of differentiation allowed between the minimum rights standards applicable in Europe and those applicable in the receiving states (Jordan and Algeria).

[178] Immigration Act 1971, sch 2, para 22(1); Special Immigration Appeals Commission Act 1997, s 3 and sch 3. For a description of the statutory framework behind SIAC's power to grant bail to a person who is detained pending deportation on grounds of national security, see *R (on the application of BB) v Special Immigration Appeals Commission* [2012] EWCA Civ 1499, [3] (Lord Dyson).

nature and extent of the conditions that can be imposed upon release on bail are not constrained in the manner of TPIMs.[179] Soon after the introduction of control orders, the JCHR expressed concern about the use of onerous bail conditions under the Immigration Act 1971 against former controlees.[180] In the debates on the TPIM Bill, it was suggested that SIAC bail conditions had been used as a substitute for control orders, and should rightly have been included in the review of conditions to which the control order regime was subject: 'SIAC bail conditions will still permit forced relocation, forced curfews, monitoring with the same level of secrecy and the lack of access, all without any charges being brought.'[181]

The grant of bail assumes the power to detain and so is constrained by the *Hardial Singh* principles,[182] the topic of the next section. Accordingly, TPIMs remain relevant for non-citizens to the extent that deportation is not a realistic prospect.[183]

To summarise the above discussion of the current operation of the 'exit model', *Belmarsh*'s achievement in dislodging preventive detention from the immigration context and requiring equality between citizens and non-citizens has had little direct benefit for non-citizens, as assessed with reference to the successor regimes under the POTA 2005 and the TPIM Act 2011. This is despite the fact that it is arguable that *Belmarsh* had the democracy–reinforcing effect anticipated by Jackson J in the passage from *Railway Express.* The extension of preventive measures to citizens contributed to the antipathy they aroused and the attention they received, with the legislative and jurisprudential history of the measures charting a restriction of powers and the development of procedural protections. But non-citizens were increasingly only marginal and occasional beneficiaries of this diminution in the extent of obligations that could be imposed on the subjects of orders and the strengthening of procedural protections. The liberalising trend evident in the successor regimes to Part 4 of the ATCSA 2001 has been accompanied by the deployment of an increasing armoury of other measures directed at the removal and exclusion of non-citizens determined to pose a risk to security.

[179] See eg *AP* (n 98) [8]: 'since 20 July 2009, AP has been on bail pending deportation on conditions, including residence in the Midlands, similar to those of the control order [he was previously on] save that the curfew period is now 18 hours.'

[180] JCHR, 2006 Report (n 50) paras 43–44; see Appendix 4 to that report, 'Submission from Campaign Against Criminalising Communities'.

[181] Richard Fuller, HC Deb 7 June 2011, vol 529 col 122. See also Fuller's earlier statements at HC Deb 7 June 2011, vol 529 col 109.

[182] See eg *R (Omar Othman) v SIAC* [2012] EWHC 2349.

[183] For a statement to this effect see Anderson (n 62) para 5.27.

7.8 Development of the *Hardial Singh* Principles

7.8.1 Confirmation and Elaboration of the Principles

The main legal limitation on the discretion to detain pending deportation contained in the Immigration Act 1971 remains the *Hardial Singh* principles.[184] These principles have been reaffirmed and refined in a number of authorities over recent years, the most significant of which is *Lumba*.[185] In addition to the issue of non-compliance with the *Hardial Singh* principles, *Lumba* was directed to whether a breach of a public law duty could have the consequence that detention became unlawful.

In *Lumba*, the United Kingdom Supreme Court reaffirmed the *Hardial Singh* principles. I examine the decision's affirmation of those principles by way of analysis of a challenge to them. In his dissent Lord Phillips mounted an extended attack on the prevailing understanding of the *Hardial Singh* principles. If accepted, his alternative account of the principles would shift them from the rights-protecting model, towards its rights-precluding competitor. Lord Phillips' dissent on the *Hardial Singh* principles, and Lord Hope's response to him, go to the lawful purposes of immigration detention and their relation to national security. *Lumba* not only affirmed but elaborated on the principles, with Lord Dyson giving extended consideration to factors going to whether detention was for a 'reasonable time'. Finally, I flag the existence of other limitations on the lawfulness of detention, arising from breach of public law duties, as discussed in *Lumba* and *Kambadzi*.

Lumba reaffirmed the principles as they were summarised in *R(I) v Secretary of State for the Home Department*,[186] namely:

> (i) the Secretary of State must intend to deport the person and can only use the power to detain for that purpose; (ii) the deportee may only be detained for a period that is reasonable in all the circumstances; (iii) if, before the expiry of the reasonable period, it becomes apparent that the Secretary of State will not be able to effect deportation within a reasonable period, he should not seek to exercise the power of detention; (iv) the Secretary of State should act with reasonable diligence and expedition to effect removal.[187]

This account of the *Hardial Singh* principles was endorsed by eight of the nine members of the bench in *Lumba*,[188] with Lord Phillips dissenting.

[184] *R v Governor of Durham Prison, ex parte Singh* [1983] EWHC 1 (QB), [1984] 1 All ER 983 (*Hardial Singh*). See ch 5, s 5.2.

[185] *R (on the application of Lumba) v Secretary of State for the Home Department* [2011] UKSC 12, [2012] 1 AC 245.

[186] *R(I) v Secretary of State for the Home Department* [2003] INLR 196.

[187] *Lumba* (n 185) [22] (Lord Dyson), citing *R(I) v SSHD* (n 191) [46] (Lord Dyson).

[188] ibid, [22] (Lord Dyson), [171] (Lord Hope), [189] (Lord Walker), [250] (Lord Kerr), [347] (Lord Brown, Lord Rodger in agreement), and see [258] (Lord Phillips, dissenting): 'Lord Dyson . . . rightly

One proposition underlying the above principles is that the initial authority to detain cannot 'be regarded as comprehensive of the issues which are germane to the continued lawfulness of detention'.[189] '[D]etention which is lawful initially can be transformed to a condition of illegality.'[190] This proposition is fundamental to any variant of a rights-protecting approach to immigration detention. A second proposition implicit in the discussion of the principles in the judgments is that it is for the courts, not the Secretary of State, to determine whether the *Hardial Singh* principles have been complied with.[191]

In elaborating on the *Hardial Singh* principles, the contrast between the majority opinion and that of Lord Phillips delineates points of distinction between the rights-protecting and rights-precluding approaches to detention pending removal outlined in chapter one. The majority's reading of the four principles instantiated a variant of the rights-protecting approach. By way of contrast, Lord Phillips proposed an approach best characterised, in terms of the models outlined in chapter one, as rights-precluding. To introduce the differences, Lord Phillips argued that the first two of the four principles listed in *R(I)* cannot be derived from *Hardial Singh*. He challenged the continued application of these two principles. The majority defended all four of the listed principles.

To begin with the area of agreement between Lord Phillips and the majority, in his dissent Lord Phillips accepted the third principle, the need for a realistic possibility of removal, but gave it a very different function from the majority. In the leading judgment, Lord Dyson emphasised that this principle is the threshold question for authority to detain. If there is no realistic prospect of removal, continued detention is unlawful, regardless of whether or not a 'reasonable time' has elapsed.[192] This expresses the purposive orientation of the rights-protecting approach. Lord Phillips instead spoke in terms of deportation being a 'practical possibility'.[193] Lacking the support of the first two principles on Lord Phillips' approach, the need for a realistic possibility of removal appears to allow for detention for an inordinate length of time, provided that the possibility of deportation is not conclusively foreclosed. The fourth principle, which requires the Secretary of State to act with reasonable diligence and expedition to effect removal, was uncontroversial. It was accepted by Lord Phillips (and is consistent with both rights-protecting and rights-precluding models of detention pending removal).

It was the first two principles with which Lord Phillips took issue. He accepted that detention is only authorised where removal is a 'practical possibility', but rejected the requirement that detention be for a reasonable time. The reasonable

states that it has been common ground in these appeals that he correctly summarised the effect of *Hardial Singh* . . . in the four principles he set out in [*R(I) v SSHD*].'

[189] *R (Kambadzi) v Secretary of State for the Home Department* [2011] UKSC 23, [2011] 1 WLR 1299, [82] (Lord Kerr). See also [50] (Lord Hope).

[190] ibid, [82] (Lord Kerr).

[191] *R (on the application of Anam) v Secretary of State for the Home Department (No 2)* [2012] EWHC 1770 (Admin), [32] (Walker J).

[192] *Lumba* (n 185) [103] (Lord Dyson).

[193] ibid, [283], and see [337] (Lord Phillips).

time requirement is a direct expression of the detainees' liberty interest and the proportionality analysis anchored by that liberty interest. Finally, Lord Phillips unequivocally departed from the rights-protecting approach in stating that concerns such as national security, independent of any relationship of proportionality with removal, might justify the continued detention of a non-citizen so long as removal remains in prospect. Reflecting on the position of the applicant in *Chahal*,[194] Lord Phillips stated:

> Provided that he was being detained with a view to his removal as soon as reasonably possible I consider that the Secretary of State was entitled to detain him pending that removal on the ground that he would pose a terrorist threat if released.[195]

Lord Hope responded to Lord Phillips that to release the Secretary of State from limitations as to the purpose of the power would be 'regrettable', in that it would reduce the protections the *Hardial Singh* principles were designed to give the detainee.[196] It would allow for the utilisation of detention pending removal for national security purposes, independent of, and so not constrained by,[197] a proportionate connection with deportation. Though not stated by Lord Hope, Lord Phillips' argument here challenged a central achievement of the *Belmarsh* decision, namely the clear distinction it drew between detention for deportation purposes and preventive detention confined to non-citizens.

Lord Hope correctly identified the fundamental connection between the limit as to purpose and the limit as to time:

> It is hard also to see how the limitation as to time which Lord Phillips PSC accepts can be read into the statute can be tested without having regard to the purpose for which the detainee is being held. The limitation as to time and the limitation as to purpose are really two sides of the same coin. They cannot be separated from each other.[198]

The viability of removal, assessed by a system of review, is determinative of whether or not the period of detention has continued beyond what is 'reasonable', and so whether or not it is authorised.[199]

The basic proposition underlying the *Hardial Singh* principles is that a non-citizen issued with a deportation order retains a right to liberty. That right can be infringed for the purpose of facilitating removal, but it remains, weighing more heavily with the passage of time. 'There must come a time when, however grave the risk of absconding and however grave the risk of serious offending, it ceases to be lawful to detain a person pending deportation.'[200] Or, as stated by Baroness Hale:

> the Secretary of State may genuinely be doing all that she can to effect deportation, and deportation may still be a realistic possibility, but even so the deportee may have been

[194] *Chahal* (n 15).
[195] *Lumba* (n 185) [269] (Lord Phillips).
[196] ibid, [174] (Lord Hope).
[197] Other than the overarching need for deportation to remain a 'practical possibility'.
[198] *Lumba* (n 185) [174] (Lord Hope).
[199] See ibid, [250] (Lord Kerr).
[200] ibid, [144] (Lord Dyson).

> detained for so long that it is no longer lawful to keep him there. That this has never until now [by Lord Phillips in dissent] been questioned indicates how strong are the objections to indefinite detention by order of the executive.[201]

The response of these members of the majority to Lord Phillips on the purposes of detention captures the way in which it is differences as to the legitimate purposes of detention pending deportation that separate the rights-protecting and rights-precluding approaches. Both Lord Dyson and Baroness Hale endorsed the submission of Michael Fordham QC that the *Hardial Singh* principles simply express the basic public law duties to act consistently with the statutory purpose (*Padfield*)[202] and reasonably in the *Wednesbury*[203] sense.[204] The disagreement with Lord Philips turned on what the statutory purpose is.

In addition to affirming the centrality of purpose of facilitating removal, *Lumba* elaborated on the nature of the inquiry the *Hardial Singh* principles require. In an extended passage in his reasons, Lord Dyson discussed a range of circumstances bearing on authority to detain and the length of detention, with a view to addressing the question of 'how long is a reasonable period' of detention pending removal.[205] Lord Dyson's treatment has been accepted as determinative of the issues he covered.[206] Judicial determination of a reasonable period involves the weighing of a number of factors that

> include at least: the length of the period of detention; the nature of the obstacles which stand in the path of the Secretary of State preventing a deportation; the diligence, speed and effectiveness of the steps taken by the Secretary of State to surmount such obstacles; the conditions in which the detained person is being kept; the effect of detention on him and his family; the risk that if he is released from detention he will abscond; and the danger that, if released, he will commit criminal offences.[207]

In elaborating on the principles, Lord Dyson's focus was on the risk of absconding, and the inferences going to that risk that could, or could not, be drawn from particular facts. Animating the discussion was the view that detention pending removal is a practical measure, the infringement of liberty justified by, and proportionate to, the purpose of ensuring a person's presence at the time of removal. The idea that initial authority to detain is 'comprehensive of the issues which are germane to the continued lawfulness of detention' was rejected.[208] The approach outlined by Lord Dyson allows for the development of case law and doctrine that begins to address the complexity of detention pending deportation, aspiring to accommodate both the detainee's rights and the reasonable needs of immigration control.

[201] ibid, [200] (Baroness Hale).
[202] *Padfield v Minister of Agriculture, Fisheries and Food* [1968] AC 997.
[203] *Associated Provincial Picture Houses Ltd v Wednesbury Corporation* [1948] 1 KB 223.
[204] *Lumba* (n 185), [30] (Lord Dyson), [199] (Baroness Hale).
[205] ibid, [102]–[148].
[206] See eg *R (Anam)* (n 191).
[207] *Lumba* (n 185) [104], quoting *R(I)* (n 186) [48].
[208] *Kambadzi* (n 189) [82] (Lord Kerr).

7.8.2 The Consequences of Breach of a Public Law Duty

The confirmation and elaboration of the *Hardial Singh* principles is an important feature of *Lumba* and *Kambadzi*. Another aspect of the decisions' significance lies in the finding that a breach of public law duty by the Secretary of State could (and in both cases did) render that detention unlawful, giving rise to a claim in damages for false imprisonment.[209] As to which public law errors render detention unlawful, the test is whether the breach of public law bears on or is relevant to the decision to detain.[210] The error must be capable of affecting the decision to detain or not to detain.[211] In *Lumba*, the application of an unlawful, unpublished policy to the plaintiff's detention was held to have the effect of rendering the Home Secretary's exercise of the power to detain unlawful. In *Kambadzi*, the relevant error of public law was the failure to adhere to published policy on the review of detention.

The proposition that breach of a public law duty can render detention unlawful adds to the law that limits the Secretary of State's authority to detain under the statute.[212] 'The requirements of the 1971 Act and *Hardial Singh* principles are not the only applicable law with which the Secretary of State must comply.'[213] He or she must also be mindful of the normal public law duties insofar as they bear on the decision to detain, or not to detain.

When breach of a public law duty can render detention unlawful, this situates such detention more firmly within the body of generally applicable public law principles. In *Kambadzi*, the government argued that authority to detain under the original authority of the statute was unassailable on public law grounds other than the *Hardial Singh* principles.[214] The government allowed that the facts under dispute might have violated public law principles, giving rise to legal remedies. But it denied that these errors of public law could affect the authority to detain. The United Kingdom Supreme Court's rejection of this government submission challenges and qualifies the idea that authority to hold a person in immigration detention is not subject to the same legal constraints as other public powers. The Supreme Court reasoned: 'Where there is an executive discretion to detain someone without limit of time, the right to liberty demands that the cause of action [false imprisonment] should be available if the discretion has not been lawfully exercised.'[215]

[209] *Lumba* (n 185), [196] (Baroness Hale), [340] (Lord Brown, Lord Rodger concurring).

[210] ibid, [68] (Lord Dyson). Confirmed in *Kambadzi* (n 189) [30], [33] (Lord Hope), [69] (Baroness Hale).

[211] *Lumba* (n 185), [68] (Lord Dyson).

[212] *Kambadzi* (n 189) [31]–[33] (Lord Hope).

[213] ibid, [40] (Lord Hope).

[214] ibid, [32] (Lord Hope).

[215] ibid, [40] (Lord Hope).

7.9 Conclusion

In *Belmarsh*, the House of Lords held that the confinement of indefinite detention measures to non-citizens was irrational, arbitrary and discriminatory. It further held that the fact that the detention measures had not been seen as strictly necessary for British terrorist suspects raised the question of the need for indefinite detention more generally. The government did not explain why it was necessary only for non-citizens, leading to the ruling that the indefinite detention measures were arbitrary and unnecessary. The House of Lords removed a national security power of indefinite detention from the range of options having the sanction of the courts. An additional factor shaping the parliamentary and governmental response was Lord Bingham's comments on the adequacy of bail conditions to meet the security threat.[216] To the extent that these comments shaped the preventive regimes that followed, Lord Bingham may have failed to fully anticipate the intrusiveness of such regimes or their adverse impact on those subject to them.

As highlighted in the parliamentary debates, the parliamentary response could have ceased to detain without trial,[217] or have enacted a more limited and less intrusive set of constraints. Parliament and the government instead enacted the control order regime discussed in this chapter. In operation that regime gave rise to substantially the same harms as the regime of indefinite detention it replaced, namely an intolerable level of intrusion and control over a detainee's life.

The control order and TPIM regimes, and the jurisprudence they have generated, give rise to a sense of dissatisfaction: the various judicial holdings that a particular condition infringes a particular right seem too piecemeal and reactive, and leave the basic iniquity of a system of preventative constraint without charge largely unaffected.[218] The rights rulings do not appear to be unified by any overarching understanding of how control orders could be transformed into a coherent, rights-respecting practice.[219] Another way of expressing this dissatisfaction is that the control order regime seems to offend against fundamental assumptions of autonomy and responsibility that underpin the various rights, but are not captured by any of them.

The intrusiveness of preventive detention measures has declined in the period since their introduction in 2005. The most significant legal development in relation to the content of the relevant orders was the adoption of the TPIM Act 2011. I have proposed in this chapter that a reason for this legislative development was the extension of the measures to citizens. The basic thesis is that an insistence on the general application of the law tempers the tendency to sanction harsh and disproportionate laws in the confidence that they are only applicable to others.

[216] *Belmarsh* (n 2) [35] (Lord Bingham). This connection is discussed in ch 6, s 6.5.
[217] See above, s 7.4.1, text to n 69 and following.
[218] See Ewing and Tham (n 93) 688–90.
[219] For a discussion on this theme see Zedner (n 52), especially 183–87.

The fact that a burden is shared by citizens and non-citizens alike provides non-citizens with a measure of political protection. The application of the measures to British subjects was cited in parliamentary arguments for reducing the intrusiveness of the measures. The TPIM Act 2011 introduced a two-year limit for measures of preventive detention and constraint, and authorised a more limited list of measures than under the POTA 2005.[220]

While these changes have improved the regime in rights terms, they have also reduced its attractiveness to government, at least as a means of addressing the security risk posed by foreigners. Preventive detention has fallen from government favour as a means of dealing with unwanted non-citizens. Other means of pursuing an 'exit' strategy have come to prominence. The means before the House of Lords in *Belmarsh* – indefinite detention of non-citizens – is only one option for a government intent on removing from the community non-citizens believed to pose a risk. Other means, attended by fewer rights protections, are available.[221]

Turning from national security to the use of immigration detention more generally, a number of key decisions, notably *Lumba*,[222] have maintained *Belmarsh*'s commitment to the proposition that the purpose of facilitating removal defines and limits the duration of detention pending removal.[223] In addition, *Lumba* and *Kambadzi* held that an error of public law can render detention unlawful, expressing an understanding of immigration detention as continuous with the wider body of public law, subject to its rules and constraints.[224]

[220] A new TPIM can be issued where there is 'new terrorism related activity': see n 144 above.

[221] See s 7.7.

[222] *Lumba* (n 185).

[223] Lord Phillips' dissent in *Lumba* highlights the ever-present possibility of a reversal or attenuation of this commitment.

[224] *Kambadzi* (n 189).

Canada

8

The Charter and Security Certificates

> [A]liens seem to suffer under an extended, severe handicap when they seek to apply elements of fundamental rights to domestic law immigration processes . . . Permission to enter Canada is not viewed as a right, but a privilege to be granted on whatever terms are deemed appropriate by the state. While courts do often speak of aliens having statutory rights, or those rights which are extended by the State in relation to the administration of immigration, the underlying presumption seems to be that aliens have no cause for complaint if legislative rights do not measure up to an objective standard offered by a concept of overriding fundamental rights. This anomaly seems to suggest that aliens may not be able to point to a bill or Charter of rights as a source of protection from infringing provisions of immigration statutes, because the presence of aliens within the jurisdiction is a matter of privilege.
>
> Christopher J Wydrzynski, *Canadian Immigration Law and Procedure* (1983)[1]

8.1 Introduction to the Canadian Chapters

Charkaoui upheld the constitutionality of the indefinite detention of non-citizens subject to a deportation order.[2] The decision was a legal challenge to Canada's security certificate regime, dedicated to the deportation and detention of foreign terrorist suspects and others certified as inadmissible to Canada. The Supreme Court upheld the regime, subject to changes to its procedures mandated by the Charter.[3] The security certificate regime has proved dysfunctional when assessed against its ostensible statutory purpose of facilitating the removal of foreign terrorist suspects. It has resulted in indefinite detention or constraint, not removal. The Supreme Court accepted the regime's characterisation as detention pending deportation, so justifying its confinement to non-citizens.

This chapter provides the background needed to situate *Charkaoui* in its legal context, with the decision itself the subject of chapter nine. In sections 8.2–8.4, I examine approaches to the Charter that have led to the extension, and withholding,

[1] Christopher J Wydrzynski, *Canadian Immigration Law and Procedure* (Aurora, Canada Law Book, 1983) 458–59.

[2] *Charkaoui v Canada (Minister of Citizenship and Immigration)* 2007 SCC 9, [2007] 1 SCR 350.

[3] Canadian Charter of Rights and Freedoms, Part I of the Constitution Act, 1982, being Schedule B to the Canada Act 1982 (UK), c 11 (Charter).

of legal protections to non-citizens. The immediate legal context for *Charkaoui* is the subject of sections 8.5–8.7. The statutory detention regime in issue, the security certificate regime, is the subject of section 8.5. In section 8.6 I introduce a key precursor to *Charkaoui*, *Suresh*.[4] Canadian Federal Court cases on security certificates, detailing the detention regime's operation prior to *Charkaoui*, are the subject of section 8.7.

8.2 Citizenship in the Constitution

In Canada, as in Australia and the United Kingdom, the national government's competence regarding immigration is grounded in legislation, not the prerogative.[5] The Constitution Act 1867 provides authority for legislation relating to aliens and immigration. Like the Australian Constitution, it contains separate heads of federal legislative power in relation to immigration,[6] and aliens and naturalisation.[7] Older pre-Charter legal disputes centring on issues of discrimination against foreigners and race were litigated with reference to the division between federal and provincial competencies.[8] But in the debates covered in this book, issues concerning discrimination against non-citizens have been fought in different legal terrain. They have largely become Charter disputes, and not only in the sense that legal challenges to alleged discrimination rely on Charter rights. The textual justification for differential treatment has also been grounded in the Charter.

'Citizenship' is not defined in the Canadian Constitution. As in Australia, this is attributable to Canada's original status as a Dominion of the British Empire. At the time the Constitution was drafted, the relevant personal status was not 'Canadian citizen' but British subject. As a statutory concept, it was only with the passing of the Citizenship Act in 1976 that 'alien' was dropped as the relevant statutory concept and replaced by 'person who is not a Canadian citizen'.[9]

With the advent of the Charter, citizenship took on constitutional implications. Canadian citizenship entitles the holder to voting rights (section 3),[10] mobility

[4] *Suresh v Canada (Minister of Citizenship and Immigration)* 2002 SCC 1, [2002] 1 SCR 3.

[5] See Wydrzynski (n 1) 25–26.

[6] Constitution Act 1867, s 95. This section is a rare Canadian instance of a concurrent power, conferred on both the federal Parliament and the provincial legislatures. It is qualified by the requirement that any provincial law shall have effect 'as long and as far only as it is not repugnant to a federal law': see WH McConnell, *Commentary on the British North America Act* (Toronto, Macmillan of Canada, 1977) 304–07.

[7] Constitution Act 1867, s 91(25). In *Law Society of BC v Mangat* 2001 SCC 67, [2001] 3 SCR 113, [35], the Supreme Court of Canada stated that the Canadian case law was unhelpful on the tensions '*within* the federal domain between ss 91(25) [aliens and naturalisation] and 95 [immigration]'. This is distinct from the Australian situation, where at most points in time there was a clear reliance on one or the other power, with a historical shift from the immigration power to the aliens power: see ch 2, s 2.2.1.

[8] See eg *Union Colliery v Bryden* [1889] AC 580; *Cunningham v Tomey Homma* [1903] AC 151.

[9] Citizenship Act RSC 1985.

[10] Section 3 only regulates voting for the federal Parliament.

rights (section 6),[11] and minority language educational rights (section 23). Section 6(1) of the Charter reads: 'Every citizen of Canada has the right to enter, remain in and leave Canada.' In the Supreme Court's 1992 decision in *Chiarelli*,[12] discussed in section 8.4.3 below, the fact that section 6(1) of the Canadian Charter confers a right to remain only on citizens was drawn upon to support an argument for the differential treatment of non-citizens.

The legal challenge to indefinite administrative detention of non-citizens in *Charkaoui* engaged a range of Charter rights: equality, liberty, freedom from cruel and unusual treatment, and the right not to be arbitrarily detained. In chapter eight I provide legal context in respect of only the first two of these sections: section 15, the right to equality; and the right to liberty under section 7. I discuss section 15 as it most directly addresses the issue of discrimination against non-citizens. I analyse section 7 jurisprudence as it has performed most of the 'jurisprudential heavy lifting' with respect to the liberty and security of the person of non-citizens.[13]

Rights under the Charter are qualified by section 1, the limitations clause, which provides that the Charter 'guarantees the rights and freedoms set out in it subject only to such reasonable limits prescribed by law as can be demonstrably justified in a free and democratic society.' Section 1 is the home of a proportionality analysis under the Charter, most famously given expression in the *Oakes* test.[14] As summarised in *Charkaoui*, the *Oakes* test

> requires a pressing and substantial objective and proportionate means. A finding of proportionality requires: (a) means rationally connected to the objective; (b) minimal impairment of rights; and (c) proportionality between the effects of the infringement and the importance of the objective.[15]

In addition, the Charter contains a notwithstanding clause (section 33), a mechanism which allows Parliament or a legislature to declare, in enacting a law, that that law overrides a nominated right in section 2 or sections 7–15 of the Charter.[16]

8.3 Section 15 of the Charter

I examine statements of the Supreme Court on section 15 and non-citizens' susceptibility to removal from Canada in order to introduce and situate the question

[11] Only s 6(1), relating to mobility across the Canadian national border, is restricted to citizens. The rights under sub-ss 6(2)–(4), relating to mobility between provinces, are conferred on both citizens and permanent residents.

[12] *Canada (Employment and Immigration) v Chiarelli* [1992] 1 SCR 711.

[13] Audrey Macklin, 'Transjudicial Conversations about Security and Human Rights' in Mark Salter (ed), *Mapping Transatlantic Security Relations: The EU, Canada and the War on Terror* (Oxford, Routledge, 2010) 212, 216.

[14] *R v Oakes* [1986] 1 SCR 103.

[15] *Charkaoui* (n 2) [67].

[16] s 33 of the Charter limits the operation of any such declaration to a maximum of five years (s 33(3)), though a declaration can be renewed (s 33(4)).

of how equality of treatment is reconciled with a non-citizen's vulnerability to removal in Canadian constitutional law. Section 15 of the Charter reads, in part,

> (1) Every individual is equal before and under the law and has the right to the equal protection and equal benefit of the law without discrimination and, in particular, without discrimination based on race, national or ethnic origin, colour, religion, sex, age or mental or physical disability.

In its very first judgment on section 15, *Andrews v Law Society of British Columbia*, the Supreme Court declared non-citizen status to be a ground of discrimination analogous to those explicitly set out in section 15. An analogous ground stands as 'a constant marker of potential legislative discrimination'.[17] From the outset, differential treatment of non-citizens was subject to an equality rights analysis under the Charter.

In *Andrews*, the Supreme Court established non-citizen status as an analogous ground by emphasising the historical disadvantage suffered by members of the class. Expanding on the understanding that non-citizens are a 'discrete and insular minority',[18] the Court emphasised the vulnerability and political powerlessness of non-citizens. In Wilson J's words: 'Relative to citizens, non-citizens are a group lacking in political power and as such vulnerable to having their interests overlooked and their rights to equal concern and respect violated.'[19] Quoting John Hart Ely, she stated that non-citizens are among 'those groups in society to whose needs and wishes elected officials have no apparent interest in attending.'[20]

It is not clear what work this characterisation of aliens as a relatively defenceless group needing judicial protection did in *Andrews. Andrews* struck down provincial legislation restricting the right to practise law to Canadian citizens. The reasoning that did the work focused not on the fact that aliens were downtrodden, but on an analysis not dissimilar to that which was successful before the House of Lords in *Belmarsh*, that is, the state could offer no legitimate reason for singling them out. The Supreme Court framed the question as one of whether citizenship was a proxy for good lawyering, understood as being knowledgeable about

[17] *Lavoie v Canada* 2002 SCC 23, [2002] 1 SCR 769, [2] (McLachlin CJ, L'Heureux-Dubé and Binnie JJ dissenting), [41] (Gonthier, Iacobucci, Major and Bastarche JJ) affirming *Corbiere v Canada (Minister of Indian and Northern Affairs)* [1999] 2 SCR 203, [7]–[10]. Cf *Egan v Canada* [1995] 2 SCR 513, [47]–[54].

[18] *Andrews v Law Society of British Columbia* [1989] 1 SCR 143, 183 (McIntyre J) and 152 (Wilson J). The phrase originated in *United States v Carolene Products*, 304 US 144 (1938), 152–53 fn 4.

[19] *Andrews* (n 18) 152.

[20] ibid, citing John Hart Ely, *Democracy and Distrust* (Cambridge, MA, Harvard University Press, 1980) 151. La Forest J's language was stronger again. He stated: 'non-citizens are an example without parallel of a group of persons who are relatively powerless politically, and whose interests are likely to be compromised by legislative decisions', before referring to historical instances of discrimination on grounds of nationality as the companion of discrimination on the basis of race and national or ethnic origin: 195, [76]. As the author of *Disallowance and Reservation of Provincial Legislation* (Ottawa, Department of Justice, 1955), a work documenting provincial immigration legislation targeting 'Asiatics and other orientals', he was well placed to comment on this history. His references to historical instances underline how the place of alienage as an analogous ground was underwritten by historical injustice based on racial or ethnic background, not on non-citizenship as such.

Canadian political and social affairs and committed to the country. The majority held that it was not a good proxy.[21]

Andrews did not address the potential tension between the section 15 guarantee of equality of treatment and the fact that non-citizens do not have an express constitutional right to remain in Canada.[22] The Supreme Court had an opportunity to consider that tension in *Canada (Employment and Immigration) v Chiarelli*.[23] One of the constitutional questions stated in *Chiarelli* was whether section 15 prohibited the mandatory deportation of a non-citizen convicted of an offence carrying a punishment of five years or more.[24] It was not disputed that non-citizens were vulnerable to deportation and citizens were not. It was the particulars of procedures attending the deportation power that were in issue. Sopinka J's response for the Court consisted of a single paragraph, which reads in part:

> As I have already observed, s 6 of the Charter specifically provides for differential treatment of citizens and permanent residents in this regard . . . only citizens are accorded the right to enter, remain in and leave Canada in s 6(1). There is therefore no discrimination contrary to s 15 in a deportation scheme that applies to permanent residents, but not to citizens.[25]

Here, it is simply registered that in Canadian law post-Charter the tension between vulnerability to deportation and limits on differential treatment ancillary to that deportation is inscribed within the Charter, as a relationship between section 6 and section 15.

The Supreme Court reinforced a view of deportation, and more generally mobility rights, as an exception to section 15 in obiter dicta in *Lavoie*.[26] The three claimants in *Lavoie* challenged as discriminatory an express and regulated preference for citizens within the appointment process for the federal public service. Four members of the Court held that the preference in question did violate section 15(1), but was justified under section 1,[27] and two members held that there was no violation.[28] Accordingly, the preference withstood constitutional challenge.[29] After expressing the 'rule' that 'non-citizens are equally vital members of Canadian society and deserve tantamount concern and respect', the majority held: 'The only recognized exception to this rule is where the Constitution itself withholds a benefit from non-citizens, as was the case in *Chiarelli* . . . In such a case it may be said that the Charter itself authorizes differential treatment.'[30]

[21] This characterisation of the decision is informed by Denise Réaume, 'The Relevance of Relevance to Equality Rights' (2006) 31 *Queen's Law Journal* 696, 710.

[22] Certain comments in *Andrews* anticipated that tension: see eg *Andrews* (n 18) 196 (La Forest J). See also *Miron v Trudel* [1995] 2 SCR 418, [139] (McLachlin J) and *Egan* (n 17) [50].

[23] *Chiarelli* (n 12).

[24] ibid, 736.

[25] ibid, [34]. The respondent did not make any submissions on s 15.

[26] *Lavoie* (n 17).

[27] Bastarache J with Gonthier, Iacobucci and Major JJ.

[28] Arbour and LeBel JJ.

[29] McLachlin CJC, L'Heureux-Dubé and Binnie JJ dissented.

[30] *Lavoie* (n 17) [44].

Section 15 is also relevant to the approach taken to section 7 of the Charter. As stated by L'Heureux-Dubé in *New Brunswick (Minister of Health and Community Services) v G (J)*, 'These equality interests should be considered in interpreting the scope and content of the interpretation of the rights guaranteed by s 7'.[31] Section 7 is to be viewed through the 'interpretive lens' of the equality right in section 15.[32]

8.4 Section 7 of the Charter

The Charter provision at the centre of the Canadian jurisprudence on the security certificate regime is the right to 'life, liberty and security of the person' in section 7. The tension between fundamental rights and the idea of their conditional extension to non-citizens has been a marked feature of the section 7 Charter jurisprudence on non-citizens' rights under immigration statutes. One strand of the jurisprudence has welcomed section 7 as marking a break with the presumptions Christopher Wydrzynski complains of in the passage at the beginning of this chapter, that 'aliens have no cause for complaint if legislative rights do not measure up to an objective standard offered by a concept of overriding fundamental rights'.[33] There is, however, another strand of the jurisprudence that fully bears out Wydrzynski's concerns about the tenacity and possible continuing significance of the rights/privilege distinction under the Charter.

8.4.1 Relationship between Section 7 and Section 1 of the Charter

Section 7 of the Charter provides: 'Everyone has the right to life, liberty and security of the person and the right not to be deprived thereof except in accordance with the principles of fundamental justice.' To reiterate, section 7 is subject to the general limitations clause in section 1 of the Charter, which states: 'The [Charter] guarantees the rights and freedoms set out in it subject only to such reasonable limits prescribed by law as can be demonstrably justified in a free and democratic society.'

The submissions in *Charkaoui* devoted considerable space to the appropriate relation between section 7 of the Charter and the limitations clause in section 1.[34] At issue is the point at which societal interests and justificatory policy goals enter

[31] *New Brunswick (Minister of Health and Community Services) v G(J)* [1999] 3 SCR 46, [112] (L'Heureux-Dubé J for Gonthier and McLachlin JJ).

[32] ibid, [112] (L'Heureux-Dubé J for Gonthier and McLachlin JJ).

[33] Wydrzynski (n 1) 458–59. See text to n 1.

[34] eg Factum of Appellant – Mohamed Harkat, *Charkaoui et al v Minister of Citizenship and Immigration*, Supreme Court of Canada File No 31178 (Harkat Factum), [38]–[42]; Factum of Intervener, Amnesty International, *Charkaoui et al v Minister of Citizenship and Immigration*, Supreme Court of Canada File Nos 30929, 30762 and 31178 (Amnesty International Factum), [8]–[19].

the analysis. Two competing approaches to this relation have been discerned in the Canadian Charter jurisprudence: an 'internal balancing' approach, and a 'two-step' approach.[35]

The textual foundation for the internal balancing approach is understanding the phrase 'in accordance with the principles of fundamental justice' in section 7 to qualify the protected interests of 'life, liberty and security of the person'. The two distinct parts of section 7 are seen to create a vehicle for limitation and justification within the section.[36] Societal interests can be factored into an analysis of the 'principles of fundamental justice' to determine their scope. The protection afforded to 'life, liberty and security of the person' waxes and wanes according to the scope given to the principles of fundamental justice. The internal balancing approach has the potential to render section 1 of the Charter redundant in its application to section 7 infringements.

La Forest J offered a rationale for the internal balancing approach in *Godbout v Longueuil*:

> looking to 'the principles of fundamental justice' often involves the more general endeavour of balancing the constitutional right of the individual claimant against the countervailing interests of the state . . . To my mind, performing this balancing test in considering the fundamental justice aspect of s 7 is both eminently sensible and perfectly consistent with the aim and import of that provision, since the notion that individual rights may, in some circumstances, be subordinated to substantial and compelling collective interests is itself a basic tenet of our legal system.[37]

This passage suggests the deferential nature of the internal balancing approach. The balancing exercise is a means by which the requirements of justice are recalibrated so as to accommodate 'compelling collective interests'. The deferential nature of the internal balancing approach is developed in the discussions of *Chiarelli*, *Suresh* and *Charkaoui* in sections 8.4.3, 8.6 and chapter nine respectively.

By way of contrast, the critical feature of the two-step approach is the sequential and separate analysis of (i) whether the protected interests have been violated in a way that does not accord with the principles of fundamental justice; and (ii) whether there is any 'societal' justification for that violation. On this approach, under section 7 one determines, independently of 'substantial and compelling collective interests', whether the protected interests are impinged on in a way that breaches the requirements of justice. When a breach of section 7 has been established, one then goes on to consider whether the breach is nonetheless justifiable in a free and democratic society given the collective interests at issue. A classic expression of the two-step approach is contained in *R v Swain*:

[35] See Elissa M Goodman, 'Section 7 of the Charter and Social Interest Justification' (winner of the Department of Justice/Canadian Bar Association National Essay Contest marking the Twentieth Anniversary of the Charter 2002) (unpublished, on file with author). Ms Goodman analysed 53 section 7 cases from the Canadian Supreme Court. She refers to a 'Balancing' rather than 'Internal Balancing' approach.

[36] ibid, 14.

[37] *Godbout v Longueuil (City)* [1997] 3 SCR 844, [76].

> It is not appropriate for the state to thwart the exercise of the accused's right by attempting to bring societal interests into the principles of fundamental justice and therefore limit an accused's s 7 rights. Societal interests are best dealt with under s 1 of the Charter, where the Crown has the burden of proving that the impugned law is demonstrably justified in a free and democratic society. In other words, it is my view that any balancing of societal interests against the individual right guaranteed by s 7 should take place in the confines of s 1 of the Charter.[38]

The two-step approach constitutes an instance of the 'exception' theory of the Charter voiced in *Oakes*:

> limits on the rights and guarantees enumerated in the Charter are exceptions to their general guarantee. The presumption is that rights and freedoms are guaranteed unless the party invoking s 1 can bring itself within the exceptional criteria, which justify their being limited.[39]

The case law discussed in this chapter evidences a correlation between the Supreme Court's adoption of the internal balancing approach and a lack of success in claiming a violation of section 7. Conversely, where the Supreme Court adopts the latter, two-step, approach to section 7, this has correlated with successful claims for breach of the Charter. Under the two-step approach, the Court is more likely to find an infringement of section 7 and it has been rare for such an infringement to be justified under section 1. This pattern aligns with the findings of broader studies of the section 7 jurisprudence.[40] Common awareness of this correlation is evident in the submissions in *Charkaoui*, in which the appellants and interveners (all of whom supported the appellants) all argued in favour of the adoption of what is here called a two-step approach.[41]

The immediate salience of the internal balancing approach to the present inquiry is that it allows for a 'contextualisation' of the principles of fundamental justice with reference to the 'immigration' context. Conversely, the two-step approach works against recalibration of the scope of the right, placing the onus on the government to justify the infringement. Under the two-step approach, the government's justification is subjected to a proportionality analysis under section 1 of the Charter.

8.4.2 *Singh*

The Supreme Court first considered the application of section 7 to non-citizens in *Singh*.[42] The decision has become emblematic of the principle that Charter rights

[38] *R v Swain* [1991] 1 SCR 933, 937–38.

[39] *Oakes* (n 14) 137.

[40] See Goodman (n 35); Christopher J Bredt and Adam M Dodek, 'The Increasing Irrelevance of Section 1 of the Charter' (2001) 14 *Supreme Court Law Review* (2d) 175, 179. The low success rate for section 1 justifications of section 7 infringements suggests a sense in which the 'two-step' approach reduces to a single step, as a finding of infringement is dispositive.

[41] See n 34 above.

[42] *Singh v Canada (Minister of Employment and Immigration)* [1985] 1 SCR 177.

are for 'everyone' regardless of citizenship status. It exemplifies a strand of section 7 jurisprudence that requires rights extended to non-citizens under immigration legislation to measure up to Charter standards. The decision involved a challenge to the refugee determination procedures under the Immigration Act 1976.[43] Only one of the two concurring judgments, that of Wilson J (Dickson CJ and Lamer J concurring), applied a section 7 analysis, and it is that judgment that I will discuss.[44]

It was not disputed by the Minister in *Singh* that the term 'everyone' in section 7 was sufficiently broad to encompass the appellants. As to *what* was secured to them by section 7, the appellants did not assert a constitutional right to enter and remain in Canada analogous to the right accorded to citizens by section 6(1) of the Charter. The substance of their case was that they did not have a fair opportunity to present their claim for refugee status, or to know the case they had to meet.[45] The appellants had not been granted the status of Convention refugees; their claim was that they were entitled to fundamental justice in the determination of whether or not they were Convention refugees.[46] Any finding of refugee status would see significant rights conferred by legislation.[47] A wrong decision could have dire consequences, including the risk of being sent back to a country where one had a 'well-founded fear or persecution' on Convention grounds. [48] These factors led Wilson J to hold that it was 'unthinkable that the *Charter* would not apply to entitle them to fundamental justice in the adjudication of their status'.[49]

Wilson J presented the Charter as a clear step away from assumptions that non-citizens are in some sense strangers to constitutional protections. She considered an argument that 'might be suggested' by cases under the Canadian Bill of Rights,

[43] The procedures provided for a refugee applicant to be interviewed by an immigration officer as to the basis for his or her claim. The decision whether or not to grant refugee status was made by the Minister's delegate on the basis of a transcript of this interview together with other material that was not disclosed to the applicant. A decision against the applicant could be appealed to the Immigration Appeals Board (IAB), but to get an oral hearing on the merits, the applicant had first to satisfy the IAB, on the balance of probabilities, that there were 'reasonable grounds to believe that a claim could, upon the hearing of the application, be established'. All seven appellants in *Singh* had had their claim rejected by the Minister and had been denied an appeal to the IAB. The question of their refugee status arose in the context of removal proceedings.

[44] Beetz J (Estey and McIntyre JJ concurring) refrained from considering the applicability of s 7 of the Charter to the facts of the case, preferring to analyse the procedures through the earlier Canadian Bill of Rights. He was concerned that existing rights instruments should not be eclipsed by the Charter, holding that the protection of rights would be better served by the cumulative effect of multiple instruments: *Singh* (n 42) 223–24. He read s 2(e) of the Canadian Bill of Rights (see n 50 below) as better serving rights conferred by legislation: 228. He found that the procedures were in conflict with s 2(e) of that instrument.

[45] ibid, 201 (Wilson J) (Dickson CJ and Lamer J concurring).

[46] ibid, 208 (Wilson J) (Dickson CJ and Lamer J concurring). 'Convention refugees' means individuals meeting the requirements for refugee status under the Convention relating to the Status of Refugees 189 UNTS 150 (opened for signature 28 July 1951, entered into force 22 April 1954) (Refugee Convention) and Protocol 606 UNTS 267 (opened for signature 31 January 1967, entered into force 4 October 1967).

[47] *Singh* (n 42) 210. See also the earlier discussion at 204.

[48] Refugee Convention (n 49) Art 1A(2).

[49] *Singh* (n 42) 210 (Wilson J) (Dickson CJ and Lamer J concurring).

a 1960 federal statute,[50] that whatever procedure is provided under statute exhausts the 'due process' and 'fundamental justice' to which an alien subject to immigration control is entitled.[51] Wilson J stated: 'The creation of a dichotomy between privileges and rights played a significant role in narrowing the scope of the application of the Canadian Bill of Rights.'[52] And she concluded that the 'restrictive attitude' expressed through the dichotomy between privileges and rights under the Canadian Bill of Rights had no place under the new Charter regime, in particular in its 'application to the adjudication of rights granted to an individual by statute'.[53]

Wilson J held that there had been a breach of section 7. Her account of what section 7 requires speaks to later procedural issues encountered in the context of the security certificate regime in Canada and under the control order regime in the United Kingdom. Wilson J held that the procedures did not accord with fundamental justice as they denied a refugee claimant the opportunity to make an 'effective challenge' to the information or policies that underlay the Minister's decision.[54] The problem with the procedures was that a refugee claimant had to establish that the Minister's decision not to accord refugee status was wrong 'without any knowledge of the Minister's case beyond the rudimentary reasons which the Minister has decided to give him in rejecting his claim'.[55]

8.4.3 *Chiarelli*

In *Singh* Wilson J suggested that the Charter had inaugurated the end of a 'restrictive attitude' to the constitutional rights of non-citizens expressed in terms of the rights/privilege distinction and effecting 'the adjudication of rights granted to an individual by statute'.[56] This prediction was qualified by the Supreme Court's unanimous decision in *Chiarelli*.[57] *Chiarelli* was a decision on the then security certificate process, a predecessor to the regime challenged in *Charkaoui*.

Mr Chiarelli was a permanent resident, having emigrated to Canada when he was 15. Upon being convicted, at the age of 24, of an offence for which a sentence of more than five years could be imposed, the government sought his removal.

[50] The Canadian Bill of Rights 1960 applies only to federal laws. It remains in force, but has largely been overtaken by the Charter. One of the provisions of the Canadian Bill of Rights not replicated in the Charter was the guarantee in s 2(e) of a fair hearing for the determination of rights and obligations. Section 2(e) was relied upon by Beetz J in *Singh*: see n 44 above.

[51] *Singh* (n 42) 208 (Wilson J) (Dickson CJ and Lamer J concurring). The immediate reference for these phrases was sub-ss 1(a) and 2(e) of the Canadian Bill of Rights.

[52] ibid, 209 (Wilson J) (Dickson CJ and Lamer J concurring).

[53] ibid.

[54] *Singh* (n 42) 216 (Wilson J) (Dickson CJ and Lamer J concurring).

[55] ibid, 215 (Wilson J) (Dickson J and Lamer J concurring). Wilson J concluded (at 216–21) that the section 1 justification was not established in this case. She lamented the paucity of material offered by the government on the section 1 justification and expressed doubt that any argument of administrative convenience could suffice as a section 1 justification, at least in the present case.

[56] ibid, 209 (Dickson J and Lamer J concurring).

[57] *Chiarelli* (n 12).

The relevant ministers made a joint report to the Security Intelligence Review Committee (SIRC)[58] indicating that they were of the opinion that Mr Chiarelli was involved in 'organized criminal activity'.[59] SIRC consisted of five Privy Councillors chosen by the Prime Minister in consultation with the Leader of the Opposition in the House of Commons.[60] The format of deportation hearings before SIRC was largely governed by procedural rules promulgated by SIRC pursuant to its authority under the Canadian Security Intelligence Service Act 1984.[61] Following an investigation into the report on Mr Chiarelli, SIRC concluded that a security certificate should be issued. Issuance of a security certificate authorised the exclusion or removal of the non-citizen named in it from Canada.

The *Chiarelli* decision addressed a number of different issues with reference to section 7. The relevance of the decision for the present discussion lies in what it says about the legal constraints on issuance of a deportation order, and the power to exclude a non-citizen from deportation hearings on confidentiality grounds. In relation to the first issue, the judgment advocated a 'contextual' approach to the requirements of fundamental justice, particular to the immigration context. This contextual approach has become the main vehicle for arguments for differential and more limited protections for non-citizens in the immigration area.

Sopinka J, writing for the Court, stated:

> in determining the scope of the principles of fundamental justice as they apply to this case, the Court must look to the principles and policies underlying immigration law. The most fundamental principle of immigration law is that non-citizens do not have an unqualified right to enter or remain in the country.[62]

This statement is known as the '*Chiarelli* principle'. The distinction between citizens and non-citizens is grounded in section 6(1) of the Charter, in the provision of mobility rights 'to enter, remain in and leave' Canada.[63] It has been held to establish that deportation of a non-citizen cannot 'in itself' implicate the liberty

[58] Established under the Canadian Security Intelligence Service Act 1984 (CSIS Act 1984), the Security Intelligence Review Committee (SIRC) initially reviewed all decisions on deportation for reasons of national security. SIRC's involvement in the deportation review process came to an end in 2002 with the entry into force of the Immigration and Refugee Protection Act 2001. SIRC's jurisdiction over the deportation of non-citizens who were not permanent residents had been removed many years earlier under amendments made to the Immigration Act in 1988, in response to the arrival of 174 Sikh refugee claimants off the east coast of Canada. In both cases, review was transferred to a single Federal Court judge, and limited to review of the 'reasonableness' of the certificate: see Rayner Thwaites, 'Deportation on National Security Grounds', (LLM thesis, University of Toronto, 2004) Appendix 1. As with the parliamentary debates on rights of appeal from the United Kingdom Special Immigration Appeals Commission, discussed in ch 5, s 5.4, it was assumed that the courts would 'correct' any lack of deference on the part of the specialist body.

[59] Immigration Act 1976, s 82.1(2).

[60] CSIS Act 1984, s 34.

[61] See Murray Rankin, 'The Security Intelligence Review Committee: Reconciling National Security with Procedural Fairness' (1989–1990) 3 *Canadian Journal of Administrative Law and Policy* 173, 179.

[62] *Chiarelli* (n 12) 733.

[63] ibid. Earlier, the same point was made, also with reference to *Chiarelli*, in relation to s 15 of the Charter: see text to n 25 above.

and security interests protected by section 7.[64] The question is how far the effects of the *Chiarelli* principle radiate beyond deportation.

A second aspect of the Supreme Court's judgment is its reasoning on powers to conduct in *camera* proceedings on deportation. Mr Chiarelli argued that the SIRC procedures contravened section 7 of the Charter as he and his legal representative were excluded from the portion of the hearing conducted *in camera*, and were only supplied with a summary of the government case against him. The government claimed that these restrictions were necessary to protect the police's investigatory processes.[65] Mr Chiarelli objected that the provisions gave SIRC complete discretion to exclude him from the Minister's case, and not simply from those portions of it where his exclusion was necessary to safeguard protected information. He argued that the relevant statutory provisions were too broad.

The Federal Court of Appeal agreed with Mr Chiarelli. It held that there had been a breach of section 7 of the Charter. Section 7 requires a meaningful opportunity to be heard, where this was in turn held to require that the affected person knew the information before SIRC (in order to be able to contradict it), and also the sources of the information (to challenge its credibility).[66] Applying a 'two-step' approach to section 7 of the Charter, and proceeding from a finding of a section 7 infringement to a section 1 analysis, a majority of the Federal Court of Appeal held that the statutory powers granted to protect confidentiality were disproportionate, as they did not meet the minimal impairment requirement.[67] Stone JA held that the relevant provision, rather than balancing the state's interest in confidentiality against the certified individual's interest in procedural justice, 'opts for a complete obliteration of the individual's rights in favour of the state's interests'.[68]

The Federal Court of Appeal held that the confidentiality provisions contravened section 7. The Supreme Court reversed this decision and did not progress to a section 1 proportionality analysis. It emphasised the fact that SIRC's rules, devised by SIRC, expressly directed that it exercise its discretion with regard to the competing state and individual interests.[69] The Supreme Court also detailed the options that had been available to Mr Chiarelli in the course of his hearing.[70] The distinction between the Supreme Court judgment and that of the Federal Court is that the former did not require that the *statute itself* mandate a balancing of the state's interest in the confidentiality of the information against the individual's rights under section 7. The Federal Court's criticism was directed not to SIRC's actual practices, but to the statutory framework in which it operated.

[64] *Medovarski v Canada (Minister of Citizenship and Immigration)* 2005 SCC 51, [2005] 2 SCR 539, [46] (McLachlin CJ for the Court).

[65] *Chiarelli* was the first Royal Canadian Mounted Police (RCMP) case to appear before SIRC, its previous cases originating with the Canadian Security Intelligence Service (CSIS).

[66] *Chiarelli v Canada (Minister of Employment and Immigration)* [1990] 2 FC 299, 67 DLR (4th) 697 (*Chiarelli* FCA), [30] (Stone JA, Urie JA concurring).

[67] ibid.

[68] ibid, [43].

[69] *Chiarelli* (n 12) 745, [51].

[70] ibid, 745–46, [52]–[53].

The Supreme Court's *Chiarelli* decision came to be regarded as authority for the proposition that the security certificate process was consistent with the Charter even if it did not allow any adversarial challenge to the intelligence that ministers submitted to justify the issuance of a security certificate.[71] Absent from the Supreme Court's reasoning in *Chiarelli* was any sense, given the existence of a statutory framework ostensibly concerned with affording a permanent resident some measure of procedural fairness, that the Charter might require that the statutory framework mandate certain procedural standards.[72]

The Supreme Court's decision in *Chiarelli* was shaped by deference to government decision-making in national security and crime control. It referred to the need for 'delicate balancing' between the interests of the individual and the state,[73] before offering a number of generalisations concerning the desirability of the state 'effectively conducting national security and criminal intelligence investigations and . . . protecting police sources'.[74] These generalisations were held to sanction an unqualified power to exclude the applicant and his legal representative, and to license the non-disclosure of evidence to them. In a classic statement of the internal balancing approach, the Supreme Court held that its reasoning was directed at a 'just accommodation between the interests of the individual and those of the state, both of which factors play a part in assessing whether a particular law violates the principles of fundamental justice'.[75]

The divergent approaches represented in the Supreme Court decisions of *Singh* and *Chiarelli* define the poles of section 7 jurisprudence on non-citizens' procedural rights under immigration statutes. *Singh* provides a particularisation of decisions and rights that carefully demarcates the relevance or otherwise of a non-citizen's vulnerability to removal. On the other hand, *Chiarelli* supports the proposition that a non-citizen's conditional presence colours the existence and weight of any rights he or she may have.

8.5 The Security Certificate Regime

In Canada, the question of the legality of indefinite detention of non-citizens has arisen in the context of a statutory regime that provides for the removal of

[71] See eg *Re Charkaoui* (2005) FC 149, (2005) 261 FTR 1, [17] (Noël J).

[72] On the contextualisation of s 7 with reference to the immigration context in *Chiarelli*, see Ninette Kelley, 'Rights in the Balance: Non-Citizens and State Sovereignty under the *Charter*' in David Dyzenhaus (ed), *The Unity of Public Law* (Oxford, Hart Publishing, 2004) 253, 264–68.

[73] *Chiarelli* (n 12) 744, [49], citing *Thomson Newspapers v Canada (Director of Investigation and Research)* [1990] 1 SCR 425 (La Forest J).

[74] ibid, [50], citing Lord Denning in *R v Secretary of State for the Home Department, ex parte Hosenball* [1977] 3 All ER 452, 460.

[75] ibid, quoting *Thomson Newspapers* (n 73), citing *R v Lyons* [1987] 2 SCR 309 (La Forest J). Goodman (n 35) argues that the internal balancing approach was mainly developed by La Forest J in a series of cases in the mid-to-late 1980s, of which *R v Lyons* is one: Goodman (n 35) 9–10.

non-citizens on security grounds and detention pending removal. The security certificate regime is found in Part 1, Division 9 of the Immigration and Refugee Protection Act 2001 (IRPA 2001).[76] An analogous process has, however, operated over a longer period, encompassing two pre-IRPA 2001 decisions discussed in this chapter, *Chiarelli* and *Suresh*. This section describes the statutory framework in place at the time of hearing and judgment in *Charkaoui*.[77] The regime described here continues down to the present. A number of aspects of the regime were changed in 2008 in response to the *Charkaoui* decision and are discussed in the next chapter.[78]

Under the IRPA 2001, two ministers initiate the procedure by signing a certificate stating that a named permanent resident, refugee or other non-citizen is inadmissible to Canada on one or more of a range of grounds, including organised criminality and security.[79] At the centre of the process is usually a risk profile that the intelligence services have prepared in respect of the individual involved. Once signed, the security certificate goes to the Federal Court, where a judge determines whether it is reasonable.[80] The aim of the procedures attending any such reasonableness hearing that are provided for under statute is primarily to protect against disclosure of information, where that disclosure might be injurious to national security or to a person's safety.[81] A judge can convene *ex parte* hearings at the request of the government and rely on material disclosed in such a hearing without providing it to the named individual or his or her representatives.[82] A judicially approved certificate constitutes an order for removal from Canada.[83]

The IRPA 2001's security certificate regime permits the minister to detain a non-citizen on the issuance of a certificate.[84] A certified individual can apply to the Federal Court for review of his or her detention. Detention is to be continued if the judge is satisfied that release on conditions would be injurious to security, or that the non-citizen would be unlikely to appear at a proceeding or for removal if he or she were released.[85] Under the statute, a finding that release would be a risk to security is a sufficient ground for continued detention. Where that determination is made, the only limit on the period of detention arises from any constitu-

[76] Immigration and Refugee Protection Act 2001, as amended by SC 2002, c 8, SC 2005, c 38 (IRPA 2001). This was the version of the IRPA considered in *Charkaoui* (n 2).

[77] The footnoted references that follow are to the substance and numbering of the statutory provisions in place at the time of hearing and judgment in *Charkaoui* (n 2).

[78] See ch 9, s 9.9.

[79] IRPA 2001, s 77(1).

[80] ibid, s 80.

[81] eg ibid, s 78.

[82] s 78 was the central procedural provision challenged in *Charkaoui* (n 2).

[83] IRPA 2001, s 81.

[84] A warrant issued by the Minister was required for the arrest of a permanent resident (IRPA 2001, s 82(1)), while no warrant was required for the arrest of other non-citizens (s 82(2)).

[85] IRPA 2001, s 84(2). On the timing and frequency of detention review the IRPA 2001 distinguished between permanent residents (s 83) and other non-citizens (foreign nationals) (s 84(2)). This feature of the statute was amended in response to *Charkaoui*, with the fuller procedural protections previously afforded only to permanent residents extended to all non-citizens.

tional requirement that detention must be for the purpose of removal from Canada.[86]

A further feature of the security certificate regime is relevant to the discussion. The IRPA 2001 prohibits the return of 'protected persons'[87] to a country where they would be at risk of persecution or torture.[88] There is an exception to this prohibition in the case of any protected person

> who is inadmissible on grounds of security, violating human or international rights or organized criminality if, in the opinion of the Minister, the person should not be allowed to remain in Canada on the basis of the nature and severity of acts committed or of danger to the security of Canada.[89]

This ministerial discretion is exercised through 'danger opinions' which weigh the risk to the named individual against the danger to the security of Canada. A danger opinion may be quashed on judicial review. Where this occurs, the protected person's removal is precluded by the IRPA 2001 unless and until there is a new administrative determination that there is no risk of persecution or torture; or where there is a risk but a 'danger opinion' establishes that the exception to the rule against removal operates.

8.6 *Suresh*

Suresh determined a challenge to the 'danger opinion' provision in existence prior to the enactment of IRPA 2001.[90] As noted above, a 'danger opinion' is a statutory provision allowing for the removal of a non-citizen facing a risk of persecution or torture, where the Minister determines that the risk to the non-citizen is outweighed by the 'danger to the security of Canada' he or she poses. *Suresh* concerned the constitutionality of this ministerial discretion, and the attendant process.[91]

[86] See the discussion of *Charkaoui* in ch 9.

[87] IRPA 2001, s 95(2) defines a protected person as a person on whom refugee protection has been conferred under s 95(1) and whose claim or application has not been deemed to be rejected pursuant to a number of listed statutory provisions.

[88] ibid, s 115(1): 'A protected person or a person who is recognized as a Convention refugee by another country to which the person may be returned shall not be removed from Canada to a country where they would be at risk of persecution for reasons of race, religion, nationality, membership in a particular social group or political opinion or at risk of torture or cruel and unusual treatment or punishment.'

[89] ibid, s 115(2)(b).

[90] *Suresh* (n 4). In *Suresh*, the order for deportation was made under Immigration Act 1985, s 53(1)(b). The relevant IRPA provision came into force on 27 June 2002.

[91] For earlier commentaries on *Suresh*, see eg Kent Roach, 'Did September 11 Change Everything? Struggling to Preserve Canadian Values in the Face of Terrorism' (2002) 47 *McGill Law Journal* 893; David Mullan, 'Deference from *Baker* to *Suresh* and Beyond: Interpreting the Conflicting Signals' in Dyzenhaus (n 72) 21; Kent Roach, 'Constitutional, Remedial, and International Dialogues about Rights: The Canadian Experience' (2005) 40 *Texas International Law Journal* 537.

Mr Suresh, originally a citizen of Sri Lanka, was granted refugee status by Canada in 1991. In early January 1998, the Minister issued an opinion that Mr Suresh constituted a danger to Canada's security, on the basis of his membership of, and connections with, an organisation alleged to engage in terrorism in Sri Lanka, and that on those grounds he should be deported. No reasons were required under the statutory provision and none were given. Mr Suresh argued that he faced a substantial risk of torture if returned to Sri Lanka, and that section 7 of the Charter precluded deportation to torture. He further argued that the statutory scheme for deportation on security grounds contained inadequate procedural safeguards against deportation to torture. In a decision handed down on 11 January 2002, the Supreme Court held that the statutory provision for deportation on security grounds where there is a risk of torture was constitutional, but that in exercising his discretion the Minister had failed to meet the procedural requirements demanded by section 7 of the Charter.[92] The decision to deport was remanded to the Minister for reconsideration.

Suresh holds that section 7 of the Charter does not place an absolute prohibition on deportation to torture. The Supreme Court gave extensive consideration to Canadian and international authority on the question of deportation to torture. Notably absent from the Canadian Supreme Court's review of the authorities was the European Court of Human Rights' decision in *Chahal*.[93] The Court in *Suresh* seemed to be reasoning its way towards an absolute prohibition on the practice of deportation to torture, only to veer away from this conclusion at the last moment.[94] The Supreme Court stated: 'We do not exclude the possibility that in exceptional circumstances, deportation to torture might be justified, either as a consequence of the balancing process mandated by section 7 of the Charter or under section 1.'[95] The Supreme Court's reference to 'the balancing process mandated by section 7 of the Charter' refers to the internal balancing approach to section 7 discussed in section 8.4.1. The possibility of deportation to torture in exceptional circumstances has become known as 'the *Suresh* exception'. It is not apparent from the judgment why the Supreme Court accepted the possibility of an 'exceptional discretion' to deport. It appears that the Court could not bring itself to say that rights under the Charter could operate to serve as an absolute bar on a non-citizen's removal to his or her country of nationality. Rather than follow the absolute prohibition under Article 3 of the Convention Against Torture,[96] the Supreme Court opted to assess matters on a 'case-by-case basis' against 'the fun-

[92] *Suresh* (n 4) [130].

[93] *Chahal v United Kingdom* (1997) 23 EHRR 413. On the absence of reference to *Chahal* in *Suresh* see Macklin (n 13) 228–29.

[94] See *Suresh* (n 4) [58], [78] (the Court) in relation to the constitutional and international law reasoning respectively. See Roach, 'Dialogues about Rights' (n 91) 569–72, 575–76.

[95] *Suresh* (n 4) [78] (the Court). The 'balancing process' refers to the 'internal balancing' approach described in s 8.4.1.

[96] Convention against Torture and Other Cruel, Inhuman or Degrading Treatment (opened for signature 10 December 1984, entered into force 26 June 1987) 1465 UNTS 85, Art 3.

damental justice balance under section 7 of the Charter'.[97] The Court stated: 'As the matter is one of balance, precise prediction is elusive. The ambit of an exceptional discretion to deport to torture, if any, must await future cases.'[98]

The Supreme Court acknowledged that 'the better view is that international law rejects deportation to torture, even where national security interests are at stake'.[99] Rather than responding directly to the position at international law, the Court treated international law as a factor to be rolled into constitutional interpretation. International law 'informs the content of the principle of fundamental justice under section 7 of the Charter'.[100] It was at this point that qualifications to any absolute prohibition began to appear.[101] The rejection of deportation to torture was 'virtually categoric'; it will 'almost always' be a disproportionate response, and 'barring exceptional circumstances' will violate section 7.[102] The reluctance to commit to an absolute prohibition expressed here was justified with reference to a passage from the House of Lords' judgment in *Rehman* on the superior institutional competence of the executive in evaluating matters of future risk.[103] The Canadian Supreme Court then arrived at the exceptional discretion to deport to torture, which it held could not be ruled out as a possible, if remote, outcome of constitutional balancing.[104]

In *Suresh*, the Supreme Court reduced an international law prohibition on deportation to torture to a factor in a constitutional balancing exercise. This raises questions for theories on the legitimacy of judicial review that rely on the courts' role as 'expert balancers'. The international lawyer Eyal Benvenisti has written on what he sees as the increasing confidence of national courts in challenging executive unilateralism in the wake of 9/11.[105] He argues that the 'most far reaching explanation' for these courts' assumption of an authority to intervene is their assertion of a role as 'expert balancers'.[106] This explanation for authority to intervene is presented as a component of judges' view of themselves as guardians of human rights.[107] But in *Suresh*, it was the Court's insistence on balancing that *qualified* what had at international law been treated as an absolute prohibition on

[97] *Suresh* (n 4) [78].

[98] ibid.

[99] ibid, [75].

[100] ibid.

[101] The qualifications were arguably already evident in the Court's use of deformalised language: eg 'rejects' rather than 'prohibits', 'norm' rather than 'rule'.

[102] *Suresh* (n 4) [76].

[103] ibid, [77]. *Rehman* (n 118) is discussed in ch 5, s 5.6.

[104] *Suresh* (n 4) [78]. A number of European governments have referenced *Suresh* to argue for the insertion of a '*Suresh* exception', allowing for deportation to torture, in European jurisprudence. *Saadi v Italy* (2009) 49 EHRR 30 constituted a conclusive rejection of these arguments. Placing *Saadi* against *Suresh* reiterates the continuing divergence between Canadian and European law on the issue of deportation to torture: see Macklin (n 13) 229–30.

[105] Eyal Benvenisti, 'United We Stand: National Courts Reviewing Counterterrorism Measures' in Andrea Bianchi and Alexis Keller (eds), *Counterterrorism: Democracy's Challenge* (Oxford, Hart Publishing, 2008) 251. Benvenisti's views on the use of comparative and international law in the counterterrorism context are discussed in ch 10, s 10.2.

[106] ibid, 265.

[107] ibid, 266–68.

deportation to torture. Some rights are not qualified, the prohibition on deportation to torture under the Convention against Torture being a clear example.[108] In such instances, holding that a right is appropriately made subject to judicial expertise in balancing weakens, rather than strengthens, the protection afforded by the right,[109] as happened in *Suresh.*

The *Suresh* exception is troubling for a variety of reasons. It allows for deportation where a real risk of torture is established. Even if one holds that there are circumstances where such deportation should be allowed, the Supreme Court's legal analysis does not channel the government's response through a section 1 proportionality analysis, a mechanism devoted to justifying the infringement of, or departure from, rights.[110] Nor does it require the government to have recourse to the notwithstanding clause in section 33 of the Charter.[111] The Supreme Court allowed that deportation to torture *may not even infringe section 7* of the Charter.[112] The *Suresh* exception places a limitation on section 7, allowing for deportation to torture, that does not require the government to invoke any mechanism to suspend or depart from the Charter framework.

A further problem with the *Suresh* exception lies in the complicated, and somewhat ambiguous,[113] landscape of review of 'danger opinions' outlined by the Supreme Court. The Court held that the 'threshold question' of whether there is a substantial risk of torture in the receiving country is factual.[114] It indicated that the most deferential standard of review should be applied to this 'threshold question', though the inquiry is mandated by section 7 of the Charter.[115] If the 'threshold' question is answered in the affirmative, and a substantial risk of torture by the receiving country established, there is to be an abrupt shift in the standard of review. The Supreme Court will then adopt the correctness standard of review appropriate to constitutional questions, making its own assessment of the government's justification for deportation to torture.[116]

[108] Convention against Torture and Other Cruel, Inhuman or Degrading Treatment, Art 3.

[109] Tom Hickman drew my attention to this point.

[110] For a detailed criticism of the Court's failure to require a section 1 justification, see Mullan (n 91) 56–59.

[111] Insofar as the '*Suresh* exception' was meant to operate as a 'safety valve', allowing for the removal of non-citizens in extreme circumstances, the notwithstanding clause could have performed this function. On the argument that the Court in *Suresh* should have required the government to employ the notwithstanding clause if it wished to provide for deportation to torture, see Roach, 'Dialogues about Rights' (n 91) 572–73.

[112] *Suresh* (n 4) [78] (the Court).

[113] See Mullan (n 91) 43–45.

[114] Further, the onus is on the deportee to establish a prima facie case of a real risk of torture upon return. In the companion case to *Suresh*, the Canadian Supreme Court found that Mr Ahani had not established a prima facie case and so was not entitled to be told the reasons for his deportation: *Ahani v Canada (Minister of Citizenship and Immigration)* 2002 SCC 2, [2002] 1 SCR 72.

[115] *Suresh* (n 4) [27], [39]–[41]. In *Suresh* reference was made to the patent unreasonableness standard. The category of patent unreasonableness was abolished in *Dunsmuir v New Brunswick* [2008] SCC 9, [2008] 1 SCR 190.

[116] *Suresh* (n 4) [41], [76]–[78].

Through this bifurcated process, the Court attempted to accommodate both the high level of deference it thought appropriate for matters of national security and immigration and the close scrutiny appropriate where Charter rights are at issue.[117] The difficulties here are analogous to those discussed in relation to the *Rehman* decision of the House of Lords in chapter five.[118] In *Suresh*, the Supreme Court advocated a deferential approach in the area of national security. It stated that the question of whether there is a substantial risk of torture upon return involves weighing a range of issues 'largely outside the realm of expertise of reviewing courts and possess[ing] a negligible legal dimension', counselling deference to the Minister's decision.[119] But in practice, protection of the right is so dependent on factual determination of the prior factual question of risk upon return that it is impossible to show deference at this initial factual stage without effectively relinquishing the attempt to uphold the right. Subsequent Canadian Federal Court case law on 'danger opinions', discussed in section 8.7 below, shows government findings that there was no substantial risk of torture by the receiving country being consistently rejected by the courts. The courts were well aware that the only way to meaningfully protect the right against deportation to torture was to subject the government's factual claims as to (lack of) risk to close scrutiny, effectively ignoring any *Suresh* injunction to the contrary.

A separate issue in *Suresh* was whether Mr Suresh was entitled to procedural protections in relation to the exercise of the Minister's discretion to deport him to torture. The Court held that he was to be provided with reasons, 'subject to privilege and valid legal reasons for not disclosing detailed information', articulating why the Minister believed him to be a danger to Canada.[120] He was to be informed 'of the case to be met', and given 'an opportunity to challenge the information of the Minister where issues as to its validity arise'.[121] These procedures are not to apply in 'every case of deportation of a Convention refugee' but only where the refugee had successfully raised the prospect of a substantial risk of torture by the receiving country.[122] Mr Suresh was determined to have established a prima facie case of deportation to torture. The Supreme Court held that he was not provided with the necessary procedural safeguards and remanded the case to the Minister.[123] Mr Suresh remained in Canada. In 2008, new security certificates were issued under the amended legislation that responded to *Charkaoui*. No certificate was issued for Mr Suresh.

[117] For a discussion of this feature of the judgment see Mullan (n 91) 41–47, 55–60.

[118] ch 5, s 5.6 centres on Lord Hoffmann's combination of a highly deferential approach to executive decision-making in national security and his endorsement of the absolute nature of the prohibition on deportation to torture in *Secretary of State for the Home Department v Rehman* [2001] UKHL 47, [2003] 1 AC 153.

[119] *Suresh* (n 4) [39].

[120] ibid, [126].

[121] ibid, [123] and [122]. Though there was no requirement of 'a full oral hearing or a complete judicial process'. Cf *Singh* (n 42).

[122] *Suresh* (n 4) [127].

[123] ibid, [130].

8.7 Federal Court Decisions Preceding *Charkaoui*

The Canadian Federal Court jurisprudence that preceded *Charkaoui* provides a window onto the operation of the regime at the time of hearing and judgment. Against this backdrop, the issues the Supreme Court addressed, and those it avoided, can be better appreciated. Use of the security certificate regime under the IRPA 2001 has proved, and continues to be, highly problematic in counterterrorism cases.[124] Despite years of extensive litigation towards that objective, certified individuals have remained in detention, or subject to conditions analogous to those imposed under control orders in the United Kingdom. Detained or subject to such constraints, over a decade has elapsed, and the foreign terrorist suspects against whom a security certificate has been issued have not been removed.

My account of the Federal Court litigation focuses on the legal reasoning as to why these foreign terrorist suspects have not been removed, and why they were detained and were or are subject to constraints. In its pursuit of the deportation of foreign terrorist suspects, the Canadian government has sought to avail itself of the '*Suresh* exception', allowing for deportation to a real risk of torture. As the courts have acknowledged, the Canadian jurisprudence on deportation to torture has been shaped by the 'collision between the *Chiarelli* principle [that a non-citizen has no right to remain] and Canada's international obligations with respect to deportation'.[125] There has been no concerted attempt by the Supreme Court to direct traffic and provide guidance as to how to reconcile these competing imperatives. This has led to the deferral of deportation, and inertia when it comes to addressing the consequences of this deferral, notably indefinite detention and/or constraint.

Security certificates are ostensibly a deportation regime. In practice they have been converted into a mechanism of indefinite preventive detention and/or constraint. Judicial statements at both Supreme and Federal Court level evidence awareness of this,[126] but this awareness has not generated any definite response on the part of the Supreme Court directed at confronting and addressing this state of affairs. This lack of response on the part of the Supreme Court has facilitated the continuance of a system that is dysfunctional when assessed against its ostensible statutory purpose of removal. There are two components to my account. The first focuses on the operation of section 115 of IRPA 2001, the ministerial discretion to deport a non-citizen to a risk of torture on grounds of posing a danger to Canadian

[124] Compare its effective utilisation in achieving the swift deportation of an alleged Russian spy posing as a Canadian national (removed to Russia): see CBC News, 'Canada Kicks Out Alleged Russian Spy', www.cbc.ca/canada/story/2006/12/26/hampel-gone.html.

[125] *Almrei v Canada (Minister of Citizenship and Immigration)* [2005] FC 1645, (2005) 270 FTR 1, [430] (Layden-Stevenson J).

[126] On the relevant Federal Court decisions see s 8.7. The Supreme Court statements are from *Charkaoui* (n 2), the subject of ch 9.

security; and the second discusses the operation of the detention provisions in that statute.

8.7.1 Decisions on Deportation to Torture

Government attempts to remove a foreign terrorist suspect subject to a security certificate are recurrently frustrated by the existence of a prima facie case that the deportee faces a real risk of persecution or torture in the receiving state. In such cases, the Minister must determine whether there is a real risk of persecution or torture, and if so, whether a 'danger opinion' applies. The Federal Court litigation concerning the five individuals held under the security certificate regime at the time of judgment in *Charkaoui* demonstrates how complex and protracted this process can become.[127] The *Mahjoub* litigation provides an illustration. A security certificate was issued for Mr Mahjoub in June 2000, at which time he was taken into detention. In July 2004, a delegate of the Minister of Citizenship and Immigration gave a 'danger opinion', stating that Mr Mahjoub should be removed from Canada because while he could be at 'substantial risk of ill-treatment and human rights abuses' upon removal to Egypt, this was outweighed by the danger he posed to Canada's security.[128] According to the Federal Court, the delegate took the view that

> in *Suresh*, the Supreme Court of Canada 'endorsed' a procedure for making a determination under what is now subsection 115(2) of the Act. Such procedure was said to require the Minister to balance the danger posed by the person named in the security certificate against the risk to that person if removed from Canada.[129]

The delegate treated *Suresh* as mandating a simple balancing process in which the prospect of Mr Mahjoub's ill-treatment and abuse upon return was weighed against the danger he would pose to national security if he remained in Canada. The delegate determined that the latter weighed more heavily. In January 2005, the Federal Court's Dawson J quashed this decision,[130] on the ground that it was not based on cogent evidence. The delegate had relied on a narrative provided by the Canadian Security Intelligence Service, without the documents and appendices referred to in that narrative, and she had relied on documents prepared for purposes other than assessing Mr Mahjoub's risk of torture or ill-treatment upon return to Egypt.[131]

A little less than a year later, in January 2006, a delegate for the Minister issued a second danger opinion, indicating that Mr Mahjoub would *not* face any

[127] Hassan Almrei, Adil Charkaoui, Mohamed Harkat, Mahmoud Jaballah and Mohammad Mahjoub. Manickavasagam Suresh was also subject to the security certificate regime at that time.

[128] *Mahjoub v Canada (Minister of Citizenship and Immigration)* [2005] FC 156, (2005) 261 FTR 95 (*Mahjoub, First Danger Opinion*), [12], [35].

[129] ibid, [12].

[130] ibid, [67].

[131] ibid, [48]–[49] and more generally [44]–[58].

substantial risk of torture upon return to Egypt. In December 2006, the Federal Court's Tremblay-Lamer J quashed this second danger opinion, on the ground that it was patently unreasonable in its 'selective reliance on one piece of evidence that held that human rights abuses were not a systemic problem in Egypt, against the overwhelming bulk of the evidence which essentially pointed to the contrary'.[132]

In *Mahjoub, Second Danger Opinion*, Tremblay-Lamer J recognised the possibility of continuing deportation attempts, and continuing legal resistance to deportation:

> I am cognizant that in redetermining this matter, it is possible for the subsequent decision-maker to conclude that Mr Mahjoub faces a substantial risk of torture and that he continues to pose a danger to the security of Canada. This would inevitably lead to the issue of whether the present circumstances justify deportation to face torture.[133]

The pattern of alternating government arguments in Mr Mahjoub's proceedings based on the propositions that (a) any substantial risk of torture upon return was outweighed by the danger the detainee posed to Canada and (b) there was no substantial risk of torture, was repeated in the litigation involving Hassan Almrei, one of the appellants in *Charkaoui*.[134] This pattern exposes the artificiality, and lack of workability, of the Court's injunction in *Suresh* to combine a deferential approach to the factual question of the risk of torture with a correctness standard of review where such risk is established.

8.7.2 Consequences of the *Suresh* Exception

The Canadian Federal Court jurisprudence falling between the Supreme Court's decisions in *Suresh* and *Charkaoui* indicates the problems to which the *Suresh* exception gives rise. In practice, the ongoing debate around the use of the exception has deferred resolution of whether deportation is possible. This deferral has made it easier for the courts to indefinitely postpone answering the question whether detention consequent on issuance of a security certificate, in circumstances where there is no real prospect of removal, is properly authorised as detention pending removal.

The Supreme Court in *Suresh* sent mixed messages regarding the possibility of deportation to torture. Having allowed for the possibility, the Court offered little encouragement for the view that 'exceptional circumstances' justifying deportation to torture might ever be established. It emphasised that deportation to torture was an *extraordinary* possibility given that 'torture and violations of human rights [are matters] in which Canada can neither constitutionally, nor under its

[132] *Mahjoub v Canada (Minister of Citizenship and Immigration)* [2006] FC 1503, [2007] 4 FCR 247 (*Mahjoub, Second Danger Opinion*), [82].

[133] ibid, [110].

[134] *Almrei v Canada* [2005] FC 355, (2005) 262 FTR 7 (*Almrei, Second Danger Opinion*).

international treaty obligations, be complicit'.[135] In the period between *Suresh* and *Charkaoui* there was no case law development to suggest that courts would ever find the *Suresh* exception applicable. In all but one case, the Federal Court had quashed 'danger opinions' on administrative law grounds that made it unnecessary to determine whether the *Suresh* exception was made out.[136] And in the one case that did consider the application of the *Suresh* exception, *Re Jaballah, Second Reasonableness Decision*, Mackay DJ held that, in the circumstances of the case, the Minister could not exercise his discretion to deport Mr Jaballah to any country where there was a substantial risk of torture.[137] In reaching his determination on the *Suresh* exception, Mackay DJ was aware that his decision on the exception's applicability to Mr Jaballah would simply be another step towards a 'definite judicial or legislative response'.[138] Thankfully, the *Suresh* exception has not enabled deportation to countries where the detainee faces a substantial risk of torture.

The real, practical significance of the *Suresh* exception has been that it has prolonged a continuing judicial debate on the *possibility* of removing the subject of a security certificate to his country of nationality. The Canadian Federal Court case law on danger opinions preceding *Charkaoui* registered an impasse between the courts and the government. This impasse is most charitably attributed to unresolved, and opposing, readings of the legal framework supplied by *Suresh*.[139] The government has repeatedly argued that deportation to a substantial risk of torture was warranted in the circumstances. And the Federal Court has rejected every single government attempt to rely on the *Suresh* exception, in all bar one case on the basis of administrative law considerations.

The impasse has had the effect of preserving the use of detention and constraint pursuant to the security certificate mechanism. It is enabled by the fact that the *Suresh* exception leaves open diametrically opposed possibilities and can be read in light of fundamentally divergent values. As succinctly stated in an article on 'case-management risk':

> any form of risk assessment, irrespective of context is dependent on the ascription of value, not just probability, to potential outcomes . . . In other words, decision outcomes are inevitably conditioned by the degree of weight decision-makers are willing to place on the protection of foreign nationals relative to that of maintaining immigration control.[140]

[135] *Suresh* (n 4) [120]. And see the summary of the *Suresh* exception in *Re Jaballah* [2006] FC 1230, (2006) 148 CRR (2d) 1 (*Jaballah, Second Reasonableness Decision*), [80]–[81] (Mackay DJ).

[136] See eg *Mahjoub, First Danger Opinion* (n 128); *Mahjoub, Second Danger Opinion* (n 132); *Almrei, Second Danger Opinion* (n 134).

[137] *Jaballah, Second Reasonableness Decision* (n 135) [85].

[138] ibid, [78].

[139] On a less charitable reading, the problems that the Federal Court identified in the evidential foundation of decisions to deport are more suggestive of the government testing how far it could push the exception than a considered attempt to determine its scope.

[140] Robert Thomas, 'Risk, Legitimacy and Asylum Adjudication' (2007) 58 *Northern Ireland Legal Quarterly* 49, 70.

The case law surveyed evidences that the Canadian government and the Canadian Federal Court attached different weight to the protection of foreign nationals relative to national security concerns. This divergence generates the toing and froing between the government and the Federal Court on the preliminary 'factual' questions under the security certificate regime, where the risk the refugee poses to Canada and the risk the receiving country poses to the refugee are to be balanced.

Prior to *Charkaoui*, with the exception of *Jaballah, Second Reasonableness Decision*, the Federal Court did not directly address whether the *Suresh* exception was or was not established in the particular case, despite the fact that the applicability of the exception was determinative of the possibility of removal to the deportee's country of nationality (and there did not appear to be an available prospect of removal elsewhere). While not foreseeing a case in which the exception could be employed, the Federal Court was not able to ignore it. Use of the *Suresh* exception was regarded as an ever-present possibility whose uncertain application awaited clarification from the Supreme Court. On Mr Mahjoub's second application for release, Dawson J stated: 'I find on the balance of probabilities that Mr Mahjoub is unlikely to be removed from Canada until the Supreme Court authoritatively decides whether circumstances will ever justify a removal to torture.'[141] At the time of writing, the Supreme Court has yet to authoritatively decide this question. And Mr Mahjoub has yet to be removed from Canada or exit the security certificate regime. Keeping the *Suresh* exception open keeps the possibility of deportation open, and that provides a slender thread of justification for characterising the detention as detention pending deportation. Closing off the *Suresh* exception would make it harder to avoid the question, can such a regime of detention or constraint be confined to non-citizens when deportation is precluded?

8.7.3 Review of Detention

In parallel with the administrative process relating to danger opinions, Mr Mahjoub made three applications to the Federal Court for release from detention.[142] Giving judgment on his second application for release, Dawson J was 'mindful that issues of significant concern to Canadian society are posed . . . This is so because detention of uncertain duration is anathema to the principles which

[141] *Canada (Minister of Citizenship and Immigration) v Mahjoub* [2005] FC 1596, (2005) 270 FTR 101 (*Mahjoub, Second Application for Release*) (n 146) [29]. Even in the decision on his first application for release under s 84(2), in which it was determined that Mr Mahjoub could be removed within a reasonable time, one of the reasons given for the acknowledged 'uncertainty' as to when was the difficulty of deporting him without violating the Charter given that he had asserted a risk of torture upon return: see *Canada (Minister of Citizenship and Immigration) v Mahjoub* [2004] 1 FC 493, [52], [54]–[59].

[142] *Canada (Minister of Citizenship and Immigration) v Mahjoub* [2003] FC 928, [2004] 1 FCR 493; *Mahjoub, Second Application for Release* (n 141); *Mahjoub v Canada (Minister of Citizenship and Immigration)* [2007] FC 171, (2007) 309 FTR 72 (*Mahjoub, Third Application for Release*).

govern our judicial system.'[143] On the third application for release that the judge ordered Mr Mahjoub's release on conditions. In his reasons for judgment, Mosley J stated as follows:

> the fact that Mr Mahjoub has now been detained for six and a half years cannot be ignored. As was stated by Justice Marshall Rothstein in *Sahin v Canada*, '. . . *when any number of possible steps may be taken by either side and the times to take each step are unknown, I think it fair to say that a lengthy detention, at least for practical purposes, approaches what might be reasonably termed "indefinite"*'. In the present instance, the practical reality is that there is no fixed time period for a conclusion of the proceedings or for Mr Mahjoub's removal from Canada. In that sense, his detention might reasonably be described as indefinite.[144] (emphasis added)

In practice, the Federal Court has ordered the release of individuals held on security certificates on the second, third or fourth periodic review of their detention provided for under the IRPA 2001. The periods spent in detention prior to release on conditions have ranged from 21 months to over 7 years: Mr Charkaoui spent 21 months in a detention facility; Mr Harkat was detained for almost 3½ years; Mr Mahjoub for 6½ years; Mr Jaballah 5½ years; and Mr Almrei for more than 7 years.[145] And these periods are misleading in that they suggest the cessation of constraints on the subject of a security certificate, whereas the orders for release were given on onerous conditions amounting to house arrest. The Court's judgments granting release have accepted the government's claim that the individuals still pose a threat to national security, but have held that the threat can be 'neutralized or contained' by an extensive series of restrictive conditions.[146] The informing assumption was that release on conditions improved the position of the detainee. The judges acknowledged that 'Stringent release conditions seriously limit personal liberty', but these conditions were viewed as 'less severe than incarceration'.[147] The practice of release on conditions developed by the Canadian Federal Court has, since *Charkaoui*, been endorsed by statute.[148]

In practice, as with the discussion of control orders in the United Kingdom,[149] there is a real question as to which is worse: detention in a facility or release on conditions amounting to, or approaching, house arrest. As with control orders, a

[143] *Mahjoub, Second Application for Release* (n 141) [92].

[144] *Mahjoub, Third Application for Release* (n 142) [103] (citations omitted).

[145] Release on conditions was ordered in the following judgments: *Re Charkaoui* [2005] FC 258, (2005) 252 DLR (4th) 601 (*Charkaoui, Fourth Application for Release*) (17 February 2005, after 21 months in a detention facility); *Harkat v Canada (Minister of Citizenship and Immigration)* [2006] FC 628, [2007] 1 FCR 321 (*Harkat, Second Application for Release*) (23 May 2006, after almost 3½ years in a detention facility); *Mahjoub, Third Application for Release* (n 142) (15 February 2007, after 6½ years in a detention facility); *Jaballah v Canada (Minister of Public Safety and Emergency Preparedness)* [2007] FC 379, (2007) 296 FTR 1 (*Jaballah, Third Application for Release*) (12 April 2007, after 5½ years in a detention facility); *Re Almrei* 2009 FC 3, (2009) 337 FTR 160 (2 January 2009, after more than 7 years in a detention facility).

[146] See the language in, for example, *Charkaoui, Fourth Application for Release* (n 145) [78]; *Harkat, Second Application for Release* (n 145) [82]; *Mahjoub, Third Application for Release* (n 142) [139].

[147] *Jaballah, Third Application for Release* (n 145) [70].

[148] See IRPA 2001 as amended by SC 2008 (Bill C-3), s 82(5).

[149] See ch 7, s 7.4.1.

significant factor in assessing the impact of orders on release under the Canadian security certificate regime is the effect they have on the family of the certified individual. Family members effectively find themselves sharing in the house arrest of the certified person. Following his release on conditions, Mr Mahjoub requested readmission to detention, due to the impact the conditions were having on his family, with whom he shared the home to which he was largely confined.[150]

The Federal Court decisions on release were intended to ameliorate the burden of detention. They leave unresolved the impasse between courts and government on the use of the security certificate regime as a *mechanism of removal* in circumstances where there is no real prospect of removal within a reasonably foreseeable period. Notwithstanding the Federal Court's orders for release on conditions, the security certificate regime is still an onerous, rights-infringing regime. The regime is confined to non-citizens on the basis that non-citizens are subject to a deportation order, in circumstances where, after more than a decade, deportation has not been effected.

[150] *Canada (Minister of Citizenship and Immigration) v Mahjoub* [2009] FC 439. Blanchard J confirmed by order Mr Mahjoub's request to return to detention (ordering the immediate cessation of all monitoring of the family home). For a detainee and his wife's own perspective on life under security certificate conditions, see Mike Larsen, Sophie Harkat and Mohamed Harkat, 'Justice in Tiers: Security Certificate Detention in Canada' (2008) 17(2) *Journal of Prisoners on Prisons* 31, 40–42.

9

Charkaoui's Procedural Solution

> The prevalence of procedural rulings in the 'war on terror' cases . . . has significant implications for substantive rights in at least two ways. First, by delaying ultimate resolution of rights claims, it has allowed serious violations of human rights to continue for years. Second, this approach has foreclosed many rights-based challenges without actually considering the merit of those challenges.
>
> Jenny Martinez, *Columbia Law Review* (2008)[1]

9.1 *Charkaoui* Introduced[2]

The three appellants in *Charkaoui*,[3] Mr Almrei, Mr Harkat and Mr Charkaoui, had been certified 'inadmissible' on grounds of national security and detained under the Canadian security certificate regime established by the Immigration and Refugee Protection Act 2001 (IRPA 2001).[4] Mr Charkaoui and Mr Harkat had been released on onerous conditions prior to hearing and judgment, having been detained for 21 months and for almost three and half years respectively.[5] Mr Almrei remained in detention, where he had been for over five years. As expressly acknowledged in the Canadian Supreme Court's judgment, on Mr Almrei's last application for release, the Federal Court judge had found that his removal would not occur within a reasonable time, but that she was obliged to keep him in detention because she found that his release would pose a danger to national security.[6]

The appellants challenged the constitutionality of the security certificate regime on a number of grounds.[7] They argued that the procedures for 'reasonableness'

[1] Jenny S Martinez, 'Process and Substance in the "War on Terror"' (2008) 108 *Columbia Law Review* 1013, 1031.

[2] This section draws on material published as Rayner Thwaites, 'Process and Substance: *Charkaoui I* in the Light of Subsequent Developments' (2011) 62 *University of New Brunswick Law Journal* 13.

[3] *Charkaoui v Canada (Citizenship and Immigration)* [2007] SCC 9, [2007] 1 SCR 350 (*Charkaoui*).

[4] See ch 8, s 8.5.

[5] *Re Charkaoui* [2005] FC 258, (2005) 252 DLR (4th) 601; *Harkat v Canada (Minister of Citizenship and Immigration)* [2006] FC 628, [2007] 1 FCR 321.

[6] *Almrei v Canada (Minister of Citizenship and Immigration)* [2005] FC 1645, (2005) 270 FTR 1, referred to in *Charkaoui* (n 3) [102].

[7] The Supreme Court's decision in *Charkaoui* (n 3) was an appeal from three cases of the Federal Court of Appeal involving Messrs Charkaoui, Almrei and Harkat: *Charkaoui* – Leave to Appeal to the

review of a decision to issue a security certificate and the procedures for reviewing detention infringed their right to liberty under section 7 of the Charter. Further, the incidence of detention review did not meet the requirements of section 9, which provides that 'Everyone has the right not to be arbitrarily detained or imprisoned', or the section 10 rights activated upon arrest or detention.[8] They also argued that detention under the regime constituted 'cruel and unusual treatment or punishment' under section 12, and was discriminatory under section 15.[9]

The Supreme Court gave a unanimous judgment, which was delivered by Chief Justice McLachlin. It devoted most of its reasoning to deficiencies in the statutory requirements for the Federal Court's review of certification and detention.[10] The Supreme Court held that the procedures under the security certificate regime did not comply with section 7 of the Charter and, further, they were not justified under section 1.[11] The Court issued a declaration of invalidity (suspended for one year) on this ground. The certification decisions made under the IRPA 2001 would lose their 'reasonable' status one year after judgment.[12]

The Canadian Federal Court's practice of release on conditions was well established at the time of *Charkaoui*, and was endorsed in that judgment.[13] In the case of release on conditions, the Canadian Supreme Court endorsed an existing practice. It made a more active contribution in relation to the procedures to be applied on review of certification and detention. The IRPA 2001 had provided that non-citizens who were not permanent residents were only eligible for detention review 120 days after a decision had been made on the reasonableness of the certificate, presumably on the assumption that the reasonableness decision would be made swiftly. This did not prove to be the case. For example, Mr Harkat was taken into detention in December 2002. A reasonableness decision was not delivered until 22 March 2005.[14] In the period between these two dates (plus 120 days) he was ineligible for detention review. In *Charkaoui*, the Supreme Court severed certain phrases and provisions, and read in terms, so as to ensure that judicial review

Supreme Court granted in August 2005, from Federal Court of Appeal decision of 10 December 2004, [2004] FCA 421, 247 DLR (4th) 405; *Almrei v Canada (Minister of Citizenship and Immigration)* – Leave to Appeal to the Supreme Court granted in October 2005, from Federal Court of Appeal decision of 8 February 2005, [2005] FCA 54, 251 DLR (4th) 13; *Harkat v Canada (Minister of Citizenship and Immigration)* – Leave to Appeal to the Supreme Court granted in January 2006, from Federal Court of Appeal decision of 6 September 2005, [2005] FCA 285. The Supreme Court heard the matters together over three days in June 2006.

[8] Section 10 of the Charter states: 'Everyone has the right on arrest or detention (a) to be informed promptly of the reasons therefor; (b) to retain and instruct counsel without delay and to be informed of that right; and (c) to have the validity of the detention determined by way of habeas corpus and to be released if the detention is not lawful.'

[9] A challenge was also mounted based on the constitutional principle of the rule of law. See n 146 below.

[10] *Charkaoui* (n 3) [12]–[87].

[11] ibid, [85]–[87].

[12] ibid, [140].

[13] ibid, [101]. On the practice of release on conditions see ch 8, pp 248–49. The legislation enacted in response to *Charkaoui*, Bill C-3, put that practice on a statutory basis: see Immigration and Refugee Protection Act 2001 (as amended by SC 2008 – Bill C-3) (IRPA 2001 as amended 2008), s 82(5).

[14] *Re Harkat* [2005] FC 393, (2005) 261 FTR 52.

commenced within 48 hours of the beginning of detention, and at least once during each six-month period following the preceding review.[15]

The rationale for a detention regime confined to non-citizens was that it was detention pending deportation. The Supreme Court did not identify the point at which the 'hinge' between detention and deportation would be broken, but held that it remained intact in relation to the appellants.[16] The Court also held that, subject to the procedural changes it required, continuing detention pending removal under the security certificate regime did not contravene section 12 (cruel or unusual treatment) or section 15 (equality) of the Charter.[17] It reasoned that the augmented procedural protections required under its section 7 analysis 'answered' the substantive Charter challenges under sections 12 and 15.[18]

9.2 Submissions of the Parties and Interveners

The government and the three appellants each filed a factum, together with ten facta filed by various interveners, all of which were in support of the appellants.[19] *Charkaoui* is a judgment that is characterised by the issues that remain unaddressed, leading a reader of the judgment back to the facta to see what was before the Court. Issues that were not substantially addressed in the judgment include the indeterminate duration of detention under the security certificate regime and whether that detention was disproportionate with removal and so was discriminatory against non-citizens. These issues were argued in the facta, helping to rule out a characterisation of *Charkaoui*'s silence on those issues as inadvertence.

The facta raised issues of discrimination against non-citizens and detention of indeterminate duration by a variety of doctrinal routes. I start with Mr Almrei's factum, as it squarely addressed issues of arbitrary and indeterminate detention and discrimination against non-citizens.[20] Mr Almrei's argument on the principles of fundamental justice proceeded by way of the prohibition on arbitrary detention in section 9. He argued that his detention was discriminatory on the basis of citizenship status, and so was arbitrary, in breach of section 9 and so section 7. He further argued that detention cannot comply with principles of

[15] *Charkaoui* (n 3) [141]–[142]. In doing so it extended to all non-citizens the procedural protections that were previously only available to permanent residents.

[16] ibid, [131].

[17] ibid, [123], [131].

[18] ibid, [3], [123], [131].

[19] I was engaged by those preparing the (joint) Factum of Interveners Canadian Council for Refugees, African Canadian Legal Clinic, International Civil Liberties Monitoring Group and National Anti-Racism Council of Canada to provide legal research assistance. *Charkaoui et al v Minister of Citizenship and Immigration*, Supreme Court of Canada File Nos 30762, 30929 and 31178 (Canadian Council of Refugees et al Factum). The facta in the above proceeding are available at www.aspercentre.ca/constitutional-cases/scc-facta.htm

[20] The Constitutional Questions stated in Mr Almrei's appeal challenged the detention provisions in the security certificate regime, as opposed to the provisions on certification or deportation.

fundamental justice if it is grounded in discrimination. His argument for discrimination referenced *Belmarsh* in making the point that citizens 'about whom there may be similar security concerns are not treated the same'.[21] He advanced the proposition that deportation was effectively barred by the real risk of deportation upon return, with reference to *Suresh*.[22] Mr Almrei's lack of control over his release and the indeterminate nature of his detention were emphasised.[23]

The issue of discrimination against non-citizens was also raised in Mr Charkaoui's factum,[24] and by a number of the interveners. The appropriate comparator group was argued to be 'citizens suspected of being security threats', with *Belmarsh* cited for this proposition.[25] A distinction between a non-citizen's acknowledged vulnerability to deportation on the one hand and equality between citizens and non-citizens with regard to national security procedures on the other was made with reference to *Singh*.[26] In a corresponding move, the factum of the Canadian Council of Refugees argued against the view that *Chiarelli* barred the application of section 15 in the immigration context.[27] It closed its argument on section 15 by quoting an extended passage from Baroness Hale's judgment in *Belmarsh*, to the effect that valuing each person equally means that 'the will of the majority cannot prevail if it is inconsistent with the equal rights of minorities'.[28] And the Council opened its argument on sections 7 and 12 with reference to the need to view these provisions through the interpretive lens of equality, in particular the need to avoid 'a specialized, more onerous regime' for the preventive detention of non-citizens.[29] The analogy between the Canadian security certificate

[21] Appellant's Factum on Appeal, *Hassan Almrei v Minister of Citizenship and Immigration*, Supreme Court of Canada File Number 30929 (Almrei Factum), para 38. In addition to *Belmarsh*, the point on discrimination is referenced to the Report of the UN Working Group on Arbitrary Detention, Visit to Canada, E/CN.4/2006/7/Add.25 December 2005. See also the Factum of Amnesty International, *Charkaoui et al v Minister of Citizenship and Immigration*, Supreme Court of Canada File Nos 30762, 30929 and 31178 (Amnesty International Factum), paras 58, 59, 62; Factum of the Canadian Council on American-Islamic Relations et al, *Charkaoui et al v Minister of Citizenship and Immigration*, Supreme Court of Canada File Nos 30762, 30929 and 3117, para 70. For an extended discussion of *Belmarsh* on this point see University of Toronto, Faculty of Law – International Human Rights Clinic Factum, *Charkaoui et al v Minister of Citizenship and Immigration*, Supreme Court of Canada File Nos 30762, 30929 and 31178 (University of Toronto Factum), paras 55–63.

[22] Almrei Factum (n 21) para 40. See also University of Toronto Factum (n 21) paras 31–38: 'Administering IRPA in compliance with *Suresh* creates the possibility of indefinite detention' (para 33). The argument that *Suresh* effectively barred deportation, despite leaving it open as a possibility, is consistent with the findings of the review of Federal Court case law on security certificates in ch 8, pp 246–48.

[23] Almrei Factum (n 21) para 74.

[24] The Constitutional Questions stated in Mr Charkaoui's appeal included a challenge under s 15 of the Charter.

[25] Canadian Council of Refugees et al Factum (n 19), para 14. Cf the current approach to comparator groups in *Withler v Canada (Attorney-General)* 2011 SCC 12, [2011] 1 SCR 396.

[26] Canadian Council of Refugees et al Factum (n 19) para 17; *Singh v Canada (Minister of Employment and Immigration)* [1985] 1 SCR 177. On *Singh* see ch 8, pp 232–34.

[27] Canadian Council of Refugees et al Factum (n 19), para 17. *Chiarelli*: *Canada (Employment and Immigration) v Chiarelli* [1992] 1 SCR 711, 744. On *Chiarelli* see ch 8, pp 234–36.

[28] Canadian Council of Refugees et al Factum (n 19) para 18, quoting *A v Secretary of State for the Home Department* [2004] UKHL 56, [2005] 2 AC 68 (*Belmarsh*), [236], [237], [238] (Baroness Hale).

[29] Canadian Council of Refugees et al Factum (n 19), para 22.

regime and British control orders was put to the Court, with attention drawn to the fact that the latter were applicable to non-citizens and citizens alike.[30]

A number of the facta also made extensive reference to Canada's obligations under international law, including the absolute prohibition on deportation to torture and obligations relating to detention set out in the Convention against Torture.[31] Statements from international bodies going to non-discrimination against non-citizens, some with a particular focus on non-discrimination in the counterterrorism context, were cited.[32] *None* of this international law material was engaged with in *Charkaoui*, whether to accept, distinguish, or refute it.

In Mr Almrei's factum, a range of comparative authorities were marshalled to argue for a temporal limitation on detention pending removal, determined by reference to the purpose of facilitating removal. Mr Almrei submitted as follows:

> National jurisdictions comparable to Canada as well as international human rights tribunals have recognised that detention pending removal on immigration grounds must be limited to such time as is reasonable to enable the removal process to be carried out, and that removal should follow promptly on the making of a removal order.[33]

The comparative authorities for this point included *Zadvydas*, *Belmarsh* and *Tan Le Tam* (the last applying the *Hardial Singh* principles). A presumption of release where detention has exceeded a reasonable time was advanced with reference again to *Zadvydas*, *Tan Le Tam*, and decisions of the UN Human Rights Committee and the European Court of Human Rights.[34]

Notwithstanding the arguments raised in the facta and rehearsed in this section, the submissions as a whole emphasised procedural issues going to review of deportation and detention, as opposed to substantive limits on those practices. In this, the Supreme Court's emphasis on procedures, analysed in the subsequent sections of this chapter, is reflective of the argument before it.

9.3 Section 7 Analysis of the Statutory Procedure

The reasons in *Charkaoui* focused on section 7 of the Charter. To reiterate, section 7 provides that 'Everyone has the right to life, liberty and security of the

[30] ibid, para 25.

[31] See eg Almrei Factum (n 21) para 44; Amnesty International Factum (n 21); University of Toronto Factum (n 21) para 37.

[32] See eg Canadian Council of Refugees et al Factum (n 19) para 15. Canada's treaty obligations with respect to non-discrimination were listed, including the United Nations Committee on the Elimination of All Forms of Racial Discrimination (CERD) General Recommendation 30 on Discrimination Against Non-Citizens, paras 1, 3, 4 and 10. Paragraph 10 calls upon states to ensure that measures taken against terrorism do not discriminate on grounds of national origin. These paragraphs from CERD Recommendation 30 were quoted in *Belmarsh* (n 28) [62] (Lord Bingham).

[33] Almrei Factum (n 21) para 46; see also paras 43 and 44.

[34] ibid, para 43.

person and the right not to be deprived thereof except in accordance with the principles of fundamental justice'.

The Supreme Court held that detention ancillary to deportation engages the protected interests under section 7 of the Charter. While deportation does not 'in itself' engage section 7,[35] 'some features associated with deportation, such as detention in the course of the certificate process or the prospect of deportation to torture, may do so'.[36] This is a welcome rejection of 'immigration exceptionalism' in relation to detention pending removal, though it transpires that the rejection was only partial. In the Court's reasoning, the consequences of section 7 being engaged were exclusively procedural.

In relation to procedure, the Court reasoned from a principle of general application, namely: 'a person whose liberty is in jeopardy must be given an opportunity to know the case to meet, and an opportunity to meet the case.'[37] Its central objection to the procedures under the IRPA 2001 concerned the lack of 'informed participation' by the detainee,[38] and the judges' resulting dependence on 'what the ministers put before him or her'.[39] The Court concluded that under the security certificate regime the judge is

> not in a position to compensate for the lack of informed scrutiny, challenge and counter-evidence that a person familiar with the case could bring. Such scrutiny is the whole point of the principle that a person whose liberty is in jeopardy must know the case to meet. Here that principle has not merely been limited: it has been effectively gutted. How can one meet a case one does not know?[40]

The Court rejected the idea that section 7 rights are to be sharply contextualised downward in the immigration context. The statutory scheme did not allow for adversarial challenge to the intelligence Ministers submitted in secret *ex parte* hearings. The Supreme Court held that such limitations were contrary to 'fundamental justice'.

In chapter eight, I outlined the 'internal balancing approach' to section 7, according to which the phrase 'in accordance with the principles of fundamental justice' serves as a vehicle for the qualification and limitation of the protected interests of 'life, liberty and security of the person'.[41] In the immigration context,

[35] The Supreme Court cited *Medovarski* for this proposition: *Medovarski v Canada (Minister of Citizenship and Immigration)* [2005] SCC 51, [2005] 2 SCR 539, [46] (McLachlin CJ for the Court). *Medovarski* in turn cited *Chiarelli*: *Canada (Employment and Immigration) v Chiarelli* [1992] 1 SCR 711; see ch 8, pp 234–36.

[36] *Charkaoui* (n 3) [17].

[37] ibid, [61] (McLachlin CJ for the Court). The Court's endorsement of this principle was reminiscent of Wilson J's position in *Singh*. She had focused on the ability of the appellants to make an 'effective challenge' to the information or policies underlying the minister's case: see *Singh* (n 26) 215–16; see ch 8, pp 232–34.

[38] *Charkaoui* (n 3) [62].

[39] ibid, [63]. The Court further addressed the dependence of judges on the government's characteristion of intelligence information in *Charkaoui v Canada (Minister of Citizenship and Immigration)* [2008] 2 SCR 326 (*Charkaoui II*). This case is discussed in section 9.10.1.

[40] *Charkaoui* (n 3) [64].

[41] See ch 8, pp 230–32.

there is the danger that the requirements of the principles of fundamental justice will be contextualised downward, resulting in attenuated protections for non-citizens. Chapter eight also outlined competing strands of the Charter jurisprudence on section 7, allowing or resisting this downward contextualisation, represented by *Chiarelli* and *Singh* respectively.[42]

In its reasoning on procedures, the Supreme Court rejected the internal balancing approach to the relationship between sections 7 and 1,[43] and as a consequence rejected government arguments for a 'delicate balancing' between the right to a fair hearing and national security confidentiality at the section 7 stage.[44] The Court's stance on non-citizens' procedural rights is reminiscent of that adopted in the early Charter case of *Singh*.[45] In both *Charkaoui* and *Singh*, the motivation behind the application of Charter rights was the potentially dire consequences of the denial, or ascription, of status.[46] In both cases, the central point at issue was the need for each appellant to mount an effective challenge to the case against him or her. In its reasoning on procedure, the Court contributed to the line of section 7 authority which holds that immigration legislation must measure up to objective standards offered by Charter rights.[47]

The Supreme Court held that the procedures under the security certificate regime violated section 7 of the Charter.[48] Accordingly, the Court shifted its attention to the question of whether the government had a principled justification under section 1 for violating section 7. The issue to be justified was the non-disclosure of evidence on grounds of national security. The test applied in determining whether a violation could be justified under section 1, the *Oakes* test,[49] required '(a) means rationally connected to the objective; (b) minimal impairment of rights; and (c) proportionality between the effects of the infringement and the importance of the objective'.[50] In *Charkaoui*, the Court did not doubt that non-disclosure was rationally connected to a pressing and substantial objective: national security. What remained at issue was whether the procedures under the security certificate regime minimally impaired the rights of non-citizens.

In considering the question of minimal impairment, the Supreme Court outlined a range of alternative means for addressing confidentiality issues in the national security context. This section of the judgment effectively set the parameters of the legislative response. The alternative means discussed by the Court include the role that used to be played by the Security Intelligence Review

[42] *Canada (Employment and Immigration) v Chiarelli* [1992] 1 SCR 711; *Singh v Canada (Minister of Employment and Immigration)* [1985] 1 SCR 177.

[43] *Charkaoui* (n 3) [21]–[23], [62]–[63].

[44] See ibid, [62], and see [63]. See also *Chiarelli* (n 35) 744. Discussed in ch 8, pp 236–37.

[45] *Singh* (n 26) 210 (Wilson J) (Dickson CJ and Lamer J concurring).

[46] In *Singh* (n 26) the status in question was refugee status. In *Charkaoui*, the relevant status was certification as inadmissible on grounds of security.

[47] See ch 8, s 8.4 first paragraph, referencing Christopher J Wydrzynski, *Canadian Immigration Law and Procedure* (Aurora, Canada Law Book, 1983) 458–59.

[48] *Charkaoui* (n 3) [65].

[49] *R v Oakes* [1986] 1 SCR 103.

[50] *Charkaoui* (n 3) [67].

Committee (SIRC) in reviewing security certificates.[51] SIRC had developed its own investigative procedures.[52] In *Chahal*, the European Court of Human Rights had referred to these procedures as the 'Canadian technique'.[53] *Chahal's* reference to the procedures had been influential in the development of the 'special advocate' role before the United Kingdom's Special Immigration Appeals Commission (SIAC).[54] In *Charkaoui*, in addition to discussing the home-grown procedures of SIRC, the Canadian Supreme Court made separate mention of the SIAC 'special advocate' process in the United Kingdom.[55] The Court characterised the procedures developed by SIRC and SIAC, and other alternatives canvassed,[56] as 'less intrusive' upon the procedural rights of those certified than security certificates.

The smorgasbord of less intrusive approaches set out by the Supreme Court has occasioned discussion of the dangers of 'judicial pre-approval of legislative responses'.[57] The spur for this discussion was the fact that the eventual Canadian legislative response, discussed in section 9.9 below, was closely modelled on the role of 'special advocates' before SIAC, and this has been assessed as 'the one alternative [discussed by the Court] that arguably achieves the worst job of all the alternatives in ensuring fair treatment of the affected person'.[58] Here, the basic line of criticism, with which I agree, is that it would have been preferable for the Supreme Court to confine itself to pointing out the legal shortcomings of the current system. Laying out alternatives arguably sends the signal that any one of them will be 'Charter compliant'. In *Charkaoui*, this issue was exacerbated by incomplete and inaccurate summaries of the available alternatives.[59] Against this, there was clearly pressure on the Court to substantiate its view that there were workable, 'less intrusive' alternatives available in the national security context. Reconciling the dangers of 'judicial pre-approval' with the need to demonstrate

[51] ibid, [71]–[76]. Established under the Canadian Security Intelligence Service Act 1984 (CSIS Act 1984), the Security Intelligence Review Committee (SIRC) initially reviewed all decisions on deportation for reasons of national security. SIRC's involvement in the deportation review process came to an end in 2002 with the entry into force of the Immigration and Refugee Protection Act 2001: see Rayner Thwaites, 'Deportation on National Security Grounds' (LLM thesis, University of Toronto, 2004), Appendix 1.

[52] Pursuant to its authority under the CSIS Act 1984. On the procedures see Murray Rankin, 'The Security Intelligence Review Committee: Reconciling National Security with Procedural Fairness' (1989–90) 3 *Canadian Journal of Administrative Law and Policy* 173, 179.

[53] *Chahal v United Kingdom* (1997) 23 EHRR 413, paras 144 and 131: see ch 5, pp 132, 135.

[54] See ch 5, s 5.4.

[55] *Charkaoui* (n 3) [80]–[84]. On SIAC see ch 5, s 5.4.

[56] The other alternative means discussed by the Court were the procedure under s 38 of the Canada Evidence Act; the reliance placed on undertakings by counsel in the Air India trial; and the role of amicus curiae in the Arar Commission. See *Charkaoui* (n 3) [77]–[79].

[57] Kent Roach, '*Charkaoui* and Bill C-3: Some Implications for Anti-Terrorism Policy and Dialogue between Courts and Legislatures' (2008) 42 *Supreme Court Law Review* (2d) 281, 304–06. See also David Dyzenhaus, 'Cycles of Legality in Emergency Times' (2007) 18 *Public Law Review* 165, 175–76.

[58] Roach (n 57) 305. See also David Jenkins, 'There and Back Again' (2011) 42 *Columbia Human Rights Law Review* 279.

[59] Roach (n 57) 293–06; Audrey Macklin, 'Transjudicial Conversations about Security and Human Rights' in Mark B Salter (ed), *Mapping Transatlantic Security Relations: The EU, Canada, and the War on Terror* (Oxford, Routledge, 2010) 212, 223–26.

workable alternatives counsels that the Court register the 'less intrusive' measures with little attendant assessment or exposition.

There is much to welcome in the Supreme Court's reasoning on procedure. It found that section 7 was engaged, and its reasoning on the provision drew clearly and convincingly on generally applicable principles of public law. The Court did not treat invocations of national security confidentiality as a bar to analysis in accordance with those general principles. But the clear reasoning from principles of general application, characteristic of the Court's reasoning on procedure, did not extend to the Court's reasoning on the substantive rights claims.

Before considering those substantive rights challenges, I note the lulling effect of the Court's extended discussion of procedure. Having sharply segregated procedural issues from any substantive concerns, the Court devoted the first half of its judgment to the application of section 7 to the statutory procedures and, having found a violation of section 7, a proportionality analysis of the government's justification under section 1.[60] At no point in the discussion did the Supreme Court raise as problematic the fact that the regime was in effect a regime of indefinite preventive detention or constraint, confined to non-citizens. The prolonged discussion of the merits and demerits of the procedure under the security certificate regime proceeded as though the regime itself was otherwise legally and constitutionally sound. Long before undertaking a cursory consideration of whether the regime discriminated against non-citizens, the Court had signalled its decision on this question by focusing on the secondary issue of whether the procedures for review passed constitutional muster.

9.4 Unanswered Questions

9.4.1 Substantive Limits on Indefinite Detention?

The Supreme Court's focus on procedural review left two broad questions unaddressed: What are the substantive limits on the practice of preventive detention? And is the regime of preventive detention or constraint discriminatory against non-citizens, by reason of an insufficient connection between detention and deportation? The Court's response to the first question was to put its faith in a case-by-case review of each detainee's individual circumstances. The Canadian Supreme Court's approach to this issue stands in marked contrast to the substantive position adopted by the United States Supreme Court in *Zadvydas*.[61] In that decision, a majority held that,

[60] *Charkaoui* (n 3): [12]–[65] are devoted to the application of s 7 to the procedures, and [66]–[87] to the attempted s 1 justification for the violation of s 7, in a judgment of 143 paragraphs.

[61] *Zadvydas v Davis*, 533 US 678 (2001).

> for the reasons we have set forth, we believe that an alien's liberty interest is, at the least, strong enough to raise a serious question as to whether, *irrespective of the procedures used* . . . the Constitution permits detention that is indefinite and potentially permanent.[62] (emphasis added)

The Canadian Supreme Court's reliance on regular review also stands in marked contrast to the approach taken by the House of Lords in *Belmarsh*. There, Lord Nicholls stated:

> Nor is the vice of indefinite detention cured by the provision made for independent review by the Special Immigration Appeals Commission. The commission is well placed to check that the Secretary of State's powers are exercised properly. But what is in question on these appeals is the existence and width of the statutory powers, not the way they are exercised.[63]

Charkaoui inverted this approach. The Supreme Court left the existence and width of the indefinite detention power untouched and focused on the procedures governing its exercise. The substantive issues at the centre of the litigation – legality of deportation to torture and of indefinite detention – were left open, to be assessed on a case-by-case basis.[64]

The Supreme Court's reliance on procedural review removed the legislature's responsibility for Charter compliance.[65] Legislative grants of power that posed the clear potential to infringe Charter rights were allowed to stand. The implicit understanding appears to be that courts can respond to legal challenges to particular exercises of those powers as and when they arise. This puts the onus on those affected to bring a legal challenge through the courts. Further, the Court's failure to require explicit legislative authorisation for deportation to torture or indefinite detention means that resolution of these grave rights infringements remains a matter for the courts.[66] As Kent Roach says, 'the Court's minimalism in *Charkaoui* appears to maximize the ability of courts, not legislatures, to make important decisions in future cases'.[67]

62 *Zadvydas* (n 61) 696. The *Zadvydas* majority, in *obiter*, made clear that their comments requiring an implied temporal limitation on immigration detention were not addressed to terrorism or other circumstances where 'special arguments might be made for forms of preventive detention and for heightened deference to the judgments of the political branches with respect to matters of national security': 696; see ch 1, pp 9–10.

63 *Belmarsh* (n 28) [82]. Lord Nicholls' statement has particular bite in the Canadian context, in that the Canadian parliamentary amendments to the security certificate regime enacted in February 2008 (Bill C-3 (n 13)) sought to replicate 'the provision made for independent review by the Special Immigration Appeals Commission' to which Lord Nicholls referred.

64 See also Roach (n 57) 349–50.

65 For an argument that where a statute confers a discretion to engage in activities that may breach Charter rights, that provision should itself be struck down as failing to take adequate measures to ensure those rights, see Sujit Choudhry and Kent Roach, 'Racial and Ethnic Profiling: Statutory Discretion, Constitutional Remedies and Democratic Accountability' (2003) 41 *Osgoode Hall Law Journal* 1.

66 The legislature did not attend to these issues in responding to *Charkaoui*: see Bill C-3 (n 13) and, for commentary, Roach (n 57).

67 Roach (n 57) 349.

Federal Court judges supervising the security certificate regime were aware that procedural steps under the IRPA 2001 could continue indefinitely.[68] The Canadian Supreme Court shared this awareness: 'while the IRPA in principle imposes detention only pending deportation, it may in fact permit lengthy and indeterminate detention or lengthy periods subject to onerous release conditions.'[69] The issue is why the Court did not address this feature of the statutory regime.

In Charter terms, the Court's response to indefinite detention was framed in terms of the requirements of sections 7 and 12 of the Charter. The issue of substantive limits on indefinite detention was funnelled through consideration of whether 'extended' detention under the IRPA 2001 violated the guarantee against cruel and unusual treatment under section 12 of the Charter. Section 7 only featured in the reasoning by way of the impact of 'the mechanisms available to the detainee to regain liberty' (a section 7 matter) on the 'psychological stress' and 'indefiniteness' of detention.[70] Raising the issue of indefinite detention under section 12 had the effect that it was not 'the detention itself, or even its length, that is objectionable.'[71] The issue under section 12 was whether detention 'violated accepted norms of treatment'.[72]

In response to the challenge under section 12 of the Charter, the Court held that the 'robust ongoing review' of detention demanded by the Court's application of section 7 to the security certificate regime meant that the 'extended' detention allowed under the statute did not contravene section 12.[73] The Court emphasised 'the possibility of a judge concluding at a certain point that a particular detention constitutes cruel and unusual treatment'.[74] This possibility of a future ruling on 'cruel and unusual treatment', confined to the facts of the case at hand, was all the Court was prepared to commit to on the question of indefinite detention and the Charter. It avoided defining what would constitute indefinite detention and did not determine whether indefinite detention would constitute cruel and unusual punishment.[75]

The only guidance provided by the Court on what conduct would infringe the substantive rights at issue was implicit in what it did not find. It declined to reach a finding of cruel and unusual punishment in relation to any of the appellants. One of the appellants, Mr Almrei, had been detained for over five years and remained in detention at the time of hearing and judgment. Of that period, more than three years had been spent in solitary confinement. He was held in a remand facility intended for short-term detention pending criminal trial and had made

[68] See eg *Mahjoub v Canada (Minister of Citizenship and Immigration)* [2007] FC 171, (2007) 309 FTR 72. See ch 8, p 248.

[69] *Charkaoui* (n 3) [105], and see more expansive discussion at [99].

[70] ibid, [96].

[71] ibid.

[72] ibid.

[73] ibid, [123].

[74] ibid.

[75] ibid, [102]: The Court noted: 'Mr Almrei argues that as far as he is concerned, his detention is indefinite', but abstained from comment.

complaints about harassment, problems with practising religion, access to reading materials, the right to wear shoes, having adequate heat in winter and maintaining contacts with the outside world.[76] Further, a Federal Court judge had found that Mr Almrei would not be removed within a reasonable time.[77] The Supreme Court, by its silence, held that over five years' administrative detention without charge, without an end in sight, did not breach section 12.[78]

The Supreme Court clearly endorsed the Federal Court practice,[79] established at the time of judgment in *Charkaoui*, of ordering release from detention on onerous conditions.[80] It recognised that just as detention itself called for regular review, the conditions on which release was ordered would themselves need to be subject to regular review.[81] What the Court did not do was indicate any limits to the continued deployment of this system of preventive detention and/or restraint without charge.

9.4.2 Discriminatory against Non-Citizens?

The existence of a review process was also relied upon to address the discrimination argument under section 15 of the Charter. The Court in *Charkaoui* devoted a cursory three paragraphs of reasoning to the section 15 discrimination claim. It is clear that the Court held that the constitutionality of the security certificate regime rested on its characterisation as a regime of detention for the purposes of deportation.[82] The relevance of the deportation context is bluntly illustrated in the way the Court distinguished *R v Lyons*.[83] In that case, the Court had indicated that 'a sentence of indeterminate detention, applied with respect to a future crime or a crime that had already been punished, would violate section 7 of the Charter'.[84] The Court's basis for distinguishing *R v Lyons* from *Charkaoui* was the 'immigration context' in the latter, attended by review.[85]

After registering that deportation was legitimately confined to non-citizens, the court noted that detention pending deportation may nonetheless be discriminatory:

> First, detention may become indefinite as deportation is put off or becomes impossible, for example because there is no country to which the person can be deported.

[76] See Almrei factum (n 21) paras 12, 13 and 85, citing earlier Federal Court security certificate proceedings and a habeas action before the Ontario courts.

[77] *Charkaoui* (n 3) [102], citing *Almrei v Canada (Minister of Citizenship and Immigration)* [2005] FC 1645, (2005) 270 FTR 1 (Layden–Stevenson J).

[78] *Charkaoui* (n 3) [95].

[79] On that Federal Court practice see ch 8, pp 249–50.

[80] See *Charkaoui* (n 3) [101]: 'courts have read [s 84(2) of the IRPA] as allowing the judge to inquire whether terms and conditions could make the release safe. This is an invitation that Federal Court judges have rightly accepted.'

[81] ibid, [122].

[82] ibid, [131].

[83] *R v Lyons* [1987] 2 SCR 309.

[84] As summarised by the Court in *Charkaoui* (n 3) [106].

[85] ibid, [107].

> Second, the government could conceivably use the IRPA not for the purpose of deportation, but to detain the person on security grounds. In both situations, the source of the problem is that the detention is no longer related, in effect or purpose, to the goal of deportation.[86]

The Court went on to find that the detentions at issue had not become 'unhinged from the state's purpose of deportation'.[87] It concluded its review of section 15 with the statement that 'the answer to these concerns lies in an effective review process that permits the judge to consider all matters relevant to the detention'.[88] The Supreme Court's preceding statements on discrimination and deportation give rise to a series of questions. Why did the Court find that deportation remained possible, and that the detentions (and constraints) at issue had not become unhinged from the state's purpose of deportation? There were judicial findings that there was no prospect of an appellant's removal within a reasonable time, if ever. Is it accurate to say that the government was not detaining the appellants on security grounds? The legislative basis for ongoing detention was that release would pose a danger to national security.[89] Why, in the circumstances, did the Court repose confidence in review as a complete answer? And finally, what was the Court's understanding of detention pending removal such that these findings and holdings appeared tenable to it?

The last question – the Court's position on detention pending removal – underlies the others. The Court held that detention was authorised for the purposes of deportation if the government still intended to deport the non-citizen and deportation remained a future possibility. This characterisation of the Canadian Supreme Court's reasoning is developed below through a review of the Court's use of comparative authority.

9.5 The Court's Use of Comparative Authority[90]

9.5.1 'Reasonably Necessary for Deportation Purposes'

The Supreme Court in *Charkaoui* held that 'extended periods of detention pending deportation' did not violate the Charter provided that such detention was attended by periodic reviews, whose procedures accorded with the strictures laid down by the Court. The Court's phrase 'extended periods of detention pending deportation' encompassed, for example, Mr Almrei's case, in which there had

[86] ibid, [130].
[87] ibid, [131].
[88] ibid.
[89] See IRPA 2001, s 84(2).
[90] This section draws on and develops Rayner Thwaites, 'A Coordinated Judicial Response to Counterterrorism? Counter-Examples' in Mark B Salter (ed), *Mapping Transatlantic Security Relations: The EU, Canada, and the War on Terror* (Oxford, Routledge, 2010) 236.

been a judicial finding that the appellant would not be removed within a reasonable time.[91] Mr Almrei had spent more than five years in preventive detention without anything more than a speculative prospect of removal.[92] In relation to the holding that such detention did not violate the Charter, the Court stated:

> These conclusions are consistent with English and American authority . . . Courts in the United Kingdom and the United States have suggested that detention in this context can be used only during the period where it is reasonably necessary for deportation purposes: [*Hardial Singh*]; *Zadvydas*.[93]

Contrary to the Canadian Supreme Court's claim, *Charkaoui* is not consistent with the English and American authorities referenced.

In *Hardial Singh*, the onus was on the government to prove that there was a real prospect of removal within a reasonable time.[94] It was clear that in the absence of such evidence, the judge was to order release. If removal was not a real prospect, the purpose of detention no longer obtained and could not be used to justify that detention. If the legal reasoning in *Charkaoui* was, in fact, consistent with the '*Hardial Singh* principles', the Federal Court's finding that Mr Almrei would not 'be removed within a reasonable time'[95] would bring authority to detain to an end. Under the *Hardial Singh* principles, this factual finding in Mr Almrei's case would sever the requisite connection with the purpose of removal.

The *Zadvydas* majority directed reviewing courts to

> measure reasonableness primarily in terms of the statute's basic purpose, namely assuring the alien's presence at the moment of removal. Thus, if removal is not reasonably foreseeable, the court should hold continued detention unreasonable and no longer authorized by statute.[96]

On the basis that it would assist in the uniform administration of the detention period in the courts, the US Supreme Court went on to state that detention was presumptively valid for six months. As it was no more than a presumption, a non-citizen could be held for longer 'until it has been determined that there is no significant likelihood of removal in the reasonably foreseeable future'.[97]

In *Zadvydas*, the United States Supreme Court directly considered, and rejected, a position analogous to that accepted by the Canadian Supreme Court in

[91] See *Almrei v Canada (Minister of Citizenship and Immigration)* [2005] FC 1645, (2005) 270 FTR 1 (*Almrei, Second Application for Release*), [255] (Layden–Stevenson J): 'I am satisfied, on a balance of probabilities, that Mr Almrei will not be removed within a reasonable time.' See also *Canada (Minister of Citizenship and Immigration) v Mahjoub* [2005] FC 1596, (2005) 270 FTR 101 (*Mahjoub, Second Application for Release*).

[92] Mr Almrei was released on conditions on 2 January 2009, after more than seven years in a detention facility: see *Re Almrei* 2009 FC 3, (2009) 337 FTR 160, and pp 280–82 below.

[93] *Charkaoui* (n 3) [124].

[94] *R v Governor of Durham Prison, ex parte Singh* [1983] EWHC 1 (QB), [1984] 1 All ER 983 (*Hardial Singh*), 985 (Woolf J). See ch 5, s 5.2. See also ch 7, s 7.8 on the development of the *Hardial Singh* principles.

[95] *Almrei, Second Application for Release* (n 91) [255].

[96] *Zadvydas* (n 61) 699–700.

[97] ibid, 701.

Charkaoui. Mr Zadvydas appealed from a decision of the Fifth Circuit, which held that his detention did not violate the United States Constitution because 'eventual deportation was not "impossible", good faith efforts to remove him from the United States continued, and his detention was subject to periodic administrative review'.[98] This description of the Fifth Circuit's decision reproduces the essential features of the Supreme Court of Canada's ruling in *Charkaoui*. The United States Supreme Court reversed the decision of the Fifth Circuit. The *Zadvydas* majority held that the features relied upon by the Fifth Circuit did *not*, in the absence of an implied temporal limitation, suffice to address the 'serious constitutional problems' posed by continuing detention pending removal when removal was not in prospect.[99]

In *Charkaoui*, the Court abstracted the phrase 'reasonably necessary for deportation purposes' from the meaning it possessed in the comparative judgments cited. It arrived at a criterion for limiting detention that proved capable of accommodating not only the positions adopted in *Hardial Singh* and *Zadvydas*, but their opposite, the competing position against which the ratio of these decisions was defined. The need for there to be a real prospect of deportation in the reasonably foreseeable future, central to the reasoning in *Zadvydas* and *Hardial Singh*, was absent in *Charkaoui*, effecting a fundamental change in the nature of the detention. The phrase was switched from identifying a rights-protecting approach to identifying a rights-precluding approach.

As accurately described by John Finnis, *Charkaoui* allows that detention, in circumstances characterised by an ongoing threat and ongoing efforts to deport, might '*reasonably* last even, in principle, indefinitely'.[100] This is a qualitatively different proposition from those at the heart of *Hardial Singh* and *Zadvydas*. The Canadian Supreme Court's claim to consistency with United Kingdom and United States authorities is misleading on the central point at issue, namely whether a deportation rationale supplies ongoing authority to detain non-citizens in the circumstances before the Court. The Canadian Supreme Court's use of the phrase 'reasonably necessary for deportation purposes' in *Charkaoui* was closer to the reasoning relied upon by the *Al-Kateb* majority than the reasoning of the authorities it cited in support.[101]

The Canadian Supreme Court structured its consideration of the appellants' detention by reference to a passage from *Sahin* on detention pending deportation.[102] There Rothstein J outlined a list of factors going to whether detention

[98] ibid, 685.

[99] The analogy with *Zadvydas* is complicated by the *Zadvydas* majority's allowance for a 'terrorism exception': see ch 1, pp 9–10. The Canadian Supreme Court in *Charkaoui* did not reference this aspect of *Zadvydas* in drawing an analogy with that judgment.

[100] John Finnis, 'Nationality, Alienage and Constitutional Principle' (2007) 123 *LQR* 417, 430 fn 61, citing *Charkaoui* (n 3) [105], [110].

[101] *Al-Kateb v Godwin* 2004 HCA 37, (2004) 219 CLR 562. On this aspect of the reasoning in *Al-Kateb*, the nature of the 'possibility' of deportation required to sustain authority to detain, see ch 3, s 3.2, and in particular Hayne J in *Al-Kateb* [229].

[102] *Charkaoui* (n 3) [107], citing *Sahin v Canada (Minister of Citizenship and Immigration)* [1995] 1 FC 214, 231–32 (Rothstein J).

'constitutes a deprivation of liberty that is not in accordance with the principle of fundamental justice'.[103] The *Sahin* factors were no different in kind from Lord Dyson's elaboration of the *Hardial Singh* principles in *R(I)* and *Lumba*.[104] Again, the primary distinction between *Charkaoui* and the comparative authorities cited lay not in the formulation of the principles, but in a qualitative difference in their application. The substantive rights at issue were not found to be breached in *Charkaoui*. The Court did not clarify what it meant by 'indefinite detention', except to hold that the appellants were not presently subjected to it. In *Charkaoui*, the point at which the hinge between deportation and detention will break, rendering detention discriminatory, is uncertain, except to the extent that the hinge holds, after five years and with no sure end to detention in sight. The Canadian Supreme Court held out the prospect that ongoing detention may yet breach substantive rights, but that day never arrived.

9.5.2 'The IRPA . . . Does Not Authorise Indefinite Detention'?

The Canadian Supreme Court's reference to *Hardial Singh* and *Zadvydas* led it into discussion of a case 'raising similar issues', *Belmarsh*.[105] The Court's treatment of *Belmarsh* is characterised by the same problem that marks its use of *Zadvydas* and *Hardial Singh*. The Court claimed that its reasoning was compatible with that of the House of Lords. But upon examination the claim of compatibility is shown to be unsustainable, papering over a fundamental divergence of reasoning of the Canadian Supreme Court from that of the House of Lords. I agree with John Finnis's assessment of the divergence between the two decisions:

> But in truth the Canadian decision differs substantially from the Lords by accepting that there *need* be no breach of human or constitutional rights in open-ended detention for the purposes of deportation, provided that regular review keeps all factors in view.[106]

The Court's discussion of *Belmarsh* straddled its discussion of sections 12 and 15 of the Charter, effectively unifying the discussion of the two provisions.

The Canadian Supreme Court did not take issue with the reasoning of the *Belmarsh* majority. It asserted a factual distinction between the cases. It distinguished *Belmarsh* on the basis that the British legislation, the Anti-Terrorism, Crime and Security Act 2001 (ATCSA 2001), expressly authorised permanent detention.[107] Section 23 of the ATCSA 2001 provided for a certified person to be detained under the Immigration Act 1971 'despite the fact that his removal or departure from the United Kingdom is prevented (whether temporarily or

[103] *Charkaoui* (n 3) [107], citing *Sahin* (n 7) 229.

[104] *R(I) v Secretary of State for the Home Department* [2003] INLR 196; *R (on the application of Lumba) v Secretary of State for the Home Department* [2011] UKSC 12, [2012] 1 AC 245. On these decisions see ch 7, s 7.8.

[105] *Charkaoui* (n 3) [125].

[106] Finnis (n 100) 440 fn 91 (emphasis in original), citing *Charkaoui* (n 7) [110], [126]–[127].

[107] *Charkaoui* (n 3) [127].

indefinitely)'.[108] By way of contrast, the Canadian Supreme Court stated: 'The IRPA, unlike the UK legislation under consideration in [*Belmarsh*], does not authorize indefinite detention and, interpreted as suggested above, provides an effective review process that meets the requirements of Canadian law.'[109]

But the IRPA 2001 does authorise indefinite detention. There is nothing in the legislation to preclude it. As the Canadian Supreme Court acknowledged at another point in its reasoning, 'It is thus clear that while the IRPA in principle imposes detention only pending deportation, it may in fact permit lengthy and indeterminate detention or lengthy periods subject to onerous release conditions'.[110] To render the Court's statement on IRPA 2001 true, one has to add the qualifier that 'The IRPA . . . does not *explicitly* authorise indefinite detention . . .'. The requirement of explicit authorisation is, in the factual and legal context in which the Supreme Court found itself, best regarded as a distinction without a difference. What matters is that the IRPA 2001, like the UK legislation, authorises indefinite detention. As stated in Mr Almrei's factum before the Court, 'He is indefinitely detained under a statutory scheme which permits this'.[111] Previous Federal Court judgments on the security certificate regime had also characterised the IRPA 2001 as permitting indefinite detention.[112]

The Canadian Supreme Court characterised the House of Lords' reasoning in *Belmarsh* as follows: 'Absent the possibility of deportation, [the provision authorising detention] lost its character as an immigration provision, and hence constituted unlawful discrimination.'[113] There is every indication that the Canadian Supreme Court held that this proposition was equally applicable in Canada. Again, the distinction between the two jurisdictions was allegedly a factual one. The distinction the Court relied on was that in Canada there remained a possibility of deportation, a possibility that was absent in the United Kingdom. However, this factual distinction turned on a legal distinction that the Canadian Supreme Court both created and maintained. The difference between the two jurisdictions on the 'possibility of deportation' is a function of a divergence in the jurisprudence on deportation to torture, between *Chahal* in Europe,[114] and *Suresh* in Canada.[115]

[108] On the statutory context see ch 6, s 6.1.
[109] *Charkaoui* (n 3) [127] and see [130].
[110] ibid, [105].
[111] Almrei Factum (n 21) para 92.
[112] See *Canada (Minister of Citizenship and Immigration) v Mahjoub* [2005] FC 1596, (2005) 270 FTR 101 (*Mahjoub, Second Application for Release*), [92] (Dawson J). See also *Mahjoub v Canada (Minister of Citizenship and Immigration)* [2007] FC 171, (2007) 309 FTR 72 (*Mahjoub, Third Application for Release*), [103] (Mosley J). See further ch 8, pp 248–50.
[113] *Charkaoui* (n 3) [126]. See also [130].
[114] *Chahal* (n 53).
[115] *Suresh v Canada (Minister of Citizenship and Immigration)* [2002] SCC 1, [2002] 1 SCR 3.

9.6 Deportation to Torture and the *Suresh* Exception

Belmarsh and *Charkaoui* raised 'similar issues'.[116] In both cases, the deportation of foreign terrorist suspects was blocked by the prospect of a real risk of torture if the detainees were returned to their country of nationality. In the British case, the possibility of deportation to a real risk of torture was foreclosed by the decision of the European Court of Human Rights in *Chahal*.[117] *Chahal* read Article 3 of the European Convention on Human Rights (ECHR) as imposing an absolute prohibition on deportation to torture.[118] This absolute, non-derogable prohibition was the reason for the United Kingdom's derogation from Article 5(1)(f) of the ECHR and its express authorisation of the indefinite detention of non-citizens.[119]

Moving across the Atlantic, the issue of deportation to torture is no less pervasive in the Canadian context. The Canadian Federal Court stated that removal to torture 'is an issue in virtually all security certificate cases'.[120] The Federal Court jurisprudence on deportation to torture was shaped by *Suresh*,[121] as described in chapter eight, sections 8.7.1 and 8.7.2. As detailed in those sections, the operation of the *Suresh* exception effectively imposed a prohibition on deportation to torture. But by qualifying any absolute prohibition on deportation to torture with an exceptional discretion to deport, *Suresh* preserved, at least as a matter of legal fiction, the *possibility* of deportation in circumstances characterised by a real risk of torture upon return.[122]

The Canadian Supreme Court distinguished *Belmarsh* on the grounds that the United Kingdom legislation in that case expressly provided for indefinite detention. To focus on this legislative distinction is to focus on a secondary phenomenon. The primary distinction between the two jurisdictions, which shaped the different legislative responses, is that in Canada there was and is no absolute prohibition on deportation to torture. In this context, there was no need to make express provision for indefinite detention. The Canadian government could, and did, achieve the same objectives the British government sought under section 23 of the ATSCA 2001 without such a provision. Unlike the British government, notwithstanding a real risk of deportation to torture, the Canadians could continue

[116] *Charkaoui* (n 3) [125].

[117] *Chahal* (n 53).

[118] Convention for the Protection of Human Rights and Fundamental Freedoms (opened for signature 4 November 1950, entered into force 3 September 1953) 213 UNTS 211, Eur TS 5 (ECHR).

[119] See ch 6, s 6.1.

[120] *Re Jaballah* [2006] FC 1230, (2006) 148 CRR (2d) 1 (*Jaballah, Second Reasonableness Decision*), [76] (Mackay DJ).

[121] *Suresh* (n 115).

[122] This is an example of the way in which a failure to take a principled position on one issue (deportation to torture) can have a domino effect, undermining surrounding legal principles (opposition to indefinite detention) that rely on it in reasoning and argumentation. On the general phenomenon see Jeremy Waldron, 'Torture and Positive Law: Jurisprudence for the White House' (2005) 105 *Columbia Law Review* 1681, especially 1736.

to entertain the possibility of deportation and so continue to detain for that purpose. The Canadian Supreme Court endorsed the House of Lords' conclusion that explicit provision for indefinite detention is incompatible with fundamental rights commitments. But when a practice of indefinite detention developed in Canada, authorised, but not explicitly provided for, under statute, the Canadian Supreme Court held that it did not necessarily infringe any Charter rights.

There were additional reasons for the Supreme Court to close off the *Suresh* exception, or at least to resolve its application to the cases before it. The lower courts were clearly seeking guidance on how to apply the *Suresh* exception. In a 2005 case on a security certificate, Dawson J of the Canadian Federal Court stated: 'I find on the balance of probabilities that Mr Mahjoub is unlikely to be removed from Canada until the Supreme Court decides whether circumstances will ever justify a removal to torture.'[123] In operation, the *Suresh* exception effectively served to bar deportation. Conversely, it also served as a justification for maintaining 'detention pending deportation' by preserving the *possibility* of deportation to torture.

By the time the Court delivered its judgment in *Charkaoui*, it was readily apparent that the security certificate regime was unable to achieve its ostensible purpose of removal.[124] In 2005, in the course of an application for release, Dawson J wrote: 'Mr Almrei insists that the legislation does not contemplate the present circumstances . . . it is arguable that when prolonged detention occurs, the legislation has diverted from its stated goal [namely removal from Canada].'[125] And it was readily apparent that government attempts to utilise the *Suresh* exception could give rise to an indefinite number of procedural steps.[126] What was needed to resolve the impasse was a definitive ruling by the Supreme Court on the possibility of deportation to torture.[127]

Nonetheless, the *Charkaoui* Court left the *Suresh* exception untouched. The Supreme Court avoided the need to address this point of doctrine, central to the workability of the regime as a mechanism of removal, on the basis that a risk of torture remained to be proven in each of the appellants' cases: 'The issue of deportation to torture is . . . not before us here.'[128] This is to take a technical point. The determinations on deportation to torture had been quashed and remitted to the Minister. Whether or not it was immediately at issue, the question of deportation to torture generated and shaped the security certificate jurisprudence. It was readily apparent that the ongoing debate occasioned by the *Suresh* exception needed to be resolved by the Supreme Court, in order to resolve the impasse attending use of security certificates as a mechanism of removal. Failure to address the *Suresh* exception meant that uncertainty over the prospects of removal continued.

[123] *Mahjoub, Second Application for Release* (n 112) [29].

[124] See ch 8, ss 8.7.1 and 8.7.2, where this point is elaborated with reference to Federal Court jurisprudence.

[125] *Almrei* (n 77) [428] (Layden-Stevenson J).

[126] *Mahjoub, Third Application for Release* (n 112) [103]. See ch 8, s 8.7.

[127] See *Mahjoub, Second Application for Release* (n 112) [29]. See pp 247–48.

[128] *Charkaoui* (n 3) [15].

On the Supreme Court's understanding of detention pending deportation, this uncertainty maintained authority to detain.

9.7 The Missing Proportionality Analysis

To return to the comparison between *Charkaoui* and *Belmarsh*, in a marked divergence from *Belmarsh*, the Canadian Supreme Court did not engage in a proportionality analysis of the detention or of the decision to confine the measures to non-citizens, as opposed to the procedures and the regularity of review. The topics central to the legal discussion in *Belmarsh* – the rational connection between deportation and detention and the corresponding issue of discrimination against non-citizens – were peripheral to the Canadian Supreme Court's reasoning.[129]

If the Canadian Supreme Court had squarely confronted the real risk of torture upon a detainee's return to their country of nationality and instituted an absolute prohibition on deportation to torture, this would have severed the connection between detention and deportation. In these circumstances, to maintain consistency with the reasoning in *Belmarsh*, the Court would have had to openly acknowledge that the security certificate regime was better characterised as a preventive detention regime confined to non-citizens. Stripped of a deportation rationale, the fact that the regime discriminated against non-citizens, infringing section 15, would come into view and the inquiry would proceed to ask whether the measures were nonetheless justified under section 1 of the Charter.

The outlines of the applicable section 1 proportionality analysis are supplied by *Belmarsh*. In the absence of a deportation rationale, the Supreme Court would presumably consider whether security was a sufficient justification for detention provisions confined to non-citizens.[130] Here, there arise issues of rational connection. Why are security detention measures confined to non-citizens? In the absence of empirical evidence that non-citizens constituted the exclusive source of the threat in Canada, there is no apparent ground of factual distinction between the circumstances in *Charkaoui* and *Belmarsh* on this point.

[129] See also Maureen T Duffy and René Provost, 'Security Detention in Practice: Constitutional Canaries and the Elusive Quest to Legitimize Security Detentions in Canada' (2009) 40 *Case Western Reserve Journal of International Law* 531, 552.

[130] On the nature of a section 1 analysis in the circumstances, also outlined with reference to *Belmarsh*, see also Roach (n 57) 309.

9.8 Conclusions on *Charkaoui*

9.8.1 Principled Minimalism?[131]

A central characteristic of the Canadian Supreme Court's reasoning in *Charkaoui* was its lack of decision on the substantive issues. No one was ordered to be released. No one was ordered to be removed. The spectacle of a detention regime ostensibly facilitating deportation, under which deportation does not occur, continued. There was no discussion of the discretion to deport to torture in exceptional circumstances, nor was the question of the constitutionality of indefinite detention directly addressed. Instead, the Court provided for the possibility of such infringements being identified on a case-by-case basis, and devoted its energies to examining and ultimately strengthening the procedural protections afforded to those certified under the regime.

The Canadian Supreme Court's approach might be defended as a principled instance of constitutional minimalism.[132] In the influential accounts of constitutional minimalism offered by Sunstein and Katyal,[133] this approach is defined by a preference for narrowness over breadth and shallowness over depth.[134] The reasoning on the challenges to substantive rights in *Charkaoui* met these criteria. On the narrowness criterion, the Court adopted a 'one case at a time' approach to the key substantive points at issue. The Court allowed that a court might, in a future case, determine that the 'hinge' between detention and deportation has been broken.[135] Its reasoning on these points was also shallow in Sunstein's sense. The Court did not develop the basis for its conclusion that detention remained for the purpose of deportation in the cases before it and did not make clear how it would be determined when this purpose ceased to authorise detention.

A key motivation for the theory of constitutional minimalism is the view that it avoids 'freezing' constitutional standards in place. This concern is seen as particularly salient in the area of national security, where any substantive constitutional arrangement has to thread its way between the risks of unduly hampering the executive's response to security threats on the one hand and lending sanction to unnecessary executive powers on the other. For Sunstein and Katyal, it was the desire to avoid imposing the constraints of constitutional invalidity on the

[131] This section draws on material originally published as Thwaites, 'Process and Substance' (n 2).

[132] Kent Roach has also analysed *Charkaoui* against the minimalist position: see Roach (n 57) 307–08.

[133] Cass Sunstein, 'Minimalism at War' [2004] *Supreme Court Review* 47; Neal Katyal, 'Equality in the War on Terror' (2007) 59 *Stanford Law Review* 1365. Sunstein's article applied to emergencies the minimalist position he argued to be generally appropriate in constitutional cases, set out in Cass Sunstein, *One Case at a Time: Judicial Minimalism on the Supreme Court* (Cambridge, MA, Harvard University Press, 1999).

[134] Sunstein, 'Minimalism at War' (n 133) 48.

[135] *Charkaoui* (n 3) [131].

political branches (and future courts) that motivated avoidance of substantive positions on constitutional rights and a reliance on procedure.[136]

A key criticism of *Charkaoui* centres on how much the Court decided without discussion or supporting reasoning. This objection can be recast as stating that minimalist judgments, such as *Charkaoui*, may do more than minimalist theory assumes. Minimalism is motivated by the desire to keep legal questions open, so preserving greater space for democratic deliberation. But as applied to *Charkaoui*, this seems descriptively inadequate. Kent Roach makes a related point against minimalism in his review of *Charkaoui*, arguing that the decision's 'one case at a time' approach did not 'maximize the space for legislative policy making' in leaving the legislation intact but uncertain in its operation.[137] My focus here is on the way the decision constrains future legal argument.

What is troubling about *Charkaoui* is the range of substantive decisions that were embedded in the reasoning with little by way of justification or debate.[138] It upheld the prolonged detention of the appellants without ever clearly naming it as indefinite administrative detention, or indicating the constitutional status of indefinite detention pending removal. It allowed for the preventive detention of non-citizens on grounds of risk to national security, without indicating what the constitutional bounds of this practice were, absent review to a particular standard. In circumstances where the prospect of removal was the justification for confining detention to non-citizens, the Court raised a number of factors that break the connection between detention and removal without explaining why the appellants could not successfully invoke them in the circumstances.

It is misleading to characterise these positions as leaving the issues they touch open, because the Court's silence and avoidance gave legal sanction to the relevant practices. The Court's position on these issues forms the starting point for future argument. An argument that detention of non-citizens pending removal, in circumstances there is no reasonable prospect of removal in the reasonably foreseeable future, cannot be detention for the purposes of removal and so infringes sections 7 and 15 of the Charter now has to overcome *Charkaoui*. Critically, the Court arrived at this position while leaving the merits of the appellants' substantive Charter challenges largely unaddressed.

9.8.2 Commonalities between *Charkaoui* and *Suresh*

The underlying affinity between *Suresh* and *Charkaoui* lies in the refusal to set substantive bounds on the conduct of the executive in the area of national security. In both cases, a unanimous judgment of the Supreme Court of Canada upheld, as potentially free of constitutional limitation, a sweeping power over

136 Sunstein, 'Minimalism at War' (n 133) 53; Katyal (n 133) 1381–83.
137 Roach (n 57) 307–08.
138 See Martinez (n 1) 1058, and more generally her discussion of 'substance disguised as process'.

non-citizens. In *Suresh*, it was possible deportation to torture. In *Charkaoui*, the Court left the possibility of deportation to torture untouched and gave judicial sanction to indefinite administrative detention.[139] Further, in both cases, the Court chose to address any rights infringements on a case-by-case basis, rather than addressing the existence and width of the statutory powers in question.[140] In both cases, the preponderance of the reasoning, the legal material and the commentary on the facts was supportive of the conclusion that there was a substantive right, against deportation to torture or indefinite detention, that had been infringed. But this was, for reasons that remain unclear, not determinative, preserving an ability on the part of the government to deport or detain.

A related similarity between *Suresh* and *Charkaoui* lies in their failure to seriously engage with international and comparative law. By 'engage with' I do not mean 'follow', but rather offer a reasoned justification for either accepting or rejecting the relevant principles.[141] This avoidance took different forms in *Suresh* and *Charkaoui*. In *Suresh*, the Court's decision had the merit of laying out the relevant international law jurisprudence, though the Court offered little by way of explanation for its ultimate decision to reject a categorical prohibition on deportation to torture. In *Charkaoui* the Court ignored international law. Scant reference was made to comparative jurisprudence bearing on indefinite detention, with the exception of the few paragraphs on *Belmarsh*, discussed in sections 9.5.2 and 9.7 above. No reference *at all* was made to Canada's treaty obligations relevant to deportation and detention, despite these being rehearsed in the facta before the Court.

The Court's focus on Charter jurisprudence in *Charkaoui* was hermetic. Foreign practice or jurisprudence was considered in the Court's discussion of the United Kingdom's 'special advocate' regime,[142] and in the Court's attempts to grapple with *Belmarsh*.[143] Other than that, in the course of a judgment of 142 paragraphs, foreign or international jurisprudence was only referenced at two points, in both cases to buttress a conclusion arrived at under the Charter. It was drawn on to support a foreign national's right, sourced to section 10(c) of the Charter, to a prompt review of his or her detention.[144] And, as discussed in section 9.5.1 above, the Court (wrongly) referenced *Hardial Singh* and *Zadvydas* in support of its characterisation of the detention as for the purpose of deportation.[145]

[139] As discussed in s 9.6, the possibility of deportation to torture assisted the argument for the legal permissibility of indefinite detention.

[140] In this regard, *Suresh* and *Charkaoui* were consistent with the Supreme Court's earlier decision in *Chiarelli*. As highlighted by the comparison with the reasoning of the Federal Court in that decision, the Supreme Court focused on SIRC's actual practices as opposed to the powers granted under the statute: see ch 8, pp 236–37.

[141] On the concept of 'engagement' of national constitutional judges with transnational law, see Vicki C Jackson, *Constitutional Engagement in a Transnational Era* (New York, Oxford University Press, 2010) 8–10, ch 3.

[142] *Charkaoui* (n 3) [80], [83], [84]. See s 9.3.

[143] ibid, [125]–[127] and [130]. See pp 266–67 and 270.

[144] ibid, [90].

[145] ibid, [124].

Charkaoui is a decision whose legal reference points are almost exclusively Charter jurisprudence.[146]

The Supreme Court's near-exclusive focus on the Charter in *Charkaoui* sits uncomfortably with both the novelty of the circumstances before the Court and the level of contemporaneous legal attention that has been paid to such circumstances in the comparative jurisprudence.[147] The absence of engagement with international law is particularly striking given the extensive reference to international law in the facta before the Court,[148] and the adverse comment of various international bodies on the very security certificate regime before the Court.[149] Further, as discussed in section 9.5 above, when the Court did reach for comparative authority (*Hardial Singh*, *Zadvydas*, *Belmarsh*), it did so to support conclusions arrived at under the Charter, and in a way that distorted the meaning of those comparative authorities.

The Supreme Court's hermetic focus on the Charter can be read as avoiding confronting or engaging with legal reasoning at odds with its own, whether from comparative or international law sources.[150] In *Charkaoui* the attempt to answer, address or learn from the problems posed by other sources of legal authority, international or comparative, was marginal. The Court did not try to justify or defend its rejection or variation of other legal sources; it simply ignored them (in the case of international law), or inadvertently distorted them (in the case of comparative authorities).

9.9 Bill C-3

The remainder of this chapter is concerned with the consequences of the Court's holdings in *Charkaoui*. The immediate consequence was amending legislation, Bill C-3. The Bill's primary innovation was the introduction of special advocates into the Canadian security certificate regime. They were modelled on the United

[146] This extends to the dismissal of attempts to rely on Canadian case law not focused on the *Charter*. In relation to the constitutional challenge premised on unwritten constitutional principles bearing on the rule of law, the Court held that the 'constitutional protections surrounding arrest and detention are set out in the Charter, and it is hard to see what the rule of law could add to these provisions': *Charkaoui* (n 3) [137]. The Court did, however, discuss procedural practices developed by a range of Canadian bodies in response to issues of national security confidentiality, at the minimal impairment stage of the section 1 analysis of the procedures under the security certificate regime (held to have violated s 7).

[147] As attested to by the extensive discussion of international law and comparative authority in *Belmarsh*, a decision to which the Canadian Supreme Court referred in *Charkaoui*.

[148] See s 9.2 above.

[149] See eg United Nations Working Group on Arbitrary Detention, *Report of the Working Group on Arbitrary Detention – Visit to Canada (1–15 June 2005)*, E/CN.4/2006/7/Add.2, 5 December 2005.

[150] For a similar point made in relation to *Suresh* see Audrey Macklin, 'Mr Suresh and the Evil Twin' (2002) 20(4) *Refuge* 15, 18.

Kingdom institution of the same name, introduced in chapter five.[151] The role of the special advocate is to 'protect the interests' of the certified person in security certificate proceedings whenever, for reasons of confidentiality, evidence is heard in his (or his counsel's) absence.[152] The special advocate is intended to counterbalance the lack of full disclosure and the lack of a full, open, adversarial hearing, by testing the evidence and putting arguments on behalf of the certified person during closed hearings.

Bill C-3 also put the existing practice of release on conditions on a legislative basis. The Canadian system of release on conditions shares many similarities with the control order regime introduced in the United Kingdom subsequent to *Belmarsh*.[153] A persisting point of distinction between developments in Canada and the United Kingdom is that *Charkaoui*, unlike *Belmarsh*, did not dislodge the preventive detention regime in question from the immigration framework. The following statement was made in support of Bill C-3:

> We must always remember that we are not dealing with Canadians. We are dealing with non-Canadians. The security certificate provisions do not involve Canadians, only non-Canadians. The non-Canadian category includes people with no status and people who have permanent resident status but are not citizens.[154]

As this passage emphasises, the legislative response to *Charkaoui* continued to focus on non-citizens alone. And as the passage implies, and the context for it confirms, the fact that it was confined to non-citizens was important to its political acceptability.

In *Charkaoui*, the Supreme Court ruled that certification decisions made under the IRPA 2001 would lose their 'reasonable' status one year after judgment.[155] The government accordingly quashed the earlier certification decisions and, on 22 February 2008, the day the amendments introduced by Bill C-3 came into effect, the Ministers signed new security certificates for five foreign terror suspects previously certified, referring those certificates to the Federal Court for reasonableness review.[156] All of those re-certified under the modified security certificate regime in February 2008 were later released from detention, subject to conditions. And two of those re-certified exited the regime entirely. This last development is detailed in the following section.

[151] Bill C-3 received extended consideration in three lengthy commentaries in vol 42 of the *Supreme Court Law Review* (2d): Roach, '*Charkaoui* and Bill C-3' (n 57); Craig Forcese and Lorne Waldman, 'A Bismarckian Moment: *Charkaoui* and Bill C-3' (2008) 42 *Supreme Court Law Review* (2d) 355; David Dunbar and Scott Nesbit, 'Parliament's Response to *Charkaoui:* Bill C-3 and the Special Advocate Regime under IRPA' (2008) 42 *Supreme Court Law Review* (2d) 415.

[152] IRPA 2001 as amended 2008, s 85.

[153] See ch 7, s 7.3.

[154] Canada, HC Deb 20 November 2007, vol 42, no 20, 1085 (Derek Lee).

[155] *Charkaoui* (n 3) [140].

[156] The five persons certified were Mr Almrei, Mr Charkaoui, Mr Harkat, Mr Jaballah and Mr Mahjoub.

9.10 Exits from the Security Certificate Regime[157]

9.10.1 *Charkaoui II*

I have criticised the Canadian Supreme Court's reasoning in *Charkaoui* on the basis that it used procedure to avoid the substantive issues of primary concern to the appellants. These criticisms need to be leavened by an acknowledgment that *Charkaoui* instigated a cycle of developments that strengthened the procedural protections afforded to the subjects of security certificates.[158] And these heightened procedural protections resulted in tangible benefits for the certified subjects, most notably the exit of two of the appellants in *Charkaoui* – Mr Charkaoui and Mr Almrei – from the regime.

In the last months of 2009, the security certificates issued against Mr Charkaoui and Mr Almrei were ruled to be void, and quashed, respectively. The circumstances leading to their exit from the security certificate regime are detailed in sections 9.10.2 and 9.10.3 below, following an examination of a Canadian Supreme Court decision bearing on the security certificate regime, *Charkaoui II*.[159] *Charkaoui II* confirmed the Supreme Court's commitment, initially evidenced in *Charkaoui*, to trying to ensure meaningful judicial review in a context characterised by secret evidence.

In *Charkaoui II*, the Supreme Court sought to address certain problems arising from the use of secret evidence and, in particular, the judge's dependence on the executive's selection and characterisation of secret evidence.[160] *Charkaoui II* did not address the interpretation of Bill C-3, nor its constitutionality.[161] The facts of the case were that, prior to the fourth periodic review of Mr Charkaoui's detention, government counsel informed the judge that it had failed to disclose a document at the outset of the proceedings, namely a summary of two Canadian Security Intelligence Service (CSIS) interviews with Mr Charkaoui in 2002. The judge ordered that the documents be immediately disclosed.

Following a review of the interview summaries, Mr Charkaoui requested disclosure of the complete notes and recordings of the CSIS interviews. The government responded that there were no recordings on file and that CSIS interview notes were, in accordance with CSIS policy, systematically destroyed once the

[157] This section draws on material originally published as Thwaites, 'Process and Substance' (n 2).

[158] On the idea of 'cycles of legality', both virtuous and harmful, see Dyzenhaus (n 57). See also Graham Hudson, 'Whither International Law? Security Certificates, the Supreme Court and the Rights of Non-Citizens in Canada' (2009) 26 *Refuge* 172, 183.

[159] *Charkaoui II* (n 39).

[160] Gus Van Harten, 'Charkaoui and Secret Evidence' (2008) 42 *Supreme Court Law Review* (2d) 251 (Postscript), 278. For commentary on the decision see Kent Roach, 'When Secret Intelligence becomes Evidence: Some Implications of *Khadr* and *Charkaoui II*' (2009) 47 *Supreme Court Law Review* (2d) 147.

[161] *Charkaoui II* (n 39) [18].

officers had completed their reports. Mr Charkaoui argued that he was entitled to the notes and applied for a stay of proceedings, requesting that the security certificate against him be quashed.[162] The trial judge dismissed the application, drawing a distinction between the work of an intelligence agency and a police force, and holding that the former was not subject to the disclosure obligations of the latter under the criminal law.[163] He also cautioned against the application of criminal justice standards in the immigration context.[164] His decision was upheld by the Federal Court of Appeal.[165]

The Supreme Court allowed Mr Charkaoui's appeal in part.[166] It held that CSIS's policy of destroying interview notes breached its duty to retain and disclose information under the Canadian Security Intelligence Service Act 1984 (CSIS Act 1984).[167] The Court interpreted the relevant provision, section 12 of the CSIS Act 1984,[168] in the light of section 7 of the Charter. It rejected the claim that section 7 rights were confined to the criminal justice system or were to be aggressively contextualised downward in the immigration context:

> whether or not the constitutional guarantees of section 7 of the Charter apply does not turn on a formal distinction between the different areas of law. Rather, it depends on the severity of the consequences of the state's actions for the individual's fundamental interests of liberty and security and, in some cases, the right to life. By its very nature, the security certificate procedure can place these rights in serious jeopardy, as the Court recognized in *Charkaoui*. To protect them, it becomes necessary to recognize a duty to disclose evidence based on section 7.[169]

In adopting this position, the Court confirmed the approach it took in *Charkaoui* to review of the security certificate regime's procedures. The decision in *Charkaoui II* shows that the Court was well aware of the procedural deficiencies that remained following *Charkaoui*, chief among them being the judge's dependence on the executive to characterise and select the material introduced as secret evidence.[170] In *Charkaoui II*, the Court took steps to address this issue. It held that 'Retention

[162] ibid, [10]–[11].

[163] *Re Charkaoui* (2005) FC 149, (2005) 261 FTR 1, [17] (Nöel J).

[164] In making this point he relied on the *Chiarelli* decision discussed in ch 8, s 8.4.3: *Canada (Employment and Immigration) v Chiarelli* [1992] 1 SCR 711.

[165] *Re Charkaoui* (2006) FCA 206, (2006) 272 DLR (4th) 175.

[166] It held that the only appropriate remedy was to confirm the duty to disclose Mr Charkaoui's entire file to the designated judge, who would then act as a filter on what was disclosed to Mr Charkaoui and his counsel. As an appeal on an interlocutory point, it was held to be premature to determine how the destruction of the notes impacted on the reliability of the evidence. That assessment was left with the reviewing judge.

[167] Canadian Security Intelligence Service Act 1984 (CSIS Act 1984), s 12.

[168] Section 12 of the CSIS Act 1984 provides: 'The Service shall collect, by investigation or otherwise, to the extent that it is strictly necessary, and analyse and retain information and intelligence respecting activities that may on reasonable grounds be suspected of constituting threats to the security of Canada and, in relation thereto, shall report to and advise the Government of Canada.'

[169] *Charkaoui II* (n 39) [53].

[170] Van Harten (n 160) 278, 279.

of the notes will make it easier to verify the disclosed summaries and information based on those notes'.[171]

The Court held that while the CSIS is not a police agency, it is subject to duties of disclosure that go beyond provision of mere summaries of information.[172] It took care not to treat the security certificate process as equivalent to a criminal trial.[173] Nonetheless, starting from the proposition that 'The consequences of security certificates are often more severe than those of many criminal charges',[174] the Court reasoned that section 7 of the Charter required 'a procedure for verifying the evidence adduced against [the individual]' that centred on the reviewing judge.[175] It stated: 'If the original evidence was destroyed, the designated judge has access only to summaries prepared by the state, which means that it will be difficult, if not impossible, to verify the allegations.'[176] This was held to 'compromise . . . the very function of judicial review'.[177] CSIS was required to retain all the information in its possession, disclosing it to the ministers and the designated judge.

In its ruling on disclosure, the *Charkaoui II* Court referred back to the procedural problems identified in *Charkaoui*:

> Despite the judge's best efforts to question the government witnesses and scrutinize the documentary evidence, he or she is placed in the situation of asking questions and ultimately deciding the issues on the basis of incomplete and potentially unreliable information.[178]

The disclosure requirements insisted upon by the Court in *Charkaoui II* were an attempt to ameliorate this state of affairs. The disclosure in question was disclosure to the designated judge and Minister. This information was to be provided to the special advocates, but not to the detainees or their lawyers.

The focus on disclosure *to the designated judge and Minister* in *Charkaoui II* is to be contrasted with the focus on disclosure *to the controlee* outlined in the United Kingdom and European authorities detailed in chapter seven.[179] I do not claim that the United Kingdom and European decisions have necessarily resulted in greater disclosure to the controlee relative to the Canadian cases. It has been suggested that in practice the summaries released to certified individuals under the Canadian security certificate regime provided fuller disclosure than was the

[171] *Charkaoui II* (n 39) [39].

[172] ibid, [50]. Earlier in the judgment, the Court stated that the activities of Royal Canadian Mounted Police and CSIS had been converging: see [25]–[28].

[173] ibid, [47] and [50]–[63].

[174] ibid, [54]. Lord Bingham made a similar point in his judgment in *MB*: see *Secretary of State for the Home Department v MB* [2007] UKHL 46, [2008] 1 AC 440, [24] (Lord Bingham); see ch 7, s 7.5.

[175] *Charkaoui II* (n 39) [56].

[176] ibid, [61].

[177] ibid, [62]. See also [42].

[178] *Charkaoui* (n 3) [63] quoted in *Charkaoui II* (n 39) [60].

[179] See ch 7, s 7.5.

norm under the British control order regime.[180] The implications of *Charkaoui II*, and the way in which it builds on *Charkaoui*, are best appreciated in the light of Mr Almrei's 2009 reasonableness decision, examined below, following a discussion of Mr Charkaoui's own exit from the security certificate regime.

9.10.2 Exit 1 – Mr Charkaoui

The security certificate issued against Mr Charkaoui was declared void in October 2009. The litigation described here arose in the course of the reasonableness review of the certificate naming Mr Charkaoui issued in February 2008.[181] By way of background, to initiate the reasonableness review of those certified in February 2008 under the newly amended 'post-*Charkaoui*' provisions, the Ministers filed a Notice of Referral of Certificate together with a top-secret Security Intelligence Report (SIR) and supporting reference materials. The SIR was a narrative report prepared by CSIS, setting out its grounds for believing that a person was inadmissible to Canada. A public summary of the SIR entitled 'Statement Summarizing the Information' with the corresponding open-source reference material was served on each of the certified individuals and filed with the Court.[182]

In the course of *in camera* proceedings for Mr Charkaoui in April and May 2009, special advocates challenged 'the Minister's claim that the disclosure of information or other evidence would be injurious to national security or endanger the safety of any person'.[183] As a consequence, the Court was persuaded that the disclosure of certain evidence would not be injurious to national security or the safety of a person, and it issued a number of orders requiring its disclosure. The Ministers disagreed with the Court's determinations, and decided to withdraw that evidence rather than disclose it in accordance with the Court's orders, as they are entitled to do under the IRPA 2001.[184] On 31 July 2009, the Ministers stated that, in their opinion, the evidence remaining in the file was not sufficient to meet their burden of showing that the certificate was reasonable. Nevertheless, they asked the Court to determine whether the certificate was reasonable in order to force an appeal on the required disclosure.[185] On 5 August 2009 the Court stated the following question for the parties:

[180] Discussion between Tom Hickman, who has served as a lawyer for controlees in the United Kingdom, and John Norris, Canadian special advocate, attended by the author: Tom Hickman, 'Secret Justice?', University of Toronto, Constitutional Round Table, 9 September 2009.

[181] On the recertification of certain foreign terrorist suspects, including Mr Charkaoui, in 2008 see the text accompanying n 156 above.

[182] *Re Almrei* (2009) FC 1263, [2011] 1 FCR 163 (*Almrei 2009 Reasonableness Decision*), [17] (Mosley J).

[183] IRPA 2001 as amended 2008, s 85.1(2)(a). The facts are taken from *Re Charkaoui* (2009) FC 1030, [2010] 4 FCR 448 (*Charkaoui 2009*).

[184] IRPA 2001 as amended 2008, s 83(1)(j) provides that the judge determining the reasonableness of a security certificate 'shall not base a decision on information or other evidence provided by the Minister . . . if the Minister withdraws it'.

[185] *Charkaoui 2009* (n 183) [30] (Tremblay-Lamer J).

> Given the Ministers' admission that the evidence is not sufficient to meet the burden of proof imposed by the IRPA, is it appropriate for the Court to determine whether the certificate is reasonable, or should the certificate simply be *withdrawn* by the *Ministers* without further formalities?[186]

The Ministers reiterated that they were not prepared to withdraw the certificate, and certified two questions on disclosure to the Federal Court of Appeal.[187] Following further submissions by the parties, media reports indicate that in a public hearing in Montreal on 24 September 2009, the judge ordered Mr Charkaoui's immediate release without conditions, with reasons to follow.[188] Those reasons were provided in a judgment of 14 October 2009, in which the judge held that the security certificate was ultra vires and void.[189] Accordingly, Tremblay-Lamer J did not proceed to determine the reasonableness of the certificate. Further, she refused to certify the appeal question proposed by the Ministers, on the basis that they were in truth just seeking to re-open the court's assessment of the facts.[190]

9.10.3 Exit 2 – Mr Almrei

As with Mr Charkaoui, on 22 February 2008 a new security certificate was issued in respect of Mr Almrei and referred to the Federal Court for reasonableness review. The 'reasonableness' decision for Mr Almrei, reviewing the Minister's 'post-Bill C-3' certification decision of 22 February 2008, was handed down on 14 December 2009,[191] following public hearings and *in camera* hearings spread over 40 days between March and September 2009. At the end of a lengthy judgment, Mosley J concluded that the certificate issued against Mr Almrei was not reasonable and must be quashed.[192] The judge determined that Mr Almrei was not, at the time of judgment, a danger to the security of Canada and that none of the grounds of inadmissibility required for certification had been established.[193]

The *Almrei 2009 Reasonableness Decision* shows the practical effects of the combination of the holding on disclosure in *Charkaoui II* and the procedural reforms required by the Supreme Court's decision in *Charkaoui*, in particular the intro-

[186] ibid, [17] (Tremblay-Lamer J) (emphasis in original).

[187] ibid, [18]. In accordance with IRPA 2001 as amended 2008, s 79.

[188] Andrew Chung, 'Charkaoui to be Freed' *Toronto Star* (Toronto, 24 September 2009), www.thestar.com/news/canada/article/700356; Les Perreaux and Colin Freeze, 'Al Qaeda Suspect Freed, Ottawa's Terror Law Shattered' *Globe and Mail* (Toronto, 24 September 2009), www.theglobeandmail.com/news/national/judge-lifts-charkaoui-restrictions/article1299943.

[189] *Charkaoui 2009* (n 183) [36], [23]–[45].

[190] ibid, [92] (Tremblay-Lamer J). The Ministers were found to be seeking an '*item-by-item re-assessment of the specific summaries to the disclosure of which the Ministers object.* This objection pertains to the facts of this case. It does not transcend the parties' interests and is not of general importance. It raises no question that meets the criteria of section 79 of the IRPA' (emphasis in original).

[191] *Almrei 2009 Reasonableness Decision* (n 182).

[192] ibid, [504].

[193] ibid.

duction of special advocates. Mosley J held that the production of *Charkaoui II* information allowed for comparison of the reports provided by human sources with other information held by CSIS. That comparison exercise identified 'serious contradictions'.[194] These contradictions only came to light when put to the CSIS witness in cross-examination by the special advocates.[195] The increased disclosure of information under *Charkaoui II* and cross-examination by the special advocates combined to undermine the credibility of key human sources relied upon by CSIS. The *Almrei 2009 Reasonableness Decision* conveys that the cumulative effect of Canadian judicial decisions on security certificates has been more effective judicial scrutiny of national security matters.

The findings also raise serious concerns about the Canadian government's use of the security certificate process. Mosley J found that information presented to the court through the SIR was inconsistent with information 'produced in conformity with the Service's *Charkaoui II* obligations',[196] and concluded that CSIS and the Ministers had breached their duty of candour to the court. Mosley J also found that the government had made little effort to revise or review the basis on which Mr Almrei was held in the eight years that he was subject to the Canadian security certificate regime.[197]

In the course of his judgment, Mosley J spoke of shifts in the standard of review of national security matters over the preceding eight years. The Minister had submitted that the government was entitled to deference on the dangerousness posed by Mr Almrei, citing the following statement from *Suresh*: 'Provided the Minister is able to show evidence that reasonably supports a finding of danger to the security of Canada, courts should not interfere with the Minister's decision.'[198] Mosley J noted that the Court in *Suresh* had supported its position with reference to Lord Hoffmann's statements in *Rehman* on the relative expertise and access to special information possessed by the executive. He continued:

> Much has changed in the past eight years, including the Supreme Court's decision in *Charkaoui I* and the House of Lords decision in the *Belmarsh* case in which they resiled from the *Rehman* dictum where the question to be determined is legal as opposed to political: [*Belmarsh*].

The shift between *Rehman* and *Belmarsh* is presented as emblematic of a trajectory away from blanket deference to the executive in the area of national security, to a higher standard of review where rights are implicated.[199] A parallel is drawn

[194] ibid, [163].
[195] ibid, [163].
[196] ibid, [502]. See also [164].
[197] ibid, [413], [426].
[198] ibid, [102], citing *Suresh* (n 115) [85].
[199] *Rehman and Belmarsh* do not neatly line up in the way suggested by Mosley J. *Rehman* concerned the level of deference to executive decision-making in the area of national security, *Belmarsh* with line-drawing between Parliament and the courts in the national security area. It still makes sense to speak of the need to read *Rehman* in the light of the subsequent House of Lords decision in *Belmarsh*, but the influence is indirect. On the relation between the judgments see Adam Tomkins, 'National Security and the Role of the Court: A Changed Landscape?' (2010) 126 *LQR* 543, 565.

between the shift in understandings of judicial deference in the area of national security in the United Kingdom and that in Canada,[200] with the Canadian parallel substantiated with reference to *Charkaoui* and *Charkaoui II*.

> In *Charkaoui* . . . the Supreme Court observed that Judges were correct to eschew an overly deferential approach in security certificate cases given the nature of the proceedings. And . . . it was stated that '[t]he IRPA does not ask the designated judge to be deferential, but, rather, asks him or her to engage in a searching review.'
>
> Here, the Court is making a fresh determination based on all of the information and other evidence presented including additional material which was not before the Ministers. The Court, as a result of *Charkaoui II*, has had access to operational and human source management information not previously made available. In the closed sessions, the information relied upon by the Ministers was called into question and the Court heard evidence about the manner in which the SIR was prepared. Having reviewed all of the information and evidence, I consider that little deference is owed to the Ministers['] decision.[201]

This statement evidences the procedural contribution made by the decisions in *Charkaoui* and *Charkaoui II*. These decisions resisted the downward contextualisation of a detainee's procedural rights, reasoning from the detainee's liberty interest to principles of general application. And the *Almrei 2009 Reasonableness Decision* evidences the real effects of the procedural rulings in *Charkaoui* and *Charkaoui II* on the disposition of subsequent cases.

9.11 Conclusion

The Canadian security certificate process operates as a preventive detention regime confined to foreign terrorist suspects. Non-citizens have been subject to detention and/or constraint under the regime for over a decade and it remains unclear where the constitutional boundaries of the practice lie. The primary problem is the deferred resolution of the issues generating the security certificate litigation and the consequences of this for detainees. The second problem, potentially of more lasting damage to the legal system, is that by avoiding engagement with the substantive rights the Court has been shaping their scope and nature. *Charkaoui* saw the range of arguments available in rights-based challenges diminished by avoiding those challenges and acquiescing in the continuance of the practice under challenge. The rights-based challenges to ongoing legal authority to detain, or to the constraints imposed as conditions on release, were determined unfavourably for the claimant, with scant argument as to the nature of, or justification for, that legal authority.

[200] On the relevant shift in the United Kingdom context see ch 6, pp 167–71.
[201] *Almrei 2009 Reasonableness Decision* (n 182) [103]–[105].

The procedural protections secured by the decision are valuable. But the proposition that these procedures are part of a preventive detention regime that is fundamentally 'unfixable' in its present form, discriminating against non-citizens and disconnected from general principles of law on preventive detention, needs to be confronted.

Conclusion

10

Conclusion

> To hold that a foreigner who comes here, and who is answerable to our laws, is at the same time not to have their protection, would, it appears to me, altogether carry us back to the days of barbarism.
>
> Windeyer J, *Ex parte Lo Pak*, NSW Supreme Court (1888)[1]

10.1 Introduction

Why is it that three final courts of appeal, sharing legal traditions of the common law, came to such very different conclusions on the legality of indefinite detention pending removal? I have argued, in relation to Australia, the United Kingdom and Canada, that there was nothing in the legal framework of those jurisdictions to prevent the adoption of a rights-protecting approach to detention pending removal. The legislation authorising detention did not require the courts to sanction a rights-precluding outcome. In each jurisdiction either a tenable interpretation consistent with the rights-protecting approach was available, as in *Al-Kateb* and arguably *Charkaoui*,[2] or a formal means of registering the legislation's incompatibility with rights was available, as with the declaration of incompatibility in *Belmarsh*.[3] In both Australia and Canada the stronger argument was that the legislation, if read as requiring a rights-precluding approach, was invalid for reasons grounded in the constitutional separation of powers and the Canadian Charter respectively.

In this chapter I argue that what underpins the different rulings on the legality of indefinite detention, within and across the national jurisdictions surveyed, are

[1] *Ex parte Lo Pak* (1888) 9 NSWLR 221, 245 (Windeyer J).

[2] *Al-Kateb v Godwin* [2004] HCA 37, (2004) 219 CLR 562; *Charkaoui v Canada (Minister of Citizenship and Immigration)* 2007 SCC 9, [2007] 1 SCR 350. In *Charkaoui*, the legal challenges were directed to the validity of the law under the Charter and other sources. The Immigration and Refugee Protection Act 2001 did not expressly provide for indefinite detention (this was the Court's ground of distinction with *Belmarsh*: see ch 9, s 9.5.2). As interpreted by the Canadian Supreme Court, the Act allowed for indefinite detention. If the Charter was read to preclude indefinite detention pending removal then presumptions of compliance with the Charter, conjoined with presumptions in favour of common law rights and of consistency with international law, would militate against reading the Act as authorising extended, indefinite detention of the form sanctioned by the Canadian Supreme Court.

[3] *A v Secretary of State for the Home Department* [2004] UKHL 56, [2005] 2 AC 68 (*Belmarsh*).

different understandings of the extent to which non-citizens are entitled to the protection of the law.

10.2 Divergent Responses to a Common Issue[4]

10.2.1 The Decisions of Courts of Other States

Do courts within the common law family of the Commonwealth exert a strong mutual influence on each other, drawing on a shared commitment to liberty rooted in the common law and international human rights? An extensive use of comparative law in counterterrorism cases more generally has grounded the claim that national courts have been united in their response to counterterrorism. Eyal Benvenisti argues that courts from prominent democratic states have been consistent in their judgments on counterterrorism measures, coordinating outcomes across national jurisdictions.[5] He also claims that the availability of identical or similar norms, grounded in international human rights law, has facilitated this coordination effort.[6] Benvenisti's claim of a coordinated judicial response is not simply a methodological one. He argues that the coordinated response benefits individual liberties,[7] domestic democratic processes,[8] and the rule of law in the global sphere.[9] Furthermore, when faced with major challenges, the courts have risen to meet them. Looking at each other's jurisprudence they have inclined to a similar result. The cases surveyed in this book both attest to an extensive use of comparative law, and refute the application of Benvenisti's thesis to the areas of counterterrorism law under review.

Al-Kateb was delivered in August 2004, the House of Lords' *Belmarsh* decision in December of that year, and *Charkaoui* in February 2007. As discussed, critical passages of the judgment in *Charkaoui* are framed as a response to *Belmarsh*.[10] Furthermore, all three authorities make reference to the earlier decision of the

[4] Material in this section is developed from Rayner Thwaites, 'A Coordinated Judicial Response to Counter-Terrorism? Counter-Examples' in Mark B Salter (ed), *Mapping Transatlantic Security Relations: The EU, Canada, and the War on Terror* (Oxford, Routledge, 2010) 236.

[5] Eyal Benvenisti, 'United We Stand: National Courts Reviewing Counterterrorism Measures' in Andrea Bianchi and Alexis Keller (eds), *Counterterrorism: Democracy's Challenge* (Oxford, Hart Publishing, 2008) 251; Eyal Benvenisti, 'Reclaiming Democracy: The Strategic Uses of Foreign and International Law by National Courts' (2008) 102 *American Journal of International Law* 241; Eyal Benvenisti and George W Downs, 'National Courts, Domestic Democracy, and the Evolution of International Law' (2009) 20 *European Journal of International Law* 59. Benvenisti's thesis is not limited to common law courts.

[6] Benvenisti, 'United We Stand' (n 5) 273; Benvenisti, 'Reclaiming Democracy' (n 5) 252; Benvenisti and Downs (n 5) 66–67. This second claim, about international law, is considered in s 10.2.2.

[7] Benvenisti, 'United We Stand' (n 5).

[8] Benvenisti, 'Reclaiming Democracy' (n 5).

[9] Benvenisti and Downs (n 5).

[10] See ch 9, s 9.5.2.

United States Supreme Court in *Zadvydas*, delivered in June 2001.[11] *Hardial Singh* is likewise a constant presence in this case law.[12] The cross-referencing continued, with both the House of Lords in *MB* and the European Court of Human Rights (ECtHR) in *A v United Kingdom* referring to *Charkaoui*.[13]

The references recorded in the judgments may only be the tip of the iceberg. There is also the (admittedly speculative) phenomenon of 'background influence'.[14] Hayne J's majority judgment in *Al-Kateb* bears the strong imprint, in reasoning and rhetoric, of the minority judgments in *Zadvydas*.[15] Gleeson CJ's analysis of Mr Al-Kateb's detention replicates a human rights law analysis of the problem.[16] In neither case is the apparent source of influence acknowledged. The increasingly widespread availability of submissions and transcripts of argument makes evident the extent of the comparative and international law material accessible to the relevant courts.[17] In some cases the courts ignore this material, a theme developed in the discussion of *Charkaoui*.[18] In the context of the extensive jurisprudence from other states on the legality of indefinite detention, the Canadian Supreme Court's lack of engagement with comparative material constituted a lost opportunity for it to test, justify and clarify its own position.

Despite extensive references to comparative law, a review of the case studies on the legality of indefinite detention refutes, or at least constitutes a strong counterexample to, Benvenisti's suggested phenomenon of a 'globally coordinated

[11] *Zadvydas v Davis*, 533 US 678 (2001). The reference to *Zadvydas* in *Belmarsh* (n 3) does little real work in the reasoning, receiving only a glancing reference at [69] of Lord Bingham's judgment. *Zadvydas* is referred to in every substantive judgment in *Al-Kateb* (n 2), either in the text or footnotes: see eg [145], [159] and [193] (Kirby J in dissent, endorsing the majority position in *Zadvydas*); [283]–[286] and [290] (Callinan J in the majority, endorsing the dissenting position in *Zadvydas*). As discussed in ch 9, s 9.5.1 *Zadvydas* is referred to in *Charkaoui* (n 2) [124].

[12] *R v Governor of Durham Prison, ex parte Singh* [1984] 1 All ER 983 (*Hardial Singh*). For reference to *Hardial Singh* in *Minister for Immigration & Multicultural & Indigenous Affairs v Al Masri* [2003] FCAFC 70, (2003) 126 FCR 54 see [97]–[101] (and [102]–[108] on the operation of the *Hardial Singh* principles in other cases), [118], [129] and [133]. For reference to *Hardial Singh* in *Al-Kateb* (n 2) see at [3] (Gleeson CJ); [53] (McHugh J); [160] (Kirby J); [240]–[241] (Hayne J); [296] (Callinan J) (all bar Kirby J doubting the decision's relevance to the dispute). The United Kingdom's intention to override *Hardial Singh* (and more centrally *Chahal v United Kingdom* (1997) 23 EHRR 413) motivated the derogation order at the centre of the *Belmarsh* litigation. See also *Charkaoui* (n 2) [124] (as discussed in section 9.5.1).

[13] *Secretary of State for the Home Department v MB* [2007] UKHL 46, [2008] 1 AC 440, [30]; *A v United Kingdom* (2009) 49 EHRR 29, para 111.

[14] Brun Otto-Bryde, 'The Constitutional Judge and the International Constitutionalist Dialogue' in Sir Basil Markesinis and Jörg Fedtke (eds), *Judicial Recourse to Foreign Law: A New Source of Inspiration?* (Oxford, Routledge, 2006) 295, 298.

[15] See ch 3, pp 74, 77–78.

[16] See ch 3, s 3.4.

[17] See eg Submissions on behalf of the Australian Human Rights Commission, *Plaintiff M47/2012 v Director General of Security* (High Court of Australia, filed 8 June 2012), paras 47–53, citing *Secretary of State for the Home Department v AF* [2009] UKHL 28, [2010] 2 AC 269, *A v United Kingdom* (n 13), *Charkaoui* (n 2). None of these decisions were referred to in the judgments. On *Plaintiff M47* see ch 4, s 4.4.

[18] See ch 9, pp 273–74.

move'[19] on the part of the 'national courts from prominent democratic states'.[20] The *Al-Kateb* majority upheld a sweeping power of detention pending removal. In *Belmarsh*, the House of Lords rejected a government argument that the power of detention pending removal could be stretched, by way of derogation, to accommodate the indefinite detention of non-citizens. In *Charkaoui*, the Canadian Supreme Court gave legal sanction to an indefinite detention regime confined to non-citizens, characterising it as detention pending removal. *Charkaoui* also reasoned from the liberty interests of the detainees to hold that further procedural protections were required under the Charter. The courts diverged markedly in result on a key question of immigration and counterterrorism law and policy. Cases enlisted by Benvenisti as examples of this inter-judicial coordination effort, such as *Charkaoui* and the House of Lords' decision in *Belmarsh*, do not support his judicial coordination thesis.

Furthermore, where the courts have looked at each other's case law, they have often gone in different directions.[21] The use of comparative authority in *Charkaoui*, while not simply decorative, did not maintain the level of consistency between national courts needed to support the thesis of an 'inter-judicial coordination effort' in response to state counterterrorism measures.[22] In particular, the Canadian Supreme Court's efforts to distinguish *Belmarsh* were unconvincing.[23] The two cases were patently on the same issue, namely the legality of the indefinite detention of non-citizens 'pending removal'.

Benvenisti's articles did arguably pick up on a shift, observable in the case law analysed in this book, in judicial attitudes to review of national security. As stated by Mosley J at the end of 2009, in the *Almrei 2009 Reasonableness Decision*:

> much has changed in the past eight years, including the Supreme Court's decision in *Charkaoui* and the House of Lords decision in the *Belmarsh* case in which they resiled from the *Rehman* dictum where the question to be determined is legal as opposed to political.[24]

There has been a discernible shift in attitudes toward judicial review in the area of national security in the period from 11 September 2001 up to the time of writing, away from blanket deference to the executive where national security concerns are invoked. A commonly referenced example of the shift is that offered in the above passage: the shift between *Rehman* and *Belmarsh*.[25] This British shift has a

[19] Benvenisti, 'United We Stand' (n 5) 254.

[20] Benvenisti and Downs (n 5) 72.

[21] See eg the *Al-Kateb* majority's endorsement of the minority position in *Zadvydas* in ch 3, pp 77–78.

[22] See eg the Canadian Supreme Court's erroneous claim that its reasoning was consistent with *Zadvydas* and *Hardial Singh*: ch 9, s 9.5.1.

[23] See ch 9, pp 266–67, 270.

[24] *Re Almrei* (2009) FC 1263, [2011] 1 FCR 163 (*Almrei 2009 Reasonableness Decision*) [103]. Discussed in ch 9, pp 280–82.

[25] For discussions referencing the shift between *Rehman* and *Belmarsh* as indicative of broader changes in attitude toward judicial review of national security, see eg Jack Beatson et al, *Human Rights: Judicial Protection in the United Kingdom* (London, Sweet & Maxwell, 2008) paras 3-254, 3-269; Benvenisti, 'United We Stand' (n 5) 252–55; Roger Masterman, *The Separation of Powers in the*

Canadian counterpart. In the *Almrei 2009 Reasonableness Decision*, Mosley J concluded that the deference to executive risk assessments recommended by the Supreme Court in *Suresh* had been eschewed in *Charkaoui*, and was not appropriate with regard to the ministerial decision before him.[26] As the preceding extract from Mosley J's judgment indicates, a changed understanding of the judicial deference appropriate to national security matters where it is alleged that fundamental rights are infringed has become part of how the judiciary understands itself. As such it can be expected to influence the way in which they perform their role.

To return to the comparison between *Belmarsh* and *Charkaoui*, both decisions arguably depart from a 'traditional' position of judicial acquiescence to political demands in the area of national security.[27] But even if they do share a common judicial ethos in this respect, it manifests to very different degrees and in very different ways. In the *Belmarsh* litigation, a majority of the House of Lords, and the Special Immigration Appeals Commission and the European Court of Human Rights, refused to accept the government's characterisation of the measures as detention pending removal, or the proposition that non-citizens are intrinsically vulnerable to detention in times of threat in a way that citizens are not. In *Charkaoui*, the Canadian Supreme Court reached a diametrically opposed position on these issues, but held that greater procedural protections were required to strengthen a detainee's ability to meet the case against him. Allowing that common law courts have made a discernible shift from 'traditional' approaches to judicial review of national security matters in the period from 11 September 2001, the resulting legal norms are far from uniform. In the United Kingdom, indefinite detention of non-citizens could not be effected through a derogation from the European Convention on Human Rights (ECHR). In Canada, such detention did not even infringe section 7 of the Charter.

10.2.2 The Influence of International Law

Benvenisti's claim of coordination between national courts refers to international human rights. He argues that in making available identical or similar norms, international human rights facilitate this coordination effort.[28] Pausing to consider his claim, one can start with the commonalities before descending to the

Contemporary Constitution: Judicial Competence and Independence in the United Kingdom (Cambridge, Cambridge University Press, 2011) 98–99. As Tomkins notes, *Rehman* concerned deference to the executive, while *Belmarsh* was concerned with relations between the legislature and the courts: Adam Tomkins, 'National Security and the Role of the Court: A Changed Landscape?' (2010) 126 *LQR* 543, 565.

[26] *Almrei 2009 Reasonableness Decision* (n 24) [103]–[105]. The shift identified by Mosley J in the *Almrei 2009 Reasonableness Decision* exists alongside deep continuities between *Suresh v Canada (Minister of Citizenship and Immigration)* [2002] SCC 1, [2002] 1 SCR 3 and *Charkaoui* (n 2): see ch 9, pp 272–74.

[27] For an exemplar of the 'traditional' approach to national security, see the comments of the United Kingdom courts in the *Chahal* litigation, quoted in ch 5, pp 129–30.

[28] Benvenisti, 'United We Stand' (n 5) 273; Benvenisti, 'Reclaiming Democracy' (n 5) 252; Benvenisti and Downs (n 5) 66–67.

basic fact of difference. It is generally agreed across the three jurisdictions surveyed that recourse can be had to international law in cases of statutory ambiguity. There is, at that high level of abstraction, general agreement as to the starting point – there is a shared set of obligations at international law – and some agreement as to international law's point of entry into the domestic legal system. Yet there is a diversity of result. What explains it? The review of the case law raises a number of issues of judicial method.

(a) Australia – The Point of Entry for International Law

As with the presumption against the abrogation of fundamental common law rights, there was general agreement among the *Al-Kateb* majority and minority as to the existence of a presumption that statutes should be interpreted and applied in conformity with international law, so far as the language of the statute permits. As stated by McHugh J in *Al-Kateb*, albeit with some reluctance, this rule of construction was 'too well established to be repealed now by judicial decision'.[29]

Despite the general acceptance of this presumption of consistency with international law, the difference between the Australian rights-precluding and rights-protecting judgments on the legality of indefinite detention correlates with the respective rejection and use of international law in statutory interpretation in those judgments. International law entered into interpretation on the rights-protecting approach, on the coat tails of arguments about common law presumptions and constitutional doctrine.

The presumption of consistency with international law is triggered by ambiguity.[30] In the rights-protecting judgments, the ambiguity necessary to 'access' the presumption of consistency with international law was generated by the operation of common law presumptions and by constitutional reasoning, the latter by way of the presumption that statutes should be read as constitutional to the extent possible. There was no reliance on international law to read an unexpressed exception into the statutory language. Rather, international law was held to fortify the conclusion, arrived at by way of common law presumptions and/or a presumption of constitutional validity, that the detention power was subject to an implied temporal limitation.[31] The relegation of international law in the Australian rights-protecting authorities to a secondary role, supporting conclusions already arrived at by other means, reflected a jurisdiction in which recourse to international law remained deeply contested, as evidenced in McHugh J's response to Kirby J's advocacy of international law.[32]

[29] *Al-Kateb* (n 2) [65] (McHugh J).

[30] See eg *Chu Kheng Lim v Minister for Immigration, Local Government and Ethnic Affairs* [1992] HCA 64, (1992) 176 CLR 1, 38: courts 'should in a case of ambiguity, favour a construction of a Commonwealth statute which accords with the obligations of Australia under an international treaty'. See *Minister for Immigration and Ethnic Affairs v Teoh* (1995) 183 CLR 273, 287 (Mason CJ and Deane J).

[31] This was clearest in *Al Masri* (n 12), analysed in ch 2, pp 59–63.

[32] See ch 3, s 3.6.

International human rights norms filtered into legal analysis in the Australian rights-protecting judgments in other ways, sometimes without express acknowledgment.[33] The international law materials were influential in their emphasis on the need for proportionality between the stated goal of deportation and the duration of detention ancillary to that goal.[34] International human rights law is best understood as having not only buttressed, but also shaped, common law and constitutional doctrine, in terms of such a proportionality analysis.[35]

Conversely, in the Australian rights-precluding judgments, neither common law presumptions nor presumptions of constitutionality were held to have generated any ambiguity in the statute, with the result that the presumption of consistency with international law could find no purchase. In this way, openness to rights-protecting interpretations sourced in common law and constitutional doctrine and openness to such interpretations sourced in international law, stood or fell together. The latter influence, international law, depended on the work of the former, domestic, influences to gain a place in the legal analysis.

(b) The United Kingdom – The Meaning of Treaty Texts

Under the Human Rights Act 1998 (HRA 1998), there is necessarily a supranational aspect to the jurisprudence. The Convention rights are drawn from the ECHR, and section 2 of the HRA 1998 provides in part that a court determining a question which has arisen in connection with a Convention right 'must take into account' any ECtHR judgment relevant to the proceedings. Of more immediate relevance to the *Belmarsh* litigation, the parties proceeded on the basis that the validity of the derogation in domestic law depended on whether the derogation to which it gave effect was lawful under Article 15 of the ECHR.[36] Further, European jurisprudence both led to, and shaped, the statutory provisions and derogation at issue in *Belmarsh*, most notably with reference to the ECtHR's rulings in *Chahal* on the purpose and scope of immigration detention and on deportation to torture.[37]

[33] See the discussion of Gleeson CJ's dissent in *Al-Kateb* (n 2), ch 3, s 3.4. In both *Al Masri* (n 12) (ch 2, s 2.4.3) and Kirby J's dissent in *Al-Kateb* (ch 3, ss 3.5, 3.6), reference to international human rights law was express.

[34] As discussed, in the Australian authorities where proportionality is applied by means of a 'reasonably necessary' test, it is not applied to the prior question of the need for detention to secure the non-citizen's availability for removal (or during processing); it is applied only to the duration of detention authorised.

[35] For example, in *Al Masri* (n 12) it was clear that international human rights law did not just 'buttress' conclusions arrived at on the basis of common law and constitutional sources; it also solidified confidence in the existence and strength of the common law right to liberty: see ch 2, p 60. For a study charting similar patterns of judicial reasoning in the United Kingdom prior to the advent of the HRA 1998 see Murray Hunt, *Using Human Rights Law in English Courts* (Oxford, Hart Publishing, 1997).

[36] See ch 6, s 6.2.

[37] See ch 5, ss 5.3, 5.4 and ch 6, s 6.1. Another prominent example of European jurisprudence determining the British position is the procedural rulings of the ECtHR in *A v United Kingdom* (n 13) which were determinative of the procedural requirements on control orders required in *AF* (n 17): see ch 7, pp 204–07.

In the United Kingdom material surveyed, issues were raised by the diametrically opposed conclusions that emerged from Brooke LJ's review of international law in the Court of Appeal and that of Lord Bingham in the House of Lords. Brooke LJ upheld the government's argument that international law permitted the differential treatment of non-citizens in times of emergency. For Brooke LJ, this argument was determinative of his holding that the government's derogation was lawful. Lord Bingham roundly rejected Brooke LJ's assessment of the position at international law, holding the materials to be 'inimical to the submission that a state may lawfully discriminate against foreign nationals by detaining them but not nationals presenting the same threat in a time of public emergency'.[38]

In chapter six I described the differences in judicial approach that generated these very different evaluations of the position at international law.[39] In summary, Brooke LJ focused on particular treaty provisions and comparative cases, considering each in relative isolation from the others. In the House of Lords, the government advanced an argument similar to that accepted by Brooke LJ in the Court of Appeal. Lord Bingham criticised the government's failure to properly represent the context in which the relevant treaty provisions came to be interpreted. He pointed out that the government had selectively cited treaties, failed to take qualifications within treaties into account, and failed to consider subsequent relevant treaty obligations. In contrast to Brooke LJ, Lord Bingham considered the relevant provisions and cases as part of a unified and dynamic body of international law, and worked to elucidate the relationship between the sources.

Lord Bingham's reading of the treaties also had a wider frame of reference than that of Brooke LJ. Lord Bingham made use of the commentary of treaty bodies, in a way that both acknowledged their role in interpreting the application of the relevant treaty to changing conditions, and sought to work towards consistency in the treaty's application and understanding. In all its aspects, the difference between the two judgments is one of judicial methodology.

The central contribution of international law to Lord Bingham's judgment was to highlight the wrong of discrimination, and more particularly to deny any presumptive reasonableness to differential treatment of non-citizens. In *Belmarsh*, the proportionality test was taken not from public international law, but from the Privy Council's Commonwealth jurisprudence,[40] as informed by other comparative authorities.[41] Here, in effect, proportionality was applied *to* the international law materials. The general tenor of the international law materials, questioning the 'reasonableness' of the differential treatment of non-citizens, was solidified and enhanced by the application of a proportionality test derived from the common law cases. Viewed collectively, the Australian and British rights-protecting authorities testify to the ability of international law to influence the application of

[38] *Belmarsh* (n 2) [63] (Lord Bingham).

[39] See ch 6, pp 176–79.

[40] *de Freitas v Permanent Secretary of Ministry of Agriculture, Fisheries, Lands and Housing* [1999] 1 AC 69.

[41] Notably the *Oakes* test: *R v Oakes* [1986] 1 SCR 103.

domestic law, and vice versa, strengthening a common legal commitment to scrutinise the differential treatment of non-citizens.

Further, in chapter seven I showed how the British government's arguments before the ECtHR in *A v United Kingdom* attempted to use international legal avenues to circumvent its domestic courts.[42] This highlights that greater reference to, and use of, international law should not in itself be assumed to benefit non-citizens or the protection of rights more generally.

(c) Canada – How Seriously are International Law Obligations Taken?

Benvenisti claims that the availability of identical or similar norms (grounded in international human rights law) has facilitated coordination between national courts in the counterterrorism area.[43] The *Suresh* exception, and its continued authority, constitutes one of the clearest possible counter-examples. The rejection of an absolute bar on deportation to torture under the Charter in *Suresh*[44] is inconsistent with the evolving ECtHR jurisprudence, as constituted by *Chahal*[45] and reaffirmed in *Saadi*.[46] *Suresh* furnished an example of two jurisdictions, Canada and the members of the Council of Europe, failing to coordinate around a common norm drawn from international human rights law, here the United Nations Convention against Torture.[47] *Charkaoui* continued this divergence between Canada and Europe, giving sanction to the indefinite detention of non-citizens subject to a deportation order, in contrast to the European position reaffirmed in *A v United Kingdom*.[48]

In *Suresh*, the Canadian Supreme Court used a national constitutional rights regime to dilute the force of Canada's obligations under international human rights law. The categorical rejection of deportation to torture at international law simply became a factor in Charter interpretation, to be balanced against national security.[49] In *Charkaoui*, the Court effectively treated the Charter as a complete and self-sufficient source of law on the relevant fundamental rights. Human rights jurisprudence sourced outside the Charter only appeared at the very margins of the reasoning.[50] In both cases the national rights framework was applied to weaken or simply shut out reference to international human rights jurisprudence.

[42] See ch 7, s 7.2.1.

[43] Benvenisti, 'United We Stand' (n 5) 273; Benvenisti, 'Reclaiming Democracy' (n 5) 252; Benvenisti and Downs (n 5) 66–67.

[44] *Suresh v Canada (Citizenship and Immigration)* [2002] SCC 1, [2002] 1 SCR 3.

[45] *Chahal* (n 12).

[46] *Saadi v Italy* (2009) 49 EHRR 30.

[47] Convention against Torture and other Cruel, Inhuman or Degrading Treatment or Punishment (opened for signature 10 December 1984, entered into force 26 June 1987) 1465 UNTS 85. On the contrast between the Canadian and European jurisprudence on deportation to a real risk of torture see Audrey Macklin, 'Transjudicial Conversations about Security and Human Rights' in Mark Salter (ed), *Mapping Transatlantic Security Relations: The EU, Canada, and the War on Terror* (Oxford, Routledge, 2010) 212, pp 227–32.

[48] *A v United Kingdom* (n 13). On the relationship between *Suresh* (n 26) and *Charkaoui* (n 2) see ch 9, s 9.6.

[49] See ch 8, pp 240–42.

[50] See ch 9, pp 273–74.

From a shared set of legal references, judgments from across the three jurisdictions end up at very different points. These differences, both between national jurisdictions and between judges within a national jurisdiction, are variously attributable to differences in international law's point of entry into the domestic legal system, differences as to how to establish the meaning of treaty texts, and differences as to the appropriate weight to be given to a state's international law obligations, as evidenced in the Australian, British and Canadian judgments respectively. Again, the divergence between the judgments is attributable to differences in judicial methodology.

10.3 The Purpose(s) of Detention

How do those judgments that uphold the indefinite detention of non-citizens justify and articulate the basis for that decision against the background of existing public law approaches and protections? The case law discloses two general ways in which the legality of indefinite detention is upheld in the judicial reasoning, both of which refer to the purposes of immigration detention. The first is to extrapolate from an expansive conception of the permissible purposes of immigration detention. An expansive conception of immigration detention obviates the need for any test for the sufficiency of the connection between detention and deportation. The second means of upholding indefinite detention is to accept the need for a sufficient connection between detention and deportation, but to adopt a test of sufficiency of connection that effectively empties the requirement of any content.

10.3.1 'Segregation from the Community' or 'Dangerousness'

The rights-precluding authorities, either expressly or implicitly, adopt purposes such as 'segregation from the community',[51] 'dangerousness',[52] or preventing 'danger to national security'[53] as stand-alone, self-sufficient rationales for the indefinite detention of non-citizens. The adoption of such purposes constitutes a 'complete' answer to the issue of the legality of indefinite detention, obviating the need for any proportionality test.

Repeatedly, the case law surveyed in this book provides legal reasons against adoption of expansive justifications for the indefinite detention of non-citizens

[51] *Al-Kateb* (n 2) [255] (Hayne J), [247] (Heydon J concurring), and see [45] (McHugh J). See ch 3, s 3.3.

[52] *Zadvydas* (n 11) (Kennedy J, dissent). This rationale was also spoken of in terms of protection of the community. See ch 1, pp 7–8.

[53] Under the Canadian security certificate regime, a judge is not to order release of a non-citizen in detention pending deportation if satisfied that release on conditions would pose a danger to security. Where there is no temporal limit on authority to detain pending deportation, this effectively sees a non-citizen detained indefinitely on the basis that they are a danger to security.

such as segregation from, or protection of, the community. Opposition to such purposes is contained, for example, in the presentation of United States constitutional doctrine in the Opinion of the Court in *Zadvydas*,[54] the Australian separation of powers analysis in the judgments of Gummow and Kirby JJ in *Al-Kateb*,[55] and Lord Bingham's review of international law in *Belmarsh*.[56] Woven through this opposition to the use of expansive purposes to justify indefinite detention are a number of interrelated points.

As a starting point, we can register that indefinite detention 'is anathema to the principles which govern our judicial system'.[57] A standing purpose of 'segregation' from the community, as adopted by members of the *Al-Kateb* majority,[58] negates a non-citizen's right to liberty. The equation of exclusion from the country with exclusion from the community is indifferent to the fact of the non-citizen's physical presence. The segregation purpose is activated by the presence of a non-citizen who does not have permission to be in the country. It constitutes a near total denial of the detainee's autonomy. There may well be nothing the detainee can do, ever, to extricate herself or himself from indefinite detention. This results in the debilitating feeling of helplessness recorded by so many long-term detainees.[59]

'Segregation from the community', or indeed any justification for indefinite detention measures confined to non-citizens, also constitutes a blow to equality of persons in its sweeping distinction between the liberty rights of citizens and those of non-citizens. A purpose such as 'segregation' extends much further than is required by a non-citizen's vulnerability to removal. Indeed, it has an odd relationship to removal, being totally indifferent to its viability. It is a purpose of detention that is indifferent to everything about the detainee apart from their removable status. Gleeson CJ was rightly dismayed by the *Al-Kateb* majority's judgment that 'a person, regardless of personal circumstances, regardless of whether he or she is a danger to the community, and regardless of whether he or she might abscond' could be indefinitely detained on the basis of an implication drawn from the general words of a statute.[60] Authority to detain fixes on an ascribed status – that of unauthorised non-citizen. This is pure status-based discrimination.

This discrimination against non-citizens is not resolved if detention is justified by reference to 'dangerousness' or 'risk to national security'. There is no inherent

[54] See ch 1, s 1.1.

[55] See ch 3, s 3.5.

[56] See ch 6, pp 176–79.

[57] *Canada (Minister of Citizenship and Immigration) v Mahjoub* [2005] FC 1596, (2005) 270 FTR 101 (*Mahjoub, Second Application for Release*), [92] (Dawson J). See also, eg, Kirby J in dissent in *Al-Kateb* (n 2) [146]: 'indefinite detention at the will of the executive, and according to its opinions, actions and judgments, is alien to Australia's constitutional arrangements.'

[58] A purpose endorsed by three of the four majority judges in *Al-Kateb* (n 2) [45] (McHugh J), [255] (Hayne J), [303] (Heydon J, agreeing with Hayne J). See ch 3, s 3.3.

[59] See eg the research into the health of long-term detainees in Australian immigration detention discussed in ch 4, pp 102–03. See also the adverse impact of control orders on controlees' mental health, discussed in ch 7, s 7.4.1.

[60] *Al-Kateb* (n 2) [21].

reason for such a purpose to single out non-citizens. As identified in the Opinion of the Court in *Zadvydas*, such rationales reduce to no more than a stark assertion of difference – the fact of the non-citizen's 'removeable status' – irrespective of whether the non-citizen can be removed.[61] A national security rationale for indefinite detention measures confined to non-citizens is, as the House of Lords held in *Belmarsh*, arbitrary, irrational and discriminatory.[62]

Under a rights-protecting approach, the liberty right of the non-citizen is expressed in the idea that the legitimate purposes of immigration detention provide only a *limited* justification for detention, which has to be weighed against that right. The nature of this assessment follows from the purpose of detention, namely facilitating removal. Detention is predicated on the viability of removal as ascertained on judicial review.[63]

10.3.2 'Detention Pending Removal'

There is another means of rationalising indefinite detention confined to non-citizens, which is to define 'detention pending removal' as requiring only the government's continued intention to deport. The *Al-Kateb* majority applied this approach in their interpretation of the Migration Act 1958. The Canadian Supreme Court's reasoning in *Charkaoui* is no different in kind. The 'hinge' between detention and deportation does not appear to require any real prospect of removal. If the point at which liberty is held to be unjustifiably infringed never arrives, as in *Charkaoui*, or if it will never arrive because there always remains an unverifiable and unchallengeable future 'possibility' of removal, as held by the *Al-Kateb* majority,[64] then the category of 'detention pending removal' becomes a euphemism for indefinite detention on grounds of a person's 'removeable status'.

In both *Al-Kateb* and *Charkaoui* the characterisation of detention as 'pending removal' rested on the executive's intention to deport the relevant detainees. On the assumption that the 'viability of removal' has *some* bearing on the characterisation of detention as 'pending removal' (an assumption rejected by the *Al-Kateb* majority), Gummow J's criticisms of the *Al-Kateb* majority made with reference to the *Communist Party Case* have real bite.[65] One does not have to enter into the

[61] See ch 1, pp 5–7.

[62] Unless it can be factually demonstrated that the threat emanates exclusively from non-citizens, hence the importance of SIAC's factual finding in the *Belmarsh* litigation that the threat was from both citizens and non-citizens: see ch 6, pp 153–54.

[63] No objection is made to this assessment being conducted by a body independent of the executive that is not a court. But in the legal systems discussed, the independence and proper operation of that body will ultimately be secured by judicial review. Care has to be taken that this review supports the body's purpose in independently assessing the viability of removal, rather than curtailing it in the manner of the House of Lords' review of SIAC's operation in *Rehman*, on which see ch 5, s 5.6.

[64] *Al-Kateb* (n 2) [231] (Hayne J): 'Because there can be no certainty about whether or when the non-citizen will be removed, it cannot be said that the Act proceeds from a premise (that removal will be possible) which can be demonstrated to be false in any particular case.'

[65] See ch 3, pp 82–85.

detail of Australian constitutional law to understand the import of his objection that, if constitutional authority to detain requires a nexus to removal, 'The continued viability of the purpose of deportation or expulsion cannot be treated by the legislature as a matter purely for the opinion of the executive government'.[66] To do so is effectively to cede to the executive the power to determine the length and legality of a person's detention.

Sweeping purposes that constitute a complete reason for indefinite detention, such as 'segregation from the community', and notions that 'detention pending removal' can be stretched to accommodate indefinite detention, both ultimately rest on the proposition that a person's 'removable status' places them outside the normal legal objections to indefinite administrative detention. I discuss the reasons why this proposition has some purchase in the case law in section 10.4.

10.3.3 The Rights-Protecting Approach

In contrast to the *Al-Kateb* majority and *Charkaoui*, the rights-protecting approach maintains the integrity of 'detention pending removal' as a limited exception to the law's presumptive antipathy to administrative detention. The starting position is that there is a right to liberty, or a constitutional immunity from administrative detention,[67] and an exception to that right or immunity arising from a non-citizen's vulnerability to deportation. The proportionality requirement that recurs through the 'rights-protecting' jurisprudence is, at its simplest, a tool to reconcile the right, namely liberty, and the exception derived from vulnerability to removal. In the task of determining the scope of the exception, 'proportionality would appear to be a useful criterion to use'.[68]

For the proportionality test to serve as a meaningful limit on detention pending removal, authority to detain has to rest on the viability of removal, as assessed on independent review.[69] Where there is no real prospect of removal in the reasonably foreseeable future, authority to detain is suspended. This requirement ensures that authority to detain remains properly tethered to its purpose.

Under a rights-protecting approach, a commitment to the non-citizen's liberty right is evident at two points in the legal reasoning. It serves to define the permissible purposes of detention, and it informs a proportionality analysis of detention for that purpose. The two elements go together because a permissible immigration purpose will always be amenable to proportionality analysis.[70]

[66] *Al-Kateb* (n 2) [140].

[67] See *Lim* (n 30). Discussed in ch 2, pp 48–52.

[68] Leslie Zines, *The High Court and the Constitution*, 5th edn (Sydney, Federation Press, 2008) 289.

[69] See eg Lord Hope's comments on the connection between the limitation as to the purpose of facilitating removal, and the limitation as to time in *R (on the application of Lumba) v Secretary of State for the Home Department* [2011] UKSC 12, [2012] 1 AC 245, [174]; see ch 7, pp 217–18.

[70] See Daniel Wilsher, *Immigration Detention: Law, History, Politics* (New York, Cambridge University Press, 2012) 335: 'In order for proportionality to re-enter the picture, we must make some value judgments about the *reasonable* goals of detention policy.' My argument is that these value judgments are built into the legal doctrine and principles applied.

10.4 Non-Citizens in Times of Threat

An underlying theme of the rights-precluding judgments is to cast non-citizens as a threat of a different order to citizens. This theme is express in Kennedy J's reasons in *Zadvydas*,[71] and is also evident in the reasons of the *Al-Kateb* majority[72] and the government arguments in both *Al Masri*[73] and the *Belmarsh* litigation.[74] More pervasive and influential than the idea of non-citizen as heightened threat is the related but distinct idea that 'our' tolerance of risk is, and should be, lower in the case of risk presented by non-citizens.

Security concerns underlie the perceived reasonableness and plausibility of expansive justifications for indefinite detention such as 'protection of the community'. They also motivate a stretching of the connection between detention and deportation. The latter phenomenon is illustrated by *Charkaoui*. In chapter nine, I criticised the Canadian Supreme Court's claim in that case that its reasoning was consistent with *Hardial Singh* and *Zadvydas*. The Court held that all three authorities limited authority to detain to 'the period where it is reasonably necessary for deportation purposes'.[75] I argued that the Court's claim to consistency with the comparative authorities was unsustainable.[76]

Charkaoui stretched the understanding of a 'reasonable period' for detention pending deportation so as to render it qualitatively distinct from the comparative authorities. Finnis describes the open-ended concept of 'reasonableness' employed in *Charkaoui*:

> To grant that the phrase 'within a reasonable period' imports a 'temporal restriction' is by no means to concede that, in the concrete circumstances of an ongoing threat involving the deportee and ongoing efforts to deport, there is some identifiable length of time beyond which detention has exceeded 'a reasonable period'. In circumstances of such a kind, such detention might reasonably last even, in principle, indefinitely: see *Charkaoui*.[77]

The temporal restriction described is no restriction at all.

There is a shift in the understanding of the limits on detention pending removal from *Zadvydas* to *Charkaoui*. In *Zadvydas*, the limits on detention pending removal were understood as the bounds of permissible differentiation between the rights of citizens and those of non-citizens. They set the bounds on detention that could legitimately be confined to non-citizens. And this boundary line

[71] See ch 1, p 7.

[72] See ch 3, pp 76–77 and Matthew Zagor, 'Judicial Rhetoric and Constitutional Identity: Comparative Approaches to Aliens' Rights in the United Kingdom and Australia' (2009) 19 *Public Law Review* 271, 282.

[73] *Al Masri* (n 12). See ch 2, p 62.

[74] Covered in ch 6 and ch 7, 7.2.

[75] *Charkaoui* (n 2) [124].

[76] See ch 9, s 9.5.1.

[77] John Finnis, 'Nationality, Alienage and Constitutional Principle' (2007) 123 *LQR* 417, 430 fn 61.

between a legitimate focus on non-citizens, and arbitrarily singling them out, was understood to be consonant with deep-seated constitutional imperatives.[78] The boundary was set with reference to a criterion independent of government intention and intended for judicial assessment, namely the viability of removal. *Zadvydas* defined what was 'reasonably necessary for deportation purposes' in terms of the reasonable foreseeability of removal.

Charkaoui dropped the reasonable foreseeability requirement. The category of 'detention pending removal' was stretched beyond previous bounds to accommodate national security concerns. This constituted a revision of the comparative authorities' understanding of what counts as discrimination against non-citizens. It increased the permissible differentiation in treatment between citizens and non-citizens. The effect of this was to cast the previous understanding of the limits on permissible differentiation between the liberty rights of citizens and non-citizens as a luxury, slipping away to disclose the 'true', more fundamental, division between citizens and non-citizens under the pressure of security concerns.

By way of contrast, the House of Lords in *Belmarsh* rejected the idea that detention pending removal is an elastic concept, expanding in times of threat. If a threat to national security is the true rationale for detention and it is a threat posed by both citizens and non-citizens, then non-citizens cannot be singled out to bear the burden.

10.5 The Importance of Membership[79]

The rights-precluding judgments are permeated by understandings of the legal position of non-citizens. What are those understandings? To begin to address that question, I return to John Finnis's clear and influential exposition of the principle of 'nationality-differentiated risk-acceptability' as underlying what I have called the rights-precluding approach.[80] Finnis explicitly advances that principle to counter the influence that the principles of liberty and equality exert on the reasoning in *Belmarsh*.[81] He argues that a misguided application of these principles to non-citizens in *Belmarsh* led to a deeply unsatisfactory and troubling result. In chapter one, I argued that Finnis's principle neither explains the shape of contemporary law in the area nor has a solid historical foundation.[82] Here, I consider the normative argument for the principle.

[78] *Hardial Singh* was also 'constitutional' in the sense that it drew on a common law presumption in favour of liberty to read the relevant statutory discretion as subject to an unexpressed temporal limitation.

[79] This section draws on Rayner Thwaites, 'The Security of Citizenship? Finnis in the Context of the United Kingdom's Citizenship Stripping Provisions' in Fiona Jenkins et al, *Allegiance and Identity in a Globalised World* (Cambridge, Cambridge University Press, forthcoming 2014).

[80] Finnis (n 77). See ch 1, ss 1.4 and 1.5.

[81] Finnis (n 77) 417.

[82] See ch 1, s 1.5.

Looking to Finnis's motivations for advocating 'nationality-differentiated risk-acceptability' helps to identify a principled, though I argue mistaken, case for the legal understanding of non-citizens that informs the rights-precluding judgments. The core of his case for the differential treatment of non-citizens, affording them a lower level of rights protection, is contained in the following paragraph:

> Much recent political theory shows how equal laws, public probity, impartial government, social justice, an democratic deliberation towards the undertaking of collective commitments and obligations and international action all depend upon – and in turn foster – a generalised trust sufficient to outweigh *competing* bonds of kin, caste, religion or ethnicity, a level of trust and common sympathies attainable only within bounded national communities, nation states . . . The distinction between nationals and aliens is an indispensable framework for articulating, expressing, ratifying and demanding such willingness to share, such awareness of being part owner of a shared inheritance and future, such integration in and assimilation to *this* nation state rather than some other.[83] (footnotes omitted)

In essence, Finnis argues that citizenship and the state constitute themselves through exclusion. The concept of citizenship set out in the passage is doubly exclusionary. It 'designates non-members by defining members' and it 'recognizes an association that is expected to exercise power in the interests of members with less concern for the interests of non-members'.[84]

Both Finnis and his foil, namely the majority in *Belmarsh*, reason from the proposition that non-citizens are vulnerable to removal and citizens are not. Finnis argues that the distinction between the two classes of person suffices to justify the indefinite detention of non-citizens when they present

> some genuine risk, even relatively slight, to the rights of others, national security, public safety, the prevention of crime, the protection of health or morals or the maintenance of l'ordre public, or to anything else of 'public interest in a democratic society' . . .[85]

He pushes for an expansion of the *extent* of differentiation between the rights of citizens and non-citizens beyond what was accepted by the *Belmarsh* majority.

Finnis's treatment of citizenship as membership, and membership as determinative of legal rights, resonates with the rights-precluding approach to detention pending deportation. A notable feature of the reasoning of the *Al-Kateb* majority was the proposition that granting release from detention would constitute the grant of de facto membership to a person who had no right to be in Australia.[86] Conversely, indefinite detention was justified on the basis that the detainee had 'no permission to be at liberty'.[87] In the rights-precluding judgments the absence of a 'legal right' to be in the country is treated as determining questions of

[83] Finnis (n 77) 444.

[84] Alexander Aleinikoff, 'Citizens, Aliens, Membership and the Constitution' (1990) 7 *Constitutional Commentary* 9, 14. See also Alexander Aleinikoff, *Semblances of Sovereignty: The Constitution, the State, and American Citizenship* (Cambridge, MA, Harvard University Press, 2002) 168.

[85] Finnis (n 77) 423.

[86] *Al-Kateb* (n 2) [46] (McHugh J), [189] (Callinan J). See ch 3, pp 76–77.

[87] *Al-Kateb* (n 2) [254] (Hayne J). See ch 3, s 3.3.

liberty.[88] This conflation of a right 'to be here' with a right to liberty was persistently objected to by Gummow J in the cases surveyed.[89]

On the rights-precluding approach the legal analysis is largely determined by an initial classification exercise: citizen or non-citizen, with or without legal authority to remain. There is little, if any, place in the legal analysis for an inquiry into the impact of detention on the non-citizen, how its effects might change over time, or detention's relation to the ostensible rationale for singling out non-citizens in the first place, namely their vulnerability to removal.

What might drive the importance ascribed to citizenship in determining the fundamental right to liberty? Finnis's underlying claim is that a sharp division between the rights of citizens and those of non-citizens is needed to secure solidarity between citizens. He argues that the 'generalised trust' necessary for 'equal laws, public probity, impartial government, social justice, and democratic deliberation' is best secured by constituting a bounded and exclusive citizenry.[90] Ultimately, it is this solidarity and the social goods it enables that Finnis defends against what he sees as an over-zealous extension of principles of equality and liberty to non-citizens.

In talking of 'willingness to share' and elsewhere in the article of the need to 'call upon their members' sense of identification with fellow members',[91] it is apparent that Finnis wishes to 'harness the motivational power of shared identity to the ends of the democratic state'.[92] Citizenship is proposed as the obvious candidate for the shared identity of those in the modern nation state, in some sense above the other, divisive, candidates for identity ('kin, caste, religion or ethnicity').[93] The exclusive conception of citizenship he advances is allied with a project to valorise citizenship. The stark distinction between citizen and non-citizen is taken to render citizenship a meaningful concept.

I agree that the state remains vital to redistributive welfare and democratic politics. However, I am not convinced by Finnis's argument that these public goods are lost if close scrutiny for violation of legal norms is extended to immigration detention and to arguments for the differential treatment of citizens more generally. The rights-protecting approach means that persons the government has ordered to be removed will have a right to be released. But the release of some non-citizens against whom removal orders have been issued merely describes

[88] See *Al-Kateb* (n 2) [254] (Hayne J). See also *Zadvydas* (n 11) 702–03 (Scalia J in dissent, joined by Thomas J), 717 (Kennedy J in dissent, joined by Rehnquist CJ); see ch 1, s 1.1. See *Plaintiff M47/2012 v Director General of Security* [2012] HCA 46, (2012) 86 ALJR 1372 (*Plaintiff M47*) [228] (Heydon J in the minority); see ch 4, pp 114–15.

[89] *Re Woolley, ex parte Applicants M276/2003 (by their next friend GS)* [2004] HCA 49, (2004) 210 ALR 369, [146] and more generally [137]–[148]; see ch 3, pp 85–87. See also *Plaintiff M47* (n 88) [88] (Gummow J).

[90] Finnis (n 77) 444.

[91] ibid.

[92] Melissa S Williams, 'Nonterritorial Boundaries of Citizenship' in Seyla Benhabib et al (eds), *Identities, Affiliations and Allegiances* (Cambridge, Cambridge University Press, 2007) 226, 233. Williams is addressing the general phenomena, not Finnis's writing.

[93] Finnis (n 77) 444.

present reality. In the harshest of the detention regimes surveyed, Australia, the entire structure of 'removal pending bridging visas' and other executive mechanisms for release testifies to the reality that removal may be an extremely protracted process, if it ever occurs, and release must be contemplated as a consequence.[94] A review of 419 cases of Australian long-term detention between July 2005 and March 2009 found that in 85 per cent of the cases, detainees were eventually provided with permanent protection in Australia.[95] The question is not whether non-citizens without a 'legal right' to remain should be released. They are and will be. It is whether their release should be left to 'the opinion of the executive government',[96] or whether the law sets meaningful limits on the duration of their detention. The latter response is consistent with recognition of a right to liberty and a commitment to equality of persons before the law. In the national security context, the fixed time limit of two years for British terrorism prevention investigation measures is explained by the view that preventive or protective detention must be subject to legally enforceable limits.[97]

Finnis does not offer any empirical foundation for his view that a stark distinction between nationals and aliens is necessary to social solidarity. Melissa Williams's comments are apposite:

> a further difficulty in these arguments is that they present the necessity of shared identity for democratic citizenship as a normative-theoretical claim derived from a conceptual analysis of citizenship, when it fact it only makes sense as an empirical claim – or, rather, several empirical claims bundled together.[98]

Finnis's work of political theory supports the observation that liberal political theorists, while fascinated by issues of membership, have not 'greatly explored what level of hardship may be imposed on "outsiders" for the sake of achieving any given level of control over borders'.[99] The primacy Finnis gives to issues of membership places questions about how to reconcile the enforcement of membership rules with a commitment to human rights in soft focus. In this, his article reflects that portion of the jurisprudence I have characterised as rights-precluding, in which issues of membership predominate over rights, and questions about the limits on what we can do to non-citizens remain largely unaddressed.

[94] See ch 4, s 4.2.

[95] Melissa Bull et al, 'Sickness in the System of Long-Term Immigration Detention' (2013) 26 *Journal of Refugee Studies* 47, 59. See ch 4, s 4.2.

[96] *Al-Kateb* (n 2) [140] (Gummow J, in dissent), criticising this view.

[97] Under the Terrorism Prevention Investigation Measures Act 2011: see ch 7, s 7.6.

[98] Williams (n 92) 235.

[99] Wilsher (n 70) 259.

10.6 The Integration of Rights and Immigration Control

Finnis argues that unless one is prepared to concede a wider zone of selective, and attenuated, application of principles of equality and liberty to non-citizens than was countenanced in *Belmarsh*, the power to 'admit, exclude and expel aliens' will 'crumble'.[100] He presents a stark choice between a power protective of the citizenry, and the assertion and enforcement of general legal principles of equality and liberty to non-citizens. This way of framing the issue should be rejected. What is at issue is whether an older, 'spatial' conception of judicial deference is maintained in the areas of immigration and national security, or whether these areas are integrated with the general body of legal principle by taking seriously the rights of those who bear the burdens of policy in these areas.[101] An insistence on the rights of non-citizens, and the applicability of general legal principles to them, requires a more particularised application of immigration powers, alive to the interplay of rights and purposes obscured by the assertion of sweeping governmental powers.

Finnis argues that the House of Lords' assertion of equality and liberty in *Belmarsh* imposes unduly simplistic claims on a complicated reality.[102] On the contrary, acknowledgment of the rights of non-citizens has, time and again, opened up questions of immigration and national security previously addressed with reference to generalities. At its best, an advantage of litigation is that once a beachhead is formed, the set of issues is relentlessly exposed to view and explored.[103] Claims founded in non-citizens' rights have allowed judicial discussion to 'condescend to the particular'.[104]

The rights-protecting approach draws on established public law doctrines. Human rights instruments and case law can supply cogent reasoning to support an analysis that there is no justifiable reason for distinguishing between citizens and non-citizens. Once this point is established, public law doctrine operates in the normal way to protect non-citizens. Human rights reasoning can serve as a valuable means of getting to that starting point, but there are other means of

[100] Finnis (n 77) 417.

[101] On a 'spatial' conception of deference see Murray Hunt, 'Sovereignty's Blight: Why Contemporary Public Law Needs the Concept of "Due Deference"' in Nicholas Bamforth and Peter Leyland (eds), *Public Law in a Multi-Layered Constitution* (Oxford, Hart Publishing, 2003) 337. See ch 5, s 5.6.

[102] See eg Finnis (n 77) 423–29.

[103] Campbell McLachlan, 'The Allocative Function of Foreign Relations Law' (2012) 82 *British Yearbook of International Law* 349, 359.

[104] See Dominic Grieves, HC Deb 21 Feb 2008, vol 472 col 567, commenting on a speech by Tony McNulty arguing for the continuance of control orders. McNulty's speech concluded as follows: 'We must protect the public while ensuring that our fundamental rights and values are protected, and we must do that overwhelmingly within the body of the rule of law, our statutes and the terrorism legislation framework. There are and will be very small matters of exception in that regard, of which control orders are a part. I say freely that they are part of the delicate balancing act between security and human rights.' Dominic Grieves commented: 'The Minister delivered one of his characteristic speeches. He tends to look at the general rather than condescend to the particular.'

getting there. In the rights-protecting judgments under review, human rights have been conjoined with, or replaced by, commitments to liberty and equality of persons rooted in common law and constitutional doctrine other than express rights protections. Whether rooted in common law, constitutional doctrine or international law, a commitment to these principles has served to dislodge the 'thought-blocking, definitional weight that the citizenship-as-membership perspective throws up against constitutional [and legal] questions'.[105]

To return to the reasoning of the *Belmarsh* majority, the commitment to human rights dislodged government arguments for a deferential approach. The legal analysis that followed can be characterised in terms of formal legal principles, statutory purposes, rational connection and a formal concept of equality.[106] But this does not show that the reasoning was 'really' the application of formal legal doctrine, understood as in some way independent from a substantive conception of rights. These two characterisations are not so easily distinguished. It took a lot of work to reveal the lineaments of the dispute in such a way that it was amenable to a legal analysis in terms of statutory purposes, rational connection and a formal concept of equality. There was an impressive marshalling of the material, very much within the common law tradition, in order to dispel obfuscatory claims to deference based on the government's 'immigration' characterisation of the detention and the national security context. Lord Bingham and others in the *Belmarsh* majority would not have done that work if it had not called on their sense of what the law is *for*.

10.7 Conclusion

The central theme of the comparative work in this book is that differences in judicial mindset, rather than any difference in legal structure, have determined the legality of the indefinite detention of non-citizens who are subject to a removal order. Within each jurisdiction the question arose as to whether the administrative detention of non-citizens, in circumstances where there was no real prospect of removal in the reasonably foreseeable future, constituted detention for the purposes of deportation. A rights-protecting approach was available in each national jurisdiction. Under the rights-protecting approach, in the absence of a real prospect of removal in the reasonably foreseeable future, authority to detain was suspended. The detention could not be said to be for the purpose of deportation and

[105] Aleinikoff, 'Membership' (n 84) 27.

[106] See Christopher Forsyth, 'Showing the Fly the Way Out of the Fly Bottle: The Value of Formalism and Conceptual Reasoning in Administrative Law' (2007) 66 *Cambridge Law Journal* 325, 344–46. For another example of the way in which a set of principles going to 'rights' can be understood in terms of formal legal doctrine, the *Hardial Singh* principles were understood simply to express the basic public law duties to act consistently with statutory purpose (*Padfield*) and reasonably in the *Wednesbury* sense: *R (on the application of Lumba) v Secretary of State for the Home Department* [2011] UKSC 12, [2012] 1 AC 245, [30] (Lord Dyson), [199] (Baroness Hale). On *Lumba* see ch 7, s 7.8.1.

confined to non-citizens on that basis. Further, reasoning justifying the indefinite detention of non-citizens on the basis of additional purposes, independent and distinct from facilitating removal, was to be rejected as incompatible with fundamental tenets of the relevant legal systems, centrally a commitment to the equality of persons.

In the case law of each jurisdiction, the distinction between the legal models centred not on fundamentally different understandings of the legal context in general, but rather on fundamentally different understandings of the rights of non-citizens. The rights-protecting judges reasoned on the basis that there was a persisting right to liberty, one that survives a removal order, while the rights-precluding judges did not.

The relationship between state and non-citizen that informs the rights-protecting model is that expressed in epigraph to this chapter – a foreigner answerable to our laws is entitled to their protection.[107] The obligation to afford the legal subject, the detainee, the protection of the law is bound up in the very notion of what it means to exercise power through law. Specifically, this excludes the arbitrary selection of non-citizens to bear a burden, the successful basis for the challenge in *Belmarsh*. It is also opposed to the view that a non-citizen's right to liberty can be readily negated through law, as in the majority's reasoning in *Al-Kateb*, or be endlessly deferred as a legal issue, as in *Charkaoui*. In the areas of immigration and/or national security detention, the government is subject to constraints of legality no different in kind from those that operate in less contested areas of administration, and should be subject to equally close judicial scrutiny where grave rights infringements are involved. A commitment to equality before the law has deep roots in the common law, in national constitutional doctrines and in international law. Freed of the perspective that membership determines rights, a richer conception of law is exposed to view.

[107] *Ex parte Lo Pak* (n 1) 245 (Windeyer J). See text to n 1.

BIBLIOGRAPHY

Aleinikoff, T Alexander, 'Detaining Plenary Power: The Meaning and Impact of *Zadvydas v Davis*' (2002) 16 *Georgetown Immigration Law Journal* 365.

——, *Semblances of Sovereignty: The Constitution, the State, and American Citizenship* (Cambridge, MA, Harvard University Press, 2002).

——, 'Citizens, Aliens, Membership and the Constitution' (1990) 7 *Constitutional Commentary* 9.

Allan, James, '"Do the Right Thing" Judging? The High Court of Australia in *Al-Kateb*' (2005) 24 *University of Queensland Law Journal* 1.

Allan, TRS, 'Deference, Defiance and Doctrine: Defining the Limits of Judicial Review' (2010) 60 *University of Toronto Law Journal* 41.

——, *Constitutional Justice: A Liberal Theory of the Rule of Law* (Oxford, Oxford University Press, 2001).

Andenas, Mads and Fairgrieve, Duncan, 'There is a World Elsewhere – Lord Bingham and Comparative Law' in Mads Andenas and Duncan Fairgrieve (eds), *Tom Bingham and the Transformation of the Law: A Liber Amicorum* (Oxford, Oxford University Press, 2009).

Aronson, Mark, Dyer, Bruce and Groves, Matthew, *Judicial Review of Administrative Action*, 3rd edn (Sydney, Law Book Co, 2004).

Basten, John, 'Book Review of *The Ultimate Rule of Law* by David M Beatty' (2005) 29 *Melbourne University Law Review* 930.

Beatson, Jack et al, *Human Rights: Judicial Protection in the United Kingdom* (London, Sweet & Maxwell, 2008).

Beatty, David M, *The Ultimate Rule of Law* (Oxford, Oxford University Press, 2004).

Benvenisti, Eyal, 'Reclaiming Democracy: The Strategic Uses of Foreign and International Law by National Courts' (2008) 102 *American Journal of International Law* 241.

——, 'United We Stand: National Courts Reviewing Counterterrorism Measures' in Andrea Bianchi and Alexis Keller (eds), *Counterterrorism: Democracy's Challenge* (Oxford, Hart Publishing, 2008).

—— and Downs, George W, 'National Courts, Domestic Democracy, and the Evolution of International Law' (2009) 20 *European Journal of International Law* 59.

Blackshield, Tony and Williams, George, *Australian Constitutional Law & Theory*, 4th edn (Sydney, Law Book Co, 2010).

Bonner, David, *Executive Measures, Terrorism and National Security: Have the Rules of the Game Changed?* (Aldershot, Ashgate, 2007).

Bosniak, Linda, *The Citizen and the Alien: Dilemmas of Contemporary Membership* (Princeton, Princeton University Press, 2006).

——, 'A Basic Territorial Distinction' (2002) 16 *Georgetown Immigration Law Journal* 407.

Boughey, Janina, 'The Use of Administrative Law to Enforce Human Rights' (2009) 17 *Australian Journal of Administrative Law* 25.

Bredt, Christopher J and Dodek, Adam M, 'The Increasing Irrelevance of Section 1 of the Charter' (2001) 14 *Supreme Court Law Review* (2d) 175.

Bryde, Brun-Otto, 'The Constitutional Judge and the International Constitutionalist Dialogue' in Sir Basil Markesinis and Jorg Fedtke (eds), *Judicial Recourse to Foreign Law: A New Source of Inspiration?* (Oxford, Routledge, 2006).

Bull, Melissa et al, 'Sickness in the System of Long-Term Immigration Detention' (2013) 26 *Journal of Refugee Studies* 47.

Campbell, David, 'The Threat of Terrorism and the Plausibility of Positivism' [2009] *PL* 501.

Cane, Peter, *Administrative Law*, 5th edn (Oxford, Oxford University Press, 2011).

——, *Administrative Tribunals and Adjudication* (Oxford, Hart Publishing, 2009).

Choudhry, Sujit and Roach, Kent, 'Racial and Ethnic Profiling: Statutory Discretion, Constitutional Remedies and Democratic Accountability' (2003) 41 *Osgoode Hall Law Journal* 1.

Clark, DJ, 'Jurisdiction and Power: Habeas Corpus and the Federal Court' (2006) 32 *Monash University Law Review* 275.

Clark, David and McCoy, Gerard, *The Most Fundamental Legal Right: Habeas Corpus in the Commonwealth* (Oxford, Clarendon Press, 2000).

Cole, David, 'Enemy Aliens' (2002) 54 *Stanford Law Review* 953.

Craig, Paul, *Administrative Law*, 7th edn (London, Sweet & Maxwell, 2012).

Crock, Mary, *Immigration and Refugee Law in Australia* (Sydney, Federation Press, 1998).

——, 'A Legal Perspective on the Evolution of Mandatory Detention' in Mary Crock (ed), *Protection or Punishment: The Detention of Asylum Seekers in Australia* (Sydney, Federation Press, 1993).

——, 'Climbing Jacob's Ladder: The High Court and the Administrative Detention of Asylum Seekers in Australia' (1993) 15 *Sydney Law Review* 338.

—— and Ghezelbash, Daniel, 'Due Process and Rule of Law as Human Rights: The High Court and the "Offshore" Processing of Asylum Seekers' (2011) 18 *Australian Journal of Administrative Law* 101.

Curtin, Juliet, '"Never Say Never": *Al-Kateb v Godwin*' (2005) 27 *Sydney Law Review* 355.

Dauvergne, Catherine, 'Security and Migration Law in the Less Brave New World' (2007) 16 *Social & Legal Studies* 533.

Dicey, AV, *The Law of the Constitution*, 8th edn (London, Macmillan, 1915).

——, *Lectures on the Relation between Law and Public Opinion in England during the Nineteenth Century*, 2nd edn (London, Macmillan, 1904).

Duffy, Maureen T and Provost, René, 'Security Detention in Practice: Constitutional Canaries and the Elusive Quest to Legitimize Security Detentions in Canada' (2009) 40 *Case Western Reserve Journal of International Law* 531.

Dunbar, David and Nesbit, Scott, 'Parliament's Response to *Charkaoui*: Bill C-3 and the Special Advocate Regime under IRPA' (2008) 42 *Supreme Court Law Review* (2d) 415.

Durkin, Mary and McMillan, John, 'External Scrutiny of Immigration Administration: The Changing Role of the Commonwealth and Immigration Ombudsman', National Administrative Law Forum, Surfers Paradise, June 2006.

Dutton, David, *Citizenship in Australia: A Guide to Commonwealth Government Records* (Canberra, National Archives of Australia, 1999).

Dyzenhaus, David, 'Cycles of Legality in Emergency Times' (2007) 18 *Public Law Review* 165.

——, *The Constitution of Law: Legality in a Time of Emergency* (Cambridge, Cambridge University Press, 2006).

——, 'Intimations of Legality Amid the Clash of Arms' (2004) 2 *International Journal of Constitutional Law* 244.

——, Hunt, Murray and Taggart, Michael, 'The Principle of Legality in Administrative Law: Internationalisation as Constitutionalisation' (2001) 1 *Oxford University Commonwealth Law Journal* 5.

Elliott, Mark, *Administrative Law: Text and Materials*, 4th edn (Oxford, Oxford University Press, 2011).

——, 'United Kingdom: The "War on Terror", UK-Style – The Detention and Deportation of Suspected Terrorists' (2010) 8 *International Journal of Constitutional Law* 131.

Ely, John Hart, *Democracy and Distrust* (Cambridge, MA, Harvard University Press, 1980).

Evans, Simon, 'The Meaning of Constitutional Terms: Essential Features, Family Resemblance and Theory Based Approaches' (2006) 29 *University of New South Wales Law Journal* 207.

Ewing, Keith, 'The Futility of the Human Rights Act: A Long Footnote' (2005) 37 *Bracton Law Journal* 41.

—— and Tham, Joo-Cheong, 'The Continuing Futility of the Human Rights Act' [2008] *PL* 668.

Feldman, David, 'Case and Comment: Proportionality and Discrimination in Anti-Terrorism Legislation' [2005] *Cambridge Law Journal* 271.

——, 'Public Law Values in the House of Lords' (1990) 106 *LQR* 246.

Finnis, John, 'Nationality, Alienage and Constitutional Principle' (2007) 123 *LQR* 417.

Forcese, Craig and Waldman, Lorne, 'A Bismarckian Moment: *Charkaoui* and Bill C-3' (2008) 42 *Supreme Court Law Review* (2d) 355.

Forsyth, Christopher, 'Showing the Fly the Way Out of the Fly Bottle: The Value of Formalism and Conceptual Reasoning in Administrative Law' (2007) 66 *Cambridge Law Journal* 325.

Foster, Michelle, 'Membership in the Australian Community: *Singh v Commonwealth* and its Consequences for Australian Citizenship Law' (2006) 34 *Federal Law Review* 161.

Gearty, Conor, 'Human Rights in an Age of Counter-Terrorism: Injurious, Irrelevant or Indispensable?' (2005) 58 *Current Legal Problems* 25.

Geiringer, Claudia, 'Sources of Resistance to Proportionality Review of Administrative Power under the New Zealand Bill of Rights Act 1990' (2013) 11 *New Zealand Journal of Public and International Law* 123.

Glass, Arthur, '*Al-Kateb* and *Behrooz*', Gilbert + Tobin Centre of Public Law 2005 Constitutional Law Conference, Sydney, 18 February 2005.

Gleeson, Murray, 'The Meaning of Legislation: Context, Purpose and Respect for Fundamental Rights' (2009) 20 *Public Law Review* 26.

——, *The Rule of Law and the Constitution: Boyer Lectures* (Sydney, ABC Books, 2000).

Glenn, HP, *Legal Traditions of the World*, 3rd edn (Oxford, Oxford University Press, 2007).

Goodman, Alex and Leslie, Justin, 'The Limits of Detention: Case Law since *Hardial Singh*' [2010] *Judicial Review* 242.

Goodman, Elissa M, 'Section 7 of the Charter and Social Interest Justification' (winner of the Department of Justice/Canadian Bar Association National Essay Contest marking the twentieth anniversary of the Charter 2002) (unpublished, on file with author).

Gross, Oren, 'Chaos and Rules: Should Responses to Violent Crises Always be Constitutional?' (2003) 112 *Yale Law Journal* 1011.

Groves, Matthew, 'Chapter 14 – Habeas Corpus' in Mark Aronson, Bruce Dyer and Matthew Groves (eds), *Judicial Review of Administrative Action*, 3rd edn (Sydney, Law Book Co, 2004).

Hampshire, James, 'Disembedding Liberalism? Immigration Policies and Security' in Terri E Givens, Gary P Freeman and David L Neal (eds), *Immigration Policy and Security* (New York, Routledge, 2009).

Hancock, Moffatt, 'Discharge of Deportees on Habeas Corpus' (1936) 14 *Canadian Bar Review* 116.

Harlow, Carol, 'The Political Constitution Reworked' in Rick Bigwood (ed), *Public Interest Litigation* (Wellington, LexisNexis NZ, 2006).

Harris, Max, 'Public Law Values in the House of Lords – In an Age of Counter-Terrorism' (2011) 17 *Auckland University Law Review* 119.

Henkels, Caroline, 'Mandatory Detention of Asylum Seekers in Australia: Would a Bill of Rights Make a Difference?' (2006) 4 *Human Rights Research Journal* 1.

Hickman, Tom, *Public Law after the Human Rights Act* (Oxford, Hart Publishing, 2010).

——,'Between Human Rights and the Rule of Law: Indefinite Detention and the Derogation Model of Constitutionalism' (2005) 68 *MLR* 655.

——,'Constitutional Dialogue, Constitutional Theories and the Human Rights Act 1998' [2005] *PL* 306.

Hogg, PW, *Constitutional Law of Canada*, looseleaf, vol 2 (Scarborough, ON, Carswell, 2000).

Hudson, Graham, 'Whither International Law? Security Certificates, the Supreme Court and the Rights of Non-Citizens in Canada' (2009) 26 *Refuge* 172.

Hunt, Murray, 'Sovereignty's Blight: Why Contemporary Public Law Needs the Concept of "Due Deference"' in Nicholas Bamforth and Peter Leyland (eds), *Public Law in a Multi-Layered Constitution* (Oxford, Hart Publishing, 2003).

——, *Using Human Rights Law in English Courts* (Oxford, Hart Publishing, 1997).

Ip, John, 'The Rise and Spread of the Special Advocate' [2008] *PL* 717.

Irvine of Lairg, Lord, 'The Development of Human Rights in Britain under an Incorporated Convention on Human Rights', Tom Sargant Memorial Lecture, Law Society Hall, London, December 1997.

Jackson, Vicki C, *Constitutional Engagement in a Transnational Era* (New York, Oxford University Press, 2010).

——and Greene, Jamal, 'Constitutional Interpretation in Comparative Perspective: Comparing Judges or Courts?' in Tom Ginsburg and Rosalind Dixon (eds), *Comparative Constitutional Law* (Cheltenham, Edward Elgar, 2011).

Jenkins, David, 'There and Back Again: The Strange Journey of Special Advocates and Comparative Law Methodology' (2011) 42 *Columbia Human Rights Law Review* 279.

Johns, Fleur, 'Human Rights in the High Court of Australia, 1976–2003: The Righting of Australian Law' (2005) 33 *Federal Law Review* 287.

Jowell, Jeffrey, 'Judicial Deference: Servility, Civility or Institutional Capacity?' [2003] *PL* 592.

Katyal, Neal, 'Equality in the War on Terror' (2007) 59 *Stanford Law Review* 1365.

Kelley, Ninette, 'Rights in the Balance: Non-Citizens and State Sovereignty under the Charter' in David Dyzenhaus (ed), *The Unity of Public Law* (Oxford, Hart Publishing, 2004).

Kiefel, Susan, 'Proportionality: A Rule of Reason' (2012) 23 *Public Law Review* 85.

Kirk, Jeremy, 'Constitutional Guarantees, Characterisation and the Concept of Proportionality' (1997) 21 *Melbourne University Law Review* 1.

Knop, Karen, 'Citizenship, Public & Private' (2008) 71 *Law & Contemporary Problems* 309.

La Forest, GV, *Disallowance and Reservation of Provincial Legislation* (Ottawa, Department of Justice, 1955).

Larsen, Mike, Harkat, Sophie and Harkat, Mohamed, 'Justice in Tiers: Security Certificate Detention in Canada' (2008) 17(2) *Journal of Prisoners on Prisons* 31.

Leckey, Robert, *Contextual Subjects: Family, State and Relational Theory* (Toronto, University of Toronto Press, 2008).

Lester, A and Pannick, D (eds), *Human Rights Law and Practice* (London, Butterworths, 1999).

Lindell, Geoffrey, 'Reflections on the Tampa Affair' (2002) 4(2) *Constitutional Law and Policy Review* 21.

McConnell, WH, *Commentary on the British North America Act* (Toronto, Macmillan of Canada, 1977).

McDonald, Stephen, 'Involuntary Detention and the Separation of Judicial Power' (2007) 35 *Federal Law Review* 25.

MacDonald QC, Ian A and Toal, Ronan, *MacDonald's Immigration Law & Practice*, 7th edn (London, LexisNexis, 2008).

McHugh, Hon Michael H, 'A Human Rights Act, the Courts and the Constitution' (2009) 11 *Constitutional Law and Policy Review* 86.

——,'The Strengths of the Weakest Arm', Australian Bar Association Conference, Florence, 2 July 2004.

——,'Tensions between the Executive and Judiciary' (2002) 76 *Australian Law Journal* 567.

McLachlan, Campbell, 'The Evolution of Treaty Obligations in International Law' in Georg Nolte (ed), *Treaties and Subsequent Practice* (Oxford, Oxford University Press, 2013).

——,'The Allocative Function of Foreign Relations Law' (2012) 82 *British Yearbook of International Law* 349.

McMillan, John, 'Judicial Restraint and Activism in Administrative Law' (2002) 30 *Federal Law Review* 335.

Macklin, Audrey, 'Transjudicial Conversations about Security and Human Rights' in Mark Salter (ed), *Mapping Transatlantic Security Relations: The EU, Canada and the War on Terror* (London, Routledge, 2010).

——,'Mr Suresh and the Evil Twin' (2002) 20(4) *Refuge* 15.

Maitland, FW, *The Constitutional History of England* (Cambridge, Cambridge University Press, 1919).

Marr, David and Wilkinson, Marian, *Dark Victory* (Sydney, Allen & Unwin, 2003).

Martinez, Jenny S, 'Process and Substance in the "War on Terror"' (2008) 108 *Columbia Law Review* 1013.

Masterman, Roger, *The Separation of Powers in the Contemporary Constitution: Judicial Competence and Independence in the United Kingdom* (Cambridge, Cambridge University Press, 2011).

Meagher, Dan, 'The Common Law Principle of Legality in the Age of Rights' (2011) 35 *Melbourne University Law Review* 449.

——,'The Significance of *Al-Kateb v Godwin* for the Australian Bill of Rights Debate' (2010) *Constitutional Law and Policy Review* 15.

Mole, Nuala, *Asylum and the European Convention on Human Rights*, 4th edn (Strasbourg, Council of Europe Publishers, 2007).

Moran, Mayo, 'Authority, Influence and Persuasion: *Baker*, Charter Values and the Puzzle of Method' in David Dyzenhaus (ed), *The Unity of Public Law* (Oxford, Hart Publishing, 2004).

Mullan, David, 'Deference from *Baker* to *Suresh* and Beyond: Interpreting the Conflicting Signals' in David Dyzenhaus (ed), *The Unity of Public Law* (Oxford, Hart Publishing, 2004).

Nash, Kate, *The Cultural Politics of Human Rights: Comparing the US and UK* (Cambridge, Cambridge University Press, 2009).

Nazfiger, James AR, 'The General Admission of Aliens under International Law' (1983) 77 *American Journal of International Law* 804.

Neuman, Gerald, *Strangers to the Constitution* (Princeton, Princeton University Press, 1996).

Phillips, Janet and Spinks, Harriet, *Immigration Detention in Australia*, Parliamentary Library Background Note, updated 20 March 2013.

Plender, Robert, *International Migration Law*, 2nd edn (Dordrecht, Martinus Nijhoff, 1988).

Rankin, Murray, 'The Security Intelligence Review Committee: Reconciling National Security with Procedural Fairness' (1989–90) 3 *Canadian Journal of Administrative Law and Policy* 173.

Réaume, Denise, 'The Relevance of Relevance to Equality Rights' (2006) 31 *Queen's Law Journal* 696.

Roach, Kent, 'When Secret Intelligence becomes Evidence: Some Implications of *Khadr* and *Charkaoui II*' (2009) 47 *Supreme Court Law Review* (2d) 147.

——, '*Charkaoui* and Bill C-3: Some Implications for Anti-Terrorism Policy and Dialogue between Courts and Legislatures' (2008) 42 *Supreme Court Law Review* (2d) 281.

——, 'Constitutional, Remedial, and International Dialogues about Rights: The Canadian Experience' (2005) 40 *Texas International Law Journal* 537.

——, 'Did September 11 Change Everything? Struggling to Preserve Canadian Values in the Face of Terrorism' (2002) 47 *McGill Law Journal* 893.

Rolls, Alice, 'Avoiding Tragedy: Would the Decision of the High Court in *Al-Kateb* have been Any Different if Australia had a Bill of Rights like Victoria?' (2007) 18 *Public Law Review* 119.

Rose, Dennis, 'The High Court Decision in *Al-Kateb* and *Al Khafaji*: A Different Perspective' (2005) 8(3) *Constitutional Law and Policy Review* 58.

Rubenstein, Kim, *Australian Citizenship Law in Context* (Sydney, Law Book Co, 2002).

——, 'Citizenship and the Centenary: Inclusion and Exclusion in 20th Century Australia' (2000) 24 *Melbourne University Law Review* 576.

——, 'Citizenship and the Constitutional Convention Debates: A Mere Legal Inference' (1997) 25 *Federal Law Review* 295.

Runciman, David, 'The Precautionary Principle: Tony Blair and the Language of Risk' (2004) 26(7) *London Review of Books* 12.

Saul, Ben, 'Dark Justice: Australia's Indefinite Detention of Refugees on Security Grounds under International Human Rights Law' (2012) 13 *Melbourne Journal of International Law* 685.

——, 'Australian Administrative Law: The Human Rights Dimension' in Mathew Groves and HP Lee (eds), *Australian Administrative Law: Fundamentals, Principles and Doctrines* (Melbourne, Cambridge University Press, 2007).

Saunders, Cheryl, 'Constitution as Catalyst: Different Paths within Australasian Administrative Law' (2012) 10 *New Zealand Journal of Public and International Law* 143.

Selway, Bradley, 'The Rise and Rise of the Reasonable Proportionality Test in Public Law' (1996) 7 *Public Law Review* 212.

Sharpe, RJ, *The Law of Habeas Corpus*, 2nd edn (Oxford, Clarendon Press, 1989).

—— et al, *The Law of Habeas Corpus*, 3rd edn (Oxford, Oxford University Press, 2011).

Steyn, Lord, '2000–2005: Laying the Foundations of Human Rights Law in the United Kingdom' (2005) 4 *European Human Rights Law Review* 349.

Stubbs, Matthew T, 'Arbitrary Detention in Australia: Detention of Unlawful Non-Citizens under the Migration Act 1958 (Cth)' (2006) 25 *Australian Year Book of International Law* 273.

Sunstein, Cass, 'Minimalism at War' [2004] *Supreme Court Review* 47.

——, 'Beyond the Precautionary Principle' (2003) 151 *University of Pennsylvania Law Review* 1003.

——, *One Case at a Time: Judicial Minimalism on the Supreme Court* (Cambridge, MA, Harvard University Press, 1999).

Tavan, Gwenda, *The Long, Slow Death of White Australia* (Melbourne, Scribe Publications, 2005).

Taylor, Savitri, 'Sovereign Power at the Border' (2005) 16 *Public Law Review* 55.

Thomas, Robert, 'Risk, Legitimacy and Asylum Adjudication' (2007) 58 *Northern Ireland Legal Quarterly* 49.

Thwaites, Rayner, 'The Security of Citizenship? Finnis in the Context of the United Kingdom's Citizenship Stripping Provisions' in Fiona Jenkins et al, *Allegiance and Identity in a Globalised World* (Cambridge, Cambridge University Press, forthcoming 2014).

——, 'Process and Substance: *Charkaoui I* in the Light of Subsequent Development[s]' (2011) 62 *University of New Brunswick Law Journal* 13.

——, 'A Coordinated Judicial Response to Counterterrorism? Counter-Examples' in Mark B Salter (ed), *Mapping Transatlantic Security Relations: The EU, Canada, and the War on Terror* (Abingdon, Routledge, 2010).

——, 'Discriminating against Non-Citizens under the Charter: *Charkaoui* and Section 15' (2009) 34 *Queen's Law Journal* 669.

——, 'Deportation on National Security Grounds' (LLM thesis, University of Toronto, 2004).

Tilmouth, Sydney, 'Citizenship as a Constitutional Concept: *Singh v Commonwealth of Australia* and *Rasul v Bush, President of the United States*' (2005) 26 *Australian Bar Review* 192.

Tomkins, Adam, 'National Security and the Role of the Court: A Changed Landscape?' (2010) 126 *LQR* 543.

——, 'The Rule of Law in Blair's Britain' (2007) 26 *University of Queensland Law Journal* 255.

——, 'Readings *of A v Secretary of State for the Home Department*' [2005] *PL* 259.

Tooze, Jennifer, 'Deportation with Assurances: The Approach of the UK Courts' [2010] *PL* 362.

Tushnet, Mark, 'Defending Korematsu? Reflections on Civil Liberties in Wartime' in Mark Tushnet (ed), *The Constitution in Wartime: Beyond Alarmism or Complacency* (Durham, NC, Duke University Press, 2005).

Van Harten, Gus, '*Charkaoui* and Secret Evidence' (2008) 42 *Supreme Court Law Review* (2d) 251.

Vincenzi, Christopher, 'Aliens and the Judicial Review of Immigration Law' [1985] *PL* 93.

Waldron, Jeremy, 'Torture and Positive Law: Jurisprudence for the White House' (2005) 105 *Columbia Law Review* 1681.

——, 'Security and Liberty: The Image of Balance' (2003) 11 *Journal of Political Philosophy* 191.

Walker, Clive, *Terrorism and the Law* (Oxford, Oxford University Press, 2011).

——, 'The Threat of Terrorism and the Fate of Control Orders' [2010] *PL* 4.

——, 'Keeping Control of Terrorists without Losing Control of Constitutionalism' (2007) 59 *Stanford Law Review* 1395.

Walker, Clive, 'The Treatment of Foreign Terror Suspects' (2007) 70 *MLR* 427.
——,'Prisoners of "War all the Time"' [2005] *European Human Rights Law Review* 50.
—— and Horne, Alexander, 'The Terrorism Prevention and Investigations Measures Act 2011: One Thing but Not Much the Other? [2012] *Criminal Law Review* 421.
Warbrick, Colin, 'The European Response to Terrorism in an Age of Human Rights' (2004) 15 *European Journal of International Law* 989.
Weisselberg, Charles D, 'The Exclusion and Detention of Aliens: Lessons from the Lives of Ellen Knauff and Ignatz Mezei' (1995) 143 *University of Pennsylvania Law Review* 933.
Williams, Melissa S, 'Nonterritorial Boundaries of Citizenship' in Seyla Benhabib, Ian Shapiro and Danilo Petranovic (eds), *Identities, Affiliations and Allegiances* (Cambridge, Cambridge University Press, 2007).
Willis, John, 'Statute Interpretation in a Nutshell' (1938) 16 *Canadian Bar Review* 1.
Wilsher, Daniel, *Immigration Detention: Law, History, Politics* (Cambridge, Cambridge University Press, 2012).
Winterton, George, 'The Communist Party Case' in HP Lee and George Winterton (eds), *Australian Constitutional Landmarks* (Cambridge, Cambridge University Press, 2003).
Woolf, Lord, 'Human Rights: Have the Public Benefited?', British Academy, Thanks-Offering to Britain Fund Lecture, 15 October 2002.
Wydrzynski, Christopher J, *Canadian Immigration Law and Procedure* (Aurora, ON, Canada Law Book, 1983).
Zagor, Matthew, 'Judicial Rhetoric and Constitutional Identity: Comparative Approaches to Aliens' Rights in the United Kingdom and Australia' (2008) 19 *Public Law Review* 271.
——,'Uncertainty and Exclusion: Detention of Aliens and the High Court' (2006) 34 *Federal Law Review* 127.
Zedner, Lucia, 'Preventive Justice or Pre-Punishment? The Case of Control Orders' (2007) 60 *Current Legal Problems* 174.
Zines, Leslie, *The High Court and the Constitution*, 5th edn (Sydney, Federation Press, 2008).

Official Publications

Anderson, David, *Terrorism Prevention and Investigation Measures in 2012: First Report of the Independent Reviewer on the Operation of the Terrorism Prevention and Investigation Measures Act* (London, The Stationery Office, 2013).
——, *Control Orders in 2011: Final Report of the Independent Reviewer on the Prevention of Terrorism Act 2005* (London, The Stationery Office, 2012).
Carlile, Lord, *Sixth Report of the Independent Reviewer Pursuant to Section 14(3) of the Prevention of Terrorism Act 2005*, 3 February 2011 (London, Stationery Office, 2011).
——, *Third Report of the Independent Reviewer Pursuant to Section 14(3) of the Prevention of Terrorism Act 2005*, 18 February 2008 (London, Stationery Office, 2008).
Comrie, Neil, *Inquiry into the Circumstances of the Vivian Alvarez Matter*, Report No 03/2005 (Canberra, Commonwealth Ombudsman, September 2005).
Conservatives, *Resilient Nation: National Security Green Paper* (Policy Green Paper No 13, 2009).
Home Office, *Review of Counter Terrorism and Security Powers* (Cm 8004, 2011).
——,'Tackling Terrorism – Behaviours Unacceptable in the UK', Press Release 124/2005, 24 August 2005.
——, *Counter-Terrorism Powers: Reconciling Security and Liberty in an Open Society* (Cm 6147, 2004).

House of Commons, *Statement of the Changes in Immigration Rules* (HC 251 1990).
Liberal Democrat Party Manifesto (2010).
Joint Committee on Human Rights, *Counter-Terrorism Policy and Human Rights (Sixteenth Report): Annual Renewal of Control Orders Legislation 2010* (2010–12, HL 64, HC 395).
——, *Counter-Terrorism Policy and Human Rights (Fourteenth Report): Annual Renewal of Control Orders Legislation 2009* (2008–09, HL 37, HC 282).
——, *Counter-Terrorism Policy and Human Rights (Ninth Report): Annual Renewal of Control Orders Legislation 2008* (2007–08, HL 57, HC 356)
——, *Counter-Terrorism Policy and Human Rights: Draft Prevention of Terrorism Act 2005 (Continuance in force of sections 1 to 9) Order 2006, Twelfth Report of Session 2005–06* (2005–06, HL 122, HC 915).
——, *Anti-Terrorism, Crime and Security Act 2001: Statutory Review and Continuance of Part 4 (Sixth Report)* (2003–04, HL 38, HC 381).
McMillan, John, *Lessons for Public Administration: Ombudsman Investigation of Referred Immigration Cases* (Canberra, Commonwealth Ombudsman, August 2007).
Ministry of Justice, *Responding to Human Rights Judgments: Report to the Joint Committee on Human Rights on the Government Response to Human Rights Judgments 2011–2012* (Cm 8432, 2012).
National Human Rights Consultation Committee, *Report on the Consultation into Human Rights in Australia* (September 2009).
Palmer, Mick, *Inquiry into the Circumstances of the Immigration Detention of Cornelia Rau: Report* (Commonwealth of Australia, July 2005).
Parliament of Australia, *Immigration Detention in Australia* (Parliamentary Library Background Note, updated 20 March 2013).
Privy Counsellor Review Committee, *Anti-Terrorism, Crime and Security Act 2001 Review: Report* (HC 2003–04, 100-I).
Revised Explanatory Memorandum to the Migration Legislation Amendment (Judicial Review) Bill 2001 (Cth).
Special Immigration Appeals Commission (Procedure) Rules 2003, SI 2003/1034 (SIACR 2003).
UN Working Group on Arbitrary Detention, Report of Working Group on Arbitrary Detention, Visit to Canada, E/CN.4/2006/7/Add.25 (December 2005).

UK Parliamentary Debates

Betts MP, Clive, HC Deb 23 February 2005, vol 431 col 352
Blunt MP, Crispin, HC Deb 28 February 2005, vol 431 cols 749–50
——, HC Deb 23 February 2005, vol 431 col 353
Brake MP, Tom, HC Deb 7 June 2011, vol 526 col 88
Campbell, Sir Menzies, HC Deb 28 February 2005, vol 431 col 653
Clarke MP, Charles, HC Deb 23 February 2005, vol 431 cols 345–7
Clarke MP, Kenneth, HC Deb 28 February 2005, vol 431 col 726
Cook, Robin, HC Deb 28 February 2005, vol 431 col 715
——, HC Deb 23 February 2005, vol 431 col 338
Davis MP, David, HC Deb 23 February 2005, vol 431 cols 364–65
Dismore MP, Andrew, HC Deb 3 Mar 2009, vol 488 col 758
Dobson MP, Frank, HC Deb 23 February 2005, vol 431 col 389
Fuller MP, Richard, HC Deb 7 June 2011, vol 529 cols 109 and 122
Johnson MP, Boris, HC Deb 23 February 2005, vol 431 cols 386–90

Grieves MP, Dominic, HC Deb 21 Feb 2008, vol 472 col 567
Greenway MP, John, Special Immigration Appeals Commission Bill Deb (11 November 1997)
Hogg MP, Douglas, HC Deb 23 February 2005, vol 431 col 386
——, HC Deb 3 March 2009, vol 488 col 755
Huhne MP, Chris, HC Deb 3 Mar 2009, vol 488 col 752
McDonnell MP, John, HC Deb 15 February 2006, vol 442 col 1518
Marshall-Andrews, Robert, HC Deb 23 February 2005, vol 431 cols 415–16
Mercer MP, Patrick, HC Deb 7 June 2011, vol 529 col 98
O'Brien, Mike, Parliamentary Under-Secretary of State for the Home Department, on the Third Reading of the Special Immigration Appeals Commission Bill, HC Deb 26 November 1997, vol 301 col 1033
Pound MP, Stephen, HC Deb 5 September 2011, vol 532 col 112
Raab MP, Dominic, HC Deb 7 June 2011, vol 529 col 111
Williams of Mostyn, Lord HL Deb 5 June 1997, vol 580 col 752

Other Media

'Bill of Rights: One Way to Defeat Indefinite Detention' (Greens Media Release, 6 August 2004).
Bibby, Paul et al, 'Deported Refugee Shot Dead' *Sydney Morning Herald* (Sydney, 2 August 2008).
Chung, Andrew, 'Charkaoui to be Freed' *Toronto Star* (Toronto, 24 September 2009).
Colman, Elizabeth and Lewis, Steve, 'PM Eases Stance on Detainees' *The Australian* (Sydney, 23 March 2005).
Dodson, Louise, 'Set them Free: PM's Big Shift on Boat People' *Sydney Morning Herald* (Sydney, 23 March 2005).
Georgiou, Petro, 'Protection should be Paramount' *The Age* (Melbourne, 31 July 2008).
Howard, John, 'Election Policy Speech' (City Recital Hall, Sydney, 28 October 2001).
Marr, David, 'Escape from a Life in Limbo' *Sydney Morning Herald* (Sydney, 27 October 2007).
Perreaux, Les and Freeze, Colin, 'Al Qaeda Suspect Freed, Ottawa's Terror Law Shattered', *Globe and Mail* (Toronto, 24 September 2009).
Shaw, Meaghan, 'Ban indefinite detention: Lawrence' *The Age* (Melbourne, 12 August 2004).

INDEX

A v UK (ECtHR):
analysis, 186–93, 204–5
article 5(1), 188–92
fair balance, 190–1
findings on the facts, 191–2
scope of immigration detention, 188–90
article 5(4), 204–5
assessment, 192–3
comparative context, 289, 295
confirming House of Lords decision, 148–9
damages, 192
facts and background, 186–8
Finnis theory and, 21, 180, 186
new government argument, 21, 186
subsidiarity, 187
Aleinikoff, Alexander, 12, 302, 306
Al-Kateb (Australia):
Al Masri and, 38, 56, 64, 66, 98
aliens power, 72–6, 86–7
analysis, 65–119
assessment, 95–8
common law rights, 45, 68–71, 78–81
comparative context, 77–8, 97, 289
constructional choice, 38
effect, 95–8
facts and context, 65–6
indefinite detention of aliens, 37, 65–119
justification, 296-9
international law and, 87–91, 292–5
Lim and, 54, 56, 72–6, 79–80, 82–4, 95–6,114
majority judgments, 10, 37, 66–78
comparative law, 77–8, 97–8, 303
constitutionality of indefinite detention, 71–8
de facto citizenship, 76–7, 302
interpretation of detention legislation, 67–71
separation of powers, 72–6, 96
WWII analogy, 77, 90–1
minority judgments, 66, 78–87
community: concept, 86–7
constitutional fact doctrine, 82–5
Gleeson CJ, 78–81
Gummow and Kirby JJ, 82–7
principle of legality, 79, 81, 90, 111–13
Offshore Processing and, 103, 107, 119
Plaintiff M47 case and, 109–17
release conditions, 81
rights-precluding approach, 10–11, 96
segregation from community, 74–8, 85–6, 114–15, 296–8
separation of powers, 66, 72–6, 82–5, 95–6
status, 99, 111, 119
Al Masri (Australia):
Al-Kateb and, 38, 56, 64, 66, 98
analysis, 55–64
assessment, 63–4
common law presumptions, 59–61
comparative approach, 58, 61, 63
confidentiality claims, 57–8
constitutionality presumption, 59–60
facts and context, 55–7
first instance judgment, 57–8
Full Court judgment, 59–63
implied time limits, 58, 61–2
international obligations, 62–3, 64
rights-protecting model, 56
suspension of detention, 58, 76
aliens
see also specific countries
enemy aliens, 25
equality before the law and, 11, 12–14
importance of membership, 301–4
indefinite detention *see* indefinite detention of aliens
integrating rights and immigration control, 305–6
nationality-differentiated risk-acceptability, 20–8
significance of non-citizenship, 12
threat from, 300–1
vulnerability to removal, 13, 24-8
Allan, TRS, 14, 180n176
Almrei's release, 280–2, 290
Australia:
administrative detention
common law and, 44–6
exception to constitutional immunity, 31, 43, 50–4, 72–6, 83–5, 95–7
aliens power
Al-Kateb, 72–6, 85–7
immigration power and, 40–2, 86–7
Lim, 49
meaning, 40
bridging visas, 100–1, 304
citizenship
Constitution and, 40–1
de facto citizenship, 76–7

Australia (*cont*):
citizenship (*cont*):
legislation, 41
common law presumption of liberty, 44–6, 60–64, 68–71, 78–81, 111–3, 292–3
Communist Party case, 82–5
community: concept, 42, 86–7
Constitution
see also specific cases
citizenship and, 40–1
constitutionality presumption, 59–60
federal legislative powers and, 39–43, 63–4
indefinite detention of aliens and, 37, 71–8, 82–5, 95–6, 111–17
no Bill of Rights, 29, 31, 38, 39, 87–91
separation of powers, 43, 46, 48–54, 64, 66, 72–6, 82–5, 95–6, 114
detention conditions: *Behrooz & SBEG*, 91–5
statutory authority: need for, 39
federal legislative powers
aliens power, 40–2, 72–6, 85–7
overview, 39–44
immigration power, 40–2, 86–7
habeas corpus, 44–5
immigration detention
damages, 48, 92–5
exception to constitutional immunity, 31, 43, 50–4, 72–6, 83–5, 95–7
legislation, 47–8, 55, 56–7, 67
Lim, 46–55
time limits, 48, 52
turn-around provision, 47
Immigration Ombudsman, 101–3, 119
immigration power
aliens power and, 40–2, 86–7
indefinite detention of aliens
administrative oversight, 101–3, 118–19
Al-Kateb see *Al-Kateb*
Al Masri, 55–64
ASIO security clearance and, 109–18
ASIO security clearance & procedure, 106, 108, 117–18
detention conditions, 91–5
international law and, 87–91, 108, 162, 292–3
mental health, 102–3
Offshore Processing, see *Offshore Processing*
outcomes, 304
Plaintiff M47 see *Plaintiff M47*
survey, 65–119
WWII, 77, 90–1
legal context, 31, 39–46
migration zone, 104
non-refoulement obligations, 110
offshore processing, 103–5
presumptions *see* common law presumptions *and* principle of legality
principle of legality, 45–6, 59–64, 68–71, 78–81, 111–3, 292–3
proportionality analysis, 14, 51–2, 54–5, 75–6, 80–1, 116, 299
right to liberty
see also common law presumptions
Al-Kateb, 71, 74, 77, 79, 96–7, 119
Al Masri, 59, 60–1
Offshore Processing case, 106
security: ASIO Act, 109–10, 115–6, 117
statutory interpretation: fundamental rights *see* common law presumptions
Tampa incident, 103–4

Belmarsh litigation (UK):
assessment, 182–4, 214
certification proceedings, 163, 166, 220
Chahal and, 134, 154, 157, 192–3, 293
Charkaoui (Canada) and, 255, 260, 266–7, 268–9, 270, 273, 288, 290–1
Court of Appeal judgments
aliens in time of public emergency, 161–2
analysis, 156–63
assessment, 162–3
Brooke LJ, 161–2, 176–7, 179, 294
deference, 156, 160
discrimination, 156–61
international law, 156, 161–2, 176–7, 179
Woolf CJ, 156–61, 182–3
derogation from ECHR, 143, 146–8, 155, 164–6
ECtHR case *(A v UK) see A v UK* (ECtHR)
extension of detention to citizens and, 180–1, 210
facts and context, 145–9
Finnis on, 21, 27–8, 180–1, 186, 189, 301, 305
Hardial Singh and, 153, 156–7
House of Lords judgments
analysis, 164–81
assessment, 182–4
declaration of incompatibility, 179–81
deference, 124–5, 167–71, 184, 306
deportation as solution, 213
discrimination, 17, 125, 173–9,182–4, 294
existence of public emergency, 164–5
immigration powers: choice of, 173–6
international law, 176–9, 293–5
no case-by-case analysis, 166–7, 260
proportionality *see* standard of review
standard of review, 165–6, 171–3, 182, 294
legislative response to, 181, 193–5
see also control orders (UK); TPIMs (UK)
measures at issue, 145–7
Rehman and, 140, 141, 142, 151, 168, 281, 290–1
rights-protecting model and, 17, 30, 301, 307
SIAC appeal
analysis, 149–55

assessment, 154–5
deference, 155
derogation from ECHR, 149–50, 155
discrimination, 149, 151–2, 153–5, 157, 159
fair balance argument, 152–3, 190
proportionality, 149–53, 172
rational connection, 149–50, 170
'strictly required', 150–1, 155, 157, 173
Benvenisti, Eyal, 241, 288–92, 295–6

Canada:
aliens
Charter s 15 and, 228–30
discrimination, 253–5, 262–3
Bill C-3, 274–5
Bill of Rights (1960), 233–4
Charter of Rights
see also specific cases
citizenship rights, 226–7, 229
s 1 (limitations clause), 32, 227, 230–2
s 7 (life, liberty and security), 32, 230–7, 240–3, 255–9
s 7 and s 1, 230–2
s 7 and s 12, 261–2
s 9 (arbitrary detention), 252, 253
s 12 (cruel and unusual treatment), 252–4
s12 and s15, 266–7
s 15 (equality), 227–30, 253, 262–3
s 33 (notwithstanding clause), 227, 242
citizenship
Charter, 226–7, 229
Chiarelli principle, 235–6
Constitution, 32
citizenship, 226–7
danger opinions, *see under* security certificates (Canada)
detention pending deportation on security grounds
see security certificates (Canada)
indefinite detention of aliens
authorised by statute?, 266–7
international law and, 295–6
substantive limits on, 259–63
internal balancing approach, 230–2, 237, 240–2, 256–7
review of detention *see* security certificates (Canada),
reasonableness review
right to liberty *see* Charter of Rights, s 7
rights-protecting model, 30
security certificates *see* security certificates (Canada)
SIRC, 235
Chahal on, 258
procedures, 236, 257–8
two-step approach, 231–2
Carlile, Lord, 208–9
Chahal v UK (ECtHR):
analysis, 128–35
Belmarsh and, 134, 154, 157, 192–3, 293
'Canadian technique,' 132, 135, 258
Commission decision, 129, 132–3
control order jurisprudence and, 203
detention limits, 130, 132–5
facts, 128–9
lack of effective remedy (ECHR Art 13), 131–2, 135
procedural requirements (ECHR Art 5(4)), 134–5
prohibition on deportation to torture, 130–2, 268, 295
SIAC creation in response to, 135–7
Charkaoui I (Canada):
analysis, 251–70
appellants, 251
assessment, 271–4
Charter rights and, 227
s 7, 252–3, 255–9, 261, 307
s 7 and s 12, 261–2
s 9, 252, 253
s 12, 252–4
s 12 and s15, 266–7
s 15, 253, 262–3
comparative authorities
Belmarsh, 255, 260, 266–7, 268, 270, 273–4, 288, 290–1
failure to engage with, 273–4
Hardial Singh (UK), 264–6, 273–4
judicial use of, 263–7
submissions, 253, 254
Zadvydas, 264–6, 273–4
deportation to torture and *Suresh* exception, 268–70, 272–3
discrimination *see* equality
equality before the law and, *see also* Charter rights, s 15
submissions, 253–5
discrimination claim, 262–3
facts and background, 251–3
indefinite detention
justification, 298–9
periods of detention, 249
substantive limits on, 259–63
international law and, 255, 273, 295
legislative response, 238, 258, 274–5
missing proportionality analysis, 270
Oakes test, 227, 232, 257
parties' submissions, 253–5
comparative authorities, 253, 254
discrimination, 253–5
international law, 255, 273
principled minimalism as explanation for, 271–2, 282
release on conditions, 249–50, 252, 275
rights-protecting model, 30, 299

Charkaoui's release, 279–80
Charkaoui II, (Canada), 276–9, 282
Chiarelli (Canada):
  Charter s 6(1), 227, 229
  Charter s 7, 234–7, 257
  Charter s 15, 229
  Chiarelli principle, 235–6, 244
  facts and background, 234–5
  fair hearing, 236–7
citizenship
  see also specific countries and cases
  constitutional positivism and, 19
  exclusion as constitutive of, 302
  membership and, 301–4
  nationality-differentiated risk-acceptability, 20–8, 301–6
Commonwealth:
  choice of jurisdictions, 28–30
  divergent responses, 4, 15–20, 30, 288–96
  shared legal tradition, 28–33
  shared principles, 12–15
  structural differences, 30–3
comparative authority, approach to:
  A v UK (ECtHR), 289, 295
  Al-Kateb (Australia), 77–8, 97, 289
  Al Masri (Australia), 58, 61, 63
  Charkaoui (Canada), 253–5, 260, 263–7, 268, 270, 273–4, 288, 290–1
  overview, 288–91
constitutional positivism, 18–19, 69n17, 90
control orders (UK)
  see also TPIMs (UK)
  A v UK and, 188, 204–7
  AF (No 3), 205–7, 213
  AP case, 201
  bail conditions, 163
  bail from immigration detention as alternative, 213–4
  case law, 196–207
  curfew length, 199–201
  definition, 193
  derogating control orders, 194
  disclosure requirements, 202–7, 278–9
  duration, 195, 198–9
  effect on controlee, 196–9
  family life and, 197–9, 201
  JJ case, 199–201
  legislative response to *Belmarsh,* 193–5
  MB case, 202–4, 205, 207, 213, 289
  mental health impact, 197–9
  non-discrimination and, 210–11, 214, 254–5
  non-nationals: declining usage against, 211
  operation, 194–5
  parliamentary debate, 181, 196–9, 211
  procedural fairness, 202–7
  punishment for breach, 198
  relocation, 198, 201
  renewal debates, 196–9
  repeal, 194
  special advocates, 202–5

deference *see* judicial deference
Dicey, AV, 24, 28, 112, 181
Dyzenhaus, David, 17–19

equality before the law
  see also specific cases and countries
  nationality-differentiated risk-acceptability compared, 20–8
  political protection and, 210
  non-citizens' vulnerability to removal and, 12–5, 305–7
European Convention on Human Rights:
  deportation exception to liberty (Art 5(1)(f)) 125, 132, 133–4, 156–7, 160–1, 188–93
  derogations (overview) (Art 15), 142–4, 148
    A v UK, 186–7
    Belmarsh, 147–9, 154–60, 164–73
    control orders (UK) and, 194
    standard of review under, 143–4, 149–50, 157, 159–60, 171–3
    United Kingdom and, 146–8, 186
  liberty (Art 5), 63, 123, 125, 132, 194
  margin of appreciation, 170
  non-discrimination (Art 14), 151–5, 157–61, 173–6
  review of detention (Art 5(4)), 134–5, 186, 192, 204–5
  torture, absolute prohibition on deportation to (Art 3), 130–2, 134, 140, 146, 160–1, 191–3, 212, 268
  UK Human Rights Act and, 31–2, 137–8
European Court of Human Rights:
  A v UK see A v UK
  Chahal see Chahal
  HRA, 'must take into account', 31, 137

Finnis, John, 3, 12, 20–8, 115, 180, 186, 189, 265, 266, 300–5

Geneva Conventions, 177
Gleeson, Murray (extrajudicial), 18

Hardial Singh (UK):
  analysis, 126–8
  Belmarsh and, 156–7, 162
  Chahal and, 153, 157
  Charkaoui and, 264, 265, 273, 274
  comparative authority, 58, 61, 289
  development of principles from, 215–18
  facts, 127
  principles, 126–8, 133, 162, 215–8, 255
Hickman, Tom, 142–3, 241–2
Hunt, Murray, 141, 169 n115, 305

immigration detention
see also specific countries
indefinite detention see indefinite detention of aliens
models see rights-precluding model; rights-protecting model
indefinite detention of aliens
see also specific countries and cases
deference to executive see judicial deference
international law and, 291–6
judicial divergences, 4, 15–20, 30, 288–96
perception of threat and, 300–1
proportionality, 11, 13–14, 299
purposes of detention, 296–9
rights-precluding model see rights-precluding model
rights-protecting model see rights-protecting model
shared legal traditions?, 28–33
shared principles, 12–15
wartime detention, 25, 77, 90–1, 161–2, 170
Independent Reviewer of Terrorism Legislation (UK), 195, 198, 199, 209, 210, 211
International Covenant on Civil and Political Rights, 62–3, 178n163
international law and indefinite detention of aliens:
assessment, 291–6
Australia, 59, 62–3, 87–91, 108, 292–3
Canada, 240–3, 255, 273, 295–6
United Kingdom, 156, 161–2, 176–9, 188–9, 293–5
Irvine of Lairg, Lord, 138

Joint Committee on Human Rights (UK), 175, 185, 194, 197, 199, 209, 214
Jowell, Jeffrey, 168–9
judicial deference and national security
Belmarsh, 153, 155, 156–60, 167–71
Rehman, 138–42, 159
Suresh, 243, 281

Katyal, Neal, 271–2

Lauterpacht, Hersch, 3, 174
Liberty (organisation), 156n44, 197
Lim (Australia):
Al-Kateb and, 54, 56, 72–6, 79–80, 82–4, 95–6, 114
Al Masri and, 56, 59, 64
analysis, 46–54
assessment, 54–5
constitutional limits on detention, 43, 50–4
facts and context, 47–8
Plaintiff M47 case and, 114, 116
proportionality test, 46–7, 52, 54–5, 73–6
request for removal provision, 48, 53–5, 95–6
separation of powers, 48–54, 64, 72–6, 114

McLachlan, Campbell, 178
Macklin, Audrey, 26n118
Martinez, Jenny, 251, 272n138

national security
see also Canada; United Kingdom
aliens and, 300–1
nationality-differentiated risk-acceptability, 20–8, 115, 186, 189, 301–4
see also Finnis, John
overview, 20–8, 301–4
explanatory & historical elements, 20–8
normative elements, 301–4
rights-precluding model and, 20–3, 301–3
Nazfiger, James AR, 26–7
Newton Committee (UK), 172, 175, 213
non-citizens see aliens

Offshore Processing case (Australia):
Al-Kateb and, 103, 107, 119
background, 103–6
limits of discretion, 106–8, 119
non-refoulement obligations, 110
overview, 103–8
procedural fairness, 106, 108

Pierce, Gareth, 197
Plaintiff M47 (Australia):
Al-Kateb and, 99, 109–16
overruling, 111–13
segregation from the community, 114–16
separation of powers, 114
upholding, 113–16
assessment, 119
facts and background, 109–11
Lim and, 114, 116
majority decision, 116–18
procedural fairness, 117–18
security, 109–10, 115, 117
Plender, Robert, 26–7
prerogative powers, 24, 26–8, 39–40
proportionality
see also specific countries and cases
indefinite detention of aliens, 11, 13–14, 299
purposes of detention:
overview, 296–9
see also rights precluding model and rights protecting model

Railway Express, passage from, 158, 174, 210, 214
Rehman (UK):
Belmarsh and, 140–2, 151, 168, 281, 290–1
democratic principle, 168–9
facts, 138
judicial deference, 138–42, 159
overview, 138–42
SIAC review function, 138–42, 150–1

right to liberty
 see specific countries, cases, and provisions
rights-precluding model:
 Al-Kateb (Australia): majority, 96, 296–9
 Charkaoui (Canada), 265, 298–9
 Hardial Singh (UK), 265
 international law and, 292–3
 Lumba (UK), 215–8
 meaning, 15–18
 national security justification, 300–1
 nationality-differentiated risk-acceptability, 20–3, 115, 301–3
 purposes and, 296–9
 Zadvydas (US), 265, 296–8
rights-protecting model:
 Al Masri (Australia), 56
 Belmarsh (UK), 17, 30
 Charkaoui (Canada), 30
 international law and, 292
 meaning, 15–18
 purposes, 299
 Zadvydas (US), 15
Roach, Kent, 260, 272
Rose, Dennis, 70n26
rule of law:
 Al-Kateb (Australia), 81, 113
 aliens' detention and, 12
 Belmarsh (UK), 167–8
 models and, 17–20
 constitutional positivism, 18–19
 equality and, 14
 Lim (Australia), 50
 substantive conception, 18

Saul, Ben, 81, 118
security certificates (Canada):
 amendments (2008), 252–3, 274–5
 Chiarelli, 234–7
 conditional release from, 249–50, 252, 275
 danger opinions,
  pre-*Charkaoui* decisions, 244–8
  Suresh, 239–43, 268–70
 disclosure requirements, 236–7, 243, 276–82
 indefinite detention and, 244, 247–8, 259–62, 265–7, 269, 272–3, 282–3, 298–9
 introduced, 237–9
 pre-*Charkaoui* federal decisions, 244–50
 reasonableness reviews, 279–82
  amendments 2008, 275
  Charkaoui and, 252–3
  post-*Charkaoui*, 279–82
  pre *Charkaoui*, 248–50
 Suresh exception and, 239–48, 268–70, 272–3
 special advocates, 274–5, 280–1
segregation from the community:
 Al-Kateb, 74–8, 85–7, 297–8
 Plaintiff M47, Heydon J, 114–6
 purpose of detention overview, 296–8
 Zadvydas, related concepts, 5–9, 16, 77–8, 297–8
Shaughnessy v Mezei (US), 6, 9, 68–9, 77–8, 97–8, 179
SIAC (UK):
 bail powers, 163, 213–14
 see also Belmarsh litigation (UK), SIAC appeal
 Chahal and, 126, 135–7, 139
 creation of, 126, 135–7, 139
 introduced, 135–7
 members, 136
 Rehman and, 138–42
Singh (Canada):
 Charter s 7, 232–4, 237, 257
 equality of rights, 232–3, 254
sovereignty:
 exclusions of aliens and, 3, 20–1, 27–8, 51, 301–4, 305
Sunstein, Cass, 271–2
Suresh (Canada):
 overview, 237–43
 Charkaoui and, 268–70, 272–4
 effect, Federal Court decisions, 244–8
 international law and, 273, 295
 Suresh exception, 240–3, 244–8, 268–70, 272–3

Tampa incident, 103–4
Thomas, Robert, 247
Torture Convention, 240–2, 255, 295
torture prohibition:
 Canadian cases, 240–3, 244–8, 268–70, 272–3
 ECHR absolute prohibition on deportation to torture, 130–2, 140–2, 146, 192–3, 212, 268, 295
 international law, 293, 295–6
TPIMs (UK):
 bail from immigration detention compared, 213–4
 change from control orders, 207–9
 curfews, 208
 duration, 208–9
 evidentiary standard, 208
 introduction, 193, 194, 207–8
 non-discrimination, 210, 211, 214, 220–1
 parliamentary debates, 211
 scope of conditions, 208

United Kingdom:
 ATCSA Part 4 introduced, 146–7
 Belmarsh see Belmarsh
 Chahal see Chahal
 citizenship deprivation, 212–13
 constitutional position, 29, 31–2, 181
 control orders *see* control orders
 detention pending removal
  development of *Hardial Singh* principles, 215–19

Hardial Singh, 125–8
Lumba, 215–19, 221, 266, 306n106
sanctions for breach of public duty, 219
ECHR and,
Human Rights Act, 31–2, 137–8
UK derogation from Art 5(1), 146
UK revocation of derogation, 186
exit model and, 210–14
Human Rights Act
introduction, 31–2, 137–8
declarations of incompatibility, 31–2, 179–82
Joint Committee on Human Rights, 175, 185, 194, 197, 199, 209, 214
judicial deference *see* judicial deference
London bombings (2005), 211, 212
national security deportation
recourse to, 211–14
bail conditions, 213–14
Belmarsh see Belmarsh
Chahal see Chahal
deportation to torture *see* European Convention on Human Rights, torture
non-statutory advisory procedure (previous), 128
Rehman, 138–42
SIAC, creation of, 135–7
Newton Committee, 175, 213
SIAC *see* SIAC (UK)
United States:
Carolene Products, 228
Commonwealth tradition compared with, 29
comparative authorities in Australia, 27n126, 58, 61, 68–9, 74, 77–8, 85–6, 97–8, 289
comparative authorities in Canada, 255, 259–60, 264–6, 273
comparative authorities in UK, 179
(no-)entry fiction, 6, 77–8, 85–6, 179
Railway Express see *Railway Express*
Shaughnessy v Mezei see Shaughnessy v Mezei
Zadvydas see Zadvydas

Vattel, Emmerich de, 27n126
Vincenzi, Christopher, 267

Walker, Clive, 194, 201–2, 211–13
wartime detention, 25, 49, 77, 90–1, 170
Williams, Melissa, 303–4
Wilsher, Daniel, 13, 299n70, 304
Wydrzynski, Christopher, 225, 230

Zadvydas (US):
analysis, 4–10
Australian citations, 58, 61, 74, 77–8, 82
Charkaoui and, 255, 259–60, 264–6, 273
comparative authority, 288–9
minority opinions, 7–9, 16
Opinion of the Court, 5–7
rights-protecting model, 15, 297–8
terrorism exception, 9–10
Zedner, Lucia, 200, 220
Zines, Leslie, 52, 72

9 781849 464314

Printed by Libri Plureos GmbH in Hamburg,
Germany